The Movie Mom's® Guide to Family Movies

NELL MINOW

AVON BOOKS NEW YORK

AVON BOOKS, INC.
1350 Avenue of the Americas
New York, New York 10019

Copyright © 1999 by Nell Minow
Cover photograph by David Apatoff
Cover illustrations by Julie Johnson
Interior design by Kellan Peck
Published by arrangement with the author
ISBN: 0-380-78839-X
www.avonbooks.com

Library of Congress Cataloging in Publication Data:
Minow, Nell, 1952–
    The movie mom's guide to family movies / Nell Minow.
        p.   cm.
    Includes indexes.
    1. Motion pictures Catalogs. 2. Video recordings Catalogs. I. Title.
PN1998.M43   1999   99-14406
016.79143'75—dc21   CIP

First Avon Books Trade Paperback Printing: April 1999

AVON TRADEMARK REG. U.S. PAT. OFF. AND IN OTHER COUNTRIES, MARCA REGISTRADA, HECHO EN U.S.A.

Printed in the U.S.A.

QPM 10 9 8 7 6 5 4

*

In this book, I salute the leading men of the classic movies:

The acrobatic ebullience of Cary Grant in *Holiday*;

the quiet integrity of Gregory Peck in *To Kill a Mockingbird*;

the poetic sweetness of Gary Cooper in *Ball of Fire*;

the irresistible rascality of Clark Gable in
It Happened One Night;

the elegant tenderness of William Powell in *I Love You Again*;

the literate discernment of Jimmy Stewart in
The Philadelphia Story;

the impeccable grace of Fred Astaire in *Shall We Dance?*;

the athletic exuberance of Gene Kelly in
It's Always Fair Weather;

the courage and loyalty of Humphrey Bogart in
To Have and Have Not;

the optmistic resilience of Mickey Mouse in *The Band Concert*;

the legal skills of Spencer Tracy in
Adam's Rib and *Inherit the Wind*;

the heartbreaking sensitivity of James Dean in *East of Eden*;

the inspirational persuasiveness of Robert Preston in
The Music Man;

the romantic patience of Buster Keaton in *The General*;

the strength and commitment of John Wayne in
The Quiet Man; and

the anarchic irreverence of all of the Marx brothers.

This book is for David, my own leading man, who is all of
that and more.

Contents

Note to the Reader   xi

Introduction   1

✳

Part One
MOVIES ABOUT VALUES

Duty and Responsibility 33

Honesty and Integrity 41

Empathy and Compassion 49

Courage 56

Courtesy 65

Fairness and Justice 73

Helping Others 89

Respect 99

Tolerance 105

Loyalty 135

Education 149

Peace (and War) 155

Making Moral Choices 167

✳

Part Two
MOVIES ABOUT GROWING UP

Ambition 201

Competition 209

Dreams and Reality 215

Money 230

Solving Problems 237
Families: Functional and Dys 252
Finding the Hero Within 289
Understanding Emotions 306
Loss 313
Women Worth Watching 324
School Days 337
It's Tough to Be a Teenager 356
Making Life Choices 386

✳

Part Three
JUST FOR FUN

Action and Adventure 413
American Lives 422
Animals 434
Animated Classics 446
Books on the Screen 466
Comedy 493
Fantasy and Science Fiction 515
Musicals 543
Mystery and Suspense 567
Romance 580
Sports 587
Westerns 592

✳

Part Four
SPECIAL OCCASIONS, SPECIAL KIDS

A Calendar of Movies 601
Homebound 619
The Best Videos for Kids from Ages 2—6 626
The Best Videos for Kids from Ages 6—12 634
The Best Movies for Parents About Being a Parent 656

The Movie Mom's Television and
Video Watching Guidelines   663
Film Lingo   666
Sources for Hard-to-Find Videos   670
Recommended Reading   671
Acknowledgments   673
Title Index   675
Age Group Index   683

Note to the Reader

- When the title of a movie appears in boldface, this means it is discussed in another part of the book. The easiest way to find the entry for that movie is by consulting the title index at the end of the book.

- Running times may not be exact because sources disagree with one another when it comes to length.

- The abbreviation NR stands for Not Rated and indicates that a movie was not submitted to the MPAA for a rating.

The Movie Mom's® Guide to Family Movies

Introduction

"**I** know *Cliffhanger* is rated R, but it's only for violence, not for sex, Dad!"

The boy in the video store added that all his friends had seen it and said it was no worse than several other gruesome titles he had already seen. His father sighed and gave in.

This kind of exchange goes on in just about every family. The same technology that has enabled us to have a range of entertainment broader than anyone could have imagined has created tough challenges for families. Too often parents end up grabbing videos from the "Just Released" shelf or watching the same ones over and over. This electronic baby-sitting has nothing to do with engaging the mind or heart. Instead, we use it as something of a video pause button, parking kids in front of a numbing cavalcade of explosions and jump cuts. The messages of these movies are never consciously considered, yet they sink in. Too often, parents feel unable to impose any kind of control.

In 1961, when I was nine years old, my father, Newton Minow, made headlines around the world (and ultimately became a Trivial Pursuit answer) by calling television a "vast wasteland." As President Kennedy's new, thirty-five-year-old Chairman of the Federal Communications Commission, he was the first person ever to hold that position to tell the National Association of Broadcasters that he would not allow their licenses to be renewed unless they met their obligation to serve the public interest. He has been fighting for better television ever since. He and my mother did their best to teach their three children to think critically about what we saw on television, and they were always looking for movies and television shows we could watch together and talk about afterward. They never hesitated to tell us that we were not allowed to watch something they considered inappropriate. Most important, they made me think very hard about what I was watching.

My parents both love movies, and I always have, too, even as a very small child. When I was sixteen, the last week of my sophomore year in high school, I came down with a very bad case of mononucleosis, and was confined to bed for the entire summer. My eyes were infected, which made it difficult for me to read, so my mother allowed me the unprecedented privilege of having a television set in my bedroom. While my friends were off at camp and the beach, I spent an entire summer watching movies on our small black-and-white television set. This was long before the days of cable and the VCR, so I was pretty much stuck with whatever came on. It was a great education in the movies of the 1940s and 1950s, and when I got better I began to read books (and later take classes) about film history and criticism. And I kept watching every movie I could.

All of this paid off years later, when I had two small children on a rainy vacation. We had made cookies, worked on puzzles, and played board games and were all looking for something new. I sat them down on the sofa and said, "Some mothers can do sports, and some can do craft projects. I am not one of those moms, but there is one thing I can do better than any other mother—I can do a MomFest!" Once I explained that this meant a movie festival, they were delighted. Every day we watched a movie and did a related project. We saw *1776* and took the train to Philadelphia to see where it all took place. We saw *State Fair* and visited a county fair. We saw *The King and I* and looked up the history of Thailand in the encyclopedia and made Thai puppets. The MomFest was such a success that it became an annual tradition.

Knowing a lot about movies also helped me find movies that related to my children's interests. Probably my greatest challenge was on the day when my son wanted a movie about boxing and my daughter wanted a musical. I remembered the Gene Kelly musical *It's Always Fair Weather* has a song with the names of every heavyweight champion in it, and both of my children got a big kick out of it. Sharing my favorites with the kids was like seeing them for the first time. I tried to teach them what my parents had taught me about thinking critically about what we watched and I tried to protect them from inappropriate material.

Unfortunately, in that respect I had a tougher challenge than my parents did. When I was a child parents could sit their children down in front of the television set confident that what they saw might be boring or even dumb, but that the most dangerous thing they might see would be tobacco commercials. Violence was confined to a few cowboy shoot-outs. Sex was just about nonexistent: Rob and Laura Petrie slept in twin beds, Lucy was not allowed to use the word "pregnant," and Jeannie's harem pants had to cover her belly button. When we came home from school, we watched *The Mickey Mouse Club*. Today's kids can come home from school and watch television talk shows with topics like, "Men who have sex with their baby-sitters"; "I don't know which of my lovers is the father of my child"; and "My mother is a stripper." Early evening sitcoms have jokes about wife-swapping and premature ejaculation. Cable television shows naked people making love. We baby boomers spent afternoons speculating on the lyrics to "Louie Louie"; today's kids hear Alanis Morissette asking whether her former boyfriend's new girlfriend performs the same sexual favors that she did. The average child spends 15,000 hours in front of a television set by age fifteen, 4,000 more hours than in school, far more than he or she spends with parents. And nowhere is really safe. I took my kids to see a G-rated movie and sat through a coming attraction in which a woman said to a man, "I am going to give you lots of sex." I do not advocate a return to the repression and ignorance of the past. But this is not a healthy situation for kids. And it is so pervasive that parents feel overwhelmed.

Yet it is still possible to protect kids from the media onslaught, to find videos that exercise the mind and spirit and bring families closer together. Classic movies that once were available only on scratchy prints in art houses or shot through with commercials on the "Late Late Show" now appear in video stores, public libraries, and mail-order houses—pristine new prints, as timeless as Rembrandts. Films that enchant, inspire, thrill, even teach, are there for parents who know where to look.

It can be a challenge, once you have found these movies, to get kids to watch them. Children love the familiar. That's why they want to hear the same books over and over when they are small and see the same videos (or almost-carbon-copy sequels) over and over when they are bigger. Mental exercise, like physical exercise, is not as easy as watching a movie that is, to use Frank Lloyd Wright's description of television, "chewing gum for the eyes." Furthermore, the style of moviemaking has changed, so that older movies can at first seem unfamiliar and slow-moving. Kids accustomed to movies like *Home Alone* and *Teenage Mutant Ninja Turtles* or even television shows like *Sesame Street* are used to kaleidoscopic images and nonstop action. But be patient—and persistent. Just as important as their exposure to wonderful stories, beautifully presented, is the stretching they have to do to adjust to quieter, subtler storytelling. Although introducing these movies to today's children can be a challenge, it can be done, and it is worth the effort. These hints will help:

Entice them. Get children curious and interested before the movie begins. Tell them what the challenge or conflict is in the movie, but don't tell them how it turns out. "This is a movie about a girl who dreams of owning the fastest and most beautiful horse in the world." "This is a movie about a teacher who goes to a country far from home to teach the children of a king." Children are also curious about the movies that were their parents' (and grandparents') favorites when they were young.

Engage them. Movies should not be background noise for whatever else they happen to be doing. If they wander off, bicker, or start to play with toys, turn off the television set and tell them they can see the movie when they are ready to watch. Stretch their attention spans. Don't let them zone out between explosions and car chases.

Challenge them. Make sure that every movie they see is one you genuinely feel is worth the two hours it takes away from books, music, talking with you and with each other, homework, making something, or helping around the house. Be aware that older movies are more slowly paced, and some children will complain that black-and-white movies are boring. Just reply with a slight tone of regret that you are sorry to have made a mistake in thinking they were old enough for these movies, and maybe they can try again next year, and that for now they can go to their rooms and read or draw while you watch it.

Challenge them to challenge the film, as well. Make sure they are thinking about what is happening. Ask them what they would do if they were in that situation. Ask why the character is behaving that way. Ask them what the people who made the movie wanted them to think about the characters, and how they can tell. How does the movie spring its surprises? How does it make you feel the suspense? This not only teaches them about narrative and point of view, it also helps to teach them critical thinking.

Prepare them. No matter how bright and well-educated a child is, a child under age twelve is unlikely to be able to follow and understand and truly enjoy a full-length movie's plot, especially one set in another time or place, without some kind of introduction. This is another reason children like to watch the same movie over and over; each viewing allows them to understand it better.

Give children a general overview to make sure they understand the situation, the issues, and the characters. If they ask questions, give them more details. But don't tell them how it turns out. Instead, say: "That's just what the guy in the movie is trying to decide! Watch to see what he does!" Sometimes, with younger children, it helps to read together a book on the same or a related subject. With musicals, it helps to listen to the music a few times before seeing the movie; it usually sparks kids' curiosity, too. Sometimes a classic movie will seem like a cliché to children who have seen the imitations. There is no way to make a John Ford Western seem new to a child who has already seen a dozen shoot-'em-ups. But it can be fun to tell them that this movie was so popular, it was copied over and over again, and let them try to catch the original inspiration and see if they can figure out why it had such an impact.

Connect with them. Pick a movie that relates to the child's interests or experiences in some way. If you have visited (or plan to visit) New York City, try *On the Town,* in which three sailors have only one day to see the city. If the child loves baseball, try *The Pride of the Yankees* or *It Happens Every Spring.* Many classic children's books have been made into movies. Children who have read *The Secret Garden, Little Women, Anne of Green Gables, The Diary of Anne Frank, Tuck Everlasting,* or *The Phantom Tollbooth,* will especially enjoy the movie versions. A child who has learned about Abraham Lincoln, Thomas Edison, Malcolm X, Charles Lindbergh, or

Helen Keller in school can see movies about their lives. Children also love movies that feature a child as a major character. Try *The Secret Garden, Heidi, The Canterville Ghost, Oliver!, Annie, Lassie Comes Home,* or *The Prince and the Pauper.*

Everyone watches *A Christmas Carol, Miracle on 34th Street,* and *It's a Wonderful Life* at Christmas, but other holidays have movies, too. For example: *1776* for the Fourth of July, *The Long Walk Home* for Martin Luther King Day, *I Remember Mama* for Mother's Day, *Life with Father* or *To Kill a Mockingbird* for Father's Day, *The Pajama Game* or *Norma Rae* for Labor Day and *Sergeant York* or *To Hell and Back* for Memorial Day (for more, see the Calendar chapter on page 601).

If a child likes a particular genre (Westerns, pirates, detective stories, adventure), seek out movies in that category. Some children get attached to particular actors and will want to see all of their films. One movie can lead to a related one: *The Wizard of Oz* to *The Wiz, West Side Story* to *Romeo and Juliet, Rudy* to *Knute Rockne, All American.* Movies can teach a child about the careers or backgrounds of family members or friends. A child dealing with challenges like courage, loss, growing up, moving, confidence, or tolerance can find them easier to talk about (or even think about) after seeing them in a movie.

Warn them. Older movies do have the advantage of telling their stories without the kind of language, violence, or nudity that led to the development of the rating system in the late 1960s. But the disadvantage is that they sometimes reflect assumptions or attitudes that are insensitive or even offensive by today's standards, particularly in their treatment of women and minorities.

This creates an important opportunity for discussions with children about those attitudes, about the history they were a part of and the history since, and, most importantly, about being able to identify prejudice and its impact, to make sure it is eradicated.

Protect them. Examine the ratings carefully and make sure the movie is suitable for children before you bring it home. Never rely on the information on the box, which is designed to sell, not inform. One mother brought home *Sirens* for her son, not realizing that most of the movie features three naked women discussing sex very explicitly—the box made it look like something from *Masterpiece Theatre.* Many parents have allowed their children to see *The Good Son* or the *Ace Ventura* movies because they seemed like children's movies. If you are watching a movie with the children and decide it is not appropriate, turn it off. This has nothing to do with how smart or sophisticated they are for their ages; it has to do with your communicating to them your views on what is appropriate. Showing it to them implies your endorsement. It is very tough, in this era, to protect children from inappropriate material, but they will appreciate every effort, if not now, later.

Join them. Sharing a movie with your children shows them you are not seating them in front of the television set to give yourself a break; you are sharing something with them that you think is worthwhile. It gives you the chance to answer their questions and tell them what you think of characters or issues. Even a movie with some inappropriate material can have some value if it prompts a discussion about the objectionable behavior. It gives you a chance to point out aspects of your past ("I used to dress like that!"; "You see, all airplanes had propellers!") or places you have been. It gives you a chance to talk about values without sounding as though you are preaching to them. And it gives you a chance to win the Grand National Steeplechase with Velvet, save King Richard with Robin Hood, learn to communicate with Helen Keller, and climb the Alps with Heidi. You'll fall in love with the movies along with your children, and the movies will be a part of your shared experience and frame of reference that you will always treasure.

THE MOVIE MOM'S FREQUENTLY ASKED QUESTIONS

These are the questions parents most often ask me.

Is there really a problem, or are you overreacting?

Literally thousands of studies show that kids are harmed by premature exposure to portrayals of sex, violence, substance abuse, and other inappropriate material. They become desensitized and get a distorted view of adult life. As one college student said to me, "My parents pretty much let me watch anything I wanted. At the time I thought it was great, but now I'm sorry. I feel like someone took something from me that I wish I'd been able to keep longer."

The boomer generation is in something of a bind. We rebelled against repression, but forgot there is a difference between repression and protection, and we threw out the babies with the bathwater. I am not saying we should repress a child's natural curiosity about adult issues and concerns; on the contrary. Some movies provide an exceptionally good context for initiating discussions on these issues. Others, however, do not, and parents can need some help in establishing limits.

Why does it matter? It's only a movie.

Movies are our sagas, our myths, our touchstones, our collective cultural heritage. They illuminate and shape our culture, and they transmit it as well. Think back to when you fell in love: the movies you went to together, the movies you discovered that only the two of you appreciated or hated in just the right way. Think of the way that movies create a cultural language for us: Bogart telling the cop that the Maltese falcon is "the stuff that dreams are made of"; Claude Rains saying, "Round up the usual suspects," or, "I'm shocked . . . shocked to find gambling going on in Casablanca"; Gene Kelly singing in the rain; Vivien Leigh as Scarlett O'Hara, saying, "As God is my witness, I'll never be hungry again!"; or Orson Welles murmuring "Rosebud" as he drops the snow globe.

Movies are one important way that we teach ourselves and our children cultural norms. Movies give kids their first exposure to the world outside the family and school. How do we behave with the opposite sex? How do we behave in the workplace? How do we behave when our parents are not there to tell us what to do?

Movies give our children their first glimpse of these worlds, teaching how a couple moves closer to show their attraction, then how a woman holds her head when she wants to be kissed; how people evaluate risk and set their priorities; how people make decisions about work; how people follow their dreams and how they react when they fail.

More than 40 percent of children in America today grow up in families that have no particular religious affiliation. This means that unless families sit down together on a regular basis to talk about values, there is no one place where children go to learn moral lessons and confront ethical dilemmas. Thus, they are going to get it from television and the movies, whether you like it or not. You can either play a part in that process or not, but it will happen.

Movies show us the modern equivalent of parables or *Aesop's Fables*. Characters confront moral dilemmas, they evaluate risk, establish priorities, adapt to change, learn important lessons, overcome loss and fear, grapple with responsibility, face consequences, solve problems, and find redemption, and in doing so, they teach your child how to do those things as well. They provide a superb opportunity for family discussions of values and feelings.

And there are advantages to using movies to initiate discussions about these issues. Like parables and fables, stories told to us through movies have the power of distance. For kids, especially for very young kids and teens, it can be much easier to talk about what is going on with the people on the screen than it is to talk about what is going on inside them. The difference between movies and life is that life doesn't have to make sense. But movies do, and thus they give us a manageable starting point for a discussion of the most sensitive and painful topics.

Do you ever lighten up?

Of course I do. I love to watch movies just for fun with my family, and this book includes hundreds of these movies.

How do you determine whether a child is old enough for a particular movie?

As any parent knows, this is a very complex issue. The key is whether the child is ready from a *developmental* standpoint. No matter how intelligent he or she is, a child follows a path of comprehension-development that is directly related to age. Age-based development matters above all else, including intelligence, in a child's comprehension of the messages of movies and television. So it really does not make sense for a parent to say, "It says ages five and up, but my child is very bright, so she can watch even though she is only three." A three-year-old might be so bright that he can read at the second-grade level, but that does not necessarily mean that he can follow a story line that involves changes in time and location, or one that turns on some characters knowing a secret that others do not.

Children are less cynical than adolescents and adults are about what they see, more prone to confuse important issues raised by what they view, less able to see actions in light of motives and consequences, more apt to confuse fantasy and reality, and more ready to accept screen characters as behavior models. As a result, children are more vulnerable to the potential negative messages in what they watch, including violence and other inappropriate behavior.

The nature of film and television lies in fast-paced action and cuts that are difficult for young children to follow, often causing them to miss the consequences and motives that are central in understanding and analyzing actions. In one study, kindergartners, second, fifth, and eighth graders were shown an edited version of an aggressive television program. Afterward, they were asked to recount the plot, their understanding of the main characters' motives, and the consequences of the main characters' actions. Kindergartners typically remembered only the aggressive actions and didn't mention any motives or consequences. However, older children associated consequences first, then motives, and finally the full complex of motives *and* consequences as they described aggressive action. Thus, younger children are prone to see actions such as violence as stand-alone deeds. Children are more likely than adolescents or adults to act on violence they witness on the screen if it is portrayed as rewarding (which it often is). By watching violence or other aggressive behavior with an underdeveloped ability to see the relevant painful consequences or reasoned motives, children get a distorted impression of what actions mean in the real world.

A definitive shift in viewing sophistication generally occurs around the age of nine. For example, before the age of nine, children tend not to understand the difference between a television program and the commercials that interrupt it. This is made even more difficult by programs that are essentially half-hour-long commercials for action figures and other toys, such as *Mighty Morphin Power Rangers*.

The MPAA ratings (G, PG, PG-13, R, and NC-17) are based on a fairly narrow definition of "objectionable material" rather than on age-appropriateness, so they are not necessarily a good guide. The ratings are formulaic, based on particular body parts, words, and the amount of blood and guts, rather than on situations. In this book, each listing specifies the ages that are most likely to appreciate and enjoy the movie. I have not recommended any full-length features for kids under four. While most kids under four will find one or more features they like, these are exceptions.

These are the Motion Picture Association of America ratings, with my comments.

G
General Audiences. All ages admitted.
Suitable for all ages. These movies are usually designed for children.

PG
Parental guidance suggested.
Some material may not be suitable for children.
This rating generally means that the movie contains a few swear words, some violence, or particularly tense material.

PG-13
Parents strongly cautioned.
Some material may be inappropriate for children under 13.
This rating generally means that the movie contains stronger language, nudity and sexual refereces, and/or more graphic violence. This is the most treacherous category for parents. It is something of a catch-all. Parents should be very cautious because there is wide disparity between the movies that are included. Just because a child handled one PG-13 movie well, that does not mean that all PG-13 movies are suitable. Parents of kids from 8-15 in particular should read the reviews of PG-13 movies, particularly those that highlight issues of parental concern, before making a decision to let children see them.

R
Restricted. No one under age 17 is admitted to the theater without an accompanying parent or adult guardian.
Of course, these restrictions mean nothing with regard to videos and cable television. R-rated movies generally have more nudity and violence, but occasionally they will get this rating just for extensive use of the F-word. Again, parents should read the reviews carefully to determine whether an R-rated movie is appropriate for their children.

NC-17
No one under 17 admitted.
It is very rare for any of the major distributors to exhibit a movie with this rating, and Blockbuster and other "family" video stores will not carry them. These movies are not intended to be viewed by children and teenagers and are not appropriate for them.

In this book, I also use:

NR
Not rated.
Either because the movie was made before the rating code or because the producer decided not to seek a rating, the MPAA has not assigned a rating to it.

In general, very young children are not developmentally ready to appreciate a full-length story, and will tend to watch a feature as a collection of unconnected pieces, drawing on their own limited knowledge of the world to help them figure it out. For example, my son, then about four, seemed to have an unusual amount of trouble following a simple "good guys–bad guys" plot in a Disney movie. Finally, just before the end, he said in utter astonishment, "You mean the bad guy drives the big car?" At that point, his passion for vehicles of all kinds was so overwhelming that it was simply impossible for him to believe that a bad guy would have a great car.

My recommendation is that preschoolers watch material designed for that age group. And, as with kids of any age, I recommend that viewing of television or videos be strictly limited. The important "work" of the preschool years is the development of interpersonal skills and imagination, and that is best accomplished away from television. While movies and television can stimulate daydreams, studies show they can depress creative imagination by providing a plethora of ready-made mental pictures, sounds, and actions that can later be called up at will. This store of knowledge seems to hurt abilities integral to creative imagination such as the ability to dissociate oneself from existing information, a reflective style of thinking, sustained effort, and the peace and quiet necessary to give a matter careful thought.

For school-age children and teens, a parent's primary concerns are likely to be sex, violence, and scariness. There, the MPAA ratings are a starting point (especially since they now explain the basis for the rating: e.g., *Titanic* is rated PG-13 for "disaster-related peril and violence, nudity, sensuality and brief language"), though they cannot always be counted on. Context is crucial. There is a big difference between a character having a glass of wine at dinner and drunkenness used for comic effect. And there is a big difference between sexual references concerning an exploitative relationship and one concerning two people committed to one another. In this book, I make distinctions between sexual and other material that seems to me disturbing and material that seems innocuous. The information is there so that parents can decide for themselves what is appropriate, based on their own values and their knowledge of their child.

How do you determine if a movie is too scary or too upsetting for kids?

First of all, it is simply impossible to predict the reaction of any child under age five. One almost three-year-old I know was so terrified when she saw the Disney version of **Cinderella** that she talked about it constantly for weeks. What scared her? Not the wicked stepmother, and not the mean stepsisters. It was Lucifer the cat, who preyed on Cinderella's friends, the mice.

My niece Alexandra, a very smart, funny, tough kid who is not easily scared, showed me the ultimate folly of trying to predict how scary a movie will be for a child. When she was about four, her mother took her to see *Bambi,* with a favorite toy, a box of candy, and a seat by the exit in case the movie became too upsetting. Her mother even spoke to several friends ahead of time, so that she knew exactly what the scary parts were (Bambi's mother getting shot, and the forest fire) and when they occurred. Alex did just fine through both, and her mother was breathing a sigh of relief when, just before the movie ended, Alex burst into tears, crying, "Where's Bambi? Where's Bambi?" As her mother assured her, Bambi was right there on the screen. But to Alex, it did not look or sound like Bambi. He was now a young stag. "That's not Bambi! Bambi has the white spots on his back!" Nothing her mother could say would change Alex's mind. At that age, she was barely able to understand that children become adults, and Bambi appeared so different (and sounded so different because his voice had changed) that she was simply unable to comprehend it was the same character.

Very young kids react in ways we cannot predict because their fears tend to focus on a part of the story that is more understandable to them. It is better to err on the side of caution and keep them away from movies that may scare them, especially those that feature major characters in peril, menacing bad guys, or the death of any character.

By the time children are older, they will have a sense of what they can handle and may be able to talk about something they find upsetting. Just as some kids love roller coasters and some would rather die than go near them, some kids enjoy grisly movies, some like intense suspense, some love crashes, explosions, and shoot-'em-ups, and some never like them, even as adults. Always respect a child's choices about what he or she does not want to see, and do not hesitate to impose limits that you feel are appropriate on what he or she does want to see.

My child got scared—now what do I do?

First, respect the child's fears. Never say that what they think is scary is not scary for them. But that does not mean you should admit that it scares you, too (even if it does). Someone has to be the grown-up, and the thing about being a parent is that it has to be you. You cannot always protect a child from getting scared, but you can teach your child some important skills for dealing with fear.

There are some excellent books to read together. My favorite is *Annie Stories* by Doris Brett. Brett created these stories to help her own child deal with nightmares, starting school, loss, scary animals, and other childhood fears. She explains how parents can adapt the stories for their own children. Kids also love *There's a Nightmare in My Closet* by Mercer Mayer, *Go Away, Big Green Monster,* by Ed Emberly, and *There's a Monster Under My Bed* by James Howe.

You can also teach children to take some action that will help them feel more powerful than what they fear. Remind them they can always turn off the VCR and television if something upsets them, and make sure they know how to do it. If it makes them feel better, they can put the video on a high shelf or in a locked box or somewhere else safely out of reach. Some parents have had success using a spray bottle filled with water to "spray away" bad dreams. Encourage kids to use their imagination: "Can you draw me a picture showing you putting Lucifer the cat in jail?" "Can you sing me a song about what you will do to the bad guy?" "If you had magical powers, what spell would you cast on Cruella De Vil?"

What do I say when my child says, "Everyone but me has seen it?" Won't I harm his/her social standing?

We don't raise kids by lowest common denominator. One of the greatest gifts you can give your kids is the lesson that appeals based on what everyone else does *never* work. Parents who are susceptible to such appeals teach kids that they can justify their behavior by saying, "Everyone else smokes pot (or shoplifts, or has sex) and everyone else will think I'm a dork if I don't." If you hold firm, your kids may not agree with you, but they will understand that you love them enough to establish limits to protect them.

If other kids' parents permit their kids to see inappropriate films, we feel sorry for them, but we don't sink down to their level. Teach your kids that cultivating an expression (and a feeling) of smug superiority when other people try to make you feel bad for not doing something you shouldn't be doing, anyway, is a wonderful skill to develop, and now is a great time to start. You can use some of the movies in this book to provide excellent examples of individuals who do the right thing despite peer pressure (**12 Angry Men, The Nasty Girl,** or **High Noon,** for example).

What do I do when my child goes to someone else's house?

Talk to the parents hosting your child ahead of time and say, "My child is not allowed to watch television or videos. Will that be a problem for you?" This may sound overly harsh, but the complaints I hear most often are from parents who tell me how careful they are, only to find that their six-year-old has seen *Dumb and Dumber* or their twelve-year-old has seen *The House That Dripped Blood* at someone else's house. If a parent replies, "Oh, that's a shame, because we were hoping to make popcorn and watch *Babe,*" you can say, "Oh, just this once," and show your flexibility and good judgment. Or, you can take on the challenge of approving in advance whatever they intend to show the kids. But I think it is wise to establish clear and firm limits when your child visits friends or when a baby-sitter takes charge in your own home.

Is it okay if the objectionable material is just "over their head"?

No. Item number one in the job description of being a kid is trying to figure out everything, and they don't distinguish between the stuff we want them to figure out and the stuff we don't. That wonderful natural curiosity and persistence that enables them to learn language and understand the notion of gravity and figure out how many times they can ask us for something after being put to bed before we get angry does not discriminate. They will puzzle about whatever they do not understand until they figure it out, and when it comes to sexual values, a little information (or misinformation) can be very disturbing.

Even when they think they do understand, it is no better. A twelve-year-old who told me that *Clueless* is her favorite movie and that she has seen it more than thirty times repeated to me a joke she particularly liked, where a high school-aged character says she can't play tennis because her plastic surgeon "doesn't want her to do anything where balls might fly at [her] face." The heroine's comeback is, "There goes your social life." The twelve-year-old thought that was funny because if the girl could not play tennis, she would not have a social life—in other words, the insult was that tennis was the only social life she was likely to have. She will continue to repeat that "joke" until someone tells her what it is really about. Imagine how she will feel.

Many young kids have seen the Ace Ventura movies. Five minutes into the first one, a woman client asks Ace if he would prefer to be paid in cash or by having her pull down his zipper. He then gets oral sex—off camera, but we see his facial contortions. At the end of the movie, a woman's dress is torn off, and it turns out she has a penis (a *Crying Game* joke). In the sequel, there is a prolonged masturbation sequence and a joke about a gorilla raping a person. Will six-year-olds "get" this humor? No, but on some level it will register, and it will teach them concepts of sex and sexual values for which they have no context, and that therefore may be very disturbing.

How do I get my children to talk to me about what they see?

Watch with them. Listen to their questions, but first let them try to answer them by asking them, "What do you think?" Model the behavior you are looking for by commenting on the action yourself: "Wow, she looks happy!"; "Why do you think he decided to do that?" Vote on a rating for the movie afterward, or get the kids to pretend to give reviews at the dinner table, explaining to someone who has never seen the movie what was good or bad about it.

What if my children say old movies are boring?

Kids (and adults) tend to use television more to numb their thoughts than to engage them. Studies show that while adults think of watching television as relaxing for themselves and their kids, it is quite the opposite. What it is instead is superficially anesthetizing, providing us with the illusion of relaxation, but in reality it jazzes us up. We can see that by the way we tend to click the remote from show to show.

Kids who grow up putting their minds on hold this way will look for more dangerous ways to zone out in the future. Make sure they learn that watching should be active exercise for their minds and spirits. And make sure they learn the difference between pleasure and happiness, both from the way that you and they use and watch movies and from the characters and stories themselves. There is a big difference between fun and distraction, and the way you use entertainment in your home is an important way to teach that to your children.

Sometimes kids who have been saturated in media need to be "detoxed" before they can begin to learn about watching a movie with the intellect and the heart instead of mainlining it into the pleasure center. The best thing to do for these kids is to go cold turkey, with a week (or more) of no television or video games. (It is harder on the parents than the kids, but it can be done.) After that, make it clear there is to be no television watching unless chores and homework are done, and make sure whatever they plan to watch is genuinely worthwhile. Even the best movies on video should not be the "default protocol" in the house.

It is important, too, not to make a particular rating a badge of maturity. Otherwise, kids want to see R-rated movies just because they are not allowed to, because it will make them feel grown up. And they reject G-rated movies as babyish. One day when my son was about five, he asked me how old my grandmother was. "Almost ninety," I replied. "Wow," he said. "I'll bet she can go to any movie she wants to!" Make sure kids know that the ratings are just one of the factors you consider in making the decision about whether a particular movie is appropriate.

How do I find the movies in this book?

Begin at your local public library, which may have the movies or be able to get them for you. If that does not work, check out the sources listed in the Sources for Hard-to-Find Videos section at the end of the book.

My child wants to watch the same movie over and over, as much as two or three times a day. What do I do?

Many parents have this problem. In some cases, children rewatch movies to help them understand the story. In others, like a security blanket or a favorite toy, a particular video becomes almost a "transitional object" for some children, especially when they are facing some unusual stress, either from external sources (family changes, illness, starting preschool) or internal (going through some developmental stage). I recommend respecting a child's attachment, but imposing limits, such as watching the movie no more than once a day and then only if there is time. This stage will pass.

Why is it that in most movies featuring a child in the lead role, the child is missing one or both parents?

This is often much more troubling for parents than for kids, though some children will ask what happened to Heidi's parents or Dorothy's parents or become upset when the parents are killed in **The Witches** and **James and the Giant Peach.** Even in movies where the child has loving parents, they are physically separated for the course of the movie, as in **Home Alone, Peter Pan,** and **Pinocchio.**

Adults who watch these films (and are at a stage of life when they have reason to be concerned about losing their own parents) are sometimes upset at this consistent theme and wonder if there is some sort of maliciousness behind it. There isn't. Parents are missing in children's films for two reasons. First, it is very hard to place a child in the middle of the action if a parent is there to protect and warn him. It removes most of the narrative momentum. Second, it is impossible to inject romance into a movie about a child. And a single parent provides the potential for a romantic happy ending to appeal to a broader audience.

How did this all happen? Why are movies so different now from the ones that I watched as a child?

The idea of appealing to a larger audience with sex and violence is not new. Some of the movies of the late silent and early talkie eras were quite frank. Responding to objections from moviegoers and the threat of some kind of censorship, the movie industry developed the Production Code, adopted in 1934. It required that evildoers be punished, and prohibited plotlines like interracial romances and the portrayal of clergymen as comic characters or villains. The restrictions on sex and language were very explicit (there was a memorable fuss over whether Rhett Butler would be permitted to use the word "damn" in **Gone With the Wind**), but the rules about violence were more general, essentially requiring that it be in "good taste." These rules remained in effect until the mid-1960s, when they were amended and then abandoned in favor of the rating system in use today. Similarly, television's National Association of Broadcasters adopted a standards and practices code in 1952 that lasted until the 1980s, when government concerns about antitrust (and competition from cable) intervened. The television ratings system adopted in 1997 is designed to work with a V-chip, which will be included in new televisions and enable a parent to limit inappropriate programs.

WHAT THIS BOOK IS (AND IS NOT)

This is not a book of movies "for kids." It is a book of movies for families with children from ages two through eighteen to watch together, to use as a starting point for discussions of values, feelings, and consequences, to provide a common experience, to share something that will be fun for everyone. Although most of these films can be watched by children and older kids without adults present, they are selected because they are family films, not just "kids' films."

This is not a book of movie reviews, or of film criticism. Reviews are written to give you enough information so you can decide if you want to see the movie, without giving away so much information that you don't need to see it. Film criticism, like literary criticism, usually assumes that you have seen the movie and want to explore some additional insights, and often assumes or gives away important details. A review of **Citizen Kane** won't tell you what Rosebud is, but criticism will. Plenty of works of both kinds are available, and I have listed some of my favorites in the Recommended Reading section.

This book has a different purpose. All of the movies I recommend are "good" in some sense, meaning that they are worth watching. While many of the films in this book are classics that no one should grow up—or be a grown-up—without seeing, some others are selected less for inherent artistic merit than for the likelihood that they will be enjoyed by families and provide a good starting point for discussions of issues. These write-ups are designed to give you the information you need to determine whether this film suits your values and the interests and needs of your child.

This book is also not intended to compete with encyclopedias that have thousands of thumbnail sketches to give you just enough information to jog your memory about whether you have seen a particular film or give you some sense of whether you might like it. Those books are great (I especially like Leonard Maltin's), but they do not provide the information that a parent needs to decide whether a particular movie is appropriate for a particular child or teenager. For that reason, I do include "spoilers" in many write-ups, meaning that I let you know how the movie comes out. (An exception is the Mystery and Suspense chapter.) Only you know how your child will react to plot developments like the death of one of the characters. "Happier" endings may also raise concerns. Many children will be delighted when the twins's parents get back together in **The Parent Trap.** Some children, who are still having problems dealing with divorce in their own families, may find it upsetting. So I try to alert parents to anything in the movie that could create problems for a child.

Most important, this is a supplement, not a substitute, for moral instruction by parents. They learn from you, and from your example, not from stories you tell them. This book can only illuminate and supplement that example by exposing them to stories and situations to compare to their own experience, that allow them to imagine how they might react, to better understand the reactions of others.

You are their moral teacher, and not just when you talk to them about values, but every waking moment. There is no movie that can teach a child the importance of integrity when a parent says, "You don't need to buy pencils; I'll bring some home from the office"; or, "Tell the man you are only ten so we can get a discount"; or, "If we don't get a new car, people will think we are worthless"; or, "Good thing no one saw me scrape that parked car—let's leave now before anyone comes." You can show them a dozen movies about tolerance, but it means nothing if you have never entertained friends from other races or religions in your home. There is no movie that can teach children about the dangers of substance abuse or disrespect or violence if they live in a home where that behavior is accepted.

This book is not a lesson plan. The discussion and question sections included for each of the main entries are not intended to make every family viewing session into a seminar. Rather, they are intended to give parents an idea of the issues raised by the movie so that parents can decide whether it is one that is appropriate for a particular child at a particular stage, based on the issues he or she is dealing with. Sometimes they can be used to get children interested before the movie. And they can provide a starting point for talking about what you have seen.

It is likely that parents will think of better questions on their own; it is inevitable that children will. The most important thing is for families to watch together so that parents can see how their children react, so children can see how their parents react, so that the movies are something to think about instead of something to put one's mind on hold.

About two hundred of the movies have full-length write-ups. The rest have briefer descriptions, including notes about any areas of special sensitivity or connections to particular interests or to other movies. A shorter write-up does not mean that the film is less good or less important or less instructive; it just means that it was less complex, or that illustrated issues were included in the discussion of another film. The longer write-ups include details of the plot, a discussion of topics raised, bullets detailing any profanity, nudity/sexual references, alcohol/drug abuse, violence/scariness, or tolerance/diversity issues, questions that could be prompted by the movie, "connections" and activities. For movies aimed at younger children, the activities are usually connected to some aspect of the movie (i.e., "Find Thailand on a map" after watching *The King and I*). For movies likely to be viewed by middle school or high school kids, the connections are more likely to be other movies featuring the same performers or director, or with related themes. But the "connections" tend to be somewhat free-associative on my part, with a little of everything, including some of my favorite bits of film trivia.

This is a book of family movies, so it does not include movies kids like that are just about impossible for parents to sit through, like *Teenage Mutant Ninja Turtles*. Regretfully, I have left out all but a few subtitled films, because they do not lend themselves well to family viewing.

If I have left out your family's favorite movie, it was probably for lack of time and space or availability; send me an email at moviemom@usa.net so I can include it in the next edition.

The movies listed in this book are organized by themes, in three categories or parts. The first part contains value-related themes like Honesty and Integrity, Tolerance and Making Moral Choices.

The second part contains themes relating to "growing up," movies about issues that all kids must learn how to handle. It includes movies about evaluating priorities and risks in making choices, about issues like ambition, competition, and money. It also includes movies illustrating different kinds of families, and has a section focusing on the special challenges faced by teenagers.

The third and final parts help families find movies their families will enjoy with topic-related themes like Animals, American Lives, and A Calendar of Movies, with movies for every holiday and season. There are also six Just for Fun topics, with the best in musicals, fantasies, comedies, romance, adventure, and mystery and suspense. There are lists like The Best Videos for Ages 6–12, The Best Videos for Children from 2–6, and a chapter with movies to watch on rainy or snowy days, or when a child (or a parent) is sick in bed. There is even a section on the best movies for parents about being a parent and guidelines for family television and video watching.

Finally, there are indexes by title and age range at the end of the book, to make sure you find what you are looking for. When a movie could have fit just as easily into more than one category, I list the title in both sections (and sometimes discuss it in the introductions to both sections), the briefer summary a pointer to the fuller discussion elsewhere.

TALKING WITH KIDS ABOUT WHAT THEY WATCH

Watching Movies with a Young Child

Movies can provide a wonderful opportunity to help young children in their development, particularly in understanding emotions. Ask them about the characters ("Is she happy or sad?"; "Is he angry or frightened?") and encourage them to talk with you about what the characters are feeling. Movies can also help children develop empathy by teaching them to understand and even identify with the perspective of others.

One of the great advantages of watching a movie with children is their freshness of perspective. They don't know that if an orphan boy meets a rich man whose beloved child was once mysteriously kidnapped, chances are he will turn out to be that child. They don't know it's corny, or a cliché. Never allow anyone (including an older sibling) to make them feel dumb for being surprised by what happens. Enjoy the freshness it brings to your own appreciation of the film, and encourage them to begin to recognize patterns.

Watching Movies with an Older Child

School-age kids are ready to identify more complex patterns and predict consequences. Teach them that every story is like a mystery, and that as they watch, they should ask why each character and each event is in the story, and what they add to the narrative or the atmosphere. If the difference between story and life is editing, why were these characters and events chosen to illustrate this story? What makes it a story?

Normally, the hero is changed at the end of a story; he or she learns something or loses something. Teach kids to look for this, and try to understand what writers call the "arc" of the story. Ask them to predict what will happen, and to comment on the characters' behavior, on consequences, and on the reactions of other characters. Ask them to summarize the movie, an excellent mental challenge. Anyone who has ever spent time with eleven-year-olds knows that they love to tell you the entire movie, scene by scene. To help them learn organization and communication skills, teach them to pick the most important parts to tell someone unfamiliar with the story. Kids at this age love to share movies with their friends, and it can be fun to have a group of families share a monthly movie and discussion.

Almost every movie falls into one or more of the following thirteen plot patterns. Kids ages ten and up enjoy learning to recognize them and categorize the movies they see.

- **Road movies.** People who start out not knowing or even disliking each other learn to respect, like, and even love each other, often while traveling together to accomplish some goal (examples: *The Wizard of Oz, Toy Story, It Happened One Night*). Sometimes it is a group of diverse people who must confront some challenge together. Another variation features people who are somehow connected but have not seen each other for a while or do not know each other well, like family members or former classmates.
- **The reluctant hero.** A cynic or a callow youth discovers or rediscovers the hero within. These movies often provide a chance to observe moral judgments and choices (examples: *Casablanca, Star Wars*).
- **Fish out of water.** Someone outside our culture or society throws our cultural assumptions and personal foibles into stark relief by highlighting a fresh perspective (examples: *The Gods Must Be Crazy, The Jungle Book, King of Hearts*).
- **Boy who cried wolf.** People who don't tell the truth have to deal with the consequences. This theme is often found in romantic movies (examples: *Alice Adams, Daddy Long Legs*), and it is also very popular in comedies (example: *Mrs. Doubtfire*).
- *Cat in the hat.* An ordinary person's life is disrupted by a wacky but exciting and lovable outsider, revealing to the ordinary person how much more there is to life (examples: *Bringing Up Baby, Ball of Fire*).
- **Rise and Fall.** A character with ambition and vision (and, usually, good intentions) achieves success, and then wants too much or forgets his original purpose. This popular theme goes back to the ancient Greek dramas and myths, where it was called "hubris," a human's attempt to be like the gods (examples: *Yertle the Turtle, Citizen Kane*).
- **Growing up.** One or more young people come of age, learning sometimes painful lessons about loss and responsibility. This is often combined with one of the other plot patterns (examples: *Little Women, The Yearling*).
- **Redemption.** People who have lost their self-respect or integrity find it. People who never had it develop it (examples: *Bad Day at Black Rock;* Doc Holliday in *Gunfight at the OK Corral* and other versions of the same story). We often see the hero overcoming a tragic flaw—or learning his lesson but being felled by the flaw (example: *The Gunfighter*).
- **Triumph of the underdog.** Someone no one believes in, who does not believe in him/herself, grows, learns, and achieves an all-but-impossible goal (examples: *Rocky* and countless movies about ragamuffin sports

teams, as well as *The Solid Gold Cadillac, The Nasty Girl, Mr. Smith Goes to Washington*).

- **Boy meets girl; boy loses girl; boy gets girl.** This, of course, is the classic romance (examples: *On the Town, Top Hat, His Girl Friday*).
- **The quest for the MacGuffin.** "MacGuffin" was Alfred Hitchcock's word for whatever it is that the hero and heroine are so eager to get. These movies involve a search for treasure, solving a mystery, or saving the world. Sometimes the hero is a professional (examples: James Bond movies; *The Thin Man*), but more often, the hero is an ordinary person thrust into terror and intrigue and called upon to exercise extraordinary courage and skill (examples: *Raiders of the Lost Ark;* most Hitchcock movies).
- **Biography.** These movies allow us a peek into the life of an interesting or unusual person. They often include elements from the underdog or coming-of-age genre as well (examples: *The Spirit of St. Louis, Young Tom Edison, Abe Lincoln in Illinois, The Great White Hope*).
- **Explosion movie.** And then there are movies with lots of explosions. Something in the impact of hot weather on brain cells seems to require everyone to attend at least one of these each year (example: *Independence Day*).

Some good questions to ask intermediate and middle school kids: With so few plots used over and over, what is the difference between a good and a bad movie? What does the main character learn? What problem does he solve? What does he lose? What does he gain?

Watching Movies with a Teenager

Surprisingly, teens are a lot like toddlers. Both are going through stages in which oppositional behavior is a temporary substitute for genuine independence. Just as a toddler's brain is optimally constructed to be able to absorb information, a teenager's is optimally constructed to absorb rules of interaction and behavior. For the first time, they are looking outside the family for guidance on how to behave, and they learn a lot from the movies. Like toddlers, they are more comfortable talking about what is going on with the characters on-screen than they are talking about themselves. So movies can be an important way to help you connect with them about issues like communication, values, priorities, and evaluating risk.

Teens are busy and often prefer to go to movies with their friends. But parents should continue to impose limits (just because your child is over thirteen does not mean that any PG-13 movie is appropriate), get a sense of what movies they are watching, and do their best to watch with them as often as possible. Child development specialists encourage parents to have "floor time" with toddlers, to get down on their level and let them lead the play. For parents of teens, the equivalent of "floor time" is letting them pick the movies you watch together part of the time (within your own guidelines for appropriateness), maybe taking turns. Watch the movies they love, without criticism, as a way to connect with them. Teens love to express their views of morality, and so they may be willing to talk with you about issues raised by the movies.

WARNING: SOME MOVIES ARE NOT WHAT THEY SEEM

It is almost impossible to appreciate just how damaging today's movies can be. Movies today are not just different in content, they are also more readily available. Kids may not be able to buy tickets to R-rated movies in a theater, but they can see R-rated movies playing on the screens at the video store, or at home on cable or the VCR.

It is hard for adults to think of this kind of material from the perspective of a child, because we have something they do not—context, based on our experience. In *Four Weddings and a Funeral,* for example, a couple has sex after perhaps two dozen words of conversation, and she describes her thirty-one other lovers before they decide that they are deeply in love. Adults may find the movie witty, charming, and fairly tongue-in-cheek, rather than sordid. We know that the world does not really work that way. But a twelve-year-old, or even a seventeen-year-old, is likely to view it in much more literal terms.

When parents in the 1990s were growing up, it was unthinkable for heroes and heroines to engage in casual sex; now it is assumed in movies that any two people who feel warmly toward each other will sleep together. If parents bring their children to a popular romantic comedy like *While You Were Sleeping,* they will see a prolonged (and presumably humorous) reference to a missing testicle as well a number of sexual references. *The Truth About Cats and Dogs* has an extended phone-sex sequence. As delightful as these movies are, or, indeed, because they are so delightful, they can teach our kids lessons we do not want them to learn, especially if parents are uncomfortable discussing their own values.

Kids (and parents) often grab videos based on the titles or packaging, and the teens behind the video store counters are not much help. But just because the title or cast makes it appear to be acceptable does not mean that it is. Beware of movies like *Kindergarten Cop* (explicit violence, bedroom scene, and a genuinely kinky bad guy), *Problem Child* (crude and gross, and the sequel is even worse), *Killer Klowns From Outer Space* (violent and scary—the Klowns drink blood), the Ace Ventura movies (numerous sexual references), *Bebe's Kids* (animated but not for kids, very raunchy), and *The Good Son* (a thriller with Macaulay Culkin playing a murderous child). *The Brady Bunch Movie* may be based on a thoroughly G-rated television series, but the movie is rated PG-13 for innuendo. The Eddie Murphy version of *The Nutty Professor* is rated PG-13, and has very explicit sexual humor—for example: "Your mother is so fat that after I had sex with her, I rolled over twice and was still on top of her".

Nor is it safe to assume that you can't go wrong with a comedy. Movies made by Jim Carrey, the Zuckers (the *Airplane!* and *Naked Gun* movies) and Mel Brooks (*Robin Hood: Men in Tights*) and their "slob comedy" imitators are filled with raunchy and scatalogical references, and should be screened by parents before allowing kids to watch them.

Movie are often marketed to the broadest possible audience. Be careful of promotional tie-ins (like fast-food giveaways) designed for young children advertising movies that may not be appropriate for them. Big media conglomerates do a lot of cross-promotions that may be deceptive. For example, when *Clueless* was released, the company that produced it came out with a series of books directed at ten-to-thirteen-year-olds, who were much too young to see the movie. Television cartoons based on **The Mask** and **Beetlejuice** are directed at a much younger audience than the movies that inspired them.

Beware of knockoffs. Low-budget producers market videos in packaging designed to be easily confused with popular movies. A documentary about the Apollo 13 mission was repackaged to look like the Tom Hanks movie, and *Gordy* (the **bad** talking pig movie) was repackaged to look like **Babe** (the **good** talking pig movie). *Happily Ever After* was designed to look like a Disney sequel to **Snow White,** instead of the inferior Filmation Studios production that it is. Very often a dreadful movie that features a rising star in a walk-on will be repackaged to make it look as though he or she had the leading role. Read the box carefully before bringing it home.

That applies to quoted reviews as well. There are a number of critics who will give a rave to anything in order to publicize their names. Keep in mind that the box is like a commercial for the video, and read everything on it with a critical eye. But if you see *Parents' Choice award* or a good review from *Parents* magazine, you are almost certainly guaranteed a worthwhile film.

MOVIES ON TELEVISION—PROS AND CONS

It's almost always best to watch a movie in a theater. There is something about sitting there, in the dark, popcorn on your lap, that lets you give yourself to the movie in a way you cannot at home, with the laundry and the telephone close at hand. On television, scenes are cut, sound tracks are changed, and movies are almost always shown with the sides of the picture cut off, to fit the television screen. If you watch **Seven Brides for Seven Brothers** on television, you may only see five brothers dancing. (The rare exceptions are movies that are designated Letter-Box, shown with dark strips on the top and bottom to preserve the "aspect ratio" of the theatrical release.)

But there is one advantage to seeing movies on television. The Disney Channel and the broadcast networks will cut objectionable material before showing a film, and in some cases, this may make an otherwise acceptable film with one or two unacceptable scenes suitable for family viewing. Airlines do this as well, so be aware that a movie that was appropriate in any of these venues may be quite different if you rent or buy it at a video store.

WHAT CHILDREN LEARN FROM WHAT THEY WATCH

The main debate that rages about the effect of television and movie viewing on children revolves around what it teaches children about violence and sex. While this debate captures much of the attention, it is by no means the only question parents should think about when they consider what to allow their children to watch.

In fact, the debate can be made much simpler for parents when we move away from the cause-and-effect studies of violence and sex on the screen into a broader review of the impact of what kids watch. Violence and sex aside, television and movies provide characters that teach children about actions, motives, consequences, and character; overall, how to act in the adult world. In many ways, it has been shown that the characters a child meets on the screen simply become part of the "environment" in which he or she grows up, as powerful a character and role model as the people the child sees at home and in school.

A child's developmental capacity for abstraction is a crucial factor in appreciating his or her capacity to understand a movie. A related but separate factor is the child's capacity for moral reasoning. Jean Piaget discovered that children younger than eight or nine had trouble judging people on their intentions. Rather, when read hypothetical stories, younger children would judge people on the final outcome of their actions. One story concerned a boy who broke a cookie jar while helping his mother clean the kitchen. The other was about a boy who stole a cookie when his mother was not looking, but did not break the cookie jar. Before the developmental shift at around age eight or nine, children almost always saw the child who broke the cookie jar as the one who did something wrong. They were far less inclined to take into account a character's intentions than the ten- and eleven-year-olds were. Once children begin to understand motives and consequences, it is safer for them to see more sophisticated programs and movies.

The same susceptibility of children to the negative effects of television and movies means that, conversely, the right kind of material can have very positive effects on children. Programs like *Sesame Street, Barney & Friends, The Puzzle Place,* and *Mister Rogers' Neighborhood* have taught many children not just numbers and letters but also problem-solving, tolerance, and interpersonal skills. In one experiment to test *Mister Rogers'* effectiveness, preschool children were observed in a classroom for twelve days. They were observed for four days without television, four days during which they watched *Mister Rogers' Neighborhood* or another less positive show, and for four postviewing days. The children who watched *Mister Rogers' Neighborhood* were found to have significant increases in positive social behavior and in total social contacts, and the positive social behaviors were maintained during the follow-up days when the children were no longer viewing the program. As former Federal Communications Commissioner Nicholas Johnson said, "All television is educational. The only question is what we are learning from it."

SENSITIVITY TO GENDER AND DIVERSITY ISSUES

Social attitudes toward women and minorities have changed dramatically over the past few decades. Although I have tried to flag instances of sensitivity (or insensitivity) to issues of gender, race, religion, or nationality, I have not tried to judge movies made decades ago by today's standards. So, unless otherwise noted, it is fair to assume that any movie more than thirty years old will have a cast that is all white (and all physically able, and all of some undefined Christian religion) and that women (if any) will be relegated to the jobs of secretary, teacher, or nurse and will wait to be rescued by the hero.

I have, however, noted particularly troublesome dialogue or plot developments. For example, in the Shirley Temple movie, **Poor Little Rich Girl,** a black railroad porter is respectfully but stereotypically portrayed, and her father says, "That's white of you." In the Disney animated movie **Peter Pan** (originally released in 1953), the song "What Makes the Red Man Red" now seems embarrassingly racist and sexist. I have also pointed out movies that display sensitivity to these issues. The boxing classic **Body and Soul** is a rare example of a movie made before 1960 (indeed, it is rare in any movie of any era) that treats a black character with both equality and dignity. Even in that movie, however, he dies tragically.

For some reason, the films of the 1950s and early 1960s were far worse in terms of the portrayal of women than earlier movies, which featured dozens of feisty heroines played by Rosalind Russell, Bette Davis, Katharine Hepburn, Joan Crawford, and Barbara Stanwyck. I have noted dialogue or plot developments that seem especially egregious (e.g., "Girls can't do that;" or "You're so much smarter than I am"). The Women Worth Watching, chapter offers a more extended discussion of the issue of role models for adolescent girls and suggests ways to work with them to discern the messages in movies and find heroines they can be inspired by.

It is beyond the scope of this book to mention every moment in every movie that is insensitive to gender or diversity issues, or even racist or sexist. One of the reasons it is so important for parents to watch movies with their children is so that they can point out that in the days these movies were made (in our parents' childhoods, and even in our own), opportunities were very limited ("Look—there is not one kid in that classroom who is not white!"; "There isn't one woman doctor in that hospital—isn't that strange?"). It is absolutely essential to the development of a child's critical thinking skills—as well as to his or her tolerance and appreciation for diversity—that we challenge the portrayal of American life in the movies we watch and teach our children to challenge it as well.

A FEW WORDS ABOUT TASTE

Profanity and Obscene Language

If it were up to me, I would not want my children to see any movie that contains language I don't want them to use. Any parent knows it is much more difficult to teach children that certain words are not permitted in the house if you then show them a movie where even the good guys use those words.

Why is such language in the movies at all? The first reason is the one your mother always told you: lack of imagination. Even today, when we are less easily shocked, four-letter words provide an easy thrill. The second reason is more cynical: It sells tickets. A four-letter word is an easy way to get a PG or PG-13 rating, crucial for getting sixteen-year-olds to buy tickets for repeated showings. This point is addressed explicitly in the underrated *Last Action Hero,* where the young hero uses a magic ticket to step into the latest movie featuring his favorite star, played by Arnold Schwarzenegger. At one point, trying to convince the action hero that he is just a character in a movie, he shows him a piece of paper and asks him to say the word on it aloud. Schwarzenegger refuses. "You see?" the kid says triumphantly. "You can't say it, because this is a PG-13 movie!" The distributors of the lovely **Fly Away Home** literally insisted that a four-letter word be added so that the movie would avoid a G rating, telling the director that kids will not go to a G-rated movie except for a Disney cartoon.

A movie from a more innocent era that addresses the issue of profanity is the original **Angels in the Outfield** (1951). Baseball manager Paul Douglas cannot receive the help of the angels for his team unless he cleans up his behavior—and his language. His use of profanity is amusingly left to the imagination. He must find a whole new vocabulary for expressing his feelings about the acuteness of the umpire's vision, and he ends up using Shakespeare as a guide. In **A Christmas Story,** the little boy's father is described as an artist of profanity, but the actual words are muffled. When the boy himself uses one four-letter word (never spoken aloud), he is punished.

The fact is that most modern movies use language we do not permit in our homes. Even the adorable G-rated **Babe** uses the term "butt-head." Many movies reflect the modern tolerance for terms like "bullshit" and "damn," and many otherwise worthwhile movies contain even stronger language. Even more troubling is the use of nonprofane epithets to get around the ratings. For some reason, the traditional four-letter words relating to sex and excretory functions are factored into the ratings while insults like "vomit-breath" or "butt-head" are not, despite the fact that most families are no more comfortable with them than they are with the old favorites. I have done my best to alert parents to the type of language used in the movies in this book with "mild expletives" referring to the kind of language routinely heard in public ("damn"; "shit").

Although older movies do not contain these words, they often include words that are considered unacceptable in today's society—usually racial terms, and usually not intended to be demeaning or insulting. Katharine Hepburn refers to "darkie stories" in **Alice Adams,** and Ingrid Bergman calls Dooley Wilson "boy" before she asks him to "play it" in **Casablanca.** I have tried to alert parents about the use of these kinds of terms as well.

I find the best way to handle this issue is to tell my children that I think they are old enough to hear this language without imitating it, and that if I find out otherwise, I will stop letting them see movies until they are.

Alcohol and Drug Abuse

I am concerned about the way alcohol is used in movies. I am especially concerned about movies where people react to stress by reaching for a drink (for some reason, this is particularly prevalent in movies made in the 1950s and 1960s), or movies where people become drunk without any adverse consequences. If drunken behavior is portrayed as funny or even fun, I question whether the movie is appropriate for children. Illegal drug use without consequences can also make a movie inappropriate. In the case of an otherwise worthwhile movie like *Field of Dreams,* where there is a reference to past drug use, I have included the movie but alerted parents to the reference so they can make their own decision about its appropriateness and be prepared to discuss it if they decide that the movie is one they want their children to see. Some of the movies about teenagers include alcohol use; it is worthwhile for parents and teens to view these films together to share their views.

Sex and Sexual Behavior

When it comes to sex, I am more concerned with the values shown in the movies than I am with the body parts. It isn't that I am entirely comfortable with nudity in movies seen by children and teenagers; it is that I am far more uncomfortable with behavior that gives viewers a dangerously inaccurate idea about sex—especially casual sex—and its consequences. In an otherwise innocuous movie of the "slob comedy" genre, *Revenge of the Nerds,* there is some behavior that is deeply disturbing, especially since it is presented in a comic context. First, a group of unattractive girls are matched up with unattractive nerds, who happily have sex with the girls and then never see them again. Later in the movie, one of the male leads has sex with a campus beauty queen by wearing a mask so that she thinks he is her boyfriend. When she discovers she has been tricked, she is delighted. It turns out that the nerd is so much more expert a lover than her boyfriend that she immediately becomes his girlfriend.

All of this may seem trivial from an adult perspective. We are so thoroughly aware of the reality of sexual behavior and politics that it is almost impossible to understand what it is like to view this material from the more limited and literal perspective of a child or teen. I am not saying that a thirteen-year-old who sees this movie will inevitably conclude it is all right to trick a woman into having sex. But I do think a scene like this is incorporated in an adolescent's sexual values, influencing notions of what is appropriate.

Someone once said that well over 95 percent of the sex shown in movies is of people who are having sex with each other for the first time. I have no idea how this data was compiled, but it is very hard to think of a counter-example. The only one that comes to mind is the famous scene in *Don't Look Now,* legendary for its eroticism in part because it involves a couple who so clearly are deeply intimate and have profound knowledge of each other and a history together.

A Martian trying to understand American sexual behavior from a study of our movies would conclude that everybody has sex with everybody else, but only once, and that it is always magnificent that one time. In sexual terms, a child is a Martian. Thanks to the luxury of the latency period, children come upon the whole notion of sex overpoweringly as they enter adolescence. They may be able to recite the facts about where babies come from at age seven or eight, but that is a long way from being able to understand sexual desire, much less passion and the risks of intimacy. When a twelve-year-old says that she thinks you have a baby every time you have sex, it is not because she does not understand all of the factors that go into procreation; it is because she is still not quite sure why people would have sex other than to have babies. In the 1950s, girls were encouraged to seem to know less about sex than they really did; these days, they are encouraged to seem to know more. As shown in films like *Smooth Talk,* that can be very dangerous.

Today's children, tragically, learn about AIDS before they learn about sex. So often they are terrified of this powerful desire that makes people take such terrible risks and suffer such dire consequences. And when an eleven-year-old says that men can't have sex with each other because there is "no place to put it," he is not asking for a diagram; he is asking for some more time to grow up before dealing with the details.

Yet all around us, and especially in the movies, people seem to be having exciting, wonderful, completely fulfilling sex with each other all the time. This is a message that is hard for parents to compete with. Few even try, either because they don't know how or because they mistake superficial sexual precocity for genuine understanding.

A movie that might otherwise be fun for kids, like *The Cutting Edge,* begins with the leading man waking up with a woman whose name he does not quite recall. This is presented simply as evidence of his charming disorganization, like being late to the Olympic hockey match. Later, frustrated sexually and otherwise by his spoiled ice-skating partner, he goes off for a weekend with the specific goal (apparently successful) of having sex with anyone he can find. And this is portrayed sympathetically—what else should anyone expect? Because there are no bare breasts in this movie, it gets a PG rating. But I think this portrayal of sexuality is inappropriate for children, and even for teenagers. The often delightful *Clueless,* a huge hit among young teenagers, also has a disturbingly casual attitude toward sex. The heroine and her friend are virgins, but the friend airily explains that she takes care of her boyfriend's sexual needs in other ways. The heroine impulsively decides to have sex with a boy she has just met (ultimately she does not, because he is unwilling—because he is gay).

There are two movies that do attempt to portray teenage sex honestly. Despite the movies' considerable other limitations (like poor scripts and uneven performances), parents might want to watch them with their adolescents to begin a discussion of sexual values. In *Little Darlings,* summer campers Tatum O'Neal and Kristy McNichol make a bet over who will be the first to lose her virginity. It is a dreadful concept, and the movie is not very good. But the scene in which McNichol is reacting to her first sexual experience is very real. She says, "I feel so lonely," and, "God, it was so personal—like you could see right through me." She clearly regrets having been so casual about sex, and about herself. She later finds out that all of the girls at camp lied about being sexually experienced, because they were ashamed to tell the truth.

The other movie is *Fast Times at Ridgemont High,* loosely based on the real-life experiences of a young journalist who enrolled in high school, pretending to be a teenager. Like *Porky's* and other teenage sexual farces, the kids in this movie are obsessed by sex. But in *Fast Times,* as in *Little Darlings,* a girl (Jennifer Jason Leigh) is disappointed and embarrassed after her first sexual encounter. I do not recommend this movie, however. Parents should know that there is also a boy in the movie who is perpetually stoned (played by Sean Penn, one of many outstanding young actors who appear), and this is portrayed as kind of lovable and charming. And one of the other young girls in the movie (Phoebe Cates) is a sexual sophisticate, also portrayed as an admirable quality in a teenager.

Every generation insists that it faces an entirely new world that the previous generation cannot begin to understand. In this case, on this subject, they are right. When I was eleven, driving cross-country with my parents, we stopped in a small town that had one theater. I remember very well my parents asking the woman in the box office whether the movie *Island of Love* was okay for children, and I remember her answer: "It doesn't have anything you don't see in the papers." I asked my mother what that meant, and she said that sometimes newspaper ads showed girls in their underwear. The movie, a romantic farce, did have a character who became pregnant without being married (this was supposed to be funny), though it was presented so mildly that I did not realize it until I saw the movie again as an adult.

When I was in high school, I went to one of the smarmiest movies ever made (with my boyfriend's parents!), *The Impossible Years.* The entire plot revolved around a middle-aged psychology professor's obsession with whether his daughter had had sex with her hippie-ish boyfriend. There are two points to make about this miserable so-called comedy. First, she had not had sex with the boyfriend; at the end it turned out that instead she had had sex with the father's hip young colleague, but only after they secretly had gotten married. Second, to give you some idea of how it rates according to today's standards, this movie is rated G.

Today, movies about drag queens are considered suitable for all ages, and television sitcom reruns on during the "family hour" feature Peg Bundy's complaints and insults about her husband's sexual performance. Even shows designed for family viewing, like *Full House* and *The Nanny* depend on children's sexually precocious wisecracks for many of their laughs. Today's children know why Mike Tyson went to jail, how Magic Johnson got AIDS, what Michael Jackson was accused of, why Monica Lewinsky is on the cover of *Time* and *Newsweek* and that RuPaul is really a man. In the 1960s, episode after episode of *That Girl* reiterated that Ann Marie (Marlo Thomas) was saving herself for her wedding night. In today's television shows, fiction and nonfiction, it is a rare teenager who has not had sex, and in today's movies, every warm moment between a man and a woman is consummated sexually.

We used to watch *The Mickey Mouse Club* after school, while our moms gave us Twinkies and milk. Many of today's kids come home to empty houses and watch afternoon talk shows, where teenagers brag about how many people they have slept with. Or they turn on cable, or rent videos, or log online for even worse. Even *The New Mickey Mouse Club* has come a long way from the days of Annette and Spin and Marty: It looks like a Las Vegas extravaganza. Somewhere, in this sensory overload, we must help our children find values that will help them treat themselves and others with respect.

Violence and Gore

As with sexual references and alcohol, the issue of violence/gore is one of context. Seeing a man shot on a battlefield is entirely different from seeing the same man shot in his own home by a professional hit man, or seeing a child hit by an adult. Even the battlefield scene could be portrayed a number of different ways, depending on whether the man was on "our" side or the enemy's, and on whether the director and screenwriter were making an action movie or an antiwar movie.

And there are many different kinds of violence. Wile E. Coyote always emerges unscathed from his perpetual catastrophes. There are the guts-on-the-floor special effects of *Scream.* In "action" (i.e., cartoon-style) violence, many punches are thrown but no one gets seriously hurt. Someone may get shot, but we never see blood spurting from the wound. Movies like the *Home Alone* series distort the consequences of violence with wildly exaggerated "comic" bobbytraps that thwart the bad guys without real harm. By importing cartoon conventions to live action they make it seem more believable for children.

Individual family members of all ages will have different interests in and tolerance for violence. Many kids enjoy this kind of fantasy violence (and imitate it), but should be warned that it is just pretend. More disturbing are more explicit violence, unprovoked violence, violence with sadistic undertones, and violence directed toward children. Movies featuring this kind of violence are not included in this book. A few movies showing more realistic violence (like **Glory,** a Civil War movie) are included. One of the biggest problems caused by violence in films (and the "if it bleeds, it leads" school of local television news broadcasts) is the completely unrealistic picture of the world it creates. Surveys show that kids believe that the crime rate and especially the rate of violent crime is many times higher than it actually is. Make sure they compare what they see to the real statistics, and that they recognize the real consequences of violence.

HOW TO TALK TO CHILDREN AND TEENAGERS ABOUT MORALITY AND VALUES

The rules and goals you establish for your children—even basics like wearing seat belts, not going off with strangers, not taking drugs, not having promiscuous sex (or any sex outside of marriage, if those are your values)—have to be presented in a moral context or they have no meaning. And there is no more powerful teacher than your own behavior.

One way to set an example for your child is to be explicit in your own moral choices and the processes you use to evaluate them. "Oh, the clerk gave me too much change. I can't keep that. Let's go back and return it to her." Or, "Someone at work wants me to tell him something that I promised to keep secret, but of course I can't do that." Or, "One of our neighbors made a racist joke. I had to tell him I don't find that acceptable." Invite them to make the decisions with you. "I found this wallet on the street. What do you think I should do with it?"

Parents should also be explicit about views on the choices and behavior of others. "I'm glad that politician is going to jail. That's what he deserves for taking that bribe." Or, "I have never felt the same about that man since he told me how he cheated on his taxes." Or, "I don't respect the way she treats her husband, criticizing him in front of other people." Or, "That man spends a lot of money on his boat, but never gives a penny to charity." Or, "I hated seeing that kid smoking cigarettes. What a stupid choice." You do not need to send a message that violation of the rules makes someone a bad person; but it does mean that violation of the rules is a bad moral choice. Explain the ways you evaluate the political candidates, what you like and respect about your friends, family, and colleagues, what you are proud of in your own life, and how you decide which issues are most important to you. And there is nothing that makes more of an impression on a child than hearing (or overhearing) you telling someone else about something they did right.

Movies illustrate every possible kind of choice and lesson that can be imagined. They show us characters resolving conflicts about money, love, work, community, and friendship. Again, it helps to provide a context for discussion of these issues if parents are explicit about their own choices ("I could make more money in that job, but it would take too much time away from the family"), the choices of others ("I really respect the way she has gone back to school because she loves learning new things"), and the choices of the people on the screen ("Why do you think Robin Hood decided to oppose Prince John? Why did the other nobles decide to support him?").

Now, let's go to the movies!

Part 1

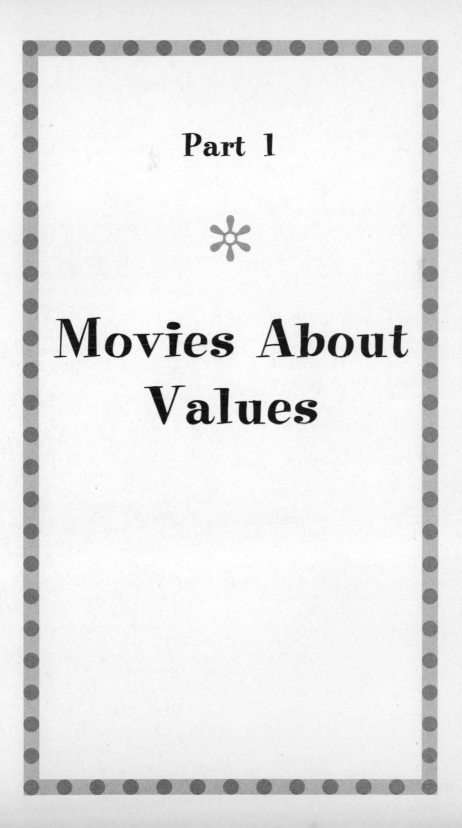

Movies About Values

DUTY AND
RESPONSIBILITY

"Duty is a very personal thing. It is what comes from knowing the need to take action and not just a need to urge others to do something."

—MOTHER TERESA, OF CALCUTTA

These days, there is a lot of emphasis on doing whatever makes us feel good and a reluctance to tell others what their obligations are, which makes duty a rather neglected virtue. These movies give us examples of thoughtful people making principled choices, contrary to their own pleasure, because of a sense of responsibility to others.

It's a Wonderful Life
1946, 129 min, NR, b&w, 10 and up
Dir: Frank Capra. Jimmy Stewart, Donna Reed, Lionel Barrymore, Henry Travers

❋ **PLOT:** George Bailey (Jimmy Stewart) has had a tough time. All he ever wanted was to leave his hometown of Bedford Falls and his family's business, the Bailey Building and Loan, to travel the world free of responsibility. But he has stayed on, and it has become too much for him. Everything he has worked for is about to unravel, and he is thinking about suicide.

Clarence, his guardian angel (Henry Travers), materializes and reviews George's life up to that moment. Growing up, George was a good boy who prevented the pharmacist, distraught over the death of his son, from sending the wrong medication, which would have killed the patient. But before the pharmacist understood what he was doing, he boxed George's ear, leaving him hearing-impaired. George saved his brother, Harry, in a sledding accident. He gave up his dream trip so his father could use that money to send Harry to college. Harry becomes a war hero, but George stays at home, ineligible to serve because of his deaf ear. After their father dies, George runs the Bailey Building and Loan, waiting for Harry to come home. When the Building and Loan is in trouble, George uses the money for his honeymoon to save it. Harry gets another job, and George stays on. But George's foolish Uncle Willy has lost several thousand dollars of the company's money, and it looks like the business will have to be taken over by the wicked Mr. Potter (Lionel Barrymore), who cares only about money and power.

Clarence, afraid George might jump into the river, jumps himself, and George jumps in to rescue him. When George says he wishes he had never been born, Clarence shows him what Bedford Falls would have been like without him. The pharmacist would have become a vagrant after losing his job for poisoning someone with the wrong medication. Harry would have died—and so would all of the sailors he saved during the war. George's wife, Mary (Donna Reed), would have become a terrified and lonely woman. And Potter would own the town.

George sees that he has had a wonderful life after all. He races home to his family, where the whole town has gathered to replace the missing money and remind him that he's the richest man they know.

✻ **DISCUSSION:** The head of production at RKO Studios found the story of this movie in a Christmas card and had it made into a script. Of all the films they worked on, this perennial Christmas classic was the favorite of both its star, Jimmy Stewart, and its director, Frank Capra. For both of them, it was their first movie following service in WWII, and it said much about what they had been fighting for.

It features not only the famous "Capra-corn," (Capra's own term for his sentimental stories) but also Capra's other trademark: vivid character portraits from the bit players. In the scene where the people are taking their money out of the building and loan, Ellen Corby (later, Grandma Walton on the TV series) almost gives you the story of her life in the way she asks whether she can take just what she needs.

It is very difficult to know how far our duty extends to those around us. Today George would be called an "enabler" because of the way he keeps his alcoholic uncle on the payroll. But George keeps taking care of everyone because he knows that he is the only one who can do it.

It is a very healthy exercise for each of us to think about what we would see if someone were to show us the effect we have had on those around us. George is far from perfect. He is angry, even bitter, at not being able to follow his dream. He is not able to share his fear of not being able to keep it all together for his family. It keeps him alone, no matter how loving and devoted his family. This may be why suicide seems an option for him. Like George, we would all like to have our contributions recognized. This movie reminds us that we would all like to have made contributions worthy of this recognition.

PROFANITY: None.

NUDITY/SEXUAL REFERENCES: Oblique references to Violet as something of a party girl; Mary stuck in the bushes without clothes.

ALCOHOL/DRUG ABUSE: Uncle Willy has a drinking problem.

VIOLENCE/SCARINESS: George contemplates suicide; George is hit by pharmacist.

TOLERANCE/DIVERSITY ISSUES: Without George, Mary is portrayed as a skittish spinster.

✳ **QUESTIONS FOR KIDS:**
- Why does George seem mad at Mary when they are on the phone with Sam?
- Why does George stay in Bedford Falls?
- Why doesn't George insist that Harry keep his promise?
- Why does Mr. Potter want to destroy George's business?

✳ **CONNECTIONS:** This movie has become a touchstone of American culture. Almost everyone recognizes "Every time a bell rings, an angel gets his wings." A literary newsletter is called *Zuzu's Petals* in honor of the flower petals from his daughter that George finds in his pocket, confirming that he is back in the Bedford Falls he knows. The creators of *Sesame Street* say that the names "Bert and Ernie" do not come from this film, but one can't help wondering if those two wonderful characters didn't have some subliminal impact.

✳The Pirates of Penzance
1983, 112 min, G, 6 and up
Dir: Wilford Leach. Kevin Kline, Linda Ronstadt, Angela Lansbury

✳ **PLOT:** This is the Gilbert and Sullivan operetta about Frederic (Rex Smith), the "slave of duty." Mistakenly indentured to pirates as a child (his nanny, Ruth, having misunderstood when his parents asked that he be apprenticed to a pilot), he parts from his pirate friends on his twenty-first birthday, noting regretfully that his honor and sense of duty will now require him to devote his life to vanquishing them.

   No sooner is he taken in by Mabel (Linda Ronstadt), the ward of a "very model" Major General (George Rose), than he finds to his horror that he has not yet reached the age of majority. Because he was born on February twenty-ninth, he has lived twenty-one years, but has had only five birthdays. He must remain a pirate until he has celebrated twenty-one birthdays, which will not occur until he is eighty-four. Therefore it is his duty to remain a pirate. Meanwhile, according to Mabel, it is the duty of the local constabulary to go fight the pirates, even though they are likely to be killed. Despite all of this duty, and despite the tenderhearted pirates' unwillingness to fight anyone who is weaker than they are, or anyone who is an orphan (or claims to be), after some glorious musical numbers, all is happily resolved.

✳ **DISCUSSION:** Even young children can become big fans of Gilbert and Sullivan's delicious humor and gorgeous melodies, but it may take some preparation. Play the music for them a few times before you watch the movie (most public libraries have the music on tapes or CDs) and tell them the main outline of the plot to prepare them. Explain that it was the custom in those days to apprentice children so that they had to work until they turned twenty-one, as portrayed more dramatically in **Johnny Tremain** and **Oliver!**. And make sure they understand that Gilbert and Sullivan enjoyed making fun of some of the silly things they saw going on around them.

This movie can provide the basis for a gentle inquiry into the issue of duty. Frederic is torn between two duties: one to the pirates, to whom he owes his energies until he reaches the age of majority (and for whom he has great affection), and one to his sense of honor, which is opposed to their violation of the law. What should he do?

PROFANITY: None.

NUDITY/SEXUAL REFERENCES: None.

ALCOHOL/DRUG ABUSE: None.

VIOLENCE/SCARINESS: None.

TOLERANCE/DIVERSITY ISSUES: None.

✳ **QUESTIONS FOR KIDS:**
- Do you remember the last leap year? When is the next leap year? Why do we have a leap year? Would you like to have your birthday on February twenty-ninth?
- How do the Pirate King and the Major General figure out their misunderstanding about the word "orphan"?
- Why is Frederic called "a slave of duty"? How does he decide what his duty is? What about the policemen? What do they think their duty is? Why do they keep singing that they are going, and then not go?
- Can you sing as fast as the Major General?

✳ **CONNECTIONS:** Note Angela Lansbury (of **National Velvet** and TV's *Murder, She Wrote*) as Ruth. Kids might also like to listen to the music of Linda Ronstadt, who plays Mabel, especially her wonderful CD for children, *Dedicated to the One I Love*. There is a rather odd but engaging video of *The Mikado*, featuring Eric Idle of Monty Python, that kids might enjoy.

✳ **ACTIVITIES:** Most communities have live productions of Gilbert and Sullivan plays in schools or local theaters. Try to find one (especially *The Mikado* or *H.M.S. Pinafore*) and take the children to it (prepare them by playing the music for them first). Have them try to write a song about what they are proudest of about themselves, like the Major General does.

✳Roman Holiday

1953, 119 min, NR, b&w, 8 and up
Dir: William Wyler. Audrey Hepburn, Gregory Peck, Eddie Albert

✳ **PLOT:** Princess Anne (Audrey Hepburn) stops in Rome in the middle of an exhausting goodwill tour. Overcome with the restrictions that govern every moment of her life, she becomes very upset and says she cannot stand it anymore. She is given something to help her sleep, but as soon as her guardians leave, she slips out of the hotel to wander around on her own. She falls asleep and is found by Joe (Gregory Peck), a reporter about to lose his job. At first he does not recognize her, but when he realizes who she is, he knows that the story of her escapade would save his job and make his career. He arranges for his photographer friend, Irving (Eddie Albert), to come along as they explore the city. They have a wonderful time, but as they begin to fall in love, Anne realizes she must go back, and Joe realizes he cannot betray her by writing the story.

The next morning, as she appears before a large group of reporters, he hands her an envelope containing all of Irving's pictures of their day together, and she departs from her careful diplomacy to say that Rome was her favorite city on the tour.

✳ **DISCUSSION:** The movie seems almost quaint—neither journalists nor princesses behave this way anymore. In addition to the many delights of its story and its stars (Audrey Hepburn's luminous appearance in her first major role won an Oscar), this movie provides an opportunity for a discussion of duty, loyalty, and priorities.

PROFANITY: None.
NUDITY/SEXUAL REFERENCES: None.
ALCOHOL/DRUG ABUSE: None.
VIOLENCE/SCARINESS: A minor scuffle.
TOLERANCE/DIVERSITY ISSUES: None.

✳ **QUESTIONS FOR KIDS:**
• Why was it so important that Anne behave so strictly?
• What made Joe change his mind about the story?
• What made Anne go back?
• When Anne has a chance for freedom, she first eats ice cream and has her hair cut. What would you do?

✳ **CONNECTIONS:** Fleeing a life that is pampered yet restrictive is a popular theme in movies, possibly because we are reassured to see that people of wealth and position are not as "free" as we are. In his autobiography, director Frank Capra said it was this theme that led to the success of *It Happened One Night.* The character played by Claudette Colbert was just a spoiled rich girl in the original story. But by changing the script to have her run away from an overly protective father because she is longing for a taste of real life, Capra made her sympathetic not just to traveling companion Clark Gable, but also to the audience. Teenagers and their parents might be interested to know that the story for *Roman Holiday* is credited to Ian McLellan Hunter, who won an Oscar for it. He was actually a "front" for distinguished writer Dalton Trumbo, blacklisted from Hollywood during the McCarthy era, who won another Oscar for *The Brave One* screenplay written under a pseudonym during this period. John Dighton and Ben Hecht (uncredited) also worked on the screenplay.

☀ A Thousand Clowns

1965, 118 min, NR, b&w, high schoolers
Dir: Fred Coe. Jason Robards, Barbara Harris, Martin Balsam, William Daniels,
Barry Gordon

✳ **PLOT:** Murray Burns (Jason Robards) is a free spirit, whimsical and spontaneous. He has quit his job as a writer for a silly kids' television show; in fact, he has quit the entire world of work and spends his days making wisecracks and doing whatever strikes him at the moment. His twelve-year-old nephew, Nick (Barry Gordon), reads him the want ads and tries to persuade him to go back to work, but Murray sees work as hypocritical and soul-destroying. Murray has taken care of Nick since he was five, and they love each other very deeply, though Murray's parenting style is so casual that the child does not even have a name. "Nick" is just the most recent of the dozens of names he has tried out over the years.

Two social workers visit Murray, explaining that they are evaluating him to determine whether he is providing a suitable home for Nick. Albert Amundson (William Daniels) is stiff and formal, but Sandy Markowitz (Barbara Harris) is very warm and sympathetic. When she and Albert argue over the case, he dismisses her and leaves. It turns out she and Albert were engaged, and she is very upset about the collapse of both her personal and professional plans. Murray cheers her up, they go out together to enjoy some of his favorite haunts, and she spends the night.

The next day, Sandy explains that Murray has to get a job immediately if he wants to keep Nick. His brother, Arnold (Martin Balsam), arranges for some interviews. Meanwhile, Sandy is redecorating the apartment, getting rid of the odd knickknacks and putting up chintz curtains.

Murray cannot bring himself to accept any of the jobs. Nick, Arnold, and Sandy are all deeply disappointed that Murray has failed. When Murray's former boss, the demanding Leo of the Chuckles the Clown show (Gene Saks), comes to offer Murray his old job, Nick begs him not to accept, because it is a humiliating return to everything he hates. Murray takes the job.

✳ **DISCUSSION:** Murray, like everyone else, must find a way to balance the need for compromise with the importance of personal integrity. Teenagers identify readily with Murray because he has an adolescent's easy contempt for the hypocrisy and burdens of society, and especially for having to deal with those who accept those burdens and are therefore lacking in wit, or sensitivity, or appreciation of irony. When asked to return to reality, he replies, "I'll only go as a tourist." He also appeals because as an adult, he has no parents to make him conform.

But in addition to its wit and the appeal of its characters, one of this movie's strengths is the way it shows that a certain amount of compromise is necessary to have the things that matter most to us. Murray could decide never to work again and spend all of his days playing the banjo and watching ocean liners depart—if he is willing to lose Nick. When he realizes how much he needs Nick, he realizes he will do whatever is necessary to keep him.

Murray describes Nick as a "forty-year-old midget named Max." Nick has had to become precociously mature. (Gordon's exceptional performance shows us the child inside the precocity.) The fact is that no one avoids responsibility without imposing its costs on someone else. This is another reason for Murray to change.

The other great strength of the movie is the way it presents all of the points of view and all of the characters with sympathy. Albert easily could have been a stock character created simply to act as a straight man for Murray's "I am much more hip and sensitive than you will ever be" humor. But in a deeply affecting moment, Albert confesses he regrets that he is not "one of the warm people," and envies Murray's ability to be so relaxed and likable. Leo is certainly obnoxiously needy and self-absorbed, but insecure and clearly also envious of Murray's self-assurance.

Murray's brother, Arnold, understands his responsibility to himself and his family to mean that he has had to give up some of the wild anarchy of his youth. He responds to Murray's criticism by explaining that he does not have the luxury of that life anymore, and that he feels good about the choices he has made, and about his "talent for surrender." It isn't that he is less sensitive than Murray, less aware of the "quiet desperation" of the working world; it is that he realizes that accepting and coping with that world is what he has to do.

PROFANITY: None.

NUDITY/SEXUAL REFERENCES: Murray and Sandy spend the night together the day they meet (and have an awkward conversation the next morning); it is clear that Murray does this often, as Nick has a routine for packing his things and going somewhere else to sleep. Nick has a "doll" whose breasts ("boobies") light up. Discussion of Nick's illegitimacy, and his mother's promiscuity.

ALCOHOL/DRUG ABUSE: None.

VIOLENCE/SCARINESS: None.

TOLERANCE/DIVERSITY ISSUES: Issues of tolerance of those with different outlooks. Sandy sees her role in the relationship in very traditional terms. When Murray fails to get a job, her reaction centers on what it says about his feelings for her rather than about its importance to Murray and Nick ("That means I have had no effect on you at all!").

✳ **QUESTIONS FOR KIDS:**
- What can you tell about Nick from the names he has picked?
- What do you think about what Albert said about not being "one of the warm people"? How do you get to be "one of the warm people"?

- What did Arnold mean about the "talent for surrender"?
- Would you like to live with someone like Murray? Why?
- Do you agree with Murray's decision to go back to work for Leo?

✳ **CONNECTIONS:** The theme of responsibility for those who depend on you is explored in a different context in *To Have and Have Not,* as Humphrey Bogart claims to have no strings but finds himself tied to sidekick Walter Brennan. In that movie, acknowledging that sense of connection enables him to develop a relationship with Lauren Bacall and also find a sense of connection to his community, and therefore a willingness to fight to protect it. It is also a part of *The Magnificent Seven,* when O'Reilly tells the boys that their fathers are braver than he is.

Martin Balsam won an Oscar for his performance as Arnold Burns. You can see William Daniels as the "obnoxious and disliked" John Adams in *1776.* He also appeared in the television program *St. Elsewhere* and as the voice of KITT the car in the television series *Knight Rider.*

✳ THE PRISONER OF ZENDA

1952, 101 min, NR, 8 and up
Dir: Richard Thorpe. Stewart Granger, Deborah Kerr

Rudolf Rassendyll, a dashing Englishman who looks just like the king of a small European country (he is a distant relative), takes the king's place to foil an assassination attempt. Stewart Granger plays both the king and his cousin, and Deborah Kerr plays the beautiful Princess Flavia, who is engaged to the king. She and Rassendyll fall deeply in love, and for a moment they consider his staying on as king or her leaving with him. But they know that duty requires them to part, and they do, knowing that their love will always connect them, even though they will never see each other again.

SEE ALSO:

Casablanca At first, Rick says, "I stick my neck out for nobody." But he later becomes someone who believes that his problems do not "amount to a hill of beans" in comparison to the importance of working to fight facism, and he ends up sticking his neck out quite a lot.

Judgment at Nuremberg This movie, and the real-life trials that inspired it, pose this question: When orders from your superior are fundamentally immoral, and failure to follow orders risks death for you and your family, what is your duty?

Now, Voyager Two people who love each other deeply resolve to stay apart because it is best for a child they both love.

HONESTY AND
INTEGRITY

"An honest man's the noblest work of God."
—ALEXANDER POPE

Even though most movies feature at least one character telling at least one lie, it is hard to find a good illustration of the importance of honesty. One of the most popular movie plots has a character tell a lie, then fall in love with the person he/she lied to, then deal with the problem of telling the truth without losing the trust of the person he/she loves. Usually the loved one finds out the truth just as our hero/heroine was about to come clean, and it takes the third act of the movie to straighten it all out in time for the big clinch. This is a popular dramatic (and comic) structure because allowing the audience to know something a character does not know automatically provides a lot of narrative energy and audience interest.

But this classic plotline is not so much about telling the truth as it is about issues of intimacy, the lie merely a metaphor for the overarching issue of the conflicts we face in wanting to be known and loved for our true selves but being wary of the risk. We ask ourselves: "What if I do let him/her know me and he/she rejects me? Maybe it's better if they just reject this false image I put up to protect myself instead." Although these stories may enable parents to begin to discuss the importance of honesty, they do not really address the central issue of integrity.

The movies in this chapter present those issues more directly. Of course, the classic is *Pinocchio.* For over a century its unforgettable graphic depiction has aided parents in talking to very young children about the importance of telling the truth. In *These Three,* an impetuous lie told by a young girl destroys the lives of her teachers and her own grandmother. In those movies, a child and a puppet lie to protect him/herself from getting in trouble. In *The Fallen Idol,* one of the tensest suspense dramas of all time, a child innocently lies to protect his dearest friend, only to get him more deeply into trouble. These films illustrate the incentives for—and the consequences of—dishonesty.

Some movies give us heroes who illustrate the importance of integrity by insisting on telling the truth, even under the worst kind of pressure to lie. In *Citizen Kane,* Jedediah gives up his job and his lifelong friend by telling the truth about Susan's poor performance in his review. In *Mr. Smith Goes to Washington,* Jefferson Smith tells the truth until his voice gives out, and his honesty so shames Senator Paine that he admits his corruption. Laura Partridge in *The Solid Gold Cadillac* topples the management of a major corporation by telling the truth to the shareholders. In *The Nasty Girl,* based on a true story, a young German woman insists on uncovering the truth about her community's complicity with the Nazis during World War II, despite the most horrible reprisals. These provide a basis for a discussion of the challenge of integrity, and the risks and consequences of failing to attain it. And movies like *The Man Who Shot Liberty Valance* and *Keeper of the Flame* require us to think about what happens "when the legend becomes the fact (*The Man Who Shot Liberty Valance*)," and it seems that it may be best for people to believe something that may not be true.

*The Man Who Shot Liberty Valance

1962, 123 min, NR, b&w, 10 and up
Dir: John Ford. John Wayne, Jimmy Stewart, Lee Marvin, Vera Miles

✳ **PLOT:** An aging and distinguished senator, Ransom Stoddard (Jimmy Stewart), returns to the sleepy Western town of Shinbone to attend the funeral of an old friend, Tom Donathan (John Wayne). In a flashback, Senator Stoddard recounts the early days of the Wild West when Shinbone was new and Stoddard first came to town as a young lawyer. There, he met Donathan—a tough, two-fisted, sharp-shooting wrangler. Stoddard and Donathan have very different views about how to tame the West. Stoddard sets out to practice law and teach classes, while Donathan runs a ranch outside of town. In particular, the two differ about how to deal with the vile and depraved criminal, Liberty Valance (Lee Marvin), who terrorizes the town.

Both men's beliefs are sorely tested. Stoddard, who believes in nonviolence, education, and the rule of law, buys a gun to face Liberty Valance in the street. Donathan, the only man in town bigger and tougher than Liberty Valance, finds that the old ways of doing things will no longer work as civilization comes to Shinbone. There are no easy answers and a number of surprises as Stoddard and Donathan fight Liberty Valance, clash among themselves, and compete for the affections of the beautiful waitress Halley (Vera Miles).

✳ **DISCUSSION:** This movie has enough gunfire, excitement, and humor to hold restless young viewers spellbound. Yet, in a very accessible and relevant way, it deals with problems of identity and civilian courage: When Liberty Valance challenges Stoddard to a gunfight on Main Street, should Stoddard leave town or defend his beliefs with a gun? Where do you turn when the town marshal responsible for law and order is a bumbling oaf who lives in fear of the criminals? Stoddard believes that "education is the basis for law and order," and holds classes trying to teach cowboys to read and write, but Donathan maintains (with some justification) that "when force threatens, talk is no good anymore." Stoddard and Donathan embody different notions of what it means to be a man; Stoddard wears an apron and waits on tables to pay for his room and board until he is humiliated by Liberty Valance. Donathan steps in and protects Stoddard in one of the great "tough guy" confrontation scenes of Western films. Yet, Stoddard manages to salvage his own dignity and masculinity with his pacifism.

The struggle between Stoddard and Donathan is played out against a backdrop of the same, larger struggle for the soul of the country. As towns become more settled and the structures required to support them become more complex, law and order grapples with the Wild West, cattle barons clash with farmers, and statehood advocates clash with those supporting open territory. Early elections are portrayed with humor and insight, but underneath it all remains Donathan's deadly serious admonition: "votes won't stand up against guns."

A parallel struggle takes place in the competition for the affections of Halley. When Donathan gives her a cactus rose, Stoddard asks whether she has ever seen a "real rose." Stoddard offers her reading and writing and exposure to the larger world outside. Donathan offers her rough love in the Wild West, where her roots and heart are. Which one will she choose? And will she come to regret it?

PROFANITY: None.

NUDITY/SEXUAL REFERENCES: None.

ALCOHOL/DRUG ABUSE: The editor of the town newspaper is a drunk who gives long speeches when inebriated. Several scenes in saloons.

VIOLENCE/SCARINESS: In addition to standard gunfight scenes, younger children might be frightened by two or three short scenes in which Liberty Valance demonstrates his vicious nature by beating up innocent people.

TOLERANCE/DIVERSITY ISSUES: Donathan has a black ranch hand whom he treats well but refers to as "my boy, Pompy." In Stoddard's classroom, he calls on Pompy to explain Thomas Jefferson's lines about all men being created equal. In a bar, the bartender tries to refuse service to Pompy and incurs Donathan's wrath.

✳ **QUESTIONS FOR KIDS:**
• Who was a greater force for good, Donathan or Stoddard? Or are both kinds of people necessary?

- Who ended up happier? Who was more successful, and why?
- Why did it matter who was the one who shot Liberty Valance?
- In light of its title, who was the movie about?
- Did Halley make the right choice? Did she think so?
- What do you think the editor meant when he said, "When the legend becomes the fact, print the legend"? How does that relate to how the director has portrayed the characters?

✷ **CONNECTIONS:** There is an excellent documentary about director John Ford, called *The Man Who Shot The Man Who Shot Liberty Valance*. Ford was the great cinematic poet of the West, and his movies *She Wore a Yellow Ribbon*, **Stagecoach,** and **The Searchers** helped to define the American image of the West and of the American spirit.

✷Pinocchio

1940, 88 min, NR, 6 and up
Dir: Ben Sharpsteen, Hamilton Luske. Voices of Dickie Jones, Cliff Edwards

✷ **PLOT:** Gepetto is a wood-carver who lives with his cat, Figaro, and his fish, Cleo, and dreams of having a child of his own to love. When he wishes on a star, the Blue Fairy comes to his workshop to make his little wooden puppet come to life. She tells the puppet, Pinocchio, that if he can prove himself brave, unselfish, and able to tell right from wrong, he will become a real, live boy. She appoints Jiminy Cricket as his conscience.

Gepetto is overjoyed with Pinocchio. The next day, on the way to school, Pinocchio meets con men Honest John and Gideon, who promise Pinocchio fame and fortune on the stage. He ignores Jiminy's warning and goes with them. They sell Pinocchio to the evil Stromboli, who puts Pinocchio in his puppet show and locks him in a cage. The Blue Fairy finds him and asks for an explanation, and as he lies to her, his wooden nose grows longer and longer. She helps him escape and tells him to do better.

But Pinocchio listens to Honest John again and goes to Pleasure Island, where boys can do anything they like. The boys behave so foolishly that they turn into donkeys and are sold. Pinocchio grows a donkey's ears and tail, but Jiminy rescues him before the transformation is complete. They go back to Gepetto's workshop only to find that Gepetto has gone to search for them and has been swallowed by Monstro the whale. Pinocchio and Jiminy go to rescue Gepetto and are swallowed by Monstro, too. Inside the great whale they light a fire, causing Monstro to sneeze them out. They get away, but Monstro follows, smashing their raft. Pinocchio saves Gepetto, at the cost of his own life. Back in the workshop, the Blue Fairy arrives, saying that Pinocchio has proved himself worthy and can now be a real boy. And for Jiminy there is a gold badge that reads OFFICIAL CONSCIENCE.

✷ **DISCUSSION:** This is the most gorgeous, splendid, and fully realized of all of the Disney animated films, the high point of painstakingly hand-painted animation, before the use of photocopiers and computers. Every detail is brilliantly executed, from the intricate clocks in Gepetto's workshop to the foam on the waves as Monstro thrashes the water. It also has one of Disney's finest scores, featuring "When You Wish Upon a Star," which has become the Disney theme song. "I've Got No Strings," "Give a Little Whistle," and "An Actor's Life for Me" are also memorable.

Pinocchio is a natural for the first discussions with kids about telling the truth (especially admitting a mistake) and not talking to strangers. Talk to them, too, about how to find their own conscience and listen to it as if it were Jiminy Cricket. The trip to Pleasure Island may also lead to a discussion of why things that feel like fun may be harmful, and the difference between fun and happiness.

PROFANITY: None.

NUDITY/SEXUAL REFERENCES: None.

ALCOHOL/DRUG ABUSE: The boys smoke cigars and drink on Pleasure Island.

VIOLENCE/SCARINESS: The scenes with Monstro are scary.

TOLERANCE/DIVERSITY ISSUES: None.

✳ **QUESTIONS FOR KIDS:**
- Why does Pinocchio listen to Honest John and Gideon?
- Why does Lampwick turn into a donkey before Pinocchio does?
- If you were going to wish upon a star, what would you wish?

✳ **CONNECTIONS:** The *Faerie Tale Theater* version of the story is also worth seeing. The idea of "becoming real" is also the theme of the classic children's story, *The Velveteen Rabbit*, which is read by Meryl Streep in the Rabbit Ears production. The book, by Carlo Collodi, is also worthwhile.

These Three
1936, 93 min, NR, b&w, 12 and up
Dir: William Wyler. Miriam Hopkins, Merle Oberon, Joel McCrea

✳ **PLOT:** Martha Dobie (Miriam Hopkins) and Karen Wright (Merle Oberon) are close friends who run a girls' school with the help of Martha's foolish and pretentious Aunt Lily. One of the students, Mary Tilford (Bonita Granville), is selfish and cruel. To protect herself from being disciplined, she tells her grandmother that she saw Martha in a compromising position with Dr. Joseph Cardin (Joel McCrea), Karen's fiancé. Mary blackmails another girl, Rosalie Wells, into supporting her story. Mary's grandmother withdraws her from the school and informs the other parents that it is an improper environment. The school is ruined. Martha and Karen try to bring a libel action, but they lose. Too late, Mrs. Tilford finds out that Mary lied. She goes to see Martha and Karen to offer to pay any damages they will accept and to offer her humblest apologies, but Martha and Karen know that nothing anyone can do can make up for all they have lost.

✳ **DISCUSSION:** There is no better depiction of the destructiveness of a lie than this movie. A selfish and impetuous girl tells a lie to distract attention from her own transgressions and ruins the lives of at least four people: Martha, Karen, Joe, and her own grandmother. Kids find this movie especially interesting because it takes place in a school and the chief villain is a child, who is responsible for the downfall of all of the powerful adults in her life. It also presents an interesting ethical dilemma for Rosalie, who does not want to lie but who feels that she must to protect herself from getting in trouble for stealing a bracelet. The impact of the lie on Martha and Karen, not only in the way they see the world but in the way they see each other and Joe, is depicted with insight and sensitivity.

An interesting element of the story is that the lie reveals an underlying truth. Martha is in love with Joe, as revealed in a very moving scene in which the exhausted doctor falls asleep while they are talking, and she allows her feelings for him to show while he cannot be aware of them. Mary's ability to manipulate others suggests that she was aware of the vulnerability created by this undercurrent of feeling when she decided on this particular lie to tell.

PROFANITY: None.

NUDITY/SEXUAL REFERENCES: Mary's charge that Joe and Martha were sexually intimate is considered shocking in a way hard to understand for today's kids.

ALCOHOL/DRUG ABUSE: None.

VIOLENCE/SCARINESS: None.

TOLERANCE/DIVERSITY ISSUES: None.

✳ **QUESTIONS FOR KIDS:**
- Why did Mary tell the lie? Why did Rosalie?
- How did the lie make Karen and Martha feel differently about each other? About Joe?
- What should Mrs. Tilford do for Karen and Martha when she finds out that Mary lied?
- How should Mary be punished?
- In most movies, the person who does something wrong feels bad about it by the end of the movie. That is not the case in this movie. Why?

✳ **CONNECTIONS:** Lillian Hellman adapted her play *The Children's Hour* for the screen, making one major change. In the play, Mary's charge was that Martha and Karen were lesbians. This was considered much too shocking for the movies in 1936, so it was changed to an allegation of heterosexual sex between two people who were unmarried. The same director did a remake in 1961 restoring the original plot. Despite fine performances by Audrey Hepburn, Shirley MacLaine, Fay Bainter (nominated for an Oscar as Mrs.

Tilford), James Garner, and Miriam Hopkins (the original Martha) as Aunt Lily, it is heavy-handed and not as effective as the original. Oddly, today that version seems even more dated than the first, due to increased openness about homosexuality. Parents also should know that the remake has a much more somber ending, with Martha committing suicide and Joe and Karen splitting up.

Older kids may want to see another movie based on one of Hellman's plays, *The Little Foxes,* in which family members lie, scheme, steal, and worse. They may also want to read Hellman's memoirs, *Pentimento* (which provided the basis for the movie *Julia*) and *Scoundrel Time.* In light of the theme of these three, it is interesting to examine the charges that Hellman lied in these supposed works of nonfiction, most memorably by Mary McCarthy, who said that "every word is a lie, including the 'ands' and the 'thes.' "

✳ THE FALLEN IDOL
1948, 94 min, NR, b&w, 12 and up
Dir: Carol Reed. Ralph Richardson, Bobby Henrey
This tense thriller is about a young boy, the son of the French ambassador to England, whose only friend is the family's butler, Baines (Ralph Richardson). The boy adores Baines and only dimly understands that Baines is in love with a woman other than his shrewish wife. When the wife is accidentally killed, however, the boy, projecting his own dislike and fear of Mrs. Baines, believes Baines must have been responsible. He lies to protect Baines, but inadvertently implicates him instead, and when he tells the truth, no one listens to him.

✳ THE NASTY GIRL
1990, 92 min, PG-13, subtitled, mature high schoolers
Dir: Michael Verhoeven. Lena Stolze
This German movie is the true story of a young girl who, inspired by a prize for her historical essay, decided to write another, called "My Hometown in the Third Reich." She expected to find evidence of her community's resistance to the Nazis, as she had always been told. But, as she examined the evidence, she learned that, on the contrary, people in her community, many still there in prominent positions, had aided Hitler. Despite every effort to stop her, interfering with her ability to get the records of the era from the library, threats, harassment, and even assault of the young woman and her family, she spent ten years documenting the truth. NOTE: Contains nudity and sexual explicitness and should be previewed by parents before viewing by teens. The surreal tone of parts of the movie may seem peculiar to viewers accustomed to more traditional and straightforward storytelling.

SEE ALSO:

The Emperor's New Clothes All three versions of classic fairy tale are about the pressures to lie and the power of telling the truth, with a child as the triumphant truth-teller.

Keeper of the Flame The widow of a beloved statesman must decide whether it is better to allow him to continue to be seen as a hero or to be honest about his hidden fascist agenda.

The Solid Gold Cadillac A woman discovers the power of asking honest questions when she topples the corrupt management of a large corporation.

EMPATHY AND COMPASSION

"If you want others to be happy, practice compassion. If you want to be happy, practice compassion."
—THE DALAI LAMA

If we are not careful, movies can deaden our sense of empathy. The average child sees 4,000 murders a year on television, and it is natural to respond by becoming less sensitive. But movies also give us a wonderful opportunity to develop our ability to understand the feelings, perspectives, and challenges of others. Every time we watch, we are caught up in the lives and concerns of the characters. As we talk about them afterward and try to understand their motives and their choices, we are developing our empathy and insight. And that leads to compassion.

Movies are superb on matters of empathy for individuals. They do less well in terms of different cultures and races, and tend to promote a sense of "us and them" by portraying nonwhite cultures as exotic people who are backward, even childish. It is important to be sensitive to this in viewing movies with kids and to make sure they see some of the very few films that acknowledge the cultures and traditions of people other than white Americans. These issues are sometimes well-presented in movies specifically dealing with bigotry and intolerance.

Empathy is necessary for cooperation, and it is cooperation that really makes a difference. It is important to point out that being sensitive to others' feelings is not enough; what matters is action.

The Gods Must Be Crazy
1981, 109 min, PG, 6 and up
Dir: Jamie Uys. N!xau, Jamie Uys, Sandra Prinsloo, Marius Weyers

PLOT: Botswana Bushmen are gentle and generous, "the most contented people in the world." They have "no crime, no punishment, no laws, no rulers, no judges." They have no concept of individual ownership, because there is nothing to own. When a pilot flying overhead drops an empty Coke bottle on them, for the first time they see something new, and something that only one person can have at a time, "something that they could not share because there was only one of it." And so, for the first time, they experience selfishness and jealousy. This unique item is so interesting that suddenly "everybody needed it most of the time." A man named Xi (N!xau) says that the gods must have been crazy to send them this awful thing, and he will take it to the end of the world and throw it off.

Meanwhile, in "civilization," a botched coup results in several deaths on both sides. And journalist Kate Thompson (Sandra Prinsloo), decides she cannot stand city life anymore and quits her job to become a teacher out in the bush. But the only car available to go meet her has no brakes and is impossible to start. The reverend (director and scriptwriter Jamie Uys) is afraid to drive it, so he sends scientist Andrew Steyn (Marius Weyers), who is very bashful around women.

Kate and Andrew have a number of mishaps and misunderstandings on the way back. When they run into Xi and the rebel forces, the result is chaos, but it all ends happily.

✳ **DISCUSSION:** This gentle, low-budget comedy broke the record for the highest-grossing foreign film in U.S. history. In addition to some wonderful slapstick (including a jeep that gets strung up in a tree), it has a lot to teach us about other cultures, about ourselves, and about empathy. Children are, after all, strangers to our culture, trying to understand it and learn its rules. They can identify with Xi as he tries to figure out the odd behavior of the people he meets, because, like anyone else exposed to a new situation, he makes very logical conclusions based on the limited information and experience he brings to it. When he picks up the odd "stick" he sees, and the man runs away, he thinks it is because the man saw the evil Coke bottle; Xi does not know that the "stick" is a rifle. His amazement at seeing the trappings of modern life, the Coke bottle, motorized vehicles, the pipe that Andrew smokes, the clothes that "looked as if they were made with cobwebs," help us see our world instead of taking it for granted. Notice that in the first interaction between Kate and Xi, they each conclude that the other is "rude." Each culture thinks that the other can't "speak"; to each, the language of the other sounds like chattering noises and clicks. There is further confusion because the Botswanas shake their head to mean "yes" instead of "no." Our assumptions of what is beautiful are questioned: Xi thinks that the blond, blue-eyed Kate is very ugly.

In Xi's society, there is no word for "guilt." There is no concept of individual "ownership." The Bushmen apologize to an animal before killing it for food. This movie provides a wonderful opportunity to talk about some of our "civilization's" underlying principles, and the way that other cultures give us a chance to look at things differently, and to determine what is inherently human and what we have created, and why.

PROFANITY: None.

NUDITY/SEXUAL REFERENCES: The Bushmen are nearly nude. Various mishaps lead Kate to conclude that Andrew is trying to make a rather aggressive pass at her. Several of the gags result in Kate's being out in her underwear and very embarrassed, as a way of showing one of the sharp contrasts between the "civilized" and "uncivilized" people in the story.

ALCOHOL/DRUG ABUSE: None.

VIOLENCE/SCARINESS: Machine-gun shooting; main characters in peril.

TOLERANCE/DIVERSITY ISSUES: A major theme of the movie.

✳ **QUESTIONS FOR KIDS:**
- How many differences can you find between Xi's culture and ours? In what ways do you think Xi's is better? In what ways is ours better?
- In Xi's culture, "they never punish a child or even speak harshly to it, so of course their children are well-behaved." Do you think these two things go together?
- Can you imagine a culture without ownership or guilt?
- Why does Xi think Kate is rude? Why does she think he is rude?
- Why does Andrew have such a hard time making a good impression on Kate? Have you ever felt that way? Why does she change her mind about him?

✳ **CONNECTIONS:** The sequel, *The Gods Must Be Crazy II,* is not very good. **The Jungle Book** is another "fish out of water" story, though Mowgli is not a part of an established culture, as Xi is here. A more dramatic (and tragic) treatment of some of these themes is in an Australian movie, *Walkabout* (for mature teens), in which two white children, abandoned in the outback, are saved by an Aborigine boy.

✳ **ACTIVITIES:** Kids can try to write or act out a story about what would happen if Xi came to their house. They might be amused to see how the actor's name is spelled; the "!" in N!xaus's name stands for a clicking sound.

✳The Philadelphia Story
1940, 112 min, NR, b&w, 10 and up
Dir: George Cukor. Katharine Hepburn, Cary Grant, Jimmy Stewart

✳ **PLOT:** Tracy Lord (Katharine Hepburn), the daughter of an upper-class Philadelphia family, is preparing for her wedding when her ex-husband, C. K. Dexter Haven (Cary Grant), appears with a reporter, Macauley (Mike) Connor (Jimmy Stewart), and a photographer, Elizabeth (Liz) Imbrie (Ruth Hussey). Though Tracy loathes publicity, she agrees to let them stay so that their magazine will not publish a story about her father's affair with a Broadway dancer, which would humiliate her family. Tracy's fiancé, George

Kittridge (John Howard), a "man of the people" who hopes for a political career, is pleased to have them there.

At first, Tracy and her young sister, Dinah (Virginia Weidler), behave outrageously to shock Mike and Liz. But Tracy reads Mike's book of short stories and discovers they have a lot in common. She is hurt when he rejects her offer of help, and even more hurt when Dexter tells her she acts like a "goddess," rigid, unforgiving, and without compassion. Her father, who was not invited to the wedding, returns. She is hurt further when he says she does not have an understanding heart, and she feels oddly betrayed when her mother forgives him.

That night, at the prenuptial party, Tracy deliberately gets drunk. She and Mike have a romantic moonlight swim, and when he carries her back to the house, George and Dexter are waiting for them. The next morning, she is hung over and does not remember what happened the night before. George assumes that she and Mike had an affair and insists on an apology and a pledge that she will never drink again. She turns him down, saying that she knows she would disappoint him. Mike offers to marry her, but she turns him down, too, because "Liz wouldn't like it." She goes in to tell the guests that the wedding has been called off, but Dexter tells her to tell them that she will marry him again instead. As her father prepares to escort her down the aisle, she tells him that she feels "like a human being."

✳ **DISCUSSION:** One of the glossiest romances ever made, with splendid dialogue and three of the greatest movie stars ever, this film is a pure pleasure to watch. At the beginning of the movie (after a brief prologue showing the end of Dexter and Tracy's marriage), Tracy is rigid and judgmental, but only because she thinks it is the way to make sure she will never be hurt again. She tells her mother they both "picked the wrong first husbands," and she is sure that this time, in marrying someone who is the opposite of Dexter in every way, she will make up for her past mistakes.

Tracy likes to be in control. She insists on preventing her father from coming to her wedding and even renames her sister. In her first conversation with George in the movie she has to be gently reminded that their home together will be "ours," not "mine." If she cannot prevent reporters from covering her wedding, she will behave outlandishly to give herself control over the story, making sure they cannot have access to the real Tracy (or the real family situation—she introduces her uncle as "Father").

But she is moved by Mike's writing and admits that she, too, understands what it's like to put on a tough veneer to protect a vulnerable spirit. And it is Mike who is able to give Tracy back a vision of herself as "lit from within" that enables her to accept her own faults and those of others. It enables her to accept her own feelings, too, and realize it is Dexter she has loved all along. It was really herself she was hardest on. Forgiving herself frees her to feel compassion for others.

PROFANITY: None.

NUDITY/SEXUAL REFERENCES: Very mild, by today's standards—references to Mr. Lord's affair with a dancer; an off-screen nude swim; George's assumption that Tracy and Mike slept together. Uncle Willie's pinches would be classified today as sexual harassment. Note Mike's famous line that "there are rules about that" in explaining why he did not sleep with a willing Tracy because she was "the better" for alcohol.

ALCOHOL/DRUG ABUSE: Tracy and Mike get very drunk (and have terrible hangovers); references to Dexter's past alcohol problem (which he calls his "deep and gorgeous thirst").

VIOLENCE/SCARINESS: None (Dexter shoves Tracy in a brief prologue).

TOLERANCE/DIVERSITY ISSUES: Class issues.

✳ **QUESTIONS FOR KIDS:**
- Why does Tracy want to marry George? Why does George want to marry Tracy?
- Why was it hard for Tracy to see George's stuffiness? Why do they feel differently about publicity?
- How does Tracy make Mike and Liz uncomfortable? How does Mike make Tracy uncomfortable?
- What does Tracy learn from her father? From Mike? From Dexter?
- Why does Tracy want George to think better of her than she did of herself? What is the meaning of Mike's quote about "with the rich and mighty, always a little patience'?

✳ **CONNECTIONS:** This movie is based on a play written for Katharine Hepburn by Philip Barry. She had a huge success with it on Broadway, and bought the movie rights herself so she could be assured of starring and selecting her own director and costars when it was made into a film. Hepburn and Cary Grant appear together in *Holiday* (also directed by Cukor and based on a play by Barry adapted by Donald Ogden Stewart) and *Bringing Up Baby.* Jimmy Stewart won a Best Actor Oscar for his performance, and Donald Ogden Stewart won one for his screenplay, a deft improvement over the already excellent play. There was a musical remake in 1956 called *High Society,* with Grace Kelly, Frank Sinatra, and Bing Crosby. Despite good performances and some good songs by Cole Porter (including "True Love"), it is not in the same class. At the time of this movie, there was no *Spy* magazine, but in the 1980s it seemed just the right name for a bratty, wickedly insouciant publication, and was adopted by a monthly satire magazine.

✳The Prince and the Pauper
1937, 120 min, NR, b&w, 6 and up
Dir: William Keighley. Errol Flynn, Claude Raines, Billy and Bobby Mauch

✳ **PLOT:** The heir to the throne of England is young Prince Edward, son of Henry VIII (Bobby Mauch). He meets a beggar boy (Billy Mauch) who looks exactly like him, and they decide to trade places so that each can find out what it feels like to live the life of the other.

They exchange clothes. Through a mistake, the prince is thrown out of the castle grounds, and no one believes him when he tells them who he is. He makes many discoveries about the world outside the castle, the most disturbing being the poverty of some of his subjects, and the most terrifying the realization that his enemies inside the court have discovered his secret and are hoping to kill him, and make Tom Canty, the beggar boy, their pawn.

He finds a defender, Miles Hendon (Errol Flynn), who at first befriends him because he feels sorry for him, and then realizes that the boy really is Edward, now the king, because Henry VIII has died. With the help of Miles, Edward makes it back just in time to prevent Tom from being coronated King, and takes the position himself, with the greater understanding he gained from trying life as Tom Canty.

✳ **DISCUSSION:** This exciting story (based on the book by Mark Twain) has a lot of appeal because we get to experience the fantasy of feeling what it would be like to be royalty. And we get to think about what our lives would seem like if a prince or princess took over from us for a day or two. The young prince had not had a chance to develop compassion because he had simply not been aware of the realities of poverty and abuse until he went out into the world without the protection of his position. Edward has to find out how to prove his worth to people who are not impressed by his title, power, or wealth, and how to solve his problems on his own. The young pauper develops understanding as well when he masquerades as the prince, learning that even wealth and power cannot prevent loss or loneliness or protect him from the wickedness of others. Both boys learn that rich and poor people can be lonely and afraid, but that both can also find true friends.

PROFANITY: None.
NUDITY/SEXUAL REFERENCES: None.
ALCOHOL/DRUG ABUSE: None.
VIOLENCE/SCARINESS: Sword fights.
TOLERANCE/DIVERSITY ISSUES: Class issues.

✳ **QUESTIONS FOR KIDS:**
- How will Edward do a better job as king than he would have if he had not had this experience?
- Compare Edward to Chulalongkorn, who becomes King of Siam at the end of *The King and I.* How are their relationships with their fathers alike or different? How are their plans for ruling alike or different?
- Who would you change places with if you could?

✳ **CONNECTIONS:** The movie was remade for television by Walt Disney, with one boy playing both parts, using the same special effects used in both versions of *The Parent Trap.* Miles was played by dashing Guy Williams, star of the "Zorro" television series, and the video is well worth seeing if the original is not available. In 1990, Disney made an animated version, starring Mickey Mouse, and it is delightful. Older kids might like to see some of the movies featuring Edward's father, Henry VIII, such as **A Man for All Seasons** and *Anne of the Thousand Days.*

✳ **ACTIVITIES:** Look up Prince Edward in an encyclopedia to find out about his brief reign, and about the long and influential reign of his half sister, Queen Elizabeth I. Older children who are good readers might like to read the book by Mark Twain.

✳ EMMA
1996, 111 min, PG, 8 and up
Dir: Douglas McGrath. Gwyneth Paltrow, Jeremy Northam
Emma (Gwyneth Paltrow) is a beautiful and wealthy young woman whose attempts to "help" others cause more trouble than good. She tries to elevate an awkward girl (Toni Collette) to the upper classes, preventing her marriage to the farmer she loves and encouraging her to try to win a snobbish clergyman. She learns she has completely misread (and disrupted) the romantic intentions of at least four people and finally, when she thoughtlessly insults a silly but well-meaning lady (Sophie Thompson), she begins to learn how to be truly sensitive to others. When Jane Austen was writing this book, she predicted that she was creating a character no one would like. But it is impossible not to like Emma, despite her disastrous attempts to arrange the lives of everyone around her.

✳ FREAKY FRIDAY
1977, 97 min, G, 6 and up
Dir: Gary Nelson. Jodie Foster, Barbara Harris
The first of the recent spate of "body-switching" movies, this is the story of a mother and teenage daughter who each make the mistake of wishing for the other one's life, at the same moment, and find that they got what they wished for. Jodie Foster and Barbara Harris are both terrific as the mother/daughter who each learn a great deal about the challenges faced by the other.

✳ **CONNECTIONS:** This is based on the popular book by Mary Rodgers, daughter of composer Richard Rodgers (**The Sound of Music**).

SEE ALSO:
Gentleman's Agreement A reporter pretends to be Jewish to investigate anti-Semitism.

A Little Princess Every material possession is taken from Sara, and yet she continues to feel empathy for others and try to help them.

Mr. Deeds Goes to Town Deeds's empathy for the poor farmers, and empathy from Babe and the judge for Deeds are the turning points in the movie.

COURAGE

"The chief activity of courage is not so much attacking as enduring, or standing one's ground against dangers."
—SAINT THOMAS AQUINAS

Movies almost always have heroes, and heroes are almost always coura-geous. Think of Indiana Jones in **Raiders of the Lost Ark,** entering the booby-trapped cave, racing from poisoned darts, and then confessing that he is terrified of snakes (and later facing thousands of them in the buried tomb).

In comedies, we see cowards. Bob Hope and Woody Allen are two arche-typal examples. But in Westerns, adventure sagas, mysteries, sword and sorcery epics, and war movies, we see the most thrilling depictions of physical courage. It is important to talk to kids about the other kinds of courage. Movies give us that chance with examples of moral courage, as when Sir Thomas More stands up to the King in **A Man for All Seasons** or the *Washington Post* takes on the President in **All the President's Men.** As Adlai Stevenson said, "It is often easier to fight for principles than to live up to them." The best films show that courage is never easy, and that even the bravest people get scared. It is a lot of fun to watch a movie hero run toward the guys who are shooting at him, but it is these other films that give us a chance to think about—and talk about—what courage really means.

Invasion of the Body Snatchers
1956, 80 min, NR, b&w, 12 and up
Dir: Don Siegel. Kevin McCarthy, Dana Wynter, Carolyn Jones

✳ **PLOT:** Dr. Miles Bissell (Kevin McCarthy), under restraint and being evaluated for possible commitment to a mental hospital, insists he is not crazy and tells the admitting doctors his story.

Called home early from a medical conference because a number of patients wanted to see him urgently, he finds that all have canceled their appointments. A small boy insists that his mother is not really his mother, and a woman insists that her uncle is not really her uncle. He looks and sounds like him, and has all of the uncle's memories, but he seems emotionless. It turns out that many people in the town have made similar complaints.

Becky (Dana Wynter), an old girlfriend of Miles's, is back in town, newly divorced. Miles and Becky are called to the home of friends, Jack (King Donovan) and Theodora (Carolyn Jones), who found a mysterious body in a pod in their greenhouse. It grows to resemble Jack as the night goes on, even down to the cut he had received that evening on his palm. Miles fears for Becky and runs to her house. In her basement, he finds a huge pod with a Becky-duplicate growing inside. He runs to her bedroom to wake her up, and they call the police. Everywhere they turn for help, they find the people have been taken over by emotionless pod duplicates who complete the final possession when the humans are asleep.

Becky and Miles hide out in his office. They see trucks filled with pods going off in all directions. At last Jack comes, and they are relieved—until they realize that he, too, has been replaced by a pod. He has brought the others with him, telling Miles, "You're reborn into an untroubled world." "Where everyone's the same?" "Exactly."

Miles races to the highway, begging anyone to stop and help him. He is brought to the mental hospital. His story complete, the doctors conclude he is insane—until they hear of an accident involving a truck filled with mysterious pods. As the movie ends, they are calling for help.

✳ **DISCUSSION:** This has been called the most frightening film ever made. What makes it so scary is the absence of special effects and disgusting-looking aliens. The enemy is within those we trust and rely on most. The slow realization of the ultimate horror—complete annihilation of the individual personality and ability to feel—in everyone around Miles and Becky, and finally in Becky herself, is genuinely terrifying.

People have argued about the political meaning of this movie since it was made. Some believe that the emotionless pod people were supposed to represent the Communists. Others argue the opposite, that the references to conformity mean that the movie is a criticism of Joe McCarthy and those who were threatened by any challenges to their way of thinking. In that light, it can be compared to **High Noon,** made four years earlier. Its appeal is enduring because it can serve as a metaphor for whatever pressures for conformity exist at the time we view it.

Miles says to Becky, "In my practice, I've seen how people have allowed their humanity to drain away, only it happened slowly and not all at once. They didn't seem to mind . . . All of us, a little bit, we harden our hearts, grow callous. Only when we have to fight to stay human do we realize how precious it is to us, how dear, as you are to me." One of the pod people says, "Love, desire, ambition, faith—without them, life is so simple, believe me." The pod people have "no feelings, only the instinct to survive." But Becky says, "I don't want a world without love or grief or beauty—I'd rather die." It is just her ability to feel that makes her so precious to Miles. (It also gives them away when, trying to pass as one of the pod people, she can't help crying out as she sees a dog run in front of a truck.)

Kids will not understand that the reference to "Reno" means that Becky was just divorced. The need to use an operator to make a long distance call will also be a surprise to them.

PROFANITY: None.

NUDITY/SEXUAL REFERENCES: None.

ALCOHOL/DRUG ABUSE: Social drinking.

VIOLENCE/SCARINESS: No violence or gore, but very scary.

TOLERANCE/DIVERSITY ISSUES: The importance of respecting individual differences is a subtext of the movie (though everyone in the movie is white and middle class).

❋ QUESTIONS FOR KIDS:

- The pod people believe that survival is more important than feelings, but Becky says she would rather die than live without feelings. Why does Becky include "grief" as one of the feelings she would rather die without?
- What does Miles mean when he says he has seen people let their humanity drain away?
- When do people have to "fight to stay human"? When this movie was made, it did not have the prologue (which lets you know right away that he is going to get away from Santa Mira) or the epilogue (which assures you that the invaders will be beaten). Do you think it is better with those additions?
- What does this movie say about the pressure to conform?

❋ CONNECTIONS: This movie seems to get remade about once every twenty years, and each version reflects something of its era. The 1978 version (rated PG) was directed by Philip Kaufman (*The Right Stuff*) and features Donald Sutherland and Brooke Adams. Watch for Kevin McCarthy and director Don Siegel from the original in brief appearances. In 1994, another version, this time called *Body Snatchers* (and rated R) was released. This version is less a political analogy than a reflection of a teenager's conflicts over identity and separation.

Carolyn Jones, who plays Teddy, later played Morticia in television's *The Addams Family*. If Becky's cousin looks vaguely familiar to older viewers, it is because actress Virginia Christine went on to play "Mrs. Olson" in the long-running series of Folger's coffee commercials. She also appeared as Katharine Hepburn's bigoted business partner in *Guess Who's Coming to Dinner*. The eerie music is by Carmen Dragon, father of "the Captain" of the musical group the Captain and Tennille.

The Magnificent Seven

1960, 126 min, NR, 8 and up

Dir: John Sturges. Steve McQueen, Yul Brynner, James Coburn, Charles Bronson, Eli Wallach

✳ **PLOT:** Farmers in a small Mexican village are being robbed by Calvera (Eli Wallach), a bandit, who takes all of their crops to feed his men. The village wise man advises the farmers to buy guns.

The farmers ask Chris (Yul Brynner) to help them buy guns. He agrees instead to help them try to find someone who can defend them. The first candidate is Chico (Horst Buchholz), who is "very young and very proud." Chris rejects him, explaining that "The graveyards are full of boys who were very young and very proud." The next candidate is Harry (Brad Dexter), who is too experienced to fall for Chris's test trap. He is an old friend and insists that if Chris is involved, there must be a lot of money in it somewhere. Chris offers Vin (Steve McQueen) the job, but he refuses at first, saying that the fee "wouldn't even pay for my bullets." But Vin is drawn to being a gunman "for the competition." The farmer asks, "With whom does he compete?" Chris answers, "Himself." Vin agrees to join them.

They find O'Reilly (Charles Bronson) chopping wood for food. Britt (James Coburn) is challenged to prove that he can outdraw a gun with a knife. He proves it without saying a word. Lee (Robert Vaughn), a laconic southerner, says, "I'll have the money before I go." He is on the run and needs it to pay off the people who have been hiding him. The six of them ride off together. Chico follows them. Now there are seven.

They arrive at the small farm village, where the farmers are afraid of them. Calvera sends three spies to see what is going on. Lee, Britt, and Chico go after them and kill them. The next day, they begin to prepare the villagers, teaching them to shoot and building new walls. Chico finds Petra, one of the girls the villagers have hidden because they were afraid to let the gunmen near them. O'Reilly tells the gunmen they have been given all the food in the village, so they share it with the villagers.

Calvera comes into the town. There is a gunfight, and Calvera retreats. As the villagers celebrate, Calvera returns. Snipers shoot at the town. The villagers and the gunmen go to their battle positions. Three boys stay with O'Reilly, telling him they got him in a lottery. This means that if he dies, they will avenge his death and see to it that there are always fresh flowers on his grave. Chico tells Petra that he is one of the gunmen, and cannot be confined to a small, quiet farm village like this one.

Chris kills all the snipers, but Calvera comes back again. The seven are vastly outnumbered, and Calvera is desperate. He will fight to the finish. Some of the villagers want to give up. Chris says he will kill the first man who even so much as whispers about giving up. But some of the gunmen are thinking about it, too. Calvera traps the gunmen, with the help of the frightened villagers. He will let them go, with food and water and even their guns. "I know you won't use those guns against me. No one is crazy enough to make the same mistake twice." Chico wants to fight, but Chris knocks his gun away. They retreat.

Outside the town, they debate going back. They know they will most likely be killed. All but Harry go back. There is one last massive shoot-out. Harry comes back and is shot badly. He begs Chris to tell him treasure was really there after all: "I hate to die a sucker." Chris tells him he was right, and he dies happy. Britt and Lee are killed. O'Reilly is killed pushing the boys to safety. Chris shoots Calvera, who says as he dies, "A place like this, why? A man like you, why?"

With the village safe, Chris, Vin, and Chico ride off, but Chico returns. His place is in the village. He goes back to Petra and takes off his gun belt. Chris says, "The old man was right. Only the farmers won. We lost. We'll always lose." As Chris and Vin ride off, the boys are tending O'Reilly's grave, just as they promised.

✳ **DISCUSSION:** The Western is American mythology, and this one features many of the archetypal characters and issues. The gunmen are tough, cool outsiders, their speeches brief and ironic. They know they have more in common with Calvera than they do with the villagers they are protecting. Their skills are necessary to make it safe for the villagers, but once it is safe, the villagers will be relieved to see them go. And although they know that a quiet life is not for them, that Vin could never be a "crackerjack" grocery clerk, a part of them yearns for it, which is what makes it so important to them to protect it.

O'Reilly spanks the boy who says his father is a coward. "You think I'm brave because I carry a gun. Your fathers are much braver because they carry responsibilities. . . . This responsibility is like a big rock that weighs a ton. It bends and it twists them until it buries them under the ground. . . . I have never had this kind of courage." This is an opportunity to talk about kinds of courage, and about the commitment to honor that ultimately places Calvera and the seven on opposite sides.

You can see this in an exchange between Chris and Vin: "We took a contract." "Not the kind any court would enforce." "That's just the kind you have to keep." There is also a scene in which Chico asks, "Your gun has got you everything you have, isn't that true?" and the gunmen answer with an evenhanded assessment of what the gun has got them. Vin: "Yeah, sure, everything. After a while you can call bartenders and Ferro dealers by their first name, maybe two hundred of them. Rented rooms you've stayed in, maybe five hundred. Meals you've eaten in hash houses, maybe one thousand. Home, none. Wife, none. Kids, none. Prospects, zero. Suppose I left anything out?" Chris: "Yeah. Places you are tied down to, none. People with a hold on you, none. Men you step aside for, none." Lee: "Insults swallowed, none. Enemies, none." Chris: "No enemies?" Lee: "Alive."

One of the movie's greatest strengths is the way that each of the gunmen has his own history and destiny. Lee is particularly interesting, as he understands that now only he can see his skill is less than it was, but that soon others will see it and he will be vulnerable. His nightmares belie his efforts to appear fearless.

Calvera says to Chris, "We're in the same business . . . Can men of our profession worry about things like [farmers]? It may even be sacrilegious. If God did not want them sheared, he would not have made them sheep." But the seven are different. A farmer tells Vin that the feeling he had when Calvera's men ran away was a feeling worth dying for. "Have you ever felt like that?" "Not for a long time. I envy you." Vin later tells Chris that both of them have made a gunman's worst mistake in caring about the villagers. But he knows it is that feeling that is worth dying for, and that he no longer has to envy anyone.

PROFANITY: None.

NUDITY/SEXUAL REFERENCES: The farmers hide the young women because they are afraid the gunmen will rape them.

ALCOHOL/DRUG ABUSE: None.

VIOLENCE/SCARINESS: Shoot-outs.

TOLERANCE/DIVERSITY ISSUES: The villagers are Mexican, and the gunmen are Anglo except for Chico and O'Reilly.

✳ QUESTIONS FOR KIDS:

- Many different kinds of courage are depicted and discussed in this movie. How many did you see?
- What are the answers to Calvera's questions: "A place like this, why? A man like you, why?"
- The gunmen each had different reasons for being there. What were they?
- What did Vin mean when he said he did it for the competition?
- Do any of the gunmen regret their choices? How can you tell? Why did Chris lie to Harry?
- What did Calvera mean when he said that if God did not want them sheared, he would not have made them sheep?
- How does the music help tell the story?

✳ CONNECTIONS: *The Magnificent Seven* is a remake of a terrific Japanese movie called *The Seven Samurai,* which is well worth making an effort to see. Virtually the entire cast can be seen in other outstanding movies. Brynner, of course, is best known for his Oscar-winning performance in **The King and I**. McQueen starred in **The Great Escape** and *The Reivers*. The score, one of the most memorable in the history of movies (thanks in part to its use in Marlboro ads) was composed by Hollywood veteran Elmer Bernstein, whose compositions have been featured in movies that include **Ben-Hur, The World of Henry Orient,** *The Blues Brothers,* **Airplane!** and *Stripes*.

The Red Badge of Courage

1951, 70 min, NR, b&w, 12 and up
Dir: John Huston. Audie Murphy, Andy Devine, Bill Mauldin

✳ **PLOT:** During the Civil War, a young Union soldier named Henry Fleming (Audie Murphy) worries that he will embarrass himself by being a coward, afraid of getting the "red badge" —a wound in battle. At first, he does run away, but returns to his battalion, lying about where he has been and pretending to have been wounded. He goes into battle the next day and loses himself in the fury of the moment, charging into the fray without regard to his safety. After the battle is over (with another group getting the credit, though Henry is personally recognized by the colonel), Henry knows that he can fight, but feels his spirit reaching out for the sunlight and the birds' singing, "images of peace."

✳ **DISCUSSION:** Based on the book by Stephen Crane, this is as much a story of the battle within Henry as of the battles without. At first he feels isolated, "alone in space," the only one who is afraid. What frightens him is not the battle itself, but how he will respond to it. To him, it appears that his comrades are "so sure of their courage." He is so scared that he cannot admit it. His friend Jim confesses that "I am, a mite," but Henry insists that he is sick of drill and looking forward to battle.

After he runs from battle, he feels "betrayed." His worry is how his fellow soldiers wll react. He envies the wounded, who have their "red badge of courage." He swears to help his friend Jim, who has been wounded, but is helpless when Jim collapses and dies. When he returns to the camp, he says he fought in another section of the battle and is relieved that they believe him. "He had performed his mistakes in the dark. So he was still a man." His view of "manhood" is still dependent on the way he is seen by others.

But after he loses "every sense but his sense of hate" in the next day's battle, he is sure enough of his own manhood to confess to Wilson that he had run the day before (though not to tell him the complete truth). When Wilson tells him that he ran, too, until the captain ordered him back, Henry says that confession is good for the soul.

The stark black-and-white cinematography, by Harold Rosson, recalls the images of the Matthew Brady photographs of Civil War soldiers and perfectly matches the mood of the story.

PROFANITY: None.

NUDITY/SEXUAL REFERENCES: None.

ALCOHOL/DRUG ABUSE: None.

VIOLENCE/SCARINESS: Intense battle scenes; some characters killed and wounded.

TOLERANCE/DIVERSITY ISSUES: Definition of "manhood."

✳ **QUESTIONS FOR KIDS:**
- What does Henry think constitutes "manhood"? How does that change over the course of the movie?
- What do we learn from the scene where the general promises to eat with all the different platoons?
- How do the different characters react differently to the dangers of battle? Which do the authors of the book and screenplay approve of most? Do you agree?

✳ **CONNECTIONS:** Compare this to the antiwar classic about the young German WWI soldier, *All Quiet on the Western Front,* brilliantly filmed in 1930 (and winner of the Oscar for Best Picture), and remade for television in 1979, with Richard Thomas, who, coincidentally, also appeared in the television remake of *The Red Badge of Courage* as well. High school kids may also appreciate *Captain Newman, M.D.,* a comedy-drama based on the Leo Rosten novel about an Army psychiatrist who must take those sensitive enough to be deeply disturbed by war and heal them so they can be sent back to battle.

Henry is played by Audie Murphy, the most highly decorated American soldier of WWII, who knew a great deal about courage and battles. His autobiography, *To Hell and Back,* was made into a movie with himself in the lead role. Another expert on war is cartoonist Bill Mauldin, who plays Wilson. Mauldin created the WWII soldier characters Willie and Joe. A book called *Picture,* by Lillian Ross, documents the making of this movie, which included its own off-screen battles. Director John Huston (**The African Queen, The Maltese Falcon, The Treasure of the Sierra Madre**) also wrote the screenplay.

✳ **ACTIVITIES:** Kids from ages ten to fourteen will like *Charlie Skedaddle,* by Patricia Beatty, also about a young soldier who runs away from battle, then finds his courage and returns. Older kids may want to read Stephen Crane's book, which was written when he was only twenty-two years old and had never seen a battle. He was also the author of some poetry that has a lot of appeal to teenagers.

✳ THE CANTERVILLE GHOST
1944, 96 min, NR, b&w, 6 and up
Dir: Jules Dassin. Robert Young, Margaret O'Brien, Charles Laughton

An American soldier (Robert Young) named Cuffy is billeted at the castle of six-year-old Lady Jessica de Canterville (Margaret O'Brien). The ghost of her cowardly ancestor (Charles Laughton) is cursed to haunt the castle until one of his descendants demonstrates bravery. Cuffy (who turns out to be a distant relative) and Lady Jessica triumph over their fears to discover the courage inside them. There is also a nice discussion of noblesse oblige and the duty of those to whom much has been given to give much back to the community.

SEE ALSO:

High Noon Told that a man he put in jail is coming back to kill him, a just-retired marshal must decide whether to run or stay to fight, and keep safe the people who have refused to help him.

The Nasty Girl A young woman persists in uncovering the truth about her neighbors' complicity in Nazi war crimes, despite threats, insults, and abuse.

COURTESY

Of Courtesy—it is much less
Than courage or heart or holiness;
Yet in my walks it seems to me
That the Grace of God is in Courtesy.
                        —HILLAIRE BELLOC

Courtesy is a neglected virtue, often dismissed as old-fashioned or even hypocritical. But courtesy is crucial, requiring us to be sensitive to the feelings of others and to show respect for them and for ourselves. And this is particularly important because so many of today's movies seem to depict lack of courtesy as somehow brave, honest, or funny. The movies in this chapter teach us that being treated with courtesy—or acting courteously—can be a transforming experience.

Babe

1995, 92 min, G, 4 and up
Dir: Chris Noonan. James Cromwell

✳ **PLOT:** "This is a tale about an unprejudiced heart, and how it changed our valley forever." So begins this lovely story about a pig who lives his dream (and saves his life) by learning to herd sheep. Farmer Hoggett (James Cromwell) wins the little pig at a fair. Back at his farm, Babe is adopted by Fly, the sheepdog, who treats him like one of her puppies. Babe learns the ways of the farm and the barnyard and is very distressed to hear from Maa, the sheep, that she thinks Fly is cruel, and even more distressed to learn from Ferdinand, the duck, that humans eat animals.

Babe gets in trouble when he goes into the house to help Ferdinand. They are scheduled to be slaughtered for Christmas dinner. But both he and Ferdinand escape the knife when another duck is killed instead. And Hoggett calls

Babe a "watch pig" when Babe alerts him to some thieves who make off with some of the herd. He thus earns the privilege of going with Fly and her spouse, Rex, to guard the sheep. At first, Babe tries to herd the sheep as Rex and Fly do, threatening them and biting them on the legs. But Maa tells him to ask them nicely, and when he does, they comply. Rex is furious and fights with Fly. With Rex tied up and sedated and Fly injured, Babe becomes a "sheep pig."

Maa is killed by a wolf, and Hoggett, blaming Babe, decides to shoot him. Fly, desperate to save Babe, talks to the sheep for the first time to ask them to help Babe by telling her what really happened to Maa. Hoggett discovers the truth and unloads his gun.

The jealous cat tells Babe that the other animals are laughing at him and that he is going to be eaten. But Hoggett now believes in Babe and brings him inside the house, nursing him. Hoggett enters Babe into competition at the fair, submitting him as the best sheepdog. At first, the sheep at the fair won't listen to Babe, but when Rex finds out the sheep password (by promising to be kind and respectful to sheep in the future), Babe uses it, along with his unique style of courteous friendliness, to manage the sheep so brilliantly that he wins the competition.

✳ **DISCUSSION:** This movie is a delight for the eye, heart, and spirit. Hoggett's small farm is a picturesque ideal of country life. The screenplay is witty without being cynical and tender without being soppy. The combination of real animals, animation, and puppetry is flawless, down to the tiny Greek chorus made up of mice, who chirp about the "Pig of Destiny."

And it deals very well with many important issues. Babe and some of the other characters make mistakes, some serious, when they draw conclusions from insufficient information. Ferdinand thinks that the Hoggetts like his "crowing" in the morning. Babe thinks that the "shiny tube" (gun) produces food. The sheep call all dogs "wolves." The pigs think that they are going to "pig paradise." And Hoggett thinks that Babe killed Maa. It can be very useful to discuss wrong judgments you or your children have made, and how to tell if you have enough information to draw the right conclusion.

The movie is really a tale of *two* "unprejudiced hearts." Hoggett's belief in Babe is contrasted with Mrs. Hoggett's hysteria at the thought of having him in the competition. Babe treats all species as friends, while they show a great deal of prejudice toward each other and against him. The sheep say that the dogs (whom they call wolves) are ignorant, and the dogs say that the sheep are stupid. There is a great deal of jockeying for status, as determined by the affection and approval of "the boss" (the Hoggetts).

It is also the story of a dream, as Babe dreams of being useful in a way that will be more important than any value he could have as food.

The movie provides an opportunity for the discussion of some other issues as well. Rex and the cat both behave badly because of jealousy. Rex is also very sensitive about his hearing loss and, in one of the movie's most touching moments, confesses it for the first time when he asks the sheep for their password so he can help Babe. There are issues of trust (Babe has to decide whom to trust when he is learning how the farm works and what the relationships are) and loyalty (the animals' to Hoggett; Babe's to the sheep, to Hoggett, and to Ferdinand, for whom he breaks the rule about not entering the house). There is the issue of honesty, as Hoggett commits some lies of omission in filling out the entry form (the movie makes it clear that he would not lie if the entry specified "dog"). And there is the importance of kindness—Hoggett's to Babe, Fly's to Babe, Babe's to the sheep, and ultimately Rex's to Babe—and how it transforms both the giver and the recipient.

PROFANITY: None (Babe uses the word "butt-heads," which is actually rather apt when applied, as it is here, to sheep!).

NUDITY/SEXUAL REFERENCES: Oblique reference to male dog being "snipped" and its effect on his ability to breed.

ALCOHOL/DRUG ABUSE: None.

VIOLENCE/SCARINESS: The issue of animal slaughter for food is dealt with very directly. Babe is alone because his family was slaughtered for food. Ferdinand says, darkly, "Christmas means carnage." It at first appears that Babe's friend Ferdinand has been killed for Christmas dinner, but it later turns out that it was another duck.

TOLERANCE/DIVERSITY ISSUES: A theme of the movie.

✳ **QUESTIONS FOR KIDS:**
- Why does Babe feel differently about the sheep than Fly and Rex do?
- How does Babe decide what to believe (and whom to believe)?
- Why is the cat so mean to Babe?
- Why is Rex so angry at Babe? What makes Rex change his mind? How will Rex get along with the sheep, now that he has had to ask for their help and promise not to bite?
- Why is Babe so polite to the sheep? Why does that matter to them?

✳ **CONNECTIONS:** Children may recognize "The Dance of the Hours" music from *Fantasia*. Children who enjoy this movie will also enjoy that other barnyard classic, ***Charlotte's Web***, by E. B. White, which every family should read aloud at least once. Like *Babe*, it is the story of a pig's fight to be more than bacon and pork chops (these movies may create more vegetarians than *Bambi*). The animated movie version, with Debbie Reynolds as Charlotte, lacks White's beautiful language, but is a pleasant diversion.

✳ **ACTIVITIES:** Children who enjoy this movie might like to visit a petting zoo or farm.

✳ My Fair Lady
1964, 170 min, NR, 6 and up
Dir: George Cukor. Rex Harrison, Audrey Hepburn, Wilfrid Hyde-White

✳ **PLOT:** On a rainy night in Covent Garden, Professor Henry Higgins (Rex Harrison) meets Colonel Pickering (Wilfrid Hyde-White), a fellow linguistics scholar, as he is correctly identifying accents of all those around him. Off-handedly commenting that in England people are defined by their accents, Higgins says that he could even teach a poor *Cockney* flower girl to speak like a lady. The next day, the flower girl (Audrey Hepburn) comes to see him to offer to pay Higgins for language lessons. She wants to be "a lady in a flower shop," and that requires a more bourgeois accent and manner.

Higgins says that he can do better, even teach her to speak and act like a lady of wealth and breeding, well enough to fool everyone at an upcoming ball. Pickering makes him a bet, and they agree. Eliza is overwhelmed, but her hope for something more out of life, and the kindness of Colonel Pickering (and the promise of chocolates), persuade her to stay.

Her father, dustman Alfred Doolittle (Stanley Holloway), arrives, looking for a handout. Higgins, charmed by Doolittle's cheerful amorality, gives him some money and jokingly recommends him to an American philanthropist as an astute social thinker.

Higgins and Pickering work Eliza very hard and finally think she is ready for a trial run. They bring her to the ultraelegant Ascot races, where her uncertain veneer of refinement and her irrepressible directness appeal to Freddie Eynsford-Hill (Jeremy Brett), a poor, unskilled, but impeccably upper-class gentleman.

Meanwhile, the American philanthropist has died, leaving a substantial amount of money to Doolittle, based on Higgins's recommendation. Understanding that money requires a level of respectability he had thus far happily ignored (as described in the song "With a Little Bit of Luck"), he agrees to marry his longtime companion.

After much more work, Eliza is ready for the ball and appears, a vision of grace and beauty. She is the belle of the ball, enchanting even the prince, and speaking with such exquisite diction and manners that Higgins's rival declares she must be Hungarian royalty. Back at Higgins's home, the men are exultant over "their" success. But they ignore Eliza, and she leaves, hurt. She goes to Higgins's mother, and when Higgins realizes how much he misses her and comes after her, she explains that she wanted to be seen as a person. He tells her he is relieved; that now she is showing independence, he does not need to feel responsible for her. But she has nowhere to go; those with upper-class bearing (like Freddie) are not employable. Higgins and Eliza cannot come to an agreement, but finally she returns to his house, and with the question "Eliza, where the devil are my slippers?" he lets her know how much he has missed her.

✳ **DISCUSSION:** This musical was based on *Pygmalion,* written in 1912 by George Bernard Shaw. In this era, and in this country, it is hard to imagine how genuinely revolutionary it was for Shaw to say that the only difference between the classes was accent and demeanor. It is worth discussing the way that language and accent defined people in this era, and asking children about the conclusions people draw from accents today.

This story has its parallels to *Cinderella*: It has its climax at a ball, which our heroine attends in borrowed finery. But Higgins and Pickering are far from fairy godfathers. Their interest is not in rewarding Eliza for a virtuous life; they want to show off their own achievement and play something of a joke on high society. And Higgins is not a prince. In a way, he reveals the princess inside of Eliza, though he never intended to. He never even took the time to imagine it to be possible.

One of Shaw's most important insights in this story is of the role of courtesy, and the different characters' ideas of its importance provide an excellent opportunity for discussion. Pickering's treating Eliza like a lady has as much to do with her becoming one as all of the training about diction and appropriate topics for conversation. As she says, he treats a flower girl like a duchess. When she says that Higgins treats a duchess like a flower girl, Higgins says that "the great thing" is to treat everyone the same way. That may be, but Pickering is able to treat everyone (even Eliza at her Cockney-est) with equal courtesy, instead of equal brusqueness. Mrs. Higgins is also courteous to everyone (with the exception of her son); her concern over having Eliza at Ascot is at least as much for Eliza's comfort as her own.

> PROFANITY: Eliza shocks everyone at the Ascot races by saying, "Move your blooming arse!" (In the play, she says, "Not bloody likely," considered not shocking enough by the time the musical was written.)
> NUDITY/SEXUAL REFERENCES: None.
> ALCOHOL/DRUG ABUSE: Liquor is used to celebrate triumph; Mr. Doolittle happily drinks a great deal.
> VIOLENCE/SCARINESS: None.
> TOLERANCE/DIVERSITY ISSUES: Class issues are a theme of the movie.

❋ **QUESTIONS FOR KIDS:**
- Eliza says that Pickering treats a flower girl like a lady, and Higgins treats a lady like a flower girl. Higgins says that what is important is treating everyone exactly the same. What do you think about this?
- Eliza sings "I Could Have Danced All Night," but she also sings "Just You Wait." Why does she feel so differently about Higgins at different points in her lessons?
- What does Higgins mean when he says that the English don't teach their children how to speak?
- Do you know people who have accents? How do accents change the way people react to those who have them? Can you imitate different accents?

❋ **CONNECTIONS:** See the play *Pygmalion,* on which this musical was based. There is an excellent movie version, with an Oscar-winning screenplay by Shaw himself, starring one of Shaw's favorite actresses, Wendy Hiller. Note that in the Afterword to the play, Shaw makes it very clear that Eliza marries Freddie. But in both filmed versions, the strong implication is that Eliza and Higgins become romantically involved.

Fans of *Sherlock Holmes* on PBS will enjoy a young Jeremy Brett as Freddie (his songs and Hepburn's were sung by others).

❉ To Kill a Mockingbird

1962, 129 min, NR, b&w, 10 and up
Dir: Robert Mulligan. Gregory Peck, Robert Duvall, Brock Peters

❉ **PLOT:** The story is about prejudice and injustice, seen through the eyes of a little girl, the daughter of a lawyer who defends a black man against a trumped-up rape charge in 1930s Georgia. The lawyer, Atticus Finch (Gregory Peck), is the essence of quiet dignity, integrity, and courtesy. His efforts to teach his son and daughter the values he believes in, which the community they live in does not always honor, are moving and inspiring.

Scout (Mary Badham), her brother Jem (Philip Alford), and their friend, Dill (John Megna), are fascinated by the stories about Arthur "Boo" Radley (Robert Duvall), the man who lives in the house next door and has not been seen in many years. They have heard that he stabbed his father with a pair of scissors and that he comes out at night to peer in people's windows. They dare each other to make contact with him, and once manage to run all the way to his porch, where they are terrified by an ominous shadow and run off by Boo's father's shotgun.

Their father, Atticus, has been appointed to defend Tom Robinson (Brock Peters), who has been charged with raping Mayella Ewell (Collin Wilcox). Atticus asks Scout not to fight with the children who call him a "nigger-lover." And he tells Mayella's father, Bob (James Anderson), that he intends to give Tom the best possible defense. When members of the town come to jail to lynch Tom, Scout's arrival and her friendly greeting to the father of her classmate dissipates the crowd's hostility.

At the trial, Atticus shows that Mayella's injuries indicate a left-handed assailant. But Tom's left arm is useless, having been injured years before in a cotton gin. Bob Ewell, though, is left-handed, supporting Atticus's implication that Ewell is the culprit. Though it is clear that Tom is innocent, he is convicted. And though Atticus promises an appeal, Tom is killed trying to escape.

Still, Bob Ewell is furious and swears revenge. He attacks Jem and Scout, but they are rescued by Boo Radley, who carries Jem home, stays to see that he is all right, and walks back to his house with Scout without saying a word.

❉ **DISCUSSION:** The sense of time and place in this movie is extraordinary—not just the time in history, but the time in the lives of the little girl and her brother. In addition to the power of the story and the appeal of the characters, this is one of the best movies about childhood ever made.

There is a great deal of emphasis in the movie on courtesy and sensitivity to the feelings of others. In the first scene, Atticus tells Scout not to embarrass a client named Walter Cunningham when he comes by to drop off some food as payment for legal services. Later, when Scout brings Walter, Jr., home for lunch, she is told not to say anything when he pours syrup all over his food. Atticus treats mean old Mrs. Dubose with gallantry, disarming her. Atticus's courtesy in cross-examining Mayella Ewell is so unfamiliar to her that she assumes it is some new sort of insult. The black people in the courtroom balcony stand as a courtesy to Atticus. And Sheriff Heck Tate explains why the official record will show that Bob Ewell fell on his knife. He wants to protect Boo "with his shy ways" from the well-meaning gratitude (and curiosity) of the "good ladies" of the town.

Of course, a central theme of the movie is racism. By virtue of their slovenly way of life and contempt for society, the Ewells would have been at the bottom of the town's social strata, except for the conviction that any black person was less worthy of respect than any white person. The word of a white person with a terrible reputation would automatically outweigh the word of any black person, no matter how fine his reputation. And, in this case, the movie makes it clear that the deciding factors in Tom Robinson's conviction were the community's uneasiness and embarrassment over two of his statements: that Mayella tried to hug and kiss him, and that he felt sorry for her. Both of those statements struck at the very foundations of the community's sense of appropriate behavior, possibly because the foundation was already cracked. These statements made it much more difficult for the community to deny that blacks were capable of seeing themselves—and being seen by whites—as appealing or even superior, and that made it necessary to get rid of Tom.

It is also worthwhile to examine the structure of this story. Unlike, for example, *Destry Rides Again,* which has a very tight, linear, construction, or *Meet Me in St. Louis,* which is just a series of separate incidents, this Oscar-winning screenplay is a magnificent example of a story that appears episodic and yet whose parts all turn out to be essential not just to the mood but to the theme and climax. This is even more true in the book. Both book and movie also do a superb job of presenting the story from the perspective of the child, but with the insight of the adult.

PROFANITY: None.

NUDITY/SEXUAL REFERENCES: The plot centers on a rape trial; no explicit language.

ALCOHOL/DRUG ABUSE: None.

VIOLENCE/SCARINESS: Scary expedition to Radley house; suspense over threatened lynching; children in peril.

TOLERANCE/DIVERSITY ISSUES: A theme of the movie.

✳ **QUESTIONS FOR KIDS:**
- How can you tell Tom is innocent? Why does the jury vote to convict him?

- Why does everyone get upset when Tom says he felt sorry for Mayella?
- Why does Mr. Cunningham change his mind about lynching Tom?
- Why is the incident about Atticus shooting the mad dog in the movie? What does it tell us about Atticus and about his relationship with his children?
- Why do the people in the balcony stand and tell Scout, Jem, and Dill to stand as Atticus leaves the courtroom?
- Why is courtesy so important to Atticus? How is that shown?

✳ **CONNECTIONS:** This movie is based on the outstanding book by Harper Lee, strongly recommended as a read-aloud before seeing the movie. Although they learn about Martin Luther King, Jr., and other civil rights leaders in school, children and teenagers who see this movie may be unaware of the open bigotry of that era. They should go to the library for more information, and see documentaries like the two *Eyes on the Prize* series and dramas like **The Long Walk Home,** *Ghosts of Mississippi,* and **The Autobiography of Miss Jane Pittman.**

✳ **ACTIVITIES:** The character of Dill is based on Lee's childhood friend, Truman Capote, whose story of his childhood, **A Christmas Memory,** is also well worth reading aloud. It was beautifully filmed with Geraldine Page and was remade for television starring Patty Duke.

✳ TO SIR, WITH LOVE

1967, 105 min, NR, mature high schoolers
Dir: James Clavell. Sidney Poitier, Judy Geeson, Lulu

Released the same year as **Up the Down Staircase,** this is also the story of a new teacher in an inner-city school, although this time the city is London and the teacher is Mark Thackeray (Sidney Poitier). An outsider by virtue of his country (West Indies) more than his color, Poitier becomes impatient with the insolence and narrow-mindedness of his students and imposes his own set of rules, foremost of which is courtesy to him and to each other. At first, they are embarrassed and awkward, as though they don't want to believe they could deserve such treatment. The other teachers make it quite clear they don't think the students deserve it. But soon the exaggerated sarcasm of "Miss Dare" and "Sir" falls away, and we see a superb example of the transforming nature of being treated with—and treating others with—respect.

✳ **CONNECTIONS:** Judy Geeson, who plays Pamela Dare, is an occasional guest star on the television show *Mad About You* as the Buchmans' English neighbor.

FAIRNESS AND
JUSTICE

"Injustice anywhere is a threat to justice everywhere."
—THE REVEREND DR. MARTIN LUTHER KING, JR.

A ny high school English teacher will tell you that the first requirement for a story is conflict. The challenge for the storyteller, whether a writer or a filmmaker, is to involve us in that conflict. As a result, many movies present us with issues of fairness and justice. Many of them do so directly, by taking us into the judicial system. Because every lawsuit represents a conflict, every one is automatically a story, or perhaps more of a play, with the lawyers and witnesses the clients, and the jury the very important audience.

Because the opposing sides often take extreme positions and use colorful language and creative approaches to persuade the judge and jury, it is hard to watch a lawsuit without feeling strongly about it, even though we may change our minds more than once as we hear both sides. There are a number of outstanding movies that feature courtroom battles at the center of the story.

Compare, for example, two courtroom dramas, **Miracle on 34th Street** and **Inherit the Wind.** They could not be more opposite in tone—one is a delightful fantasy-comedy, almost a fairy tale, and the other is a very serious play, based on a real case argued by the foremost lawyers of their time, and dealing with issues that are still the subject of bitter controversy today. Yet in a very real sense, both plays are about the same thing. Both are about how we know what we know, and whether it will be based on what we can prove or what we know through faith. Do we listen to our heads or our hearts? Do we believe what we are told, or do we challenge it, asking questions and evaluating the evidence?

The two films deal with the theme in sharply contrasting ways. But both include consideration of issues like relevance and probity of evidence to help decide the case. One crucial element in common is that in both the decision is strongly, even definitively, influenced by political considerations—both have judges whose political advisers tell them how to decide the cases. Both have characters who are confronted with their rigidity, though one is rigidly committed to faith and one to rationality. But the cases have very different conclusions. In both, the side representing the filmmaker's point of view puts his opposition on the stand (in one case, the opposing counsel; in the other, the opposing counsel's son). One movie comes out in favor of empiricism, and the other in favor of faith—yet in both cases, the resolution is one that most of the audience will find highly satisfying. Watching these movies can lead to a discussion not just of the issues they pose, but also of point of view and tone in storytelling.

Some movies use the judicial system to show its fairness, while others show how it can be subverted. Some show its complexity and its limits, as when the side who won the war judges the side that lost in *Judgment at Nuremberg.* Other movies depict people trying to devise their own systems of justice, either because the system has failed or because they are so removed from it that they have no alternative. Then there are also movies that lead us to consider larger notions of fairness, like those concerning issues of bigotry and equality, wealth and poverty, or war and peace. These movies make us think about the injustice of our world and give us an opportunity to think and talk with each other about how it happens and how we can make it better.

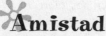 **Amistad**

1997, 152 min, R, high schoolers
Dir: *Steven Spielberg. Anthony Hopkins, Djimon Hounsou, Matthew McConaughey, Morgan Freeman, Nigel Hawthorne*

✳ **PLOT:** In 1839, a group of Africans sold into slavery were being transported to the United States on a Spanish ship. Off the coast of Cuba, they escaped from their shackles and attacked the crew, leaving two crew members alive to take them back to Africa. The Spanish sailors tricked the Africans and sailed up the coast of the United States until an American naval ship off the coast of Connecticut captured them. The Africans were brought into court to determine their fate. They were claimed as property ("like livestock") by both the Spanish crew and by the American captors.

Roger Baldwin (Matthew McConaughey), a property lawyer, persuades abolitionists Theodore Joadson (Morgan Freeman) and Lewis Tappan (Stellan Skarsgård) that he has a theory that will help the Africans. He argues that it is not a property case at all. The law provides that only the child slaves can be a slave. Since the Africans were not born slaves they are free, and their actions were merely self-defense in aid of restoring their freedom. If Baldwin can prove that they were born as free people in Africa, and not, as their captors alleged, slaves in the West Indies, they would not be considered property; they would be considered human beings.

The trial attracts the attention of President Martin Van Buren (Nigel Hawthorne), who is in the midst of a campaign for re-election and very aware that he will need the support of Southern voters to win. He is under additional pressure from the eleven-year-old queen of Spain, Isabella II, and her ambassador, who raise claims on behalf of the Spanish fleet. When the judge and jury appear sympathetic to the Africans, Van Buren arranges for a new judge to hear the case without a jury.

Meanwhile, the Africans try to understand what is going on around them. Baldwin and Joadson are able to find a man who speaks Mende, the language of Cinqué (Djimon Hounsou) and some of the other Africans. They win in court and the government appeals. Former President John Quincy Adams (Anthony Hopkins) represents them before the U.S. Supreme Court, where seven of the nine Justices are slaveholders. In a moving and eloquent argument, he persuades the Justices (with one dissenter) that the Africans were free, and that if they had been white, they would have been called heroes for rebelling against those who tried to take that freedom away.

✻ **DISCUSSION:** Adams explains that in court the one with the best story wins. Indeed, we hear many different stories in the course of the movie as each character tries to explain why his view is the right one. In the first courtroom scene we hear several different "stories" about what happens to the Africans. All of those stories assume that the Africans are property; the only question is whose property they are. Interestingly, as "property," they cannot be charged with murder or theft. One cannot be both property and capable of forming criminal intent. The only issue before the court is where the Africans will go and not the question of homicide.

As Baldwin begins to tell Joadson and Tappan his story of the case, we see them slowly becoming aware of what had always been obvious to us. The Africans cannot be property. They were free, in which case their actions were not only honorable but heroic, in the same category as America's founding fathers, whose rebellion is central to our own story about who we are as Americans. Despite the attempts of Van Buren to subvert the legal system established just decades before, the essential commitment to freedom is so much a part of the story that, at least in this one brief moment, justice triumphed. Adams, the son of the second President, made that his story.

PROFANITY: None.

NUDITY/SEXUAL REFERENCES: Slaves are nude in brief scenes.

ALCOHOL/DRUG ABUSE: None.

VIOLENCE/SCARINESS: Very violent opening scene with slave uprising and other violent scenes in flashbacks (including whipping, beating, and drowning) and when the slave fortress is liberated (including shooting).

TOLERANCE/DIVERSITY ISSUES: A theme of the movie.

✻ **QUESTIONS FOR KIDS:**
• Why was it important to prove where the Africans were from?
• What was Calhoun's justification for slavery?

- Why does Tappan say that the death of the Africans may help the cause of abolition more than their freedom?
- Why does Spielberg organize his story as he does, taking the audience from the confrontation to the courtroom and only later providing the background about the capture of the Africans?
- What does it mean that there is no Mende word for "should"?

✳ **CONNECTIONS:** Chief Justice Storey is portrayed by real-life former Supreme Court Justice Harry Blackmun.

✳Anatomy of a Murder

1959, 160 min, NR, b&w, 12 and up
Dir: Otto Preminger. Jimmy Stewart, Ben Gazzara, Arthur O'Connell, George C. Scott, Lee Remick, Eve Arden

✳ **PLOT:** This classic courtroom drama was written by a lawyer (later a judge), based on one of his own cases, and the judge is played by a real-life lawyer-judge, Joseph Welch. That lends this story of a murder trial some extra authenticity, and the dazzling performances and electric direction make it unforgettable.

Frederick Manion, an Army lieutenant (Ben Gazzara), is on trial for murder for shooting Barney Quill, the owner of a bar. Paul Biegler (Jimmy Stewart), a former district attorney returning to law practice after losing his bid for reelection, agrees to defend him. Manion says he killed Quill because he raped Manion's wife, Laura (Lee Remick). With a strong hint from Biegler, Manion says he must have been crazy.

Biegler, aided by legal research by an old friend with a drinking problem (Arthur O'Connell) and his loyal secretary (Eve Arden), puts together a defense strategy based on a ruling by another court in the state that "irresistible impulse" is a defense to a murder charge. All they must do is prove that it was irresistible impulse for Manion to shoot Quill. Manion is acquitted, but another "irresistible impulse" causes him to leave town without paying his bill.

✳ **DISCUSSION:** The use of precedent, the role of the expert witness, the advice to Laura about how to appear for her testimony, the evidentiary rulings, the cross-examination, and the acknowledgment by Biegler that the jury can never "disregard" what they have heard are all real-life legal details that are also compelling drama. The courtroom presentation is almost a play within a play, as we see when Biegler tells Laura how to dress for her testimony as though he was directing her in a part. There is a great deal of moral complexity as well. Biegler never seems interested in the issue of Manion's guilt or culpability; all he cares about is winning the case (and beating the man who defeated him at the polls). Yet there is morality and redemption in the movie in the dedication to the law and to at least some form of truth and fairness.

> PROFANITY: None.
> NUDITY/SEXUAL REFERENCES: Frank discussion of the rape.
> ALCOHOL/DRUG ABUSE: Manion and his wife drink a lot; McCarthy has a drinking problem.
> VIOLENCE/SCARINESS: Only described.
> TOLERANCE/DIVERSITY ISSUES: None.

✳ QUESTIONS FOR KIDS:
- What does the title tell us? Is it a murder if the jury finds that it isn't?
- How did Paul get Manion to say that he must have been crazy without telling him to say it?
- Should Manion have gone to jail? What is the relevance to his culpability or credibility of whether Laura was in fact raped or not? Shouldn't the issue be what he believed, since his defense was insanity?
- How does the filmmaker make you want Paul to win? How could he make you want Manion to be convicted?
- What do you think of the ending? What is that supposed to show us?

✳ **CONNECTIONS:** Joseph Welch, who plays the judge, was a real American hero, the man who put a stop to Joseph McCarthy. Try to get the videotape of his famous confrontation of McCarthy, where he asked, "Have you no shame?" It might lead you to watch *Tail Gunner Joe,* a made-for-television movie about McCarthy's life.

✳ **ACTIVITIES:** Read Stephen Becker's novel *A Covenant with Death,* which has a similar tone and some of the same themes.

✳ Inherit the Wind
1960, 127 min, NR, b&w, 10 to adult
Dir: Stanley Kramer. Spencer Tracy, Fredric March, Gene Kelly

✳ **PLOT:** In the famous Scopes "monkey" trial, three-time presidential candidate and Wilson administration Secretary of State William Jennings Bryan argued that Darwin's theory of evolution should not be taught to high school students. Clarence Darrow, the most renowned trial lawyer in American history, argued that it should. In this movie, the names and some of the facts are changed, but some of the dialogue is taken from the transcripts of the real Scopes trial.

At first, some of the town leaders are concerned that the trial will be bad for the town, but when they hear that Matthew Harrison Brady (Fredric March playing the character based on William Jennings Bryan) has volunteered to come to Hillsboro to prosecute the case, they decide to accept. The merits of the law aside, Brady's presence will "fill up the town like a rain barrel in a thunderstorm," which is good for business. Bertram Cates will be defended by Henry Drummond (Spencer Tracy as the character based on Clarence Darrow).

One of the first people to arrive is E. K. Hornbeck (Gene Kelly as a reporter, based on acidic newspaper correspondent H. L. Mencken), whose newspaper is paying Drummond's fee.

At the trial, Drummond tries to present a series of distinguished scientists to testify in favor of Cates. Brady objects; their testimony is not relevant to the issue of whether Cates violated the law. The judge agrees. Drummond is so furious, he asks for permission to withdraw from the case. Cates won't let him cross-examine Brady's witness, Cates's own girlfriend, Rachel, and the judge won't let Drummond present his own. For him, the issue is not whether Cates violated the law, but whether the law violates a larger law. "I warn you that a wicked law, like cholera, destroys everyone it touches, its upholders as well as its offenders."

Drummond says, "What I need is a miracle." Kelly sardonically hands him the Bible. "Here's a whole bag full, courtesy of Matthew Harrison Brady." For Drummond, the Bible does provide the answer. The next morning, Drummond calls Brady to the witness stand as "one of the world's foremost experts on the Bible and its teachings." Drummond says that he thinks one thing is holy: "The individual human mind. In a child's power to master the multiplication table there is more sanctity than in all your shouted 'Amens!' 'Holy Holies!' and 'Hosannas!' An idea is a greater monument than a cathedral. And the advance of man's knowledge is a greater miracle than all the sticks turned to snakes or the parting of the waters . . . The Bible is a good book, but it is not the only book . . . How do you know God didn't speak to Charles Darwin?"

Drummond keeps pressing Brady on how he knows what he knows. When Brady finally says in frustration that God tells him what to support, the crowd for the first time turns against him, frightened by his arrogance and fervor. Brady is beside himself.

The next day, the mayor warns the judge that the lieutenant governor wants the publicity to "simmer down." Elections are coming. The jury finds Cates guilty, but the judge imposes only a token fine, one hundred dollars. Brady wants to make a speech, but the judge adjourns the trial and the crowd leaves. It has been too much for him. He collapses, and shortly after he dies. Drummond is deeply saddened. "A giant once lived in that body. But Matthew Brady got lost because he looked for God too high up and too far away." Hornbeck looks at Drummond and says, "You're just as religious as he was." Drummond holds both books, the Bible and Darwin's, one in each hand, then puts them together and walks out of the courtroom.

✳ **DISCUSSION:** In 1925, the two greatest lawyers in America went to court to argue what was called the trial of the century. It wasn't about a famous person like O. J. Simpson, or a famous crime like Lorena Bobbitt's or Jeffrey Dahmer's. It wasn't even one of the lawsuits that changed American life, like abortion or desegregation. It was the Scopes trial, a case about how we decide what we teach our children in school. At the heart of the case, though, was a fight about how we know what is true. Do we listen to our heads or our hearts? Do we believe what we are told, or do we insist on asking questions and evaluating the evidence?

As in any courtroom drama, the question of fairness arises over and over, but in this case it both surrounds and exemplifies the core issue of the case. How do we know what is true? If that depends, in some sense, on making it a "fair trial," what does that mean? How do we make a trial fair?

Note the issue of jury selection. A juror who says, "I believe in the holy word of God, and I believe in Matthew Harrison Brady" is excused. Apparently, even in a case that challenges the right of teachers and students to question the Bible, some notion of fairness requires that the issue be judged by a juror who has a more open mind. Drummond objects to the fact that Brady is addressed in court by the honorary title of Colonel, just bestowed on him by the town. He believes it adds more weight to Brady's comments and lends him a greater aura of respect and authority. How is it resolved? Surprisingly, not by addressing both attorneys as "Mr.," but by bestowing the same honorific on Drummond, albeit temporarily. Drummond asks that a sign outside the courtroom with the exhortation READ YOUR BIBLE should either be removed or be augmented with a sign telling people to READ YOUR DARWIN. The sign is removed.

The trial is about keeping one kind of information out of the classroom. But, as in any trial, a significant amount of time is spent keeping certain kinds of information out of the courtroom, and it is very interesting to contrast the justification for excluding information raised in both contexts. In science, all information is evaluated on the basis of its accuracy and relevance; in law, these are also important. For example, the scientific testimony Drummond wants to present is excluded for reasons of relevance— whatever the scientists have to say is judged to have no relation to the issue of whether or not Cates violated the law.

But there are concerns besides accuracy and relevance. Some of the challenges to information in the courtroom relate to fairness, as with Drummond's request that prayer meetings not be announced by the judge for fear it will prejudice the jury. Another example is the objection to certain testimony as "hearsay," the staple of any courtroom drama. The legal system has determined that hearsay (reporting on what someone else said) is just not reliable enough to be used in court, with certain narrow exceptions. In other words, the likelihood that it will help us find out the truth is outweighed by the likelihood that it will be inaccurate and lead us to the wrong conclusions.

Sometimes a lawyer will object to something a witness or the opposing lawyer has said, and the judge will tell the jury to pretend they didn't hear it, as happens here when Brady refers to Cates as having "gone astray." Of course, the jury can't really forget about it (as Jimmy Stewart notably acknowledges in *Anatomy of a Murder,* a courtroom drama actually written by a lawyer), but the point is that they can be reminded not to rely on it in coming to a decision. Finally, some information is kept out of the courtroom because Cates won't let Drummond cross-examine Rachel. He decides he would rather go to jail than see her put through that difficult experience. Some things are more important than the truth, even to him.

Drummond is not permitted to read from Darwin in order to be able to ask Brady about it during the trial. Just as it is considered too dangerous and inflammatory for the students to hear, it is too dangerous for the jury, and perhaps even the members of the community in the courtroom, to hear. Drummond cannot put Darwin on trial; his only alternative is to put the refusal to consider Darwin on trial, and he does that in his cross-examination of Brady.

In this movie about skepticism, science, and faith, Drummond does have faith in one thing. He believes in the ability of the human mind to think, to question, and to know. When he is examining one of Cates's students during the trial, he asks, "Did you believe everything Mr. Cates told you?" When the boy answers, "I don't know, I gotta think about it," Drummond responds, "Good for you! Good for you!" Drummond is not there on behalf of Darwin; he is there on behalf of open-mindedness. It is not Drummond who is the nonbeliever in this case; it is Hornbeck, the most cynical of newspapermen.

What does Brady believe in? Brady is not there on behalf of the Bible or even faith as much as he is on behalf of a narrow and rigid view that prizes certainty above anything else. His world is composed of platitudes and facile retorts. He is described by Hornbeck as "the only man I know who can strut sitting down." When Drummond shows him a fossil determined by geologists to be millions of years old, Brady says he is "more interested in the Rock of Ages than in the age of rocks." And when Drummond questions Brady, he shows just how easy that kind of faith is to crack, and how devastating the consequences are when it does. Drummond demonstrates that his method of finding the answers is able to prove one fact—that Brady's faith is superficial, based on fear, not strength. As Mrs. Brady says to Rachel, "Maybe it meant too much to him."

It may be said that the filmmakers stacked the deck, and presented the story less than completely evenhandedly. It is clear throughout whose side they are on. A courtroom must be fair and objective; a movie can seldom get away with that without being static and a little boring. Just as Cates/Scopes had ideas he wanted to teach his students, and Brady/Bryan and Drummond/Darrow had ideas they wanted to persuade the jury about, the writers and director of this movie had their story, too, their own version of what they thought was true, and like each of the characters and their real-life counterparts, they did their best to persuade their audience. Their audience's challenge is to do their best to determine what the truth really is.

PROFANITY: In keeping with his character as something of a heretic, Drummond uses some mild language, at one point censoring himself when he is about to say "damn."

NUDITY/SEXUAL REFERENCES: None.

ALCOHOL/DRUG ABUSE: None.

VIOLENCE/SCARINESS: Threats by crowd.

TOLERANCE/DIVERSITY ISSUES: None, beyond an accurate historical representation of traditional notions of "a woman's place."

✳ **QUESTIONS FOR KIDS:**
- Who won this case? Brady, who was able to persuade the jury to convict Cates, or Drummond, whose view ultimately prevailed?
- Both Drummond and Brady say, at different points in the case, that all they are interested in is the truth. Is that right? Do they mean different things when they use the word "truth"?
- Who should decide which version of the facts is taught to children: parents, teachers, or lawmakers?
- How do we know what is the best way to find the truth: the Brady way (to have faith) or the Drummond way (to question)? Which is each good for? Which is each bad for? What truth does the Drummond method show about Brady?
- In this movie, Drummond acknowledges that Cates broke the law, but argues that it is a bad law and should not be enforced. Should a jury do that? Under what circumstances?

✳ **CONNECTIONS:** This movie features three of the most talented and versatile actors in Hollywood history. All three were superb in dramatic or comedic roles, and of course Kelly is a legend for his dancing in the finest MGM musicals. It might be special fun to compare the two versions of *Dr. Jekyll and Mr. Hyde,* one with March (1932) and one with Tracy (1941). Fans of the early episodes of *Bewitched* will recognize Dick York (Cates) as the original Darrin Stephens (1964–69), and fans of TV's *The Rockford Files* will recognize Noah Beery, Jr. (Stebbens), as Jim Rockford's father, Rocky.

The director, Stanley Kramer, made a number of movies about political and social controversies, including **Judgment at Nuremberg** and **Guess Who's Coming to Dinner** (both with Tracy) and *On the Beach,* about people in Australia waiting to die after nuclear bombs have destroyed everything else.

✳ **ACTIVITIES:** High school kids can do research on controversies over the curriculum in local schools. They may also want to learn something about Darwin and his theories, or something about Clarence Darrow's colorful career.

✳The Ox-Bow Incident
1943, 75 min, NR, b&w, 10 and up
Dir: William Wellman. Henry Fonda, Dana Andrews

✳ **PLOT:** Two drifters, Gil Carter (Henry Fonda) and Art Croft (Harry Morgan), ride into a small town in Nevada in 1885. A rumor spreads that a well-liked cattle rancher named Kinkaid has been killed by rustlers, and the people in the town make up a posse to go after them. A shopkeeper named Davies (Harry Davenport) tries to stop them, warning, "We want to act in a reasoned and legitimate manner and not like a lawless mob." The judge asks them not to act in "this same spirit of lawlessness that begot this foul crime." But his pomposity and equivocation ("Of course, you can't flinch from what you believe to be your duty, but certainly you don't want to act hastily") are unpersuasive. He reminds them that the sheriff is away, and his deputy has no legal authority to deputize others. But he does, anyway. One of the group jeeringly invites Sparks (Leigh Whipper), a black handyman and preacher, to come along, telling him that praying will be needed, and he gently replies that they are "accidentally right," and he will go with them.

Some in the group are going along to revenge the death of their friend. Some go because they are bored and looking for excitement. Some are frustrated with the delays and "lawyer's tricks" of the legal system. One man is just a bully who enjoys feeling powerful at others' expense. A former Confederate major longs to be a leader again and to teach his son to be a man, "which I haven't been able to do." Carter and Croft go along in part because when they resist, suspicion falls on them.

As the group is about to give up, they find three men traveling with cattle that belonged to Kinkaid. Donald Martin (Dana Andrews) says that he has bought the cattle, but they do not have a bill of sale, and one of them has Kinkaid's gun, which he says he found. This is enough for the group, who sentence the three men, by a vote of twenty-one to seven, to be hanged immediately. Martin asks for a trial, or for a delay while his story is checked out, and when the major turns him down, he asks that the other two men, a Mexican (Anthony Quinn) and a feebleminded old man (Francis Ford), be allowed to go free. All the mob will grant him is a reprieve until dawn so that he may write a farewell letter to his wife.

Martin gives the letter to Davies, who begs to read it aloud in hopes that it will make the mob understand that Martin is innocent, but Martin refuses. The men are hanged. The major's son cannot bring himself to hit the horse out from under one of the condemned man, so the major strikes him and orders one of the other men to finish the job. Sparks kneels by the men to pray for them.

On the way back to town, the mob meets up with the sheriff, who tells them that Kinkaid has not been killed and will recover. Furthermore, the sheriff caught the men who shot him. When he hears what the mob has done, the sheriff says, "The Lord better have mercy on you. You won't get it from me." The major, in disgrace, kills himself. The rest raise $500 for Martin's widow. Carter reads aloud Martin's letter about conscience and the law, and then he and Croft leave town to deliver the letter and the money to Martin's widow.

✳ **DISCUSSION:** This film was made at a time when lynchings were still going on in the United States. The Tuskegee Institute documented nearly 2,000 from 1882 to 1943. Lynchings took place in every state, and although victims were of all races, the vast majority were black. The subject was so controversial that this film was not released until almost two years after it was filmed.

While lynchings have been all but eradicated in this country, the lesson of this movie—that ordinary, moral persons can be induced to commit acts of terrible cruelty and injustice—is still valid. This is not a wild-eyed mob acting out of hysteria. This is a combination of revenge, boredom, cruelty, cowardice, moral weakness, demagoguery, and irrationality overcoming humanity and fairness.

Compare this movie to **Stagecoach,** in which a sheriff in the Wild West combines traditional legal procedures with very rough ad hoc notions of "justice" (giving the Ringo Kid the opportunity for a shoot-out with the men who killed his family).

PROFANITY: None.
NUDITY/SEXUAL REFERENCES: Very oblique reference to Carter's past relationship with a young woman they meet on the road.
ALCOHOL/DRUG ABUSE: Drinking.
VIOLENCE/SCARINESS: Major strikes his son; a hanging and a suicide, both off camera.
TOLERANCE/DIVERSITY ISSUES: Sparks is the only person of faith in the movie; his deferential manner of speaking to whites is typical of the period.

✳ **QUESTIONS FOR KIDS:**
- Why was it so easy for these people to abandon the legal system's way of handling questions of guilt and innocence?
- What is the evidence that convinces the crowd that the men are guilty? How would that evidence be treated in court?
- Why is it important that the people in the mob have so many different reasons for going along?
- What does Martin mean about all consciences being part of one big conscience? Do you think he was right?

✳ **CONNECTIONS:** The book, by Walter Van Tilburg Clark, is worth reading for high schoolers. *Fury,* with Spencer Tracy, is a powerful film about lynching in a more contemporary setting. There are also references to lynching in some of the movies set in the early Civil Rights era, like **The Autobiography of Miss Jane Pittman.** Compare this community to the one in **High Noon,** where the people in the town would not act. In *The Ox-Bow Incident,* they are too willing to act, with disastrous consequences. Compare it, too, to **Lord of the Flies** on the issue of the disintegration of concepts of fairness and equality in a mob setting.

✳12 Angry Men

1959, 95 min, NR, b&w, 10 and up
Dir: Sidney Lumet. Henry Fonda, Lee J. Cobb, Ed Begley, Martin Balsam, Jack
Klugman, Jack Warden

✳ **PLOT:** Twelve jurors, hot and tired after a six-day murder trial, file into the jury room. They begin with a vote—eleven vote for a guilty verdict, but one (Henry Fonda), juror number eight, votes to acquit. The others are impatient, and there are mutters of "there's always one." Juror number eight says he is not convinced that the boy, accused of killing his father, is innocent, but that he believes they owe him more than one quick vote. They should talk about it before they find him guilty, which means an automatic sentence of death.

We never hear the men's names, but we learn a great deal about them as they deliberate. The boy admitted arguing with his father. He admitted buying a switchblade with a distinctive handle, exactly like the one the man was stabbed with. One witness says she saw the boy stab his father with the knife in the brief moment when an El train sped by the window. Another witness says he heard a body fall to the floor and then saw the boy run out of the apartment. But the boy says that he wasn't there, that he went to a movie, though on that night he could not remember the name of the movie or any of the details. He said the knife must have fallen out of his pocket.

After an hour, juror number eight says they should vote again, and if the eleven are still in favor of a guilty verdict, he will vote with them. But another juror changes his vote, and they continue to debate. They examine each piece of evidence, each word of testimony carefully. And they examine themselves, uncovering prejudices and blind spots that interfere with their ability to be impartial. One by one, each finds a flaw in the evidence that persuades him of the boy's innocence.

✳ **DISCUSSION:** The men are impatient to come to a conclusion not just because they are hot and tired, but also because they are uncomfortable sentencing a boy to death. They want it to be easy and clear-cut, and they want it to be quick, so they do not have to think too hard about what they are doing. Juror number eight's most difficult challenge is to get each of them to think independently and objectively about the evidence. One of the last jurors to change his mind is the ultralogical juror number four (E. G. Marshall). When a new fact is introduced that calls the logic of his calculations into question, he is willing to change his vote. But for most of the others, the issue is emotional as well as logical. Families should try to identify the way that each juror brings his background, personal or professional, into the deliberations. In some cases, that background provides insight that was helpful, as when juror number five (Jack Klugman) speaks of his experiences growing up in a slum. In others, the background is an obstacle that has to be overcome, as in the bigotry of juror number ten (Ed Begley) or the displaced anger of juror number three (Lee J. Cobb).

Notice in particular the way that juror number eight listens to everyone else, even when it does not relate to the case, as when the foreman tells him about the time his big game was rained out. Compare that to the energy juror number three devotes to refusing to listen, and to juror number seven's (Jack Warden) constant efforts to deflect or push away any engagement, intellectual or emotional, with wisecracks. Juror number seven's use of humor is in sharp contrast to that of some of the others, like juror number eleven, who use humor to make a point, to take the discussion further, as in the comment about the use of proper English. This is also an outstanding example of different approaches to problem-solving, an especially important subject for family discussion.

PROFANITY: None.
NUDITY/SEXUAL REFERENCES: None.
ALCOHOL/DRUG ABUSE: None.
VIOLENCE/SCARINESS: Tense, but not violent.
TOLERANCE/DIVERSITY ISSUES: A theme of the movie.

❋ **QUESTIONS FOR KIDS:**
- What would have happened if juror number eight had not been on the jury?
- Why didn't they use their names during the deliberation (or in the credits), and why did two of them introduce themselves before they left the courthouse?
- Why do you think juror number three's son won't see him? How did that affect his judgment?
- Why do we have juries, instead of just letting the judge decide every case? Why do we have twelve, and not fewer or more?
- Does this movie make you feel better or worse about the jury system? How will it affect you when you serve on a jury?

❋ **CONNECTIONS:** This film includes outstanding character actors Martin Balsam, Ed Begley (both Oscar-winners for other performances), E. G. Marshall (from television's *The Defenders*), Jack Klugman (from televison's *The Odd Couple* and *Quincy*), and Jack Warden (Harry Rosenfeld in **All the President's Men**). One of the best books ever written about filmmaking is Sidney Lumet's *Making Movies*, which includes a fascinating explanation of the making of this, his first feature film. Watch the way that he uses camera angles to create different impressions within the confines of the one-room set. The movie was remade for cable television in 1997, starring Jack Lemmon and George C. Scott, also very worthwhile.

❋ **ACTIVITIES:** Talk to the kids about your own service on a jury, or, if you have not had the chance to serve, see if someone else they know can tell them what it was like. Take them to sit in on a trial, or pick one suitable for them to watch a bit of on Court TV. Ask them how they would handle serving on a jury deciding the outcome of the O.J. Simpson case or some other trial in the news.

The Winslow Boy

1948, 117 min, NR, b&w, 10 and up
Dir: Anthony Asquith. Robert Donat, Margaret Leighton

✳ **PLOT:** This is the story of a real court case that was, in its, day, almost as notorious as the Dreyfus affair. In 1912, a fourteen-year-old boy was "sacked" (expelled) from a naval academy school for stealing a five shilling postal order (worth less than a dollar). At enormous cost—financial, emotional, and personal—the family challenges this decision until, granted a special right to have a barrister (Robert Donat) present their evidence in court, Ronnie Winslow is exonerated.

✳ **DISCUSSION:** Ronnie Winslow was kicked out of school without a chance to review the evidence against him or get any kind of hearing. The school refused to permit his father to see the evidence, and the goverment prohibited any kind of challenge, arguing that to permit people to sue a government agency would create a dangerous precedent. But Ronnie's father insists on pursuing it with the help of the country's top barrister (trial lawyer). The issue of what is "fair" is presented from several different perspectives.

As the case drags on, Ronnie's brother must leave school and get a job, and his sister's engagement is broken. But Ronnie's father and sister never waver in their support of his right to a hearing to establish his honesty. The members of the family (including the erstwhile fiancé) and Sir Robert react to the situation differently, which reveals the character as well as the perspective of each one.

Families should discuss the way that Ronnie's family decided to make considerable sacrifices to support his exoneration, as well as Sir Robert's comment that his goal was "right," rather than "justice."

PROFANITY: None.

NUDITY/SEXUAL REFERENCES: None.

ALCOHOL/DRUG ABUSE: None.

VIOLENCE/SCARINESS: None.

TOLERANCE/DIVERSITY ISSUES: Ronnie's sister, Catherine, is a suffragist, though she explains more than once she is not "militant." (When Sir Robert tells her it's a lost cause, she replies, "How little you know women.") A female reporter says that she expects people to be surprised when they find a woman journalist, then she conforms to stereotype by acting like a fluttery scatterbrain.

✳ **QUESTIONS FOR KIDS:**
- Were you surprised when Sir Robert agreed to represent Ronnie and, after questioning him, said he was innocent? How do you think that he made up his mind?
- Sir Robert admits that some of what he does is more like putting on a play than arguing a case. When does he do that?
- What can you tell about John by the way he reacts to Ronnie's dis-

missal from school? What do the scenes in the music hall add to the movie?

- Ronnie's sister tells Sir Robert that she and her father have different goals. What are they? What do they tell you about each of the characters?
- Everyone in the Winslow family made enormous sacrifices to pursue the case. How would your family evaluate their options in such a case?

✳ **CONNECTIONS:** The movie was remade for British television in 1988, with Emma Thompson as Catherine.

✳ **ACTIVITIES:** The issue of who has the right to sue the government is still an important one. Look up the Magna Carta (which is referred to in the movie) in an encyclopedia to see how the question was first raised in Britain, and look up "sovereign immunity" to find out how it has been addressed in the United States. The issue of children's rights is also a continuing controversy. Kids will like to read about the case of *Tinker v. the School Board of Des Moines*, in which the Supreme Court upheld the right of a high school student to exercise free speech by wearing a black armband to protest the Vietnam War, and *In re Gault*, in which the Court found that children and teenagers had a right to the same fair treatment as adults, despite arguments that these rights were suspended for their "protection."

✳Judgment at Nuremberg

1961, 178 min, NR, b&w, high schoolers
Dir: Stanley Kramer. Spencer Tracy, Burt Lancaster, Maximilian Schell

✳ **PLOT:** One of the most fascinating explorations of moral choices ever filmed, this movie focuses on the Nuremberg trials that followed World War II. When this movie begins, the trials of the highest-ranking war criminals are over, and the men now on trial are the judges who abandoned their sworn commitment to truth and justice to follow the orders of Hitler and provide legal authority for his atrocities. Spencer Tracy plays the American judge assigned to preside over the trial of his German counterparts, one of whom is portrayed by Burt Lancaster. Richard Widmark plays the prosecuting attorney, and Maximilian Schell (who won an Oscar) plays the lawyer for the defense.

The judges say that they were "just following orders," and that if they had done anything else they would have been imprisoned or killed. Tracy must confront his own moral dilemma when he is pressured to be lenient with the judges to protect American political interests. Though he has some reason to be especially sensitive on this point, having lost a reelection to his position in America, he insists on issuing a judgment based on upholding "justice, truth, and the value of a single human being."

Every family with teenagers should make an effort to watch this film together, to talk about the history involved and how to evalute the necessity for disobeying orders, even at the direst risk to oneself and one's family. NOTE: The movie includes description and explicit documentary footage of concentration camp atrocities.

✳ **CONNECTIONS:** There are many excellent books to read about the Nuremberg trials and the era, including *Night,* by Elie Wiesel, and *Ordinary Men,* by Christopher R. Browning. *Schindler's List,* and the play *The Andersonville Trial,* by Saul Levitt (about a Civil War prison camp), raise related issues.

✳ WITNESS FOR THE PROSECUTION
1957, 114 min, NR, b&w, 10 and up
Dir: Billy Wilder. Tyrone Power, Marlene Dietrich, Charles Laughton

Handsome and likable Leonard Vole (Tyrone Power), accused of killing his wealthy benefactor, is defended by a choleric barrister (Charles Laughton) in this Agatha Christie courtroom classic that raises many questions of fairness and justice. Marlene Dietrich plays the enigmatic Mrs. Vole, and Elsa Lanchester (Laughton's wife) plays the barrister's fluttery nurse.

✳ **CONNECTIONS:** The movie was remade for British television in 1982 with Ralph Richardson and Diana Rigg.

HELPING OTHERS

"The best of alms is that which the right hand giveth, and the left hand knoweth it not."

—MUHAMMAD

Compassion and empathy are important, but they are not enough. Those feelings must be translated into action that makes a difference. In these films, characters try several different ways of helping others, and sometimes find that it takes more than enthusiasm and good intentions. The first challenge is to understand what the problem is. As the movie director hero finds in **Sullivan's Travels,** the poor people he wants to help are more grateful for funny movies than they would be for the turgid dramas he wanted to make to show his sensitivity to their suffering. And Major Barbara learns that handouts at the mission are not as helpful to people as jobs.

It is also important to help others in a way that preserves, or better yet enhances, their sense of dignity. These films show us that helping others—and being able to accept help ourselves—give our lives meaning and resonance, and help our spirits grow and deepen.

Bells Are Ringing
1960, 127 min, NR, 6 and up
Dir: Vincente Minnelli. Judy Holliday, Dean Martin

* **PLOT:** Ella Peterson (Judy Holliday) works for an answering service. Her job is to "take and deliver messages" to the clients. But she can't help trying to solve their problems, too. Shy in person, over the phone she plays Santa Claus for one mother who wants help persuading her son to eat his spinach, prescribes a mustard plaster for an opera singer with a chest cold, and provides motherly advice to Jeffrey Moss (Dean Martin), a playwright who is struggling with his first solo effort following a split with his longtime

partner. She has a crush on Jeffrey and says they have a "perfect relationship," where "I can't see him, he can't see me, he thinks that I am eighty-three." But when he oversleeps on the day of an important appointment, she goes to his apartment to make sure he wakes up, intending to leave before he sees her. He does see her, and she makes up a different name and identity for herself and stays to help him get his work done. He falls in love with her. Ella also visits two other clients, an out-of-work actor and a dentist who wants to be a songwriter. Based on what she has learned from her other clients, she gives them advice about how to get jobs and disappears before they can ask who she is.

In the meantime, Ella's cousin, Sue (Jean Stapleton), the owner of the answering service, has a new boyfriend, Otto (Eddie Foy, Jr.), who tells her she is accepting record orders for him when she is really placing illegal bets. Two detectives are following Ella to investigate the answering service as a possible call-girl operation. And Ella agonizes over how to tell Jeffrey that she is not "Melisande Scott" but just the answering service operator he calls "Ma." All of this is resolved as the dentist, the actor, Jeffrey, the detectives, and the bookie show up at Ella's office, and everyone lives happily ever after, even Otto, whose arrest saves him from a worse fate at the hands of mobsters.

✻ **DISCUSSION:** In these days of Voicemail and answering machines, it is a good idea to begin by explaining to children what an answering service is. They may also find it hard to understand the "Drop a Name" scene, in which Ella is taught how to succeed at a snobbish party by acting as though she knows anyone who is famous. It is unlikely they will recognize any of the names in the song, other than Lassie.

The movie begins with a "commercial" for Susansaphone, amusingly followed by a scene that shows that the real operation is far less elegant than portrayed in the ad. The story and the music are wonderful (including the standards "Just in Time" and "The Party's Over"), and there are a lot of good issues to talk about with children, including the importance of being yourself, dealing with feelings of shyness and inadequacy, and the way a person can transform the lives of others with a sympathetic ear and the willingness to get involved.

PROFANITY: None.

NUDITY/SEXUAL REFERENCES: Suspicion that the answering service is a call-girl operation.

ALCOHOL/DRUG ABUSE: Jeffrey drinks (off camera) to avoid having to work on his own.

VIOLENCE/SCARINESS: None.

TOLERANCE/DIVERSITY ISSUES: None.

✻ **QUESTIONS FOR KIDS:**
• Why does Ella find it easier to talk to people on the phone than in person?

- Why is Jeffrey afraid to work on his play?
- What does Ella do to help Blake and Dr. Kitchell?
- What makes Ella so special? Do you know anyone who helps people the way she does?

✳ **CONNECTIONS:** Jean Stapleton of TV's *All in the Family* plays Ella's cousin, Sue. Frank Gorshin (The Riddler on television's *Batman*) plays Blake Barton (a parody of 1950s actors who liked to imitate Marlon Brando by mumbling their lines). Eddie Foy, Jr.'s, real-life show business family was portrayed in the movie *The Seven Little Foys,* starring Bob Hope as vaudevillian Eddie Foy, Sr. You can also see Foy, Jr. playing his own father in **Yankee Doodle Dandy** and *Wilson.* Ella's disastrous blind date in the beginning of the movie is with her real-life love, jazz great Gerry Mulligan.

✳ **ACTIVITIES:** See if the kids can learn the cha-cha along with Ella. Try to come up with names that might fit in the song "Drop That Name" if it were written today.

✳Lilies of the Field

1963, 93 min., NR, b&w, 10 to adult
Dir: Ralph Nelson. Sidney Poitier, Lilia Skala, Stanley Adams

✳ **PLOT:** Homer Smith (Sidney Poitier), a black itinerant handyman driving through the Arizona desert, stops at a farm to ask for some water. The farm is the home of a small group of nuns, recent refugees from Eastern Europe. He stays on to do some work for them, but resists when the flinty Mother Superior (Lilia Skala) wants him to build a chapel, especially when it is clear that they are not going to pay him. "I ain't no contractor. I don't need all that work," he says.

Ultimately, for his own reasons, the chapel becomes his dream, too. The skepticism and prejudice of the local builder makes him want to prove himself. He tells Mother Maria, "All my life, I wanted to really build something, you know? Well, maybe, if I had an education, I would have been an architect or even an engineer and throw the Golden Gate Bridge across San Francisco Bay. And even maybe build a rocket ship to Venus or something." As fiercely independent as Mother Maria, he wants to do it himself. But he learns how to accept the help of the community and to become their leader. When the chapel is complete, he writes his name in the cement in the bell tower and drives on.

✳ **DISCUSSION:** When this movie was made in the midst of the early 1960s civil rights battles for integration and tolerance, a black man in the leading role made it seem that the movie was about race. Now, more than thirty years later, we see that race is just one of many differences the characters must understand in order to be able to work together. A black

Baptist, a group of nuns who have just escaped from East Germany, a Mexican-American atheist, a group of Mexican-American Catholics, and an Irish priest find themselves building a chapel together in the Arizona desert. Until Smith takes over, it is like the Tower of Babel, but with his leadership they all work together as a community.

More important than the cultural and religious differences between Smith and Mother Maria are their temperaments and personalities, especially their insistence on independence, a theme throughout this movie. Both are fiercely independent and refuse to accept help, and both, in this story, learn to do so. Smith, who puts a sign saying DON'T TOUCH ANYTHING on the bricks, finally accepts the help of the members of the community when they begin handing him bricks. At first he sulks, but when it becomes clear that they need him, he takes over. Mother Maria refuses to acknowledge his contribution, saying, "I thank Him—you couldn't help yourself." When she criticizes him for bringing candy to the nuns, Smith says to her, "You are very large on religion and all of that, but you don't even know how to accept a gift from somebody without making him feel small." But as he is getting ready to go, he says, "Sank you," gently mocking her accent, and as she corrects him, showing off the English he has helped her improve, she says, "Thank you," and they both realize that she is acknowledging his contribution.

PROFANITY: None.

NUDITY/SEXUAL REFERENCES: None.

ALCOHOL/DRUG ABUSE: The priest has an (off-screen) drinking problem. Smith has an off-screen escapade that leaves him hung over and is hung over again the night after the fiesta celebrating the completion of the chapel.

VIOLENCE/SCARINESS: None.

TOLERANCE/DIVERSITY ISSUES: The issue of race is sensitively handled in this movie. Smith, teaching the nuns to speak English, uses his own skin to illustrate the word "black." Ashton, the local builder, calls Smith "boy," prompting Smith to prove himself to Ashton, to the nuns, and to himself. Later on, Ashton humbly asks "Mr. Smith" to come back to work for him. Without Smith's leadership, the chapel becomes something of a Tower of Babel, with all of the different cultures and languages spoken by the members of the community. Once he takes over, they all work together cooperatively.

❋ QUESTIONS FOR KIDS:
• In what ways are Mother Maria and Homer alike?
• In what ways are they different?
• What did the chapel mean to each of them?
• How will Homer's life be different from now on?

❋ CONNECTIONS: Poitier, the first black movie star to play leading roles, became the first black man to win an Oscar for his performance in this movie. A made-for-television movie sequel, *Christmas Lilies of the Field*, starred Billy Dee Williams.

Magnificent Obsession
1954, 108 min, NR, 10 and up
Dir: Douglas Sirk. Rock Hudson, Jane Wyman, Agnes Moorehead

✳ **PLOT:** Bob Merrick (Rock Hudson), a careless playboy, is injured in an accident, and critical medical equipment is used to save his life, making it unavailable to save the life of a beloved doctor. The doctor's widow, Helen Phillips (Jane Wyman), discovers that the doctor left no money, but she receives mysterious messages from many people he had helped by lending them money. He never had allowed them to pay him back because "it wasn't used up yet."

Bob inadvertently causes an accident that blinds Helen. Overcome with guilt, he meets an artist who explains the doctor's secret, his "magnificent obsession." He had devoted his life to helping others, with two requirements: It must be a secret, and he must not be repaid. Instead, he had urged them to pass it along by helping someone else the same way. Bob finds this foolish. But, using another name, he befriends Helen, and they fall in love. He begins to see the satisfaction in helping others. He returns to the medical studies he had abandoned and is able to develop an operation to restore Helen's sight.

✳ **DISCUSSION:** This is by no means a good movie in terms of its literary qualities. Though gorgeously produced, it is hopelessly melodramatic. But for someone young enough not to know how corny and melodramatic it is, it can be very affecting, and the point it makes about finding meaning in life through helping others without any repayment, and without boosting one's reputation, is very worthwhile.

PROFANITY: None.

NUDITY/SEXUAL REFERENCES: None.

ALCOHOL/DRUG ABUSE: Social drinking; references to Bob's drinking too much in his playboy days.

VIOLENCE/SCARINESS: Helen hit by car.

TOLERANCE/DIVERSITY ISSUES: None.

✳ **QUESTIONS FOR KIDS:**
- What did the doctor mean when he told the people he helped that he hadn't "used it up yet"?
- Why was it important that they were not allowed to tell anyone?
- Why was it important that they were not allowed to pay him back?
- Why could Bob show his real self to Helen only after she was blind?

✳ **CONNECTIONS:** This is a remake of a 1935 version starring Robert Taylor and Irene Dunne, based on a novel by Lloyd C. Douglas, whose books includes *The Robe.* Jewish philosopher Moses Maimonides created a hierarchy of charity, with the lowest level a contribution in which the donor and the recipient know each other, and the highest level the creation of a society in which charity is no longer necessary. His emphasis on the dignity of the recipient and the genuineness of the charity from the donor (without expectation of thanks or reward) fits well with this movie. The idea of finding cheer and happiness through helping others is a part of many religions and philosophies.

*Mr. Deeds Goes to Town
1936, 115 min, NR, b&w, 10 and up
Dir: Frank Capra. Gary Cooper, Jean Arthur

* **PLOT:** Longfellow Deeds (Gary Cooper), of Mandrake Falls, Vermont, is a quiet bachelor who writes rhymes for birthday cards and plays the tuba for concentration. Informed that he has inherited twenty million dollars, he goes to New York City to collect it.

Swarms of people come after him to try to get some of the money, but the only one he will talk to is Babe Bennett (Jean Arthur), who attracts his attention by fainting. She tells him she is an unemployed secretary, but in reality she is a tough journalist out for a good story. He has a lot of fun feeding doughnuts to hungry cab horses and chasing fire engines. When some snooty poets make fun of his rhymes, he says, "I know I must look funny to you. Maybe if you came to Mandrake Falls, you'd look just as funny to us. . . . But nobody'd laugh at you and make you ridiculous—'cause that wouldn't be good manners." He tells Bennett his impressions of the city, explaining that the wealthy people in New York "work so hard at living, they forget how to live . . . They've created a lot of grand palaces, but they forgot about the noblemen to put in them."

Bennett writes a newspaper story making fun of him, calling him "The Cinderella man," and he becomes a figure of ridicule. But she realizes she has fallen in love with him, with his innate goodness and sincerity and his ability to have fun.

Heartbroken by her betrayal, and disgusted with life as a wealthy man, Deeds makes plans to give the money away to help poor farmers. But unscrupulous relatives take him to court, arguing that he is not competent and that they should have control of the money.

He is too miserable to defend himself. But Bennett persuades him that she loves him and that he must try. And the judge concludes, "In my opinion, you are not only sane, you are the sanest man who ever walked into this courtroom."

* **DISCUSSION:** This is one of Frank Capra's populist classics, and its Depression-era sensibility is still appealing. Finding meaning in life through

helping others is well-presented, as are the issues of what makes people important (Deeds says, "All famous people aren't big people"). The public policy issue of how much help we give to those "who can't make the hill on high" is something that teenagers with an interest in politics might like to pursue.

The issue of the role of the press is even more timely now, as public figures and even private ones are considered fair game. More important, and more relevant to kids, especially teenagers, is the issue of cynicism as a mode of approaching the world. Bennett says, "He's got a lot of goodness, Mabel. Do you know what that means? No, of course you don't. We've forgotten. We're all too busy being smart alecks." That's a good description of teenagers who put on a cynical demeanor to protect themselves from being vulnerable. A thoughtful journalist once said that a reporter's responsibility was to be skeptical without being cynical, and that statement is a good way to open a discussion of this issue. Deeds's statement that "It's easy to make fun of someone if you don't care how much you hurt 'em" is also something for kids to think about.

It is also worthwhile to consider how the same facts can be interpreted differently. Deeds plays the tuba, feeds doughnuts to horses, and wants to give money away. Those actions can be seen as foolish (as portrayed in Bennett's newspaper), crazy (as portrayed by the lawyer), or endearing (as portrayed by Cooper and Capra). What does that tell us about being careful to challenge "spin"?

PROFANITY: None.

NUDITY/SEXUAL REFERENCES: None.

ALCOHOL/DRUG ABUSE: Deeds gets drunk (which is one of the charges against his competency).

VIOLENCE/SCARINESS: Deeds punches some people.

TOLERANCE/DIVERSITY ISSUES: Tolerance for different kinds of people, especially those in need.

✲ QUESTIONS FOR KIDS:

- Why did Babe Bennett's editor want her to make fun of Deeds?
- What do you do to help you concentrate?
- If Mr. Deeds inherited the money today, what group do you think he would give it to?
- What would you do if you inherited twenty million dollars?

✲ CONNECTIONS: This movie popularized two words: "doodle" and "pixilated." As Deeds points out, doodling is highly individual.

✲ ACTIVITIES: Let the kids "doodle" while watching the movie, and see what they come up with. They might also like to try making up some words of their own.

Sullivan's Travels

1941, 91 min, NR, b&w, 10 and up
Dir: Preston Sturges. Joel McCrea, Veronica Lake

❋ **PLOT:** "Sully" Sullivan (Joel McCrea) is a successful director of silly comedies, including *Ants in Your Pants* and *Hey, Hey in the Hayloft.* The studio wants him to make more, but he wants to make a movie with a serious message about the Depression and man's inhumanity to man. He plans on calling it *O Brother, Where Art Thou?* When he lists all the things that are wrong with the world, the studio executive replies, "Maybe they'd like to forget that." His own butler advises him that "the subject is not an interesting one. The poor know all about poverty, and only the morbid rich find the subject glamorous. . . . It is to be stayed away from, even for the purpose of study. It is to be shunned." But Sullivan is determined. Before he can make the movie, he has to see what life is like as a "bum." His first efforts fail, as the luxurious studio trailer follows him around. He meets "the Girl" (Veronica Lake), a would-be actress, and she persuades him to let her go with him, dressed as a boy, and they start over again.

This time he discovers the sadness and lack of dignity among the homeless. But before he can go back home, he and the Girl are separated, and he is hit on the head, becomes disoriented, and loses his memory. He punches a railroad guard and is sentenced to six years on a chain gang. Meanwhile, the hobo who has stolen his shoes is killed and, through the studio identification card sewn into the shoes, is identified as Sullivan. One night, the prisoners are taken to a small church, where they see a Mickey Mouse cartoon. Sullivan realizes the joy that laughter gives to these men who have nothing else.

When Sullivan regains his memory, he gets out of jail by "confessing" to his own murder so he can contact his lawyer and be properly identified. He goes home to find that his wife has remarried, leaving him free to marry the Girl. And he resolves to make more funny movies, because he realizes that is the best contribution he can make, concluding, "There's a lot to be said for making people laugh. Did you know that's all that some people have? It isn't much, but it's better than nothing in this cock-eyed caravan."

❋ **DISCUSSION:** Sensitive teenagers often make the mistake of thinking they cannot care deeply and still find humor, or that those around them cannot appreciate their pain and still find anything funny, even something that has no relation to the situation they are struggling with. This movie makes it clear that laughter and insight go together, that humor is never an insult to a serious situation, indeed that humor can be the highest form of awareness and perception, and that making people laugh can be a good way to help them. Sullivan himself is funny, with his pretensions and his misguided attempts to find out what poverty is like.

PROFANITY: None.
NUDITY/SEXUAL REFERENCES: Very mild.

ALCOHOL/DRUG ABUSE: None.

VIOLENCE/SCARINESS: Fighting; a hobo is killed; Sullivan is sent to jail.

TOLERANCE/DIVERSITY ISSUES: Class issues are a subtext.

❋ QUESTIONS FOR KIDS:

• Why does Sullivan want to make a different kind of movie?

• Why don't the studio executives want him to? How do they try to persuade him?

• What is the difference between the ways that the two servants try to find out how Sullivan can board the train? Why does the second one work?

• What does the Girl mean when she says, "The nice thing about buying food for a man is that you don't have to laugh at his jokes"?

• What does Sullivan learn from the Mickey Mouse cartoon?

• Do you think this is the kind of movie that Sullivan would make when he gets back to the studio?

❋ CONNECTIONS: Woody Allen echoed the sentiments of this movie

when he had aliens inform his character in *Stardust Memories* (not for kids), "You want to help humanity? Write funnier jokes!" In *No Time for Comedy*, Jimmy Stewart plays a character somewhat like Sully, the author of a series of very successful comedies on Broadway, starring his wife, played by Rosalind Russell. In his case, another woman persuades him that he is too sensitive and important to write comedies, and with her "inspiration" he writes a serious play that is a disaster. Poet W. H. Auden said it best: "The funniest mortals and the kindest/are most aware of the baffle of being/don't kid themselves our care is consolable/but believe that a laugh is less heartless than tears."

Screenwriter/director Preston Sturges described the movie this way: "Bit by bit I took everything away from (Sullivan)—health, fortune, name, pride, and liberty. When I got down to there, I found he still had one thing left: the ability to laugh. So, as a purveyor of laughs, he regained the dignity of his profession and returned to Hollywood to make laughter."

Sturges himself was one of Hollywood's best "purveyors of laughs," with a unique combination of satire and slapstick that enabled him to get away with angrier and even more savage messages than any other director of his time. In 1944, for example, when all of America was patriotically starry-eyed, he attacked hero worship and war heroes in *Hail the Conquering Hero*. His satire skewered the rich (*Easy Living*, *The Lady Eve*, *The Palm Beach Story*) and the not-so-rich (*Christmas in July*, *The Miracle of Morgan's Creek*), the clever (**The Great McGinty**), and the not-so-clever (*Christmas in July*), the honest (*The Lady Eve*) and the not-so-honest (*The Lady Eve* again), and, always, anyone with any pretensions. In his best movies, including this one, he allowed his characters to learn something and, in learning, achieve intimacy.

SEE ALSO:

Awakenings A doctor who tries to help patients no one thought could be helped has to question whether it was the right thing to do when his efforts result in only a brief improvement.

Hello, Dolly! Dolly finds a way to help everyone around her discover their dreams and then make them come true.

Major Barbara A central theme of the movie is the best—meaning most moral and most effective—way to help people who need it.

White Christmas The issue of finding a way to help a general without hurting his pride is sensitively handled.

RESPECT

The greatest good you can do for another is not just to share your riches but to reveal to him his own.
—BENJAMIN DISRAELI

As with education, respect has a transformational effect. Over and over, movies show us that being treated with respect makes people feel differently about themselves and about the people around them. Interestingly, respect for oneself and respect for others are closely linked. Some films show us characters so transformed by respect that they are able to allow themselves to fall in love and to feel worthy of being loved. In some cases, the characters find that they have been worthy of respect all along; in others, they change their behavior to earn it and find more meaningful changes in themselves than they had hoped. Courtesy is linked to this value because it implies respect for others.

Bus Stop

1956, 96 min, NR, b&w, 10 and up
Dir: Joshua Logan. Marilyn Monroe, Don Murray, Arthur O'Connell, Hope Lange

* **PLOT:** Bo (Don Murray) is a rough cowboy who comes to the city for the first time with his more worldly friend, Virgil (Arthur O'Connell), to compete in a rodeo. They meet Cherie (Marilyn Monroe), a good-hearted girl who sings and hustles drinks in a saloon. Cherie's casual affection persuades Bo that she is the one he wants to marry, and he carries her off, without her permission, on the bus.

The roads are snowed in, and they get stuck at a bus stop. Bo will not listen when Cherie insists she is not going with him. With the help of the others at the bus stop, she persuades him that he cannot make her marry him. But then it emerges that she is afraid she cannot live up to the vision he has of her. She has had "many boyfriends." He is crushed at first but, after talking to Virgil, tells her that since he has never had any girlfriends, they balance each other out. After a gentle kiss, she tells him she would go anywhere with him. He wraps her in his warm coat and puts her back on the bus, at first objecting when Virgil says he is not going with them because it is time for him to move on, but finally accepting it. He does not need Virgil to take care of him anymore; he has to take care of Cherie.

❋ **DISCUSSION:** This is probably Marilyn Monroe's finest performance as a dramatic actor. The way she sings "That Old Black Magic" tells us a lot about Cherie's dreams of herself as a singer, and Monroe has the courage to make Cherie a far less talented performer than Monroe was herself. In her dealings with Bo, Cherie insists on her right to make her own choices, but Monroe also lets us see how much she longs to be loved the way Bo wants to love her, how much she wants to deserve it.

The movie also shows nicely the way that people must allow themselves to be vulnerable by being honest in order to be known and loved. Bo adds to his natural bluster because he does not want to let Cherie see how panicked he is by his overwhelming feelings for her. He longs to be close to her, but is afraid that she won't want to be with him if he lets her see that he is not always strong and confident. He finds out that she responds to his vulnerability because it is honest, because it allows her to play an equal role, and because she wants to be needed. Cherie fears that she does not deserve the level of devotion he offers. When he is willing to love her after hearing what she is ashamed of, she can allow herself to love him.

PROFANITY: Mild.

NUDITY/SEXUAL REFERENCES: References to Cherie's past (subtle by today's standards).

ALCOHOL/DRUG ABUSE: Drinking in a bar.

VIOLENCE/SCARINESS: Fistfight.

TOLERANCE/DIVERSITY ISSUES: Tolerance of differences.

❋ **QUESTIONS FOR KIDS:**
- Why is Bo so insistent on making Cherie come with him? Why doesn't he listen to her?
- How can you tell she has mixed feelings about him? What are they?
- What purpose do the other characters in the movie serve?
- What makes Cherie change her mind?
- What does it show us when Bo gives Cherie his coat?
- Why does Virgil decide to leave Bo?

❋ **CONNECTIONS:** The movie is based on a play by William Inge, author of *Splendor in the Grass*. Older kids might like to read the play, which takes place entirely at the bus stop, to see how it was expanded and adapted for the screen.

*Captains Courageous

1937, 116 min, NR, b&w, 7 and up
Dir: Victor Fleming. Spencer Tracy, Freddie Bartholomew, Lionel Barrymore,
Melvyn Douglas, Mickey Rooney

* **PLOT:** Harvey Cheyne (Freddie Bartholomew) is a spoiled rich boy who thinks that the way to succeed is to be a bully and a show-off. He tries to buy his way to success at boarding school. His father (Melvyn Douglas), preoccupied and indulgent, believes that Harvey is thriving at school. When Harvey gets in trouble at school, Mr. Cheyne takes him on an ocean liner to Europe. Harvey tries to show off to the other children onboard and bets that he can drink six sodas. He succeeds but, feeling sick, he falls overboard. He is not heard by anyone on the ship, but he is rescued by Manuel (Spencer Tracy), one of a crew of Portuguese fishermen. No matter how much Harvey tries to bribe or threaten the sailors, they tell him they cannot take him back until they complete their fishing expedition.

Harvey finds he wants their approval and learns he can only get it on their terms, which means competent, responsible, hard work. The other fishermen ignore or belittle him, but Manuel, feeling responsible for the "fish" he caught, befriends Harvey. As Harvey works to gain Manuel's respect, Manuel pays him the compliment of inviting him to share his dory, the first person to be invited since Manuel's father died. On the way home, as they race a rival ship, Manuel is in an accident. Knowing he will die, he says good-bye to Harvey, who is heartbroken. Later, back home, Harvey's father goes with him to the memorial service, and together they throw memorial rings of flowers into the water. As they drift out to sea, the rings intertwine.

* **DISCUSSION:** This is an exciting and touching story. There is always something very satisfying about seeing a spoiled brat get his comeuppance (see also *The Magnificent Ambersons* and *Private Benjamin*). But what is shown especially well here is the way that with Manuel, Harvey for the first time learns to respect others and himself. It is clear how unhappy, even desperate, Harvey is at school and on the ocean liner. He wants to be respected and liked but has no idea of how to go about it because no one has been there to teach him. As soon as he meets someone who is willing to tell him what he must do, he is eager to learn and is thrilled with the results. This movie shows that work is good for the spirit, that spoiled kids are unhappy (an astonishing concept for children), and that making friends is a skill that can—and must—be learned.

PROFANITY: None.
NUDITY/SEXUAL REFERENCES: None.
ALCOHOL/DRUG ABUSE: None.
VIOLENCE/SCARINESS: An accident that kills Manuel.
TOLERANCE/DIVERSITY ISSUES: None.

* **QUESTIONS FOR KIDS:**
  • What does Harvey try to do to get other kids to like him? Why doesn't it work? Have you ever seen a kid behave that way? What did you do?

- Who does Harvey like? Why?
- Why does Manuel's approval mean so much to Harvey?
- Why does Manuel talk to Harvey when no one else will?
- What does it mean when Manuel invites Harvey to share his dory?
- What does Harvey learn from Manuel? Do you think Harvey's relationship with his father will change? How?
- Will Harvey have to teach his father anything? What?

✱ **CONNECTIONS:** This movie has an outstanding cast, featuring some of MGM's finest actors. Freddie Bartholomew was the Macaulay Culkin of his day, one of the most popular child stars in film history. He appears here with Mickey Rooney, who was the most popular star, child or adult, in Hollywood from 1939–41. They also appeared together in **Little Lord Fauntleroy.** Spencer Tracy won the first of his Academy Awards for his performance as Manuel, an uncharacteristic performance for an actor who did not like to use accents or makeup to create a character. The following year, he won again for his portrayal of Father Flanagan in *Boys Town,* also starring Mickey Rooney. Lionel Barrymore, brother of movie stars John and Ethel, was an MGM stalwart. Families will enjoy his performance in *On Borrowed Time* as the grandfather who traps Death in a tree, and in **You Can't Take It With You** as the patriarch of the lovably nutty Sycamore family. Of course, he also plays the evil Mr. Potter in **It's a Wonderful Life,** in the wheelchair to which he was confined for the last fifteen years of his life. The director, Victor Fleming, went on to direct **The Wizard of Oz** and **Gone With the Wind.** The movie is based on a book by Rudyard Kipling, the author of **The Jungle Book** and the *Just-So Stories.*

✱Johnny Belinda

1948, 103 min, NR, b&w, 12 and up
Dir: Jean Negulesco. Jane Wyman, Lew Ayres

✱ **PLOT:** Belinda (Jane Wyman) lives with her father and aunt on a farm on an island off the coast of Nova Scotia. Her father, Black McDonald, is hard and angry. He resents Belinda because her mother died when she was born, and he treats her like an animal because she is deaf and mute. People in the town refer to her as "the dummy." Dr. Robert Richardson (Lew Ayres) teaches Belinda to communicate through sign language, and for the first time, her sweet and loving personality emerges. She is raped by Locky McCormick, a drunken brute, and becomes pregnant. The baby is named Johnny Belinda.

Everyone assumes that Robert is the father, and he must leave the community. Belinda's father finds out Locky was responsible and confronts him. Locky kills Black, making it look like an accident. When Locky's wife cannot have children, he wants Belinda's baby, knowing it is the only child he will ever have. The people in the town believe that Belinda cannot take care of the baby and decide to take it away from her.

Locky goes to Belinda's house and tries to take the baby, but she thinks he means to harm him. Trying to protect herself and the baby, she kills Locky. She is charged with murder. It looks as though she will be convicted, until Locky's widow comes forward and tells the truth. The community understands that even though Belinda cannot speak, she is loving, devoted, brave, and intelligent. Robert returns to be with Belinda and her child.

✳ **DISCUSSION:** Jane Wyman spoke of trying to achieve an "anticipation light" when she was preparing for this role, the look of interest and attention she saw in deaf people who were trying to understand what hearing people were trying to communicate. See if the kids can recognize this look and even try to create it themselves. They also may want to wear earplugs, as Wyman did, to help adjust her reactions to those of someone who does not respond to auditory cues and signals.

This movie does a good job of showing that learning a little bit can make a person hungry to learn more, and that having even one person believe in someone can make that person feel capable of achieving anything. The key themes of this movie, recognizing the humanity in those who are different and the impact that having that humanity recognized has on people and everyone around them, are well worth discussing.

Some kids may want to know more about rape, as well, and this provides an opportunity to discuss it as a crime of power and aggression rather than of sex. Young girls often misunderstand and worry about somehow sending a signal that invites rape. It is important to make sure they understand that, as shown in this movie, rapists are not accepting an invitation and that, on the contrary, it is the idea of overpowering someone who does not want to consent to sex that is exciting to them.

PROFANITY: None.

NUDITY/SEXUAL REFERENCES: Belinda is raped.

ALCOHOL/DRUG ABUSE: Locky is drunk when he rapes Belinda.

VIOLENCE/SCARINESS: The rape scene is sensitively handled, but still scary.

TOLERANCE/DIVERSITY ISSUES: A theme of the movie.

✳ **QUESTIONS FOR KIDS:**
- Why is Belinda's father so hard on her?
- How much do you think Belinda understands before she learns sign language? How can you tell?
- What makes her decide to be more aware of her appearance?
- Why does Aggie change in the way she treats Belinda? What does she mean when she says their family may fight with each other, but they support each other when any one of them needs it?
- How is this movie similar to *The Miracle Worker*? How is it different?

- Why does Locky's widow decide to tell the truth?
- Why does the ability to communicate make such a difference in the way people see Belinda?

✳ **CONNECTIONS:** The defense attorney is played by Alan Napier, later Alfred on television's *Batman* series.

✳ **ACTIVITIES:** Belinda learns American Sign Language, rather than the more laborious finger-spelling that Annie Sullivan teaches to Helen Keller in **The Miracle Worker,** because Belinda can see. Most libraries have good books or videos to teach beginners sign language, and kids will enjoy learning some of the signs.

✳ IT SHOULD HAPPEN TO YOU

1954, 87 min, NR, b&w, 8 and up
Dir: George Cukor. Judy Holliday, Jack Lemmon

Judy Holliday plays a young woman who feels so thoroughly ignored by the world that she spends every penny she has left to have her name put on a billboard. Somehow this manages to turn her into a celebrity. All of a sudden, she is treated with great respect by a range of people who want things from her, which changes the way she thinks about herself. She ends up having to choose between the glamorous life (with Peter Lawford) and a quieter existence (with a documentary filmmaker played by Jack Lemmon, in his very appealing debut performance).

SEE ALSO:

Funny Girl Both Fanny and Nick have problems with self-esteem that ultimately make it impossible for them to stay together.

TOLERANCE

"Human diversity makes tolerance more than a virtue; it makes it a requirement for survival."
—RENÉ DUBOS

Movies reflect our society. Most have careless, insensitive, or even overtly bigoted portrayals of everyone who is not white, Protestant, and male. The best we can do is try to be alert enough to teach our children to be aware of the subtle messages these movies send. It is especially important, as I have tried to point out through this book, to encourage kids to compare the way that minorities and women are portrayed (and the way they are simply omitted) in films of the 1930s, 40s, and 50s with those of more recent times. Kids today are lucky enough to find it hard to understand the explicit prejudice demonstrated by the characters in these movies, as well as by the filmmakers themselves. They need to understand that these movies are time capsules that enable us to get a glimpse of the wounds for which they may be able to see only the scars. And it is essential for parents to make sure that children receive a broad exposure to stories and characters from a variety of cultures, through series like Rabbit Ears's *We All Have Tales*. We are fortunate, too, that contemporary movies offer a broader assortment of heroes and heroines than in any time in movie history, but we are still far from equality.

Some movies explicitly reflect the painful grappling with issues of race, religion, class, nationality, disability, and gender discrimination that our nation has faced since its earliest days. The films in this chapter all provide starting points for family discussions of tolerance and prejudice. Some present the issue metaphorically. Some portray real-life conflicts. Some explore the reasons for prejudice, which include ignorance, displaced anger, fear, and a need to feel superior and powerful stemming from insecurity and self-hatred. Some show that even people who mean well can perpetuate the devastating effects of bigotry. Mature high schoolers may appreciate movies that show the devastating self-hatred that can result from living in a bigoted world.

Adam's Rib

1949, 101 min, NR, b&w, 10 and up
Dir: George Cukor. Spencer Tracy, Katharine Hepburn

✳ **PLOT:** Doris Attinger (Judy Holliday) shoots her husband, Warren (Tom Ewell), in the middle of a tryst with Beryl Craighn (Jean Hagan). He is wounded in the shoulder, and Adam Bonner (Spencer Tracy), of the district attorney's office, is assigned to prosecute Mrs. Attinger.

Adam's wife, Amanda (Katharine Hepburn), also a lawyer, thinks it is unfair that Doris has been charged, because she thinks there is a double standard that is tougher on women—social prejudices will cause Doris to be convicted of a crime for which a man would go free. She becomes Doris's defense lawyer over Adam's strong objection. She refuses to let Doris plead guilty, intending to turn the case into an argument over equal rights.

At first, Adam and Amanda are able to keep their court battle out of their relationship. But it soon becomes personal. Amanda brings in witnesses to show that women can do anything that men can do, and even has a circus strong-woman lift Adam in the courtroom. Adam moves out of their apartment.

Amanda's argument to the jury asks them to think of the case as if Doris were the faithful husband who found his wife in a compromising position with a predatory playboy. Adam tells the jury that anyone who shoots at another person should be punished. But the jury is persuaded by Amanda, and Doris is acquitted.

That night, Amanda shares a drink with her neighbor, composer Kip Lurie (David Wayne), who has a crush on her. Adam bursts in and points a gun at them, saying that the decision of the jury proves that he has a right to use it. Amanda cries out that no one has that right. Adam, gratified that she has accepted his argument, puts the nozzle of the gun in his mouth and, as Amanda screams, bites off the end. It is licorice.

The next day, Adam and Amanda meet in their lawyer's office to talk about their separation. Amanda is touched when she sees tears in Adam's eyes, and they leave together. That night, Adam explains that he can turn on the "waterworks" whenever he wants to. Amanda says this proves that there is very little difference between men and women, and Adam reminds her of the French saying *"Vive la différence!"* which means, "Hurray for that difference!"

✳ **DISCUSSION:** Adam and Amanda agree that men and women should be treated equally. Adam believes that anyone—male or female—who shoots at someone else should be prosecuted. Amanda believes that as long as men go free for that crime, women should, too. In keeping with the movie's theme of equality, each wins and each loses. Amanda wins the court case, but loses on the overall point by agreeing that "no one has the right" to shoot someone, no matter what the provocation. Adam loses the court case, but wins overall.

It will be hard for kids (or even their parents) to imagine how revolutionary this movie was half a century ago. Many of those who watched this movie when it came out could remember when women did not have the right to vote. It would be more than a decade before women would have a legal right to equal treatment in the workplace. The idea of a woman's ability to have the same professional achievements as a man was still something that had to be proven in court—in a romantic comedy. It was a long way from being taken seriously. Yet Adam and Amanda are a completely belivable couple who have worked out a partnership of equals that makes them both very happy.

PROFANITY: None.

NUDITY/SEXUAL REFERENCES: References to infidelity.

ALCOHOL/DRUG ABUSE: Social drinking.

VIOLENCE/SCARINESS: Doris shoots Warren; Adam threatens Kip and Amanda with what they think is a real gun.

TOLERANCE/DIVERSITY ISSUES: A theme of the movie.

✻ **QUESTIONS FOR KIDS:**
- What do Adam and Amanda disagree about? What do they agree on?
- Who is right?
- Who do the filmmakers think is right?

✻ **CONNECTIONS:** Jean Hagan (***Singin' in the Rain***), Tom Ewell; David Wayne; and Judy Holliday (***Bells Are Ringing*** and ***Born Yesterday***) all made their debuts in this movie. The song Kip writes, "Farewell, Amanda," is by Cole Porter. For a brilliant analysis of this movie, see the book *The Pursuit of Happiness,* by Stanley Cavell.

✻The Bingo Long Traveling All-Stars & Motor Kings
1976, 110 min, PG, 12 and up
Dir: John Badham. James Earl Jones, Billy Dee Williams, Richard Pryor

✻ **PLOT:** Leon (James Earl Jones) and Bingo (Billy Dee Williams) are two of the brightest stars of baseball's Negro National League, during segregation. Unhappy with their treatment by the owners of the teams, they join together to establish their own team, to be owned by the players, so they can "control the means of production." Other players join them, including Charlie Snow (Richard Pryor), who insists he will be able to join the white league by pretending to be Cuban, and Esquire Joe Calloway (Stan Shaw), a shy young player. Told by a local promoter that they have to be in show business as well as baseball to attract paying customers, they become adept at flamboyant entrances and razzle-dazzle. The Negro National League's owners decide to shut them out and will not allow their teams to play with them. So the All-Stars start to play white teams, using humor and humility to keep racial tensions under control. The Negro National League's owners get even tougher, stealing the All-Stars's money and attacking Charlie, who is badly hurt. Paying for Charlie's hospital stay all but bankrupts the team, and Bingo ends up stealing a car. Leon cannot work that way, so he quits.

The Negro National League's owners make them an offer—they will play one game. If the All-Stars win, they can join the league on their own terms. If they lose, all the players have to go back to their old teams. Just to make sure they will win, the owners lock up Leon, but he escapes in time to hit the winning run out of the park.

Their jubilation becomes bittersweet when Esquire Joe brings them some news. He has been invited to play for a white team. Bingo and Leon know that the era of the Negro National League is coming to an end.

✳ **DISCUSSION:** Parents should be aware that there is some material they may consider inappropriate even for older kids in this movie, including sexual references and strong racial epithets. But for many parents, that will be outweighed by its rare and sympathetic look at a part of baseball history—and American history.

In addition to the issues of racism and the contest for control between the owners and the players, it is worth pointing out the extraordinary loyalty of most of the players to each other and discussing Bingo's decision to steal a car and Leon's reaction.

PROFANITY: Some, especially racial epithets (used mostly by blacks).

NUDITY/SEXUAL REFERENCES: Scenes of characters (dressed or covered) in bed with women (including one in bed with the team owner, with the implication that it is a condition of employment); some locker-room comments.

ALCOHOL/DRUG ABUSE: Drinking.

VIOLENCE/SCARINESS: One character is pushed around by thugs; another is badly cut; a chase scene.

TOLERANCE/DIVERSITY ISSUES: Racial tolerance is a theme of the movie; bias against the woman owner.

✳ **QUESTIONS FOR KIDS:**
- What did "controlling the means of production" refer to? Where does that term come from?
- Why did Bingo lie about getting concession money to hand out to the players? Why was it important that Esquire Joe was an equal partner from the first day? Why did the promoter tell them they had to understand they were in "show business" as well as baseball?
- How did Bingo justify stealing the car?

✳ **CONNECTIONS:** Jones plays a character based on Josh Gibson, the only baseball player ever—black or white—to hit a ball out of the park in Yankee Stadium. Williams's character is based on Satchel Paige. The screenplay is based on a novel by William Brashler. The PBS series *Baseball,* by Ken Burns, provides some of the history of the Negro National League. *Soul of* the Game (also known as *Baseball in Black and White*), a more historically accurate drama about the careers of Gibson and Paige, and their hopes of playing the role given to Jackie Robinson as the first black man to play in the major leagues, was produced by HBO in 1996. Jackie Robinson played himself in **The Jackie Robinson Story.**

Director John Badham (who also directed *Saturday Night Fever* and **War-Games**) is the brother of Mary Badham, who played Scout in **To Kill a Mockingbird.**

✳ **ACTIVITIES:** A nonfiction book called *Josh and Satch: The Life and Times of Josh Gibson and Satchel Paige,* by John B. Holway, describes their lives and careers. Every family should take a look at Paige's famous rules for living, available in many collections of quotations and anthologies.

✳The Defiant Ones
1958, 97 min, NR, b&w, 12 and up
Dir: Stanley Kramer. Tony Curtis, Sidney Poitier

✳ **PLOT:** Two convicts shackled together, one black (Sidney Poitier as Cullen), one white (Tony Curtis as Jackson), must overcome their hostility to work together when they escape from a chain gang. When we first see them, they are about to get into a fistfight as they are being transported with other prisoners in a truck. But when Jackson pulls back his fist to hit Cullen, it swings Cullen's fist along with it.

At first, after they escape, they try to break the chain with rocks, Jackson calling Cullen "boy," and Cullen saying, "No more 'yassah boss' " each time he smashes the rock down. But they realize they cannot break the chain. Though Jackson wants to go South, Cullen knows that is too risky for him. "Get off my back—I ain't married to you! What do I care?" But Jackson has no choice. He can't drag Cullen, and until the shackle is broken, they have to go together.

They go through a river to throw the dogs off their trail, and Cullen is almost swept away. When Cullen thanks Jackson for pulling him out, Jackson says, "I didn't pull you out. I kept you from pulling me in."

When they sneak into a town at night, Cullen puts dirt on Jackson's face to make it harder to see them. But they are captured, and the men in the town organize a lynching party, sending the women and children home. At first, Jackson tries to save them both, then, desperate, he says, "You can't lynch me—I'm a white man!" They are freed by a man whose scar on his wrist shows that he was once a chain-gang convict, too.

Now Cullen is bitter and angry. They start to have the fight they have promised each other, until a boy appears and points a gun at them. Working together, they knock the gun away from him, and he falls, hitting his head on a rock. He is unconscious. Jackson wants to run, but Cullen insists they make sure the boy is all right. When the boy comes to, he runs to Jackson for protection; he fears Cullen because he is black. They go to the boy's home, and his mother (Cara Williams) gives them food. She is clearly attracted to Jackson, and is a bit surprised and almost amused when he insists that she feed Cullen as well. They remove the chain, and Jackson collapses from his infection. She nurses him all night, and they talk about their feelings of loneliness and their longing to get away.

The next morning, she tells Cullen his best route is through the swamp, and she and Jackson plan to travel as husband and wife. But after Cullen leaves, she confesses that she has sent him to certain death to make sure that he won't lead anyone to them. Jackson cannot stay with her. As he leaves, the boy shoots him in the shoulder. He catches up with Cullen. Cullen makes it onto the train and reaches for Jackson but, in trying to pull him on, they both fall off, tumbling back down. Cullen holds the wounded Jackson and sings softly to him as the sheriff walks over to them.

✷ **DISCUSSION:** It is impossible to recreate the pre–Civil Rights era atmosphere that made this movie appear to be so radical when it was released, but it is worthwhile for kids to see how accepted and casual racism was— from calling Cullen "boy" to lynching—only a few decades ago. They also may be interested in hearing that chain gangs have been reinstituted recently in one state, after several years in which they were banned.

This movie is exceptionally well-constructed, making it especially well-suited for discussion with teenagers, who can trace the development of the relationship between Jackson and Cullen from the beginning, where their fight causes the accident that allows them to escape, to their first discussion about themselves and the crimes they committed, to their wordless cooperation in disarming the boy, to the decision by each of them to sacrifice a chance at freedom to help the other.

PROFANITY: None.
NUDITY/SEXUAL REFERENCES: Implication that Jackson and the woman sleep together.
ALCOHOL/DRUG ABUSE: None.
VIOLENCE/SCARINESS: Tension; some fighting.
TOLERANCE/DIVERSITY ISSUES: A theme of the movie (includes racial slurs and epithets).

✷ **QUESTIONS FOR KIDS:**
- Cullen and Jackson share some details of their lives before prison. In what way were they similar? In what way were they different? What is different about their views of the world, and about what they want from life?
- What can you tell about their relationship from what they call each other?
- Why do they still "feel" chained, even after the chain is broken? Why does Jackson go after Cullen to save him? Why does Cullen risk falling off the train for Jackson?

- What do the screenwriters and director want to show you with the scenes of the posse? With the treatment of the dogs, compared to the treatment of the prisoners? With the attitude of the sheriff? With the music?

✳ **CONNECTIONS:** Other movies featuring chain gangs include *Cool Hand Luke,* **Sullivan's Travels,** and *I Am a Fugitive from a Chain Gang.*

Carl "Alfalfa" Switzer of *Our Gang* plays Angus, television star Claude Akins plays Mack, and Lon Chaney, Jr., plays Big Sam, the man who sets them free.

Screenwriter Nedrick Young was billed under a pseudonym because he was blacklisted.

✳ Enemy Mine

1985, 108 min, PG-13, 12 and up
Dir: Wolfgang Petersen. Dennis Quaid, Louis Gosset, Jr.

✳ **PLOT:** One hundred years in the future, a war is going on between humans and aliens called Dracs, so far from Earth that the humans fighting can barely remember it. In an aerial battle, two aircraft are shot down over a deserted planet. The only survivors are Davidge (Dennis Quaid) and Jerry (Louis Gossett, Jr.). Enemies at first (Jerry captures Davidge), they begin to depend on one another for survival. They learn each other's language and customs. Jerry saves Davidge's life. When Davidge asks why, he replies, "I like to see another face, even your ugly one." They ultimately develop respect and even affection for one another.

Davidge explores the planet to find evidence only of scavengers, human thieves who enslave the Dracs and use them to mine ore. He returns to find that Jerry is pregnant; Dracs are both male and female. Jerry dies in childbirth, and Davidge raises the baby, named Zammis, with great tenderness.

The scavengers return and capture the Drac child. Davidge is shot trying to rescue him and is brought back to a space station for burial. But he comes to and steals a plane to go back to get Zammis. He rescues Zammis with the help of the Drac slaves and his colleagues from the spaceship, who followed him to provide support. He is able to fulfill his promise to Jerry to take Zammis home and sing the song of his lineage before all the Dracs.

✳ **DISCUSSION:** The war going on all around them loses its meaning very quickly when it is just two creatures on an inhospitable planet who need each other to survive. At first sworn enemies because they have been trained to be so by their cultures, these two individuals have a more personal hatred: It was their fury in battle over seeing friends killed that led to the reckless behavior that stranded them. At first, they hold on to their identities as soldiers at war. But when it becomes clear that they must depend on each other to survive, they overcome their prejudices and ultimately develop respect and affection for each other. They also learn respect for one another's culture, as is poignantly demonstrated when Davidge responds to Zammis's wish to be a human instead of a Drac.

PROFANITY: Some.

NUDITY/SEXUAL REFERENCES: None.

ALCOHOL/DRUG ABUSE: None.

VIOLENCE/SCARINESS: Jerry and Davidge in peril; space-age shooting; Drac slaves whipped and beaten; evidence that slaves have been killed and eaten by scavengers.

TOLERANCE/DIVERSITY ISSUES: A theme of the movie.

❋ QUESTIONS FOR KIDS:
- Why were the humans and Dracs fighting? Who was right? Why do you think so?
- What surprised Jerry and Davidge most about each other? How were they alike?
- How were they different? How did they change? Why was Zammis so important to Davidge?
- What do you think about the importance of lineage to Dracs? What does it tell you about their culture?

❋ CONNECTIONS: This story is similar to *Robinson Crusoe on Mars* as well as other stories of people from different cultures being forced to cooperate, developing respect and ultimately affection for one another. Louis Gossett, Jr., won an Oscar in the R-rated *An Officer and a Gentleman*. Always an actor of arresting presence and focus, his performance in this movie is particularly impressive, given the challenges of conveying an alien creature with both male and female elements while his face is completely covered.

❋ ACTIVITIES: The Drac culture's focus on lineage is a good way to begin a discussion of family history with your children. Compare the comfort Jerry draws in being able to name his ancestors and his pride in his heritage with Davidge's "thin" history of a grandfather who might have been a farmer and a grandmother who was a good cook. Ask children what they would say if a Drac asked about their lineage, and tell them stories about your family.

❋ Fiddler on the Roof

1971, 181 min, G, 6 and up
Dir: Norman Jewison. Topol, Molly Picon, Paul Michael Glaser

❋ PLOT: Tevye (Topol), a poor milkman; his wife, Golde; and their five daughters live in a small Jewish community in rural Russia. They are bound by tradition, which decrees all aspects of their lives. But each of his daughters presents Tevye with a new challenge. The oldest one, Tzeitel, wants to pick the person she marries, not the wealthy widower Lazar Wolf, whom her parents and the matchmaker have chosen, but the poor tailor Motel, whom she loves.

Tevye approves and, by faking a message from a dream, gets Golde to agree, too. The second daughter tests him further by telling him she will marry Pertchik, a student with revolutionary ideas, whether Tevye approves or not. He accepts the marriage. But when his third daughter, Chava, falls in love with a Christian, Tevye cannot accept it. They get married, and he refuses to speak to them.

Anti-Semitism is growing, and Cossacks ride through the town destroying everything they can. The residents sadly make plans to leave, hoping their traditions will continue to sustain them. Tevye says, "God be with you" to Chava before they go.

❋ **DISCUSSION:** This is one of the all-time great Broadway musicals, with a score filled with standards ("Sunrise, Sunset"; "If I Were a Rich Man"; "To Life"; "Matchmaker, Matchmaker"). It will have special meaning for the descendents of the Eastern European Jewish immigrants it depicts, but will resonate for anyone whose parents came to the United States to find something better for their families. The themes are universal—keeping a family together in a world that often tries to tear it apart and maintaining traditions while adapting to changing circumstances.

PROFANITY: None.
NUDITY/SEXUAL REFERENCES: None.
ALCOHOL/DRUG ABUSE: None.
VIOLENCE/SCARINESS: Pogrom.
TOLERANCE/DIVERSITY ISSUES: A theme of the movie.

❋ **QUESTIONS FOR KIDS:**
- What does the song "Tradition" tell you about the community?
- How do Tzeitel and Motel persuade Tevye to let them get married? How does Tevye persuade Golde?
- Why can't he accept Fyedka? Does Tevye's reaction to Fyedka show any less prejudice than that which Fyedka's people show the Jews?
- What traditions are important to your family? How is that different from your grandparents or great-grandparents? How do traditions change? How do we know when it is time to change? What does the title refer to?

❋ **CONNECTIONS:** Pertchik is played by Paul Michael Glaser of the television show *Starsky and Hutch,* now a director. Younger kids will enjoy **An American Tail,** a Steven Spielberg animated feature about an immigrant Jewish family (of mice).

❋Gentleman's Agreement
1947, 118 min, NR, b&w, 10 and up
Dir: Elia Kazan. Gregory Peck, Dorothy McGuire, Celeste Holm, John Garfield

❋ **PLOT:** Journalist Phil Green (Gregory Peck) is a feature writer for a *Time-*like publication called *Smith's Weekly.* Assigned to write a series on anti-

Semitism, he has a hard time coming up with an approach until he remembers the success of previous articles when he went "undercover." He decides to find out what anti-Semitism is like from the inside by letting people think he is Jewish.

After his secretary (June Havoc) tells him she could not get a job at the magazine until she changed her name, he sends identical letters applying for jobs and making hotel reservations, one signed with a neutral name, one with a "Jewish-sounding" name. The difference in the responses shocks him. Even more shocking is the reaction of Kathy (Dorothy McGuire), the editor's niece, the woman he is beginning to love. Phil says, "I've come to see that lots of nice people who aren't [anti-Semites]—people who despise it and deplore it and protest their innocence—help it along and then wonder why it grows . . . That's the biggest discovery I've made about this whole business, Kathy, the good people, the nice people." His friend, Anne (Celeste Holm), says, "The Krays everywhere are afraid of getting the gate from their little groups of nice people. They make little clucking sounds of disapproval, but they want you and Uncle John to stand up and yell and take sides and fight. But do they fight? Oh, no!"

Phil's support through all of this comes from his wise, strong mother (Anne Revere), his oldest friend, Dave (John Garfield), a Jewish former GI, and Anne. His story is published and opens up a deeper dialogue. Kathy confronts her own weakness in opposing bigotry and helps Dave and his family move to the restricted area where she has a home.

✳ **DISCUSSION:** This movie, an Oscar-winner for best picture and director, is dated now, but that is part of what makes it so interesting. Kids today will find it hard to imagine that there was a time within the lives of their parents and grandparents when laws in some areas prohibited the sale of property to Jews and blacks. (Explain to them that the term "gentleman's agreement" referred to an implicit agreement by people in the community where there were no such laws.) Perhaps what is most dated is the way the movie finally pulls its punch by allowing Phil to end up with Kathy instead of Anne. The Motion Picture Academy showed its support for Anne by giving an Oscar to Celeste Holm.

The central message of *Gentleman's Agreement*—that the greatest injury comes from people who think the right things but are afraid or unwilling to act on their views—is still valid. Kathy tells Phil that she felt sick when she heard a bigoted joke, but admits that she didn't say anything about it. Anne says, "Kathy and Harry and all of them . . . think they've fought the good fight for democracy in this country. They haven't got the guts to take the step from talking to action. One little action on one little front. Sure, I know it's not the whole answer, but it's got to start somewhere. And it's got to be with action—not pamphlets, not even with your series. It's got to be with people—nice people, rich people, poor people, big and little people."

PROFANITY: None.

NUDITY/SEXUAL REFERENCES: None.

ALCOHOL/DRUG ABUSE: None.

VIOLENCE/SCARINESS: None.

TOLERANCE/DIVERSITY ISSUES: A theme of the movie.

✳ **QUESTIONS FOR KIDS:**
- What do you think of Phil's "angle" on the story? What did that enable him to find out that he would not have otherwise discovered? Who was it hardest on?
- What was wrong with Kathy's response when Tommy was taunted by anti-Semitic kids?
- What do you think Kathy would have to do to help Dave?
- What is better today? What is worse?
- Why are people so surprised when Phil says he is Jewish? How is he different from what they expected?
- What kind of prejudice have you seen or experienced?
- Did you ever hear someone tell a bigoted joke, as Kathy did? How did you react? How do we make sure that "nice people" do more than talk?

✳ **CONNECTIONS:** Anne Revere, who also appears in *National Velvet* and *Body and Soul,* turns in another memorable performance as a mother with great strength and wisdom. Ironically, shortly after this movie was made, she was blacklisted, an example of exactly the kind of prejudice the movie was trying to abolish. Phil's secretary, Miss Wales, is played by June Havoc, the real-life "Baby June" who was Gypsy Rose Lee's older sister. Their life together is portrayed in *Gypsy.* You can see her perform a brief dance in *Brewster's Millions.*

John Howard Griffin, a reporter inspired by this fictional account, went a step further and had his skin darkened to find out what it was like to be black. His book, *Black Like Me,* was made into a movie in 1964. More recently, a black Harvard Law School graduate named Lawrence Otis got a job as a busboy (he was not permitted to be a waiter) in an all-white country club in the same area in which the fictional Kathy in this movie lived. He wrote an essay about his experiences (included in his book *Member of the Club: Reflections on Life in a Racially Polarized World*) showing that the approach author Laura Z. Hobson created for Phil Green can still give us insight into the hypocrisies and failures of "nice people."

✳ **Glory**

1989, 122 min, R, 14 and up
Dir: Edward Zwick. Denzel Washington, Matthew Broderick, Morgan Freeman, Cary Elwes

✳ **PLOT:** This is the deeply moving story of the first black battalion of the Civil War, led by Robert Gould Shaw (Matthew Broderick), the twenty-five-year-old son of abolitionists. Shaw, already a wounded veteran of battle, volunteers to lead the battalion. The Confederate army announces they will immediately enslave any captured blacks and execute any wearing a uniform of the North. Nevertheless, the men stay, even when they are offered a chance for a discharge. They include Trip (Denzel Washington), a tough and bitter runaway slave who endures a brutal beating when he goes AWOL to get some much-needed boots; the bookish Searles (Andre Braugher); and Rawlins (Morgan Freeman), whose wisdom and courage result in his becoming one of the first black noncommissioned officers.

They are told they will be paid less than the white soldiers, and they protest. Shaw and his fellow officers join in the protest by refusing their own pay. The blacks are not permitted to fight. Instead, they are assigned menial tasks and told to loot the captured villages. One of the other white officers assigned to a black battalion says that this is an ideal assignment for blacks. Shaw does everything he can to have his men treated with respect, finally blackmailing a superior officer into giving them a chance to go into battle. Their performance is outstanding, and they are next assigned an impossible mission, against overwhelming odds. Most of them are killed and buried together with the white officers in a common grave.

✳ **DISCUSSION:** The performance of the black soldiers encouraged the Union generals to recruit more, which may have been responsible for keeping this nation united. The black soldiers are asked to fight with greater risk (worse conditions and immediate death if caught by the Confederates) and less money, under the command of people who treat them with contempt. Although theoretically fighting for the freedom of the slaves, most of the white Union soldiers are racist bigots who do not even want to give the soldiers guns, arguing that they are "little monkey children" who will drop the guns and run under fire. Even Shaw has to be persuaded that the black soliders can fight. Once he is, he is tortured, as all commanding officers are, by the thought of sending such brave and capable men into battle.

This is an outstanding film, one of the best ever made about war in general, insightful about the most devastating war in American history in particular, and simply about the human spirit. Like *Cry Freedom* and *The Long Walk Home,* this film was criticized for presenting the black story through white eyes. We can hope very much that someone will tell the story through the eyes of the black soldiers themselves. But this movie is very meaningful on its own terms. Based in part on the letters written by Shaw, the movie is partly his story as well. He and his fellow officer Cabot Forbes (Cary Elwes) have a lot to learn from these soldiers. So do the viewers, which should include every American.

PROFANITY: None.
NUDITY/SEXUAL REFERENCES: None.
ALCOHOL/DRUG ABUSE: Some drinking.
VIOLENCE/SCARINESS: Very powerful and bloody battle scenes.
TOLERANCE/DIVERSITY ISSUES: A theme of the movie.

✳ **QUESTIONS FOR KIDS:**
- Who changes the most in this movie? Why?
- Why was equality such a difficult idea during a war that was supposed to be about equality?
- What is the meaning of the title?

✳ **CONNECTIONS:** Denzel Washington won an Oscar for his performance, and another should have gone to Freeman, who is unforgettable as Rawlins. The music is performed by the Boys Choir of Harlem.

✳ **ACTIVITIES:** Check an encyclopedia to read about the controversy following President Truman's order to integrate the troops after World War II. Older teens may be interested in reading Shaw's letters in *Blue-Eyed Child of Fortune: The Civil War Letters of Colonel Robert Gould Shaw,* edited by Russell Duncan, Peter Burchard's book *One Gallant Rush,* or Lincoln Kirstein's *Lay This Laurel,* all sources for the screenplay.

✳Home of the Brave
1949, 86 min, NR, b&w, 10 and up
Dir: Mark Robson. James Edwards, Lloyd Bridges

✳ **PLOT:** A black engineer named Moss (James Edwards) volunteers for a dangerous reconnaissance mission on an island during World War II. The four white soldiers also on the mission express a range of reactions, from bigotry to ignorance to warm friendship—the last from Finch (Lloyd Bridges), who went to high school with Moss and knew him well. On the island, tensions mount, and the intolerance adds another layer of stress to the already difficult and dangerous mission. Under fire, Finch almost calls Moss "nigger." Then he is shot and captured. He escapes, but dies in Moss's arms.

Moss becomes amnesiac and paralyzed from the anxiety of the experience. An Army psychiatrist gives him a drug to help him remember what happened. The psychiatrist helps him realize that, like all soldiers, a part of him felt glad and relieved when someone else got hit. It wasn't because Finch revealed some inner core of vestigial racism; Moss knew Finch genuinely cared about him, and knew himself well enough to recognize his own barriers to seeing whites without prejudice. It was because of a natural and universal human impulse for survival. Moss goes back to the United States with one of the other soldiers from the mission, Mingo, who lost an arm. Mingo proposes that he take Finch's place in the restaurant and bar Moss was planning.

✳ **DISCUSSION:** First, kids who watch this movie will have to be told that during WWII the armed services were still completely segregated. Moss would have come from an all-black division. Finch, Mingo, and the rest would not have had any experience in training alongside or working with black soldiers.

This very early attempt to deal with racism (and with psychiatry) in a mainstream Hollywood movie is awkward and dated, but that is part of what makes it particularly interesting to watch. As a period piece, it helps to put current issues into sharper perspective. And yet its own issues remain valid, especially Moss's most painful fear—that his ambivalence over Finch's being shot was somehow even more inhuman because it stemmed from hostility over a racist remark. When he is able to connect those feelings to the experience of other soldiers of all races, he is able to accept them in himself. (A parallel is his recognition that T. J., the soldier who insults him the most, is just as insulting to everyone.) This is a reflection of racism's most virulent impact, its ability to make the objects of prejudice doubt themselves. The movie is also courageous in making Finch imperfect. Under extreme stress, he starts to call Moss a "nigger," and is even more shocked and horrified than Moss to hear that word in his mouth. This is still particularly valid in a world where we need to be taught over and over again the difficulty of eradicating racism and bigotry.

Perhaps the movie's most poignant reminder of racism is in the subsequent careers of the actors who appeared in it. Bridges, who played Finch, went on to a long and distinguished career, while it would be decades before actors like Edwards would have the same opportunity.

PROFANITY: None.

NUDITY/SEXUAL REFERENCES: None.

ALCOHOL/DRUG ABUSE: None.

VIOLENCE/SCARINESS: Shooting; Finch shot and killed; Mingo shot (loses arm).

TOLERANCE/DIVERSITY ISSUES: The theme of the movie.

✳ **QUESTIONS FOR KIDS:**
- How do each of the white soldiers react differently to Moss?
- Why does Mingo recite his wife's poem? What does the line about "coward, take my coward's hand" mean?
- What were the feelings Moss had when Finch was shot? Why was it impossible for him to accept those feelings?
- Didn't T. J. try to say nice things about black people?
- Why did it make Moss feel differently to realize that T. J. acted as though he hated everyone?

✳ **CONNECTIONS:** *Crossfire*, a similar movie released two years earlier, was one of the first movies to address anti-Semitism, also in the context of the U.S. Army during WWII. Interestingly, the play *Home of the Brave* was about anti-Semitism, but Moss was rewritten as a black character when it was made into a movie.

In the Heat of the Night

1967, 109 min, NR, 14 and up
Dir: Norman Jewison. Sidney Poitier, Rod Steiger, Warren Oates, Lee Grant

❋ **PLOT:** Virgil Tibbs (Sidney Poitier) is waiting in a train station in Sparta, Mississippi, when he is picked up by the local police on suspicion of murder. A wealthy developer was found dead, and the police assume that Tibbs is the culprit because he was unfamiliar and black. The officers and their chief, Sheriff Gillespie (Rod Steiger), are embarrassed to learn that Tibbs is in fact a police detective from Philadelphia, an expert in homicide in town to visit family. Although his supervisor encourages him to stay to help solve the crime, Tibbs is eager to go, and Gillespie is eager to have him leave. But the murder victim's widow (Lee Grant) insists that he stay because it is clear to her that he knows what he is doing. Gillespie agrees; if Tibbs succeeds, the local police will get the credit. But if he fails, it will be his fault.

As they work together, Tibbs and Gillespie must both look beyond their prejudices. Gillespie sees Tibbs's competence and expertise. And Tibbs sees that, underneath his superficial bigotry, Gillespie is an honest policeman with a strong sense of fairness. They pursue a number of leads that turn out to be wrong but that teach them more about their own prejudices and about the town and its people, ultimately leading them to the real killer.

❋ **DISCUSSION:** This is a brilliant film in every respect—writing, directing, and acting. Though the quantity and quality of racism may have changed in this country, the film does not seem dated, partly because it has a universal quality. Anyone who has ever felt underestimated will find great satisfaction as Tibbs proves his expertise; anyone who has ever felt disrespect will feel great pleasure when Gillespie makes fun of the name Virgil and asks, "What do they call you, boy?" only to be told, "They call me MISTER Tibbs!" (Indeed, this became the name of the movie's sequel.)

In *To Kill a Mockingbird,* the black man's worst sin is to admit that he felt sorry for the poor white girl. In this movie, there is a similar scene, when Tibbs, trying to make a connection with Gillespie, says that Gillespie is lonely, which makes Gillespie furious. It is one thing for Gillespie to give Tibbs respect; it is another to accept his pity. This shows how securely bigotry rests on the need to feel superior to someone.

PROFANITY: Some, including racial epithets.
NUDITY/SEXUAL REFERENCES: Dolores Purdy accuses policeman of getting her pregnant and describes their encounter; some discussion of the way men peek into her window when she walks around in the nude; reference to (illegal) abortion.
ALCOHOL/DRUG ABUSE: Some drinking.
VIOLENCE/SCARINESS: Mostly implied or off-screen. Wealthy bigot slaps Tibbs, who slaps him back. Autopsy scene.
TOLERANCE/DIVERSITY ISSUES: A theme of the movie.

✳ **QUESTIONS FOR KIDS:**
- Tibbs and Gillespie make a number of wrong starts on the way to finding the murderer. What leads them to each of them? What do they learn from each of them that helps them go in the right direction?
- Why does Dolores Purdy lie about the man who made her pregnant?
- What makes Tibbs and Gillespie feel differently about each other?
- How have things changed since the time of this movie? What made those changes happen?

✳ **CONNECTIONS:** Kids should read about this era, including *Eyes on the Prize* by Juan Williams to understand how recently such blatant bigotry was not only permitted but accepted. This movie won five Oscars, including Best Picture and Actor (Rod Steiger).

✳Nothing But a Man

1964, 92 min, NR, b&w, mature high schoolers
Dir: Michael Roemer. Ivan Dixon, Abbey Lincoln

✳ **PLOT:** Duff (Ivan Dixon) is a black man who is a member of a railroad crew, laying track in a small Southern town. He meets Josie (Abbey Lincoln), a local black woman who is a teacher, at a church social. Neither Duff's nor Josie's parents think he is a suitable match for her (when he asks her why she is going out with him, she says, "You don't think much of yourself, do you?"). But she tells him he isn't "sad" like the men she knows, and that she thought they'd have something to say to each other. They get married, and he goes to work in the mill. But he cannot accept the hazing by the whites who work at the mill and is fired when a casual remark about "sticking together" is interpreted as an indication of labor organizing. Word gets around, and he is unable to get a job at the other mill or keep jobs picking cotton or working in a gas station.

Josie gets pregnant, and Duff's sense of despair at not being able to care for her begins to eat at him. He leaves her, saying, "I ain't fit to live with no more. It's just like a lynching. They don't use a knife, but they got other ways." He goes to see his estranged father, who dies from alcohol abuse brought on by his own despair. Duff realizes that he has to do better than that. He picks up his young son, who had been boarding in another city, and takes him home to Josie. He says, "It ain't going to be easy, but it's going to be all right. Baby, I feel so free inside."

✳ **DISCUSSION:** This thoughtful, quiet movie was not widely distributed when it was made in 1964, but it has had an enduring and well-deserved reputation as a sensitive portrayal not just of a particular moment in the tortured history of race relations in this country, but also as an intimate story of human dignity and the need for connection. In a way, Duff struggles with the same problem that Mary Kate Danaher struggles with in *The Quiet*

Man—to achieve the sense of completeness and equality necessary to be able to enter a relationship fully. Josie may be right when she tells Duff he doesn't think much of himself, but he thinks enough of himself to say to Josie's father, "You've been stooping so long, Reverend, you don't know how to stand straight. You're just half a man." When the Reverend tells him to "make 'em think you're going along and get what you want," Duff says, "It ain't in me." This is part of what Josie loves about him, part of what distinguishes him from the "sad" men she knows, like her father, who knew who was responsible for a lynching but did not say anything. Duff sees his father die, broken and alone, and he knows he will do better than that. Duff finds in his son (though he says that he doubts he is the boy's natural father) what he cannot find in his environment, a way to be more than "half a man."

The portrayal of the life of the people in this movie is harsh. None of the black characters have warm, loving, intact families. Duff's failure to be involved in the life of his son may strike some viewers as callous and others as a racist (or sexist) stereotype.

PROFANITY: Some racial epithets (including some from the black characters).

NUDITY/SEXUAL REFERENCES: Duff's friend patronizes a prostitute. Duff says he is not the father of the child he is supporting. On a date, Duff says to Josie, "Next time we'll have to hit the hay or get married, and you don't want to hit the hay and I don't want to get married." When Duff tells his friends he is going to marry Josie, one says he must have "knocked her up." White men make sexual references about Josie as a way of humiliating Duff.

ALCOHOL/DRUG ABUSE: Scenes in bar; Duff's father is an alcoholic.

VIOLENCE/SCARINESS: The abuse is verbal and economic (refusal to hire Duff).

TOLERANCE/DIVERSITY ISSUES: A theme of the movie.

✳ QUESTIONS FOR KIDS:
- Josie, Duff, and the Reverend all express views of how to interact with white people. How are they different?
- Duff calls the Reverend a "white man's nigger." Is that fair? Why or why not? When Duff asks Josie why she does not hate whites, she says, "I don't know. I guess I'm not afraid of them." What difference does that make?
- What does he mean when Duff tells her she's never "really been a nigger"? Why does the way Duff is treated make it hard for him to live with Josie?
- Why is the way the white men talk about Josie especially painful for Duff?
- What does it mean when Josie says they can't really reach her "inside"? Duff disagrees—who is right? Can Duff make it impossible for them to reach him inside?

✳ **CONNECTIONS:** Fans of television's *Hogan's Heroes* will recognize Ivan Dixon as Kinchloe. Abbey Lincoln made few movies but went on to a distinguished career as a jazz singer. Made on a very low budget, this movie has a terrific Motown sound track, including many classics.

✳Perfect Harmony

1991, 93 min, NR, 8 and up
Dir: Will Mackenzie. Peter Scolari, Catherine Mary Stewart, Darrin McGavin, Moses Gunn

✳ **PLOT:** The story takes place in Georgia, at an all-white private boys' boarding school called Blanton, in 1959. Blanton is famous for its boys' choir. The candidates for the prestigious "lead boy" position in the choir include Paul, an angry, bigoted boy, and Taylor, who remonstrates mildly when Paul plays mean pranks on a Northern boy to try to get him to leave.

Derek Saunders (Peter Scolari), a new choirmaster, arrives from Boston. And Landy, a black boy whose parents have died, arrives to live with his grandfather Zeke (Moses Gunn), a janitor at the school. Landy is entranced by the choir music, as Taylor is by the blues and gospel he hears Landy play on his harmonica. They become friends, though Taylor betrays Landy by publicly belittling the death of another black boy. Derek appoints Taylor lead boy in the choir, even though he knows it will cost him his job at Blanton and the possible affections of the headmaster's daughter. When Taylor is injured in a hate crime, he and Derek arrange for Landy to take his place as soloist for the performance.

✳ **DISCUSSION:** The strength of this movie is that it does not begin to pretend that the issues it raises can be (or were) resolved simply. Throughout the movie, the local black community tries, with increasing assertiveness, to be allowed to swim in the municipal pool. There is no resolution. Landy may have been permitted to sing with the choir for one performance, but there is no suggestion that he will ever be admitted as a student (or indeed ever be allowed on campus again). And Derek, faced with a choice between his conscience and his wish to remain at Blanton, makes Taylor lead boy and has to face the consequences.

It also shows nicely the power of music in the lives of Landy and Taylor. They share something that transcends their differences. Love for music makes Landy risk not being "invisible" so he can hear the choir rehearsal. Love for music makes Taylor take the risk of breaking the rules by leaving school to go to hear it played, even though he will be the only white person there.

Derek criticizes the choir for concentrating too much on technical perfection, and not enough on feeling the composer's exaltation and passion. And he tells Taylor that boys should risk breaking the rules and get away from school once in a while.

The movie makes it clear that Paul's bigotry and hostility are in part displaced emotions stemming from his parents' neglect. One of his roommates says, after another in a series of visiting days when Paul's parents are the only ones who don't attend, "I wish he'd get mad at them instead of us."

PROFANITY: Racial epithets.

NUDITY/SEXUAL REFERENCES: None.

ALCOHOL/DRUG ABUSE: Paul smokes cigarettes.

VIOLENCE/SCARINESS: Black boy drowns (off camera); Klan-style thuggishness.

TOLERANCE/DIVERSITY ISSUES: A theme of the movie.

✴ **QUESTIONS FOR KIDS:**
- Landy's grandfather tells him that he has lasted as long as he has at the school by "being invisible." What does that mean?
- What do you learn from the way the boys talk to Derek about the Civil War? Why do they have different views? If they were taught to believe one thing and he was taught another, how do you know which is right?
- Why does Taylor call the boy who died "some stupid kid"?
- Listen carefully to the music in this movie. Do the songs they sing relate to the story at all?
- What does the title refer to?

✴ **CONNECTIONS:** Richie Havens appears as "Scrapper Johnson," a blues musician who appears at a fund-raiser to rebuild the church after it is bombed by racists. Another movie about a boys' choir is *Almost Angels*.

✴ **ACTIVITIES:** Compare the different kinds of music in this movie—classical, gospel, and blues—to see how they are different and how they are alike. Go to a choir recital.

✴The Russians Are Coming! The Russians Are Coming!

1966, 126 min, NR, 6 and up
Dir: Norman Jewison. Alan Arkin, Carl Reiner, Eva Marie Saint, Jonathan Winters, Brian Keith

✴ **PLOT:** A Russian submarine crew, curious about the United States, accidentally gets too close to the shore and gets stuck on a sandbar near an island off the coast of New England. Lieutenant Rozanov (Alan Arkin) and a small group of sailors are assigned to go onshore as unobtrusively as possible to find a boat they can use to free the submarine. They stop at the house of Walt Whittaker (Carl Reiner), a writer on vacation, whose family is getting ready to go back home to the mainland. Unable to persuade Walt that they are friendly Norwegians, they confess that they are Russians and take him into town, leaving Kolchin (John Phillip Law) with the Whitaker family. Most of the Americans, sure that they are being attacked, react with complete hysteria. The Russian captain becomes angry and is about to attack for real when both sides have to stop and work together to rescue a child.

✳ **DISCUSSION:** Today's children may find it hard to understand just how revolutionary this Cold War comedy seemed when it was first released. But it still stands up well as both delicious slapstick and social commentary.

> PROFANITY: None.
> NUDITY/SEXUAL REFERENCES: None.
> ALCOHOL/DRUG ABUSE: None.
> VIOLENCE/SCARINESS: Child in peril on church steeple.
> TOLERANCE/DIVERSITY ISSUES: The theme is tolerance of political/cultural diversity.

✳ **QUESTIONS FOR KIDS:**
- Why were the Russians and Americans so scared of each other? What made them less afraid?
- Who in the town reacted the most rationally?
- How would you react if it were your family the sailors came to first?
- Is there a country that could scare Americans today the way the Russians did when this movie was made?

✳ **CONNECTIONS:** This movie is based on a book by Nathaniel Benchley, son of humorist Robert Benchley (in many movies, including *The Major and the Minor*) and father of Peter Benchley (author of *Jaws*). The screenplay was written by William Rose, also the author of **It's a Mad Mad Mad Mad World** and *The Secret of Santa Vittoria* as well as the more serious **Guess Who's Coming to Dinner.**

✳School Ties
1992, 107 min, PG-13, 12 and up
Dir: Robert Mandel. Brendan Fraser, Amy Locane, Peter Donat, Chris O'Donnell, Matt Damon

✳ **PLOT:** David Green (Brendan Fraser), a Jewish boy from Scranton, gets an athletic scholarship to a tony (and all-WASP) boy's prep school in the mid-1950s. He keeps his religion a secret, enduring casual anti-Semitic remarks and playing football on Rosh Hashanah. But Dillon (Matt Damon), initially friendly, becomes bitter when David replaces him as quarterback and dates the girl he likes (Amy Locane). Dillon finds out that David is Jewish, gets the other students to harass him, and ultimately frames him in a cheating incident. Although the school honor society votes against David, based on bigotry, Dillon's roommate tells the headmaster the truth, and Dillon is expelled. The headmaster advises David to forget the incident and suggests that David may wish to leave to avoid embarrassment. David says that he will stay on as a constant reminder. "You used me for football; I'll use you to get into Harvard."

❋ **DISCUSSION:** This movie is, in a way, more effective than the much more prestigious *Gentleman's Agreement.* The prejudice is explicit (a swastika is painted in David's room), and sounds even more chilling coming from such fresh-faced and attractive young people. The most moving exchange in the movie is when Dillon tells David he envies him because "If you get what you want, you'll deserve it, and if you don't, you'll manage. You don't have to live up to anyone's expectation. You are who you are. That's what really draws people to you, David; it's not because you're the cool quarterback." The movie is smart enough to allow that envy is the real motivation for Dillon's behavior, with anti-Semitism just an excuse.

Like *Dead Poet's Society,* this film also addresses the burden of expectations the young men face. One has a breakdown after a French teacher takes him apart in class.

PROFANITY: Very rough locker-room language.
NUDITY/SEXUAL REFERENCES: Nudity in dorm showers; ugly reference to a boy's sister's promiscuity used as an insult.
ALCOHOL/DRUG ABUSE: David's secret revealed by a drunken alum.
VIOLENCE/SCARINESS: None.
TOLERANCE/DIVERSITY ISSUES: A theme of the movie.

❋ **QUESTIONS FOR KIDS:**
- What would have been different if David had told everyone he was Jewish on the first day of school?
- Compare David's playing on Rosh Hashanah to Eric Liddell's refusal to run on the Sabbath in *Chariots of Fire* (and real-life baseball great Sandy Koufax's refusal to play in the World Series on Yom Kippur).
- What are the reasons the boys use to support their prejudice?
- In movies about prejudice, sometimes viewers feel that the main character is too perfect, not allowed to have any faults. Is that the case in this movie?
- What do you think about what the boys did to the French professor? Was it fair? Did they accomplish what they wanted to?

❋ **CONNECTIONS:** Dillon is played by Matt Damon, who went on to cowrite and star in *Good Will Hunting.* Chris O'Donnell, who plays David's roommate, went on to star with Al Pacino in *Scent of a Woman* and played Robin in *Batman Forever* and *Batman and Robin.* The headmaster is played by Peter Donat, son of Robert Donat, who played a much more understanding headmaster in *Goodbye, Mr. Chips.*

Skin Game

1971, 102 min, PG, 10 and up
Dir: Peter Bogart. James Garner, Louis Gossett, Jr., Edward Asner, Susan Clark

❋ **PLOT:** Quincy (James Garner) and Jason (Louis Gossett, Jr.) are con men who travel through slave territory in the pre–Civil War era. Quincy "sells" Jason, and then they escape together with the money. Jason, who has been free all his life, is increasingly resentful about the humiliation of even pretending to be a slave. Quincy is sympathetic, but mildly reminds him, "You're the color people are buying this year."

Jason agrees to one more sale and persuades Quincy to buy Naomi, a lovely young woman who is to be auctioned off. But John Brown (Royal Dano) disrupts the action and frees all the slaves. Many of them are later captured by the cruel slave trader Plunkett (Edward Asner), including Naomi. Plunkett manages to buy Jason and chain him so he cannot escape. Plunkett sells Jason and Naomi to Mr. Calloway, who responds to Jason's claims that he is a free man by having him whipped.

Quincy and Ginger (Susan Clark), a fellow con artist, look everywhere for Jason. In the meantime, Jason must learn how to behave like a slave. Calloway keeps African slaves, purchased illegally, on his farm as well. Jason befriends them, and they think of him as their leader, even though they speak no English. When Jason and Ginger arrive, Jason insists they must arrange for the departure of Naomi and the Africans as well. Quincy is discovered to be a fraud and is whipped. Jason kills Plunkett. They all escape to Mexico. Jason stays with the Africans, and Quincy and Ginger go out West.

❋ **DISCUSSION:** The lighthearted story of the clever con artists is nicely combined with sensitively handled themes of the effect of bigotry and slavery on the human spirit. Both Jason and Quincy are con men who find it easy to diminish everyone else as marks for them to steal from. This allows them to avoid thinking too hard about slavery, except as something to exploit for easy money. Quincy in particular cannot allow himself to see the big picture and acts as though his treating of Jason as an equal should be enough. When Quincy finds Jason at Calloway's farm, he tries to soothe him by saying Jason has had worse experiences, but Jason replies firmly that slavery is the worst. As Jason points out, he and Quincy may be as alike as brothers, but the one difference means that one of them can sell a human being and the other can only be sold. After his experience of what it really means to be black in America, he cannot go back—either to his old life or indeed to America at all.

Interestingly, Jason's initial reaction to the Africans can be called bigoted. He is terrified of them and runs away, yelling that they are cannibals. Quincy at first calls them "savages." By then, Jason knows that they are men, like himself, far from home.

PROFANITY: Mild.
NUDITY/SEXUAL REFERENCES: Quincy and Ginger share a bathtub (off-screen) and a bed; Ginger uses sex to get what she wants.

ALCOHOL/DRUG ABUSE: None.

VIOLENCE/SCARINESS: Off-screen whippings; some fistfights; Plunkett is shot.

TOLERANCE/DIVERSITY ISSUES: A theme of the movie.

✻ **QUESTIONS FOR KIDS:**
- When did Quincy show his loyalty to Jason? When did he show insensitivity?
- Why was Naomi's master selling her? What lets you know how he felt about it?
- Why was the way Jason spoke so important?
- What were the rules for being a slave that Jason had to learn?

✻ **CONNECTIONS:** The plot of this movie recalls an "auction" by famed antislavery leader Henry Ward Beecher (brother of Harriet Beecher Stowe, who wrote *Uncle Tom's Cabin*). It is described in a brief essay by Mrs. Beecher called "The Day Mr. Beecher Sold Slaves in Plymouth Pulpit," which originally ran in the *Ladies Home Journal* and is well worth reading. Beecher used the "auction" to buy the slaves' freedom, but also to demonstrate the inhumanity of selling human beings.

The movie was remade for television as *Sidekicks*, with Gossett and Larry Hagman.

Though listed as "Pierre Marton," the coscriptwriter was Peter Stone (*Charade, 1776*).

John Brown is played by longtime character actor Royal Dano, who appeared as the Tattered Man in **The Red Badge of Courage**, as Carey in **The 7 Faces of Dr. Lao**, and as the man who delivered the bad news to the test pilots' families in **The Right Stuff**. Louis Gossett, Jr., also starred in **Enemy Mine**. Plunkett is played by Edward Asner, later on television as *Lou Grant*.

✻ **ACTIVITIES:** Look up real-life abolitionist John Brown in an encyclopedia and compare his tactics to the nonviolent approaches of Ghandi and Dr. Martin Luther King, Jr..

✻West Side Story

1961, 151 min, NR, 10 and up
Dir: Robert Wise and Jerome Robbins. Natalie Wood, Richard Beymer, Rita Moreno, George Chakiris, Russ Tamblyn

✻ **PLOT:** Modeled on *Romeo and Juliet*, this movie puts the star-crossed lovers in two warring gangs in the slums of New York. The opening dance number brings us up to date. The Sharks (Puerto Ricans) and the Jets (Anglos) have blown up a series of petty insults and turf disputes into a war over who will rule the territory. The leader of the Jets, Riff (Russ Tamblyn), goes to see his best friend, Tony (Richard Beymer), the former leader of the gang. Riff asks Tony to come to the dance that night to support him as he negotiates fight terms with Bernardo (George Chakiris), the leader of the Jets. Tony has outgrown the gang and wants more from life, but he and Riff are friends "womb to tomb," so he agrees to go.

Meanwhile, Bernardo's sister Maria, just arrived in the United States, is getting ready for the dance, begging to have her dress cut just a little lower. Bernardo's girlfriend, Anita (Rita Moreno), watches over her protectively. At the dance, well-meaning Mr. Hand tries to get the teenagers to mix with each other, but tensions are high. As each side dances furiously, everything seems to stop for Tony and Maria, who see each other and are transformed.

Bernardo is furious when he sees them together and he takes Maria home. But that night, Tony visits her, and they declare their love for each other. She asks him to make sure there is no fighting, and he agrees. At the "war council" he persuades them to make it a fistfight only and he feels successful. But Maria wants him to make sure there is no fighting of any kind, so he agrees to try to stop them. Things get out of control, and Bernardo kills Riff with a knife. Tony, overcome with grief and guilt, grabs the knife and kills Bernardo.

Running from the police and the Jets, Tony finds Maria. They dream of a place where they could always be safe and together. Anita agrees to take a message to Tony, but when the Jets harass her, she angrily tells them that Maria is dead. Blinded by grief, he stumbles out into the night and is shot by one of the Sharks. Maria holds him as he dies, and together, the Sharks and Jets carry him away.

✳ **DISCUSSION:** The story retains its power, but the gangs are endearingly tame to us now. Can it be that once there were gangs who fought with fists and knives? This is a good opportunity to explore the reasons why people fight. Anita says the boys fight like they dance, "Like they have to get rid of something, quick." According to her, they are getting rid of "too much feeling." Kids understand that idea and may like to talk about what "too much feeling" feels like to them. The music and dances in this movie do as much to tell the story as the dialogue and plot, and they illustrate this idea especially well.

One important difference between this movie and *Romeo and Juliet* is that in Shakespeare's play, the older generation plays an important role. In *West Side Story*, the few adults who appear are ineffectual and tangential, like Mr. Hand (John Astin), who thinks he can get the kids to be friends by having them dance together. Listen to the lopsided music-box song he plays for them and see what a good job it does of expressing both what he is trying to accomplish and how hopeless it is.

And, of course, this is an important movie to use in talking about prejudice. See if you can get kids to watch carefully enough to figure out why the Sharks and Jets resent and mistrust each other.

PROFANITY: In 1960s fashion, they invented substitutes; words like "buggin'" are used to suggest four-letter words.

NUDITY/SEXUAL REFERENCES: Implication that Maria and Tony sleep together; threatened sexual attack on Anita.

ALCOHOL/DRUG ABUSE: Reference in a song to drug use; lots of cigarettes.
VIOLENCE/SCARINESS: Gang fights with knives.
TOLERANCE/DIVERSITY ISSUES: The theme of the movie.

✳ QUESTIONS FOR KIDS:
- If you were going to adapt the story of *Romeo and Juliet* today, what groups would the boy and girl come from?
- Listen to the song "America," with the Sharks and their girlfriends disagreeing about whether America has been good or bad to them. Which side do you agree with? Are they both right? Why?
- In the song "Tonight," both sides sing, "Well, they began it!" Have you ever seen people act that way?
- One of the boys tells Doc, "You was never my age." What does he mean? Do all teenagers feel like that at times?
- Listen to the song "There's a Place for Us." Have you ever dreamed of a special place where you could always be safe? What would it be like?
- Tony has to decide how he can be loyal to his friend and loyal to Maria. Why is that hard? Who else in the movie has to make a decision about loyalty?
- If you could talk to Tony and Maria, what would you tell them to do?

✳ CONNECTIONS:
This is a great double feature with **Romeo and Juliet** or the 1997 version, **William Shakespeare's Romeo + Juliet.** It is fun to see how much of the movie's structure is taken from the play. In both, the lovers see each other at a party and are immediately overcome. In both, the boy comes to see the girl later that night. Juliet speaks to Romeo from a balcony. Maria speaks to Tony from a fire escape. Romeo and Tony are both pulled back into the fight due to the deaths of their friends. In both movies, tragedy results from missed messages.

Moreno and Chakiris both won Oscars for their performances, two of the ten won by this movie, including Best Picture. The brilliant music and lyrics are by Leonard Bernstein and Stephen Sondheim.

✳ THE BUDDY HOLLY STORY
1976, 113 min, PG, 12 and up
Dir: Steve Rash. Gary Busey

Gary Busey is terrific as the seminal rock and roller who wrote and sang classics like "That'll Be the Day" and "Peggy Sue." The movie deals with tolerance of musical differences (there is prejudice against rock-and-roll music). And it also deals with race: Holly's group is booked to perform at Harlem's Apollo Theater, but when they arrive, the producers are shocked that they are not black and almost do not let them perform. The audience is shocked at first, too, but then they are completely swept up in the music. Later, when they tour with black performers, they are not permitted to check into an all-black hotel until Sam Cooke explains that they are his valets. Holly falls in love with a Puerto Rican woman and must face the prejudice of her family, as well as that of his colleagues. They are happily married until he is killed with Richie Valens and The Big Bopper in a tragic plane crash, referred to as "the day the music died," in the Don McLean song "American Pie." NOTE: Some strong language and sexual references.

✳ **CONNECTIONS:** Kids might like to know that the Beatles took their name from Holly's Crickets, that another popular group paid tribute by calling themselves "The Hollies," and that Holly's songs continue to be recorded.

✳ GUESS WHO'S COMING TO DINNER
1967, 108 min, NR, 10 and up
Dir: Stanley Kramer. Spencer Tracy, Katharine Hepburn, Sidney Poitier
    A liberal white newspaperman (Spencer Tracy) and his wife (Katharine Hepburn) must confront their hypocrisy when their daughter (Katharine Houghton) announces she is going to marry a black doctor (Sidney Poitier). This is worth watching as something of a period piece, but also for Tracy's brilliant performance (his last) as a man who wants to protect his daughter from the problems she will face, but who also wants her to experience the happiness of a life spent with someone she really loves.

✳ **CONNECTIONS:** Hepburn's daughter is played by her real-life niece, Katharine Houghton.

✳ IN AND OUT
1997, 90 min, 12 and up
Dir: Frank Oz. Kevin Kline, Tom Selleck, Joan Cusack, Matt Dillon
    In an emotional acceptance speech for his performance in *Philadelphia,* Tom Hanks thanked his high school drama teacher and announced that the teacher was gay. That teacher, now retired, was already "out" and knew Hanks planned to make that statement. But screenwriter Paul Rudnick turns this moment into a movie farce with his fictional Oscar-winner (Matt Dillon) making a similar announcement that is a surprise to everyone, especially the high school drama teacher, Howard Barrett (Kevin Kline), who thinks of himself as heterosexual and indeed is about to marry his longtime girlfriend.
    A swarm of media descends on the town, led by a tabloid reporter (Tom Selleck). The drama teacher is confused, his fiancée is hurt and angry, his parents are shocked and dismayed, and his students are uncomfortable and defensive. At first Howard denies he is gay, but he realizes he must be honest with himself and with everyone else. He stops the wedding. The principal tries to fire him, but the students and their parents support him (in a gentle parody of the "I am Spartacus" scene), with the help of his former student. NOTE: Some very strong language. Also, despite one passionate kiss, the theme of the movie is presented with such a light touch, it appears to suggest that being gay relates to dancing and caring about colors

rather than about desiring a member of the same sex. Parents should talk to kids who see this movie about the importance of rising above stereotypes, and make sure kids understand that not all gay people are like the ones portrayed in the movie.

✳ **CONNECTIONS:** Director Frank Oz is a longtime Muppeteer and provides the voice for Miss Piggy.

✳ INCLUDE ME!
1997, 30 min, 2 to 6

A group of children play together in this video, unremarkable aside from its casual inclusion of kids of all races and abilities. While the songs are sugary, one animated segment (a Noah's Ark song) is nicely done, and children who sometimes feel different will appreciate the validating message.

✳ THE LONG WALK HOME
1990, 97 min, PG, 10 and up
Dir: Richard Pearce. Sissy Spacek, Whoopi Goldberg

This is the story of the Montgomery, Alabama, bus boycott, seen through the eyes of a white child as she watches her privileged suburban mother, Miriam Thompson (Sissy Spacek), struggle to reconcile the clash between the comfort of her home life and the comfort of her conscience. At first, Miriam gives the housekeeper, Odessa Cotter (Whoopi Goldberg), a ride to work because it is the only way she can get there to do the housework. But Miriam comes to understand that she has to drive her and help the other boycotters, because segregation is not right, and she must do so publicly, no matter the cost to her way of life. There are a few stories about this era from the perspective of the black community (mostly made-for-television movies instead of theatrical releases), and more of them are needed. But this movie's depiction of the struggle with racism (and, in subtext, feminism) in the white community is also a part of the story that deserves to be told.

✳ THE POINT
1971, 73 min, NR, 6 and up
Dir: Fred Wolf

Originally made for television, this is an engaging animated musical (with songs by Harry Nilsson) about a boy named Oblio who is sent away because his head is round and not pointed like everyone else's. Ringo Starr does the narration and the voice of the boy is Mike Lookinland of television's *The Brady Bunch*. Themes include tolerance, loyalty, and resourcefulness.

✳ SESAME STREET PRESENTS FOLLOW THAT BIRD

1985, 88 min, G, 3 to 8
Dir: Ken Kwapis

In *Sesame Street*'s only feature film, Big Bird is placed in a foster home by Miss Finch, a well-meaning but misguided social worker who thinks he has to be with other birds to be happy. But he is very lonely with the Dodo family and he runs away so he can go back to be with his friends at Sesame Street. The Sleaze Brothers attempt to capture Big Bird (so they can dye him blue and display him in a carnival), but he makes it home with the help of the friends he meets on the way and all the people and creatures from Sesame Street. NOTE: Although the movie is charming and does a nice job of making the point that we can love all kinds of people and not just the ones who look like us, some parts of this film could upset children in foster or adoptive homes or those in blended families. It is important to make it clear that it may be okay for seven-foot birds to run away from home, but not for children to try it.

✳ THE SHADOW OF HATE

1995, 40 minutes, NR, 12 and up
Dir: Charles Guggenheim

This documentary, subtitled *A History of Intolerance in America,* was produced as a part of the "Teaching Tolerance" project. It will require some explanation by parents, as the narration is not extensive, but it is a worthwhile survey of many of this country's worst examples of intolerance and hate crimes. Perhaps its most important lesson is in the variety of subjects of these crimes; we see atrocities involving the Irish, Chinese, Jews, Indians, and blacks, each at some point singled out as not worthy of being included in the Declaration of Independence's assertion that "all men are created equal."

The odd assortment of incidents selected and the lack of follow-through are this tape's biggest weaknesses. Families who watch this film should read more about the incidents and their consequences, as well as about the struggle to achieve liberty for each of these groups. They should also know how the "Teaching Tolerance" program was funded: The successful lawsuit brought by the Southern Poverty Law Center against the Klu Klux Klan resulted in an award of damages that bankrupted that division of the Klan and diverted all of its assets into a program to teach kids about tolerance.

✳ THE SNEETCHES

(in *The Cat in the Hat* and *Dr. Seuss on the Loose*)
1960, 50 min, 3 and up

The classic Seuss story about prejudice (the star-bellied Sneetches and the plain-bellied Sneetches each think they are the best, even when a machine removes the stars from the star-bellies and puts them on the plain-bellies) is included on this tape, along with *Green Eggs and Ham* and *The Zax*.

✳ A SOLDIER'S STORY

1984, 101 min, PG, 12 and up
Dir: Norman Jewison. Howard E. Rollins, Jr., Adolph Caesar, Denzel Washington
    A tough black sergeant is murdered in the days when the U.S. Army was still segregated. Captain Davenport (Howard E. Rollins, Jr.,) is assigned to investigate and he must sort through many stories, many different ideas about race and equality, and many suspects before finding the murderer, a disovery that reveals a deeper truth about the self-loathing that prejudice engenders.

✳ **CONNECTIONS:** Similar themes are raised in *The Man in the Glass Booth*, which is about a man put on trial for Nazi atrocities during WWII.

SEE ALSO:

Amazing Grace and Other Stories A little black girl triumphs over prejudice to play Peter Pan in the school play, teaching everyone that her dreams are bigger than anyone's attempt to limit them.

Bad Day at Black Rock Spencer Tracy plays a man who must confront prejudice against outsiders, the disabled, and the Japanese in a small Western town.

Johnny Belinda A young deaf woman overcomes prejudice when she is taught to communicate with sign language.

The King and I A British teacher and a Siamese king learn to appreciate each other's cultures, and she helps him impress British diplomats who are inclined to see Asians as barbarians.

A League of Their Own While the baseball players were off fighting in WWII, the baseball owners sponsored a league of women players, and the women showed that they had the courage, the heart, and the skill to play—and attract an audience.

The Learning Tree A young black boy must keep his ideals even though he's surrounded by bigotry.

Mask A young boy whose illness results in enlarged and distended facial features teaches those around him that his loving heart and fine intellect are what matter.

The Phantom Tollbooth Neighboring kings feud over which is more important, numbers or words, and learn to appreciate the importance of both.

A Raisin in the Sun Lorraine Hansberry's classic play is about a black family trying to move into a white neighborhood, despite the prejudice of their new neighbors and their own fears.

To Kill a Mockingbird A white Southern lawyer defends a black man in this story of teaching children to be tolerant despite a culture of racism and intolerance.

LOYALTY

"We must not confuse dissent with disloyalty."
—Edward R. Murrow

Loyalty is more than blind devotion. Keep in mind that for every good guy in a movie, there is a bad guy who also has very loyal supporters. They most often demonstrate their loyalty by agreeing with their leader and doing whatever he asks, primarily because one of the hallmarks of the movie bad guy is that he insists on absolute obedience. Heroes, however, demonstrate a more thoughtful and complex form of loyalty. Whether it is based on admiration for an individual or devotion to a cause, true loyalty requires a willingness to put the interests of others ahead of oneself and to do whatever is necessary to protect the people and the ideals that have earned loyalty.

As viewers, our own loyalties can surprise us because part of the filmmaker's art is to capture our loyalty for the star. We tend to side with whomever in the movie provides the point of view, whether the character is the cop or the robber. And some movies succeed by taking advantage of our tendency to side with the typical hero, as in *Stalag 17*. Like Sefton's fellow prisoners, we dislike him because he is a cynical loner and we share their surprise and confusion when we find that the real traitor is someone else.

It is not a coincidence that three movies that sharply depict the challenges of loyalty are set onboard ships—closed communities in which men must make careful decisions about where their loyalty lies. The main issues to consider in viewing these different illustrations of loyalty are these: How do I determine where my loyalty lies, and how is that loyalty best demonstrated?

The Adventures of Robin Hood

1938, 102 min, NR, 6 and up
Dir: Michael Curtiz and William Keighley. Errol Flynn, Olivia de Havilland, Claude Rains, Basil Rathbone, Alan Hale

✳ **PLOT:** Errol Flynn is the definitive Robin Hood in this gloriously Technicolor version of the classic story, one of the most thrillingly entertaining films of all time.

King Richard the Lion-Hearted, off fighting in the Crusades, has been captured and held for ransom. His unscrupulous brother John schemes to make sure Richard never returns, so he can take over as king. All of the knights offer their support but one, Sir Robin of Locksley, who vows to raise the ransom money himself. He and his followers use Sherwood Forest as cover so they can steal from the rich and powerful to help the poor and raise the ransom money. They capture a group of travelers that includes the Sheriff of Nottingham (Melville Cooper), Sir Guy of Gisbourne (Basil Rathbone), and the lovely Maid Marian (Olivia de Haviland), the King's ward. Marian is at first scornful, but when she learns that Robin and his men are loyal to Richard, and sees how the Normans have abused the Saxons, she becomes sympathetic.

In order to capture Robin, the Sheriff plans an archery contest, with the prize to be awarded by Marian. They know Robin will not be able to resist. He enters in disguise, but his superb skill reveals his identity, and he is caught and put in the dungeon. With the help of his men and Marian, however, he is rescued in time to help save Richard from John's plot to have him assassinated.

✳ **DISCUSSION:** In this story, Robin is the only one of the knights to stay loyal to Richard. Though he is a Norman, he is willing to lose everything he has to protect the poor Saxons. His loyalty is not limited to his own people; rather, he sees everyone who behaves justly as his people. "It's injustice I hate, not the Normans," he tells Marian.

Robin is not only the world's greatest archer and a master swashbuckler. He has an interesting and multilayered character, revealed in his interactions with Marian and with his men. He has a strong and clear sense of fairness and honor. He is always respectful of those who deserve it, including the peasants. He is confident and direct, but also unpretentious and even irreverent. When he tells Marian that her manners are not as pretty as her looks, Prince John laughs that this is quite a contrast to Sir Guy, whose feelings for Marian leave him tongue-tied. In the scene where he meets Little John, Robin fights him for the right to cross the river first, just for the fun of it. And when Little John wins, tossing him into the water, Robin is delighted. "I love a man that can best me!" Robin is not especially concerned with goodness or piety; he even steals food from Friar Tuck. But with the poor and weak, he is gentle and considerate and he is, above all, loyal. When he finds that the people who appear to be traveling monks are loyal to Richard, he says he will only take half of what they have. And, at the end, when the king asks him what he wants as a reward, all he asks for is amnesty for his men.

This is also a good movie to use for a discussion of what makes a leader. Robin's confidence in himself inspires the confidence of others. In one of history's finest pairings of actor and role, Errol Flynn brings his own assurance, grace, and passionate enjoyment to a part that added courage, integrity, and lively dialogue, creating one of the screen's greatest heroes.

PROFANITY: None.

NUDITY/SEXUAL REFERENCES: None.

ALCOHOL/DRUG ABUSE: None.

VIOLENCE/SCARINESS: Sword fights (including the famous one on the stairs in the castle); battles with arrows; etc.

TOLERANCE/DIVERSITY ISSUES: None.

✳ QUESTIONS FOR KIDS:
• Why does Robin stay loyal to King Richard?
• How does Marian learn that Robin is not just a thief?
• What do you learn about Robin from his meeting with Little John?
• What makes the men want to follow him?
• What makes someone a leader?

✳ CONNECTIONS: This is the ultimate version of one of the most classic and enduring stories of all children's literature, flawless in every respect, from performances to art direction to the unforgettably rousing score to the gorgeous jewellike Technicolor.

The director Michael Curtiz (brought in due to studio concerns over original director William Keighley) was also the director of another classic, *Casablanca.* The stirring music is by Erich Wolfgang Korngold, one of Hollywood's greatest composers. Flynn and de Havilland made nine movies together, including *Captain Blood* (the ultimate swashbuckler) and *They Died With Their Boots On,* a completely inaccurate but very exciting portrayal of the battle of Little Bighorn.

There are at least fourteen other movies about Robin Hood (not counting silent movies). Younger children may enjoy the 1973 Disney animated retelling of the story, with animals as all of the characters and some good songs by Roger Miller. Some of the other versions are all right (including the passable 1952 Disney live-action version, *The Story of Robin Hood and His Merrie Men,* with Richard Todd), but children should not be allowed to see the 1991 Kevin Costner movie (*Robin Hood: Prince of Thieves*). Although it has some redeeming features, the plot is a dreadful mishmash, with some truly disgusting violence and behavior that is ugly to the point of kinkiness ("Who told you that you could cover yourself?" snaps Alan Rickman as the Sheriff of Nottingham to the naked young woman in his bed when they are interrupted by his henchmen with a message). I don't recommend the Mel Brooks parody *Robin Hood: Men in Tights,* either. A couple of funny moments are surrounded by dozens of tasteless jokes about chastity belts and other sexual and scatological references.

✳ ACTIVITIES: Children who like this movie will enjoy the book by Howard Pyle (try to get an edition with Pyle's magnificent illustrations). Older children and teenagers might like to know more about this era and these characters. *Ivanhoe* tells the story of another group who stayed loyal to King Richard; if you watch carefully, you will see a character called Locksley who is based on the same historical figure as Robin Hood. For a movie that shows the earlier lives of both King Richard and his brother John, see **The Lion in Winter,** with Peter O'Toole as Henry II and Katharine Hepburn as Eleanor of Acquitaine, their parents. Anthony Hopkins plays Richard. A thin and sad movie about Robin Hood's later years is *Robin and Marian* (written by James Goldman, also the author of **The Lion in Winter**), starring Sean Connery and Audrey Hepburn.

The Caine Mutiny

1954, 125 min, NR, 12 and up
Dir: Edward Dmytryk. Humphrey Bogart, Van Johnson, Fred MacMurray, Jose Ferrer

✳ **PLOT:** The USS *Caine* is a minesweeper-destroyer during WWII. The people assigned to it feel far from the "real war." The story is told through the eyes of Ensign Willie Keith (Robert Francis), who does not like working with the *Caine*'s captain and is hoping for better when a new captain is assigned.

The new man is Captain Queeg (Humphrey Bogart), career Navy, in contrast to the rest of the officers, who enlisted or were drafted for the war. He is rigid and formal and explains that he expects people to go "by the book." "You may tell the crew that there are four ways of doing things aboard ship: the right way, the wrong way, the Navy way, and my way. They do things my way and we'll get along." Keith and his colleagues, sophisticated writer Keefer (Fred MacMurray) and thoughtful, responsible Maryk (Van Johnson), contemptuous of Queeg's poor seamanship, finally take over when the ship nearly founders in a typhoon.

At Maryk's court-martial, his defense counsel, Lieutenant Greenwald (Jose Ferrer), cross-examines Queeg intensely, causing the captain to reveal his instability. But Greenwald refuses to join the others in celebration. He arrives at their party drunk and furious, telling them they had no right to judge, much less destroy, a man who was doing the dirty work of defending America. He tosses a glass of champagne in the face of the man he blames the most—Keefer.

✳ **DISCUSSION:** This is a gripping story, with a brilliant performance by Humphrey Bogart as Queeg. His testimony at the court-martial is one of the most memorable scenes ever filmed. But what gives the movie its lasting resonance is the complexity of its resolution. It dares to be more than a simple good guys versus bad guys story, with the smart guys triumphing over someone who is weaker than they are.

Talk to kids about the role of each of the main characters. Keith is there as the representative of the audience; the story is told through his eyes. Maryk at first supports Queeg, but is persuaded by Keefer that Queeg is not only incompetent but dangerously unstable. Keefer may be persuasive, but when the time comes, and Maryk is on trial, Keefer does not support him. At the celebration following the trial, Maryk says, "I didn't think you'd have the guts to come," and Keefer replies, "I didn't have the guts not to."

Queeg is there to represent those who must perform the tasks that others consider beneath them. He puts a great deal of pressure on himself and on those around him, saying, "Substandard performance is not permitted to exist; that I warn you." He finds it impossible to ask for help directly, at best saying, "A command is a lonely job. Sometimes a captain of a ship needs help." His officers could have responded, but chose not to. This drives Queeg further into rigidity as he seeks to prove to them and to himself that he does not need their help.

PROFANITY: None.

NUDITY/SEXUAL REFERENCES: None.

ALCOHOL/DRUG ABUSE: Some drinking; Greenwald gets drunk.

VIOLENCE/SCARINESS: Tension on the ship and at the trial.

TOLERANCE/DIVERSITY ISSUES: None.

✷ **QUESTIONS FOR KIDS:**
- How does Willie's relationship with his girlfriend contribute to your understanding of Willie and of the main story?
- Why were the strawberries so important to Queeg?
- If Keefer had not been on the ship, what would Maryk have done differently? Why didn't the officers respond to Queeg when he asked for help?
- Why was Greenwald so angry with Keefer?

✷ **CONNECTIONS:** The Pulitzer Prize-winning novel by Herman Wouk is worth reading. Compare this movie to *A Few Good Men*, a contemporary exploration of some of the same issues, though without the courage to pursue the problems it raises. As in *The Caine Mutiny*, the climax of *A Few Good Men* is the cross-examination of a high-ranking officer. Both movies focus on the conflict between those who must become "grotesque," as Jack Nicholson's character in *A Few Good Men* admits, in the cause of protecting those who have the luxury of making fine distinctions.

Viewers should note, as the prologue to *The Caine Mutiny* points out, that in reality there has never been a mutiny on a U.S. ship.

❋Dead Man Walking

1995, 122 min, R, mature high schoolers
Dir: Tim Robbins. Susan Sarandon, Sean Penn

❋ **PLOT:** Sister Helen Prejean, a Lousiana nun, works in an inner-city neighborhood. She receives a letter from Matthew Poncelet, a prisoner sentenced to death for raping a young woman and murdering her and her boyfriend. He is hoping she will help him with his appeal. He is hard to like, hostile, ignorant, defiantly expecting and inviting the disapproval of others. He insists it was his friend who was responsible for the rape and murders. He parrots the bigotry of the Aryan Nation prisoners, extinguishing any possibility of clemency. He tries to distance himself from Sister Helen, insisting they have nothing in common and even making a clumsy pass at her. She listens patiently, never judging him but never losing sight of the truth as her faith reveals it to her. She quietly tells him they do have something in common: They both live among the poor. She tries to get him to talk to her: "Death is breathing down your neck, and you're playing your little man-on-the-make games." She does not try to convert him. She just wants him to accept responsibility for what he has done and she wants him to see that he is loved. Both goals are connected, as he must acknowledge his crimes in order to feel that he can be loved in spite of them.

Sister Helen struggles to find the best way for her to live up to her commitment as a person of faith. She is aware that the families of Matthew's victims have suffered deeply and she wants very much to support them. When they make it clear that providing support to Matthew is unacceptable to them, she grieves for the pain she causes them, but accepts the consequences of her choice to do what she can for him.

❋ **DISCUSSION:** This is a very rare movie depicting a person of faith who is not foolish, corrupt, or one-dimensional. Sister Helen's faith is a source of strength and a guide for her. Yet she struggles with her loyalty to her friends, who are hurt by her support of a bigot, a rapist, and a killer. She wants to provide support for the families of his victims, but realizes that her connection to Matthew can only give them pain. We see Sister Helen with her family and we see her enjoy a quiet laugh with another nun over the irony of the plans to bury Matthew in a plot adjoining a nun who would have been disconcerted by the thought of spending eternity next to a man. This helps us understand that Sister Helen is a human being, struggling to do the best she can, as we do, and as Matthew does.

The struggle is often about loyalty. Sister Helen believes she owes loyalty to Matthew, to the victims and their families, to her own family, to her fellow nuns and her friends, and ultimately to Jesus. The way that she thinks about these issues and the choices she makes are deeply moving. So is the impact on Matthew of unconditional love.

Tim Robbins, who wrote and directed the movie, refuses to make any easy emotional appeals. Like Sister Helen, he sees and sympathizes with both sides, and the issue of the death penalty is raised with sensitivity and respect.

PROFANITY: Strong language.

NUDITY/SEXUAL REFERENCES: References and depiction in flashback to a brutal rape.

ALCOHOL/DRUG ABUSE: References to alcohol and drug abuse; smoking.

VIOLENCE/SCARINESS: Rape and murder depicted in flashback; execution portrayed tastefully but frankly.

TOLERANCE/DIVERSITY ISSUES: Racist statements made by Matthew; objection by Sister Jean's black friends to her work with Matthew.

✳ **QUESTIONS FOR KIDS:**
- Why does Sister Jean befriend a man who has committed such a horrible crime?
- Why doesn't she try to convert him?
- How does her faith help her make decisions?
- What do we learn from the scene with Matthew's family? From the scene with Sister Helen's family?
- Why is it important for Matthew to acknowledge what he has done before he dies?

✳ **CONNECTIONS:** Susan Sarandon won an Oscar for this performance. The director-screenwriter, Tim Robbins, is her longtime companion.

✳ **ACTIVITIES:** Read the book, by Sister Helen Prejean.

Julia

1977, 118 min, PG, high schoolers
Dir: Fred Zinnemann. Jane Fonda, Vanessa Redgrave, Jason Robards, Maximilian Schell

✳ **PLOT:** Lillian and Julia are close friends as young girls, spending a lot of time together and sharing their dreams. When they grow up, Lillian (Jane Fonda) becomes a playwright with the help of her lover, writer Dashiell Hammett (Jason Robards). Julia (Vanessa Redgrave), always deeply concerned with justice and improving conditions for those less fortunate, becomes involved with the resistance movement in pre–WWII Europe. They see each other again when Lillian visits Julia in a Viennese hospital after she is injured in a student uprising. Julia mysteriously disappears from the hospital, and Lillian waits for a message. Ultimately, a message comes through a man named Johann (Maximilian Schell), who asks Lillian to help Julia by bringing American currency into Germany to be used to rescue victims of the Nazis. Lillian is terrified, but brings the money to Julia. Their meeting in a small German café is brief and guarded, but meaningful. Lillian is concerned about Julia's health (she lost a leg in the Viennese hospital and looks worn down), but she still glows with passion, with affection for Lillian, and with tenderness for her child, named Lily, living in France for safety. Later, after Julia is killed, Lillian tries to find Lily but is unable to overcome obstacles from bureaucrats and Julia's own family.

✳ **DISCUSSION:** Families will want to discuss the contrast between Julia's deep and unswerving commitment to fighting the Nazis, Lillian's struggles to make a contribution despite her fears, and the blasé indifference of many of the other characters. They may also want to compare the impact of Lillian's and Julia's ways of fighting the Nazis. Julia becomes deeply and personally involved, at the greatest possible personal risk. Although it is not covered in the movie, in reality Lillian Hellman (perhaps influenced by Julia) made a contribution by writing an influential play, *Watch on the Rhine,* one of the first strong public anti-Nazi statements.

> PROFANITY: Mild.
> NUDITY/SEXUAL REFERENCES: Brief reference to brother-sister incest; a character suggests that Lillian and Julia had a lesbian relationship; an unmarried couple lives together.
> ALCOHOL/DRUG ABUSE: A lot of drinking and smoking.
> VIOLENCE/SCARINESS: Tension; characters in peril; character injured and later killed (off-screen).
> TOLERANCE/DIVERSITY ISSUES: The two central characters are independent, strong, capable women, committed to their work. Hammett, a successful writer, is very supportive of Lillian's efforts to write a play.

✳ **QUESTIONS FOR KIDS:**
- How are Julia and Lillian alike? How are they different?
- How did Julia and her family influence one another?
- How was Dashiell Hammett most helpful to Lillian?
- What was Julia's most important influence on Lillian?

✳ **CONNECTIONS:** The movie is based on a story in *Pentimento,* a memoir by Lillian Hellman, author of *The Children's Hour* and **The Little Foxes.** Jason Robards portrays her longtime lover, Dashiell Hammett, author of **The Maltese Falcon** and **The Thin Man.** Hammett wrote the screenplay for *Watch on the Rhine,* which starred Paul Lukas and Bette Davis as a German man and his American wife who bring the message of early Nazi atrocities to America.

Redgrave and Robards won Oscars for *Julia,* as did screenwriter Alvin Sargent. Meryl Streep makes her movie debut with a brief appearance in the bar scene. Zinnemann also directed **High Noon** and **A Man for All Seasons.**

Mister Roberts

1955, 123 min, NR, 12 and up
Dir: John Ford and Mervyn LeRoy. Henry Fonda, Jack Lemmon, William Powell,
James Cagney

✳ **PLOT:** Mister Roberts (Henry Fonda) is the second-ranking officer on a
WWII supply ship, *The Reluctant.* He is restless, feeling that he is "sailing
from tedium to apathy and back again, with an occasional side trip to
monotony" and wants desperately to serve in the "real war," in combat. He
continually petitions for a transfer, but the despotic captain (James Cagney)
refuses to approve the petition. Ensign Pulver (Jack Lemmon), the ship's
morale officer, does his best to avoid work and stay out of the captain's
way. Doc (William Powell) is the ship's weary doctor, philosopher, and
when called for, moonshiner.

Roberts does his best to protect the crew from the petty tyrannies of
the captain. They ignore a direct order from the captain to put their shirts
back on in the scalding heat, and obey only when Roberts issues the order.
This disrespect and lack of control makes the captain furious. He tells
Roberts he will only give the crew the long-overdue shore leave they want
if Roberts will stop applying for a transfer and cooperate with his orders.
Roberts agrees.

The crew has a deliriously sybaritic shore leave, but when they return,
they are disappointed by Roberts's new attitude and lose their respect for
him. It is only when they overhear the captain, furiously yelling at Roberts
for throwing his beloved palm tree overboard, that they understand what
he has done for them. They forge not only another request for a transfer,
but also the captain's approval, and the transfer order comes in.

Pulver gets Roberts's job. The captain gets two new palm trees. Pulver
and Doc find out that Roberts has been killed in action. Doc gives Roberts's
last letter to the crew, and Pulver goes to confront the captain.

✳ **DISCUSSION:** Roberts's last letter says, "I've discovered, Doc, that the
unseen enemy of this war is the boredom that eventually becomes a faith
and, therefore, a terrible sort of suicide—and I know all the ones who refuse
to surrender to it are the strongest of all." That is true in peacetime as in
war, and in a way parallels the exchange between Drummond and Brady
in **Inherit the Wind:** "Do you ever think about what you *do* think about?"
The energy that it takes to fight inertia in thinking and acting is one of the
crucial messages of this film. Doc thinks. Pulver plans. He is almost a comic
variation on Hamlet as he brags about his elaborate schemes. But Roberts
acts. It isn't until he leaves that he learns that he had been active all along,
even in combat—combat against the surrender he writes about.

Another important aspect of the movie is the issue of obeying orders
and following rules. Notice the way that Pulver, Doc, and Roberts use small
rebellions to feel more independent and alive. They are all loyal to the war
effort, to each other, and to the men, but not always loyal to the system

(with the captain as its representative). This willingness to be subversive is another way of fighting mental and emotional inertia.

It is ironic that the very qualities that make Roberts want to leave make him indispensable to the captain. Those qualities are his willingness to approach all tasks, even the delivery of toilet paper and toothpaste, with energy and integrity. Pulver, on the other hand, just wants the easiest and most risk-free life he can maneuver for himself, at least until Roberts is killed, and he understands there are greater risks than the risk of challenging the captain. Maybe, too, trying to live up to Roberts's example is a way to keep him alive and close.

PROFANITY: Mild.

NUDITY/SEXUAL REFERENCES: Much conversation about peering with a telescope into the nurses' quarters; some talk about getting nurses to go out on dates, etc.

ALCOHOL/DRUG ABUSE: Drinking (including making their own liquor).

VIOLENCE/SCARINESS: Tension rather than scariness; off-screen death of major character in battle.

TOLERANCE/DIVERSITY ISSUES: Women treated as sex objects.

✳ **QUESTIONS FOR KIDS:**
- Why did the captain resent Roberts so much?
- Why did Roberts throw the palm tree overboard?
- How is this movie like **The Caine Mutiny** and how is it different?

✳ **CONNECTIONS:** Co-playwright Thomas Heggen was one of two successful young authors whose work was influenced by service in WWII, and who died young. Their lives were explored in Ross and Tom: Two American Tragedies, by John Leggett. There is a pallid sequel (with a couple of nice moments) called Ensign Pulver, starring Robert Walker, Jr., and Burl Ives.

✳Mutiny on the Bounty
1935, 131 min, NR, b&w, 8 and up
Dir: Frank Lloyd. Clark Gable, Charles Laughton, Franchot Tone

✳ **PLOT:** This movie, based on a true story, begins in 1787, when the British ship The Bounty sets sail from Portsmouth to Tahiti under the leadership of Captain Bligh (Charles Laughton) and First Mate Fletcher Christian (Clark Gable). Bligh is demanding to the point of cruelty, imposing harsh punishment for minor infractions of the rules. He says of the crew, "They respect one law—fear." Bligh also profits at the expense of the men, sending some of the provisions of cheese to his home before sailing and reporting it as stolen by the men. The crew has a blissful sojourn in Tahiti. Christian and some of the other sailors have romances with the native women.

Back at sea, Bligh becomes even more brutally capricious. He orders sick men to stay on duty and has others whipped for drinking water. He orders the ship's doctor to the deck to witness a flogging, even though he is very ill. When the doctor dies from the effort, Christian takes over the command, announcing that he is in charge of the ship. He will not permit the men to harm Bligh, but puts him, with three sailors loyal to him, in a boat with food, water, a sextant, and some tools. When Bligh says, "You're taking my ship?" Christian replies, "The King's ship, and you're not fit to command." Bligh warns that he will get back to England, and that Christian will "hang from the highest yardarm in the British fleet."

Christian takes the ship back to Tahiti. After forty-nine days, Bligh's boat arrives at the Dutch East Indies, and he gets a ship to go after the mutineers. By this time, the mutineers have settled on Pitcairn Island. Bligh captures them and takes them back to England for a court-martial. Although they present evidence of his brutality, the crew is sentenced to death, even Roger Byam, who had remained loyal to Bligh (and is later pardoned by the king). Bligh is exonerated by the tribunal, but is an outcast among his peers.

✳ **DISCUSSION:** The question of loyalty is especially compelling in the context of the armed services, with its clearly established hierarchy. And it is possibly most compelling in a naval context because sailors live in isolated communities when they are at sea. Christian and the others are literally sworn to be loyal and obedient to their superiors. Christian has nowhere to go to report his concerns about Bligh, nowhere to seek advice or ask for a transfer, no way to avoid the constant confrontation between Bligh and the men, between what he is asked to do and what he feels is right. We see every step he is asked to take, every unjust action he must tolerate, beginning with Bligh's theft of the cheese. Christian will countenance this violation because of his larger duty of obedience, because Bligh may be a bad man but he is an effective captain, and possibly because Christian wants to keep his job. But at a certain point, he must draw the line, even at the risk of his own life and the lives of the crew. That risk is outweighed by what he perceives as a greater risk from Bligh's treatment. Christian's loyalty to the men becomes more powerful than his loyalty to Bligh. We see this same phenomenon in *The Adventures of Robin Hood* and in other dramas of mutiny or near-mutiny, as in *Mister Roberts* and *The Caine Mutiny*.

Christian draws yet another line in his treatment of Bligh, preventing another crew member from shooting him and ensuring he has a chance of piloting his boat to shore (which he in fact did, and which is still regarded as an extraordinary feat of seamanship).

PROFANITY: None.

NUDITY/SEXUAL REFERENCES: None.

ALCOHOL/DRUG ABUSE: Some drinking.

VIOLENCE/SCARINESS: Abuse of sailors; death of ship's doctor.

TOLERANCE/DIVERSITY ISSUES: Sailors have romances with native women.

✳ **QUESTIONS FOR KIDS:**
- Compare this movie to **The Caine Mutiny**. How are the situations alike and how are they different?
- What should an officer do about a superior officer who is a bad man but an effective leader?
- Why did Christian take The Bounty back to Tahiti instead of England? What does that tell you about the motive for the mutiny? Were you surprised by the outcome of the trial? Why is obedience and order so especially important onboard a ship?

✳ **CONNECTIONS:** The facts of this famous case are still in dispute. Bligh made a persuasive case in his memoirs that the real reason for the mutiny was that the crew "has assured themselves of a more happy life among the Tahitians than they could possibly have in England, which, joined to some female connections, has most likely been the leading cause of the whole business." Bligh went on to a distinguished career (despite another mutiny during his service as the governor of New South Wales) and achieved the rank of vice admiral.

The story has been filmed twice more: in 1962, with Marlon Brando as Christian and Trevor Howard as Bligh, and in 1984, with Mel Gibson as Christian and Anthony Hopkins as Bligh (called The Bounty). Each has a different viewpoint on the relationship and the issues of loyalty, based on the perspective of the writer and director and the approach of the actors, and it is very interesting to compare them. Gable's Christian is a vigorous man of action who cannot contain himself any longer; Brando's is introspective, almost like Hamlet, until he finally must act; Gibson's is more of an everyman, acting out of some deeply felt notion of decency.

Another mutiny drama, Crimson Tide (rated R for language), made in 1995, is based more on policy issues, though the dispute is strongly rooted in principle on both sides. When a message to fire a missile on Russia is followed by a garbled message that may have been to rescind the order, Denzel Washington, representing the young, idealistic "new Navy," wants to wait, while Gene Hackman, representing the traditional, by-the-book "old Navy," wants to fire. In a somewhat unsatisfying but undeniably correct conclusion, they are told that they were both right—and both wrong.

✳ To Have and Have Not

1944, 100 min, NR, b&w, 10 and up
Dir: Howard Hawks. Humphrey Bogart, Lauren Bacall, Walter Brennan

✳ **PLOT:** Harry (Humphrey Bogart) and his drink-addled friend, Eddie (Walter Brennan), make a living taking tourists out in their fishing boat in Martinique, during the early days of World War II. They meet "Slim" (Lauren Bacall), a beautiful woman whose insolent, tough demeanor does not conceal her sense of honor. Harry is asked by his friend Gerard to take his boat out to pick up a leader of the underground, and Harry refuses. When asked, "What are your sympathies?" he replies, "Minding my own business." He does not want to get involved or take a risk for any cause. But he agrees to do it when Slim tells him she wants to go home but does not have enough money. He picks up Paul de Bursac and his wife, Helene, and gets them back to Martinique, but Paul is shot. Helene is angry with Harry at first, but is impressed with his courage and his care for her husband's wound.

The Nazis come looking for the de Bursacs and, when Harry will not tell them anything, they arrest Eddie. Harry realizes he does care about Eddie and Slim and he cannot avoid fighting the Nazis anymore. He finds a way to leave and take both of them with him, knowing that they must join the fight.

✳ **DISCUSSION:** This is a classic, with crackling dialogue (including Bacall's famous lesson on whistling), an exciting story, wonderful characters, and a lot of heart. In a way, it's a variation on *Casablanca* (made two years earlier), only this time, Rick goes off with Ilsa instead of with Captain Renault (in real life, too—Bogart met the nineteen-year-old Bacall on the set of this movie, and they married soon after). Like *Casablanca,* it presents a cool, tough, independent hero with a fight he cannot walk away from.

Harry tries to explain his views in relativistic terms, saying, "You save France. I'll save my boat," and telling Slim, "You ought to pick on somebody to steal from who doesn't owe me money." But as Slim points out, he does have "strings" attached, and ultimately he realizes he cannot limit his sense of commitment.

PROFANITY: None.
NUDITY/SEXUAL REFERENCES: Very mild.
ALCOHOL/DRUG ABUSE: Eddie is an alcoholic (and in today's terms, Harry and Slim are enablers); much action takes place in a bar.
VIOLENCE/SCARINESS: Suspense; some fighting and gunplay.
TOLERANCE/DIVERSITY ISSUES: Reference to "colored man" in song.

✳ **QUESTIONS FOR KIDS:**
- Why do you think Harry is friends with Eddie?
- What does it tell us that Slim is the only one who answers Eddie's question about the dead bee "correctly"?
- Why does Harry tell Slim to walk around him? How does she bring that up later to show him he was wrong?
- What changes Harry's mind? Paul says that for Harry "the word 'failure' does not even exist." Is that right? What evidence in the movie supports your answer?

✳ **CONNECTIONS:** Cricket is played by composer Hoagy Carmichael, whose songs include the Oscar-winner "In the Cool, Cool, Cool of the Evening." Play some of his music, possibly Willie Nelson's recording of

"Stardust" (or any other recording—it is possibly the most recorded song of all time) and Ray Charles's "Georgia on My Mind." Carmichael also appears in *The Best Years of Our Lives.*

Howard Hawks said this movie was the result of his boast to Ernest Hemingway that he could make a movie from Hemingway's "worst" novel. Not much in the movie comes from the novel. Coscriptwriters Jules Furthman and William Faulkner wrote what today would be called a "back story" for the characters in the novel, about what happened to the characters that led them to the place where the book begins. But according to Pauline Kael, "the novel's ending was used to polish off John Huston's film version of Maxwell Anderson's dreary play *Key Largo*; the novel's plot was used for another movie, *The Breaking Point,* directed by Michael Curtiz, in 1950; and the short story 'One Trip Across,' which Hemingway had expanded into *To Have and Have Not,* was used for an Audie Murphy movie, *The Gun Runners,* directed by Don Siegel, in 1958."

Bacall's debut in this movie made her an instant star, despite the fact that her famous sultry "look" (looking up while holding her head down) was the result of her attempts to control her shaking from nervousness. Bogart and Bacall made three more movies together, *The Big Sleep,* *Key Largo,* and *Dark Passage.*

✳ **ACTIVITIES:** Find Martinique on a map and read about the Vichy and the French resistance. Very thoughtful teenagers who want to know more should see *The Sorrow and the Pity,* about Nazi-occupied France.

SEE ALSO:

Breaking Away Four friends just out of high school provide support for each other.

Captain Blood Blood, a doctor, risks losing his life by treating a wounded rebel. He explains that his loyalty is to his fellow man, not to the king.

Spartacus The leader of a slave rebellion demonstrates deep loyalty to fellow slaves, and they give their lives to protect him.

Stand by Me An author reminisces about the loyalty of his childhood friends.

EDUCATION

"The library is the temple of learning, and learning has liberated more people than all the wars in history."
—CARL ROWAN

After the novelty wears off, just about the time that homework begins to seem tedious, kids start to wonder what the point is of going to school, and how anything that has to do with *x*'s and *y*'s or spelling or history can ever have any relevance to their lives, which they confidently assume will consist of work on computers with calculators and spell-checkers and CD-ROM reference materials. That is where these movies come in, because they do a good job of illustrating the transformation of both mind and spirit that comes from learning.

Sometimes the hero or heroine is driven by curiosity and a longing for something more. In other cases it takes a teacher to motivate the quest by giving a student a glimpse of a wider world or just by showing him that he can learn. Several "All work and no play makes Jack a dull boy" movies provide a delightful counterpoint, with characters who spend too much time on serious things finding that laughter and music are just as important.

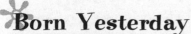Born Yesterday

1950, 103 min, NR, b&w, 10 and up
Dir: George Cukor. Judy Holliday, Broderick Crawford, William Holden

✳ **PLOT:** Harry Brock (Broderick Crawford), a loud, vulgar, thuggish man, has made a fortune in "junk" and hopes to make a bigger one if he can get some favorable legislation passed. So he comes to Washington with his full-time lawyer, Jim Devery (Howard St. John), a once-great legal mind now dissipated through alcohol and small corruptions; his cousin Eddie, a glorified gofer; and his girlfriend, Billie Dawn (Judy Holliday), a bored ex-showgirl.

When they meet Norval Hedges, the senator they have paid off to help them, Billie's lack of sophistication is an embarrassment, so Harry hires Paul Verrall (William Holden), a local reporter, to "educate" her. Paul agrees because he hopes to find out enough to expose Harry—and because he likes Billie, who may not be sophisticated but who is refreshingly direct. She agrees, even though she suspects it may be smarter not to be smart, because she has "a yen" for Paul.

But she surprises Paul and herself (and Harry) by becoming genuinely interested in what she is learning. She develops a great deal of respect for the democratic ideal—and a growing horror at the abuse of that ideal by Harry and Senator Hedges. She also develops enough self-respect that she can no longer continue as Harry's companion. She and Paul fall in love. Harry is hurt and jealous. To make things more complicated, on paper she controls much of his company—a tax and liability dodge concocted to protect Harry when it was assumed that Billie would always sign whatever was put in front of her. She agrees to sign the company back to him, a little at a time, if he will agree to behave in the future, and she and Paul go off together.

✳ **DISCUSSION:** This is a delightful comedy that includes real messages, not just about democracy and integrity, but about the transformational aspect of learning, and the importance of believing in yourself, and being with people who believe in you. At some level, Billie has been in denial. She was not proud of her life and she knew she was not living up to the ideals her father had raised her to have. She knew that if she ever thought about it, she could not stay. And yet she did stay, because she thought she knew what she wanted. Like Drummond cross-examining Brady in **Inherit the Wind,** Paul asks Billie to "think about what [she] thinks about," to question her assumptions. True to the spirit of what he is teaching her, he listens thoughtfully when she questions his assumptions and he realizes that he has been writing too ponderously and pretentiously. He helps her find the power within herself; like Alice in Wonderland, she defeats the enemy by simply calling him by name.

PROFANITY: None.

NUDITY/SEXUAL REFERENCES: Harry and Billie live together without being married (considered shocking when the movie was made); oblique references, the most explicit of which is "If he don't come across, I don't come across."

ALCOHOL/DRUG ABUSE: Devery has a drinking problem that is either the reason for his downfall or an attempt to forget it (or both).

VIOLENCE/SCARINESS: Harry slaps Billie.

TOLERANCE/DIVERSITY ISSUES: Billie is not expected (by Harry or by herself) to be able to think for herself.

❋ **QUESTIONS FOR KIDS:**
- Compare this story to **My Fair Lady,** in which a teacher and a student learn a great deal from each other. Or is it more like **Sleeping Beauty,** with the "princess" awakened by ideas instead of by a kiss?
- Why do people like Devery and Hedges behave the way they do?
- Why is Harry such a bully?

❋ **CONNECTIONS:** Mature high schoolers might enjoy *Never on Sunday,* a variation of this story involving a Greek lady of the evening and a naive scholar. In that case, he learns more from her than she learns from him.

Born Yesterday was remade in 1993 with Melanie Griffith, Don Johnson, and John Goodman. It is not nearly as good, but it is watchable and provides an interesting and perceptive update on some aspects of the original. Its best scene has Paul teaching Billie a set of all-purpose answers to any question that can be asked at a Washington cocktail party. In another scene, Billie teaches a group of high-powered Washingtonians a song celebrating the Amendments to the Constitution, set to the tune of "The Twelve Days of Christmas"—not a bad mnemonic!

Judy Holliday, who won an Oscar for this performance, can also be seen in **Bells are Ringing, The Solid Gold Cadillac, Adam's Rib,** and **It Should Happen to You.**

❋ **ACTIVITIES:** Try reading some of the books that Paul assigns to Billie and talking about how the ideas she read about changed her mind about her own life and the way she saw the people around her.

❋The Corn Is Green
1945, 114 min, NR, b&w, 10 and up
Dir: Irving Rapper. Bette Davis, John Dall

❋ **PLOT:** Miss Moffat (Bette Davis), an educated and very independent woman, arrives in a small Welsh mining village in 1895 to live in a house she inherited and start a school for the miners' children. She is told, "Down here, they're only children until they're twelve. Then they are sent away to the mine and are old men in a week." None of them can read or write, and few know any English at all. She persuades Miss Ronberry (Mildred Dunnock) and Mr. Jones (Rhys Williams) to help her, but the local landowner, called "the Squire" (Nigel Bruce), and the owners of the mine are opposed and do everything they can to stop her. She is about to give up when she sees an essay by Morgan Evans (John Dall), a young mine worker, that shows a real gift. She tells him he is "clever," which makes him "want to get more clever."

They work together for two years, but she does not realize he is becoming resentful and impatient. His friends make fun of him for learning and call him the schoolmistress's dog. He quits. But later, when Mr. Jones persuades him to come back, Miss Moffat prepares him for Oxford and even uses "soft soap and curtsying" to persuade the Squire to recommend him. He wins a scholarship. But Bessie, the dishonest and slatternly daughter of Miss Moffat's housekeeper, is pregnant with Morgan's child. Miss Moffat adopts the child so that Morgan will be able to go to Oxford. She tells him his duty is to the world. Then she tells herself, "You mustn't be clumsy this time," and resolves to be more sensitive in raising Morgan's child than she was with him.

✷ **DISCUSSION:** This movie is an adaptation of a play by Emlyn Williams, who was actually saved from the coal mines by an understanding teacher. It has a lot of parallels to **My Fair Lady** and **Born Yesterday,** which also deal with intense teacher-student relationships that transform the lives of both. Like Billie Dawn and Eliza Doolittle, Morgan is excited and disturbed by the way that learning changes him; he panics at the thought of losing everything familiar to him (including ignorance), and he gets angry and impatient. Eliza would understand Morgan's telling Miss Moffat that "I don't want to be thankful to no strange woman." Like Henry Higgins, Miss Moffat does not want thanks.

But Miss Moffat is different because of her reason for teaching Morgan. She responds to his spirit and his potential in that first essay. Perhaps because she responds so strongly, she stays very distant from him, admitting that she knows every part of his brain, but does not know him at all. She cares for him deeply. The contrast between her spirited response to the Squire when he prevents her from using the barn for a school and her "soft soap and curtsying" to get him to help Morgan shows how far she is willing to go. Ultimately, she takes on Morgan's child, knowing that it means she will never see him again, because both of them believe the child will be better off if the break is permanent.

Also worth discussing: the consequences of careless sexual involvement, the idea that there may be something more important to some women than getting married (especially in that era, when married women had so little say over what happened to them), and Bessie's statement that she only had sex with Morgan to spite Miss Moffat.

PROFANITY: None.

NUDITY/SEXUAL REFERENCES: Bessie becomes pregnant out of wedlock with Morgan's child.

ALCOHOL/DRUG ABUSE: Morgan drinks, and says the liquor gave him the courage to speak.

VIOLENCE/SCARINESS: None.

TOLERANCE/DIVERSITY ISSUES: Class issues.

✷ **QUESTIONS FOR KIDS:**
• Why didn't the Squire want the Welsh children to learn?
• Why did the miners make Morgan feel bad about learning?

- Why did telling Morgan he was clever make him want to learn more? Why did Bessie's telling him he was clever have a different effect?
- What did Miss Moffat mean by "soft soap and curtsying" and how did she use them? How did she feel about using them?
- Why was Morgan so angry about having to be grateful?

❋ **CONNECTIONS:** The real-life Morgan Evans, Emlyn Williams, became a playwright and actor and can be seen in **Major Barbara** as Snobby Price. The Squire is played by Nigel Bruce, best known as Dr. Watson in the American-made series of Sherlock Holmes movies. Bessie's mother belongs to a group like the one Sister Sarah belongs to in **Guys and Dolls,** or Major Barbara does in the film of the same name.

❋ **ACTIVITIES:** A good book about this part of the world is *On the Black Hills,* by Bruce Chatwin, and there are some outstanding books about the history of coal miners in many different parts of the world.

❋ EDUCATING RITA
1983, 110 min, PG 13, mature high schoolers
Dir: Lewis Gilbert. Michael Caine, Julie Walters
An uneducated girl from the lower class comes to see a professor, who has forgotten what the books he teaches ever meant to him, to ask him to help her pass the exams she needs to get into college. Her unpretentious joy in what she reads and her undiluted awe of him as the caretaker of wisdom make him excited about teaching. He fears, though, that she will lose her honest, unaffected, very direct responses to literature. And he knows that as she becomes better educated she will discover his limitations. Michael Caine and Julie Walters (re-creating the role she originated on the stage) are both outstanding. NOTE: Strong language and a suicide attempt.

❋ MALCOLM X
1992, 194 min, PG-13, high schoolers
Dir: Spike Lee. Denzel Washington, Angela Bassett, Al Freeman, Jr.
As a child, Malcom Little (Denzel Washington) saw his home burned and his minister father killed by racists. He becomes a street hustler and is sent to prison for theft. A fellow prisoner teaches him about Elijah Muhammad, but also about self-respect and the exhilaration and power that come from learning. He sheds his last name, the symbol of slave owners, becoming Malcolm X. When he is released from prison, he joins Elijah Muhammad as a Black Muslim minister.

Malcolm X becomes a brilliant and charismatic leader. He attracts a lot of support and a lot of controversy. Outspoken and angry, he insists that whites are responsible for the evil imposed on American blacks, and that they cannot be part of any solution. He encourages his followers to become independent and self-sufficient. When asked for a comment on President

Kennedy's assassination, he can only say obliquely that the "chickens have come home to roost." But he continues to learn and grow. His wife, Betty, nourishes his tender side. He makes a pilgrimage to Mecca and learns that people of all races can share a spiritual bond. And he discovers that his hero, Elijah Muhammad, has not always held himself to the standard he preaches. Shortly after he confronts Elijah Muhammad, Malcolm X is assassinated.

This is a thoughtful, complex, brilliant movie, with a galvanizing performance by Denzel Washington. He makes the intellectual passion and the essential integrity of Malcom X heartbreakingly touching. There is no better illustration of the transformative power of learning. It changes not just the way he sees the world, but the way he sees himself.

SEE ALSO:

Educating Rita A working-class woman is thrilled by learning.

Stand and Deliver A group of inner-city students learns calculus—and self-respect—from an inspiring teacher.

PEACE (AND WAR)

"You may not be interested in war, but war is interested in you."
—LEON TROTSKY

In movies, as in life, we see very mixed signals about the role of violence. Almost everyone would agree that violence is not a good way to resolve conflicts. Yet the powerful pull of violence continues to make violent movies among the most popular and lucrative. It is astonishing how often a movie features a hero who opposes violence but who must ultimately use it. These resolutions are undeniably satisfying. We have the best of both worlds: We get to identify with a hero who is on the right side, and we get to see him hit or shoot someone who "deserves it." In children's films like **Ferdinand the Bull** and **The Reluctant Dragon,** we see (anthropomorphic) heroes who successfully avoid violence. But in films for older kids and adults, we rarely see anyone—and never a dramatic hero—walk away from the big fight.

Some thoughtful movies show us the painful distance between those who are capable of and willing to engage in violence and those they must protect. Others show us the consequences of a life of violence or that even the best intentions can have tragic consequences when violence erupts.

Movies do a less ambiguous job of opposing violence on the largest scale, and a number of movies point out the insanity of war, some by taking us into battle. Others demonstrate the irony of war by setting the story in medical units that repair the ravages of war and send the men back into battle. Movies like **The Day the Earth Stood Still** and **20,000 Leagues Under the Sea** raise the question of the threat or use of violence to prevent greater violence through war. **WarGames** reminds us that "the only way to win is not to play," and **Gulliver's Travels** reminds us how trivial issues that inspire violence often are. Ask kids to compare movies made during WWII with those made after it was over to see how the perspective shifts and becomes more complex. The two versions of **Henry V**, one made during the war, one decades later, provide fascinating contrasts.

The use of violence, like other moral choices, is depicted in many forms.

In **High Noon,** Will Kane, having made a commitment to his new Quaker bride, at first runs away from the threat of violence. But his sense of honor and his commitment to the community (far greater, it turns out, than theirs to him), require him to turn around. In **On the Waterfront,** Terry's triumph is not in hitting anyone (he is grossly outnumbered); it is in surviving being hit, his determination and resilience an inspiration to the dockworkers.

These films provide an opportunity to get past the comic book concepts of violence promoted by *Hercules, Power Rangers, Teenage Mutant Ninja Turtles* and **Independence Day,** and to begin to talk with kids about when, if ever, violence is justified, and what the consequences are.

*The Day the Earth Stood Still
1951, 93 min, NR, b&w, 8 and up
Dir: Robert Wise. Michael Rennie, Patricia Neal, Sam Jaffe

* **PLOT:** A spaceship lands in Washington, D.C., near the Washington Monument. Surrounded by army troops, a door opens, and Klaatu steps out, looking like an elegant human male. A nervous soldier shoots at Klaatu, and his robotlike companion, Gort, shoots them. Klaatu is taken to a hospital but escapes and finds a place to stay in a boardinghouse run by widow Helen Benson (Patricia Neal). He gets to know Helen and her son, Bobby, and he and Bobby go to visit a distinguished scientist (Sam Jaffe) so Klaatu can deliver his message about the risk the earth faces from its aggressive development of weapons, jeopardizing not just the planet but the entire solar system and the universe.

Klaatu wants to find a peaceful way to deliver his message, so he shuts down all power sources on the planet, except for hospitals and other essential systems. Worried that he will be attacked again, Klaatu tells Helen the secret code to prevent Gort from attacking to protect him from harm: "Klaatu berrada nikto." Klaatu is shot and killed, and Helen delivers the message just in time. Gort brings Klaatu back to the spaceship and revives him. Klaatu speaks to the people, telling the assembled scientists that they must ensure peace, and that Gort and his fellow robots will be on guard to destroy the earth if they cannot find a way.

* **DISCUSSION:** Although this is very much a movie of the Cold War era, the "duck and cover" years when children practiced air raid drills in schools, its themes are eternal, especially for children. In addition to the themes of nonviolent conflict resolution (possibly easier for today's children to discuss in the context of this 1951 movie), there is the larger theme of making friends with those who may appear at first to be different.

PROFANITY: None.
NUDITY/SEXUAL REFERENCES: None.
ALCOHOL/DRUG ABUSE: None.

VIOLENCE/SCARINESS: Some sci-fi shooting; Klaatu gets hurt.

TOLERANCE/DIVERSITY ISSUES: A subtheme of the movie.

✳ **QUESTIONS FOR KIDS:**
- Why did some people want to kill Klaatu? Why did some want to try to talk to him instead?
- This movie was made only six years after the first atomic bombs were used to end WWII. Why is it important to know that to understand this movie? What is different now? What is the same?
- How does this compare to other movies about the importance of stopping wars, and how does it compare to other movies about visitors from other planets?
- If you could meet Klaatu, what would you say?

✳ **CONNECTIONS:** A more obscure movie with a similar theme is *The Next Voice You Hear,* a 1950 film directed by William Wellman. This time it is God who tells everyone on Earth (over the radio), including costar Nancy Reagan, that it is time to stop all war forever.

✳ Destry Rides Again
1939, 94 min, NR, b&w, 8 and up
Dir: George Marshall. Jimmy Stewart, Marlene Dietrich, Brian Donlevy, Charles Winninger

✳ **PLOT:** Bottleneck is a rough Western town. Most of the action takes place in the Last Chance Saloon, presided over by hostess-showgirl Frenchy (Marlene Dietrich) and town boss Kent (Brian Donlevy). As the movie opens, Kent is in a poker game with his cronies and a blissful sucker named Claggett, crowing over his good luck. Frenchy comes in, encourages him to bet everything he has and, when he has put the deed to his ranch on the table, spills coffee on him, allowing for a switch of the cards. Kent wins and now has all the land he needs to impose a fee on cattle driven through that part of the country. Claggett asks Sheriff Keogh for help. Keogh goes to Kent and is killed. Kent announces that Keogh has been called out of town—permanently—and that Judge Slade, the mayor (Samuel S. Hinds), will appoint a new sheriff. Slade appoints the town drunk, Washington "Wash" Dimsdale (Charles Winninger). Wash, once deputy to the famous Sheriff Tom Destry, swears he will give up drinking for the job. And he will bring Tom Destry, Jr., to town to help him.

Destry (Jimmy Stewart) arrives by stagecoach. In contrast to tough fellow passenger Jack Tyndall, he appears to be meek, even foolish. Wash, furious and humiliated, tells Destry to leave. But Destry tells Wash that his famous father's guns didn't protect him—he was shot in the back. Destry doesn't think that is the way to solve the town's troubles. "You shoot it out with 'em and for some reason or other—I don't know why—they look like heroes. But you put 'em behind bars and they look little and cheap, the way they oughta look." Wash swears him in.

Destry stops some marauders by showing his accuracy with a gun. But when Claggett and his family are barricaded on their ranch in a shoot-out with Kent, Destry insists that they leave. Kent has the deed and the legal right to the ranch. Destry promises he will get their ranch back if they give him time. Destry knows he has to prove that Kent killed Keogh. He talks to Frenchy, who lets it slip that Keogh was "taken care of."

With the help of Boris (Mischa Auer), a Russian immigrant called "Callahan" by everyone because he married a widow by that name, Destry finds Keogh's body and arrests Kent henchman Bugs Watson. Kent thinks he has nothing to fear, with the corrupt mayor acting as town magistrate, but Destry has arranged for a federal judge to hear the case. When Kent hears that, he decides to kill Wash and Destry. Frenchy sends for Destry, to protect him, but when he hears shots, he runs to find Wash, who is dying. Destry comforts Wash, saying that like his father, Wash was shot in the back. "They didn't dare face him, either." Wash dies peacefully.

Destry straps on his father's guns. With Tyndall's help, he goes to the saloon. Frenchy has brought the women of the town in to stop the fight. She sees Kent taking aim at Destry, tries to warn him, then blocks the bullet herself, wipes off her lipstick for a kiss, then dies in his arms. Destry shoots Kent. As the movie ends, the town is peaceful (except for the battling Callahans). Destry is the idol of the young Claggett boy and much admired by Tyndall's sister as well.

✳ **DISCUSSION:** Like *Shenandoah* (also starring Stewart), **High Noon,** and *Friendly Persuasion,* this movie gives us a hero opposed to fighting who reaches a point where no alternative is possible. It provides a good opportunity for a discussion of how we decide on methods of conflict resolution, and what we do when they fail. It is also a good starting point for a discussion of how people change when they get a glimpse of what they might be. Destry sees what Frenchy might be, what she is under her "mask," telling her, "I'll bet you've got a lovely face under all that paint. Why don't you wipe it off someday and have a good look—figure out how you can live up to it." He reminds her she can be that whenever she decides to. He also appreciates Wash and gives Boris a role that enables him to develop enough self-respect to insist that he be called by his own name.

Older children who enjoy a more literary approach to movies might appreciate the exceptionally tight narrative of this story, the way that each incident not only tells you something about the characters (and tells the characters about each other) but also moves the story along.

PROFANITY: None.

NUDITY/SEXUAL REFERENCES: None.

ALCOHOL/DRUG ABUSE: A lot of drinking in the bar; "manliness" measured by what a man drinks; Wash is the town drunk who reforms when he becomes sheriff.

VIOLENCE/SCARINESS: Gunfights, fistfights; two lead characters killed.

TOLERANCE/DIVERSITY ISSUES: Clara (played by Lillian Yarbo) is portrayed as a sterotyped movie black maid, a little silly. Interestingly, her comments are always accurate, though the other characters pay no attention to her. The word "nigger" is used in a song sung by an extra in the final scene.

✳ **QUESTIONS FOR KIDS:**
- Why does Destry like to pretend that the stories he tells are from a friend?
- Why do the people think that Destry is not strong or tough at first? Was that a good basis for that conclusion? What changes their minds?
- Destry is determined not to use his guns "the old way" but to use the law "the new way." Does he fail? Why or why not?
- How can you tell when you have no alternative but to use force? What did Destry say to Frenchy that made her want to be different?

✳ **CONNECTIONS:** This movie was filmed once before with Tom Mix and remade as *Destry* with WWII war hero Audie Murphy and again as *Frenchie* with Shelley Winters. Jimmy Stewart and Samuel S. Hinds (a real-life lawyer here playing a judge) also appeared together in *It's a Wonderful Life* as George Bailey and his father.

✳ **ACTIVITIES:** Look up the definition of "bottleneck" in a dictionary. Look at a bottle to discover how that term was derived. Why was that a good name for the town in this movie?

✳ Ferdinand the Bull

1938, 29 min, NR, 4 and up
(in Willie the Operatic Whale *video)*
Dir: Dick Rickard

✳ **PLOT:** The classic story by Munro Leaf and Robert Lawson is about the bull who did not want to fight. Even when he was very young, Ferdinand did not play with the others, butting heads. He just wanted to sit quietly and smell the flowers. When some men come looking for bulls for a bullfight, the others race around, trying to look fierce, but Ferdinand sits quietly. Unfortunately, he sits on a bee, gets stung, and charges the men, making them think he is the fiercest of all. They take him to the bullfight, but instead of fighting, he just smells the flowers thrown to the matador. The matador does everything he can think of to get Ferdinand to fight, and becomes so upset that he bursts into tears. "So they had to take Ferdinand home. And for all I know, he is sitting there still, under his cork tree, smelling the flowers. He is very happy." NOTE: This volume of the Walt Disney Mini Classic series includes three short cartoons about being different. I strongly recommend that you skip the first one, in which a whale sings opera. Children will not be especially interested and will not get most of the jokes (for example, the whale wears clown makeup when he sings *Pagliacci*). Furthermore, the whale is rather blithely killed off at the end, with the narrator noting that he is still singing in heaven. Children (and indeed, grown-ups) may find it hard to draw much comfort from this, especially since the whalers who harpoon him suffer no adverse consequences or remorse.

The third cartoon, *Lambert the Sheepish Lion,* is a pleasant ugly duckling tale about a lion cub mistakenly delivered (by a stork) to a ewe. She and Lambert love each other, but the lambs make fun of him because he can't baaa or butt heads. One night, while the lambs are asleep, a wolf approaches the flock. Lambert is frightened at first, but the lion in him rises to the occasion and he scares the wolf away.

✳ **DISCUSSION:** *Ferdinand the Bull* is a great movie to use to talk with children about nonviolence and about how happy Ferdinand is, even though he is different. *Lambert the Sheepish Lion* deals with the second issue as well. Note that in both, loving mothers appreciate their children and put no pressure on them to conform.

PROFANITY: None.

NUDITY/SEXUAL REFERENCES: None.

ALCOHOL/DRUG ABUSE: None.

VIOLENCE/SCARINESS: None—Ferdinand is about as antiviolent a story as has ever been written.

TOLERANCE/DIVERSITY ISSUES: The theme of all three cartoons is accepting those who are different.

✳ **QUESTIONS FOR KIDS:**
• Why doesn't Ferdinand want to fight like the other bulls?
• How does he feel about being different? How can you tell?
• How does Lambert feel about being different?
• Do you ever feel different?
• Do kids at your school tease people who are different? Why?

✳ **CONNECTIONS:** All children should read *Ferdinand the Bull*. They might also enjoy other stories about outsiders, like "The Ugly Duckling," "Rudolph the Red-Nosed Reindeer," and *Stuart Little*.

The *Ferdinand the Bull* cartoon has a Disney in-joke. The matador is none other than Walt Disney himself.

✳ Gulliver's Travels

1939, 74 min, NR, 6 and up
Dir: David Fleischer

✳ **PLOT:** The most famous episode of Jonathan Swift's classic satire is the visit of shipwrecked sailor Lemuel Gulliver to Lilliput, where no one is more than six inches tall. In this animated version, Gulliver is washed ashore, discovered by Gabby, the town crier, and captured by the Lilliputians. Their king had just been celebrating the engagement of his daughter to a neighboring prince, when a dispute over which nation's song would be played at the wedding results in a broken engagement and a declaration of war. Gulliver persuades the Lilliputians that he wants to be their friend. The king knows that having a giant on his side will keep them safe. Three silly spies for the other king try to get rid of Gulliver, but Gulliver, realizing that the prince and princess love each other, stops the fighting on both sides and brings them together, singing both songs in a duet.

✳ **DISCUSSION:** Brothers Max and David Fleischer were Disney's major competition in the early days of animation. Although they did not come close to Disney's standards for visual artistry, they made some cartoons that stand up very well (including the Betty Boop, Popeye, and Koko the Clown series). This is the better of their two full-length features, released just after Disney's **Snow White.** The use of the rotoscope (to draw over footage of real actors) for Gulliver and the prince and princess makes them seem a little out of keeping with the more "cartoony" characters like Gabby, the spies, and the king, but the story is strong, and there is some very funny slapstick as the Lilliputians use block and tackle to tie Gulliver up and transport him to the castle.

As in the book, the movie makes fun of trivial political disputes (in the book, the controversies were over heel heights on shoes and how to break an egg). Children can discuss why the Lilliputians were afraid of Gulliver, what the kings should have done about the dispute over the songs, and how Gulliver made his decision about how to resolve it.

PROFANITY: None.
NUDITY/SEXUAL REFERENCES: None.
ALCOHOL/DRUG ABUSE: None.
VIOLENCE/SCARINESS: Storm at sea; fistfights; war stopped by Gulliver.
TOLERANCE/DIVERSITY ISSUES: A theme of the story is tolerance, which in this version is represented by a war over which song will be played at the wedding of the prince and princess.

✳ **QUESTIONS FOR KIDS:**
• Would you like to visit Lilliput? What would you do?
• Why did the two kings fight about the songs? What would you tell them to do? How did Gulliiver decide what he should do?
• This movie is only about one chapter in the real book about Gulliver. In the next part of the book, he visits a place where he is as small as the Lilliputians are to him. Which one would you like better?

✳ **CONNECTIONS:** Kids who like this movie will enjoy finding out about Gulliver's other travels. A live-action 1960 version, *The 3 Worlds of Gulliver*, is very watchable and far superior to the 1977 version. In 1996, a good made-for-television miniseries version (now available on video) starred Ted Danson. Teenagers may appreciate the satire in the book by Swift.

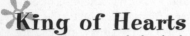King of Hearts
1966, 101 min, NR, high schoolers
Dir: Philippe De Broca. Alan Bates, Genevieve Bujold

✳ **PLOT:** Retreating WWI German troops leave a bomb in a small French village, set to explode a munitions storehouse at midnight. Word is sent to the British troops by a barber-spy, who is shot by German soldiers before he can say where the bomb is hidden. The colonel of a Scottish regiment selects Charles Plumpick (Alan Bates) to dismantle the bomb because he is fluent in French, in spite of the fact that the gentle ornithologist knows nothing about explosives.

When he arrives, the town has been evacuated, and the only inhabitants are the residents of the local "lunatic asylum" and the circus animals they have freed. The inmates are happily dressing up in outlandish costumes and acting out their delusions. Plumpick is both frustrated and enchanted by them, and tries to make them understand that they are in danger as they crown him their "King of Hearts." He tries to get them to leave the town, but they won't go, telling him, "It's too dangerous. You won't believe how wicked they are out there!"

German soldiers arrive to check on the bombs, but are chased away by the inmates, playing with the tanks. Scottish soldiers arrive to check on Charles, but they are scared away by the animals and strange behavior of everyone they meet. Charles falls in love with Coquelicot (Genevieve Bujold). At the last minute, he figures out the secret of the bomb and saves the town. Charles's regiment arrives and celebrates with the inmates, whom they take to be the town's residents. The next morning, as the soldiers are leaving, the inmates grab Charles and take him away. The German troops arrive, and in the ensuing battle all of the soldiers on both sides are killed. The town's residents return, and the inmates go back to the asylum.

Charles and his pigeon are given medals, but he cannot go back to war. In the last scene he stands nude, holding a birdcage, at the gate of the asylum, waiting to be let in.

✳ **DISCUSSION:** The "mad" people in this movie are those who are harmless, tolerant, happy, and generous. The "sane" people are those who fight suicidal battles, give medals to a bird, and mistake fireworks for gunfire.

The theme of outsiders (whether mentally ill, mentally or physically disabled, or from a different culture) as more astute than the rest of us is an enduring one. It has special appeal for teenagers who often feel that they are outside adult society. They are reassured by the portrayal of someone else who feels that way, too. For that reason, movies like *King of Hearts, Harold and Maude,* and **A Thousand Clowns** are college-town perennials.

Of course, the people in this movie bear no resemblance to those with real mental illnesses. These are fantasy lunatics, more childlike than troubled, designed to create a contrast to the real madness of the war. The "madness" of the soldiers is also exaggerated to make the point. The three Scot soldiers are so eager that they run off before they know their assignment. The soldiers are unable to see that the people in the town are "lunatics," but they conclude that Charles is mad.

Charles is in the middle. Repeatedly hit on the head, he is in a daze throughout the movie. Frustrated and helpless, he finally gets angry at the lunatics for making him care about them, but ultimately he joins them.

> PROFANITY: None.
>
> NUDITY/SEXUAL REFERENCES: Reference to whores, cuckold, and brothel; Coquelicot asks Charles to make love to her; madam sitting in bed with general tells him her girls will have babies to make soldiers for him; brief nudity (rear) in final scene.
>
> ALCOHOL/DRUG ABUSE: Some drinking.
>
> VIOLENCE/SCARINESS: Barber is shot; pigeon is shot; firing line; battle in which all of the soldiers are killed.
>
> TOLERANCE/DIVERSITY ISSUES: The "mad" people are tolerant and do not even see the kinds of distinctions that the "sane" people are killing each other over.

✳ **QUESTIONS FOR KIDS:**
- In this movie, the "mad" people act "sane," and the "sane" people act "mad." Can you give some examples?
- Is war always "insane" in some way?
- Will Charles stay in the lunatic asylum?
- Why is the mental hospital called an "asylum"?
- Charles says, "I don't need anyone," and Coquelicot replies, "Yes, you do." Does he? How can you tell?

✳ **CONNECTIONS:** Other movies that depict the insanity of war include *Catch-22, M*A*S*H,* and *Oh, What a Lovely War.*

✳ 20,000 Leagues Under the Sea
1954, 127 min, NR, 8 and up
Dir: Richard Fleischer. Kirk Douglas, James Mason, Paul Lukas, Peter Lorre

✳ **PLOT:** This is the Disney version of the Jules Verne novel that predicted the invention of the submarine. It begins with sailors reporting a "ship-killer" monster with one eye "like a lighthouse," and "breath like a furnace." Professor Aronax (Paul Lukas) and his aide, Conseil (Peter Lorre), go looking for it on behalf of the government. When their ship is sunk by the "monster," only the two of them and a harpoonist named Ned (Kirk Douglas) are saved. They find that the "monster" is really a submarine, the creation of Captain Nemo (James Mason). At first, he orders Ned and Conseil to be thrown back into the sea, but when the professor insists on joining them, Nemo allows all three of them to stay onboard, saying, "I found out what I wanted to know."

Nemo is a very cultured man, serving gourmet meals (entirely made of ingredients from the sea) and playing Bach on a pipe organ. But, as he admits, he is not a civilized man. Disgusted with humanity's destructive impulses, he refuses to share his inventions and discoveries with the world because he fears they will be used in war. Instead, he uses his submarine to blow up ships that are aiding in a war effort. He shows the professor people gathering explosive materials for weapons, and explains that he once worked there, too. Then he sinks the ship carrying those explosives so they cannot be used in war. Ned is furious: "Those were sailors, like me." The professor calls Nemo a murderer and a hypocrite, but Nemo answers, "They are the assassins, the dealers in death. I am the avenger." Ned goes on land and is chased back to the submarine by natives. Nemo flips a switch to give the natives electrical charges that send the natives back to the shore.

But Ned and Conseil used their time on land to send notes in bottles with the directions to Nemo's home base. When they return, the navy is there. Nemo blows up the submarine, rather than give it to those who might use it for war. Only the professor, Conseil, and Ned escape.

✳ **DISCUSSION:** Some of the conflict in this story stems from the fact that its characters value very different things. The professor values science. Ned values life. Nemo values independence. When Nemo is attacked by the squid, Ned saves his life. Afterward, Nemo asks why, and Ned says, "That's a good question" and goes off to get drunk. There are a lot of good issues here about the use and abuse of technology. Nemo (and Verne) were right—when the submarine was developed, it was used for destructive purposes.

PROFANITY: None.

NUDITY/SEXUAL REFERENCES: None.

ALCOHOL/DRUG ABUSE: Ned gets drunk after he saves Nemo's life.

VIOLENCE/SCARINESS: A fight with squid; sinking ships; explosions. Ned and Conseil hit each other, which somehow seals their friendship.

TOLERANCE/DIVERSITY ISSUES: None.

✳ **QUESTIONS FOR KIDS:**
- Jules Verne created a submarine long before scientists and engineers were able to make one work in real life. What invention can you think of that would make an exciting story?
- Nemo tries to stop people from destroying each other, but in order to do that, he destroys many people, too. Is that his only alternative?

- Nemo has several different motivations, including hate, revenge, and a wish for peace. How do you see each of these elements in him?
- Nemo likes being undersea because he can make his own rules. Could he do that today anywhere? Why or why not?
- Why does Ned save Nemo? Would Nemo have saved Ned?

✳ **CONNECTIONS:** This movie has terrific underwater shots and Oscar-winning special effects. Kids who are interested in submarines will also enjoy *Yellow Submarine, Operation Petticoat* (a 1959 comedy about U.S. Army nurses stuck on a submarine with Cary Grant and Tony Curtis), *The Hunt for Red October,* a Tom Clancy story about a defecting Soviet submarine commander, and *Crimson Tide* (rated R), in which Gene Hackman and Denzel Washington must decide whether to use nuclear weapons when they are cut off from communication with their commanding officers.

✳ **ACTIVITIES:** Verne wrote this book before the invention of the submarine. Look at some pictures of early submarines and try some experiments to see how one submerges and rises. Try to make a periscope with mirrors. At Disneyland and Disney World's Magic Kingdom you can take a short trip on the *Nautilus.*

Parents probably won't be able to persuade children to try any of the underwater delicacies Nemo serves in the movie (like sauté of unborn octopus), but you may be able to get them to try some seafood to get a sense of what the characters in the movie ate.

See if they recognize the music Nemo plays on the organ—it also appears in *Fantasia.* If they like it, find a recording of some other Bach organ music.

✳War Games
1983, 110 min, PG, 10 and up
Dir: John Badham. Matthew Broderick, Ally Sheedy, Dabney Coleman

✳ **PLOT:** When a test reveals that soldiers are reluctant to follow orders to launch missiles capable of massive destruction, the U.S. Defense Department creates an automatic system to launch missiles when the United States is attacked, without any possibility of human interference. Meanwhile, a teenage boy named David (Matthew Broderick) is at home, fooling around with his computer, trying to tap into the computer of a software manufacturer to try out their new games. He accidentally connects to the Defense Department instead and he "plays" something called "Global Thermonuclear War," showing it to his friend Jennifer (Ally Sheedy).

The Defense Department thinks he is a serious hacker and they come to get him. He realizes he has accidentally set in motion an unstoppable series of commands that will lead to a real thermonuclear war. David and Jennifer escape to seek out the scientist who designed the program, now a recluse. They bring him back and manage to figure out a way to teach the computer not to undertake an initiative that will leave no one a winner, concluding that "the only winning move is not to play."

✷ **DISCUSSION:** Time has caught up with the technology of this movie, and using modems to connect computers is no longer as astonishing as it was when this movie was made. But it is still an exciting story and an important issue.

> PROFANITY: Mild.
> NUDITY/SEXUAL REFERENCES: None.
> ALCOHOL/DRUG ABUSE: None.
> VIOLENCE/SCARINESS: Tension and suspense; overall anti-violence message.
> TOLERANCE/DIVERSITY ISSUES: None.

✷ **QUESTIONS FOR KIDS:**
- If it is true that humans will hesitate before launching nuclear missiles, is that a good thing or a bad thing?
- What can we do to make sure that the right decision is made?
- What are the risks, now that the technology David had is so widespread?

✷ **CONNECTIONS:** This was, at the time it was filmed, the most expensive set ever built. Ironically, the "computer graphics" on the screens were created by old-fashioned animation, at that time a more advanced and flexible technology than computer design.

✷ **ACTIVITIES:** Mathematically inclined kids might like to learn some elementary game theory, like the prisoner's dilemma, in which the simplest strategy of cooperation beats all of the complicated challenges. (See *The Evolution of Cooperation,* by Robert Axelrod.)

SEE ALSO:

Friendly Persuasion A theme of this movie is the response of people committed to nonviolence when others are fighting a war to protect their ideals and their lives and property.

The Gods Must Be Crazy The gentleness of the movie's bushman hero contrasts with the violence of the "civilized" world.

The Man Who Shot Liberty Valance A man who believes in the law finds that the law has its limits in the face of violence.

MAKING MORAL CHOICES

"Reason deceives us; conscience, never."
—JEAN-JACQUES ROUSSEAU

Even more important than talking to kids about values like integrity and responsibility is talking with them about the challenges of applying those values and the consequences of the choices we make. It is one thing to make kids understand that it is wrong to steal; it is another to give them the tools they need to resist when their friends suggest shoplifting some candy from the store and it seems to them that their reputation depends on doing it. Moral dilemmas are rarely presented to us unambiguously. A child may understand that it is wrong to cheat but may see things differently when he is desperate for the good grade his parents expect. Movies can be especially helpful in illustrating the complexity and difficulty of making these choices and in giving us a chance to see the consequences.

The most interesting moral dilemmas (and therefore the most dramatic) are those that are complex. Often this is a function of two important but clashing values. In **High Noon,** a man must weigh his commitment to his wife against his commitment to the community, a community that seems to have no commitment to him. His wife must weigh her opposition to violence against her love for her husband. In **A Doll's House,** a young wife must decide whether she should commit forgery in order to obtain the money she needs to save her husband's life. In **Major Barbara,** a woman who has devoted her life to helping others must decide whether she can ethically accept funding from people who have made their money by harming or exploiting the very people she wants to help. In **Friendly Persuasion,** a family devoted to peace must decide what to do when their neighbors are risking their lives to protect them. In **Judgment at Nuremberg,** the issue is the culpability of Nazi judges for following Nazi law, after their country has lost the war. In political movies like **All the King's Men, Advise & Consent, State of the Union,** and **The Best Man,** characters must evaluate a number of small moral compromises against the opportunity to do great good. It is not coincidental that none of these politicians gets what he dreamed of.

We see characters giving their lives for moral reasons, perhaps most heartbreakingly in *Spartacus,* where 6,000 slaves give their lives rather than betray their leader to the Romans. In *A Man for All Seasons,* Thomas More gives his life rather than lie about what he believes. Others give up their careers, as in *Mutiny on the Bounty,* or someone they care about (*The Maltese Falcon*) or a way of life (*The Adventures of Robin Hood, The Long Walk Home*). Movies like *These Three* and *Fail-Safe* show characters who must try to make up for the wreckage left by the bad choices of others.

Younger children may be especially interested in movies showing children and other characters they can identify with, like *Pinocchio, Willie Wonka and the Chocolate Factory,* and *Tuck Everlasting.*

Older kids will find interesting the movies that show careful calibration of moral choices. In movies like *The Scarlet and the Black, A Man for All Seasons,* and *Schindler's List,* characters make decisions about how far they can go in pursuit of a moral imperative. In *The Scarlet and the Black,* the priest says he will help prisoners escape but he will not help destroy anyone, even the Nazis. In *A Man for All Seasons,* More says he will stay silent, and thus avoid having to compromise himself with a lie. In *Schindler's List,* Schindler never tries to save anyone else, but puts everything he has into saving the people on his "list." In contrast, look at the unsuccessful efforts of both of the leading characters in *Quiz Show* to calibrate their choices by making distinctions that do not hold up. Charles Van Doren tells himself at first that he is not really cheating if they only give him the questions and he researches the answers. Then he tells himself it doesn't matter because he is getting kids excited about learning. Dick Goodwin tells himself that he can protect Van Doren from the hearings because the real bad guys are the people at the network. Part of what makes these four films so compelling is that all of the stories are true.

Many movies have particularly good examples of the consequences of decisions that seem quite small when they are made. For example, in *All My Sons,* a man's decision to make extra money by cheating on the specifications of airplane parts (and then framing his partner) has devastating consequences for the next generation. Small compromises by characters in *All the King's Men, The Apartment,* and *State of the Union,* become serious corruptions. In *The Apartment, On the Waterfront,* and *All My Sons,* we see how choices that seem easy to a character when considered as abstractions seem very different when they directly affect people he knows. In *Norma Rae,* what makes the character decide to act is simply learning that she can.

These are especially important points to make to help kids learn how to think about the choices they face. The movies in this section all show us characters who are confronted with a choice and who must bring their sense of morality to bear in deciding what to do. Not all of them make the right choices, though some later change their minds. These kinds of films are especially important to watch as a family, to talk about how the choices are presented, how they are evaluated, and what the impact is on the people who make the choices and the people they care about.

All the President's Men
1976, 138 min, PG, 12 and up
Dir: Alan J. Pakula. Robert Redford, Dustin Hoffman, Jason Robards

❋ **PLOT:** Based on the real-life story of the two reporters who would not give up on the story of the Watergate break-in, this is as gripping as any detective novel. Bob Woodward (Robert Redford), a junior reporter for the *Washington Post,* is sent to cover a small-time break-in of the office of the Democratic National Committee (located in the Watergate office building). He works with Carl Bernstein (Dustin Hoffman), another reporter, to find, after tediously painstaking research, that it is just part of a complex pattern of corruption in President Nixon's reelection campaign.

❋ **DISCUSSION:** Star Redford was so intent on authenticity, he even flew actual garbage from the *Washington Post* wastepaper baskets out to the set. The movie does a good job of showing how much of the work of the reporters was dull persistence, and it also does a good job of showing us what went into the decisions of editor Ben Bradlee (Jason Robards in an Oscar-winning performance) and (off-screen) publisher Katherine Graham about what they needed in terms of proof in order to be able to publish the story.

There is an interesting range of moral choices and calibrations. The famous "Deep Throat" (Hal Holbrook), still unidentified, is someone from the inside who will not allow himself to be identified or even quoted, but is willing to confirm what the reporters are able to find elsewhere.

Others involved in the scandal, both in the corruption and in its cover-up, must decide what to do and how much to disclose. "Deep Throat" will not tell them anything new, but will confirm what they find out and give them some overall direction. Most memorably, he tells them to "follow the money." One key development is the decision made by someone identified only as "the bookkeeper" (Jane Alexander) to talk to Bernstein. The participants must also deal with the consequences of their choices. Donald Segretti (Robert Walden) manages to evoke sympathy when what began as juvenile pranks leave him in disgrace. Woodward and Bernstein also make mistakes and must deal with the consequences.

As the movie ends, in 1972, Nixon is reelected, and it seems to the reporters that their work has had no impact at all. Kids who view this film may need some context in order to understand it, and will want to know what else happened before Nixon resigned in August of 1974.

PROFANITY: Some strong language.
NUDITY/SEXUAL REFERENCES: Epithets.
ALCOHOL/DRUG ABUSE: None.
VIOLENCE/SCARINESS: None.
TOLERANCE/DIVERSITY ISSUES: None.

✳ **QUESTIONS FOR KIDS:**
- Why were Woodward and Bernstein the only reporters interested in the story? Why did they insist on two sources before they would publish anything?
- What were Donald Segretti's "dirty tricks"? How was he different from Sloan? From the bookkeeper? From "Deep Throat"?
- One of the people portrayed in the movie later testified before the Watergate Committee that he had "lost his moral compass." What does that mean? How does something like that happen?

✳ **CONNECTIONS:** Look for future Oscar-winner F. Murray Abraham (*Amadeus*) as an arresting officer.

The Final Days is a made-for-television sequel, based on Woodward and Bernstein's follow-up book. For more on this era, see *Nixon,* with Anthony Hopkins, and Nixon's famous "Checkers" speech, available on video. An odd little movie, *Nasty Habits,* is an allegory of Watergate, set in a convent, with Glenda Jackson as a Nixonian nun.

✳ **ACTIVITIES:** The book this movie was based on is not much fun to read—more reporting than analysis. Older kids who want to know more can read *Breach of Faith,* by Theodore White, or the books written by participants like Judge Sirica, John Dean, and H. R. Haldeman (whose diaries are available on CD-ROM).

✳The Chocolate War

1988, 103 min, R, mature high-schoolers
Dir: Keith Gordon. John Glover, Ilan Mitchell-Smith, Wally Ward

✳ **PLOT:** While Jerry Renault (Ilan Mitchell-Smith), a freshman at Trinity Prep boys' school, is belittled by the football coach, two boys, Archie (Wally Ward) and Orbie (Doug Hutchison), sit high up in the stands watching them. Archie determines the "assignments" to be given to those boys selected for the school's elite club, the Vigils, and Orbie is the club's secretary. Jerry, whose mother has recently died, is selected for an assignment.

At home, Jerry's father is remote, still overcome by grief. In school, teacher Brother Leon (John Glover) is tough and imperious. He brutally berates an outstanding student, then tells him, "You passed the toughest test of all—you were true to yourself."

Brother Leon tells Archie the boys have to sell 20,000 boxes of chocolates for their annual fund-raiser, twice the number from previous years, and at twice the price, to help ensure that he will become headmaster. He won't refer to the Vigils by name, but acknowledges Archie's "influence." Each boy must sell fifty boxes. All of the other boys agree, but Jerry refuses. Brother Leon says that selling is voluntary ("that is the glory of Trinity"), but tells the class that "the true sons of Trinity can pick up your chocolates in the gym. The rest—I pity you."

It turns out that refusing to sell the chocolates was the "assignment" given to Jerry to prove his worth to the Vigils. But after the time period of the assignment expires, he continues to refuse to participate, despite harassment by the other boys. It gives him a feeling of strength and independence, not just from Brother Leon, but from the Vigils as well. Brother Leon says that sales are poor because the boys have become "infected" by Jerry. Brother Leon tells Archie that "if the sale goes down the drain, you and the Vigils go down the drain. We all go down the drain together."

The Vigils decide to make the chocolate sale a success by making it popular. The head of the Vigils tells Archie his position depends on his making his plan work.

At last, all of the chocolates are sold, except for Jerry's quota. Archie arranges an assembly, with a raffle; the prize is the chance to select the punches in a boxing match between Jerry and a tough boy named Janza. But Archie has to take Janza's place, and Jerry beats him. Jerry says, "I should have just sold the chocolates, played their game, anyway." Archie is now secretary, and Orbie has taken over assignments for the Vigils.

✳ **DISCUSSION:** Mature teenagers, especially fans of the popular book by Robert Cormier, will appreciate this dark story, a kind of *Dangerous Liaisons* for teenagers. Archie says that "people are two things, greedy and cruel," and devises his plans to take advantage of those qualities.

Although the story is exaggerated for satiric effect, much of it will seem true to teenagers, who often feel a heightened sense of proportion. The movie shows us some of Jerry's dreams or fantasies, which add to the surreal and claustrophobic feeling of the movie.

The movie provides a good basis for a discussion of the different ways that people get other people to do what they want, the exercise of power, and the ways that power is maintained—and lost. The interaction between Brother Leon and Archie is especially interesting because of their uneasy interdependence. As powerful as both of them seem, they ultimately lose their power without much of a struggle.

PROFANITY: Very strong language, the reason for the R rating.

NUDITY/SEXUAL REFERENCES: References to masturbation; (false) accusation of homosexuality used to taunt Jerry.

ALCOHOL/DRUG ABUSE: Smoking by teens.

VIOLENCE/SCARINESS: Jerry is beat up by a gang of smaller kids; a boxing match at the end; blackmail, harassment, and other emotional violence.

TOLERANCE/DIVERSITY ISSUES: All of the boys are white and Christian; some issues of tolerance of individual differences.

✳ **QUESTIONS FOR KIDS:**
- What are the tools that Archie uses to maintain and exercise power? What tools does Brother Leon use?
- How can anyone or any group decide to make something "popular" and "cool," as Archie does with the chocolate sale?
- Why does Archie tell Janza to "use the queer pitch" on Jerry?
- Why does the screenplay have Archie holding an impaled butterfly

when he talks to Janza on the phone? Why does Jerry tell the girl she was right?

- What is the significance of the Vigils's marble test for the person who gives the assignments?

✳ **CONNECTIONS:** Read the book by Robert Cormier, and his other popular novel, *I Am the Cheese* (filmed in 1983, and remade in Canada as *Lapse of Memory,* also known as *Memoire Tranquee,* in 1992). Compare this story to other books and movies about power struggles in a school context, including *Perfect Harmony, Lord of the Flies, School Ties* and, for mature high school and college students, *The Lords of Discipline* (1983, rated R), the surrealistic *If . . .* (1968, rated R), and one of its inspirations, the French film *Zero for Conduct* (1933).

✳Friendly Persuasion
1956, 140 min, NR, 8 and up
Dir: William Wyler. Gary Cooper, Dorothy McGuire, Anthony Perkins

✳ **PLOT:** This is the story of the Birdwells, a loving Quaker family in the midst of the Civil War. Eliza (Dorothy McGuire), a devout woman, is the moral center of the family. Jess (Gary Cooper) is a thoughtful man, not as strict as Eliza on prohibitions like music and racing his horse, but with a strong commitment to his principles. Their children are Joshua (Anthony Perkins), a sensitive young man who opposes violence but feels that he must join the soldiers; Mattie (Phyllis Love), who falls in love with Gord, a neighbor who is a Union soldier; and Young Jess (Richard Eyer), a boy who is fascinated with the talk of war and battles.

A Union soldier comes to the Quaker prayer meeting to ask the men to join the army. They tell him they cannot engage in violence under any circumstances. "We are opposed to slavery, but do not think it right to kill one man to free another." Even when the soldier points out that this means others will be dying to protect their lives and property, no one will support him.

The Confederate army approaches, and Joshua and Enoch, a freed slave who works on the Birdwells's farm, decide to join the Union. Eliza does everything she can to keep Joshua from going, even telling him that in doing so he will not only reject what he has learned in church but he will reject her, too. Jess says that Joshua has to make up his own mind. "I'm just his father, Eliza. I'm not his conscience. A man's life ain't worth a hill of beans unless he lives up to his own conscience. I've got to give Josh that chance." Joshua prays for guidance and leaves to join the army the next morning. At first Eliza won't respond, but then she runs after him to wish him well.

As the war gets closer, Jess and Eliza refuse to run away from their farm as others are doing. When Josh's horse comes back without him, Jess goes looking for him. He finds his good friend Sam mortally wounded by a sniper. When the sniper shoots at Jess, too, Jess takes his gun away but will not harm him; he tells the sniper, "Go on, get! I'll not harm thee." Josh is wounded and deeply upset because he killed a Confederate soldier. Jess brings him home.

In the meantime, the Confederates ride onto the farm, and in keeping with her faith, Eliza welcomes them and gives them all her food. But when one of the soldiers goes after her beloved pet goose, she whacks him with the broom, amusing her children and leaving herself disconcerted and embarrassed. Jess and Josh return, and the family goes off to church together to continue to do their best to match their faith to their times.

✳ **DISCUSSION:** This is an exceptional depiction of a loving family, particularly for the way that Jess and Eliza work together on resolving their conflicts. They listen to each other with enormous respect and deep affection. Jess does his best to go along with Eliza's stricter views on observance, because in his heart he believes she is right. Nevertheless, he cannot keep himself from trying to have his horse beat Sam's as they go to church on Sunday, and he decides to buy an organ knowing that she will object. In fact, he doesn't even tell her about it. She is shocked when it arrives and says that she forbids it, to which he replies mildly, "When thee asks or suggests, I am like putty in thy hands, but when thee forbids, thee is barking up the wrong tree." Having said that if the organ goes into the house, she will not stay there, she goes off to sleep in the barn. He does not object—but he goes out there to spend the night with her, and they reconcile and find a way to compromise.

All this provides a counterpoint to more serious questions of faith and conscience. In the beginning, when the Union soldier asks the Quakers if any of them will join him, one man stands up to say that nothing could ever make him fight. Later, when his barn is burned, he is the first to take up a gun. Even Eliza, able to offer hospitality to the same men who may have just been shooting at her son, finds herself overcome when one of them captures her beloved pet goose.

Jess is willing to admit that the answer is not so simple. All he asks is that "the will of God be revealed to us and we be given the strength to follow his will." He understands the difficulty of finding the right answer for himself and for Joshua. He resolves it for himself in his treatment of the sniper, and he respects Joshua and the issues involved enough to let Joshua make his own choice.

The movie is a rare one in which someone makes a moral choice through prayer, which many families will find worth emphasizing. Josh, who was able to respond without violence to the thugs at the fair, decides that he cannot benefit from risks taken by others unless he is willing to take them, too. He cries in battle, but he shoots.

The issue of how someone committed to nonviolence responds to a violent world is thoughtfully raised by this movie.

PROFANITY: None.

NUDITY/SEXUAL REFERENCES: None.

ALCOHOL/DRUG ABUSE: None.

VIOLENCE/SCARINESS: Sam killed by sniper; Jess shot at: Gord and Josh wounded (off-screen).

TOLERANCE/DIVERSITY ISSUES: Tolerance of religious differences is a theme of the movie.

✳ **QUESTIONS FOR KIDS:**
- How is the religious service in the movie similar or different from what you have experienced?
- How was the faith of the characters tested in this movie? What did they learn from the test?
- How should people who are opposed to violence respond to violence when it is directed against them? When it is directed against others?

✳ **CONNECTIONS:** The screenplay was written by Michael Wilson, who received no screen credit because he was blacklisted during the "Red Scare." His involvement makes the issues of conscience raised in the book even more poignant. The book on which the movie is based, by Jessamyn West (a Quaker, and a cousin of Richard Nixon), is well worth reading. Cooper faces some of the same issues (and has a Society of Friends bride) in **High Noon.** *Shenandoah*, with Jimmy Stewart as the father of a large family who tries to keep his sons out of the Civil War, raises some of the same themes without the religious context. It later became a successful Broadway musical.

✳ **ACTIVITIES:** Take your child to a meeting of the Society of Friends (preferred over the term "Quaker").

✳ The Gunfighter

1950, 84 min, NR, b&w, 10 and up
Dir: Henry King. Gregory Peck, Karl Malden

✳ **PLOT:** Jimmy Ringo (Gregory Peck) is the fastest gun who ever lived, which makes him a target for every young man who wants to prove himself. On his way to Cayenne, Ringo stops in a bar. A "young squirt" taunts him, and Ringo makes every possible effort to placate him, finally asking the young man's friends to make him stop, but finally he pulls his gun on Ringo, who kills him. Even though everyone saw that it was in self-defense, the witnesses tell him to move on. The dead man had three brothers, and "they won't care who drew first."

The three brothers come after Ringo, but he is waiting for them and he takes their guns and sends their horses back to town, telling them to go back on foot. But he knows they will probably follow him instead, and that once he gets to Cayenne, he will only have a brief time to do what he has in mind.

He gets to Cayenne and is surprised and pleased to find his old friend Mark Strett (Millard Mitchell) as the sheriff. Mark tells him he will have to leave; that even though Ringo does not want any trouble and has not committed any crimes, trouble will come looking for him, as there are too many young men who will risk everything to be able to claim the credit for killing Ringo. Ringo wants to see his wife, Peggy, and their child. Mark knows where they are but won't say. He does agree to ask Peggy if she will see Ringo, and tells Ringo to stay put, under the care of the sympathetic bartender (Karl Malden).

Ringo stays quietly in the corner. But every one of the boys in town plays hooky to peer in at him through the saloon window. And the local "squirt," hotheaded Hunt Bromley (Skip Homeier), comes after him. Ringo scares him off with a bluff. But Jerry is across the street with a rifle pointed out the window, sure that Ringo must be the one who killed his son. And the three brothers have found horses and guns and are approaching fast.

Peggy at first refuses to see him. She finally agrees, and when he says he wants to settle down in a place where no one knows him, she says if he can do that for a year, she will join him. He spends some time with his son and prepares to leave, happy at the thought of his new life. But Hunt is waiting for him and shoots him in the back.

As Ringo dies, he says that he drew first. He doesn't want Hunt hanged. He wants him to suffer as he has suffered, knowing that wherever he goes, there will be someone who wants to be known as the man who shot the man who shot Ringo.

✳ **DISCUSSION:** This is really a Western version of the story of King Midas. Ringo's wish came true, but at a terrible price. There was a time when he could think of nothing finer, nothing manlier, than being known as the fastest gun in the West. We see a glimmer of that again when he asks what Jimmy (who does not know that Ringo is his father) thinks of him. When he hears that Jimmy admires Wyatt Earp, he can't help telling the boy that he is far tougher than Earp. Yet now Ringo is tired. He knows that every moment he will have to watch for someone trying to kill him (as happens throughout this movie), and that someday someone will be a little less tired (or, as happens, a little less honorable) than he is.

It provides a good opportunity for a discussion of notions of manhood and courage, along the lines of the moving speech by Charles Bronson in *The Magnificent Seven.* Ringo would trade all of his fame for the chance to live with his family, as shown most poignantly when he shares a drink with a young rancher. Ringo is more successful with his intelligence than his speed—he is able to avoid shoot-outs with the brothers, with Jerry, and in the first encounter with Hunt. He arranges to have money paid to Peggy without giving away their connection, and thinks of a plausible reason to tell Jimmy why he wanted to see him so that he doesn't have to tell him the truth. His innate decency and sense of justice are shown in his dealings with Jerry, his dreams for a life with Peggy, and especially in the scene in which he talks to the ladies of the town, when they do not know who he is. His pleasure in being able to have a moment's interaction with people who are not either terrified, angry, or trying to shoot him is very moving.

This is also a good movie about the consequences of our choices. There are so many movies about redemption and triumph that it is automatically branded an "adult Western" when a gunfighter doesn't shoot the bad guy and ride off into the sunset. Unlike Alan in *The Petrified Forest,* who dies to help someone else, or Butch Cassidy and the Sundance Kid, whose deaths at the end of the movie only brighten their legend, Ringo chooses to tarnish his legend as he dies, to curse Hunt to the same fate that he suffered, and possibly also to give little boys and young squirts less reason to try to be like him.

> PROFANITY: None.
>
> NUDITY/SEXUAL REFERENCES: None.
>
> ALCOHOL/DRUG ABUSE: Much of the action takes place in bars, and there is a lot of drinking.
>
> VIOLENCE/SCARINESS: Gunfights.
>
> TOLERANCE/DIVERSITY ISSUES: None.

✳ **QUESTIONS FOR KIDS:**
- Why does every town have a "young squirt" who wants to prove he is faster than Ringo?
- Why doesn't Mark carry a gun?
- Why does Ringo insist that he drew on Hunt?
- Why was Mark able to get away and start over, when Ringo and Buck were not?
- Why does Peggy call herself Mrs. Ringo at the end?

✳ **CONNECTIONS:** One of the three brothers who come after Ringo was played by Alan Hale, Jr., who went on to play the Captain in the television show *Gilligan's Island,* and was the son of Alan Hale, who played Little John in **The Adventures of Robin Hood.**

Compare Ringo's final decision to the one made by Jimmy Cagney in *Angels with Dirty Faces.* A tough criminal on death row, he is asked by his lifelong friend, a priest, to go to his death a coward, so that the boys who look up to him will not want to follow his example.

✳Guys and Dolls
1955, 150 min, NR, 8 and up
Dir: Joseph L. Mankiewicz. Marlon Brando, Frank Sinatra, Jean Simmons, Vivian Blaine

✳ **PLOT:** The story takes place among the small-time underworld characters of New York City. Nathan Detroit (Frank Sinatra) runs a "floating crap game" (held in a different place each time) that provides entertainment and bankrolls many members of the community. His problem is that he can't find a place to have the next game. The only place available wants $1,000 up front, and he does not have it. Furthermore, his (very) long-term fiancée, Adelaide (Vivian Blaine), a showgirl, is so distressed over his failure to marry her that she has developed a psychosomatic cold.

Trying to get the money he needs, Nathan makes a bet with Sky (as in willing to bet sky-high) Masterson (Marlon Brando). After Brando brags that he can get any "doll" to go out with him, Nathan challenges him to ask Sarah Brown (Jean Simmons), the local mission worker. Sky persuades Sarah to go to Havana for dinner, and after he spikes her drink with liquor, they have a wonderful time, and she starts to fall in love with him.

When they get back, however, she finds that the crap game was held in the mission and feels betrayed. In order to persuade her that his intentions are honorable, Sky rolls the dice in the crap game against the "souls" of the other players, and when he wins, they must all go to a meeting at the mission, the two couples get married, and everyone lives happily ever after.

✳ **DISCUSSION:** This musical classic, based on the stories of Damon Runyon, is a lot of fun, despite the fact that two of the leads are not singers and none of them can dance. But Brando and Simmons do surprisingly well, especially in the scenes set in Havana, and the movie is brash and splashy enough to be thoroughly entertaining.

Themes worth discussing include honesty in relationships and in competition (Harry the Horse cheats and threatens the other players) and how people decide whether to align themselves with (or between) the two extremes presented by the mission workers and the grifters and gamblers.

PROFANITY: None.

NUDITY/SEXUAL REFERENCES: Very oblique reference to the face of the hotel clerk when an unmarried couple checks in; "Take Back Your Mink" is a song about a girl who accepts a lot of gifts from a man but is not "one of those girls."

ALCOHOL/DRUG ABUSE: Sky gets Sarah drunk in Havana by arranging for her drink to be spiked with liquor.

VIOLENCE/SCARINESS: None.

TOLERANCE/DIVERSITY ISSUES: Portrayal of Adelaide as hopelessly waiting to marry Nathan would earn her a spot on the *Sally Jessy Raphaël* show today.

✳ **QUESTIONS FOR KIDS:**
- Adelaide says she has developed a cold from waiting for Nathan to marry her. How do people get physically sick from unhappiness or worry?
- What is the meaning of Sky's father's advice about the deck of cards? Is that good advice?

• Who changes the most in this movie? How can you tell?

✳ **CONNECTIONS:** Other movies based on Runyon's colorful characters include *Little Miss Marker* (four versions, including *Sorrowful Jones,* and *Forty Pounds of Trouble.* The best one has the original title and stars Shirley Temple; the later version of that title has a nice performance by Walter Matthau, but is otherwise tedious). Additional movies based on Runyon stories are *Lady for a Day* (remade with Bette Davis as *Pocketful of Miracles*), *The Lemon Drop Kid* (also filmed twice, with the Bob Hope version the better one), and a very sad movie starring Lucille Ball and Henry Fonda called *The Big Street.*

✳ **ACTIVITIES:** Kids who like this movie may enjoy reading (or having read aloud to them) some of Damon Runyon's stories, especially "Butch Minds the Baby."

✳High Noon

1952, 84 min, NR, b&w, 10 and up
Dir: Fred Zinnemann. Gary Cooper, Grace Kelly, Lloyd Bridges, Katy Jurado

✳ **PLOT:** Marshall Will Kane (Gary Cooper) marries Amy (Grace Kelly) and turns in his badge. She is a Quaker, and he has promised her to hang up his gun and become a shopkeeper. But they get word that Frank Miller is coming to town on the noon train. Kane arrested Miller and sent him to jail, and Miller swore he would come back to kill him.

Will and Amy leave town quickly. But he cannot run away, so he turns around. He knows they will never be safe; wherever they go, Miller will follow them. And he has a duty to the town. Their new marshal will not be arriving until the next day.

Will seeks help from everyone, finally going to church, where services are in session. But he is turned down, over and over again. Amy says she will leave on the noon train. Will's former deputy, Harvey (Lloyd Bridges), refuses to help because he is resentful that Will did not recommend him as the new marshal. Will's former girlfriend, Helen Ramirez (Katy Jurado), now Harvey's girlfriend, will not help him, either. She sells her business and leaves town. Others say it is not their problem, or tell him to run, for the town's good as well as his own. The previous marshal, Will's mentor, says he can't use a gun anymore. The one man who had promised to help backs out when he finds out no one else will join them. The only others who offer to help are a disabled man and a young boy. Will must face Miller and his three henchmen alone.

At noon, Frank Miller gets off the train. The four men come into town. Will is able to defeat them, with Amy's unexpected help. As the townsfolk gather, Will throws his badge in the dust, and they drive away.

✳ **DISCUSSION:** This outstanding drama ticks by in real time, only eighty-four tense minutes long. Will gets the message about Frank Miller at 10:40, and we feel the same time pressure he does as he tries to find someone to help him. We see and hear clocks throughout the movie, and as noon approaches, the clock looms larger and larger, the pendulum swinging like an executioner's ax. In the brilliant score by Dimitri Tiomkin, the sound of the beat suggests both the train's approach and the passage of time.

This is like a grown-up "Little Red Hen" story. Will cannot find anyone to help him protect the town. Everyone seems to think it is someone else's problem (or fault). Teenagers may be interested to know that many people consider this film an analogy for the political problems of the McCarthy era. It was written during the height of the Hollywood "Red Scare." After completing this screenplay, Carl Foreman, an "unfriendly witness" before the House Un-American Activities Committee, was blacklisted. But this unforgettable drama of a man who will not run from his enemy, or his own fears, transcends all times and circumstances.

PROFANITY: None.
NUDITY/SEXUAL REFERENCES: None.
ALCOHOL/DRUG ABUSE: Drinking in a bar; bad guys drink.
VIOLENCE/SCARINESS: Shoot-out.
TOLERANCE/DIVERSITY ISSUES: Women are exceptionally intelligent and respected compared to other movies of the era. Helen speaks of the prejudice she faced as a Mexican woman, and Amy listens sympathetically.

✳ **QUESTIONS FOR KIDS:**
- Everyone seems to have a different reason for not helping Will. How many can you identify? Which reasons seem the best to you? Which seem the worst? What makes Amy change her mind?
- Why does Will throw his badge in the dirt?
- Do you think Carl Foreman, the screenwriter, chose the name "Will" for any special reason?
- How do you decide when to stay and fight and when to run? How do you evaluate the risks? What should the law be?

✳ **CONNECTIONS:** This movie was the first attempt at an "adult" Western, its stark black-and-white images a contrast to the gorgeous vistas in the Westerns of John Ford and Howard Hawks. It was included in the first group of films named to the National Film Registry, established by the Library of Congress to identify films that are "culturally, historically, or esthetically important."

It won Oscars for Cooper, best editing, best score, and best song (lyrics by Ned Washington, sung by Tex Ritter). It has had tremendous influence and has inspired many imitations and variations. *Outland,* starring Sean Connery (and rated R), is a not very good attempt to transfer this plot to outer space. *Three O'Clock High* moves it to a high school, with a new student challenged by the school bully. Despite some directorial pyrotechnics, it is not very good, either. *The Principal* has another *High Noon*–style confrontation in a school, but this time it is the title character who must show his mettle. *The Baltimore Bullet* moves the confrontation to a pool hall.

✳Major Barbara

1941, 135 min, NR, b&w, 10 and up
Dir: Gabriel Pascal, Harold French, David Lean. Wendy Hiller, Rex Harrison, Robert Morley

✳ **PLOT:** Major Barbara (Wendy Hiller) is a member of a mission devoted to saving souls and she promotes temperance, nonviolence, and socialism. Adolphus Cusins (Rex Harrison), a classics professor, falls in love with her, but before she accepts his proposal she insists he must meet her family. He is surprised to find out she is the daughter of a wealthy industrialist.

Her father, Andrew Undershaft (Robert Morley), a munitions manufacturer, returns to the family after an absence of many years. He tries to convert Barbara to his views by presenting her with an ethical dilemma: Will she accept large contributions to her mission from the makers of munitions and liquor, the very things she opposes? She cannot, and is disillusioned but understanding when her superior accepts the funds, reasoning that despite their source, the money will do some good.

Barbara visits the munitions factory and sees that she can do more to help those in need by running a business than by preaching. It does not mean much when someone accepts her views in order to get food and shelter. But if she can persuade people simply by the force of her ideas, those are converts worth having. Furthermore, she can aid the poor by providing good jobs, good wages, and good benefits. Her father says that being a millionaire is his religion. Christianity is Barbara's religion, but she will pursue it through capitalism.

✳ **DISCUSSION:** More directly political than *Pygmalion*, this provides a good opportunity for a discussion of what is now termed "corporate social responsibility," and the role of the government, the church, and the corporation in meeting society's needs.

> PROFANITY: None.
> NUDITY/SEXUAL REFERENCES: None.
> ALCOHOL/DRUG ABUSE: References to alcohol abuse.
> VIOLENCE/SCARINESS: None.
> TOLERANCE/DIVERSITY ISSUES: Class issues.

✳ **QUESTIONS FOR KIDS:**
- How socially responsible should corporations be? How should they balance the interests of employees, customers, shareholders, suppliers, and the community?

• Who is in a better position to help society: government, religion, or business? Which kinds of help are each uniquely able to provide?

✳ **CONNECTIONS:** Robert Morley, age thirty-two when this movie was made, was only four years older than the actress who played his daughter. A very young Deborah Kerr appears as Jenny Hill, and Emlyn Williams, author of the autobiographical *The Corn Is Green,* appears as Snobby Price. Wendy Hiller, picked by Shaw himself to appear in this movie and *Pygmalion,* also appears in *A Man for All Seasons* and *Murder on the Orient Express.*

Playwright and coscreenwriter Shaw was one of the twentieth century's most brilliant writers, well-known as a dramatist, essayist, critic, and social reformer. He was awarded the Nobel Prize for Literature in 1925. His play, *Pygmalion* (also filmed with Wendy Hiller) became the musical *My Fair Lady.* Among the many pleasures of his work are the superb female characters—strong, intelligent, and principled.

✳ **ACTIVITIES:** Teenagers may want to read or even act out some of Shaw's other plays, including *The Man of Destiny, Misalliance, Caesar and Cleopatra,* and *Arms and the Man,* and will also enjoy his essays and criticism.

✳The Maltese Falcon
1941, 100 min, NR, b&w, 10 and up
Dir: John Huston. Humphrey Bogart, Mary Astor, Sidney Greenstreet, Peter Lorre

✳ **PLOT:** Sam Spade (Humphrey Bogart) is a private detective. A woman who says her name is Ruth Wonderly (Mary Astor) comes to see him, asking for help in finding her sister. Sam sends his partner, Miles Archer (Jerome Cowan), to follow her when she meets Floyd Thursby, the man she thinks her sister is with, and both Archer and Thursby are killed. It turns out the woman has given him a false name. She is really Brigid O'Shaughnessy, and it turns out it is not her sister she is seeking but a small, jeweled statue of a falcon and she is mixed up with some people who will do anything to get it.

One of those people is Joel Cairo (Peter Lorre), who comes to see Sam to insist—with a gun—that he be allowed to search Sam's office to see if the falcon is there. Sam is not at all intimidated by Joel, but allows him to search. Also after the statue is Mr. Gutman, "the fat man" (Sidney Greenstreet), with his "gunsel," Wilmer. They alternately threaten and attempt to bribe Sam while Brigid appeals to his protective nature and his heart. But Sam turns them all over to the police, including Brigid, whom he loves.

✳ **DISCUSSION:** One of the most interesting aspects of this classic movie is the way that Sam Spade thinks through the moral dilemmas. When he is deciding whether to tell the police about Brigid, he is very explicit about weighing every aspect of his choices. It is not an easy decision for him; he has no moral absolutes. On the one hand, he loves her, and he did not think much of his partner. On the other, he does not trust her, he does not think she trusts him, and he knows they could not go on together, each waiting to betray or be betrayed. And he has some pride; he says that when your partner is killed, you are supposed to "do something." While it may be good for business not to appear too ethical, it is bad for business to allow a partner in a detective firm to get killed without responding. If he turns her over to the police, he loses her. But if he does not, he loses a part of himself, his own brand of integrity.

When this movie was made, moviegoers were used to cool, debonair detectives (like Philo Vance and Nick Charles, both played by William Powell), a sort of cross between Sherlock Holmes and Fred Astaire. But Sam Spade, created by Dashiell Hammett based on his experiences as a detective, was a modern-day version of the cowboy, a loner with his own sense of honor.

This was the first movie directed by John Huston, who also wrote the screenplay, but he was already a master. Watch the two scenes where Sam goes to talk to Gutman, and see how the camera angles in the first scene lead the viewer to suspect that Sam's drink is spiked (it isn't), and then how different angles are used in the second scene to make the viewer confident that it won't be (it is).

PROFANITY: None.

NUDITY/SEXUAL REFERENCES: None.

ALCOHOL/DRUG ABUSE: Some drinking.

VIOLENCE/SCARINESS: Some suspense, scuffles, threats of violence.

TOLERANCE/DIVERSITY ISSUES: Subtle prejudice against less-than-macho Joel Cairo and Wilmer, who (in the mildest 1940s terms) the movie implies are gay; implication that Spade was having an affair with Archer's wife.

✻ QUESTIONS FOR KIDS:

- What does Sam mean when he says the statue is "the stuff dreams are made of"?
- Where is Sam faced with moral conflicts? How does he resolve them? What are his reasons?

✻ **CONNECTIONS:** Note the director's father, Walter Huston, in an uncredited brief appearance as Captain Jacobi. Jerome Cowan, who appears briefly as Miles Archer, plays the prosecuting attorney who tries to prove that Kris Kringle is not Santa Claus in ***Miracle on 34th Street.*** Bogart appeared as a similarly tough detective, Philip Marlowe, in ***The Big Sleep,*** based on the novel by Raymond Chandler. The books by Hammett and Chandler are well worth reading.

A Man for All Seasons

1966, 120 min, NR, 10 and up
Dir: Fred Zinnemann. Paul Scofield, Wendy Hiller, Robert Shaw, John Hurt,
Orson Welles

✳ **PLOT:** The Lord Chancellor, Sir Thomas More (Paul Scofield), is a man of great principle and a devout Catholic in the time of King Henry VIII. The king wants to dissolve his marriage to the queen (a Spanish princess and the widow of his late brother) so that he can marry Anne Boleyn. All around him, courtiers and politicians plot to use this development to their advantage, or at least to hold on to their positions, given the conflict between the Church's position that marriage is indissoluble and the king's that it must be dissolved. For More, the choice is clear, and God comes before the king. But because of More's incorruptible reputation, his support is crucial. Every possible form of persuasion and coercion is attempted, but More will not make any affirmative statement on behalf of the divorce (though he refrains from opposing it explicitly). And More will not lend his allegiance to the new church headed by the king.

Finally, having lost his position, his fortune, his reputation (on false charges), and his liberty, More is sentenced to death. He accepts it with grace and faith, forgiving the executioner.

✳ **DISCUSSION:** This is an outstanding (and brilliantly filmed) study of a man who is faced with a harrowingly difficult moral choice. The choice remains clear to him, even at great cost not just to himself but to his family. Yet within his clear moral imperative, he does calibrate. His conscience does not require him to work against or even speak out against the divorce; he need only keep silent.

PROFANITY: None.
NUDITY/SEXUAL REFERENCES: None.
ALCOHOL/DRUG ABUSE: Some drinking.
VIOLENCE/SCARINESS: Nonexplicit execution scene.
TOLERANCE/DIVERSITY ISSUES: None.

✳ **QUESTIONS FOR KIDS:**
- What does the title mean?
- The same director made **High Noon**—do you see any similarities?
- What would you consider in deciding what to do if you were More?
- What other characters in history can you think of who sustained such a commitment to a moral principle?

✳ **CONNECTIONS:** This movie won six Oscars, including Best Picture, Director, and Actor.

Kids and teens should read some of the books about this period and see if they can find reproductions of the paintings by Hans Holbein of the real-life characters. They may want to watch some of the many movies about it as well. As history shows, the marriage that led to the establishment of the Church of England did not last. *Anne of the Thousand Days* tells the story of the relationship of Henry VIII and Anne Boleyn, including, from a different perspective, some of the events of *A Man for All Seasons.* A British miniseries, *The Six Wives of Henry VIII,* devotes one episode to each wife, and is more historically accurate and very well done. Henry VIII is such a colorful figure that he appeared in several movies, including the classic *The Private Life of Henry VIII* with Charles Laughton. His death appears in the (completely fictional) **Prince and the Pauper,** and his daughter with Anne Boleyn, Queen Elizabeth I, is featured in several movies, including *The Private Lives of Elizabeth and Essex* (with Bette Davis and Errol Flynn), *Mary, Queen of Scots* (with Glenda Jackson as Elizabeth), *Mary of Scotland* (with Katharine Hepburn as Mary and Florence Eldridge as Elizabeth), and *Elizabeth* (with Cate Blanchett).

Mr. Smith Goes to Washington

1939, 129 min, NR, b&w, 8 and up
Dir: Frank Capra. Jimmy Stewart, Jean Arthur, Claude Rains

✳ **PLOT:** Naive Jefferson Smith (Jimmy Stewart) is sent to Washington to serve the remaining term of a senator who has died. The governor (Guy Kibbee) and a businessman, Jim Taylor (Edward Arnold), believe that Smith, the leader of a Boy Scouts-type organization called the Boy Rangers, will do whatever he is told by senior Senator Joseph Paine (Claude Rains), a friend of his late father, who was an idealistic newspaper editor. Paine approves of the appointment: "A young patriot turned loose in our nation's capital—I can handle him."

At first, Smith is such a hopeless rube that he is an embarrassment. The cynical press ridicules him. He is daunted by jaded staffers Diz Moore (Thomas Mitchell) and Saunders (Jean Arthur) and reduced to stumbling incoherence by Paine's sophisticated daughter (Astrid Allwyn). But a visit to the Lincoln Memorial reminds him of what he hopes to accomplish and he returns to the Senate to promote his dream, a national camp for boys. Saunders begins to soften when he tells her what he believes: "Liberty is too precious a thing to be buried in books." She acknowledges her own idealistic roots as the daughter of a doctor who treated patients who could not pay, that idealism now buried under the practicality that resulted from her having to go to work at sixteen because her family had no money. "Why don't you go home?" she asks. "You're halfway decent."

Saunders warns him that Paine is corrupt, that he is promoting unnecessary legislation that will benefit Taylor. Smith goes to see Paine and is crushed to learn that Saunders was right. Paine tries to explain that it is just a compromise. "It's a question of give and take—you have to play by the rules—compromise—you have to leave your ideals outside the door with your rubbers." Smith promises to expose Paine, but Paine moves quickly and makes it appear that it is Smith who is corrupt. He presents a forged deed showing that Smith is the owner of the land for the proposed camp and will therefore profit from the legislation.

Smith is ready to quit, but Saunders explains that he can filibuster— take the floor of the Senate and keep speaking—while his mother and friends get out the real story. While Smith holds the floor, his Boy Rangers print up and try to distribute their own newspaper. But Taylor's henchmen stop them. After speaking for twenty-three hours, Smith sees that all of the letters and telegrams are against him. He looks over at Paine. "I guess this is just another lost cause, Mr. Paine. All you people don't know about the lost causes. Mr. Paine does. He said once that they were the only causes worth fighting for. And he fought for them once, for the only reason that any man ever fights for them. Because of just one plain simple rule, 'Love thy neighbor.' And in this world today, full of hatred, a man who knows that one rule has a great trust."

He vows to go on, but collapses from fatigue. Paine, overwhelmed with shame, runs into the cloakroom and tries to kill himself, confessing that he was the one who was corrupt.

❋ **DISCUSSION:** Frank Capra was to movies what Norman Rockwell was to illustration; he gave us a vision of our national identity that never ignored the challenges we face, although it was idealistic about our ability to meet them. This movie, made on the brink of World War II, was criticized for its portrayal of dishonesty and cynicism in Washington. But ultimately, it was recognized for the very patriotic and loyal statement that it is.

PROFANITY: None.

NUDITY/SEXUAL REFERENCES: None.

ALCOHOL/DRUG ABUSE: Diz, the press secretary, is a heavy drinker.

VIOLENCE/SCARINESS: None.

TOLERANCE/DIVERSITY ISSUES: None.

❋ **QUESTIONS FOR KIDS:**
- Paine tells Smith he has to learn to compromise. Is that wrong? How could Smith tell that this was not compromise, but corruption?
- Watch the scene where the press meets the new senator for the first time. People today often criticize the press for being unfair or too mean to politicians. Do you think they are unfair? Are they too mean? Why does the press like to make fun of politicians?
- What makes Saunders change her mind about Smith?

❋ **CONNECTIONS:** It is hard to imagine a time when Jimmy Stewart was not a major star, but this is the movie that made him one. He was a perfect choice for the shy, young idealist. Capra selected cowboy actor Harry Carey to play the vice president, who presides over the Senate during Smith's filibuster. His look of weatherbeaten integrity perfectly suited the part, and contrasted well with Rains's suave urbanity.

❋ **ACTIVITIES:** Those families who visit the Washington locations featured in the movie, the Lincoln Memorial and the U.S. Capitol building, might also want to stop by the local Planet Hollywood, which features the desk Smith stood at during his filibuster, autographed by Stewart. Those who can't get to Washington might enjoy taking a look at today's Congressional proceedings on C-SPAN and comparing them to those portrayed in the movie.

On the Waterfront
1954, 108 min, NR, b&w, high schoolers
Dir: Elia Kazan. Marlon Brando, Rod Steiger, Lee J. Cobb, Eva Marie Saint, Karl Malden

❋ **PLOT:** Based on a true story (with a less satisfying conclusion), this is the story of the men who had the courage to stand up to the corrupt longshoremen's union. The union is controlled by Johnny Friendly (Lee J. Cobb). He and his men decide who will work each day, which means they get paid off by the men and by the shipowners who rely on the union to unload their goods. "Everything moves in and out, we take our cut," Johnny brags. One of Johnny's top aides is Charley Malloy (Rod Steiger), whose brother Terry (Marlon Brando), a former prizefighter, is treated almost like a mascot by Johnny. He gives Terry errands to run and makes sure he gets the easiest and most lucrative work assignments. Terry keeps pigeons on the roof of his apartment building and is a hero to the local boys.

As the movie begins, Joey Doyle, who dared to speak out about the corruption, is killed by Johnny's thugs. Terry had unwittingly helped to set Joey up, and he is distressed. "Too much Marquess of·Queensberry, it softens him up," Charley explains, telling Johnny that Terry's exposure to the rules of fair fighting in boxing have made him idealistic. Joey's sister Edie (Eva Marie Saint) tells local priest Father Barry (Karl Malden) that he has to get out of the church to help them; "Saints don't hide in churches." Father Barry invites the longshoremen to the church to talk about what is going on. Charley tells Terry to go to the meeting to keep tabs on who is being disloyal. At the meeting, one man explains that "everyone on the dock is D&D—deaf and dumb." Everyone knows that if he speaks out, or even notices too much, he will not be allowed to work; he may even be killed, as Joey was. Thugs break up the meeting. Terry escapes with Edie. Dugan (Pat Henning) agrees to talk, and Father Barry agrees to support him. But Dugan is killed, too.

Terry and Edie fall in love. Johnny tells Charley to make sure that Terry does not tell the crime commission about his activities, because if he lets Terry tell the truth, everyone will do it, and he'll be "just another fellow." At first Charley resists, but Johnny makes it clear that if Charley can't stop Terry, Johnny will get someone else to take care of him. So Charley finds

Terry, and they talk, in the back seat of a cab. Terry tells Charley that he hates being a bum instead of a "contender" for a boxing title. He says that Charley should not have made him take a dive in the boxing ring, a "one-way ticket to palookaville." Charley lets Terry go, and then Charley is killed by Johnny's thugs. Terry is overcome with grief and swears he will get Johnny. Father Barry persuades him that the way to do it is to testify, and Terry does, while Johnny stares at him from across the room.

No one will talk to Terry. The boys who once worshipped him kill all of his pigeons. Down on the dock, at first Johnny wins, putting everyone to work except for Terry. When Terry calls him out, they have a furious battle as the longshoremen watch. Terry is badly hurt. When Johnny tells them to go back to work, they refuse, saying they are waiting for Terry to lead them to work. Father Barry whispers to Terry that "Johnny's laying odds you won't get up." Father Barry and Edie help him up, and he walks slowly to the dock. Johnny shouts, but everyone ignores him.

✳ **DISCUSSION:** This movie contrasts two conflicting ways of looking at the world and especially at responsibility. Edie and Father Barry see a world in which people have an obligation to protect and support each other. Johnny sees the world as a place where what matters is taking as much as you can. Terry is somewhere in the middle, with his kindness to the Golden Warriors and his pigeons on the one side and his willingness to take what Johnny's way of life has to offer on the other. Then Joey is killed, and Terry meets Edie.

In part, Terry falls in love not just with Edie but with the vision of another life that Edie represents. At first, when she asks, "Shouldn't everybody care about everybody else?" he calls her a "fruitcake" and says that his philosophy of life is, "Do it to him before he does it to you . . . Everybody's got a racket." He tells her, "I'd like to help, but there's nothing I can do." Like Edie, Terry is inspired to fight back by the death of his brother. When he tells Charley, "You should have looked after me," he is acknowledging the obligation brothers have for each other. He should have looked out for Charley, too.

After Terry testifies, Edie tells him to leave town, asking, "Are they taking chances for you?" Terry tells her he's not a bum, and that means he must stay. Fighting Johnny, Terry finds a way out of "palookaville."

This movie also raises some important issues about the nature of power. At the beginning, Johnny seems very powerful, and power matters more to him than money. But it is clear that the choices he makes to protect that power, more than any action taken by anyone else, are the beginning of the end. As he orders people to be killed, even Charley, his own close associate, he begins to appear desperate. The men who will kick back a few dollars and stay "D&D" about corruption will not stand for that level of violence and uncertainty.

PROFANITY: None.

NUDITY/SEXUAL REFERENCES: None.

ALCOHOL/DRUG ABUSE: Alcohol in tavern. Terry takes Edie for her first beer, which makes her a little giddy.

VIOLENCE/SCARINESS: Fighting; menacing thugs; Charley's body hung on a fence to intimidate Terry.

TOLERANCE/DIVERSITY ISSUES: None.

✳ **QUESTIONS FOR KIDS:**
- Joey's jacket is worn by three different characters in this movie. What do you think that means?
- Why do you think the director does not let you hear the conversation when Terry tells Edie about his role in Joey's death?
- Edie admits she is in love with Terry, but still wants him to leave. Why? What do you think of Edie's ideas about what makes people "mean and difficult"? Do you think that applies to Johnny?
- How does Johnny get power? How does he lose it?
- If Johnny had not killed Charley, would Terry have testified against him?

✳ **CONNECTIONS:** The music is by Leonard Bernstein, composer of *West Side Story*. This movie won eight Oscars, including Best Picture, Best Director, Best Supporting Actress, and Best Screenplay. Steiger, Malden, and Cobb were all nominated as well.

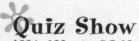

Quiz Show

1994, 133 min, PG-13, 12 and up
Dir: Robert Redford. Ralph Fiennes, Paul Scofield, John Turturro, Rob Morrow

✳ **PLOT:** This true story takes place in the early days of television. One of the most popular and successful program formats was the quiz show, in which contestants competed for huge cash prizes by answering questions. Charles Van Doren (played by Ralph Fiennes) was a member of one of America's most distinguished literary families, and he became an immensely popular contestant on *Twenty-One*. When it turned out that the quiz shows were fixed, and that contestants were supplied with the answers by the shows' producers, Van Doren became the symbol of betrayal.

In this film, Van Doren is contrasted with Herb Stempel (John Turturro) and with Congressional staff investigator Dick Goodwin (Rob Morrow). Stempel, a Jewish man from Brooklyn with "a face for radio" is bitter over being pushed aside for the impeccably WASP-y Columbia University professor. Goodwin shares the Jewish outsider's background with Stempel, and the Ivy League polish (as he frequently mentions, he was first in his class at Harvard Law School) with Van Doren. Dazzled by Van Doren, Goodwin does not want to believe that he, like Stempel, participated in the fraud. When he finds out that Van Doren did, Goodwin tries to protect him from being discovered. He wants to bring the real culprits, the network executives, to light. But when the hearings are held, the Congressmen's cozy relationships with the network executives prevent any tough questions from being asked. The producer takes the blame.

Eight years later, the producer was back in television. Stempel became a bureaucrat. Van Doren, forced to leave Columbia, lived very privately, working for Encyclopedia Britannica. Goodwin went to work for President Kennedy and later wrote highly respected books.

✳ **DISCUSSION:** This is an outstanding drama that provides an excellent opportunity for examining the way that people make moral choices. Stempel cheats because he wants to be accepted and respected, and because he believes that is the way the world works. Nevertheless, he is outraged and bitter when he finds that he has been cheated, that the producer has no intention of living up to his promise to find him a job in television. And it is important to note that his decision to tell the truth was based on vengeance, not on taking responsibility for a moral failure.

When first presented with the option of cheating, Van Doren reflects ("I'm just wondering what Kant would make of this"), and then refuses. Indeed, he concludes this is just a test of his suitability, and one that he has passed. Once on the program, however, he is given a question he had answered correctly in the interview. He knows the answer, but he also knows that it is not a legitimate competition for him to answer it. (He does not know that Stempel has agreed to fail.) At that moment, what is he thinking? What moral calculus goes through his mind? Is this the decision to cheat, or is that a separate decision, later? In the movie's most painful scene, Van Doren must tell his father what he has done. At first, Van Doren makes some distinctions between being given the questions, so he can get the answers on his own, and being given the answers. But he knows that both are equally wrong.

Why, then, did he do it? The movie suggests that it was in part a way to establish himself as independently successful, out of the shadow of his family. He enjoyed the fame and the money. He argues that no one is being hurt by it. Goodwin, on the other hand, sees that it is wrong, and never for a moment hesitates when the producer tries to buy him off. Yet, as Goodwin's wife points out, he makes his own moral compromises when he tries to protect Van Doren. In part he does it because he is after those he considers the real culprits. But in part he does it because he likes Van Doren, and because as much as he takes pride in being first in his class at Harvard, some part of him still thinks that the Van Dorens are better than he is.

PROFANITY: Some.

NUDITY/SEXUAL REFERENCES: None.

ALCOHOL/DRUG ABUSE: Social drinking and smoking.

VIOLENCE/SCARINESS: None.

TOLERANCE/DIVERSITY ISSUES: Issue of prejudice based on class and ethnicity.

❊ **QUESTIONS FOR KIDS:**
- Why did Stempel agree to cheat? Why did he tell the truth to the investigators? Why did Van Doren cheat?
- What were some of the feelings Van Doren had about his parents? How can you tell?
- In what ways was Goodwin like Stempel? In what ways was he like Van Doren? Why was Goodwin intimidated by the Van Dorens?
- Who was responsible for the "quiz show scandals"? Was the outcome fair? Who should have been punished, and how?

❊ **CONNECTIONS:** Goodwin's account of the story can be found in his book *Remembering America: A Voice from the 60s. Champagne for Caesar,* a light satiric comedy on the same subject, was produced in 1950, several years before the events portrayed in this movie. It is very funny, with outstanding performances by Ronald Colman as the professor-contestant, and Celeste Holm as the femme fatale brought in to shake his concentration. The question they find to stump him with is a lulu! Van Doren's father is played by Paul Scofield, who appeared as Sir Thomas More in **A Man for All Seasons.** Goodwin's wife is played by future Oscar-winner Mira Sorvino.

❊The Scarlet and the Black
1983, 155 min, NR, 10 and up
Dir: Jerry London. Gregory Peck, Christopher Plummer

❊ **PLOT:** Gregory Peck plays Monsignor Hugh O'Flaherty in this true story of WWII Rome. The Vatican had diplomatic neutrality, which meant that no one within its borders could be arrested. O'Flaherty used the Vatican as a base of operations to save thousands of Allied POWs in a long, elaborate, and deadly game of cat and mouse with German Colonel Herbert Kappler (Christopher Plummer).

As Italy is falling to the Allies, Kappler knows the war is over. He seeks out O'Flaherty, his bitterest enemy, to ask a favor: to draw on the same resources he used to help the POWs escape to get Kappler's family to Switzerland. Kappler does not find out until he is being interrogated by the Allies that his family is safe, and he protects O'Flaherty from charges of collaboration by refusing to give any information about his operation, even though it would have shortened his sentence.

❊ **DISCUSSION:** This movie presents us with an assortment of characters who each try to do what they believe is best to protect the values they care about. O'Flaherty and his colleagues decide that all they can do is rescue and protect; they cannot undertake or even aid anti-German activities like espionage or sabotage. A fellow priest who does become involved in these activities is captured and executed. Kappler genuinely loves his family and loves Rome. His sense of honor is clear in the sacrifice he makes to protect O'Flaherty. He is brutal only in capitulation to the orders of his superiors. The Pope preserves what politicians call "deniability" by not permitting himself to know much about what O'Flaherty is doing. Though he warns that he will not be able to protect him when the Germans come, the Pope refuses to turn him over to them. The British emissary says that he cannot help, even though the captured men are his own soldiers, explaining, "My strictest duty is to do nothing which might compromise the neutrality of the Vatican State or His Holiness the Pope." His aide, however, is one of the most important participants in O'Flaherty's efforts. This is an outstanding story of true personal moral courage and redemption, with a conclusion that is deeply moving.

PROFANITY: None.

NUDITY/SEXUAL REFERENCES: None.

ALCOHOL/DRUG ABUSE: None.

VIOLENCE/SCARINESS: Tense situations; some war casualties.

TOLERANCE/DIVERSITY ISSUES: None.

✳ QUESTIONS FOR KIDS:
• Were O'Flaherty and Kappler alike in any ways? How?
• Why wouldn't O'Flaherty do more to fight the Germans?
• Why did O'Flaherty help Kappler's family?
• Were you surprised by the ending?

✳ **CONNECTIONS:** Plummer appeared as a man who fled from the Nazis in *The Sound of Music,* another true story, and Peck appeared as a Nazi in the fantasy *The Boys From Brazil.* O'Flaherty's decision to help the prisoners but not to enter into the fight is similar to that made by Jess in *Friendly Persuasion.*

✳ Spartacus

1960, 198 min, PG-13, high schoolers
Dir: Stanley Kubrick. Kirk Douglas, Laurence Olivier, Tony Curtis, Jean Simmons, Peter Ustinov, Charles Laughton

✳ **PLOT:** Spartacus (Kirk Douglas) is a slave in the Roman empire, about seventy years before the birth of Christ. A rebellious and proud man, he is sentenced to death for biting a guard but rescued by Biatius (Peter Ustinov), who buys him and takes him to his school for training and selling gladiators. Slave women are provided to the men as rewards. Varinia (Jean Simmons), a British slave, is given to Spartacus. He is awestruck by her grace and beauty, but when he sees that Biatius is watching them, he screams, "I am not an animal!" and will not touch her.

Crassus (Laurence Olivier), a Roman dignitary, visits Biatius's home with two spoiled and decadent women who insist on seeing a fight to the death. Spartacus is paired with Draba (Woody Strode), an Ethiopian who fights with net and trident. Draba corners Spartacus but refuses to kill him and instead rushes toward Crassus, who slits his throat. Crassus buys Varinia, and when a guard taunts Spartacus about her, Spartacus kills him and leads the other slaves in a revolt.

They escape to the countryside, and other slaves join them as they make progress toward the sea, where they hope to escape. Varinia and Antoninus (Tony Curtis), a slave singer and magician, escape from Crassus and join the slaves. The Romans send troops to capture them, but the slaves defeat them, sending back the message that all they want is the freedom to return to their homes. Crassus uses the slave revolt to gain political power by promising "order" if he is given complete control. When he is successful, triumphing over his political rival, Gracchus (Charles Laughton), he cuts off the slaves' access to ships, and surrounds them with troops. Many are killed on both sides, and the slaves are recaptured. Crassus promises them their lives if they will just give him Spartacus. As Spartacus is about to step forward, each of the slaves cries out, "I am Spartacus!" The Romans crucify them all except for Spartacus and Antoninus, lining the Appian Way with 6,000 crucifixes.

Crassus takes Varinia and her new baby back to his home. If he can win her affection, it will represent the ultimate triumph over Spartacus. Spartacus and Antoninus are ordered to fight to the death, with the survivor to be crucified. Each tries to kill the other, to save him from the slow death of crucifixion. Spartacus is successful, killing Antoninus out of love and mercy, and then he is crucified. Before he dies, he is able to see Varinia and his son, now both free, thanks to Gracchus.

✳ **DISCUSSION:** This epic saga of the price of freedom is thrilling to watch, the struggles of conscience as gripping as the brilliantly staged battle scenes. When we first see Spartacus, he strikes out at an oppressor almost reflexively. He does not care that the consequence is death; as he later says, for a slave death is only a release from pain.

His life is spared when he is purchased by Biatius. His training as a gladiator gives him his first chance to form bonds with fellow slaves. His exposure to the guards and to the degenerate women from Rome, who insist on watching muscular men kill each other, shows him that power is not based on worth. When he shouts, "I am not an animal!" he is saying it to himself as much as to Biatius. When he strikes out again, he is armed not only with the fighting skills he has learned, but also with an ability to lead, founded in a new sense of entitlement to freedom.

The characters in this movie are especially vivid and interesting. Varinia has a wonderful grace and a rare humor, which adds warmth to her character. She is able to shield her emotional self from the abuse she is forced to endure without deadening her feelings. Gracchus conveys the essential decency of a man who has made many compromises, political and spiritual.

Both the author of the book and the screenwriter were blacklisted during the McCarthy era, and families should discuss how that influenced their approach to the story. Kids may also be interested to know that this was among the most popular movies shown in the former Soviet Union, and should consider what it was that appealed to the Communists.

PROFANITY: None.

NUDITY/SEXUAL REFERENCES: Implied nudity; slave women are treated as commodities, provided to male slaves as a reward; implication of homosexual advances by Crassus to Antoninus.

ALCOHOL/DRUG ABUSE: None.

VIOLENCE/SCARINESS: Very intense battle scenes, fights, crucifixions; also (off-screen) suicide.

TOLERANCE/DIVERSITY ISSUES: A theme of the movie.

❋ QUESTIONS FOR KIDS:
- Why was it important for the Romans to spread the rumor that Spartacus was of noble birth?
- What did Biatius mean when he said he had found his dignity? How was he changed?
- What did it mean when Gracchus responded that "dignity shortens life even more quickly than disease"?
- Why did Crassus say he was more concerned about killing the legend than killing the man?
- Why did each of the slaves claim to be Spartacus?

❋ CONNECTIONS:
The movie cuts back and forth between the speeches given by Crassus and Spartacus to inspire their followers. Compare the speeches to each other, and to the most famous such speech in literature, Henry V's "we few, we happy few" speech, delivered by Olivier (who also played Crassus) in the 1945 version of *Henry V,* and delivered with a very different interpretation by Kenneth Branagh in the 1989 version. The sense of community and loyalty of the slaves is reminiscent of similar scenes in *The Adventures of Robin Hood.*

This was the first screen credit for scriptwriter Dalton Trumbo after he was jailed for refusing to cooperate with Senator Joseph McCarthy's House Un-American Activities Committee, though he wrote under other names during that period and even won two Oscars for best screenplay under other names.

Peter Ustinov won an Oscar for his performance as the slave dealer who runs the gladiator school. He is a rare actor who is able to keep his character as interesting after becoming more virtuous as he was before.

All of the performances are outstanding. Jean Simmons can also be seen in *Guys and Dolls* and *Great Expectations.* Charles Laughton can be seen in *Witness for the Prosecution* and *Advise & Consent.* The movie also won Oscars for art direction, costume design, and cinematography.

In 1991, an expanded version of the film was released, which shows restored scenes that had been cut for the original release, including a bathing scene with Crassus and Antoninus with an implication of sexual interest. Because the original sound track was not available and Olivier was dead, his voice was dubbed by Anthony Hopkins.

❋ **ACTIVITIES:** Kids who like this movie might enjoy the novel by Howard Fast, also the author of a novel about the American revolution, *April Morning*.

Titanic

1997, 195 min, PG-13, 12 and up
Dir: James Cameron. Leonardo DiCaprio, Kate Winslet, Billy Zane, Kathy Bates, Gloria Stuart

❋ **PLOT:** This blockbuster movie is the winner of eleven Oscars including Best Picture and Best Director and is on its way to becoming the highest-grossing movie of all time. The real-life disaster serves as the backdrop to a fictional tragic love story between Rose (Kate Winslet), an upper class (though impoverished) girl and Jack (Leonardo DiCaprio), a lower class (though artistic) boy who won the ticket in a poker game.

❋ **DISCUSSION:** Classic Greek tragedies explored the theme of hubris as human characters dared to take on the attributes of the gods only to find their hopes crushed. This is a real-life story of hubris, as the ship declared to be "unsinkable" (and therefore not equipped with lifeboats for the majority of the passengers) sank on its maiden voyage from England to the United States.

The movie raises important questions about choices faced by the characters, as we see a wide range of behavior from the most honorable to the most despicable. The captain (whose decision to try to break a speed record contributed to the disaster) and the ship's designer (whose plan for additional lifeboats was abandoned because it made the decks look too cluttered) go down with the ship, but the owner and Rose's greedy and snobbish fiancé survive. Molly Brown (dubbed "Unsinkable" for her bravery that night) tries to persuade the other passengers in the lifeboats to go back for the rest. But they refuse, knowing that there is no way to rescue them without losing their own lives. They wait to be picked up by another ship, listening to the shrieks of the others until they are all gone.

Many parents have wondered about the appeal of this move to young teens, especially teen-age girls. The answer is that in addition to the charm of its young stars, it is an almost perfect adolescent fantasy for girls. Rose is an ideal heroine, rebelling against her mother's snobbishness and insistence that she marry for money. And Jack is an ideal romantic hero—sensitive, brave, honorable, completely devoted, and (very important for young girls) not aggressive. She has all of the power in the relationship. She makes the decision to become involved, and he is struck all but dumb when she insists on posing nude. Furthermore, if he is not quite androgynous, he is not exactly bursting with testosterone either, and, even more important, ultimately, he is not around. As with so many other fantasies of the perfect romance, from Heathcliff and Cathy in *Wuthering Heights* to Rick and Ilsa in *Casablanca* the characters have all the pleasures of the romantic dream with no risk of having to actually build a life with anyone. It is interesting that the glimpses we get of Rose's life after the Titanic show her alone, though we meet her granddaughter and hear her refer to her husband. Parents can have some very good discussions with teens about this movie by listening carefully and respectfully when they explain why it is important to them, as this is a crucial stage in their developing understanding of the adult world.

Parents should know that the movie features brief nudity (as Rose poses for Jack) and the suggestion of sex (in a steamy car). A much more serious concern is the tragedy itself, with hundreds of frozen dead bodies floating in the water, which may be upsetting or even terrifying for some kids.

PROFANITY: Several swear words.

NUDITY/SEXUAL REFERENCES: Rose poses nude for Jack. They have sex in a car (nothing shown).

ALCOHOL/DRUG ABUSE: Social drinking.

VIOLANCE/SCARINESS: Very scary and sad scenes as the ship is sinking; Rose's fiancé shoots at Rose and Jack.

TOLERANCE/DIVERISTY ISSUES: Rose rebels against the limited opportunities for women; class issues.

* QUESTIONS FOR KIDS:
* Who was to blame for the ship's sinking?
* Was there a way to prevent at least some of the deaths?
* What new rules were made as a result of the Titanic disaster?
* Why was telling Rose what to do so important to her mother and to Cal?

* CONNECTIONS: There are a number of other fictional and documentary moves about the Titanic, including *A Night to Remember* and the IMAX film *Titanica*.

* ALL MY SONS
1948, 94 min, NR, b&w, 12 and up
Dir: Irving Reis. Burt Lancaster, Edward G. Robinson

Based on the play by Arthur Miller, this is the story of the second generation's attempt to grapple with the consequences of corruption and lack of accountability of their parents. A soldier named Chris Keller (Burt Lancaster) returns from WWII to discover that his father (Edward G. Robinson) sold defective airplane parts to the U.S. Air Force. When it was discovered, he framed his partner, George Deever (Howard Duff), who was sent to jail. Keller's mother (Mady Christians) is in denial about her husband's activities and cannot accept the death of her other son in the war. With the help of Deever's daughter, Keller insists that everyone acknowledge the truth.

✳ THE APARTMENT

1960, 125 min, NR, b&w, mature high schoolers
Dir: Billy Wilder. Jack Lemmon, Shirley MacLaine, Fred MacMurray

This Oscar-winner for Best Picture, Screenplay, and Director is a biting comedy and a tender romance. A bachelor named Baxter (Jack Lemmon), whose career advancement depends on his willingness to permit senior executives to use his apartment for their assignations with their girlfriends, agrees, at first, and is delighted with his promotion. But then he finds out that one of the girlfriends is Miss Kubelik, the elevator operator he adores (Shirley MacLaine). When she tries to kill herself in his apartment after the boss (Fred MacMurray) tells her he won't marry her, Baxter takes care of her and comes to the realization that he can no longer be a part of a corrupt system. Baxter feels differently about his choices when he sees the impact they have on someone he cares about, and Miss Kubelik's decision to have the affair with the boss leads her to lose her sense of self-worth. Making the decision to change makes it possible for them to go on together in a relationship of trust and respect.

✳ AU REVOIR, LES ENFANTS (GOOD-BYE, CHILDREN)

1987, 103 min, PG, 12 and up
Dir: Louis Malle. Gaspard Manesse, Raphael Fejto
French with subtitles

This is the autobiographical story of the director's friendship with a young Jewish boy, Bonnet, at a Catholic boarding school during WWII's occupied France. The kind Fathers at the school are hiding Bonnet (Raphael Fejto) and two other boys from the Nazis. From the beginning, Julien (Gaspard Manesse) is curious about Bonnet, and takes it upon himself to discover his true identity which has been hidden from the children. In an unthinking moment, Julien inadvertently permits this knowledge to reveal Bonnet's identity to Nazi soldiers. The movie beautifully balances the beauty of childhood friendships with the realities of war and the Nazi occupation. It thoughtfully addresses religion, friendship, bravery, responsibility and loss. NOTE: This movie does not have a happy ending. It depicts what in reality happened to millions of Jews during the Nazi reign and the overwhelming guilt felt by a boy who was only dimly able to comprehend the meaning and consequences of anti-Semitism. Other parental concerns include the tension when the boys are lost; the cook's drinking problem; smoking by older boys; and the boys' discussion of sex, including examination of dirty postcards.

✳ THE DEVIL AND DANIEL WEBSTER

1941, 85 min, NR, b&w, 10 and up
Dir: William Dieterle. Walter Huston

There can be no starker or more literal moral choice than the one presented to Faust—shall a man sell his soul, whatever the price? In Stephen Vincent Benét's famous story, a New Hampshire farmer sells his soul to the devil and when the devil comes to collect, the farmer has legendary orator Daniel Webster argue his case. This version is visually striking, with outstanding performances by Edward Arnold as Webster and Walter Huston as "Mr. Scratch" (the devil).

✳ **CONNECTIONS:** This version is also known as *All That Money Can Buy.* Other representations of Faustian themes include the musical comedy ***Damn Yankees,*** the brilliant *Alias Nick Beal,* and, for mature teens and adults, the wickedly funny *Bedazzled.* Benét also wrote the story that was the basis for ***Seven Brides for Seven Brothers.***

✳ **ACTIVITIES:** The Benét story is fun to read aloud, and kids will also enjoy the poetry of his brother, William Rose Benét.

✳ KEEPER OF THE FLAME
1942, 100 min, NR, b&w, 12 and up
Dir: George Cukor. Spencer Tracy, Katharine Hepburn

The performances of Spencer Tracy and Katharine Hepburn are the highlights of this talky movie about a reporter who visits the widow of a great statesman only to find that he was secretly the head of a fascist organization that was plotting to overthrow the government. Though it is somewhat dated, the rise of the militia movement makes it relevant again, and the moral issue of whether it will better further the principles of freedom and democracy to allow people to continue to believe in the man or to expose him is still worth debating.

✳ SCHINDLER'S LIST
1993, 195 min, R, b&w, mature high schoolers
Dir: Steven Spielberg. Liam Neeson, Ralph Fiennes

This Oscar winner for Best Picture, Director, and Adapted Screenplay stars Liam Neeson as Oskar Schindler. He was a profiteer who loved luxury, but who became one of the great heroes of WWII when he saved a group of Jews by claiming that they were essential for his "munitions factory," which never produced a usable shell. By focusing on one tiny group of people who were saved, this brilliant film is able to present a more searing picture of the insanity and butchery of the Holocaust that might otherwise be unbearable. Schindler and Goeth (Ralph Fiennes), the commander of the concentration camp, are mesmerizing in their utterly different reactions to the most horrifying circumstances, showing us that everyone has the potential to be either—or both.

NOTE: The movie includes depictions of concentration camp brutality.

✳ STAR TREK II: THE WRATH OF KHAN
1982, 113 min, PG, 12 and up
Dir: Nicholas Meyer. William Shatner, Leonard Nimoy

One of the best of the venerable series has Spock and Kirk (now an admiral and no longer in active service) confronted by an old enemy (played by Ricardo

Montalban, in a reprise of his appearance on an episode of the original television show). Spock courageously sacrifices himself to save the other crew members, a choice worth discussing. It is important to note that the highly logical Spock is not the only crew member to make that choice. One of the Star Fleet captains, played by Paul Winfield, also destroys himself to save the others.

NOTE: Children may be upset by the violence in this movie, especially a particularly harrowing scene in which small snaillike creatures are inserted into the ears of two officers, causing excruciating pain.

✳ THE SURE THING

1985, 94 min, PG-13, mature high schoolers
Dir: Rob Reiner. John Cusack, Daphne Zuniga

An East Coast college student (John Cusack) is assured by a friend that "a sure thing" is waiting for him in California—a beautiful girl guaranteed to be willing to have sex with him, with no strings attached. He and a classmate (Daphne Zuniga), who is on her way to see her boyfriend, get a ride west with a relentlessly cheerful couple, but they argue so much that the couple throws them out and they have to find a way to get to California together. By the end of the trip, they trust and respect each other so much that Cusack turns down the "sure thing." The setup may be a movie cliché, but it is well-handled, with lead characters who are believably awkward (rare in movies) and believably intelligent (even more rare). This is a good movie to initiate a discussion of sexual pressures and values.

SEE ALSO:

Casablanca The famous last scene at the airport shows Rick able to make the moral choice, at great emotional and physical risk to himself, because he knows that he and Ilsa love each other.

Eight Men Out This sympathetic portrayal of the real-life story of the Chicago "Black Sox" shows how vulnerable people can make the wrong choices—and that those who are more culpable as a moral matter are not always more culpable as a legal matter.

Judgment at Nuremberg The issue of "following orders" when the orders are immoral, but the risks of disobedience are dire, is compellingly presented.

The Man Who Shot Liberty Valance Characters confront the problem of trying to use the law to stop someone who refuses to be bound to it and the problem of using a lie to help accomplish a greater good.

Part 2

Movies About Growing Up

AMBITION

"Intelligence without ambition is a bird without wings."
—C. ARCHIE DANIELSON

Movies give parents a terrific opportunity to show kids both the positive and negative consequences of ambition. One of the classic movie plots is the person with a dream who works hard to make it come true. We see that over and over again, often in the context of sports or show business but also in the context of learning and science and record-breaking or exploration. More rarely, movies address ambition in the context of politics, and even more rarely in business. These movies usually have an unhappy ending because the protagonists are defeated or corrupted by those environments.

Movies also show us the dark side of ambition, with stories of characters who sacrifice their honor or their families to achieve goals that may ultimately seem shallow to them.

There are also movies about people who struggle with another kind of ambition. They are characters who, in Joseph Campbell's famous terms, "follow their bliss." While those around them struggle for fame or money, they define success in terms of friends, family, love, learning, and creating. Perhaps most important for young people, there are movies about people their age who must fight against their own fear of failure to allow themselves to dream and to risk failure in trying to make their dreams come true.

All About Eve

1950, 138 min, NR, b&w, 12 and up
Dir: Joseph L. Mankiewicz. Bette Davis, Anne Baxter, Celeste Holm, George Sanders

✳ **PLOT:** Margo Channing (Bette Davis), a Broadway diva beginning to show her age, meets the young fan who stands outside the theater after every performance (Anne Baxter as Eve Harrington). Taken by her devotion, humility, and hard-luck story, Margo gives Eve a job as a gofer-secretary. At first, she is delighted, but later comes to realize that Eve is ruthless and will stop at nothing to steal Margo's career—not to mention her fiancé (Gary Merrill as director Bill Simpson). Eve manipulates Margo's friends and colleagues, becomes her understudy and finally, after scheming to keep her away from the theater, goes on in her place after arranging for critics to be at her performance. She takes the starring role in a new production that would have been Margo's, and wins an award for it. But by then, Margo and her friends are back together, Eve is tied to a critic who is as ambitiously manipulative as she is and, as the movie ends, she, too, meets a devoted young fan who could be another Eve.

✳ **DISCUSSION:** This movie, with one of the most literate scripts ever written (by Joseph L. Mankiewicz, who also directed) is not just the finest backstage drama ever filmed, but also a compelling parable of ambition and loyalty. Bette Davis is brilliant as Margo, bringing both the ferocity and the vulnerability of Margo to life. No one can forget her at the beginning of her party: "Fasten your seat belts, it's going to be a bumpy night." She is the first to notice that Eve is not what she seems, but her friends assume it is just petty jealousy and it only makes them want to protect Eve. That is just what Eve needs to get them to do what she wants, and it almost results in the breakup not only of Margo and Bill, but also of their best friends, playwright Lloyd Richards and his wife, Karen. Ultimately, the loyalty of all four friends keeps them together. And ultimately, Eve is reined in by someone who is her equal, acidic columnist Addison De Witt (a silky George Saunders).

This is a good movie to use to discuss how to determine what actions are appropriate to realize ambition. Compare it to movies like **Rudy,** which is also about the achievement of a dream. It is not the dream that differs here as much as how it is achieved. Eve lies and has no compunction about creating misery for others, while Rudy is scrupulous about meeting every requirement and doing everything with honor and integrity. Indeed, that is part of his dream; without that, it would not mean anything. **National Velvet** is another example. Velvet bends some rules (mostly by competing in a race in which girls are not allowed to ride) and relies on faith a good deal, but has enormous integrity in defining her dream and in her treatment of others.

PROFANITY: None.
NUDITY/SEXUAL REFERENCES: None.
ALCOHOL/DRUG ABUSE: Social drinking (sometimes to excess), some "I need a drink" responses to stress.
VIOLENCE/SCARINESS: None.
TOLERANCE/DIVERSITY ISSUES: None.

✳ **QUESTIONS FOR KIDS:**
- Who is the first one to realize that Eve is not trustworthy? Who is the second? Why?
- Why don't Margo's friends believe her when she criticizes Eve?

- Why doesn't Eve tell the truth?
- Why does Addison stop Eve? Does she get what she wants?
- What do you think will happen to Phoebe?
- Do you think Margo was like Eve? Why or why not?

✳ **CONNECTIONS:** *All About Eve* won six Academy Awards, including Best Picture, Best Supporting Actor (George Sanders), Best Screenplay, Best Direction, and Best Costume Design. There have been many other fine movies that offer a glimpse of life backstage. A very serious one is *The Country Girl*, with Grace Kelly married to alcoholic former star Bing Crosby but falling in love with director William Holden. Some of the more lighthearted backstage movies include, *Mother Wore Tights, There's No Business Like Show Business, Footlight Serenade, Royal Wedding, Footlight Parade, Kiss Me Kate* and *The Barkleys of Broadway.*

Joseph L. Mankiewicz and his brother Herman (coauthor of **Citizen Kane**) were responsible for many of the finest scripts ever produced. And that is Marilyn Monroe in one of her earliest appearances, as Miss Caswell.

✳ **ACTIVITIES:** It might be fun for kids to talk about how the theater differs from movies. Take them to a local production or get a book of plays for children from the library and help them produce one.

✳All the King's Men
1949, 109 min, NR, b&w, 12 and up
Dir: Robert Rossen. Broderick Crawford, Mercedes McCambridge

✳ **PLOT:** This is the story of the rise and fall of a Southern politician, based on the career of Louisiana's Huey Long. Here, the politician is named Willie Stark (Broderick Crawford), and the Southern state where it takes place is never named.

Stark is a poor but honest lawyer in a small town who crusades against a corrupt political machine. Newsman Jack Burden (John Ireland) is assigned to cover his campaign. No one is interested in supporting him until some children are killed when a school built by the machine collapses. The state bosses see that he is gaining support and decide to run him for governor. They figure they can control his campaign and make sure that he splits the vote so that their candidate will win. He follows their instructions, delivering dull, statistics-laden speeches. But Sadie Burke (Mercedes McCambridge), assigned to work with him by the machine, switches her allegiance and tells him he is being used. He gets drunk, then begins to deliver speeches with his own message, telling people he's a hick "just like all you hicks," abused like them by the people with power. He tells them that "Nobody ever helped a hick but a hick himself." He is exhilarated by the response from the voters.

He does not win, but four years later he runs again, promising to tax the rich to pay for better services for the poor. He wins and spends generously on new highways, schools, hospitals, and bridges. But this is accomplished through corruption and graft. At first, he insists it is the only way to accomplish what he has dreamed of for the state. But he becomes caught up in the power of the position, and soon power is his goal. He becomes ruthless, forcing Burden's girlfriend, Anne (Joanne Dru), to become his mistress, blackmailing a judge (her uncle) so that he commits suicide, even having a man murdered when he won't be bought off or bullied after his daughter is killed in an accident involving Stark's stepson. Anne's brother is shattered, and shoots Stark. He is killed by Stark's bodyguards, but Stark dies, too, saying, "It could have been the whole world."

❋ **DISCUSSION:** Jack Burden asks his editor, "What's so special about him?" when assigned to write about Stark. "They say he's an honest man," is the reply, and this puts him in the "man bites dog" category of newsworthiness. And he is an honest man, at first, motivated to study law and run for office out of a genuine desire to fight corruption and abuse of power. But, as Lord Acton famously said, "Power corrupts, and absolute power corrupts absolutely." In allowing himself to exploit the same mechanisms that he once protested, in a vain effort to use the ends to justify the means, Willie makes himself politically and spiritually vulnerable, and he does not have a trusted adviser or a moral foundation to keep him from spinning out of control.

It is interesting to watch the other characters decide how much corruption they are prepared to accept or participate in. Jack switches from being a journalist to what would now be called a specialist in "oppo" research (finding dirt on the opposing candidate). The judge agrees to support Stark, swayed in part by the "good comes out of bad" argument, but probably swayed more by the chance to be Attorney General. Still, there is a limit. When he is forbidden to prosecute a crony of Stark's, he must publicly oppose Stark. Even the prospect of blackmail will not force him to back down, only to kill himself.

This movie provides a good opportunity for a discussion of politics (and political scandals) today.

PROFANITY: None.
NUDITY/SEXUAL REFERENCES: Stark has affairs with Anne and Sadie, among others.
ALCOHOL/DRUG ABUSE: Drinking.
VIOLENCE/SCARINESS: Stark and his assailant are shot and killed.
TOLERANCE/DIVERSITY ISSUES: Class issues.

❋ **QUESTIONS FOR KIDS:**
- What changes Stark from someone who just wants to help people to someone who is willing to do anything to get and keep power?
- Why was he unable to hold on to his ideals?
- Is it possible to accomplish what he did without making deals?
- How can you establish how far to go in compromising?
- Why did the "hicks" continue to support him, in spite of all the evidence against him?

❊ **CONNECTIONS:** Read the Pulitzer Prize-winning book by Robert Penn Warren that inspired this movie, or a nonfiction examination of Long's career, such as *Huey Long*, by Thomas Harry Williams and Harry T. Williams. This movie won Oscars for Best Picture, Actor, and Supporting Actress. Ken Burns, the producer of the PBS series on the Civil War and on baseball, made an excellent documentary called *Huey Long* that is available on video. Docudramas about the colorful politician were made for TV and starred Ed Asner and John Goodman. *A Lion Is in the Streets* has James Cagney as a Long-style politician. Long's equally colorful brother Earl, who became governor of Louisiana, is portrayed by Paul Newman in the R-rated *Blaze*, which focuses on his romance with stripper Blaze Starr. A similar story in a more allegorical context, with the politician Thomas Mitchell literally selling his soul to the devil (Ray Milland), is *Alias Nick Beal*. And a wickedly satiric treament of corrupt politicians is Preston Sturges's **The Great McGinty.** Another story of the corruption of an idealist is **Citizen Kane,** though that begins before he tries to enter politics.

Crawford was the son of character actress Helen Broderick, who appears in **Top Hat** and **Shall We Dance.** Tom Stark is played by John Derek, who later married a young woman named Mary Frances Collins whom he renamed Bo Derek. Ireland and Dru, who were married at the time this film was released, also appeared together in **Red River.**

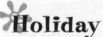

Holiday

1938, 93 min, NR, b&w, 10 and up
Dir: George Cukor. Cary Grant, Katharine Hepburn, Lew Ayres

❊ **PLOT:** After a whirlwind romance at a ski resort, Johnny Case (Cary Grant) is on his way to meet his new fiancée, Julia Seton (Doris Nolan). Overwhelmed by the mansion at the address she gave him, he assumes she must be on the staff, and goes to the back door to ask about her. But she is the daughter of the wealthy and distinguished family that occupies the house. He is surprised and amused, and enjoys meeting Julia's sister, Linda (Katharine Hepburn), and brother, Ned (Lew Ayres). They promise to help him win over their father, who is likely to object to the engagement because Johnny is not from an upper-class wealthy family.

Johnny is a poor boy who has worked hard and done very well. Julia likes him because she sees a similarity to her grandfather, who made a fortune. She wants him to do the same, and tells him, "There's nothing more exciting than making money." But Johnny, who has just taken the first vacation of his life, only wants to make enough so that he can take a "holiday," to "find out why I've been working." As the movie begins, he is about to achieve that goal.

Linda thinks this is a great idea. She is something of an outsider in the family, forsaking the huge formal rooms of the mansion for one cozy place upstairs, which she calls "the only home I've got." She tries to persuade Julia and their father that Johnny is right. Even though he completes the deal that gives him enough for his holiday, Johnny gives in and promises Julia to try it her way, and go to work for her father for a while. As her father presents them with a honeymoon itinerary and explains he is arranging for a house and servants for them, Johnny balks. He knows that if he accepts all of this, he will never be able to walk away from it. Julia breaks the engagement, and Linda joins Johnny on his holiday.

✻ **DISCUSSION:** Many kids will identify with the feeling of wanting to take a holiday, to step back from daily life and study the larger picture. The idea that other things are more important than making money and living according to traditional standards of success may also have some appeal. This is a good opportunity to talk with them about what success really means, and about finding the definition within yourself instead of putting too much weight on the definitions of others. There is nothing inherently wrong with making a fortune, of course, just as there is nothing inherently wrong with not making one.

This movie has two exceptionally appealing characters in Johnny's friends the Potters, played by Jean Dixon and Edward Everett Horton. Their kindness and wisdom contrasts with the superficial values of the Seton family.

PROFANITY: None.

NUDITY/SEXUAL REFERENCES: None.

ALCOHOL/DRUG ABUSE: Ned is an alcoholic, his method of coping with a life he considers intolerable.

VIOLENCE/SCARINESS: None.

TOLERANCE/DIVERSITY ISSUES: Theme of tolerating those who are different in background or aspirations.

✻ **QUESTIONS FOR KIDS:**
- Why was it so important to Linda that she be allowed to give the engagement party?
- Why did Johnny change his mind about trying it Julia's way?
- If you were going to take a holiday, what would you do? Remember, this is more than a vacation—it is more like a journey of discovery. Where would you go? What would you hope to find?
- How do you think people decide what jobs they want to have? Ask your parents what they thought about in choosing their jobs, and whether they ever took (or wanted to take) a "holiday."
- What do you think Johnny will do at the end of his holiday?
- If Julia thought making money was exciting, why didn't she want to do it herself?

✻ **CONNECTIONS:** Cary Grant began in show business as an acrobat, and you can see him show off some of that prowess in this movie. The same stars, director, author, and scriptwriter worked on another classic, *The Philadelphia Story*.

Rudy

1993, 112 min, PG, 11 and up
Dir: David Anspaugh. Sean Astin, Charles S. Dutton

✳ **PLOT:** In this true story of determination and courage, a young man from a blue collar family wants to play football for Notre Dame, despite the fact that he has neither the athletic nor the academic skills. Daniel "Rudy" Ruettiger (Sean Astin) is told by his family and his teachers that college of any kind is out of the question for him, and that he should be content with the good, steady work with his family at a steel mill. Only his best friend, Pete, believes in him, and when Pete is killed in an accident at the mill four years after their high school graduation, Rudy puts on the Notre Dame jacket Pete gave him and takes the bus to South Bend. A sympathetic priest helps him get into nearby Holy Cross Junior College, where with the help of a shy tutor named D-Bob (John Favreau), he is able to make the grades necessary to be accepted as a transfer to Notre Dame.

The coaches make it clear that he will never be good enough to play, but they accept him on the team to act as an opposing team player in practice sessions. His determination and commitment endear him to the team, and he is finally permitted to play for seven seconds of his last game, assuring him a place in the record books as having made it to the Fighting Irish.

✳ **DISCUSSION:** With some reservations about the language (see Profanity section), this is a good family movie for a discussion of dreams—the importance of having them and the possibility of achieving them through persistence and commitment. Rudy is contrasted not only with the athletes who have far more ability but none of the "heart," but also with his friend Fortune (Charles S. Dutton), who reveals near the end that he was once a member of the team but quit, and has regretted it every day since.

Rudy's father is afraid of dreams; his own father lost everything in the Depression by risking all he had to have a dairy farm. He insists that Notre Dame is not for people "like us." Rudy's older brother, Frank, does not want Rudy to succeed, because then he will have to confront his own failure to try for something more. Rudy's teammates want him to "tone it down a notch," not to "play every practice like it was the Super Bowl." But ultimately, his spirit and his insistence on giving everything he can every single time inspires them. Rudy becomes an indispensable part of the team, and each of his teammates goes to the coach to insist that Rudy play in his place.

> **PROFANITY:** Very strong language for a PG movie. Also, a man calls another a "pussy," and there is a reference to "busting your balls." D-Bob's girlfriend tells him not to swear anymore.
>
> **NUDITY/SEXUAL REFERENCES:** No.
>
> **ALCOHOL/DRUG ABUSE:** Beer drinking. Rudy gets a little drunk, with consequences—he makes the mistake of telling the secret he had been trying to keep, that he was not enrolled at Notre Dame.
>
> **VIOLENCE/SCARINESS:** Scuffle in a bar.
>
> **TOLERANCE/DIVERSITY ISSUES:** Subtext of class issues.

* **QUESTIONS FOR KIDS:**
  * What are some of the things Rudy has to do to be able to be on the team? Which are the hardest?
  * What are some of the things he had to give up?
  * Which do the people who made the movie think is more important, ability or determination? How can you tell?
  * Why didn't Fortune admit that he left Rudy the key? How did Fortune change Rudy's mind?
  * Why didn't the quarterback do what the coach said at the end of Rudy's last game?
  * Why did Pete's death make Rudy decide not to wait any longer?
  * Do you think determination is a talent you have to have, or can you learn it? Have you ever been determined to make something happen? What did happen?

* **CONNECTIONS:** Ideally, this movie should be seen as a double feature with *Knute Rockne, All-American*, that other great movie about Notre Dame football. Pat O'Brien appears in the title role, and Ronald Reagan plays "the Gipper," whose deathbed request inspired the most famous motivational speech of all time, memorialized on a plaque in the Fighting Irish's locker room and read aloud by Rudy.

Rudy is played by Sean Astin, son of Patty Duke (*The Miracle Worker*) and John Astin (*West Side Story*). In real life, Rudy (who appears in a photo at the end of the movie and as a fan in the stands) had a second dream—to make a movie about his time at Notre Dame. Like the first dream, it seemed impossible, and like the first dream, he made it come true. A good book for young children to read on this theme is *Ronald Morgan Goes to Bat,* by Patricia Reilly Giff. It is about a boy who has no athletic ability but "helps the team feel good."

SEE ALSO:

Major Barbara A young woman's ambition turns from saving souls through religion to saving them through jobs.

Mr. Deeds Goes to Town A man who suddenly becomes wealthy discovers that his ambition is helping others.

Red River A man is so consumed by ambition that he is unable to feel any kindness or tenderness, even toward those closest to him.

COMPETITION

"Victory is in the quality of competition, not the final score."
—MIKE MARSHALL

Like ambition, competition's best and worst aspects are vividly portrayed on film. Competition is constructive when it spurs us to perform at levels we could not otherwise have reached. It can also cause people to lose sight of values that are far more important. In these days of athlete superstars who make as many headlines for bad behavior when they are not playing as for good behavior when they are, it is worth talking to kids about which kinds of competition are worthwhile and which kinds of competitors deserve to be our heroes.

Chariots of Fire
1983, 123 min, PG, 8 and up
Dir: Hugh Hudson. Ian Charleson, Ben Cross, Nigel Havers, Ian Holm, Alice Krige

* **PLOT:** This is the true story of two athletes who raced in the 1924 Olympics, one a privileged Jewish student at Cambridge (Ben Cross as Harold Abrahams), the other a missionary from Scotland (Ian Charleson as Eric Liddell). Wonderfully evocative of the time and place, with superb performances, the movie shows us the source of the runners' determination, for one a need to prove his worth to himself and the society that discriminates against him, for the other, a way of connecting to God.

The movie begins with the memorial service for Harold Abrahams, and then goes back to his first day at Cambridge, just after World War I. A speaker reminds the entering class that they must achieve for themselves and for those who were lost in the war. Abrahams is a bit arrogant, but finds friends and impresses the whole university by being the first to meet a long-term challenge and race all the way around the quad within the twelve strokes of the clock at noon.

Liddell is deeply committed to missionary work. But when his sister asks him to give up running so that he can return to missionary work, he explains that "I believe God made me for a purpose. He also made me fast. And when I run, I feel his pleasure."

Abrahams is devastated when he loses to Liddell, saying he won't race unless he can win. But his girlfriend reminds him that he can't win unless he races. Both Abrahams and Liddell make the Olympic team. There is a crisis when Liddell's event is scheduled for a Sunday, because he will not run on the Sabbath. But Lord Lindsay (Nigel Havers) graciously allows Liddell his place in a different event, "just for the pleasure of seeing you run," and both Liddell and Abrahams win.

✳ **DISCUSSION:** Both of the athletes must make difficult choices with a great deal of opposition. One uses a coach (who isn't even English), in defiance of tradition and expectations. The other resists the urging of his sister, the person he loves most, who wants him to quit racing, and defies the Prince of Wales, who wants him to race on the Sabbath.

PROFANITY: None.

NUDITY/SEXUAL REFERENCES: None.

ALCOHOL/DRUG ABUSE: None.

VIOLENCE/SCARINESS: None.

TOLERANCE/DIVERSITY ISSUES: One of the themes of the movie is the problem that the Jewish athlete has in dealing with the prejudices of society. Liddell has to confront the conflict between the dictates of his religion and the requirements of the sport (including the entreaties of the heir to the throne) when he is asked to compete on the Sabbath.

✳ **QUESTIONS FOR KIDS:**
- Why was running so important to these men?
- Was it different for different athletes?
- Why does Harold Abrahams think of quitting when he loses to Liddell? Have you ever felt that way? What did you do?
- Why doesn't Eric's sister want him to race? Why does he race despite her objections?
- Why don't the teachers at Harold Abrahams's school think it is appropriate to have a coach? Would anyone think that today?

✳ **CONNECTIONS:** This movie deservedly won the Oscars for Best Picture, Screenplay, Costume Design, and Music.

Families who enjoy this movie will also enjoy a two-part made for television miniseries called *The First Olympics—Athens 1896,* about the American team entering the first modern Olympics in 1896. It features Louis Jourdan (of *Gigi*), David Caruso (of the original cast of television's *NYPD Blue*), and David Ogden Stiers (of Disney's **Beauty and the Beast**). While it does not have the resonance and meaning (or the production values) of **Chariots of Fire,** it is heartwarming, funny, exciting, and a lovely period piece. Not currently available on video, it usually shows up on television around the time of Olympic competitions. An extremely silly movie about the first modern Olympics is *It Happened in Athens,* with Jayne Mansfield and real-life Olympic athlete Bob Mathias.

Miracle on Ice, another made-for-television movie, is the true story of the 1980 U.S. hockey team, which astonished the world at the Olympics in Lake Placid. Yet another Olympic made-for-television movie, *The Golden Moment,* is the story of a romance between a Soviet gymnast and an American athlete. Curiously, it takes place at an Olympics in which, in real life, the U.S. never competed—that was the year the U.S. protested the Soviet invasion of Afghanistan by boycotting the Moscow Olympics. See also **Cool Runnings,** about the 1988 Jamaican bobsled team, *The Bob Mathias Story,* with the real-life decathalon champion playing himself, *The Jesse Owens Story,* with Dorian Harewood as the legendary athlete, and *Babe,* with Susan Clark as Babe Deidrickson Zaharias.

On the silly side, try *Animalympics,* an animated spoof of the Olympics with some comical moments, and the very funny *Million Dollar Legs,* with W. C. Fields as the President of Klopstockia, a country entering the Olympics. And of course Bud Greenspan's documentaries about the Olympics are always worth watching, for the stories and the personalities as much as for the athletic achievements.

The Great Race
1965, 150 min, NR, 6 and up
Dir: Blake Edwards. Tony Curtis, Jack Lemmon, Natalie Wood, Peter Falk, Keenan Wynn

✳ **PLOT:** Dedicated to "Mr. Laurel and Mr. Hardy," this movie is both a spoof of and a loving tribute to the silent classics, with good guys, bad guys, romance, adventure, slapstick, music, wonderful antique cars, and the biggest pie fight in history. The opening credits are on a series of slides like those in the earliest movies, complete with cheers for the hero and boos for the villain, apparently shown by a flickering old-fashioned projector that at one point appears to break down.

Always dressed in impeccable white, the Great Leslie (Tony Curtis) is a good guy so good that his eyes and teeth literally twinkle. His capable mechanic and assistant is Hezekiah (Keenan Wynn). The bad guy is Professor Fate (Jack Lemmon), assisted by Max (Peter Falk). Like Wile E. Coyote, Fate concocts cartoonishly hilarious stunts to stop Leslie and they inevitably backfire. After a brief prologue, in which Fate tries to beat Leslie in breaking various speed records, literally trying to torpedo him at one point, they both enter an automobile race from New York to Paris. So does a beautiful reporter (Natalie Wood as Maggie DuBois) trying to prove she can get the story, dressed in an endless series of exquisite ensembles designed by Holly-wood legend Edith Head.

The race takes them across America, through the Wild West, to a rapidly melting ice floe in the Pacific, and into a European setting that is a cross between a Victor Herbert operetta and *The Prisoner of Zenda,* where a spoiled prince happens to look exactly like Professor Fate. It takes all of the stars to foil an evil Baron (Ross Martin) who wants to use Fate to take over the throne.

✳ **DISCUSSION:** This is a perfect family movie, just plain fun from begin-ning to end. It may also provide an opportunity for a discussion of competi-tion and sportsmanship. At the end, Leslie deliberately loses as a gesture of devotion to Maggie DuBois. Professor Fate, after all, shows some sense of honor—apparently it is all right for him to cheat to win, but not all right to win by having Leslie refuse to compete. "You cheated—I refuse to accept!" Modern adults may wince a bit at DuBois's notion of how to attain equal opportunity—she ultimately succeeds by showing her leg to the editor, who becomes too dazed to argue further. But like *Mary Poppins,* it provides a chance to remind children that when their great-grandparents were children, women did not even have the right to vote.

> PROFANITY: None.
> NUDITY/SEXUAL REFERENCES: Fate and Max speculate mildly about Leslie's relationship with DuBois.
> ALCOHOL/DRUG ABUSE: The prince has a drinking problem; Leslie fre-quently has champagne as evidence of his sophistication and elegance.
> VIOLENCE/SCARINESS: Slapstick punches and, of course, the pie fight.
> TOLERANCE/DIVERSITY ISSUES: The reporter played by Natalie Wood is something of a caricature of feminism, more committed to shocking people than to any thoughtful concept of equality. But she has an un-quenchable spirit, she is courageous and resilient and, of course, she is Natalie Wood, which makes her irresistible to Leslie and to us.

✳ **QUESTIONS FOR KIDS:**
- Should Leslie have let Fate win?
- Why wasn't Fate happy when he beat Leslie?
- Why was Fate so jealous of Leslie?
- Why did DuBois want to be a reporter so badly?

✳ **CONNECTIONS:** Curtis and Lemmon also appeared together in one of the greatest comedies of all time, *Some Like it Hot.* Children who enjoy this movie might like to see some of the silent classics it saluted, like *Two Tars,* in which Laurel and Hardy create chaos in the middle of an enormous traffic jam. They might also enjoy *Those Magnificent Men in Their Flying Machines* or *Those Daring Young Men in Their Jaunty Jalopies.* Children who have enjoyed Ed Wynn as Uncle Albert (who "loves to laugh") in **Mary Poppins** may like to know that his son, Keenan Wynn, plays Leslie's assistant Hezekiah.

✳ AMADEUS
1984, 158 min, PG, 12 and up
Dir: Milos Forman. F. Murray Abraham, Tom Hulce

Antonio Salieri (F. Murray Abraham in an Oscar-winning performance), the court composer, should have been Mozart. He followed all the rules, worked hard, and cared deeply. Music was his life. Mozart (Tom Hulce) arrives, a bawdy, bratty, foolish boy whose music could enchant the angels. Salieri, ironically the only one who understands music well enough to realize Mozart's genius, is consumed with jealousy. Teens will be interested to learn that this movie was written by Peter Schaffer, a man whose twin brother Anthony Schaffer (*Sleuth*) was for a time the more commercially successful of the two, which surely influenced his choice of subject and his approach.

✳ ANNIE GET YOUR GUN
1957, 110 min, NR, b&w
Dir: Vincent J. Donehue. Mary Martin, John Raitt

This big, brassy, Irving Berlin musical is based on the story of Annie Oakley, the backwoods girl who out-shot everyone and became the star of Buffalo Bill's traveling Wild West show. The video of the theatrical release, starring Betty Hutton and Howard Keel, is not currently available, but there is a delightful video of a 1957 television production starring Mary Martin and John Raitt. The production values are far below current standards, but the singing is arguably even better than in the movie.

Annie (Mary Martin) falls in love with sharpshooter Frank Butler (John Raitt) at first sight. He is attracted to her, but finds it very difficult to cope when she beats him in a shooting contest. They are both very competitive—this movie contains the most competitive musical number of all time ("Anything You Can Do, I Can Do Better"), as well as a thunderously sexist song ("The Girl That I Marry"). Ultimately, Annie loses on purpose, to endear herself to Frank.

✳ **CONNECTIONS:** At this writing, this was the only version of the Irving Berlin musical available on video, but at some point the theatrical release starring Betty Hutton and Howard Keel may be released. Anyone who sees this musical in any form should also watch the superb Rabbit Ears video, **Annie Oakley,** which accurately points out that Frank Butler was never anything but delighted by Oakley's prowess.

✳ BRIAN'S SONG

1970, 73 min, G, 10 and up
Dir: Buzz Kulik. James Caan, Billy Dee Williams

This is the true—and heartbreaking—story of Brian Piccolo and Gale Sayers, players for the Chicago Bears, who were the first interracial roommates in pro sports, based on the memoir by Sayers. Piccolo (played by James Caan) was not as talented as Sayers (played by Billy Dee Williams), but he had enormous commitment, perseverance, and competitiveness in the most positive sense. He knew that trying to beat Sayers was what made him do his best. When Sayers was injured, Piccolo devoted himself to making sure that he recovered fully, because he wanted to beat Sayers at his best, not beat him because of the injury. Piccolo, trying to motivate Sayers to exercise his injured knee, calls him "nigger" in the hopes of getting him excited. But it is such a ludicrous insult that both men collapse into laughter.

Sayers comes back, Piccolo is added to the starting lineup, and all seems fine until Piccolo becomes ill. It turns out that he has terminal cancer. The shy and reserved Sayers must learn to handle a devastating loss by keeping the best of Piccolo inside him.

This is a touching and inspiring film (originally made for television), with an outstanding musical score by Michel Legrand. The friendship and devotion between the two friends (and their wives) is very moving, as is the treatment of racial issues.

SEE ALSO:

Breaking Away A group of local boys in a college town resents the college students, but secretly fear that they could not compete with them. They get their chance when the college's annual bicycle race is opened to outsiders for the first time.

Hoop Dreams In this documentary, two young men from poor families believe that basketball stardom is their only hope for a better life.

A League of Their Own The teammate and younger sister of the star pitcher is overwhelmed by feelings of competition.

DREAMS AND REALITY

"Hold fast to dreams
For if dreams die.
Life is a broken-winged bird
That cannot fly."

—LANGSTON HUGHES

Kipling advised memorably that we should strive to "dream, and not make dreams your master. . . ." Achieving that balance is a complicated challenge in real life. In the movies, which are, after all, a sort of collective dream to those of us to sit in darkness, we dream along with the characters, wanting Rocky to go the distance (**Rocky**), wanting Ray Kinsella to turn his corn crop into a baseball field (**Field of Dreams**), wanting Dave Stohler and the rest of the "cutters" to get on their bicycles and beat the college boys from Indiana University (**Breaking Away**), wanting the Younger family to move into that new neighborhood so that their dream doesn't dry up (**A Raisin in the Sun**), wanting Johnny Case to walk away from the house and servants (and snobbish fiancée) to find out what really matters in **Holiday.**

Some of the movies' most memorable characters are dreamers who insist on following their dreams long after any reasonable chance of achieving them seems possible. Yet sometimes those dreams are endearingly modest. Rocky just wants to go the distance. Rudy does not dream of making the winning touchdown, only of being on the field with the team. How do we form our dreams? How do we know how much we can hope for?

We love stories, too, about people who are taught how to dream, people who once had no hope of anything more than what they saw around them and who learned, in the words of Bloody Mary in **South Pacific,** that "you got to have a dream/if you don't have a dream/how you gonna have a dream come true?"

But movies also show us that dreams have a price. For every Rocky whose dream brings him Adrian and a shot at the title, there is a Fanny Brice who loses her Nicky Arnstein (**Funny Girl**). For every Ray Kinsella whose dream brings him his father, there is a Charles Foster Kane who thinks he can make some small compromises without losing the most precious part of himself (*Citizen Kane*). For every Dave Stohler who makes it across the finish line and wins for every kid who didn't have it easy, there is a Kasper Gutman and Brigid O'Shaughnessy who lie, cheat, steal, and kill for a falcon that turns out to be false, described by Sam Spade as "the stuff that dreams are made of" (*The Maltese Falcon*).

Movies give us heroes whose lives are illuminated by dreams. But they also give us characters who must learn when to put away the dreams that are shielding them from reality instead of helping them shape it. Those characters must learn J. M. Power's lesson that "The best way to make your dreams come true is to wake up."

Citizen Kane

1941, 119 min, NR, b&w, 10 and up
Dir: Orson Welles. Orson Welles, Joseph Cotton, Everett Sloane

PLOT: Charles Foster Kane (Orson Welles) dies alone at Xanadu, his enormous mansion. His last word is the mysterious "Rosebud." A newsreel gives us the highlights of his life, the wealthy young man who became an influential newspaper magnate and political candidate, who married first the niece of the president and then, after a scandal that led to the end of his political career, a singer. As the lights come up in a screening room, an editor says, "It's not enough to tell us what a man did. You have to tell us who he was." One of the reporters, Jerry Thompson, goes off to find out who Kane really was.

He meets with five different figures who were important in Kane's life to try to understand the small mystery of Kane's last word and the larger mystery of the man who was capable of both integrity and corruption, and who seemed to have no sense of peace or happiness.

Thompson begins by reading the journals of millionaire Walter Parks Thatcher (George Coulouris), now dead, the trustee who oversaw Kane's early years. He explains that Kane's mother (Agnes Moorehead) was a landlady who became wealthy when a prospector who had not paid his bill left her the deed to his mine. The mine turned out to be one of the world's richest sources of silver. Mrs. Kane believed that her son would do better if Thatcher, a bank executive, took charge of his education and upbringing. She wanted him far away from his bully of a father.

Kane was a rebellious charge, and as soon as he reached his majority, he bought a failing newspaper, which he used to criticize Thatcher and the rest of the financial elite.

Next, Thompson speaks to Mr. Bernstein (Everett Sloane), who worked with Kane at the newspaper. He talks of Kane's high ideals, and his devotion to the individual struggling against the powerful. He also speaks of Kane's first marriage and its disintegration (shown in a stunning series of scenes set at breakfasts over the years).

He then talks to Jedediah Leland (Joseph Cotton), once Kane's best friend and the drama critic for Kane's newspaper, who tells him of Kane's second marriage, to Susan Alexander (Dorothy Commingore), a nightclub singer. Kane was determined to make her a success as an opera singer. When Leland wrote a bad review of her performance, Kane finished writing it for him, printed it, and then fired him.

Thompson visits Susan Alexander, now an alcoholic. She tells him about the isolation of her life with Kane, and her decision to leave him. Neither she nor the butler at Xanadu is able to tell Thompson anything about "Rosebud."

The viewer, however, is permitted to solve the smaller mystery of Rosebud, but the answer only proves that there are never any simple answers to the complexity of the human spirit.

✳ **DISCUSSION:** Kids who watch this movie can never know how revolutionary it was. Every one of its dozens of innovations, from the flashback structure to the use of sets with ceilings for additional authenticity, has become all but standard. No problem—there is time enough for kids to study these aspects of the film's brilliance if they decide to learn more about film history and criticism. For their first viewing of this extraordinary work (and for purposes of a family discussion), just let them focus on the story, the dialogue, and the characters, which remain as compelling and contemporary as they were more than fifty years ago.

Like Willie Stark in **All the King's Men,** Kane begins as a populist and dies corrupt and alone, and we cannot help but hope for some explanation of how that happened, as Thompson does. Importantly, both Kane and Stark were based on real-life figures. Kane, of course, was based on William Randolph Hearst, the almost-impossibly wealthy heir to the largest gold and silver mine in America, who became a powerful publishing magnate. Kane might also have been based on Welles, only twenty-five years old when he cowrote, directed, and starred in this film, and then spent the rest of his life coming up with one excuse or another for why he never came close to that level of achievement again.

As we see in flashback, Kane was taken from his parents when he was six, and raised by the bank, or by Thatcher, nearly as impersonal a guardian as the bank. This created an emotional neediness and a deeply conflicted view of money and power that is one factor in his downfall. As soon as he had control over his money, Kane bought the newspaper, perhaps for the same reason Welles went to work for a Hollywood studio; he said it was "the greatest electric train set any boy ever had." A rebel by nature (as we see when he hits Thatcher with his sled, and in his glee in getting the staff to remake the paper over and over), he enjoys what H. L. Mencken referred to as the purpose of a newspaper: "To comfort the afflicted and afflict the comfortable." Afflicting the comfortable is great fun for him, especially comfortable people like Thatcher and his colleagues and his wife's uncle, the president of the United States.

Like Stark, though, Kane's taste of power makes him feel that the rules do not apply to him. He begins to feel that the ends justify the means. He does not just want to sway the electorate in favor of the candidate of his choice; he wants to be that candidate. As we see in a striking scene, with Kane in front of the enormous poster of his face, he loves the adulation of the crowd.

But as we also see, he is drawn to Susan Alexander (whom he meets as he is on his way to sit among his late mother's effects) because she responds to the private Kane, the one who can wiggle his ears and make hand shadows. When he finds that he cannot have both Susan and public acclaim, he makes the critically wrong choice of trying to make her into a publicly acceptable figure, an opera star. Leland writes an honest review (after getting drunk for courage). Kane's last shred of integrity requires him to print the review, but he cannot bear to face Leland again.

Indeed, he cannot bear to face anyone. He retreats to Xanadu, where Susan Alexander spends her nights working on jigsaw puzzles. She cannot bear it anymore, either, and finally leaves him; he hardly notices, except to become even more isolated. That private self that she responded to, and that once mattered so much to him, has become as completely inaccessible as the little house inside the snow globe that crashes to the floor when he dies.

PROFANITY: None.

NUDITY/SEXUAL REFERENCES: Scandal over Kane's affair with Susan Alexander.

ALCOHOL/DRUG ABUSE: Leland and Susan both have drinking problems.

VIOLENCE/SCARINESS: None.

TOLERANCE/DIVERSITY ISSUES: Mrs. Kane makes a mild anti-Semitic remark about Bernstein.

✳ QUESTIONS FOR KIDS:
- What do you think of Kane's pledge on the first page of the newspaper?
- How do the scenes at the breakfast table tell you what is going on in Kane's first marriage?
- Why do you think he said "Rosebud"?
- Who, if anyone, in the movie is satisfied with his or her life? How can you tell?
- Why does Kane change?

✳ **CONNECTIONS:** Fans of Phoebe Tyler on television's *All My Children* will enjoy seeing a young Ruth Warrick as Kane's first wife.

✳ **ACTIVITIES:** It is hard to say who is the more interesting real-life character, William Randolph Hearst or Orson Welles. There are many biographies of both, and they are fascinating reading. The biographies of Hearst detail his reaction to this movie. His efforts to use his newspapers to discourage people to see the movie were just what Kane himself might have done. Everyone should make an effort to see San Simeon, the model for Xanadu, now open to the public in California.

There are also volumes of material about this movie, probably the most honored ever to be produced in Hollywood, and always at or near the top of critics' surveys on the best film ever made.

The Curse of the Cat People
1944, 70 min, NR, b&w, 10 and up
Dir: Gunther von Fritsch and Robert Wise. Simone Simon

✳ **PLOT:** Despite the title (insisted on by the studio following the producer's very successful—and scary—*The Cat People*), this is a gentle story of a lonely and sensitive girl and her "friend," who may be imaginary or may be the ghost of her father's first wife. Amy (Ann Carter) is a dreamy kindergartener, not very clear about what is real and what is fantasy, and "a very sensitive and delicately adjusted child," according to her teacher. Her father, Oliver (Kent Smith), still in great pain from his first wife's tragic death, is very protective and worries about her "losing herself in a dream world."

When no one shows up for her birthday party, it turns out that Amy "mailed" the invitations in a tree, believing that it was a magic mailbox, as her father had whimsically told her years before. The party goes on with her parents and Edward, their Jamaican houseman. When she blows out the candles, she wishes to be a "good girl like Daddy wants me to be." The next day, after the other girls refuse to play with her, she finds a spooky old house, where a voice speaks to her and invites her inside. A handkerchief falls from an upstairs window, containing a ring for Amy. She wishes on the ring for a friend, and later says she got her wish, and that her friend sang to her.

Amy goes back to the spooky house and meets Julia Farren (Julia Dean), an elderly woman who was once an actress and who insists that the other woman in the house is not her daughter but her caretaker.

Amy sees a photograph of Irena, her father's first wife, and recognizes her as her "friend." Irena promises to stay "as long as you want me" but tells Amy never to tell anyone about her. But when Amy sees a picture of Irena and her father together, she tells him. He spanks her for lying, and Irena tells Amy, "Now you must send me away." Amy leaves the house in a snowstorm, looking for Irena. When she knocks on the Farrens' door, Mrs. Farren says she has to hide. Her daughter, Barbara, bitterly jealous of the affection her mother denies her but lavishes on Amy, has said she will kill Amy if she ever comes back. Mrs. Farren collapses, trying to take Amy upstairs. Barbara is furious. But Irena appears, her image flickering over Barbara, and Amy calls out, "My friend!" and embraces her. Barbara, softening, hugs her back, as her parents arrive. "Amy, from now on, you and I are going to be friends," her father tells her, and this time he says that he, too, sees Irena.

✳ **DISCUSSION:** This movie is not for everyone, but children who can identify with Amy will like it and may be able to talk about themselves in talking about her. Oliver worries that Amy's dreams will lead to madness, as he believes they did for Irena. Amy just wants someone who will be her friend and has a hard time connecting to other children. The counterpoint is Mrs. Farren, whose delusion that her child is dead is deeply upsetting to her daughter, in her own way as needy for friendship as Amy is.

This movie does a good job of showing how Amy and her parents worry about each other, and that parents make mistakes. Amy blames herself when her parents argue about her, and you may want to make it clear that children are not responsible for family conflicts.

Children may be concerned about Mrs. Farren's delusions, and how upsetting they are for her daughter. They should know that most old people are fine, but that some have an illness that makes them forgetful.

PROFANITY: None.
NUDITY/SEXUAL REFERENCES: None.
ALCOHOL/DRUG ABUSE: None.
VIOLENCE/SCARINESS: None.
TOLERANCE/DIVERSITY ISSUES: None.

✳ **QUESTIONS FOR KIDS:**
- Ever since this movie was made, people have argued about whether Amy really sees Irena or only imagines her. What do you think? Why is it hard to be sure?
- Have you ever had an imaginary friend?
- Why is it hard for Amy to make friends with the other children? What advice would you give her?
- Amy sometimes has trouble communicating with her parents. Why is that? What advice would you give her, and what advice would you give her parents?
- What do you think of Irena's Christmas present to Amy? If you were going to give that kind of present, what sight would you pick?

✳ **CONNECTIONS:** The reference to *The Legend of Sleepy Hollow* may lead children to the story by Washington Irving, or to the Disney animated movie. For a completely different story about the ghost of a first wife, try Noel Coward's sophisticated farce *Blithe Spirit* (it may scare younger children; there are some references to infidelity).

Field of Dreams

1989, 116 min, PG, 12 and up
Dir: Phil Alden Robinson. Kevin Costner, Burt Lancaster, James Earl Jones, Amy Madigan, Ray Liotta

✳ **PLOT:** Ray Kinsella (Kevin Costner), who grew up in New York and went to college at Berkeley, stands in the middle of his first Iowa corn crop and hears a voice say, "If you build it, he will come." He begins to understand that this means he must plow under the corn crop and build a baseball field so that "Shoeless" Joe Jackson, barred from baseball since 1919 and dead for years, can play on it. Ray and his wife (Amy Madigan) know this is a crazy thing to do, but they do it. And Shoeless Joe Jackson does show up, with his teammates. Jackson had been the hero of Ray's father, a former minor leaguer, with whom Ray had never been able to connect.

The voice speaks again: "Ease his pain." Ray comes to understand that this refers to an iconoclastic author of the 1960s named Terrence Mann (James Earl Jones), now a recluse. Ray finds him, and together they hear the voice say, "Go the distance." This leads them back in time to find an elderly doctor (Burt Lancaster), who had a brief career in baseball but never got a chance at bat. On their way back to the farm, they find him again, as a young man, and together, they go home, just as the farm is about to be foreclosed. The doctor gets his chance at bat. Mann gets to tell another story. And Ray gets a second chance to do what he regrets not doing as a teenager, to play catch with his father.

✳ **DISCUSSION:** The themes of this movie are dreams, family, and baseball. There are echoes of Ray's father throughout the movie. It begins with Ray's description of growing up, using his refusal to play baseball as his teenage rebellion, and as a way to test his father's love. Ray tells Mann that his father's name was used for a character in one of Mann's books. Ray builds the field to bring back Shoeless Joe, his father's hero, the hero Ray accused of being corrupt because he knew that would hurt his father. And of course at the end, it turns out that the dream all along was not bringing back the greats of baseball, but of a reconciliation with his father that was not possible before he died. "I only saw him when he was worn down by life," Ray says. His own understanding and maturity are what enable him to see his father as he really was, even before he reappears on the baseball field. Ray asks his father, "Is there a heaven?" and his father answers, "Oh, yeah. It's the place dreams come true."

PROFANITY: Some epithets.
NUDITY/SEXUAL REFERENCES: None. "Masturbation" used metaphorically to refer to self-involved and unproductive thinking.
ALCOHOL/DRUG USE: References to drug use, including pot and LSD.
VIOLENCE/SCARINESS: Costner threatens Jones to get him to go to the baseball game, but both know he does not really have a gun.
TOLERANCE/DIVERSITY ISSUES: None.

✳ **QUESTIONS FOR KIDS:**
- Why doesn't Annie's brother Mark see the baseball players at first? Why is he able to see them later?
- What did Ray mean when he talked about how he needed to insult his father's hero when he was a teenager?
- How do you know when to follow a dream that seems crazy or foolish?

✳ **CONNECTIONS:** Kids who watch this may want to know more about Shoeless Joe Jackson and the famous "Black Sox" scandal. *Eight Men Out,* with D. B. Sweeney as Jackson, tells this story sympathetically. The Ken Burns PBS documentary about the history of baseball also has a video devoted to the story. See also the discussion of baseball movies in the Calendar chapter, including *The Bingo Long Traveling All-Stars & Motor Kings* and *The Sandlot* (both also starring Jones) and *A League of Their Own.* James Earl Jones provided the voice for Darth Vader in *Star Wars.*

✳ **ACTIVITIES:** Take the kids to a baseball game. If they have attended major-league games, try a farm team or semipro. Help them with batting practice.

✳Lost Horizon

1937, 132 min (restored version), NR, b&w, 8 and up
Dir: Frank Capra. Ronald Coleman, Jane Wyatt, Sam Jaffe, Edward Everett Horton

✳ **PLOT:** "Haven't you ever dreamed of a place where there was peace and security, where living was not a struggle but a lasting delight?" Such a place exists in this movie, and its name, Shangri-La, has become a synonym for utopia. As the movie begins, distinguished and brave British statesman Robert Conway (Ronald Coleman) has been sent to China to evacuate "ninety white people." He and four others just make the last plane. They are prim paleontologist Alexander P. Lovett (Edward Everett Horton), Conway's brother George (John Howard), Gloria Stone, a blonde with a racking cough (Isabel Jewell), and Henry Barnard (Thomas Mitchell), a brash businessman. Exhausted, they fall asleep and wake to find that the plane is going in the wrong direction. After stopping for more gas at what appears to be a rebel outpost, they land on a snowy mountaintop. The pilot is dead. As Conway prepares to go for help, a group of people led by Chang (H. B. Warner) arrive to rescue them. After a long, arduous climb, they arrive in Shangri-La, a place of beauty, harmony, and peace.

Conway is strangely at home there. While the others are impatient to leave, he feels both contented and curious. Conway asks Chang, "What religion do you practice here?" Chang answers that their religion is moderation in all things—including virtue. "We rule with moderate strictness and are satisfied with moderate compliance." They have no police because they have no criminals. "There can be no crime when there is a sufficiency of anything." Conway wisely deduces, "There is something so simple and naive about all this that I suspect there has been a shrewd guiding intelligence somewhere." Sure enough, the first European to find Shangri-La, two hundred years before, is the man who created this utopia.

Conway is permitted to meet the High Lama, and discovers it is the very same man who arrived in Shangri-La two hundred years before. Part of Shangri-La's magic is that people live a very long time. The High Lama has brought Conway there to take his place. His dream was to make Shangri-La a place where all of the beauty and culture of the world could be preserved against the prospect of greed, selfishness, and destruction, and to create "a way of life based on one simple rule: Be kind."

Conway falls in love with Sondra, a teacher. It was she who read his books and knew he would be the one to lead Shangri-La. She saw his ideals, and also the emptiness he felt.

The Lama dies, telling Conway to take his place. But George and Maria (Margo), the Russian girl George loves, insist on leaving. Maria tells Conway that the High Lama is mad and cruel, that he lied when he said she'd arrived in 1888 and that she will age immediately if she leaves. Conway begins to have doubts, and agrees to leave with them. On their way down the mountain, Maria does become an old woman, and dies. George, mad with grief, falls off the mountain. Conway makes it down the mountain, barely alive. He then spends ten months finding his way back. As he arrives, the bells ring to welcome him home.

✳ **DISCUSSION:** No one can resist the prospect of describing his or her own version of Shangri-La. As the High Lama says, "There's a wish for Shangri-La in everyone's head." The original provides a good starting point. Though it has some troubling overtones by today's standards, the ideals of moderation and kindness are worth exploring with the family. Older children may be interested in talking about whether it is possible to create a society with a "sufficiency of anything" and whether there are both good and bad points of "an absence of struggle." Is it a coincidence that Shangri-La had, for example, no running water? While it may not be necessary to have running water to have a productive and creative society (look at the Renaissance), it is worth noting that Shangri-La itself produced little if any art (the children are shown singing an English song) and no scientific or technological advances.

Compare Shangri-La to the world portrayed in *The Gods Must Be Crazy*. In the latter, a real-life society based on kindness and "a sufficiency of anything" (and even more technologically rudimentary than Shangri-La) is deeply disturbed by the introduction of a Coke bottle. It is the first object in their experience that can be used or owned by one person to the exclusion of the others. Compare this movie also to *Brigadoon,* another timeless paradise found by an outsider who felt more at home there than in the "real world." (And compare it to Orson Welles's famous speech in *The Third Man,* comparing the achievements of the peaceful Swiss to the achievements of the turbulent Medicis.)

PROFANITY: None.

NUDITY/SEXUAL REFERENCES: None (children swim without suits, nothing revealed).

ALCOHOL/DRUG ABUSE: None.

VIOLENCE/SCARINESS: Scary fall from a mountain.

TOLERANCE/DIVERSITY ISSUES: Racist undertones. As the movie begins, Conway is sent to China to evacuate "ninety white people before they are butchered in a local revolution." As he loads the plane, he says, "Be sure none of the natives get in!" Conway later reflects on the irony of saying that the nonwhites "don't count." In Shangri-La, the people who are educated and in power are all white except for Chang. The servants are all natives. The High Lama speaks of a time when "the Christian ethic may be at last fulfilled." The movie is also somewhat sexist by today's standards; when Conway asks what happens when two men desire the same women, he is told that the men defer to one another, with no suggestion that the woman should play a role of any kind!

✳ **QUESTIONS FOR KIDS:**
- What was the High Lama's dream for Shangri-La? Was it different from Chang's?
- What do you think about the way Chang describes their "religion"?
- Why did Maria and George want to leave? Why did Maria lie?
- What did "Lovey" mean when he said Bernard should take off his mask?
- If you were going to collect the best examples of the world's beauty and culture, what would you pick? How would you decide?

✳ **CONNECTIONS:** Fans of Rocky and Bullwinkle will recognize Edward Everett Horton as the voice in the Fractured Fairy Tales segment on "Rocky and His Friends." He was also a supporting actor in some of the best Astaire and Rogers films, and gave a touchingly professorial performance in *Holiday.* The author of the book on which this movie is based, James Hilton, was the author or screenwriter of a number of other movies, including *Goodbye, Mr. Chips, Portrait of Jennie, Random Harvest,* and *Camille.*

Do not waste your time on the musical remake, also called *Lost Horizon.* Even with a wonderful cast, it is unwatchably bad.

✳ **ACTIVITIES:** A good book for children with a very different utopian idea is *The 21 Balloons,* by William Pene du Bois. Families might like to read about some of the other utopian ideas people have designed, either in books or in real communities, and see how they have fared, and try to design their own Shangri-Las.

Miracle on 34th Street

1947, 96 min, NR, b&w, 6 and up
Dir: George Seaton. Natalie Wood, Maureen O'Hara, Edmund Gwenn

❋ **PLOT:** Doris Walker (Maureen O'Hara), an executive at Macy's, is responsible for the Thanksgiving Day Parade. When the Santa Claus she has hired for the parade shows up drunk, she quickly subsitutes Kris Kringle (Edmund Gwenn), who is an enormous success. She hires him to serve as the store's in-house Santa. There, he is an even bigger success. He tells customers to shop elsewhere when Macy's doesn't have what they want. The employees are aghast, but it turns out to be a public relations triumph, and Macy's becomes known as "the store with a heart."

Doris has a little girl named Susan (Natalie Wood). She has decided to raise Susan without any fantasies or illusions, to help her handle "reality." Susan does not believe in Santa Claus. But Kris tells her that he really is Santa Claus, and when she sees him singing a song in Dutch to comfort a little girl who doesn't speak English, she begins to believe him. He teaches her how to use her imagination, so that the other children will enjoy playing with her. He has the enthusiastic support of lawyer Fred Gailey (John Payne), who cares deeply for Doris and Susan.

But Kris's insistence that he really is Santa Claus leads to a hearing on his mental competency. Kris is so unhappy that he does not even want to assist in his defense. Doris and Susan write to let Kris know they believe in him, and a postal clerk decides to send along with it all of the letters addressed to Santa Claus as well. Fred persuades the court that this is conclusive proof that the U.S. government believes that Kris is Santa, and the judge rules in his favor. The next day is Christmas, and when Doris, Fred, and Susan all get what they asked for, it is clear that it is Kris who made it possible.

❋ **DISCUSSION:** In a way, this is the opposite of *Inherit the Wind*. Both are courtroom dramas about how we decide what is true, based on faith or based on provable fact. They have opposite conclusions, however, and the great gift of the movies is that both seem right to us. (One similarity is that in both, the judges are warned that they must make a decision that will have favorable political consequences.)

Doris has been hurt, and thinks she can protect herself and Susan from further hurt by not letting herself believe in anything outside themselves anymore. She finds out that both she and Susan have missed a lot, not just in imagination but in the ability to trust and to allow themselves to get close to other people.

PROFANITY: None.
NUDITY/SEXUAL REFERENCES: None.
ALCOHOL/DRUG ABUSE: None.
VIOLENCE/SCARINESS: Kris bops Sawyer on the head for mistreating Albert.
TOLERANCE/DIVERSITY ISSUES: Tolerance of individual differences.

❋ **QUESTIONS FOR KIDS:**
- Why doesn't Doris want Susan to use her imagination? Why do Kris and Fred think it is important?
- Why is it important that Kris told people to go to other stores to buy things they didn't have at Macy's?
- Why doesn't Mr. Sawyer like Kris?
- Why did Fred have Mr. Mara's son testify in the trial?
- Why doesn't Kris try harder to win the case at first? What makes him change his mind?

❋ **CONNECTIONS:** Gwenn won a well-deserved Oscar, as did the screenplay. Ignore the pallid 1973 (television) and 1994 (theatrical) remakes. The original is much, much better, and the 1994 version completely ruins the courtroom denouement.

Rocky

1976, 116 min, PG, 8 and up
Dir: John G. Avildsen. Sylvester Stallone, Talia Shire, Burgess Meredith, Carl Weathers

❋ **PLOT:** Rocky Balboa (Sylvester Stallone) is a sweet-natured but not very bright boxer and small-time enforcer for a loan shark. He has a crush on Adrian (Talia Shire), the painfully shy sister of his friend, Paulie (Burt Young). Apollo Creed (Carl Weathers) is the heavyweight champion, whose big upcoming fight is cancelled when his opponent is injured. Creed and his promoters decide to give an unknown a shot at the title, and pick Rocky.

Rocky has never really committed to anything before, but this opportunity galvanizes him. He works with Mickey (Burgess Meredith), a demanding trainer. He takes Adrian on a date, and they fall in love. When her brother becomes furious over their relationship, she moves in with Rocky. Rocky knows he cannot beat Creed; his goal is to "go the distance," to conduct himself with class and dignity in the ring and still be standing at the end of the fight. Apollo, sure of himself and busy marketing the fight, neglects his own training. Apollo wins, but it is a split decision. Rocky goes the distance. Surrounded by fans and the press, he bellows over and over, "Adrian!"

❋ **DISCUSSION:** In Rocky's first fight, we get a glimpse of his potential. But it is also clear he has failed to make a commitment to anything. Mickey wants to throw him out of the gym because he doesn't take boxing seriously enough. It is less an insult to boxing than an insult to himself. He takes pride in small things, like his pet turtles, and the fact that his nose has never been broken. When he gets the call from Apollo, he assumes that he is going to be invited to be a sparring partner for the champion, the greatest honor he could imagine for himself.

But Apollo's impetuous offer gives Rocky a chance to see himself differently. That offer does for him what Paul does for Billie in **Born Yesterday,** what Miss Moffat does for Morgan in **The Corn is Green,** or Obi-Wan does for Luke in **Star Wars.** Rocky has a chance to think of himself as someone who can hold his own with the world champion, and once he has that image of himself, it is just a matter of taking the steps to get there. That image also gives him the courage to risk getting close to Adrian. Rocky also gives Adrian a chance to see herself differently. He was told when he was young that he was not smart, so he should concentrate on his physical ability; she was told she was not pretty, and should concentrate on her mental ability. Each of them sees in the other what no one else did. He sees how pretty she is; she sees how bright he is; each sees the other as lovable, as no one has before. This, as much as anything, is what allows both of them to bloom.

Rocky is realistic about his goal. He does not need to win. He just needs to acquit himself with dignity, to show that he is in the same league as the champion. In order to achieve that goal, he will risk giving everything he has, risk even the small pride of an unbroken nose. He develops enough self-respect to risk public disgrace. This is a big issue for teenagers—adolescence has been characterized as the years in which everything centers around the prayer, "God, don't let me be embarrassed today." Rocky begins as someone afraid to give his best in case it is not good enough, and becomes someone who suspects that his best is enough to achieve his goals, and is willing to test himself to find out.

It is worth taking a look at Creed as well. Like the hare in the Aesop fable, he underestimates his opponent. He is so sure of himself, and so busy working on the business side of the fight, that he comes to the fight unprepared.

It is especially meaningful that the action behind the scenes paralleled that in the movie. Stallone, a small-time actor, was offered a great deal of money for this script, which he wrote. But he insisted instead on selling it for a negligible sum, provided that he play the lead. The entire movie was made for less than $1 million. Stallone beat even longer odds than Rocky did when the movie went on to win the Oscar as Best Picture. Stallone also became only the third person in history (after Charlie Chaplin and Orson Welles) to be nominated for both Best Actor and Best Screenplay.

PROFANITY: Mild.

NUDITY/SEXUAL REFERENCES: Rocky and Adrian have (off-screen) sex and move in together; Adrian's involvement with Rocky infuriates her brother Paulie.

ALCOHOL/DRUG ABUSE: Paulie comes home drunk.

VIOLENCE/SCARINESS: Paulie becomes violent and trashes a room with a baseball bat; brutal boxing match.

TOLERANCE/DIVERSITY ISSUES: Apollo and his promoters want to pick a white unknown fighter for marketing reasons.

✳ **QUESTIONS FOR KIDS:**
  • Why did Mickey want to throw Rocky out of the gym?
  • Why didn't Rocky have higher aspirations, until after he got the offer from Apollo?
  • How is Apollo like the hare in the fable about the tortoise and the hare?
  • Why is it so hard for Rocky and Adrian to get to know one another?

✳ **CONNECTIONS:** There are four sequels, all increasingly garish and cartoonish. They are barely more than remakes, and are only for die-hard fans.

✳ THE GLASS MENAGERIE

1987, 134 min, PG, 12 and up
Dir: Paul Newman. Joanne Woodward, Karen Allen, John Malkovich

Tennessee Williams's "dream play" based on his own family is about a fragile girl and her mother, both trapped by their dreams. Amanda (Joanne Woodward) is determined that her shy and crippled daughter, Laura (Karen Allen), can will herself into a good job and a romance, but Laura prefers to stay home and tend to her collection of glass animals, especially her prized unicorn. When her brother brings a colleague home for dinner, it turns out to be the man Laura has secretly loved since high school. The women have the chance to accept reality, but choose not to.

✳ **CONNECTIONS:** This play was also filmed in 1950, with Gertrude Lawrence and Jane Wyman, and was produced for television in 1973, with Katharine Hepburn and Joanna Miles.

✳ HARVEY

1950, 104 min, NR, b&w, 12 and up
Dir: Henry Koster. Jimmy Stewart, Josephine Hull

Jimmy Stewart plays the gentle, genial, and generous Elwood P. Dowd, a modest but very friendly man who horrifies his social-climbing sister because he insists that his best friend is an invisible six-foot-high rabbit with magical powers named Harvey. She sends him to a mental hospital, where the doctor decides that he'd like to have a Harvey, too. As with *King of Hearts,* this is a movie where the crazy person is saner than the sane people. Elwood explains his view of life: "My mother always used to say to me, 'Elwood,'—she always called me Elwood, by the way—'Elwood, in this life you must be oh, so smart or oh, so pleasant.' For years I was smart. I recommend pleasant."

✳ **CONNECTIONS:** Elwood's sister is played by Josephine Hull, who also appears in *Arsenic and Old Lace.*

✳ THE PIRATE

1948, 102 min, NR, b&w, 10 and up
Dir: Vincente Minnelli. Judy Garland, Gene Kelly, Walter Slezak, the Nicholas
Brothers

Manuela (Judy Garland) dreams of falling in love with a dashing pirate,
so circus performer Serafin (Gene Kelly) pretends to be the pirate to win
her heart. When it appears that Serafin will be sentenced to death, he must
find a way to make the real pirate confess, and Manuela finds that he is
not what she dreamed of after all. This musical (with songs by Cole Porter)
was too satiric to be successful when it was first released, but now it has a
strong following. Everyone agrees that "Be a Clown" is one of the all-time
great musical numbers. It is also a chance to get a rare glimpse of the
dazzling Nicholas Brothers, the most astonishingly energetic dancers ever
filmed.

SEE ALSO:

Chariots of Fire Two very different athletes bring their dreams of
running to the Olympics.

The Music Man Professor Harold Hill, a con man, brings dreams
of music to a small Iowa town and the dream of love to a local librarian.

The NeverEnding Story A young boy learns about the power
of his imagination.

The Rainmaker Starbuck, a con man, brings dreams to an insecure
woman and a parched community.

MONEY

"Money will be slave or master."
—HORACE

Every possible kind of attitude toward money is reflected in the movies. We see adventure movies where people risk their lives for treasure. We see mystery and suspense movies in which people are willing to cheat, steal, and even murder for money. We see dramas in which people forego love or family for money or are about to do so when they learn their lesson. In dramas and in comedies we see people tempted by money to do things they would never have thought possible, losing sight of every value and every shred of self-respect. And we see people learning that having money to spend is less important than giving to the community and having the respect of those you care about.

Parents are often reluctant to talk about money with children, either because they want to protect them from family worries about money, because they do not want children to become overly mercenary or status-conscious, or because they think children do not care about it. But they do. Thanks to the latency period, most children are not interested or willing to talk about sexual values until they are nearing adolescence (if then). But they begin to think about money when they are very young and by age four or five are usually aware of "we can't afford it" as a reason for not getting something they want, or "it was a terrific bargain" as something to be proud of.

The family in *I Remember Mama* sits down together once a week to allocate the family resources, illustrating one method of involving the family in discussions of money and priorities. Other families may want to use movies like these to initiate more general discussions of how to develop a healthy understanding of and attitude toward money as well as a starting point for a discussion of things that are more valuable than money.

Brewster's Millions

1945, 79 min, NR, b&w, 8 and up
Dir: Allan Dwan. Dennis O'Keefe, June Havoc

✳ **PLOT:** This is a modern fairy tale about a man who has to spend a fortune so that he can inherit an even larger one. Monty Brewster (Dennis O'Keefe) is a GI just home from serving in WWII. He gets the news that he will inherit $8 million from his late uncle, *if* he can spend $1 million in sixty days. The theory is that this will make him sick of spending money, and thus fit for taking over the rest of the fortune. The catch is that he cannot tell anyone what he is doing, and at the end of the sixty days he must be left with nothing at all. Also, no more than 5 percent can go to charity, and he cannot give it away. While his friends and fiancée worry that he has lost his mind, he tries desperately to lose it all in the stock market, at the races, and in a range of other investments, but everything goes wrong, and he even ends up making another $25,000 in a radio contest. When he does his best to get mugged, he ends up helping capture the mugger and being given a $100 reward. Ultimately, and just in the nick of time, Brewster spends the money, tells his friends and fiancée the truth, inherits the fortune, and lives happily ever after.

✳ **DISCUSSION:** This slight comedy can provide a starting place for a discussion about money. This is one of seven different film versions of the story, with increasing amounts at stake to reflect inflation—the latest starring Richard Pryor as a baseball player in line to inherit $30 million dollars. Its enduring appeal stems from its reversal of the common problem of not having enough money to spend. Brewster has too much. Children will enjoy talking about what they would do with the money and whether they think they would have the problems that Brewster did.

PROFANITY: None.

NUDITY/SEXUAL REFERENCES: None.

ALCOHOL/DRUG ABUSE: None.

VIOLENCE/SCARINESS: None.

TOLERANCE/DIVERSITY ISSUES: Eddie "Rochester" Anderson plays Brewster's friend. He is treated with a great deal of affection, but not equality; he is called "Jackson," but calls Brewster "Mr. Brewster," for example. Similarly, when everyone is getting jobs at his new company, Brewster's fiancée is, naturally, made a secretary.

✳ **QUESTIONS FOR KIDS:**
• What would you do if you had to spend $1 million in sixty days?
• What are the problems that Brewster had?
• Did people like Brewster for himself or for the money he had to spend? How could you tell?

✳ **CONNECTIONS:** June Havoc is the real-life "Baby June," sister of Gypsy Rose Lee, whose early years in show business are the subject of *Gypsy*. She does quite a dance number in this movie—with a glass on her head! She appears in a more serious role in *Gentleman's Agreement*.

A very funny film about another mischievous bequest is *Laughter in Paradise*. Four people will inherit a relative's fortune only if they perform tasks completely contrary to their personalities: The timid man must rob a bank; the snob must get and keep a menial job; and the ladies' man must marry the first woman he talks to. The more recent film *Greedy* (rated PG-13) stars Kirk Douglas as a wealthy man whose venal relatives are after his money, and Michael J. Fox as his favorite nephew. It is uneven at best, but has some very funny moments.

*The Treasure of the Sierra Madre

1948, 126 min, NR, b&w, 12 and up
Dir: John Huston. Humphrey Bogart, Walter Huston, Tim Holt

✳ **PLOT:** Fred C. Dobbs (Humphrey Bogart) lives by panhandling in Tampico, Mexico. He accepts a job for good pay, but the boss cheats him out of his salary. When he and Curtin (Tim Holt), a coworker, find the boss again, he tries to buy them off with drinks and promises of more work, but they beat him up until they get their money. That night, Howard (Walter Huston), a grizzled prospector, tells them of the thrill and the danger of gold. They resolve to use their cash to get the equipment they need to go prospecting, ignoring Howard's warnings about what gold does to men. They are short of money for equipment until Dobbs wins the lottery and contributes the prize money.

It is hard going. Just as Curtin and Dobbs say they will give up, Howard tells them he has found gold. They build a mine so they can refine it on the site. As they start to see the gold, they become suspicious and selfish, insisting that it be meticulously divided each night. As Howard warned, they worry about hiding it from each other, and become suspicious and greedy.

In town to get supplies, Curtin meets a man who follows him to the site. They try to get him to leave, but he insists on staying, telling them that they can either kill him, run him off, or take him in as a partner from that day forward, keeping for themselves everything they have collected so far. He warns that if they decide to kill him, the one who does it will be in the power of the other two forever. They decide to kill him, anyway. Before they can, the bandits arrive. The stranger, whose name is Cody, is killed helping to fight them off. Dobbs, Curtin, and Howard read a letter from Cody's wife, saying that she hopes he comes home soon, and that finding gold is not important to her.

On their way back with the gold, they are stopped by local Indians, who need help with a boy rescued from drowning who hasn't regained consciousness. Howard goes with them and when he saves the boy, they insist on bringing him to their village to reward him. He goes with them, trusting the others with his share of the gold. That night, Dobbs tells Curtin they should split his share. When Curtin refuses, Dobbs says he will kill Curtin and take it all. They cannot go to sleep because they know whoever falls asleep first will be killed by the other. Dobbs accuses Curtin of planning to take it all, and he shoots him. He starts to unravel, unable to rest, unable to decide whether to bury the body or leave it for the buzzards. He goes to move it, and it is gone. Curtin has managed to get to Howard, who treats his wounds. Dobbs is killed by the bandits, who take the hides he was carrying for camouflage and throw the sacks away, thinking they are worthless.

The bandits are captured and executed by the police as Howard and Curtin come to town. They find the empty bags as a windstorm blows the gold dust back to the mountains. It hurts less than they expected; Howard will go back to the Indians, who revere him as a healer, and Curtin will seek out Cody's wife, who knows what treasure really is.

✳ **DISCUSSION:** This movie is almost an autopsy of greed. At the beginning, Dobbs is a feckless but fundamentally decent character. When he wins in a lottery the money they need for prospecting, he contributes it freely to the venture, refusing his right to a larger share of the proceeds because he contributed more capital. He insists they are all a team. He thinks about whether all men can be corrupted by gold as Howard has said, but decides that "it depends on the man." Yet even his awareness of the risk and his resolve not to let it happen are not able to save him from irrationality, paranoia, and abandonment of all moral principles.

Like the end of another Huston-Bogart movie, *The Maltese Falcon,* at the end the characters find that the treasure is only "the stuff that dreams are made of." And like the end of *The Wizard of Oz,* the (remaining) characters find that what they were seeking was within them all along. Howard will find the fame he was seeking among the Indians, and Curtin hopes to find his orchard with Cody's wife.

This movie includes a textbook example of projection, well worth pointing out to kids who watch it. Dobbs insists that it is Curtin who wants to murder him and take all the gold, when he is really the one fantasizing about murder.

PROFANITY: None.

NUDITY/SEXUAL REFERENCES: None.

ALCOHOL/DRUG ABUSE: Dobbs and Curtin get drunk waiting for the boss to come pay them.

VIOLENCE/SCARINESS: Fistfights; shooting.

TOLERANCE/DIVERSITY ISSUES: A wide range of Mexican and American characters; Howard shows respect for the customs of the Indians.

✳ **QUESTIONS FOR KIDS:**
- Why does Dobbs tell the man who gave him handouts that he never looked at his face, only at his hands and the money?
- What makes Dobbs change? What is the evidence of his changes?
- Why did gold become so important to him, when he had lived without money for so long?
- Which of Cody's options would you have accepted if you were one of the three men? Why?
- What do you think of the ending? How is it different from most adventure stories?

✳ **CONNECTIONS:** Director-screenwriter John Huston appears in the early part of the film as the American who gives Dobbs a handout. The director's father, distinguished matinee idol Walter Huston, was persuaded (by force, according to rumor) to play the part of Howard without his dentures. His performance earned him an Oscar for Best Supporting Actor. The boy who sells Dobbs the lottery ticket is Robert Blake, who grew up to star in *In Cold Blood* and television's *Baretta*.

Almost as interesting as the story of the movie is the story of the author of the original book, the mysterious B. Traven, who was intensely private. Huston suspected that Traven's "representative," who negotiated the rights and consulted on the film, was Traven himself. A biography, *The Secret of the Sierra Madre: the Man Who Was B. Traven,* by Will Wyatt, was published in 1980.

✳ CAN'T BUY ME LOVE
1987, 94 min, PG-13, high schoolers
Dir: Steve Rash. Patrick Dempsey, Amanda Peterson

Ronald Miller (Patrick Dempsey), a nerdy boy, pays the most popular girl in school $1,000 to pretend to be his girlfriend for a month so that he will become popular, too. She agrees, only because she is desperate for money, but finds herself liking Ronald—until the popularity goes to his head. The movie is only fair, but does have a perceptive treatment of high school social strata. Once Ronald is accepted by a popular girl, he is immediately accepted by everyone, and everything he does is automatically considered cool. NOTE: Some strong language and teen drinking, and some particularly troublesome bimbo behavior by some of the girls.

✳ THE EMPEROR'S NEW CLOTHES
Any of the versions of this classic story will help kids learn a lesson from the foolish emperor who thinks that fancy clothes are more important than kindness and generosity. The best are the videos from Faerie Tale Theatre (starring Alan Arkin and Dick Shawn) and Rabbit Ears.

❊ THE MAN THAT CORRUPTED HADLEYBURG

1980, 40 min, NR, 12 and up
Dir: Ralph Rosenblum. Robert Preston, Fred Gwynne

In this video made for the "American Short Story Collection," based on a satire by Mark Twain, a stranger (Robert Preston) comes to a town famous for the honesty of its citizens and proves that they are all greedy hypocrites. The stranger has a bag of money for whomever in the town once helped a poor man with twenty dollars and some good advice. All that is necessary is for the person to identify himself by providing that advice in a sealed envelope to the town's former clergyman. It turns out that the reward is a clever trap prepared by a man still bitter over his treatment in Hadleyburg years before. When he makes it possible for each of the town's leading citizens, the "Nineteeners," to claim credit for the good deed, each conspires to get the money and keep it away from all the others, until a final public confrontation shows each of them to be completely corruptible.

❊ POOR LITTLE RICH GIRL

1936, 72 min, NR, b&w, 4 and up
Dir: Irving Cummings. Shirley Temple, Alice Faye, Jack Haley

One of Shirley Temple's best movies is this story of a reverse Cinderella who finds happiness when she leaves her wealthy father and meets up with a poor but jolly family and a pair of vaudevillians. Shirley Temple plays Barbara Barry, the daughter of a wealthy widower, owner of a soap company. She is a curious and imaginative child, but very lonely due to her isolated upbringing. Waited on and fussed over, she is sent to bed after just one sneeze. Her father arranges to send her away to school, but the nanny is injured taking her there, and Barbara decides to take the opportunity to explore the world and meet people. Two vaudevillians (Jack Haley and Alice Faye) take her in and, once she joins their act, they get a job performing on the radio. Barbara does not realize that their sponsor is her father's biggest rival in the soap business, Simon Peck, a cranky old man who is (of course) charmed by the little girl with the ringlets. Once her father finds her again, she paves the way for a merger of the two soap companies and her father's marriage to Peck's Secretary. NOTE: A black porter is respectfully but stereotypically portrayed; Barbara's father uses the expression "white of you."

❊ **CONNECTIONS:** The secretary is played by Gloria Stuart, who was nominated for an Oscar in 1998 as Rose in *Titanic*. Jack Haley also appears as the Tin Woodsman in **The Wizard of Oz**.

❊ WHAT A WAY TO GO!

1964, 111 min, NR, 8 and up
Dir: J. Lee Thompson. Shirley MacLaine, Paul Newman, Dean Martin, Gene Kelly, Dick Van Dyke, Robert Mitchum

This wild black comedy stars Shirley MacLaine as a simple young woman who wants nothing more in life than a quiet home with the man she loves. Unfortunately, she marries a series of husbands (Dick Van Dyke, Paul Newman, Gene Kelly, Robert Mitchum) who make fortune after fortune and then die. Each marriage parodies a different style of movie, from artsy European to splashy big-budget musical. Throughout the movie, like Dorothy in Oz, she keeps trying to go "home." She finally finds happiness with a husband who makes sure that she will never be troubled with money again. NOTE: Some kids will not be comfortable with black comedy, and may find the constant deaths of the husbands upsetting, but others will find it funny and will appreciate the message.

SEE ALSO:

A Christmas Carol A man who has sacrificed love and family to make money learns that true riches come from giving to others.

It's a Mad Mad Mad Mad World The prospect of a hidden treasure of $250,000 inspires a variety of motorists to extraordinary (and hilarious) levels of greed and selfishness.

King Midas and the Golden Touch This is the classic fairy tale about the king who loves gold so much that he wishes everything he touches would turn to gold, and finds that when the wish is granted, the results are not what he expected.

Mr. Deeds Goes to Town A man who inherits a fortune finds that he is most fulfilled when he gives it away to help others.

Split Infinity A young girl who wants to be rich goes back in time to meet her wealthy grandfather as a young man, and together they find out that money is not as important as they'd thought.

SOLVING PROBLEMS

Adversity introduces a man to himself.
—ANONYMOUS

Most films present their protagonists with some kind of challenge, and most often it comes in the form of a change or crisis. Watching the characters respond can teach kids (and their parents) a great deal not just about the way people solve problems, but about the ways that people adapt to new and unexpected events and the kind of flexibility, confidence, and creativity that are required. In movies, we see characters coping with everyday changes, like going to a new school, changing technology, and changing times, to the most overwhelming, like the loss of a family member or the devastation of war and genocide. Even good news creates changes that must be assimilated. Fantasy and science fiction movies show us characters confronting astonishing and even bizarre circumstances. Yet these characters employ the same skills as those facing more familiar challenges. Make sure that kids see the way that adapting successfully changes the way the characters feel about themselves.

Help kids notice the methods the characters use to adapt. Some give up and accept whatever happens. Some are too inflexible to adapt to change. Some find themselves hemmed in by the choices they have made, and are unable to change, even though they want to. Some survive by trying different ways of achieving a sense of control over some concrete aspect of the situation, even a very small one. Some transfer the skills they had to the tasks before them. Some whose skills are not transferable look for another place where their skills are needed. Some adapt by using humor or by dreaming of ways to make things better or by becoming close to others in the same situation. Some ask for help through prayer, some through reading or learning a new skill or seeking help from a trusted adviser. Some work creatively and doggedly to solve the problem at hand. Others find one part of the problem that they can solve. Sometimes, they stay and fight. Sometimes, they leave and start a new life somewhere else. In every case, whether explicitly or intuitively, the characters recognize the change and its consequences and determine how they will respond. The ones who triumph are those who approach challenges with spirit, integrity, self-respect, and determination.

❋Apollo 13
1995, 135 min, PG, 8 and up
Dir: Ron Howard. Tom Hanks, Gary Sinise, Ed Harris, Kevin Bacon, Bill Paxton

❋ **PLOT:** This movie should be called "Smart and Smarter." In addition to the thrilling story, masterful performances, and impeccable technical authenticity, it is a heartening story of the triumph of smart guys with slide rules, a relief in this era of movies about characters who triumph by being dumb. Two-time Oscar-winner Tom Hanks plays real-life astronaut-hero Jim Lovell in this true story of the mission to the moon that almost left three astronauts stranded in space when an oxygen tank exploded. Even though we know it turned out all right, even though the technical material is dense and the action is confined to a space smaller than an elevator, the tension is breathtaking as the astronauts and the mission control team in Houston try to think their way back home. Everything from duct tape to the cover of the flight manual to one of the astronaut's socks is used in this pre-MacGyver story, where mission control asks simply, "What's good on that ship?" and builds from there.

❋ **DISCUSSION:** Because of the technical material and intensity of the story, it is a good idea to prepare younger kids beforehand by telling them what the movie is about; you also may want to reassure them, since it is a true story, that the astronauts did come home all right.

Talk to older kids about the way that Mission Control solves the problems happening thousands of miles away by recreating the conditions inside the spaceship. Point out how the adults handle the strain, sometimes losing their tempers or blaming one another (or trying to escape blame), but mostly working very well together. Lovell and Ken Mattingly (Gary Sinise) were presented with a very tough problem when exposure to the measles led Mission Control to pull Mattingly from the mission. Lovell tries to insist that Mattingly go along, but ultimately realizes that the good of the mission has to override his feelings of loyalty. Kids may have their own ideas about how this should have been handled.

The legendary "Failure is not an option," said by Gene Kranz, head of Mission Control, when most people were certain the astronauts would never make it back, is worth discussing. So are the changes since you were your children's age: Note that everyone in Mission Control is a white male (and they all smoke all the time), and that they are amazed that a computer is small enough to fit into one room. And you may have to explain why adults

who watch the movie laugh when the engineers take out their slide rules—
for kids today, they are more exotic than an abacus.

PROFANITY: A couple of mild expletives.

NUDITY/SEXUAL REFERENCES: One or two oblique references, including
one to "the clap."

ALCOHOL/DRUG ABUSE: Drinking at a party; smoking.

VIOLENCE/SCARINESS: Very tense; characters in peril.

TOLERANCE/DIVERSITY ISSUES: All of the professionals are white males.

✻ **QUESTIONS FOR KIDS:**
- What does it mean to say that "Failure is not an option"?
- Who in the movie is more worried about escaping blame than solving
  the problem?
- Describe Lovell, Mattingly, Haize, Kranz, and Swigert. What is each
  one's greatest strength?

✻ **CONNECTIONS:** Jim Lovell's book about this expedition, originally entitled *Lost Moon,* was reissued as *Apollo 13* following the release of this film.
For All Mankind is a good documentary about the Apollo expeditions, including this one. There is also a video documentary about this mission. Director
Howard (the child star of *The Music Man*) always puts his brother Clint in
his movies. Here, he plays one of the Mission Control technicians. In this
film, Howard also cast his mother, who is outstanding as Mrs. Lovell, mother
of the astronaut.

✻The Best Years of Our Lives
1946, 172 min, NR, b&w, 12 and up
*Dir: William Wyler. Fredric March, Dana Andrews, Myrna Loy, Harold Russell,
Teresa Wright*

✻ **PLOT:** Three men are returning home from service during WWII. Fred
Derry (Dana Andrews), a bombardier; Al Stephenson (Fredric March), a
middle-aged foot soldier; and Homer Parrish (Harold Russell), a sailor who
has lost both hands, fly back to their hometown of Boone City, excited, but
a little apprehensive about beginning their postwar lives. Fred is returning
to a beautiful wife, Marie (Virginia Mayo), whom he barely knows. Al is
coming back to his wife, Milly (Myrna Loy), and their two children, who
have grown up while he was gone. And Homer is coming back to face his
family and his fiancée, Wilma (Cathy O'Donnell), with hooks replacing
his hands.

Each of them has a lot of adjusting to do. Al is awkward with his wife
at first, and insists that they go out to a bar owned by Homer's Uncle Butch
(Hoagy Carmichael), where they meet Fred, who has not been able to find

his wife and Homer. Al and Fred get very drunk, and Al and Milly take Fred home with them. Al's daughter, Peggy (Teresa Wright), comforts Fred when he has a nightmare about the war, and the next morning makes breakfast for him and drops him off at his apartment. After everyone leaves the Stephensons' apartment, Al and Milly reconnect to their feelings for one another. Fred finally finds Marie, who is delighted to have him home. But Homer barely speaks to Wilma.

Al returns to his job at the bank, but when he approves loans to ex-servicemen who don't meet the bank's requirements for collateral, his boss is concerned. At a banquet, Al gets drunk and explains movingly that he learned in the war that you have to trust people, and give them a chance, and that the old rules must be changed.

Homer is still uncommunicative and withdrawn until Wilma comes to his house late one night to talk to him. He is finally able to show her the extent of his injuries, and is relieved that it makes no difference to her. They set a date for the wedding.

Fred, who was a soda jerk before the war, says that is the one job he will never do again. But he finds himself back serving ice cream when he can't find anything else, until he punches a customer who insults Homer and the other ex-servicemen. Marie, who cares about nothing but fun and money, is quickly bored with him, and starts seeing other men.

Fred falls in love with Peggy, but when Al asks him not to see Peggy anymore, he decides to leave town. At the airport, he climbs into the cockpit of one of the old bomber planes, destined to be turned into scrap metal. He meets a man who is using the metal for building and asks for a job, explaining that he knows nothing about it, but knows that he knows how to learn. He is hired.

Fred is Homer's best man. At the wedding, Fred sees Peggy, and the words of the wedding service seem to bring them together.

✳ **DISCUSSION:** Although today's families will have a hard time relating to the specifics of the postwar era, the theme of adaptation to changing circumstances and the need for genuine closeness is a timeless one. The most important scene in the movie is the one in which Fred realizes that he can use the same skills he used in the war—especially his ability to learn—to bring him what he is looking for. Fred and Homer both have a hard time believing that they deserve love, because each feels helpless and inadequate. Homer is afraid to risk rejection by Wilma, so he brusquely ignores her. Fred plans to leave town and never see Peggy again. But both ultimately take the risk and find the love they hoped for.

Al is also brusque and awkward with Milly at first, but by their first morning together he is ready to return to the relationship they had. Milly's description of marriage to Peggy is particularly important in this context, making it clear that "living happily ever after" requires commitment, courage, and work.

PROFANITY: None.

NUDITY/SEXUAL REFERENCES: Subtle references (by today's standards) to Marie's infidelity.

ALCOHOL/DRUG ABUSE: Al and Fred get drunk; Milly makes Al promise not to drink so much and checks what he is drinking at the wedding to make sure he is keeping his promise.

VIOLENCE SCARINESS: Scuffle.

TOLERANCE/DIVERSITY ISSUES: Tolerance for those with disabilities is a theme of the movie, though it's dated by today's standards, as there is no suggestion that Homer can or should get a job.

✳ **QUESTIONS FOR KIDS**
  • What were the challenges faced by each of the servicemen in adjusting to life after the war?
  • Would it have been easier for Homer if his family and Wilma had talked to him about his injuries when he first came home?
  • Why was it easier for Homer to talk to Fred and Al about his injuries than it was to talk to his family?
  • Why was Al so awkward with Milly at first?
  • What did Al mean when he talked about collateral at the banquet?
  • Why was it important for Fred to realize that he knew how to learn? How did that change the way he thought about himself?

✳ **CONNECTIONS:** Harold Russell, who lost his hands in a grenade accident in training, received both a special Oscar and the Oscar for Best Supporting Actor for his performance as Homer. He did not make another movie until *Inside Moves,* in 1980. He also served as the Chairman of President Lyndon Johnson's Committee on Hiring the Handicapped. The movie also won Oscars for Best Picture, Actor, Director, Musical Score, and Writer. Butch is played by Hoagy Charmichael, composer of "Stardust." A movie with similar themes is *'Til the End of Time,* with Robert Mitchum and Guy Madison.

✳ **Gone With the Wind**
1939, 222 min, NR, 10 and up
Dir: Victor Fleming. Vivien Leigh, Clark Gable, Leslie Howard, Olivia de Havilland, Hattie MacDaniel

✳ **PLOT:** Scarlett O'Hara (Vivien Leigh) is the beautiful and headstrong daughter of of the owner of a Southern plantation called Tara. She has "the smallest waist in three counties" and dozens of beaux clamoring for her attention. But the one she believes she loves is gentle Ashley Wilkes (Leslie Howard). At a party, just as the Civil War is beginning, she finds out that he is going to marry his cousin Melanie (Olivia de Havilland). Her fury at this news is witnessed by Rhett Butler (Clark Gable), a dashing, but cynical man who refuses to participate in hypocrisy and speaks very directly, telling Scarlett that she is "no lady" and telling the men at the party that the South cannot win a war.

Out of pique, Scarlett impulsively agrees to marry Melanie's brother Charles (her sister's beau), who dies just after he enlists. This leaves Scarlett a widow, encumbered to the point of suffocation by the mourning rituals of the era, which restrict her to elaborate black clothes and very limited social activities. She goes to visit Melanie, now married to Ashley, in Atlanta, and meets Rhett again, now a war profiteer, who shocks the community by pledging money for the war effort if she will dance with him. She is delighted to have an excuse to dance. His directness makes her uncomfortable, but also intrigues her, because she has been used to men who are both predictable and easy to control. Melanie has a baby just as Sherman comes through with his soldiers. Scarlett stays with her, then gets Rhett (staying at a bordello) to take them all back to Tara. She tells Rhett he was right not to join the Confederate army, but he has decided that now is the time to join, and leaves her at Tara.

Her mother is dead, her father has had a breakdown, and her sisters are ill. They have no food, and all but two of the slaves have left. Scarlett takes charge, swearing she will never be hungry again. When a Union deserter tries to steal her mother's jewelry, she shoots him, and Melanie helps her bury the body.

The war ends. About to lose Tara, she tries to get the money from Rhett, and when he refuses, she marries Frank Kennedy (her other sister's fiancé), a merchant, to get the money. Frank is killed in a KKK-style raid, and she marries Rhett. But she thinks that she still wants Ashley, and by the time she realizes that it is Rhett she loves, he leaves her, with the most famous exit line in the history of the movies. After he is gone, she reminds herself that she will go on and work for what she wants, that "Tomorrow is another day."

✳ **DISCUSSION:** Considered by many the definitive example of the Hollywood movie, this is by any standard one of the greatest films of all time. It could be—and should be—viewed from a dozen different perspectives, but it is, above all, a story about adapting to the most challenging circumstances possible. Interestingly, our heroine is not especially brave or smart or considerate. On the contrary, she is completely selfish. And she has very little interest or understanding of the world around her or of her own feelings. Yet the movie shows us that she has qualities like stubbornness and focus that enable her to survive, while those like Melanie and Ashley (who are thoughtful and honorable) do not. In the first scene, her father tells her that what matters most is Tara, and that becomes her symbol of survival. At the end of the movie, with her emotional life devastated, her first thought is to return there to start over again.

In the first scenes of the movie, we get a glimpse of the South before the Civil War. The lives of the landowners are similar to those of British landed gentry, with even more elaborate standards of gentility, chivalry, elegance, and refinement. Listen to Mammy (Hattie MacDaniel) before the barbecue party, reminding Scarlett of the conventions of the era, from how much it is appropriate for ladies to eat in front of gentlemen to how much skin it is appropriate to expose in the afternoon. All that is shattered when the war begins, and shattered again when the illusions about the war as an exercise in chivalry and sportsmanship are relentlessly swept away by the realities of combat with a vastly more powerful adversary. Every belief and assumption the Southerners had about themselves and their future is challenged.

Notice how much of what goes on between Scarlett and others is about power. She and Ashley have little in common; indeed, the qualities she thinks she admires in him are the ones that make her feel contempt for Melanie. Scarlett's primary interest in Ashley seems to be in making sure she can enslave him as she has the Tarleton twins and every other man she knows. In a scene that is even more controversial today than it was when it was filmed, Rhett's willingness to overpower her sexually increases her respect for and interest in him.

Scarlett and Rhett are both free from considerations of honor and duty and therefore able to think in strictly pragmatic terms about survival. The difference is that Rhett is always honest with himself and others about what is going on, while Scarlett insists on keeping her illusions about Ashley, until it is too late.

> PROFANITY: One "damn" (which was almost excised as too shocking).
>
> NUDITY/SEXUAL REFERENCES: Oblique portrayal of forced sex, character who runs a brothel.
>
> ALCOHOL/DRUG ABUSE: Drinking.
>
> VIOLENCE/SCARINESS: War scenes, including wounded soliders and the burning of Atlanta; Scarlett shoots the Union deserter; Scarlett falls down the stairs and has a miscarriage, accidental death of child and profound grief of parent.
>
> TOLERANCE/DIVERSITY ISSUES: The issue of slavery is raised in subtext. Period portrayals reflect the racial stereotypes of both the Civil War–era South and the 1930s, when the movie was made. While Mammy is a strong and loyal character, she is childishly won over with a red petticoat, and Prissy is fluttery and incompetent.

✳ **QUESTIONS FOR KIDS:**
- Why were the Southerners so wrong about their ability to win a war with the North?
- Why does Scarlett marry Charles? Why does she marry Frank? Why does she marry Rhett?
- Why is Tara so important to Scarlett?
- Why does Rhett like Scarlett? Why do his feelings about her change?
- What do you think will happen after Scarlett goes back to Tara?

✳ **CONNECTIONS:** This film, the longtime box office champion, won eight Oscars, including Best Picture, Best Actress, Best Director, Best Screenplay, and Best Supporting Actress (Hattie McDaniel, who beat Olivia de Havilland to become the first black performer to win an Oscar). Amazingly, director Victor Fleming, the fifth director assigned to the movie, directed *The Wizard of Oz* the same year. With five directors and at least twelve screenwriters, the credit for "authorship" of the movie must go to producer David O. Selznick, whose vision for the film was spelled out meticulously in long memoranda, published in *Memo from David O. Selznick*. A made-for-television movie, *The Scarlett O'Hara War*, is based on the furious efforts in Hollywood by all of the actresses (including Bette Davis, Paulette Goddard, Joan Crawford, and Tallulah Bankhead) who wanted this juiciest of parts. *Scarlett,* a television miniseries, continues the story, but with not even a fraction of the quality of the original. Read the original book by Margaret Mitchell instead.

The Great Escape
1963, 168 min, NR, 8 and up
Dir: John Sturges. Steve McQueen, James Garner, Richard Attenborough, James Coburn, Donald Pleasence, David McCallum

❋ **PLOT:** Toward the end of WWII, the Germans built a special high-security prison camp for Allied prisoners with a record of escape attempts. This is the true story of the extraordinary courage and ingenuity of the men imprisoned there, and of their plans for the greatest escape ever.

As the British ranking officer explains, when the camp commandant urges him to relax and "sit out the war as comfortably as possible," his duty is to escape, or, if escape is impossible, to force the enemy to use as many resources as possible to contain them.

Each man contributes his expertise. There are "tunnel kings" to dig the three tunnels, a "forger king" (Donald Pleasence) to forge the papers the soldiers will need when they escape, a "scrounger" (James Garner) to beg, borrow, steal, or obtain through blackmail the materials they need, and others who work as tailors and manufacturers. An American who is something of a loner, Hilts (Steve McQueen) becomes the "cooler king" for his long stints in solitary confinement, as a result of his independent escape attempts. When "Big X" (Richard Attenborough), the British officer who supervises the escape, asks Hilts to go through the tunnel to get information about the area surrounding the camp, and then allow himself to be recaptured so he can let them know what he has found, he refuses. But when his friend is killed trying to escape, his spirit broken by the camp, Hilts changes his mind.

Seventy-five of the prisoners are able to escape before the tunnel is discovered. The Germans track almost all of them down, and fifty are killed, including Big X. It is to "the fifty" that the film is dedicated.

✳ **DISCUSSION:** As in *Stalag 17* and many other films about prison camp, the prisoners in this story must adapt to the direst of circumstances, and they choose differing approaches. Hilts adapts by working on his own, or with one partner, while others work on a massive group escape. Ives and Danny begin to unravel under the stress, not so much a "choice" as an involuntary response. Unlike other prison camp movies, this one does not dwell on disputes between prisoners or on the deprivations of the prison camp, which seems almost comfortable. It is about the professionalism, courage, resourcefulness, teamwork, and loyalty of every one of the prisoners.

As in a traditional "heist" film, the story focuses on defining a problem and then solving it. They examine the restrictions imposed by their conditions, change the ones they can, and adapt to the ones they cannot. They must also adapt quickly and calmly when the plan does not go as they expected.

The story gives us an exceptional example of teamwork and loyalty. Note the way that the prisoners protect each other. When Danny (Charles Bronson) cannot take it anymore and wants to escape on his own, his friend talks him out of it. When the Forger King goes blind, Big X wants to leave him behind, for his own protection. But the Scrounger promises to take care of him.

Point out to kids what factors do—and do not—go into the prisoners' calculations and strategy. Big X is cautioned not to allow his personal wish for revenge determine their strategy. But pride (in the sense of morale) is permitted to be considered. When asked, "Have you thought of what it might cost?" he answers, "I've thought of the humiliation if we just tamely submit—knuckle under and crawl." They also consider the risk of failure, to the extent they can. At the end, when the Scrounger asks whether the escape was worth the price, the best the British Commander can do is answer truthfully, "It depends on your point of view."

PROFANITY: None.

NUDITY/SEXUAL REFERENCES: None.

ALCOHOL/DRUG ABUSE: Some drinking; smoking.

VIOLENCE/SCARINESS: Very tense moments; characters in peril and many are killed.

TOLERANCE/DIVERSITY ISSUES: People from a variety of backgrounds and countries work together toward a common goal.

✳ **QUESTIONS FOR KIDS:**
- Why are the experts called "kings"?
- What makes Hilts change his mind about getting the information they want?
- Who was right about taking the Forger out through the tunnel, Big X or the Scrounger?
- Given the results of their action in this story, should officers who have been taken prisoner feel duty-bound to try to escape?

✳ **CONNECTIONS:** The screenplay was cowritten by blockbuster novelist James Clavell (*Tai-Pan, Shogun*). His own experiences as a prisoner of war in a Japanese prison camp are the subject of *King Rat*. The outstanding musical score is by Elmer Bernstein (***The Magnificent Seven*** and ***To Kill a Mockingbird***). Sir Richard Attenborough, who played Big X, later became a director of films such as *Gandhi* and ***Shadowlands***. He continues to appear as a performer, and played Dr. Hammond in ***Jurassic Park,*** and Kris Kringle in the 1994 version of *Miracle on 34th Street*.

✳Singin' In the Rain

1952, 102 min, NR, 6 and up
Dir: Gene Kelly and Stanley Donen. Gene Kelly, Debbie Reynolds, Donald O'Connor, Jean Hagan

✳ **PLOT:** Silent movie star Don Lockwood (Gene Kelly) is paired on-screen with Lina Lamont (Jean Hagan), who would like to be paired with him off-screen as well. But Lina's personality is as grating as her squeaky, nasal voice. She is mean, selfish, arrogant, and stupid. Chased by fans following the opening of their latest movie, Don jumps into the car of Kathy Seldon (Debbie Reynolds), who tells him she is a serious actress and not at all interested in the movies. But later, at a party celebrating the new movie, Kathy appears again, jumping out of a cake. Don teases her about her "art," and she throws a pie at him, getting Lina right in the face by mistake. Lina, furious, has Kathy fired.

At the party, the guests are treated to an exhibition of the latest technology, "talking pictures." Everyone present dismisses it as a novelty. But when *The Jazz Singer* becomes a hit, everyone in Hollywood begins to make talkies. Production is halted on the latest Lockwood-Lamont movie, *The Dueling Cavalier,* while the stars are coached in vocal technique (with a delightful song mocking the exercises, "Moses Supposes"). But the movie is a disaster. Test audiences jeer and laugh.

Meanwhile, Don and Kathy have fallen in love. Don, Kathy, and Don's best friend, Cosmo (Donald O'Connor), come up with an idea. They can make it into a musical, *The Dancing Cavalier,* dubbing Kathy's voice for Lina's. Don resists at first, because it is unfair to Kathy. But they persuade him that it will be just this one time, and he goes along.

With Kathy's voice and some musical numbers, the movie is a success. Lina insists that Kathy continue to dub all her movies and, when the audience insists on hearing her sing, Lina forces Kathy to stand backstage so she can perform. But Don, Cosmo, and the beleaguered studio head reveal the secret, and Don introduces Kathy to the audience as the real star of the movie.

✳ **DISCUSSION:** This is often considered the finest musical of all time. Certainly it has it all: classic musical numbers and a witty script, unusually sharp and satiric for a musical comedy, especially one making fun of the industry that produced it. Asked to name the top ten moments in the history of movies, most people would include the title number from this movie, in which Gene Kelly splashes and sings in the rain with what Roger Ebert called "saturated ecstasy." When he swings the umbrella around and around and dances on and off the curb, his "glorious feeling" is contagious. Only in a movie containing that sequence would Donald O'Connor's sensational "Make 'Em Laugh" number be mentioned second. It is a wildly funny pastiche of every possible slapstick gag, done with energy and skill so meticulous that it appears as if it is entirely spontaneous.

Screenwriters Betty Comden and Adoph Green, asked to use some of the classic songs by Arthur Freed (later a producer of most of the great MGM musicals) and Nacio Herb Brown, decided to set the movie in the era in which they first appeared, the early talkies. This gave them a chance to use some of the Hollywood folklore of that era, when careers like John Gilbert's were destroyed overnight as audiences found out that their voices didn't match their faces. One especially funny scene has the technicians trying to find a way to record Lina's dialogue. When they put the microphone on her dress, all you hear is the sound of her pearls as she rubs them. When they put it lower down, you hear her heartbeat. When they put it near her, her voice fades in and out as she tosses her head. Note that the cameras are put inside huge boxes—that is authentic, as the cameras of that era were so loud that they had to be encased to prevent their own whirring from being recorded.

Don and Cosmo are consummate adaptors. As we see in flashback, they have already switched from vaudeville to movies, and then Cosmo from performer to accompanist (to musical director), and Don from stuntman to leading man. Lina resists change and tries to bully her way out of it, but Don, Cosmo, and Kathy all demonstrate resilience and openness to new ideas, and a willingness to be creative in solving problems.

PROFANITY: None.
NUDITY/SEXUAL REFERENCES: None.
ALCOHOL/DRUG ABUSE: None.
VIOLENCE/SCARINESS: None.
TOLERANCE/DIVERSITY ISSUES: None.

✳ **QUESTIONS FOR KIDS:**
- Why does Kathy at first lie about liking the movies?
- Why does Don lie about his background? How is that different from the way that Lina behaves?
- Have there been any new inventions that you have seen that have changed people's jobs a lot?
- What inventions do you use that your parents didn't have when they were children? Your grandparents?

✳ **CONNECTIONS:** The transition from silent movies to talkies was also lampooned in the first play by George S. Kaufman and Moss Hart, *Once in* *a Lifetime.* A silent star who has become deranged is the centerpiece of *Sunset Boulevard*—When told, "You used to be big in pictures," she says, "I'm still big—it's the pictures that got small." She also says, memorably, that in her day stars didn't need to talk: "We had *faces* then!"

❋ **ACTIVITIES:** Children might like to see some of the early silent movies to get an idea of what Hollywood was like in the days depicted in this movie. The films of Charlie Chaplin, Laurel and Hardy, Buster Keaton, and Harold Lloyd are still wonderful, and kids will enjoy learning that a story can be told without words.

❋Stalag 17

1953, 120 min, NR, b&w, 12 and up
Dir: Billy Wilder. William Holden, Otto Preminger, Peter Graves

❋ **PLOT:** As the movie opens, the narrator says that the movies he has seen about WWII are about "flyboys" in leather jackets, and do not reflect his own experience as an American prisoner of war in a German stalag (prison camp). This is that story.

Sefton (William Holden) is a cynical loner who bets (successfully) that his fellow prisoners will fail in their attempt to escape. He manages to scrounge or trade for many small luxuries, including a bar of soap and an egg. When the others show their contempt, he says, "So maybe I trade a little sharper. Does that make me a collaborator?" and sums up his philosophy: "This is everybody for himself, dog eat dog . . . You can be the heroes, the guys with fruit salad on your chest. Me, I'm staying put, and I'm going to make myself as comfortable as I can, and if it takes trading with the enemy to get me some food or a better mattress, that's okay with Sefton."

The other men in his barracks start to suspect him of trading more than cigarettes and silk stockings with the Germans. When Lieutenant Dunbar, a wealthy Bostonian who is in the barracks on his way to the officers' prison camp, is arrested for sabotage, they conclude that Sefton told the Germans that Dunbar was the one who blew up the train filled with ammunition. They beat Sefton severely. He tells them that two people know he is not the one who is telling the Germans their secrets—Sefton himself and the one who is really doing it. Sefton starts to watch the others, to find the spy, and figures out who it is. But what can he do? If he says nothing, the spy will continue to betray the Americans. If he tells the others, the spy will just be sent to another stalag. If they kill the spy, they will be killed as punishment. Sefton finds a way to reveal the identity of the spy. The prisoners use the spy as a decoy so that Dunbar can escape. Sefton insists on being the one to take him, telling the others that the risk of escaping has been outweighed by the chance at a reward from Dunbar's family.

❋ **DISCUSSION:** This is an exceptionally exciting drama, based on a play by two men who were prisoners in Stalag 17. Holden's superb performance won an Oscar for Best Actor, and the rest of the cast, some of whom were also in the Broadway play, is excellent. This movie provides a good opportunity to talk about the role of humor, especially "black" or "gallows" humor, in adapting to the harshest circumstances. A former Communist bloc comedian once said that every joke is a "tiny revolution." Here, when all control over their lives is taken from them, the prisoners try to establish some sense of control with jokes and pranks, and again, we see that, as W. H. Auden said, "a laugh is less heartless than tears" (see *Sullivan's Travels*).

Examine the other strategies and responses the prisoners had to adapt to their circumstances. Sefton adapted by trying to make whatever small improvements to his life that he could, helping him to maintain some sense of power, choice, and control. Animal and Harry use dreams to help them feel better; also giving them a sense of control, even if it is only for the future. Joey plays an ocarina and becomes completely withdrawn. Interestingly, the camp commandant, Von Sherbach (Otto Preminger), a ruthless man, is nevertheless also shown as feeling a loss of control, because he has been assigned to the backwater of the war effort. He hopes that identifying Dunbar as the one who blew up the train will bring him to the attention of those who may move him to something more prestigious.

Sefton is interesting (the narrator says he would fit into one of the *Reader's Digest* series about the "most unforgettable character") because he has none of the redeeming qualities we expect of our heroes. In contrast to Dunbar, who is rich, handsome, charming, unpretentious, modest, and brave, Sefton is selfish, cynical, and hostile. In his last words to the group as he leaves to rescue Dunbar, he says that if they should ever run into him after the war, they should pretend they don't know him. When he says he is motivated by the prospect of a reward, we believe him. Heroes are just as complicated as everyone else, possibly more so.

This movie also provides an opportunity to talk about justice and fairness. The evidence was very strongly against Sefton, and his unpleasant personality made him a natural object of hostility and suspicion. Contrast the process for finding Sefton guilty with the process the commandant uses to interrogate Dunbar (who was "guilty").

PROFANITY: None.

NUDITY/SEXUAL REFERENCES: Prisoners make a telescope to spy on the Russian women prisoners, and they often refer to their long separation from women; Sefton bribes the German guards to let him visit the women; one prisoner keeps insisting "I believe her" when he gets a letter from his wife saying that she found a baby who happens to look just like her.

ALCOHOL/DRUG ABUSE: Prisoners make their own liquor.

VIOLENCE SCARINESS: Prisoners are shot trying to escape; Sefton is beaten.

TOLERANCE/DIVERSITY ISSUES: Tolerance of individual differences and the overall issue of intolerance as the basis for war.

✳ **QUESTIONS FOR KIDS:**
- Why did Sefton give his egg to Joey?
- Why was Sefton so consumed with his own comforts and privileges?
- Why did the others suspect Sefton?
- How did the prisoners use humor to keep their spirits up? How do the filmmakers use humor to break the tension?
- How can there be "rules" like those of the Geneva Convention in a war? How can those rules be enforced?

✳ **CONNECTIONS:** Other outstanding movies about prisoners of war include **The Great Escape.** *The Rack* stars Paul Newman as a soldier accused of treason following his release from a Korean prison camp.

✳Butch Cassidy and the Sundance Kid
1969, 112 min, PG, 12 and up
Dir: George Roy Hill. Robert Redford, Paul Newman

✳ **PLOT:** This superb love letter to Western myths and Western movies is the fictionalized story of two real outlaws, played by Paul Newman and Robert Redford. When their life of robbing banks and trains is no longer possible, due to improved security, they must find a new way to survive. Like Ringo in **The Gunfighter,** their options are limited by their past transgressions, and they will not be permitted to just say they were sorry and go straight. They go to Bolivia, hoping to be able to return to what they know best—and learn that it is hard to rob a bank if you don't speak enough of the language to tell them to give you the money. They try to use their expertise as robbers to become security guards, but fail. They use a great deal of energy and ingenuity to escape capture and find a place for themselves, but ultimately they are unable to adapt, and there is no place left for them. The most they can hope for is death with honor (according to their terms).

NOTE: There is some profanity, a brief scene with a prostitute, a scene in which it appears that a woman is going to be raped at gunpoint (it turns out to be a perverse prelude to lovemaking by two people who are already intimate), and the usual level of shooting and violence for a Western.

✳ LORD OF THE FLIES
1961, 93 min, NR, b&w, 12 and up
Dir: Peter Brook.

Based on William Golding's award-winning allegorical novel, this is the story of a group of English schoolboys marooned on a remote island. At first, they operate according to the structure they are used to ("Let's make a lot of rules!" shouts one of the boys). Ralph, thoughtful and democratic, is selected as their leader. He plans for the long term, keeping a signal fire going. But when no one comes to rescue them, civilization slips further and further away. Jack and his "hunters" take over, becoming more and more savage. They paint themselves and make sacrifices to a mythical "beast," first the heads of the animals they kill for food, and then one of the boys, killed in a wild ceremonial dance. They murder Ralph's last follower, a chubby boy they call Piggy, and they are chasing murderously after Ralph when they are found by rescuers. NOTE: This has some very scary moments, and the overall theme may be particularly troubling for some kids.

✳ **CONNECTIONS:** Teenagers should read the book, by Nobel Prize—winner William Golding. This movie was remade in 1990, in color, with a contemporary setting, and the nationality of the boys changed to American. It has some power, but is not as good as the original.

✳ SWISS FAMILY ROBINSON
1960, 128 min, NR, 6 and up
Dir: Ken Annakin. John Mills, Dorothy McGuire

This handsome Disney production of the story about the shipwrecked family is a classic family film. John Mills is the optimistic father who assures his wife (Dorothy McGuire) and three sons that he will find a way to provide all the comforts of home on the island. The tree house he builds for her is a delight—and can still be visited at Walt Disney World. The family is wonderfully inventive and creative in adapting to life on the island, and the climax has a *Home Alone*-ish set of booby traps for the invading pirates. NOTE: Though she is spirited and brave, the young woman character is overly stereotyped by today's standards. It is worth discussing with kids how differently she is treated when the Robinsons think she is a boy.

SEE ALSO:

The Diary of Anne Frank Anne and her family must cope with years of confinement as they hide from the Nazis.

Fiddler on the Roof Tevye's family and community must adjust to changing times, first abandoning some of the traditions they have relied on, and then leaving their homes to start a new life.

Mike Mulligan and His Steam Shovel In this classic children's story, Mike's beloved steam shovel is about to be replaced by new technology, but together they find a way to do one last job and find a new way to continue to work together.

The Sound of Music When the Nazis invade Austria, the Von Trapp family must leave the life of wealth and prestige they had known to become a folksinging group.

FAMILIES: FUNCTIONAL AND DYS

"Family faces are magic mirrors. Looking at people who belong to us, we see the past, present, and future. We make discoveries about ourselves."

—GAIL LUMET BUCKLEY

Nothing is more fascinating to us than families, our own and others'. Despite what Tolstoy said, every family is different, happy or sad, and the endless variety of approaches to communication, power, anger, and even love is endlessly interesting. Some memorable movies have given us families so vivid that we almost feel we belong to them—or that they belong to us. Part of what makes them so vivid is that many of them are based on real families, the families of the playwrights, novelists, and screenwriters who allow us into their own families, presenting them to us sometimes with pain, but often with forgiveness, and always with insight, and with love.

Our own families are so overwhelming to us, particularly to kids, that it is especially worthwhile for them to visit with these other families, to help them see their own families in sharper relief. It can help kids with strong, intact families see how other families work well (or badly) together. It can help those dealing with difficult family problems to see movies that show families facing similar problems. It can show us the ways that different families communicate, argue, compromise, and show love, to make us think about the way we do these things, and how we can do them better.

In movies we meet happy families, families changed by loss, and characters creating their own families. We see families torn apart by greed, jealousy, and lies or by secrets and lack of trust. We see families facing some of the hardest questions of family life as they try to be supportive without being suffocating, to be tolerant without enabling destructive behavior. There are movies that show characters helping family members whose needs can be overwhelming, and movies that show characters loving those they cannot save. We see families grappling with painful issues of betrayal or abuse tri-power, and with heartbreaking tragedies. Above all, we see families triumphing. While W. C. Fields may refer to his family as "a dismal place, I admit" (*The Bank Dick*), movies more often and more accurately portray them as "that unconquerable fortress" (*Since You Went Away*). The movies in this chapter portray all kinds of families, coping with all kinds of problems, with all kinds of success and failure, all worth visiting.

Captain January

1936, 75 min, NR, b&w, 6 and up
Dir: David Butler. Shirley Temple, Guy Kibbee, Buddy Ebsen

✳ **PLOT:** Star (Shirley Temple), an orphan, lives with Captain January (Guy Kibbee), a retired sailor who runs a lighthouse. They adore each other, and she loves her life there, with the large community of sailors as her extended family and "Cap" to take care of her and teach her. A meddlesome and jealous woman, Agatha Morgan (Sara Haden), tries to prove that Cap is not a suitable guardian for Star, and that she should be in school, but when Star is tested, her performance is well ahead of her grade level.

When the lighthouse is automated, Cap loses his job, and this gives Miss Morgan another chance to take Star away. To keep her from Miss Morgan, Cap's friend Captain Nazro (Slim Somerville) tracks down Star's wealthy relatives, who come to get her. They do everything they can to make her happy, finally realizing that she cannot be happy without the people who have become her real family. They bring Cap, Nazro, and her other special friends to be the crew for their new boat so they can be together.

✳ **DISCUSSION:** This is one of Shirley Temple's best movies, and it provides an opportunity to discuss some of the most sensitive issues facing some children. Children who are home schooled will appreciate seeing the success of Shirley's home schooling with Cap. And children who are in foster homes or have had to face custody issues may appreciate the opportunity to discuss Shirley's situation as a way of addressing their own.

When Shirley is taken away from Cap, she says, "Why are they taking me away from you? What have I done?" This is a good chance to talk with children about how many kids mistakenly blame themselves for the problems that are created by the grown-ups around them. Star sings a song about how all that matters is "the right someone to love," and imagines what it would be like to be Cap's nanny. She says that he needs her to take care of him. Children need to know that it can be fun to pretend to be the caretaker, but that it is the grown-up's responsibility to take care of the child. The movie also depicts the difficulty of finding work, especially after a job has been made obsolete.

WARNING: This is a "happily ever after" movie, and any child whose own situation makes it difficult to watch an ending that ties everything up too neatly may have a hard time with it.

PROFANITY: None.

NUDITY/SEXUAL REFERENCES: None.

ALCOHOL/DRUG ABUSE: None.

VIOLENCE/SCARINESS: Very sad when Star is taken away from Cap.

TOLERANCE/DIVERSITY ISSUES: Miss Morgan is intolerant of Star's unusual home environment.

✳ **QUESTIONS FOR KIDS**
- Why does Paul try to get Mary to "bend the rules" for Star's test, and why won't she do it?
- How can you tell that Cap and Nazro are friends, even though they insult each other and argue?
- How does Star notice that Cap is sad?
- Nazro does not give Cap two important pieces of information—what are they, and why doesn't he tell Cap?
- Star and Cap both give reasons they are glad to leave the lighthouse—do you believe them? Why do they do that?
- Nazro says that children "forget quick." Is that right?

✳ **CONNECTIONS:** Television fans with sharp eyes will recognize Buddy Ebsen (of *The Beverly Hillbillies* and *Barnaby Jones*) as Star's friend Paul, who dances with her to "At the Codfish Ball."

✳ **ACTIVITIES:** Children might like to visit a lighthouse or a museum exhibit showing the way they used to operate before the automation portrayed in the movie. They might also like to learn something about the opera Shirley pretends to be in, *Lucia di Lammermoor;* the public library may have a recording you can borrow. Cap and Nazro pay pinochle, which children might like to learn. And they might like to make up a story, as Star does so well in her test at school.

✳Cat on a Hot Tin Roof

1958, 108 min, NR, 12 and up
Dir: Richard Brooks. Paul Newman, Elizabeth Taylor, Burl Ives

✳ **PLOT:** Big Daddy's (Burl Ives) family is celebrating both his sixty-fifth birthday and his medical report, which shows his health problems have proven to be minor. He has two grown sons, Brick (Paul Newman), an alcoholic former athlete, and Gooper (Jack Carson), who is constantly trying to replace Brick as Big Daddy's favorite. Gooper has five children, and Brick's wife, Maggie (Elizabeth Taylor) knows that no matter how much Big Daddy loves Brick, he will not leave Brick his property unless he provides an heir. Brick is angry at himself and at Maggie, and wants nothing more than to drink until he feels the "click" of peace when he is too drunk to feel anything else. But the "odor of mendacity" is too strong for Big Daddy, and all the lies come tumbling down like skeletons out of a closet.

✳ **DISCUSSION:** This movie, based on Tennessee Williams's play, is about a family that has been damaged more by lies than by greed. They lie to Big Daddy about the results of his medical tests. Brick lies to himself about what really went on with Skipper. Gooper and his wife lie about their feelings for Big Daddy. And Maggie lies about being pregnant. It is worth discussing the different kinds of lies and the different motivations behind them, and the impact the truth has on the characters when they are finally confronted with it. Compare this family's method of accomplishing its goals with the methods of other movie families to see which interactions make families stronger and which tear them apart.

PROFANITY: Mild.

NUDITY/SEXUAL REFERENCES: Much of the plot revolves around Maggie's attempts to get Brick to sleep with her so she can get pregnant; reference to homosexuality in the play changed to alleged heterosexual infidelity.

ALCOHOL/DRUG ABUSE: Brick has a drinking problem.

VIOLENCE/SCARINESS: Emotional violence only.

TOLERANCE/DIVERSITY ISSUES: Treatment of women typical of the period.

✳ **QUESTIONS FOR KIDS:**
- Why does Maggie compare herself to a cat on a hot tin roof? What is the roof, and what makes it hot?
- Why won't Brick agree to get Maggie pregnant? Who is he mad at? Why?
- Why does Brick have such contempt for himself? What does Skipper's death have to do with it?
- What makes Brick change his mind?

✳ **CONNECTIONS:** Compare this family to another classic Southern dysfunctional family, the Hubbards, in **The Little Foxes**. Other Tennessee Williams plays adapted for the screen include **The Glass Menagerie**, *Period of Adjustment*, and *Sweet Bird of Youth*.

✳ **ACTIVITIES:** Read the play, and you will see that Tennessee Williams wrote two different endings. Take a look at the other ending, and read his comments on it before you decide which one you prefer.

✳ Cheaper by the Dozen

1950, 85 min, NR, b&w, 6 and up
Dir: Walter Lang. Clifton Webb, Myrna Loy, Jeanne Crain, Edgar Buchanan

✳ **PLOT:** Based on the children's classic about the real-life pioneers of "motion study" (efficiency and ergonomics) and their twelve children, this movie begins with father Frank Gilbreth (Clifton Webb) coming home in 1921 Providence, Rhode Island, and whistling the signal for the children to come running. As the children race in and line up, he greets each one in a way that shows his high standards, affection, and above all his interest and involvement with each of his children. His profession is "motion study," and he applies its principles at home as well as at the factories he advises. Through a variety of inventive games and projects, he teaches the children everything from the multiplication of large numbers to Morse code.

The family is moving to Montclair, New Jersey. Frank and his wife, Lillie (Myrna Loy) make sure that all the children get into the huge Pierce Arrow "Foolish Carriage" and drive off. At the new school, Frank insists that the older children come along to help him persuade the principal that the middle children should be two grades above their age levels. They don't want to go, but he reminds them that "people with inner dignity are never embarrassed." He explains to the principal that "I'm not just dropping in." He has set aside the entire morning, and plans to stay until he gets them in the classes he thinks appropriate. As the teachers gather, he demonstrates the efficient technique he developed for taking a bath—in just the amount of time it takes to hear one side of the language records he insists that the children listen to while they are "unavoidably delayed."

The children become ill, and the doctor tells them that all but Martha must have their tonsils out. Reluctant at first, Frank becomes excited by the prospect of filming ten tonsil operations, so that he can figure out a way to make the operation more efficient. In order to get the doctor to agree, Frank promises to allow the doctor to take his tonsils out as well.

At their beach house, the Morse code and the planets are painted on the walls. The older girls are embarrassed by the old-fashioned bathing suits and hairstyles their father makes them wear. And later, back at home, when the oldest daughter, Anne (Jeanne Crain), starts to date a male cheerleader, Frank insists on going along. "What will he think of me?" "That you're a sensible, well-brought-up girl with sensible parents." When she asks if he trusts her, he says, "Of course I trust you. I trust all my daughters. It's that cheerleader I don't trust." At the school dance, he is popular with the kids. And the boy Anne likes tells her that boys respect the girls whose parents watch over them carefully.

On the way to achieve his dream of giving two important speeches in Europe, Frank dies suddenly. Lillie asks the children if she can count on them to do what is necessary to keep them together, and they promise to manage things while she goes to give the speeches for him.

✳ **DISCUSSION:** The dedication of the book on which this movie was based, written by two of the Gilbreth children, reads, "To Father, who had only twelve children, and to Mother, who had twelve only children." That is a perceptive comment about the perspectives these two wonderful people brought to their large family. When the twelfth Gilbreth child is born, Frank and Lillie have a poignant conversation about how they will miss having a baby around. And Frank pretends to get sick when the children are, because "all that quiet down there makes me nervous."

Children will be amused by the very old-fashioned swimsuits, and the fact that teenagers in every age argue with their parents about clothes and hair and dating.

The (off-camera) death of Frank Gilbreth is terribly sad. Parents should consider preparing their children ahead of time, and should reassure them (as the narrator does at the end of the movie) that the family stayed together and did very well.

PROFANITY: None. Like their real-life counterparts, Frank and Lillie have highly characteristic favorite expletives: "By jingo!" and, "Mercy Maud!"

NUDITY/SEXUAL REFERENCES: None. (There is a scene in which the local head of Planned Parenthood, as a joke, is sent to the Gilbreths to ask for their support, and is flustered by their having so many children.)

ALCOHOL/DRUG ABUSE: None.

VIOLENCE/SCARINESS: None.

TOLERANCE/DIVERSITY ISSUES: Lillian Gilbreth was a pioneer in her profession, the leading woman industrial engineer in the world, and this is pointed out with great pride at the end of the movie. It is more prominent as a theme in the sequel. Anne's heartthrob has a double standard for women, and explains that some girls are all right for fooling around with, but others are the kind he wants to marry.

✳ QUESTIONS FOR KIDS:

- Would you like to live in a family of twelve children? What would be the best thing about it? What would be the worst?
- The parents in this family spent most of their time thinking about improving the way that everything is done, making it faster and easier. What can you think of that can be improved, at home, at school, or someplace else? What would it take to improve it?
- Why is it important to save time? What do you do with the time you save?
- What do you think about their family councils? If you had one, what would you discuss?
- What does Anne mean when she says she cuts her hair and says she is "doing it for the younger kids"?

✳ **CONNECTIONS:** The movie version of the sequel features much of the same cast and is equally well done. It shows Lillian Gilbreth's struggles to be successful enough professionally to keep her family together and independent, which requires triumphing over the prejudice against women.

Clifton Webb appeared as a very fussy but effective nanny in *Sitting Pretty,* which inspired two sequels as well as the *Mr. Belvedere* television series. He also appears as the acerbic columnist Waldo Lydecker in **Laura.**

✳ **ACTIVITIES:** The book and its sequel, *Belles on Their Toes,* are both superb and great fun to read aloud. Help the children time themselves doing everyday tasks like getting dressed and making a peanut butter and jelly sandwich to see if they can find a "more efficient" way to do them. See if they can imitate Mr. Gilbreth's system for taking a bath.

A Christmas Story

1983, 98 min, PG, 8 and up
Dir: Bob Clark. Melinda Dillon, Darrin McGavin, Peter Billingsley

✳ **PLOT:** Ralphie (Peter Billingsley) is a nine-year-old boy in 1930s Gary, Indiana, whose entire life is consumed with his one wish—for a Red Ryder BB gun for Christmas. But all of the adults in his life have the same reaction: "You will shoot your eye out!" He also has to deal with his friends, his family, his teacher, with a seemingly endless wait for his Orphan Annie decoder ring, a nasty bully, and an overworked department store Santa. His father, "the Old Man" (Darrin McGavin), seems preoccupied with the neighbors' dogs (he hates them), his radio contest prize, a huge lamp in the shape of a lady's fishnet-stocking-clad leg (he loves it), the family's furnace (he engages in fervent combat with it), and the Christmas turkey (he wants it). His mother seems preoccupied with getting his brother to eat and getting the leg-lamp out of the house, but both parents manage to come through for a chaotic but very Merry Christmas.

✳ **DISCUSSION:** Part of the appeal of this movie, based on the memoirs of humorist Jean Shepard (who narrates), is the authenticity of the period detail, much of which will seem unfamiliar and even bizarre to kids today. But what is really engaging is his feel for the timeless details of childhood. Today's kids may not have Ralphie's exquisitely calibrated system of dares and double dog dares, but they will have some equivalent that is just as thoroughly understood and immutable in their own schoolyard community. And they will have a bully to deal with (and probably the bully's nasty little sidekick as well), something to send in box-tops for, a sibling to be annoyed by, an essay to dream of impressing the teacher with, the adult world to try to figure out, and, most of all, some magic dream of the ultimate Christmas present to hope for beyond all reason.

This is a nice antidote to all those Christmas television specials with perfectly harmonized carols and perfectly wrapped gifts. Because people tend to get so obsessive about every single detail at Christmas, the last scene of this movie, when the family's Christmas dinner is exactly the opposite of what they had planned, is especially sweet. Their reaction, seeing it not as a disappointment but as a delightful and funny adventure to enjoy remembering, is a lesson for all families.

PROFANITY: Some mild epithets, and episodes involving a father's and child's use of profanity (not heard). WARNING: A child is punished for swearing by having his mouth washed out with soap.

NUDITY/SEXUAL REFERENCES: Mild (episode of prize lamp in the shape of a woman's leg).

ALCOHOL/DRUG ABUSE: None.

VIOLENCE/SCARINESS: Bully; kids fight; kid touches an icy metal pole with his tongue on a dare and it freezes to the pole.

TOLERANCE/DIVERSITY ISSUES: None.

❋ QUESTIONS FOR KIDS:
- What makes people act like bullies? What makes people befriend bullies?
- How will the bully's life change after Ralphie fights him?
- Why does Ralphie's father like the lamp so much? Why does his mother dislike it?
- Why is it hard for Ralphie to talk to his parents about what he wants for Christmas?
- Why is Ralphie so disappointed by the decoder?
- Why is a "triple dog dare" so hard to resist?

❋ **CONNECTIONS:** A sequel with a different cast but the same director is not as good (*It Runs in My Family*, also known as *My Summer Story*). A third, made for television, is called *Ollie Hopnoodle's Haven of Bliss*.

❋The Diary of Anne Frank
1959, 170 min, NR, b&w, 12 and up
Dir: George Stevens. Millie Perkins, Joseph Schildkraut, Shelley Winters, Ed Wynn, Richard Beymer

❋ **PLOT:** In WWII Amsterdam, a young girl and her family must hide from the Nazis in "the hidden annex." Unimaginable horrors go on outside their tiny sanctuary. Inside, she struggles to understand, coping with both the normal confusions of adolescence and the most abnormal and terrifying circumstances.

The movie begins as Otto Frank (Joseph Schildkraut), Anne's father, returns to the annex after the war, the only one who survived. He finds her diary and begins to read it. Anne (Millie Perkins), her parents, her older sister, Margot (Diane Baker), Mr. And Mrs. Van Daan (Shelley Winters and Lou Jacobi), and their teenage son, Peter (Richard Beymer), are welcomed into the annex by two brave gentile friends. The door to the annex is hidden by a bookcase. The annex is in the attic of a spice factory, and during the day, while employees are working, the families must be absolutely silent. Their friends have only three forged ration cards, so food will be very limited. The families settle in hopefully.

But the claustrophobic living conditions, fear of discovery, and lack of food create stress, and the families bicker. Anne teases Peter and quarrels with her mother. Later, they are joined by a dentist, Mr. Dussell (Ed Wynn), who tells them that things have become much worse, and that many of the people they know have been taken off to concentration camps. They are almost discovered twice, once by a burglar who breaks into the factory, and once by the police. A radio gives them a connection to what is going on; they hear Hitler speak, and listen to music. They celebrate Hanukkah, and Anne gives everyone small gifts she has made for them. She and Peter become close and, despite the lack of privacy, are able to share their feelings. Just as they are rejoicing that the war is almost over, they are found by the Nazis and sent to concentration camps.

✳ **DISCUSSION:** This is a faithful and affecting (if long) rendition of Anne Frank's diary and of her family's experiences. Director George Stevens used the actual location (now a museum in Amsterdam) as a model for his set, and re-created every detail for authenticity. In addition to discussions of the Holocaust, this movie raises issues about the way that families work together (or don't) in times of dire adversity. Anne's famous statement that, "In spite of everything, I still believe that people are really good at heart" is also worth discussing.

> PROFANITY: None.
> NUDITY/SEXUAL REFERENCES: Anne and Peter share some chaste kisses. Peter's mother implies that more may be going on.
> ALCOHOL/DRUG ABUSE: None.
> VIOLENCE/SCARINESS: Tension as they are almost discovered; tragic ending.
> TOLERANCE/DIVERSITY ISSUES: A theme of the movie.

✳ **QUESTIONS FOR KIDS:**
- The Van Daans each have something that is very important to them: the cat, the food, the coat. Why is that? What does it tell you about each of them? What does it tell you about the impact of hiding?
- In what ways do the characters behave like anyone living under normal circumstances? In what ways do they behave differently?
- Why is Anne's relationship with her father different from her relationship with her mother?
- What do Anne's Hanukkah gifts tell you about the people she gives them to? About her?
- Is Anne's father like Pollyanna when he tells her that she should be glad there will be no more fights about wearing boots or practicing, and says, "How very fortunate we are, when you think of what is happening outside"?

✳ **CONNECTIONS:** *Anne Frank Remembered,* an outstanding documentary about Anne and her family, won an Oscar in 1996. *The Attic: The Hiding of Anne Frank* is a made-for-television drama starring Mary Steenburgen as Miep Gies, the woman who hid Anne Frank and her family from the Nazis. It provides a worthwhile opportunity to see the famous story from another perspective, and to consider the character of those who risked their lives to save others.

✳ **ACTIVITIES:** The diary itself should be read by every teenager. There is a lot of information for people of all ages about the Holocaust. Younger children should read the award-winning book by Lois Lowrey, *Number the Stars,* based on a true story, in which a little girl from Amsterdam helps some Jews escape. Children, and especially teenagers, may like to confide in a diary; remember Anne's saying that, "I can shake off everything when I write."

✳The Grapes of Wrath
1940, 129 min, NR, b&w, 12 and up
Dir: John Ford. Henry Fonda, Jane Darwell, John Carradine

✳ **PLOT:** The classic John Steinbeck novel about dust bowl farmers emigrating from Oklahoma to California became a classic film with Henry Fonda as Tom Joad, and Jane Darwell (in an Oscar-winning performance) as his mother. Tom returns home, after serving time in prison for manslaughter, to find that his sharecropper family is preparing to leave. They have lost the right to farm the land, so they are setting off to find jobs in California. Ma takes one last moment in their shack of a home, holding her earrings up to her ears, and then all twelve of them pile into the truck, including Casey, a former minister. On the way, their grandfather dies, and they bury him themselves. The grandmother dies, too, but Ma holds on to her and does not tell anyone until they get to California. Thousands of migrants have arrived for the 800 available jobs. Exploited and even robbed by the bosses, the workers are so desperate that they will do anything for any wage. They are too frightened to organize and insist on better treatment.

The bosses have hired thugs who prevent anyone from objecting to their treatment. Tom kills one to protect the people he is shooting at, and Casey takes the blame. Casey is killed, and Tom kills the assailant. Wanted by the authorities, Tom cannot stay with his family, which has now found a government-sponsored work camp with better conditions. He tells his mother farewell: "Well, maybe it's like Casey says. Fella ain't got a soul of his own. Just a little piece of a big soul. One big soul that belongs to everybody . . . I'll be around in the dark—I'll be everywhere. Wherever you can look—wherever there's a fight, so hungry people can eat, I'll be there. Wherever there's a cop beating up a guy, I'll be there. I'll be there in the way guys yell when they're mad. I'll be there in the way kids laugh when they're hungry, and they know supper's ready, and when people are eatin' the stuff they raised, and livin' in the houses they built, I'll be there, too." After he leaves, Ma says, "Rich fellers come up. They die. Their kids ain't no good and they die out. But we keep a-comin'. We're the people that live. Can't wipe us out. Can't lick us. We'll go on forever, 'cause we're the people!"

✳ **DISCUSSION:** This brilliant film shows us a family of enormous dignity and commitment. Although Ma says that they are not "the kissin' kind," and they show little emotion (except for Ma's delight in Tom's return from prison), there is clearly a great deal of love in the family.

PROFANITY: None.
NUDITY/SEXUAL REFERENCES: None.
ALCOHOL/DRUG ABUSE: None.
VIOLENCE SCARINESS: Fighting and shooting.
TOLERANCE/DIVERSITY ISSUES: Class issues.

✳ **QUESTIONS FOR KIDS:**
- Director John Ford was famous for using the landscapes in his movies to help create the mood and tell the story. How did he do that here?
- Casey is often considered to be a Christlike figure. What causes people to make that comparison?
- What do you think about Tom's comment that we all have "a piece of a big soul"? About Ma's comment that "the people will go on"?
- What is the life of migrant workers like today? To the extent that it has improved, what and who made it better?

✳ **CONNECTIONS:** John Ford won an Oscar as Best Director. Darwell can be glimpsed as "the bird lady" in **Mary Poppins**. Carradine is the father of actors David, Keith, and Robert Carradine.

✳ **ACTIVITIES:** Teens should read the book by John Steinbeck. They may also appreciate his books *Of Mice and Men* and *East of Eden*, and the films based on them.

Mask

1985, 120 min, PG-13, high schoolers (with parental warnings below)
Dir: Peter Bogdanovich. Cher, Eric Stoltz, Sam Elliott

✳ **PLOT:** This is based on the true story of Rocky Dennis (Eric Stoltz), a teenager with a genetic defect that turned his face into a huge "mask" of bone. As the movie begins, Rocky and his mother, Rusty (Cher), go to his new school, where the principal tells them Rocky cannot enroll. Rusty pulls out a file of paperwork and the name of her "lawyer"; she has been through this many times before. Rocky is enrolled. Then he is examined by a new doctor, who advises him sympathetically that he cannot expect to live more than three to six months. Rocky and Rusty have heard that before, too; they tell the doctor Rocky has already outlived all previous predictions.

Rocky does very well in school, and the principal suggests that he become a counselor's aide at a summer camp for the blind. There he meets Diana (Laura Dern) and has his first romance. They have a lovely time together, but her parents disapprove of the relationship.

Back at home, Rocky is getting impatient with Rusty. He is disappointed that she is not able to maintain a relationship with former boyfriend Gar (Sam Elliott), and loses patience with her alcohol and drug abuse. For him, she cleans up. Maybe it is because she knows on some level that he is nearing the end, and she wants him to die knowing that she will be all right.

✳ **DISCUSSION:** This is not a typical "disease of the week" movie about someone triumphing over adversity. It is a far more complex and moving story about two people who love and care for and about each other. Rusty does not work, lives on the fringes of society, uses drugs and abuses alcohol, and is sexually indiscriminate. Though in other aspects of her life she is completely irresponsible, even dissolute, with Rocky, she is the ideal of maternal strength and commitment. And Rocky is a source of strength for her, too, acting almost as her parent, trying to help her do better and (mostly) forgiving her when she fails.

The movie has several exceptionally touching moments. Rocky tries to teach Diana about colors by using her other senses, giving her a frozen rock to touch to feel "blue." Rocky peers into a fun house mirror and gets a glimpse of his features, distorted into what they might have been had he been "normal." And, moved by Rocky's academic triumph, a tough-looking biker named "Dozer" (for Bulldozer) reveals the real reason for his silence when he stutters so thickly he can barely get out the words of congratulation. The movie shows us over and over again that it is not about an "abnormal" boy in a normal world, but about a real boy in a world where everyone is different. As he says, "I look weird, but otherwise I'm real normal."

Rocky has some interesting ways of coping with his problems. He has his version of Pollyanna's "Glad Game," using happy memories to help him through hard times. And his mother, who herself uses drugs, helps him manage his headaches without drugs by "talking them away."

PROFANITY: Yes.

NUDITY/SEXUAL REFERENCES: Yes.

ALCOHOL/DRUG ABUSE: Yes.

VIOLENCE/SCARINESS: None.

TOLERANCE/DIVERSITY ISSUES: Theme of tolerance of difference, including people with disabilities (Diana's parents do not want her to associate with Rocky because of his disability, even though she is disabled herself); people with different lifestyles.

✳ **QUESTIONS FOR KIDS:**

- What do you think of the way that Rocky tries to show Diana what colors look like? If you were going to try to explain colors to a blind person, what would you do? What tastes, smells, touches, and sounds would you use to give a blind person the feelings of red, yellow, blue, pink, green?

- Why don't Diana's parents want her to see Rocky? Does that surprise you? How do Rocky and Rusty take care of each other? Give some examples.
- Why is Rusty better at taking care of Rocky than she is at taking care of herself?
- Were you surprised by the tenderness of the bikers? In what ways were they like a family?
- In what ways is it harder for Rocky to resolve his feelings of teenage rebellion than it would be for you?
- What do you think will happen to Rusty after the movie ends?

✳ **CONNECTIONS:** Families might also like to see actor Eric Stoltz without his "mask," as John Brooke in **Little Women**. And mature high schoolers may appreciate *The Elephant Man*, another true story of a man with a facial disfigurement who enlarges the understanding and compassion of those who get to know him.

✳ **ACTIVITIES:** Teenagers who see this movie might like to try helping out in a facility for the handicapped, as Rocky did at the summer camp.

✳Meet Me in St. Louis

1944, 113 min, NR, 6 and up
Dir: Vincente Minnelli. Judy Garland, Mary Astor, Margaret O'Brien, Lucille Bremer, Leon Ames

✳ **PLOT:** This episodic story of the Smith family in the St. Louis of 1903 is based on the memoirs of Sally Benson. Its pleasures are in the period detail, the glorious songs (including standards "The Trolley Song" and "Have Yourself a Merry Little Christmas"), and the loving and nostalgic look at a time of innocence and optimism, where a long-distance call was almost as thrilling as having the World's Fair come to your very own city. We see the family over the course of a year, celebrating Halloween and Christmas, riding the ice truck in the summer, and building snowmen in the winter. They face the prospect of having to leave St. Louis so that Mr. Smith can accept a promotion. They wonder whether the older girl's two boyfriends will propose. They treat each other with great loyalty and affectionate tolerance. And then they live happily ever after.

The Smiths' older daughters are Rose (Lucille Bremer) and Esther (Judy Garland). Rose is attracted to Warren Sheffield, and a bit impatient because he has not proposed. Esther has decided to marry "the boy next door," John Pruitt (Tom Drake), even though they have not yet met. When the girls have a party, their two little sisters (Joan Carroll and Margaret O'Brien as Agnes and Tootie Smith) creep downstairs. Tootie is allowed to do one song with Esther (the cakewalk "Under the Bamboo Tree") before being sent back to bed. Esther asks John to help her turn out the gas lights before he leaves, to have some time alone with him. The next day, he joins her as she and her friends ride on the trolley, and when he catches up with them, she sings "The Trolley Song." Later, Warren escorts a visiting out-of-town girl (June Lockhart) to another party, and Esther and Rose conspire to fill her dance card with the least appealing partners at the dance. When she is revealed to be so friendly and tactful that she gets Rose and Warren back together, Esther has to take all of her dances. Tootie is heartbroken about moving to New York, and while the rest of the family tries to hide it, they are, too. Mr. Smith gives up, they stay in St. Louis, and when the fair opens, they are there.

✳ **DISCUSSION:** One of the movie's most evocative scenes is Halloween, celebrated very differently in those days, but like today the one night of the year where children have the power to frighten the grown-ups. Agnes and Tootie dress up in rags and "kill" the people who answer the door by throwing flour at them. Director Minnelli skillfully shows how spooky and at the same time thrilling it is for the girls to be out after dark. When Tootie is successful at "killing" the grouchy neighbor, she is heralded by the other kids, and blissfully announces, "I'm the most horrible! I'm the most horrible!"

This is one of the most loving of all movie families. Everyone in it treats all of the other members with trust and affection, even, when it comes to Tootie, indulgence. They are interested in each other and take each other's concerns seriously, whether it is the seasoning of a sauce or choice of a future spouse. Only the poor father is rather left out. He is not told about the long-distance call, and no one is pleased with his promotion. But in a way, that is just a reflection of the family's devotion to him and to the life they have together in St. Louis. And the lovely duet he sings with his wife, "You and I," shows that it is their relationship that is the foundation of the family.

Minnelli began as an art director and designer, and his use of color is always fresh and fun. There isn't another director in history who would have thought to put Esther in purple gloves for the trolley ride, but once you see it, you can't imagine any other color.

PROFANITY: None.

NUDITY/SEXUAL REFERENCES: None.

ALCOHOL/DRUG ABUSE: None. (Tootie likes to shock people by singing a song that begins, "I was drunk last night, dear Mother . . .")

VIOLENCE/SCARINESS: None.

TOLERANCE/DIVERSITY ISSUES: None.

✳ **QUESTIONS FOR KIDS:**

- The father in this movie has a hard decision to make about whether he should take the new job, even though his family does not want

to move. What are the best reasons for going and what are the best reasons for staying? Who should make the decision? Do you agree with what he decided?
- Why does Tootie knock down her snowmen?
- Why is she proud of being "the most horrible"?
- What is most special about the town you live in?
- Would you like to live back in the time of this movie? What would you like best about living in those days?

❊ **CONNECTIONS:** Vincente Minnelli was very much in love with Judy Garland when they made this movie (they got married after it was completed), and she never looked more radiant. Judy Garland and Vincente Minnelli were, together and separately, responsible for many of the all-time best movie musicals, including *The Pirate*.

❊ National Velvet

1944, 125 min, NR, 6 and up
Dir: Clarence Brown. Elizabeth Taylor, Mickey Rooney, Anne Revere, Angela Lansbury

❊ **PLOT:** Mi Taylor (Mickey Rooney) arrives in a small English town and meets Velvet (Elizabeth Taylor) just as she and her sisters have been let out of school for the summer. They like each other immediately, and she is delighted to learn that the reason he has come to her town is that he found her mother's name in the address book belonging to his late father. He does not know what their relationship was, or what he hopes to find from her, but he has no other place to go.

At the dinner, Mi is tentative, not sure himself whether he is looking for a friend or an easy mark. That night, as Mrs. Brown goes over that day's books and puts away the cash from their butcher shop, she and Mr. Brown talk about giving Mi a job. Mr. Brown is reluctant, saying they don't need him, and that he seems to have a "sharpness" about him, but she insists. After Velvet tells him he is going to stay, he sneaks back into the house to return their money, which he had stolen.

The horse Velvet loves most is owned by a man who, angry and frustrated at his inability to control it, decides to sell it by lottery. Velvet wins and renames the horse The Pi. He won't pull the butcher shop cart, but he can jump a fence as high as the most treacherous hazard in England's biggest horse race, the Grand National Steeplechase. So Velvet decides that he must be in that race, to have a chance to be the very best he can be, the very best there is.

They hire a jockey by mail, but Velvet knows the horse must be ridden by someone who loves him, and would rather not have him race at all than have a jockey who does not believe he can win. Just as Mi is about to volunteer, Velvet decides that she will ride The Pi, even if they could have had the best jockey in the world, even if they will get in trouble because girls are not allowed to race. She rides The Pi, and he wins. But they are both disqualified because she is a girl.

They come back home in triumph, knowing that they won what was important to them. Though they were not allowed to keep the title or the prize money, all charges have been dropped, and they won't get into trouble for violating the rules. Mr. Brown is excited by all of the offers for appearances and endorsements, but Velvet knows that it would not be best for The Pi and that it is time to move on. So does Mi, who takes his knapsack and says good-bye to Mr. and Mrs. Brown. When Velvet hears that he has left, she asks if she can tell him about his father, who was Mrs. Brown's coach, and how much he meant to her in achieving her dream. Mrs. Brown consents, and Velvet races after him, just catching up to him as the movie ends.

✳ **DISCUSSION:** *National Velvet* taps into one of the oldest, deepest dreams, the dream of horses. Every child dreams of controlling these huge, powerful, loyal creatures, of flying over hurdles on their backs, of earning their devotion and of being devoted to them in return. And then there is the dream of racing, as Velvet says in this movie, until you burst your heart, and then until you burst it again, and then until you burst it twice as much as before, until the two of you explode past the finish line ahead of everyone else.

This is the story of dreams themselves, wise and foolish, big and small, realized and impossible, and about the way all of these dreams change those who are lucky enough to dream them. It is about the importance of faith—Velvet's faith in herself and in The Pi and in her dream, and her family's faith in her and in Mi—and the importance of that belief and support in making the dream come true. Mi says, "You bit off a big piece of dream for yourself, Velvet." But in one of the sweetest scenes ever filmed, Mrs. Brown takes out the 100 gold pieces she won for swimming the English Channel and gives them to Velvet. There were a thousand times the family could have used that money, but she was saving it for a dream as big as her own once was. She tells Velvet, "I too believe that everyone should have a chance at a breathtaking piece of folly once in his life."

National Velvet is also a rare movie that deals with what happens after the dream comes true. It sometimes seems that half the movies that are made, and well over half of the movies that are made for children, end with the hero or heroine triumphantly standing in the winner's circle, holding the trophy overhead as the music swells and the credits roll. One of the things I like best about this movie is that it puts the dream in perspective. After they win the race, Mr. Brown is delighted with all of the offers for appearances and endorsements for Velvet and her horse. Instead of arguing with him, Mrs. Brown asks Velvet how she feels about it. Velvet thinks it might be fun for her, but says that she would never put The Pi through all of the foolishness that would be required. Velvet and her friend Mi and those around them take what they have learned from the dream and go on with their lives, something worth discussing in this era when any achievement, good or bad, becomes a miniseries.

But most of all, *National Velvet* is the story of a loving family. It is very different in many ways from the families that the American children of today know—for example, the mother and father are so reserved that they call each other "Mr. and Mrs. Brown" until the very last scene. But it is a wonderful starting point for a discussion of the ways that families of all kinds can teach and support each other.

One of the key themes of the movie is the faith that the characters have (and don't have) in themselves and in each other. Mr. Brown is reluctant to accept Mi at first, with good reason. As Mrs. Brown says, it would be surprising for someone who had lived on the streets not to have a "sharpness about him." But, she persuades Mr. Brown to give him a chance: "What's the meaning of goodness if there isn't a little badness to overcome?" Mi does steal their money, but when he learns of their faith in him, their offer of a job and a place to stay and Velvet's acceptance of him as a friend, he puts it back. Later, when he has a chance to steal much more money from the family, he thinks about it, but decides that he can't, because "she trusts me."

Velvet's faith in both Mi and The Pi is at the center of the movie. She accepts them both immediately and irrevocably, though both are mistrusted by others. She does not believe Mi when he says he doesn't like horses, and when he says he is only interested in the race for the money. She knows that he feels as passionately for The Pi as she does, though he cannot say it.

Velvet also has faith in the future. She is certain that she will win the lottery for the horse she loves. When she tells everyone she will win, a suspicious neighbor suggests that she may have cheated by arranging for her father to pick her number in the drawing. She explains that she didn't bother with that, she just worked it out with God. Mr. Brown responds to the neighbor's accusation by having him do the drawing, and of course Velvet does win (after there is no holder of the first number picked). When the jockey they have hired by mail to ride The Pi in the race shows them that he not only does not believe that The Pi can win, he does not even care, Velvet knows that it would be wrong to let him ride her horse. Just like Mi and Velvet herself, The Pi deserves someone who believes in him.

Mr. and Mrs. Brown show their trust by risking letting Mi and their children make mistakes. "She has it in her to do the right thing," Mrs. Brown says of Velvet, and lets her decide how to respond to the offers that come in after she wins the race. Mrs. Brown also lets Velvet run to school after being up all night caring for the horse. When Mr. Brown objects, she reassures him that Velvet will be back—it's Saturday, and there is no school. But she let her go because "I like that part of her that wants to go to school after a night caring for the horse." Mrs. Brown not only lets Mi stay with the family, but she entrusts him to take her 100 gold pieces to London. Mr. Brown is certain he will steal it instead. But as the train pulls away, you can see Velvet reflected in the window of the train car. This symbolizes the way that the image of Velvet, and her faith in him, stays with Mi, and prevents him from taking the advice of his friends who get him drunk and encourage him to steal the money. As they leave for the race, Velvet says to Mrs. Brown, "You'll be proud of The Pi, mother." Mrs. Brown says, "I want to be proud of you." And she is.

Throughout the movie, Mr. and Mrs. Brown balance a spacious acceptance of their children's passions with a firm set of values and a fairly strict set of rules. Velvet is permitted to pretend to ride in bed only one night a week, and only for fifteen minutes. At his first dinner with the family, Mi is reprimanded sharply by Mr. Brown (Donald Crisp) for feeding the dog at the table ("It will turn him into a beggar," is a pointed comment made to the young man who has arrived at their door and may have some hope of being helped). But as we see during the course of the scene, each member of the family, including Mr. Brown, sneaks food to the dog when the others aren't looking. Similarly, Velvet is constantly reminded by everyone to wear her braces. When Mi does this, on the way to the race, it shows how much he has accepted the family's set of priorities and the responsibility of caring for its members. In this case, though, he lets her take the braces out until the race is over. Like Mr. and Mrs. Brown, he knows when to suspend the rules. Mrs. Brown won't tell Mi how much his father meant to her until he leaves them. As long as he had no faith in himself, that information would be no more than a way to get something from the Brown family. But once he no longer felt "soft and yellow inside," he could accept it as a heritage to build on.

PROFANITY: None.

NUDITY/SEXUAL REFERENCES: None.

ALCOHOL/DRUG ABUSE: Mi gets intoxicated with bad friends, which almost leads him to make the wrong decision and steal the money.

VIOLENCE/SCARINESS: None.

TOLERANCE/DIVERSITY ISSUES: Even though she wins the race, Velvet is deprived of the title and the prize because girls are not eligible to race. No one questions that rule or seems surprised by it; she undertakes the race knowing that this will happen. Mr. and Mrs. Brown are equal partners at home and at work, though she is the stronger character.

✳ **QUESTIONS FOR KIDS:**
- Why can't Velvet keep the prize, even though she won?
- Why didn't Mrs. Brown want to tell Mi about his father? What made her decide it was time?
- Why didn't Velvet want to make movies or do any of the other things people asked her to do after she won? What would you do?
- What did Mrs. Brown mean about goodness not meaning much unless there is a little bit of badness to overcome?

• What did she mean about everyone's being entitled to a "breathtaking piece of folly"?

✳ **CONNECTIONS:** Children who watch this movie might like to know that there is a real-life story of a little girl's dream behind it. Elizabeth Taylor wanted to play this role as much as Velvet wanted to ride The Pi. She was told she could not have the part because she was too short, and filming was scheduled to start in a few months. She promised to be tall enough by the time filming started, and fate and genes were on her side.

Anne Revere won an Academy Award for her portrayal of Mrs. Brown. She also played strong, wise mothers in many other movies, including, *Gentleman's Agreement* and *Body and Soul.* Fans of television's *Murder, She Wrote* will enjoy seeing Angela Lansbury in an early pre–Jessica Fletcher role as Velvet's older sister. Thirty-five years after **National Velvet,** Mickey Rooney played an old horse trainer in the second-best movie about a kid and a horse, *The Black Stallion.*

The sequel, *International Velvet*, with Tatum O'Neal (1978), is not very good.

✳ **ACTIVITIES:** Older children will enjoy the book *National Velvet*, by Enid Bagnold, also the author of *The Chalk Garden.*

✳Ordinary People
1980, 123 min, R, 12 and up
Dir: Robert Redford. Timothy Hutton, Judd Hirsch, Mary Tyler Moore, Donald Sutherland, Elizabeth McGovern, Dinah Manoff

✳ **PLOT:** Conrad Jarrett (Timothy Hutton) has returned home after four months in a mental hospital. He tried to kill himself following a tragic boating accident with his brother, Buck, who drowned. He is trying to find a way to fit in, both at home and at school. His father, Calvin (Donald Sutherland), tries to reach out to him, but is afraid of saying the wrong thing and is shy about his own emotions. His mother, Beth (Mary Tyler Moore), is uncomfortable with emotions and with anything else that might be "messy" or hard to control.

After some hesitation, Conrad seeks out Dr. Berger (Judd Hirsch), a psychiatrist recommended to him when he left the hospital, telling him that he is seeking "control." Berger warns him that control is tough to achieve, but says he will do what he can. He advises Conrad to start from the outside, work on his actions and let the feelings follow.

Conrad begins to reach out to a sympathetic girl at school, Jeannine (Elizabeth McGovern). He makes contact with Karen (Dinah Manoff), a friend from his hospital stay, who seems to have "control," to be busy with friends and activities and sure of herself. He is devastated when he tries to call her again and hears that she has killed herself. He calls Berger in the middle of the night and insists on seeing him. He relinquishes what he thinks of as "control" to confess to Berger—and to himself—that he can't forgive himself for surviving when his brother died, that he feels guilty and unworthy.

Calvin begins to realize that Beth's unwillingness to connect to her own emotions or anyone else's is suffocating the family. They had had the appearance of closeness, but the tragedy revealed how superficial it was. Their relationship unravels quickly, and she leaves as Cal and Conrad begin to share their feelings.

✻ **DISCUSSION:** This is a movie about emotional honesty, about the courage and emotional vocabulary that are necessary for the connections and intimacy we need to be able to survive challenges like the tragedy faced by this family. Berger says, "If you can't feel pain, then you're not going to feel anything else, either." The characters represent a wide variety of approaches and abilities to emotional openness and "control." Conrad and Calvin are both groping their way toward a better understanding of themselves and others and the ability to communicate.

Beth does not want to try. She is by no means an ogre. Indeed, it is clear that the director and writer of the movie feel sorry for her. She has chosen emptiness she can control rather than "messy" feelings. Beth preferred Buck to Conrad because Buck's easy confidence did not place any emotional demands on her. Conrad says, "I can't talk to her! The way she looks at me! She hates me!" What Conrad feels as rejection is really Beth's fear that his sensitivity and vulnerability will put demands on her that she can't or won't be able to respond to. She can't bear the thought that she might somehow be responsible for Conrad's pain, while Calvin is willing to confront that issue in order to be able to help Conrad.

Jeannine at first pulls back from Conrad's attempt to connect with her by telling her the truth about himself, but then apologizes. She wants to understand him; it was just that at first she did not know how to respond, so she retreated into the more comfortable and familiar environment of joking around. In contrast, Karen, who seems to have so much "control" and goes to elaborate pains to persuade Conrad that she is doing fine, is unable to cope.

Teenagers may know of someone who has attempted suicide, or of someone who has been successful. This movie provides an opportunity to discuss what led Conrad and Karen to consider it, how the perspective of a person about his own worth is very different from that of those around him, and what the other options are for people who are deeply depressed.

PROFANITY: Mild.

NUDITY/SEXUAL REFERENCES: Locker-room references.

ALCOHOL/DRUG ABUSE: Beth uses alcohol as an emotional anesthetic.

VIOLENCE/SCARINESS: None.

TOLERANCE/DIVERSITY ISSUES: Anti-Semitic remark by Conrad's grandmother (and lack of objection by Beth) intended to show insularity.

※ **QUESTIONS FOR KIDS:**
- Why is control so important to Conrad? Is it important to Beth and Calvin, too?
- What do you think of Berger's advice about starting from the outside?
- How does Berger help Conrad? How does Jeannine help him?
- Why does Conrad quit the swim team? Why doesn't he tell his parents?
- How do you feel about Beth? Do you dislike her or feel sorry for her or both? Why is it so hard for her to give her husband and son what they feel they need?

※ **CONNECTIONS:** This film received Oscars for Best Picture, Screenplay, and Supporting Actor (Timothy Hutton). It also popularized the lovely "Canon" by Pachelbel. Viewers of *Nick at Nite* will recognize Mary Tyler Moore from *The Dick Van Dyke Show* and *The Mary Tyler Moore Show*.

※ A River Runs Through It

1992, 123 min, PG, high schoolers
Dir: Robert Redford. Craig Sheffer, Brad Pitt, Tom Skerritt, Emily Lloyd

※ **PLOT:** Writer Norman Maclean's autobiographical story of growing up in Montana with his brother, Paul, begins, "In our family, there was no clear line between religion and fly-fishing." Their Presbyterian minister father taught them their schoolwork, religion, and fishing as though they were all one subject. All were strict and thorough. He believed that no one who did not know how to fish properly should be permitted to disgrace a fish by catching it. He used a metronome to time their four-count stroke between the positions of ten o'clock and two o'clock.

Norman, though more sober, loved the wild streak in Paul that made him "tougher than any man alive" but feared that it would destroy him. And it did. While Norman becomes a professor of English literature and falls in love with Jessie Burns (Emily Lloyd), Paul becomes a reporter and gets into trouble drinking and gambling. Norman is called by the police to get Paul out of jail, and ultimately, he is called again when Paul is killed.

※ **DISCUSSION:** One of the tragic realizations of growing up is that you can love someone without being able to understand or save them. Like Norman, Jessie has a brother who is self-destructive, though his part of the story is played more for comedy. In today's terms, Jessie's mother would be considered an enabler because she does not impose any limits on her son and does not insist that he recognize the consequences of his behavior.

PROFANITY: Mild.

NUDITY/SEXUAL REFERENCES: Jessie's brother brings a prostitute with him when he goes fishing with Norman and Paul; they fall asleep nude and are sunburned badly.

ALCOHOL/DRUG ABUSE: Paul has a drinking problem; Jessie's brother Neal and a woman become drunk and pass out.

VIOLENCE/SCARINESS: Mostly off-screen.

TOLERANCE/DIVERSITY ISSUES: Paul brings a half-Cheyenne date into a bar that does not permit Indians.

✳ QUESTIONS FOR KIDS:
- If you were Norman, what would you have said to Paul? When? Why didn't Norman say those things?
- If you were Jessie, what would you say to Neal?
- Why was it important to have Neal's story in the movie?
- What does Norman mean when he says that his father saw no difference between religion and fly-fishing?

✳ **CONNECTIONS:** Director Redford addresses the theme of loving families who do not communicate pain well, with one member of the family suffering the consequences, in *Ordinary People* and *Quiz Show*.

✳ Tex

1982, 102 min, PG, high schoolers
Dir: Tim Hunter. Matt Dillon, Jim Metzler, Meg Tilly, Ben Johnson, Emilio Estevez

✳ **PLOT:** The only one of the popular S. E. Hinton books to be filmed by Disney, this is a bit glossier than the two directed by Francis Ford Coppola (*The Outsiders* and *Rumble Fish*), but still a very frank and gritty story about two brothers who have to take care of themselves and each other while their father is on the road. Mason (Jim Metzler) is a senior, a basketball star, dedicated and responsible. Tex (Matt Dillon) is fifteen, unsure of himself, not yet ready to focus on the problems they face. His horse, Rowdy, is the center of his world. As the movie begins, they are out of money, out of food, and the gas has been turned off. It has been four months since they heard from their father, who is traveling with the rodeo. Mason sells their horses to get money for food. Tex is furious, throws things, and wrestles angrily with his brother.

Tex comes home drunk after a party with friends. The next day, his friend's harsh father, Cole (Ben Johnson), blames Tex, and threatens to call the juvenile authorities to make sure that Mason and Tex have some supervision. Mason tells Tex, "You want to stay off some youth farm somewhere? Start thinking ahead five minutes at a time now and then."

Mason is under so much pressure that he develops an ulcer. They pick up a hitchhiker on the way back from the hospital, and he turns out to be an escaped prisoner. He points a gun at them and tells them to drive him to the state line. Tex swerves into a ditch, and the hitchhiker is shot by the police.

Pop returns and promises he will stay. He tries to buy Rowdy back, but the people do not want to sell. Tex is angry and bitter. When Mason's application form for Indiana University arrives, Tex takes it.

Mason is injured in a game. Tex is suspended from school for a prank and overhears Mason say that Pop is not his biological father. Hurt and angry, he gets in the car with a small-time drug dealer friend, on his way to explain a "mix-up" to some tough characters. Tex goes along and gets shot. At the hospital, he fills out Mason's application, and Mason is accepted. Tex urges Mason to go, knowing that it is best for Mason, and that he can take care of himself.

✻ **DISCUSSION:** Tex has tougher problems than most kids, but his impulsive approach to dealing with them will seem familiar to many viewers. He knows they have no money to feed the horses, much less themselves, and yet is angry when Mason sells them. When he is angry and hurt, he makes a foolish decision to get in the middle of a fight over a drug deal, saying, "If there is any hassle, they'll be sorry, because I really feel like making somebody sorry," one of many incidents of displacement. All around Tex and Mason are the consequences of bad choices—Pop's, in going to prison and neglecting his sons; Cole's, in being too strict with his children; their own, in picking up the hitchhiker; Lem's in dealing in drugs to make money; and Lem's and his girlfriend's in getting pregnant.

The issue of responsibility is also an important one here. Mason takes on the responsibility of the household, putting enormous pressure on himself. But in "overparenting," he keeps too much from Tex, and it is only when Tex has to take some responsibility himself that he can begin to think of other people. Sexual involvement by teenagers is an issue as well. Mason's advice to Tex (that a boy should keep going until the girl tells him to stop) is worth discussing with both boys and girls. So is Jamie's ability to make it very clear to Tex that she is not ready to have sex with him.

It is also worth discussing the principal's comment to Tex: "I hope there's something you take seriously, because it's the only thing that'll save you."

PROFANITY: None.

NUDITY/SEXUAL REFERENCES: Discussion of couple getting married because the girl is pregnant; how to know how far to go with a girl; Mason's father not being Tex's father.

ALCOHOL/DRUG ABUSE: Drinking and smoking by teenagers; characters sell drugs.

VIOLENCE/SCARINESS: Characters in peril; hitchhiker killed by police; Tex shot in struggle.

TOLERANCE/DIVERSITY ISSUES: Class issues.

✳ **QUESTIONS FOR KIDS:**
- Cole and Pop have opposite reactions to the trouble Johnny and Tex get into. Is one more effective? How would you respond?
- Why didn't Mason apologize for selling the horses?
- Why did Tex take over when Johnny didn't jump his motorbike over the creek?
- Pop tells Mason to go ahead and explode and clear the air. What do you think about this approach to communication?
- Why did Johnny say it was all right for him to criticize his father, but he didn't want Tex to do it?

✳ **CONNECTIONS:** Matt Dillon also appears in **My Bodyguard.** Older teens will appreciate Francis Ford Coppola's versions of *The Outsiders* and *Rumble Fish*, both of which feature a number of future stars.

✳ **ACTIVITIES:** Read the novels of S. E. Hinton (who has a brief appearance in this movie as Mrs. Barnes).

✳ A Tree Grows in Brooklyn
1945, 128 min, NR, b&w, 10 and up
Dir: Elia Kazan. Dorothy McGuire, James Dunn, Peggy Ann Garner, Joan Blondell

✳ **PLOT:** Francie Nolan (Peggy Ann Garner), an imaginative and sensitive girl, lives with her family in a Brooklyn tenement. She adores her father, Johnny (James Dunn), a dreamer with a drinking problem, and respects but resents her down-to-earth mother, Katie (Dorothy McGuire). The family struggles to rise from poverty. Francie and her brother must each read a page aloud every night from the Bible and from Shakespeare, and their parents are intent on their becoming the first family members to graduate from grade school. Francie dreams of going to a better school in a wealthier neighborhood, and her father makes it possible by telling the principal that she is moving in with a fictitious wealthy aunt. A teacher there encourages her to pursue her love of writing. But Katie is pregnant again, and decides that Francie should leave school. When Johnny dies, Francie is devastated. She is angry with her mother, feeling that her mother did not love Johnny enough, and does not love her enough, either. But when her mother has the baby, Francie sees that she loves them both, and that Katie hates having to be practical and "hard." A kind policeman asks permission to court Katie, and Francie knows that their life will be easier, and that her father and what they shared will be with her always.

✳ **DISCUSSION:** This family has a great deal of love but a lot of difficulty showing it. Although they clearly love each other, Johnny and Katie have too many shattered expectations to accept tenderness from each other, as we see when he comes home with the food from the party and sees her with her hair down, and when she tries to tell him how much she likes hearing him sing "Annie Laurie."

They have trouble being honest and direct about their circumstances and their feelings. They have to move to a cheaper apartment, but insist— to themselves and to everyone else—that they are doing it to get more sunlight. When Katie decides that she wants her sister back in her life, she sends the message via the insurance collector. When Francie tries raising the subject of the school she wants to attend in a roundabout way, Katie tells her to speak more directly. But Johnny lets her tell him in her own way and, over Katie's objections, makes it possible for her dream to come true. Francie has a hard time understanding that Katie loves her and relies on her, until Katie is in labor and almost does not know what she is saying. This is a good opportunity to talk about the ways that families do (and do not) communicate with each other. Older kids may also want to discuss the impact that Johnny's drinking and unreliability had on Katie and why it was different for Francie.

PROFANITY: None.

NUDITY/SEXUAL REFERENCES: Aunt Sissy is involved with many different men, and at one point Katie refuses to let her see the children because she is a bad influence.

ALCOHOL/DRUG ABUSE: Johnny has a serious drinking problem.

VIOLENCE/SCARINESS: Inexplicit scene of Katie in labor may scare younger children, who should be reassured; very sad when Johnny dies.

TOLERANCE/DIVERSITY ISSUES: Issues relating to assimilation, poverty.

✳ QUESTIONS FOR KIDS:
- What does the title refer to?
- What did Francie's teacher mean about the difference between imagi-nation and pipe dreams?
- Why did the members of the family have such a hard time talking to each other about what mattered to them?
- Why does the family use the word "sick" to describe Johnny's alcohol-ism? Why does Johnny seem so sad when Francie talks with him about being "sick"?
- Why was it so important to Kate that the death certificate be changed?

✳ CONNECTIONS: James Dunn won an Oscar for his performance. Joan Blondell appeared as a brassy second lead in a number of early musicals, including Footlight Parade and Gold Diggers of 1933. Peggy Ann Garner is also lovely as the young Jane Eyre.

✳ ACTIVITIES: Kids should read the book, by Betty Smith, who based it on her own childhood.

Unstrung Heroes

1995, 93 min, PG, 12 and up
Dir: Diane Keaton. Andie MacDowell, John Turturro, Michael Richards

✳ **PLOT:** Steven Lidz is the son of Sid (John Turturro), an inventor. He is a distracted man who "believes in documentation" and empirical data. Steven is closer to his warmhearted mother, the emotional center of the family. When she becomes ill, he goes to live with his father's two brothers (Michael Richards and Maury Chaikin), both borderline (and sometimes more than borderline) mentally ill. They are hoarders, with huge piles of newspapers filling every bit of available floor space; paranoid, telling him there are only eight trustworthy people in the world (the other four have been killed); and delusional. But they love Steven very much and see in him a strength and ability to be great that he finds very comforting. They rename him "Franz" because they think it suits him better than "Steven."

Franz picks up some of his uncles' peculiarities (singing the "Internationale" in school while the other kids recite the Pledge of Allegiance), but also draws strength from what they tell him. They encourage him to connect to his heritage by studying for his bar mitzvah. And his uncle's fascination with objects inspires him to hold on to a bit of his mother by collecting small items that make him feel close to her. When she dies, he retrieves hours of "documentation" (film of experiments and family home movies) from the garbage. He and his father watch them together and, with the uncles, begin to document the family again.

✳ **DISCUSSION:** Based on the autobiographical novel by sportswriter Franz Lidz (he kept the name his uncles bestowed on him), this is a quietly moving story of a boy growing up in the midst of incomprehensible loss. Perhaps it is the very incomprehensibility of it all that makes his uncles seem understandable by comparison. Or perhaps they just have a less frightening way of being impossible to understand. To Steven, they are almost like children, the way they play with the "high-bouncers" from the collection of lost rubber balls that "hold the sounds of the children who played with them." He makes pancakes for them the way his mother made pancakes for him and his sister. He protects them from the landlord who wants to see them evicted. They have time for him, which his parents don't. They have answers for him, which no one else does. They see him as "Franz," and "Franz" is who he decides he wants to be.

This is a movie about loss, but more than that it is a movie about families, and the acceptance of family members who are not always easy to understand. This includes Sid as well as the uncles.

The movie raises the question of faith. Sid is relentlessly scientific and is furious that his brothers have encouraged Franz to study Judaism. He tells them that "religion is a crutch, only cripples need crutches." But Franz's mother, dying, says maybe Franz is right.

Franz's attitude toward his uncles is very sympathetic, even protective. But Franz and his friend Ash play a prank on Uncle Danny, slipping him a note that sends his paranoia into overdrive. Danny commits himself, and when Franz admits that he wrote the note, Danny tells him it is all right, that it made it possible for him to get help.

PROFANITY: None.

NUDITY/SEXUAL REFERENCES: None.

ALCOHOL/DRUG ABUSE: None.

VIOLENCE/SCARINESS: Scariness of mother's illness and death.

TOLERANCE/DIVERSITY ISSUES: Uncle Danny's paranoia has him seeing anti-Semitism everywhere; Steven/Franz studies for his bar mitzvah over his father's objections.

✳ QUESTIONS FOR KIDS:
- Why does Steven give up instead of giving his speech?
- Why does Steven decide to go live with his uncles? Why do his parents let him?
- Why do Sid and his brothers have different ideas about religion?
- What does "documentation" mean, and why is it important here?
- What does Sid mean by an "undisciplined mind"?

✳ **CONNECTIONS:** This was the first feature film directed by actress Diane Keaton (*Annie Hall, Reds, The Godfather,* and many others.).

✳ **ACTIVITIES:** Older kids, particularly those familiar with Lidz's sportswriting, may want to read the book. Those who are not familiar with the bar mitzvah ceremony may enjoy attending one.

✳You Can't Take It With You
1938, 127 min, NR, b&w, 8 and up
Dir: Frank Capra. Jimmy Stewart, Jean Arthur, Lionel Barrymore, Ann Miller

✳ **PLOT:** The Sycamore family, a group of loving and lovable eccentrics presided over by Grandpa (Lionel Barrymore), includes daughter Penny (Spring Byington), who writes lurid plays, and her husband Paul (Samuel S. Hinds), who makes fireworks in the basement with Mr. DePinna (Halliwell Hobbes), the iceman who came by to deliver ice nine years before and just stayed. Mr. Poppin (Donald Meek), who loves to make mechanical toys, has recently joined them. The Sycamores have two daughters. Essie (Ann Miller) loves to dance, and her husband, Ed (Dub Taylor), plays the xylophone. They sell candy to make a little money. The other daughter, Alice (Jean Arthur), is the only one in the family with a job. She works for a banking firm and has fallen in love with the boss's son, Tony Kirby (Jimmy Stewart).

A man from the IRS visits to find out why Grandpa has never paid any taxes. The neighbors are all being evicted because the land is being sold to developers who intend to build a factory. And Tony's very elegant and snobbish parents arrive for dinner on the wrong night, descending upon the Sycamore family just as Ed is arrested for enclosing seditious statements in the candy boxes and all the fireworks blow up. Various crises of finance and embarrassment and misunderstanding ensue, but all are straightened out, and everyone lives happily ever after.

✳ **DISCUSSION:** The well-loved play by George S. Kaufman and Moss Hart is given the Frank Capra treatment, which he himself called "Capra-corn." The entire populist subplot about the land being sold and the appearance of most of the characters in court are the additions of Capra and his screenwriter, Robert Riskin, and they make the film seem a bit dated. But children will enjoy the way that everyone in the family joyfully pursues his or her own dreams, and the way they all respect and support each other.

Discuss with children the way that some characters in the movie do not even seem to notice how eccentric they appear to others, while others notice and enjoy being different, and still others try desperately to appear "normal." Children may have their own ideas about what "normal" means and whether it makes them feel entertained or uncomfortable to be around people who have a different idea of normality. All children feel embarrassed by their families at times, and it is worth paying attention to the way that Alice learns, with Tony's help, that her family is not as unacceptable to the "normal" world as she'd feared.

PROFANITY: None.

NUDITY/SEXUAL REFFRENCES: None.

ALCOHOL/DRUG ABUSE: None.

VIOLENCE/SCARINESS: None.

TOLERANCE/DIVERSITY ISSUES: The two black characters, a maid and her out-of-work boyfriend, are treated with some affection but also with condescension.

✳ **QUESTIONS FOR KIDS:**
- Would you like to live in a family like this one?
- Which family member is most like you?
- Why did Tony tell his parents the wrong night for dinner at the Sycamores'?
- Notice the difference between the way that the Sycamores and the Kirbys react when they get arrested. Why?
- What does the title mean?

✳ **CONNECTIONS:** This movie won Academy Awards for Best Picture and Best Director. Kaufman and Hart were the most successful playwrights of their day, and some of their other plays have been made into movies, too. *George Washington Slept Here,* with Jack Benny and Ann Sheridan, is a very funny story about a family that moves into a ramshackle house. *The Man Who Came to Dinner* is about a nightmare dinner guest who falls and breaks his hip and is stuck in the house long enough to cause complete disruption for everyone. Kaufman was coauthor, with Edna Ferber, of *Stage Door,* about a group of young would-be actresses. It was made into a movie starring Katharine Hepburn and Ginger Rogers, and featuring Ann Miller, Lucille Ball, and Eve Arden. He was also the author of some of the Marx Brothers's most popular movies.

✲ **ACTIVITIES:** Younger kids will enjoy *Weird Parents,* by Audrey Wood, about a boy whose parents are even more outlandish than the Sycamores. Older kids can have fun getting a copy of the play and acting out some of their favorite scenes.

✲ ARSENIC AND OLD LACE

1944, 118 min, NR, b&w, 12 and up

Dir: Frank Capra. Cary Grant, Raymond Massey, Peter Lorre, Jack Carson

The most hilariously dysfunctional family in the history of the movies, this is a wildly funny black comedy about two darling old ladies who decide to help lonely old gentlemen by killing them with elderberry wine laced with arsenic. What makes it so funny is that they are not even the craziest people in the family; in addition to their nephew, Teddy (who thinks he is Teddy Roosevelt, which is pretty handy since he digs the Panama Canal in the basement to give them a place to dispose of the bodies), there is also their nephew Jonathan, a criminal with almost as many dead bodies to his credit as his aunts. In the middle of all of this is their third nephew, Mortimer (Cary Grant), who has just gotten married to the girl next door (Priscilla Lane). In the midst of a wild farce, with lots of slamming of doors (and window seats) and rushing around, there is some wicked satire. Not for all tastes, but very much to many.

✲ AUNTIE MAME

1958, 143 min, NR, 12 and up

Dir: Morton DaCosta. Rosalind Russell, Peggy Cass, Forrest Tucker

Based on the semiautobiographical Patrick Dennis novel and play, this is the story of a young boy who goes to live with his colorful aunt after his parents' death. Mame (Rosalind Russell) believes that "life is a banquet and most poor suckers are starving to death." She encourages all around her to help themselves to large portions of the banquet.

At first, it seems that she will be spending too much time going to parties and buying clothes to pay much attention to her nephew, and her grasp of a child's needs and abilities is dim at best. But she turns out to be a loving and devoted guardian, and a resilient one as well, after she loses everything in the stock market crash. She suffers an even greater loss when her husband is killed. And she questions her abilities as a guardian when Patrick seems bent on achieving the kind of conformity she has always despised. But it turns out she has taught him so well that at the end, he lets her take his young son to Europe and teach him about what really matters. NOTE: Mame encourages her secretary to be more outgoing, resulting in an (apparently) out-of-wedlock pregnancy. Lots of drinking. Anti-Semitic characters (over whom Mame triumphs by making it possible for a Jewish family to buy property near them).

✻ **CONNECTIONS:** The movie was remade as a musical *(Mame)* with Lucille Ball.

✻ THE BARRETTS OF WIMPOLE STREET
1934, 110 min, NR, b&w, 12 and up
Dir: Sidney Franklin. Norma Shearer, Fredric March, Charles Laughton
This is the thrilling real-life love story of two of the world's greatest poets, Elizabeth Barrett (Norma Shearer) and Robert Browning (Fredric March). Barrett was confined to bed with a debilitating illness, but the bigger problem was her father, a twisted, bitter man (Charles Laughton) who terrorized and humiliated his grown children and controlled every aspect of their lives, forbidding them to marry or even have close friends. Barrett and Browning first corresponded, and finally she allowed him to call on her, and they fell deeply in love. Barrett's sister, Henrietta, also fell in love with a dashing captain. Both women had to decide whether they would leave everything they had known for love and freedom.

✻ **CONNECTIONS:** The same director remade the film in 1957, with Jennifer Jones, Bill Travers, and John Gielgud as Mr. Barrett, but the original is better.

✻ BENNY & JOON
1993, 98 min, PG, high schoolers
Dir: Jeremiah Chechick. Aidan Quinn, Mary Stuart Masterson, Johnny Depp
Benny (Aidan Quinn) is devoted to his schizophrenic sister, Joon (Mary Stuart Masterson), and takes care of her lovingly. An eccentric young man named Sam (Johnny Depp) comes to stay with them to help care for Joon. Joon and Sam get along so well that Benny is able to relax for the first time, and he begins to get friendly with Ruthie (Julianne Moore). But when Joon seems to become dependent on Sam, Benny becomes very protective and throws Sam out. The stress causes Joon to have a breakdown, and she is hospitalized. Her doctor encourages Benny to let her make her own decisions about what she wants to do, and she decides to try living with Sam. Although the portrayal of mental illness in this film is sentimental and very unrealistic, the issues it raises about love and letting go are important.

✻ BOYZ N THE HOOD
1991, 107 min, R, mature high schoolers
Dir: John Singleton. Cuba Gooding, Jr., Laurence Fishburne, Ice Cube
This outstanding debut by John Singleton, who wrote and directed it at the age of twenty-three, is an enormously moving story with one of the

great fathers in the history of films—Laurence Fishburne as Furious Styles. Furious tries to raise his son Tre (Cuba Gooding, Jr.) to be strong and brave in the midst of chaos in a black neighborhood. Tre becomes friends with two brothers who live across the street, tough Doughboy (Ice Cube) and quiet Ricky (Morris Chestnut). Doughboy is sent to prison for seven years and returns devoted to his friends, but bitter and angry. Ricky, now a promising athlete with a chance for an academic scholarship, is killed by a gang, and both Tre and Doughboy want revenge. Only the intervention of Furious keeps Tre safe, and the movie ends with the admonition, "Keep the Peace." This is a rough movie, far less violent than most urban dramas, but with far more tragic power. NOTE: Strong language, substance abuse, out-of-wedlock pregnancy, and violence.

✳ DOMINICK AND EUGENE

1988, 111 min, PG-13, mature high schoolers
Dir: Robert M. Young. Ray Liotta, Tom Hulce, Jamie Lee Curtis

Dominick (Tom Hulce) and Eugene (Ray Liotta) are twins whose parents are dead. They take care of each other; Dominick takes care of Eugene by working as a garbage man to pay Eugene's way through medical school. And Eugene takes care of Dominick, who is retarded. But there is a lot of stress involved. Eugene feels overworked and overwhelmed. And Dominick worries that Eugene will leave him, especially when Eugene starts to become close to another med student (Jamie Lee Curtis). This is a touching and beautifully performed film that captures the essence of what families are about. NOTE: Theme of child abuse; one child is badly injured by his father, which prompts memories in both Eugene and Dominick about how Dominick was injured by his own father.

✳ THE FIRST OF MAY

1998, 112 min, G, 8 and up
Dir: Paul Sirmons. Julie Harris, Mickey Rooney, Charles Nelson Reilly, Joe Di-Maggio, Dan Byrd

Cory (Dan Byrd) is not enthusiastic about meeting Dan (Tom Nowicki) and Michele (Robin O'Dell), his new foster parents. Clearly, he has already decided that it makes no sense to allow himself to get close to people. He responds to their kindness and patience by thawing a little, but it is not until his choir goes to perform at a nursing home that he finds someone to feel close to. It is Carlotta (Julie Harris), like Cory unhappy and out of place. Cory buys Carlotta the ingredients she needs to make her special candy, halvah. He loves to hear about her life in the circus, and as they become close they agree to be each other's family. When Cory thinks he overhears Michelle and Dan saying that they are going to send him away, he goes to see Carlotta, and they agree to run away together. At first, they are able to support themselves by selling halvah. But when someone threatens to report Cory as truant from school, they run away. They find a circus and persuade Boss Ed (Mickey Rooney) to take them on to sell concessions. Carlotta meets up with some old friends and Cory makes some new ones (and triumphs over a jealous bully). They are very happy, until Carlotta becomes ill and has to go to the hospital. The circus has to leave without them, but Cory finds a way to have the family he dreamed of. This sweet, episodic story has many magical moments. The backstage glimpses of circus life are delightful. Cory even gets some batting advice from Joe DiMaggio, who appears as himself. Families of all kinds will respond to this story about people who triumph over a series of obstacles to create a family for themselves.

✳ THE GOOFY MOVIE
1995, 78 min, G, 8 and up
Dir: Kevin Lima.

One of the great existential questions of childhood, memorably explored in *Stand By Me,* is, "If Mickey is a mouse, and Pluto is a dog, what is Goofy?" Goofy may be in a class (and genus) of his own, as we see in this thoroughly enjoyable film. At the center of the story is Max, struggling through the torturous insecurity and self-consciousness of adolescence. Like all teens, he is humiliated by his father's goofiness. But the movie's great joke is that in this case, his father is not just goofy, he *is* Goofy, the Goof of all Goofs, the Uber-Goof!

When a prank at school gets Max in trouble, Goofy decides that what Max needs is some quality time with his father. So he takes him on a fishing trip, not knowing that Max will have to miss his first date with his adored Roxanne, and that in order to get out of the date, Max has lied to Roxanne, telling her his father is taking him to a rock concert. It takes a while (and a run-in with Bigfoot) for Goofy and Max to start talking to each other instead of at each other. But they ultimately strengthen their connection and find a satisfying resolution. Free of the pressures that sometimes smother the big Disney releases, this movie has a refreshingly casual, even insouciant feel, with some sly humor (look fast for a glimpse of Elvis at a remote lunch counter), and it even dares to poke fun at Disney itself. The teen characters are contemporary without the prepackaged feel of other Disney productions (like *The New Mickey Mouse Club*), and there are lively songs performed by Tevin Campbell.

Although the material in this movie is certainly suitable for all ages, younger kids may be uncomfortable with the strain between Max and Goofy. It's a shame that the G rating scared off the film's optimal audience, the ten-to-fourteen age group. If you can persuade them to take a look, they will find much to enjoy and identify with, and if parents and kids watch it together, it can inspire some good discussions about parent-child communication.

✳ THE LITTLE FOXES
1941, 116 min, NR, b&w, 12 and up
Dir: William Wyler. Bette Davis, Teresa Wright, Herbert Marshall
   This movie, based on the play by Lillian Hellman, presents us with probably the most greedy, vicious, and corrupt of all movie families. Regina (Bette Davis) and her brothers will do anything to get money, and if it means harming each other along the way, so much the better. In order to get the money they need to invest in a new factory, they steal bonds from the safe-deposit box owned by Regina's husband. When he tries to stop them, Regina withholds his medicine so he will die. Ultimately, however, she loses what she most wants: the love and support of her daughter.

   ✳ **CONNECTIONS:** To see how these people got the way they were, watch the prequel, *Another Part of the Forest.* Hellman also wrote *The Children's Hour,* which was also filmed as **These Three,** and the memoir that was the basis for the movie, **Julia.**

✳ LITTLE WOMEN
1994, 118 min, PG, 8 and up
Dir: Gillian Armstrong. Winona Ryder, Susan Sarandon, Christian Bale, Gabriel Byrne, Eric Stoltz, Claire Danes
   In this classic Louisa May Alcott story based on her own family, Jo March is Alcott herself, the headstrong but sensitive second daughter of the family, who dreams of being a writer. With her older sister Meg, younger sisters Beth and Amy, and friend Laurie Lawrence, and the guidance of her wise mother and father, she faces the challenges of growing up. The four girls learn patience, compassion, and the most meaningful family values. This is an exceptionally good movie for portraying sibling relationships, as the four March girls sometimes squabble but are deeply committed to each other. The story has been filmed four times. This version, produced by Winona Ryder (who plays Jo), has gorgeous period detail and spirited performances by an attractive young cast. The 1933 version, with Katharine Hepburn as Jo, is also exceptional.

   ✳ **ACTIVITIES:** Kids should read the book and its sequel, *Little Men,* as well some of Alcott's other classics, like *Eight Cousins* and *An Old Fashioned Girl.* They may also enjoy *Invincible Louisa,* or one of the other biographies of Alcott. And, if they get to Massachusetts, they can visit her home and find out more about the Alcott girls and their parents, who were the models for the Marches.

✳ LONG DAY'S JOURNEY INTO NIGHT
1962, 136 min, NR, b&w, mature high schoolers
Dir: Sidney Lumet. Katharine Hepburn, Ralph Richardson, Jason Robards, Dean Stockwell

Based on the family of playwright Eugene O'Neill, this is the searing story of four people who love each other deeply and yet cannot stop causing each other pain. Like O'Neill's father, James Tyrone (Ralph Richardson) is a well-known actor, stuck playing the same part for years just to make money. His wife, Mary (Katharine Hepburn), has just returned from a sanitorium. One son, Jamie (Jason Robards), is an alcoholic, and the other, Edmund (Dean Stockwell), is ailing with tuberculosis. Each of them suffers terribly with a weakness that hurts the others—James's miserliness; Mary's addiction to morphine; Jamie's bitterness, self-loathing, and alcoholism; Edmund's weakness. This is a brilliant portrait of a tortured family, with performances of shattering insight and vulnerability.

✳ MRS. DOUBTFIRE
1993, 125 min, PG-13, 10 and up
Dir: Chris Columbus. Robin Williams, Sally Field

Robin Williams plays Daniel, a loving but irresponsible man whose frustrated wife (Sally Field) asks for a divorce. In order to see his children, he dresses as a woman and applies for a job as their nanny. The movie's strong points are Williams's performance and the devotion of his character to his children. It will be especially reassuring to kids of divorced parents because it makes it clear that parents love their children even after divorce, and that the parents can find a way to get along with each other even after the marriage ends. This is the reason it is included in this book. Its weak points are a lazy script filled with cheap sitcom humor, often at the expense of Pierce Brosnan, as Field's new beau. NOTE: I am not a big fan of this movie, so I recommend it only with reservations because of its devoted father and its handling of the issue of divorce, and suggest that parents screen it before deciding whether it is appropriate for their children. If it is appropriate as a way to help a child deal with some difficult issues, it may be worthwhile; otherwise, skip it. Some parents will appreciate the positive portrayal of a gay couple. They are presented in such a low-key fashion that it is unlikely to spark any questions for parents who are not comfortable discussing homosexuality.

✳ RAIN MAN
1988, 140 min, R, mature high schoolers
Dir: Barry Levinson. Dustin Hoffman, Tom Cruise

Tom Cruise plays Charlie Babbitt, a self-centered young man who is furious to find that his wealthy late father left him only a car. The money has been left to a brother he did not even know he had (Raymond, played by Dustin Hoffman), who lives in an institution because he is autistic. Charlie impulsively takes Raymond with him, and as they drive across the country, Charlie moves from irritation to exploitation to understanding and love. Hoffman's Oscar-winning performance as the autistic savant attracted most of the attention, but it is Cruise's painful efforts to uncover his feelings for his brother and his understanding that he must do what is best for Raymond and let others take care of him that really matters.

✳ A RAISIN IN THE SUN
1961, 128 min, NR, b&w, 12 and up
Dir: Daniel Petrie. Sidney Poitier, Claudia McNeil

Lorraine Hansberry's classic play, its title taken from a poem by Langston Hughes ("What happens to a dream deferred? . . . Does it dry up like a raisin in the sun?"), is the story of a black family's debates about what to do with $10,000 in insurance money. The mother (Claudia McNeil) wants to use it to buy a house in a "good" (and all-white) neighborhood and send her daughter to medical school. The grown son (Sidney Poitier) wants to use it to buy a liquor store. Despite setbacks, including an offer by the neighborhood "improvement association" to buy them out, the family resolves to do whatever is necessary to move into their new home.

✳ SOUNDER
1972, 115 min, G, 8 and up
Dir: Martin Ritt. Paul Winfield, Cecily Tyson

This beautiful film offers a rare depiction of a strong and loving black family, led by Paul Winfield and Cecily Tyson, and one of the best movie portrayals ever of a family of any color. The family are sharecroppers during the Depression, and times are hard. When the father steals a ham to feed his hungry family, he is sentenced to a year in jail, and the family must bring in the crops without him. The young son is torn between his commitment to his family and his chance to go to an all-black school, where he would have a real opportunity to learn.

Note the beautiful cinematography by John A. Alonzo. Lighting and production design in movies are almost invariably designed for white actors, even in scenes with black characters. But in this movie the black actors are photographed beautifully, with loving attention to the rich range of hues of African-American skin tones.

✳ WHAT'S EATING GILBERT GRAPE
1993, 117 min, PG-13, mature high schoolers
Dir: Lasse Hallström. Johnny Depp, Leonardo DiCaprio, Juliette Lewis

Gilbert Grape (Johnny Depp) feels responsible for taking care of everyone, including his loving mother, who is all but incapacitated by her enormous weight; his retarded brother (Leonardo DiCaprio in an astonishingly perceptive and moving performance); the owners of the local grocery store, almost driven out of business by the new supermarket chain; even a lonely housewife, who orders groceries just to get him to come over to have sex. When Becky (Juliette Lewis) and her grandmother stop in town for a few days to repair their trailer, Gilbert gets a glimpse of a world in which he could have something for himself. This quirky movie is not for everyone, but it has become a cult favorite for its odd characters and their deep attachment to each other. NOTE: Mature themes. Gilbert has an affair with a married woman; Gilbert and Becky have sex; bizarre sexual comments by one character.

✻ **CONNECTIONS:** Director Hallström is also responsible for a perceptive movie about adolescence (with some mature themes), the Swedish *My Life as a Dog*.

✻ YOURS, MINE AND OURS

1968, 111 min, NR, 8 and up
Dir: Melville Shavelson. Henry Fonda, Lucille Ball, Van Johnson

This is no one's idea of a great film, but it is an enjoyable comedy on a subject literally close to home for many families—it is the real-life story of a widower with ten children (Henry Fonda) who marries a widow with eight (Lucille Ball). There is quite an adjustment period, especially after he goes off to sea not knowing that she is pregnant with number nineteen, the "ours" in the title. Fonda and Ball are always great fun to watch, and the movie has some genuinely touching moments, especially Fonda explaining to his stepdaughter why she should resist her boyfriend's advances, as he is taking Ball to the hospital to deliver.

✻ **CONNECTIONS:** You can see Fonda and Ball together twenty-six years earlier in the tragic Damon Runyon story, *The Big Street*.

SEE ALSO:

Anne of Green Gables An orphan girl and a middle-aged, taciturn brother and sister become a warm and loving family.

A Christmas Memory A little boy and his elderly cousin form a close family bond in a home where they are neglected by everyone else.

Fiddler on the Roof A strong, loving family must respond to both internal and external pressures, as the daughters insist on marrying the men of their choice, and the mounting prejudice forces the family to leave its home.

The Flamingo Kid A young man is temporarily dazzled by a wealthy and sophisticated man, but ultimately returns to his father and the values he learned at home.

Friendly Persuasion A loving Quaker family must resolve differences and find a way to keep their values while the Civil War comes literally to their doorstep.

Houseboat A widower who barely knew his children, who are hurt by his neglect and the loss of their mother, learn how much they mean to each other, and then almost lose it all again when he falls in love with their housekeeper.

Now, Voyager A woman learns how destructive family members can be, and then, with the help of a gifted therapist and the man who loves her, learns how to protect herself.

The Ramona series The videos based on this classic series of children's books offer a loving and good-humored portrait of a family dealing with aspects of everyday life, which all children will recognize.

A Thousand Clowns An iconoclastic man learns to conform enough to help him keep custody of the nephew he loves.

Where the Lilies Bloom A young girl shows determination and courage in keeping her family together after the death of her parents.

FINDING THE HERO WITHIN

The greatest obstacle to being heroic is the doubt whether one may not be going to prove one's self a fool; the truest heroism is to resist the doubt; and the profoundest wisdom is to know when it ought to be resisted and when it be obeyed.
—NATHANIEL HAWTHORNE

From Rocky to John Wayne to Indiana Jones to Mr. Smith, we love the movie heroes (mostly white men, unfortunately) who display the courage, intelligence, and persistence that we hope lies somewhere within us, too. For that reason, we are especially drawn to the characters who must find the hero within themselves, and the story of the ordinary person thrust into extraordinary circumstances (which he at first finds daunting but then masters) is one of the most popular and appealing themes of the movies. We get to watch the character evaluate the risks and, more importantly, evaluate himself. We get to see him learn and watch him be transformed as he is tested. And we get to think about what makes a hero, and what heroic qualities we can find in ourselves or in the people around us.

We often tend to think of heroism in terms of physical courage and determination, but the movies show us other kinds of heroes as well, heroes with moral courage and unshakable integrity.

The ancient Greek notion of the hero whose destiny is foretold is reflected in some movies directly based on Greek myths and in other myth-based stories. But most often in our movie mythology the hero "has greatness thrust upon him"—whether he wants it or not. And the more unlikely, the more satisfying it is for us to watch, whether the hero turns out to be a sheepherding pig, a kid who learns he can take care of himself, a drunken boatman and a prim missionary, a naive new senator, a drunken former gunfighter, or a peaceful mountain man who sets a record for achievement in battle that still stands almost a century later.

Very often, the character tries not to be a hero but is then drawn into the conflict. What leads someone to come to that choice? Also very often, the hero's biggest obstacle is his lack of faith in himself. In some cases, the hero has a flaw he must overcome, or make use of. How do these people develop enough faith in themselves to do what is necessary? How do they change in order to do what they must do, and how does the experience change them?

The most interesting heroes are the ones who are complex enough to be flawed. Oskar Schindler's whole life was one of petty crimes and careless behavior, and yet he risked everything to protect 1,100 Jews while people who had led exemplary lives were participating in the genocide.

These are movies that encourage us to think about the nature of heroism. They remind us that the heroic ideal in our hearts and dreams (probably based on some movie) is more complicated and thus more real than we think. There may even be a hero within us.

The African Queen

1951. 103 min, NR, 8 and up
Dir: John Huston. Katharine Hepburn, Humphrey Bogart, Robert Morley

❋ **PLOT:** Rose Sayer and her brother, Samuel, are English missionaries in 1914 German East Africa. Their rare contact with the outside world is through Charlie Allnut, who delivers their occasional mail on his steam-powered boat, the *African Queen*. The Germans destroy their village. Samuel is injured and dies, brokenhearted. Charlie offers to take Rose with him.

At first, they are stiffly polite to each other. He respectfully calls her "Miss," and she calls him "Mr. Allnut." She decides that they must help fight the Germans by using their explosives to blow up the powerful German gunboat, the *Louisa*. He becomes angry and frustrated by her insistence on what he sees as a dangerously reckless idea, and she becomes disgusted and furious when he gets drunk. He calls her a "crazy psalm-singing skinny old maid." She pours all his liquor overboard.

He decides that she will change her mind when she sees how dangerous the river is, and takes her over the rapids. She is thrilled, telling him that she is "filled with admiration" for his skill, and that "I never dreamed any mere physical experience could be so stimulating!" Charmed by her enthusiasm and praise, he still insists that they cannot possibly attack the *Louisa*. The river is all but impossible to navigate, and a German fort blocks their path. She insists, and as they face challenges together they learn to respect, rely on, and finally love each other. After a tender night together, she asks him, "Mr. Allnut, dear. There's something I must know. What's your first name?"

They make it past the fort and survive bugs, rapids, leeches, and the reeds that strangle the river, finally approaching the *Louisa*. But they are captured and sentenced to death by the captain. Charlie asks for a last request—that they be executed as husband and wife. The captain quickly marries them, and just as they are about to be hung, Charlie's torpedo strapped to the *African Queen* hits the *Louisa,* and Mr. and Mrs. Allnut swim to shore together.

✳ **DISCUSSION:** This is one of the finest and most satisfying of the "two diverse characters must take a journey together and learn to like and respect each other along the way" genre. Rose and Charlie are opposites. And yet they are perfectly suited to each other.

We first see Charlie hideously out of place sipping tea with Rose and Samuel and trying to hide his growling stomach. "Nature, Mr. Allnut, is what we were put in this world to rise above," she tells him later. And yet, in another sense, Rose and Samuel were out of place in Africa. Ultimately, Rose is not comfortable "rising above" nature, and indeed grows to love it as she gives up some of the strictures of civilization and appreciates the beauty and "stimulation" of the natural world. Charlie learns to appreciate some of the beauties of civilization: to take the challenge and the responsibility of participating in the fight against the Germans, to have a relationship of trust and tenderness.

> PROFANITY: None.
>
> NUDITY/SEXUAL REFERENCES: Very mild suggestion that Charlie and Rose sleep together.
>
> ALCOHOL/DRUG ABUSE: Charlie gets drunk; Rose pours all of his liquor into the river.
>
> VIOLENCE/SCARINESS: Destruction of village; characters in peril several times, from nature and from the German sailors.
>
> TOLERANCE/DIVERSITY ISSUES: Class issues.

✳ **QUESTIONS FOR KIDS:**
- What do Samuel's dying words tell you about Rose? What does her reaction tell you?
- How does Rose's experience on the first rapids change the way she feels? How does it change the way Charlie feels about her?
- Why does Charlie decide to go along with her plan to torpedo the *Louisa?*
- How does each bring out the best in the other?
- What can you tell about Rose from her prayer, asking that God "judge us not for our weakness but for our love, and open the doors of heaven for Charlie and me"?

✳ **CONNECTIONS:** Humphrey Bogart won a well-deserved Oscar for this performance. Katharine Hepburn, who was also nominated, said that her performance was based on director John Huston's suggestion that she play Rose as Eleanor Roosevelt. Compare this performance to her appearance in *Pat and Mike* a year later, in which she played a world-class athlete.

The movie is based on a novel of the same name by C. S. Forester, but the romance was added by screenwriters James Agee and John Huston. Adults who enjoy this movie might like to see *White Hunter, Black Heart,* a backstage look at the making of this film, concentrating on John Huston's elephant hunting.

❋ **ACTIVITIES:** Look at a map of Africa to see where this took place.

❋ Bad Day at Black Rock

1955, 81 min, NR, b&w, 10 and up
Dir: John Sturges. Spencer Tracy, Robert Ryan, Ernest Borgnine, Lee Marvin,
Anne Francis, Dean Jagger, Walter Brennan

❋ **PLOT:** John MacReedy (Spencer Tracy) gets off a train in a tiny, dusty little Western town. It is rare for any stranger to come to the town; it is the first time the train has stopped there in four years. The town residents move from suspicion of the one-armed man in a suit to open hostility when MacReedy enters the local hotel and asks about a local farmer named Komoko. Pete Wirth (John Ericson), the hotel manager, refuses to give him a room, saying they are all booked. When MacReedy takes a key, anyway, a bully named Hector David (Lee Marvin) insists that it is his room. MacReedy takes another room. Hector and most of the rest of the town report to Reno (Robert Ryan). When he tells them to push MacReedy without giving him information, they are happy to oblige. But the town doctor (Walter Brennan) tells MacReedy how to get to Komoko's farm, and Liz Wirth (Anne Francis), Pete's sister, rents him a jeep to get there. MacReedy finds the farm deserted. Coley Trimble (Ernest Borgnine), another of Reno's henchmen, chases Mac-Reedy back to town, driving him off the road and slamming into the jeep with his truck.

MacReedy realizes that Reno will never let him get out of town alive. He tries to make a phone call or send a telegram, but Reno has cut him off. When Trimble harasses him at the diner, he refuses to fight, then finally, when Trimble persists, MacReedy devastates him with a karate chop to the neck. That buys him some time, but MacReedy is cornered and he knows it. He persuades Liz Wirth to drive him out of Black Rock. But it is a trap. Reno is waiting for them. As Liz runs to Reno, he shoots her; he no longer trusts her to keep his secret. MacReedy puts the jeep's leaking gas into a bottle, stuffs it with his tie, lights it, and throws it at Reno, who is killed.

MacReedy had come to Black Rock to give Komoko the medal his son had been awarded by the U.S. Army for heroism. Komoko's son had saved MacReedy's life before he was killed in battle. But Komoko was also dead. Reno and his henchmen killed him at the start of World War II because he was Japanese.

The doctor asks MacReedy if he will leave the medal in Black Rock. MacReedy gives it to him, then puts out the flag so that the train will stop in Black Rock again, for the second time in four years.

❋ **DISCUSSION:** "A man is as big as what makes him mad." MacReedy says this to Reno in one of this movie's key scenes, and it is a concept children (and parents) should think about. It is also interesting that Reno killed Komoko after he was found ineligible to enlist in the army. His hostility toward Komoko was based on displaced anger and frustration as much as racism.

MacReedy did not choose this battle, but he never turns away from it. A man who had no direction, and no goal beyond the presentation of the medal to Komoko, becomes a man who will not allow Reno and his thugs to win. He is fighting them not just for Komoko, but for himself, and in doing so finds a pride and dignity that enables him to go on.

This is a good movie to use for a discussion of prejudice, not just about race, but also about disabilities.

PROFANITY: None.

NUDITY/SEXUAL REFERENCES: Mild implication that Liz Wirth and Reno are lovers.

ALCOHOL/DRUG ABUSE: Some by the bad guys.

VIOLENCE/SCARINESS: Fighting with cars, guns, and karate.

TOLERANCE/DIVERSITY ISSUES: A theme of the movie is the prejudice against the Japanese that led Reno and his men to kill Mr. Komoko. They also make fun of MacReedy (Hector David says, "You look like you need a hand") because of his disability and, more importantly, they underestimate him. MacReedy may also underestimate himself.

✳ **QUESTIONS FOR KIDS:**
- What does it mean to say, "A man is only as big as what makes him mad"? Think about a time you got mad. How big was the thing that made you mad? How do you measure?
- The people in the town had different reasons for obeying Reno. What were they?
- How did MacReedy change? What did he learn about himself?

✳ **CONNECTIONS:** Compare this to **High Noon,** another movie about a lone force for justice. Anne Francis, known to baby boomers for television's *Honey West,* plays opposite Robby the Robot in the science fiction classic **Forbidden Planet.** In both movies, she is the only woman in the cast.

Interestingly, MacReedy's handicap, so central to the story, was a last-minute addition in order to make the character challenging enough to attract Tracy to the role.

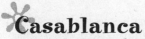

Casablanca
1942, 102 min, NR, b&w, 10 and up
Dir: Michael Curtiz. Humphrey Bogart, Ingrid Bergman, Claude Rains, Paul Henreid

✳ **PLOT:** Rick (Humphrey Bogart) owns a popular nightclub in Casablanca, in the early days of WWII. France is under the control of the Vichy government, which has close ties to the Nazis, but Casablanca still has an uneasy independence. As a result, people come from all over to try to get exit visas to countries that are still free, and corruption and chaos are pervasive. As the movie opens, the police shoot a man who does not have the proper papers, and refugees negotiate with smugglers for passage to Lisbon, from which one can get to America.

Captain Renault (Claude Rains) of the local police arrives at Rick's with Major Strasser, a Nazi. Strasser is searching for the person who killed two German couriers. Whoever killed them took their papers, including two "letters of transit," which enable the bearer to leave the country without question. Ugarte (Peter Lorre) has the letters and gives them to Rick to hide for him. Ugarte is then captured by the police. Rick makes no effort to protect him, saying, "I stick my neck out for nobody." Strasser is also looking for an escaped Czech named Victor Laszlo (Paul Henreid). Laszlo arrives at Rick's with Ilsa (Ingrid Bergman), planning to meet Ugarte.

Rick and Ilsa knew each other before, in Paris. They had planned to leave together, before the city fell to the Germans, but at the last minute, Ilsa did not come, and sent a note saying that she could never see Rick again. He is angry and bitter, and still so deeply hurt that he drinks heavily. When she returns to talk to him, he is drunk and lashes out at her, and she leaves.

The next night, they speak again, and she tells him that she is married to Laszlo, and thought he had been killed when she'd first met Rick. She found Laszlo was still alive the day she and Rick were supposed to leave Paris. She loved Rick then, and still loves him. Rick and Renault plan to trap Laszlo by giving him the letters of transit. Then Renault will arrest Laszlo, and Rick and Ilsa will leave together. But at the airport, Rick tells Laszlo that he must go and that Ilsa must go with him. In one of the most famous moments in movies, he tells her that "We'll always have Paris." Rick and Renault leave together to join the fight against the Nazis.

✳ **DISCUSSION:** This is probably the most famous Hollywood movie of all time, certainly the most quoted, and the most frequently cited as the all-time favorite, particularly by men. It is fascinating to read the story of how the film was made. The definitive rebuttal to notions of the "auteur" (director as author) in film, this movie was put together in pieces by many different sources, with script pages completed just moments before the cameras rolled. One reason that the performances by Bogart and Bergman are so subtle and complex is that the actors themselves had no idea how the movie was going to end.

Rick tries to appear cool and amoral. When Renault says he knows Rick ran guns to Ethiopia and fought for the Loyalists in Spain, Rick replies that he was well-paid. But Renault gently reminds him that the other side would have paid him better. In reality, Rick is deeply moral. He will not take any action to protect Ugarte, who does not deserve it, but when a young bride is about to sleep with Renault to get exit visas, he arranges for her husband to "win" at roulette so that they can buy the visas instead. Rick is very loyal to Sam, the piano player. And when he is able to put Ilsa's actions into a moral context, he forgives her completely and is once again able to "have Paris," to draw on the love they had for one another and the happiness they shared in order to give up all he has to get back into the fight.

Kids may need some of the political and historical context explained to them, especially the meaning of the shot at the end of the Vichy water in the garbage.

PROFANITY: None.

NUDITY/SEXUAL REFERENCES: None.

ALCOHOL/DRUG ABUSE: Much of the action takes place in a bar, Rick drinks when he is unhappy about seeing Ilsa again.

VIOLENCE/SCARINESS: Characters in peril.

TOLERANCE/DIVERSITY ISSUES: Sam, the piano player, is treated with great respect and affection, though Ilsa calls him a "boy."

❋ **QUESTIONS FOR KIDS:**
- Some of the best-remembered lines of this movie indicate the casual corruption of Casablanca. What does it mean to say, "We haven't quite decided if he committed suicide or died trying to escape," or, "I'm shocked to find gambling going on in Casablanca," or, "Round up the usual suspects"?
- What does Rick mean when he says "We'll always have Paris," and that they didn't have it until Ilsa came to Casablanca?
- How does knowing that Ilsa really loved him change the way Rick looks at the world?
- Was Ilsa right to stay with Laszlo in Paris? Was she right to leave with him to go to Lisbon? Why?
- What do you think Rick and Renault will do next?

❋ **CONNECTIONS:** This movie won Oscars for Best Picture, Director, and Writer. Almost every frame of this movie is an icon, and it has been endlessly copied and parodied. The Woody Allen movie *Play It Again, Sam* (rated PG, but not for kids since the entire plot is about seduction) is an affectionate tribute to **Casablanca** and other Bogart movies.

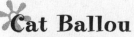

Cat Ballou

1965, 96 min, NR, 8 and up
Dir: Elliott Silverstein. Jane Fonda, Lee Marvin, Michael Callan

❋ **PLOT:** In the days of the Old West, Catherine (Cat) Ballou (Jane Fonda) takes the train home, after graduating from school. She does her best to appear proper, but peeks at potboilers about the notorious Kid Shelleen inside her book. On the train, she meets escaping cattle rustler Clay Boone

(Michael Callan) and his uncle Jed (Dwayne Hickman). She is attracted to Clay, but not interested in becoming involved with a criminal.

Cat is angry and upset when she gets home and sees that her father (John Marley) is being pressured to give up his land. He is killed by hired gun Tim Strawn. When her father's ranch hand, an Indian named Jackson (Tom Nardini), and Clay and Jed are not brave enough to help her fight back, she sends for Kid Shelleen (Lee Marvin).

Kid arrives, a hopeless drunk. But they help him pull himself together, and they get their revenge. Cat is captured and sentenced to be hung, but is saved at the last minute by her friends.

✳ **DISCUSSION:** This cheerful satire of conventional Westerns is a lot of fun, with attractive performers and an Oscar-winning performance by Lee Marvin in the dual roles of Shelleen and Strawn. Stubby Kaye (**Guys and Dolls**) and Nat "King" Cole show up as something between a Greek chorus and medieval minstrels, singing the story as it unfolds. It is good for kids to see a movie with a strong, brave, and resourceful young woman who is an effective and inspiring leader (though they all have crushes on her).

PROFANITY: None.

NUDITY/SEXUAL REFEREENCES: None.

ALCOHOL/DRUG ABUSE: Jed is drunk in first scene; Kid Shelleen has a drinking problem, comically portrayed.

VIOLENCE/SCARINESS: Shoot-outs, Cat's father is killed.

TOLERANCE/DIVERSITY ISSUES: Prejudice against Jackson Two-Bears, an Indian.

✳ **QUESTIONS FOR KIDS:**
- Why was Cat so effective at leading Clay, Jed, Kid, and Jackson?
- Do you agree with her decision to take matters into her own hands?
- How does she compare to other Western heroes, such as Shane?

✳ **CONNECTIONS:** Watch for a character named "Butch Cassidy" in a minor role, four years before Paul Newman and Robert Redford appeared in **Butch Cassidy and the Sundance Kid,** by William Goldman. Marvin appeared more often as the kind of tough guy he parodies in this movie, for example, in **The Man Who Shot Liberty Valance.** Jed is played by television's Dobie Gillis, Dwayne Hickman.

✳The Hustler

1960, 130 min, NR, b&w, 14 and up
Dir: Robert Rossen. Paul Newman, Jackie Gleason, George C. Scott, Piper Laurie

✳ **PLOT:** "Fast" Eddie Felsen (Paul Newman) is a pool hustler. He and his partner, Charlie, go into pool halls and set up the local players. Eddie pretends to be a pool player who likes to make big bets. When he beats them and takes their money, he makes it look like luck, so they can't tell they have been hustled.

Eddie's dream is to beat the legendary Minnesota Fats (Jackie Gleason), the champion. He challenges him to a contest. At first, Eddie is ahead. But he gets cocky, drinks too much, and is finally worn down by Fats. After more than twenty-four hours, Eddie realizes he can't win. He leaves Charlie the money and the car, and goes off on his own.

Eddie meets Sarah (Piper Laurie), an alcoholic, and moves in with her. When Charlie finds them, Eddie tells him to go. Charlie wants to make enough money to set up his own pool hall. Eddie wants more; he wants to win, and to be a winner.

Angry at himself and the world, Eddie hustles some young punks and shows off, humiliating them. They beat him up and break his thumbs. He has time to reflect, and to grow closer to Sarah. He agrees to go into partnership with Bert Gordon (George C. Scott), a silky gambler who sees everything in terms of dollars. Bert sets up a game with a decadent rich man. In a mirror image of the game with Fats, Eddie loses at first, and then, defying Sarah's appeal to quit, persists, and wins $12,000. At the hotel, Bert and Sarah acknowledge that in the tug-of-war for Eddie, Bert has won. Sarah commits suicide.

Bert once told Eddie that he needed more than talent to beat Fats—he needed character. Eddie shows that he has developed character when he goes back and takes Fats on again. Fats concedes, "I can't beat you." Bert says that Eddie owes him his piece of the proceeds, but Eddie refuses. Bert allows him to go, but says he will never be able to play in a big-time pool hall again. That doesn't matter. Eddie has what he wanted.

✳ **DISCUSSION:** Despite the seedy settings (so evocative that they are almost a character in the story), this is almost a traditional morality play about humility and redemption. In the beginning Eddie is, as Fats notes, as fast as his nickname, slick, cocky, superficial. He wants to win for the kick of it. But inside him, there is someone who wants to win for the beauty of the game, and the honor of doing something surpassingly well. He is really not so far removed from Eric Liddell (*Chariots of Fire*), who feels God's pleasure when he runs. But before he can be a real winner, he must get rid of the part of himself that wants to lose, that is afraid to take a real risk. For that, he has to experience real loss, the beating, the damage to his thumbs that could have ended his ability to play pool, the loss of Sarah.

As Nietzsche said, "That which does not defeat me makes me stronger." Eddie is strengthened so by these experiences and by what he has learned that he can no longer be contained by what had once been his entire world. Bert's threat that he will no longer be able to play big-time pool is meaningless to him. Even if Bert had offered him a fifty-fifty deal, he would not have taken it. That world is too small and self-contained for him now.

Most of the movie takes place in smoky, dingy bars and pool halls. The scenes at the rich man's home in Louisville are just as squalid in their own way. There is only one scene in which Eddie and Sarah are outside together. They are having a picnic. It is in that scene that they first reveal the truth about themselves to each other. Sarah confesses the real source of her money (her father) and her limp (polio), contrary to what she has told him before. And she tells him that she loves him. Eddie tells her what he barely admitted to himself, the way he loves the game of pool, the way it makes him feel to play it well. Understanding what it means to him is what enables him to begin to go back to it.

The relationship between Eddie and Sarah is a weak part of the movie, mostly because her character is the least well-crafted in the otherwise all-male story. It is hard to feel sympathetic toward her because she thinks so badly of herself. Yet her willingness to love Eddie is what causes him to recognize what is best in himself.

It is also interesting to look at this movie from Fats's perspective. He represents one direction Eddie could take. He could become the new champion and take on every tough kid who wanted to topple him, until one finally would, just as he toppled his predecessor. This is the theme of *The Gunfighter,* in a life-and-death context.

PROFANITY: None.

NUDITY/SEXUAL REFERENCES: Eddie and Sarah have (off-screen) sex; implication that Bert and Sarah have sex, a factor in her suicide.

ALCOHOL/DRUG ABUSE: A lot of drinking, much of it to excess; smoking.

VIOLENCE/SCARINESS: Eddie is beat up (in shadows); Sarah commits suicide (off-screen).

TOLERANCE/DIVERSITY ISSUES: None.

✳ QUESTIONS FOR KIDS:
- People in the movie have different ideas about what makes someone a winner or a loser. What are those ideas? How do they fit with others you have heard about, or with your own?
- What made Eddie different between his two games with Fats?
- Why didn't Sarah want Eddie to keep playing Findlay?
- How do Sarah and Bert represent two different parts of Eddie that fight with each other?

✳ CONNECTIONS: *The Color of Money,* also starring Newman as Eddie Felsen, is a sequel made twenty-six years later by Martin Scorsese (rated R). Felsen becomes a mentor for a young hustler played by Tom Cruise. Both performances are outstanding (Newman won a long-overdue Oscar), but the script is weak, especially in the second half.

✳The Last Starfighter

1984, 100 min, PG, 10 and up
Dir: Nick Castle. Robert Preston, Dan O'Herlihy, Lance Guest, Catherine Mary Stewart

✳ **PLOT:** This adventure saga mixes an update of the old system of "recruiting" sailors by shanghai with the fantasy of saving the universe by being a star at computer games. It turns out that one particular arcade game is really a test, put on Earth by very advanced beings from another planet, to find someone good enough to be "The Last Starfighter." And the only one to meet that challenge is Alex, who lives in a trailer park with his mother and younger brother, and who has just found out that he did not get the loan he needed for college.

Centauri (played with magnificent panache by Robert Preston) is the outer-space recruiter who takes Alex to the Starfighter deployment center on his planet and explains that Alex is the only one left who has the skill to be The Last Starfighter. Alex refuses, and is on his way back to Earth when all of the other Starfighters are destroyed by the evil Ko-Dan. When the bad guys come after him because they know he is the last remaining threat to them, he agrees to stay and fight.

Centauri thoughtfully leaves behind a "courtesy replacement simuloid," a robot that has Alex's looks, so his family won't worry. The simuloid, however, has no idea of how to behave like an Earthling, and gets into all kinds of trouble.

Meanwhile, Alex is paired with Grig, a reptilian-looking alien navigator (under all of that latex is a remarkably expressive Dan O'Herlihy). Alex worries, "I'm just a kid from a trailer park." "If that's all you think you are, that's all you'll ever be." Because all of the other Starfighters have been killed, Alex must face opposition leader Zor alone. "It will be a slaughter!" "That's the spirit!" "No, I mean us!" But he is successful, and returns to Earth to collect his devoted girlfriend and take her back with him.

✳ **DISCUSSION:** This movie has a lot of action and special effects. The efforts of the "simuloid" to understand life on Earth provide some good slapstick. The relationship between Alex and Grig is handled nicely. The movie is no one's idea of a classic, but kids who like space-age shoot-'em-ups will enjoy it, and with the caveats noted in the following section, it is a good family movie.

PROFANITY: One mild profanity.

NUDITY/SEXUAL REFERENCES: Teenage girl says, "Talk dirty to me," and boy reads *Playboy;* Alex's girlfriend clearly expects to engage in necking with him, and gets offended by the Simuloid because he blows a circuit every time she nibbles his ear.

ALCOHOL/DRUG ABUSE: None.

VIOLENCE/SCARINESS: Sci-fi shoot-outs.

TOLERANCE/DIVERSITY ISSUES: People of different races (species?) work together.

❋ QUESTIONS FOR KIDS:
- Why does Alex change his mind and agree to fight?
- How can he tell which are the good guys and which are the bad?

❋ CONNECTIONS: This was the last film performance by Robert Preston (*The Music Man*). Aside from Preston, the movie's greatest asset is the production design, by Ron Cobb of *Alien*, *Star Wars,* and *Conan the Barbarian*. For a much more thoughtful and mature depiction of bonding between a human and an alien, see *Enemy Mine.*

❋Shipwrecked
1990, 91 min, PG, 6 and up
Dir: Nils Gaup. Gabriel Byrne, Stian Smestad

❋ PLOT: Merrick (Gabriel Byrne) shoots an English naval officer named Howell and assumes his identity. Meanwhile, in Norway, a boy named Hakon (Stian Smestad) is being pushed around by some bullies. He warns them that his father will take care of them when he gets back from sea, and they tell him his father owes so much money, he should never come home. But his father does come home, with an injured leg, and with Jens, the man who saved his life. Hakon does not want to go to sea in his place, but when the family risks losing their home, he goes. Jens promises to look after him.

The stern captain tells him, "There is no room for children aboard this ship," and the crew initiates him by hanging him from the mast, but he watches, learns, works hard, and soon fits in well. At the first port, the captain tells him he has passed muster, and can stay on for the entire voyage. They are joined by a new First Mate—Merrick, still passing as Howell. Hakon discovers guns in a crate marked GLASS. Merrick tells him it is a secret. Just as Hakon is about to tell the captain, the captain falls ill—poisoned by one of Merrick's accomplices. The captain dies and is buried at sea. Merrick takes over.

At the next port, a brave young girl named Mary stows away. Hakon discovers her, and brings her food. She teaches him to read, using a book of Coleridge's poetry. When Merrick discovers her, Jens confesses to protect Hakon. Hakon tells Merrick that it was his fault, and Merrick orders Jens to whip Hakon. But just then, the ship is struck by lightning and sinks. Hakon is washed up on an island, where he discovers pirate treasure—and a newspaper clipping with a drawing of Merrick, leader of the pirates. Hakon knows Merrick will come for the treasure, and sets up elaborate booby traps all over the island. Seeing smoke on another island, he builds a small boat and explores it. He finds Mary and Jens, living with friendly natives. They return to Hakon's island, just before the pirates come to get the treasure.

Between the traps and Mary's liberation of the ship, they manage to get away with the treasure and return to Hakon's home in triumph.

✳ **DISCUSSION:** Neglected on its release, this is an exciting adventure, and a lot of fun to watch. Hakon does a lot of growing up. At the beginning he is a young boy who can only fight bullies by telling them to wait for his father. At the end he is a young man who is confident of his ability to protect himself.

PROFANITY: None.
NUDITY/SEXUAL REFERENCES: Very mild reference to "protecting your valuables" when prostitutes approach the sailors onshore.
ALCOHOL/DRUG ABUSE: Sailors drink ale in a tavern; teasing of Hakon about drinking milk, which he handles very well.
VIOLENCE/SCARINESS: Lead characters in exciting peril several times.
TOLERANCE/DIVERSITY ISSUES: Mary is an especially spirited and resourceful heroine.

✳ **QUESTIONS FOR KIDS:**
- How does Hakon decide whether to tell the captain about the guns he found?
- Why does Jens say that it was he who hid Mary?
- Why does Hakon tell the truth?
- Which part of the movie was the scariest? Which part was the funniest?

✳ **CONNECTIONS:** The booby traps on the island are reminiscent of the invasion of the pirates in *Swiss Family Robinson,* and of course *Home Alone.*

✳ **ACTIVITIES:** Find Norway on a map and see if you can chart the course Hakon followed. You might also enjoy reading the Coleridge poem Hakon likes, "Kubla Khan." Even if it is hard to follow, the language and rhythms are a pleasure to the ear and tongue. And it provides a good beginning for a discussion of dream or ideal places. The "pleasure dome" inhabited by Kane in *Citizen Kane* is named Xanadu, a reference to this poem.

✳Star Wars

1977, 121 min, PG, 6 and up
Dir: George Lucas. Harrison Ford, Alec Guinness, Carrie Fisher, Mark Hamill

✳ **PLOT:** The movie starts right in the middle of the action, with a battle on a spaceship. Two robots or "droids" escape, the elegant C-3PO and his counterpart, the gurgling and beeping R2D2. They carry a message from Princess Leia to Obi-Wan Kenobi, asking for help. When they arrive at a desert planet, they are bought by Luke Skywalker (Mark Hamill), who is then captured by "sand people" but rescued by Ben Kenobi (Alec Guinness).

Ben gets the message from Princess Leia and tells Luke they must go to help her fight the Empire. He tells Luke that his father was once a great fighter, a Jedi Knight, "the best star pilot in the galaxy and a cunning warrior." Luke says he cannot. Although Luke is restless and eager to explore the universe—he had begged his farmer uncle to let him go—he tells Ben, "I can't get involved. I have work to do." He will do as his uncle insisted and stay on the farm another year. Besides, this is not his fight. It all seems very far away.

But he gets back to the farm to find his aunt and uncle have been killed by Empire warriors trying to capture the droids. He and Kenobi hire Han Solo, a sometime smuggler, to get them to a planet called Alderan. Ben teaches Luke about "the force," a power within and around everyone.

They arrive only to find that Alderan has been destroyed. The Empire has a new weapon capable of eliminating whole planets. Luke, Leia, and Han, trapped on this "death star," must first escape, and then find a way to destroy it.

✳ **DISCUSSION:** George Lucas, who wrote and directed this movie, was deeply influenced by Joseph Campbell's work on myths, and by his love for the great movie classics. This movie is rich in themes from both. The scene in the bar, with all the aliens, is very much like the bar scene in a Western movie. Han Solo resembles the cowboy ideal, the loner with no loyalty to any cause but with his own sense of morality. Even his costume is reminiscent of a cowboy outfit, with boots and a gun holster at the hip.

Han and Luke must both decide whether to join the fight. At first, both are reluctant; in fact, Han leaves. But they accept the responsibility, as they must. The concept of "the force" in the movie may be something your children will want to know more about.

PROFANITY: None.

NUDITY/SEXUAL REFERENCES: None.

ALCOHOL/DRUG ABUSE: A sci-fi bar scene.

VIOLENCE/SCARINESS: A lot of comic-book-style fighting. An alien has a limb sliced off. One of the main characters is killed.

TOLERANCE/DIVERSITY ISSUES: Many different species work together well (at least with the good guys). The humans are all white males except for the princess, who is spirited but not a frontline fighter. (All of the pilots are males, for example.)

✳ **QUESTIONS FOR KIDS:**
• Why does Luke decide to fight the Empire? Why does Han?
• Why does Han leave, and why does he come back?

✳ **CONNECTIONS:** There are two sequels, *The Empire Strikes Back* and *Return of the Jedi,* both reissued in 1997 with additional scenes and special effects, and both exciting adventures. A new cycle of three movies, set a generation before *Star Wars,* is in production as of the writing of this book, with Ewan McGregor as the young Obi-Wan Kenobi.

The Sword in the Stone

1963, 75 min, G, 4 and up
Dir: Wolfgang Reighterman. Sebastian Cabot, Alan Napier

�֍ **PLOT:** Based on the book by T. H. White, this is the story of the early years of King Arthur. Nicknamed "Wart," the future King Arthur is squire to a knight when he meets Merlin the magician, who promises to take on his education. Merlin turns him into a fish, a bird, and a squirrel to teach him lessons like the importance of brains over brawn. He gets to see this in action when Madame Mim, Merlin's enemy, challenges Merlin to a duel by magic, and, though she cheats, Merlin is able to defeat her.

Wart still has his duties as a squire and, having forgotten the sword for a jousting match, he runs to get it. He sees a sword stuck in a stone and pulls it out, not knowing the legend that whomever will pull the sword out of the stone will be the rightful king. He becomes King Arthur, and listens when Merlin reminds him that knowledge is the real power.

✷ **DISCUSSION:** The King Arthur legend has fascinated people for centuries, and this story about Arthur's childhood has special appeal for children. Aside from the fun of seeing what it is like to be a bird, a squirrel, or a fish, and from having your very own wizard as a teacher, there is the highly satisfying aspect of having one's worth, unappreciated by everyone, affirmed so unequivocally.

PROFANITY: None.
NUDITY/SEXUAL REFERENCES: None.
ALCOHOL/DRUG ABUSE: None.
VIOLENCE/SCARINESS: Wizard fight.
TOLERANCE/DIVERSITY ISSUES: Symbolically, as Wart learns empathy from his experiences.

✷ **QUESTIONS FOR KIDS:**
- What made Arthur the one who could pull the sword out of the stone?
- What did he learn from his adventures with Merlin?
- How will what he learned help him to be a good king?
- How did Madame Mim cheat?
- How did Merlin fight back when she did?

✷ **CONNECTIONS:** Older kids may like to see *Camelot,* the musical by Lerner and Lowe (of *My Fair Lady*), to find out some of what happened to Arthur later (WARNING: the focus of that movie is on Guinevere's infidelity with Lancelot.) Mature teenagers might like the rather gory *Excalibur,* which has some stunning images.

✷ **ACTIVITIES:** Read aloud T. H. White's *The Sword and the Stone* and *The Story of King Arthur and His Knights,* or the other books about Camelot by Howard Pyle, which also have Pyle's magnificent illustrations.

✳ FOUR FEATHERS

1939, 115 min, NR, 8 and up
Dir: Zoltan Korda. Ralph Richardson, C. Aubrey Smith

A sensitive young man from a military family resigns his commission as his friends are about to be sent off to war in Egypt. His three friends, disgusted by what they see as his cowardice, each give him a white feather. He sees that Ethne, the woman he loves, is disappointed in him, too, so he takes a fourth white feather from her fan and leaves for Egypt, where he disguises himself as a mute native.

When his former regiment is defeated, he rescues one friend, now blind, from the battlefield, placing one of the feathers in his wallet. He then helps the two other friends escape and blow up an arsenal, only then revealing his identity and returning the feathers to them. Back in England, he is reunited with Ethne, and shows his bravery once again by interrupting an old general's war stories to set the record straight.

✳ **CONNECTION:** This exciting story was filmed five times, including a 1978 made-for-television version with Beau Bridges and Jane Seymour.

✳ NORMA RAE

1979, 113 min, PG, mature high schoolers
Dir: Martin Ritt. Sally Field, Ron Liebman, Beau Bridges

Sally Field won an Oscar for her performance as Norma Rae, an uneducated factory worker who finds herself through her efforts to unionize the mill. Based on a true story, this movie shows director Ritt's trademark feel for the South and its people.

Norma Rae is a single mother of two when Reuben, a New York City labor organizer (exceptionally well-played by Ron Liebman), comes to town, looking for a local worker to bring the union's message to the factory floor. She must confront the hostility of the managers, the fear—and worse—the indifference of her fellow workers, and the needs of her family. She must also find the strength and self-respect to allow herself to believe she can make a difference. Once she does, it becomes so important to her that she cannot quit.

Norma Rae and Reuben become very close, and care about each other deeply, but the movie has the courage and the intelligence not to give them any sexual contact (other than a brief nude swim). What matters is that Reuben sees that Norma Rae was "too smart to be doing what you're doing to yourself," and she is, indeed, smart enough to see that he is right, and do something about it. (NOTE: Some mature themes, including references to extramarital sex and an out-of-wedlock child. Norma Rae's initial lack of self-respect is reflected in her willingness to have casual sex.)

✳ **CONNECTIONS:** Sally Fields won an Oscar for her performance, which some observers felt paralleled her own journey from silly sitcoms to serious drama. The theme song "It Goes Like It Goes," also won an Oscar.

✳ A TALE OF TWO CITIES
1935, 128 min, NR, b&w, 10 and up
Dir: Jack Conway. Ronald Colman, Reginald Owen, Basil Rathbone

In this Charles Dickens story set during the French Revolution, Ronald Colman plays Sidney Carton, a British lawyer who is disillusioned and detached, settling for the friendship of the woman he loves when she marries another man. He finds meaning by taking the place of her husband, who has been sentenced to die by the guillotine because he is part of the aristocracy. He walks to his death holding the hand of another prisoner, saying, "It is a far, far better thing that I do than I have ever done; it is a far, far better rest that I go to than I have ever known."

SEE ALSO:

All the President's Men Two junior reporters with persistence and determination insist on following the story of a minor burglary to the heart of the Oval Office, despite the skepticism of their editors and colleagues.

The Hunt for Red October A CIA analyst with no field experience risks his career and his life to prove that a Soviet submarine captain is seeking asylum in the United States.

Julia A writer is drawn into the resistance effort in pre–WWII Germany by an old friend, and finds within herself unexpected courage and commitment.

A League of Their Own Women given the opportunity to do what they love and excel at (play baseball) find that it gives them self-respect and dignity. Their team manager, an alcoholic former player, is inspired by them to help them do their best.

Malcolm X A young man develops a larger vision of life through education and goes on to lead and inspire.

The Red Badge of Courage A young soldier learns that courage does not mean lack of fear; it means not letting the fear stop him from doing what needs to be done.

Sergeant York A soldier uses the techniques he learned at home on the farm to capture enemy soldiers.

The Wizard of Oz The characters all learn that what they needed was already in them.

UNDERSTANDING EMOTIONS

"Lord, teach us to take our hearts and look them in the face, however difficult it might be."
—DOROTHY L. SAYERS

A popular recent book, *Emotional Intelligence* by Daniel P. Coleman, makes a compelling argument that "EQ," or emotional intelligence, is a more important predictor of a person's success—both professionally and personally—than what is commonly thought of as intelligence, meaning mathematical and verbal ability. The stories and the characters in movies provide an ideal vehicle for families to use to develop emotional intelligence through the discussion of emotion and motivation.

First, good movies bring us believable characters in interesting situations, so we get to see the broadest possible range of people facing the broadest possible range of circumstances. Movies can show us variations and extremes of emotion that would take several lifetimes to experience firsthand.

Second, and even more important, is the opportunity that movies give us to talk about the most personal and sensitive issues in impersonal terms. It is easier for everyone, and especially for young kids and teenagers, to talk about what is going on with the people on the screen than it is to talk about what is going on inside them. A three-year-old can tell you that Big Bird feels scared and lonely—and a teenager can tell you that James Dean feels scared and lonely—when it is just too hard to acknowledge or admit those feelings in himself. Talking about the people in the movies will help them develop an emotional vocabulary that will lead them to talk about people in the news, then people they know, and then, if you're lucky, themselves.

Families can learn from the movies how to identify emotions in themselves and in others, developing a valuable approach for dealing with real-life issues. Parents watching with very young children can help them by asking questions about what the characters are feeling. Children will learn not to be afraid of feelings like jealousy, anger, and fear; accepting those feelings is the first step to moving beyond them. They will also learn about the power of analogy and making connections, an important starting point for abstract reasoning.

Older kids can learn about some of the more subtle psychological defense mechanisms, like displacement, projection, and denial, as well as about interactions like enabling behavior and about good and bad ways of resolving arguments. The best screenwriters have enormous psychological insight. We can see Paula's sense of her value, her sanity, and even her self disintegrating as her husband undermines her sanity in *Gaslight.* Watch Judith Traherne in *Dark Victory* going through Elizabeth Kubler-Ross stages in accepting her terminal illness, long before Kubler-Ross wrote about them. In *Ball of Fire,* a professor of psychology correctly deduces that Sugarpuss O'Shea really wanted to marry Bertram Potts when she "mistakenly" returns the huge diamond from her gangster boyfriend, instead of the ring that Potts gave her.

In general, movies have not done as well in portraying mental illness and its treatment, though there are some memorable exceptions.

Keep in mind that no matter what else is going on, no matter what the MacGuffin is (see page 667) or whether the story is a comedy, musical, adventure, or drama, most movies are really about characters on a psychological journey. At the end, the heroes almost always learn something about themselves or about life, and it often enables them to accomplish some goal or to become close to someone in a way that would not have otherwise been possible.

❋Dark Victory

1939, 106 min, NR, b&w, 12 and up
Dir: Edmund Goulding. Bette Davis, George Brent, Humphrey Bogart, Geraldine Fitzgerald

❋ **PLOT:** Judith Traherne (Bette Davis) is an impetuous and headstrong heiress who lives life with furious energy. Her life revolves around parties and horses. She sees Dr. Frederick Steele (George Brent) for her headaches and dizzy spells, and he tells her she has a brain tumor. He operates, and she believes she is cured. Her soul is cured as well, because she and the doctor have fallen in love, and for the first time she feels genuine happiness and peace.

But she learns that Frederick and her friends have kept the truth from her; her prognosis is negative, and she has very little time left. She breaks the engagement, telling Frederick he only wants to marry her out of pity. At first, she returns to her old life, trying to bury her fears and loneliness in a frenzy of parties. But she is terribly sad, and when Michael, her stableman (Humphrey Bogart), tells her that she should allow herself to see that Frederick really loves her, and take whatever happiness she can, in whatever time she has left, she knows he is right. She marries Frederick, and has blissful months with him on his farm in Vermont before she dies, having had a lifetime of love and happiness in their time together.

✽ DISCUSSION: This classic melodrama is also almost an encyclopedia of emotions. At first, Judith is in denial about her illness and about her feelings. She shows displaced anger when she breaks her engagement to Frederick. Most important to discuss with kids, though, is that she makes a classic mistake of confusing pleasure and happiness. The contrast between her frantic efforts to find distraction through parties ("horses, hats, and food") and fast living, and the peace and joy of her time in Vermont with love and meaningful work (okay, it's her husband's meaningful work, but this was the 1930s) is exceptionally well-portrayed by Davis and by director Goulding. This is one of the most important emotional distinctions for kids to learn, especially teenagers.

> PROFANITY: None.
> NUDITY/SEXUAL REFERENCES: None.
> ALCOHOL/DRUG ABUSE: Judith drinks and smokes too much before she learns what really matters.
> VIOLENCE/SCARINESS: No violence, but terminal illness may scare some kids.
> TOLERANCE/DIVERSITY ISSUES: Class issues in the relationship of Michael and Judith.

✽ QUESTIONS FOR KIDS:
- Why is it so hard for Judith to find happiness, even before she learns she is sick?
- How can you tell that she does not understand herself very well?
- Why does she break her engagement with Frederick?
- What does Michael tell her that makes her change her mind?
- Why doesn't she tell Frederick that she is close to the end, sending him away instead?

✽ CONNECTIONS: Bette Davis and George Brent made a number of movies together, including *The Great Lie* and *The Old Maid* (also directed by Goulding), *In This Our Life,* and *Jezebel*.

Be sure to watch for future president Ronald Reagan as a "member of [her] horsey set."

✽Gaslight

1944, 114 min, NR, b&w, 10 and up
Dir: George Cukor. Ingrid Bergman, Charles Boyer, Joseph Cotten, Angela Lansbury

✽ PLOT: Paula Alquist (Ingrid Bergman) falls in love with Gregory Anton (Charles Boyer), a musician, and once they are married, he persuades her to move into the house she lived in as a child, which has been closed since her aunt was murdered there. At first very happy, Paula soon becomes confused and insecure. While Gregory appears to be solicitous and caring, in reality he is cutting her off from all contact with anyone but himself, and making her doubt herself and her sanity. He convinces her that she is always losing things, that she sees things that are not there, that she is unstable and untrustworthy. Every night he leaves to play the piano in an apartment he has rented, and while he is gone the gaslights flicker and she hears mysterious noises from the attic. Gregory persuades her that these are just her delusions.

Just as Paula's fragile hold on reality is about to break, she is visited by Brian Cameron (Joseph Cotten) of Scotland Yard. With his help, she learns that Gregory is using an assumed name, that he is a thief, and that he had known her late aunt, a famous singer. He married Paula just to get into the house, so that he can find the missing jewels he could not get the night he murdered Paula's aunt.

Gregory is captured just as he finds the jewels. Brian ties him up and leaves him with Paula while he calls the police. Gregory tries to persuade Paula to cut the ropes and let him go, but she explains that she is insane, as he told her, so how could she help anyone? He must admit that she has been completely sane all along. She can no longer be manipulated by him. He goes off to jail. Paula and Brian have defeated him.

✳ **DISCUSSION:** This classic of suspense is a good way to begin a conversation about vulnerability and manipulation. Gregory is almost able to drive Paula mad by making her think she is mad already. By cutting her off from any outside reality, by coolly denying what she sees and hears for herself, by telling her over and over again that she is helpless and incompetent, she begins to turn into the person he tells her that she is.

PROFANITY: None.

NUDITY/SEXUAL REFERENCES: None.

ALCOHOL/DRUG ABUSE: None.

VIOLENCE/SCARINESS: Tension and suspense.

TOLERANCE/DIVERSITY ISSUES: None.

✳ **QUESTIONS FOR KIDS:**
- "Gaslighting" someone is now an accepted psychiatric term, based on this movie and its predecessor, the play *Angel Street*. What do you think it means?
- How does Gregory get Paula to doubt herself?
- How does the director help the viewer get some sense of Paula's feelings of disorientation and doubt?
- Can someone make another person doubt him or herself as Gregory did? Can someone affect other people positively along the same lines, helping them to believe in themselves? How?

✳ **CONNECTIONS:** Some of the same themes and feelings, in a more contemporary setting, are found in Alfred Hitchcock's *Dial M for Murder* (1954), with Grace Kelly as the wife whose husband (Ray Milland) plans to murder her, and in *Midnight Lace* (1960), with Doris Day and Rex Harrison. In *Ticket to Heaven* (1981), a movie about a bright young man who becomes a member of a religious cult, the techniques of mind control that cult leaders use correspond to some of Gregory's tactics for making Paula uncertain about reality.

Bergman won an Oscar for this performance, and the movie also won one for art direction. Angela Lansbury, in her first movie appearance, was nominated for an Oscar for her performance as the insolent maid.

✳ Now, Voyager
1942, 117 min, NR, b&w, 10 and up
Dir: Irving Rapper. Bette Davis, Paul Henreid, Claude Rains, Gladys Cooper

✳ **PLOT:** Charlotte Vale (Bette Davis) is the repressed and depressed daughter of an imperious mother (Gladys Cooper), head of a wealthy and socially prominent Boston family. Miserably unhappy and insecure, she spends much of her time in her room, making carved boxes and sneaking forbidden cigarettes. A sympathetic sister-in-law introduces her to Dr. Jaquith (Claude Rains), an understanding psychiatrist. Under his care, at his sanitarium, she begins to develop some sense of herself as worthy, but is still terribly insecure when she departs on a cruise ship for a rest before returning home.

On the ship, she meets Jerry Durrance (Paul Henreid), an architect. At first awkward and self-deprecating, she begins to bloom under his attention, and they fall in love. But Jerry is married to a woman whose health is too fragile for him to consider divorce. They say good-bye, and Charlotte returns home. Her mother is as tyrannical as ever, insisting that Charlotte must do as she says or she will refuse to support her. Charlotte meets Elliott Livingston (John Loder), a kind businessman who wants to marry her, and her mother approves. But when she sees Jerry again, she knows it is impossible for her to marry Elliott, and turns him down. This so infuriates her mother that she has a heart attack and dies.

Overcome with guilt, Charlotte returns to Dr. Jaquith. But at the sanitarium, she meets a troubled young girl, Tina, Jerry's daughter. In reaching out to Tina, she finds her own strength and sense of purpose. When Charlotte goes home, Tina moves in with her. Jerry at first wants to take Tina away, thinking it is too much of an imposition, but Charlotte persuades him that it is a way for them to be close, telling him, "Don't let's ask for the moon; we have the stars."

✳ **DISCUSSION:** This movie has a lot of appeal for highly romantic teenagers of both sexes, and for those who are interested in the dynamics and impact of dysfunctional families. Charlotte's mother is completely self-obsessed, consumed with power, incapable of compassion, much less love, for her daughter. As Dr. Jaquith says, "Sometimes tyranny masquerades as mother love." Never hesitating to make it clear that Charlotte was unwanted, Mrs. Vale demands that Charlotte make up for the burden she inflicted by being born by giving in to her every demand. But it is also clear that there is no way for Charlotte to be successful in pleasing her mother. Dependent and fearful at the beginning, she has her mother's contempt. But, as we see at the end, her independence and self-respect are much more threatening to her mother, who literally cannot survive Charlotte's assertion of her right to her own life.

In one sense, when Charlotte stands up for herself Mrs. Vale as ogre disappears like the Wicked Witch of the West doused with water or the Queen of Hearts when Alice tells her she is only a card. In another sense, Mrs. Vale's attack is the ultimate booby trap for Charlotte, who must then grapple with the guilt she feels for "causing" her mother's death. Both Mrs. Vale and Jerry's off-screen wife assert what F. Scott Fitzgerald called "the tyranny of sickness" or what Dr. Jaquith might call passive-agressive behavior, using powerlessness as the ultimate method of exercising power. This is a very important form of emotional blackmail to be able to identify.

The title of the movie is from a line by Walt Whitman that Dr. Jaquith gives to Charlotte: "Now voyager, sail forth to seek and find." Charlotte learns not to be afraid of what she will find, to risk getting hurt, to risk allowing herself to be known, to risk caring about someone else.

It is also worthwhile for kids to see that Charlotte must love herself before she is able to love someone else, and that just as Jerry's love helps her to bloom, she is able to do the same for Tina. Charlotte tells Jerry, "When you told me that you loved me, I was so proud, I could have walked into a den of lions; in fact I did, and the lion didn't hurt me." Just as important, helping Tina is the most enduring "cure" for her sense of being powerless and without purpose, and far better than marrying the man she did not love.

These days, the decision made by Charlotte and Jerry not to stay together seems almost quaint; we tend to think that everyone should have both the moon and the stars. Their sense of sacrifice and duty is worth talking about as well.

PROFANITY: None.

NUDITY/SEXUAL REFERENCES: None.

ALCOHOL/DRUG ABUSE: Social drinking; lots of cigarette smoking—Jerry lights two cigarettes, then gives one to Charlotte, a gesture that is highly symbolic and an icon of movie romanticism.

VIOLENCE/SCARINESS: Emotional violence only; Charlotte's mother collapses and dies in the middle of a confrontation.

TOLERANCE/DIVERSITY ISSUES: None.

✳ **QUESTIONS FOR KIDS:**
- Why did Charlotte have such a hard time feeling good about herself?
- Why did Jerry and Charlotte decide not to see each other anymore?
- Why did seeing Jerry make Charlotte change her mind about marrying Elliott?
- What did Charlotte's mother want from Charlotte? Was that fair?
- What should Charlotte have said to her mother?
- Why did helping Tina make Charlotte feel better?

✳ **CONNECTIONS:** Bette Davis and Claude Rains appeared together two years later in another movie about love, sacrifice, and lessons learned, *Mr. Skeffington*. She plays a self-centered and flighty woman who marries a man she does not love in order to protect her brother, discovering decades later how much she cares for her husband.

SEE ALSO:

All My Sons A mother refuses to acknowledge her son's death in the war (and her husband's complicity) in this example of denial.

All the Way Home A young widow and her son feel many conflicting emotions as they try to cope with their loss.

Ball of Fire A showgirl's Freudian slip reveals that the man she is marrying is not the man she loves.

Jacob Have I Loved A twin must learn to overcome her jealousy.

Perfect Harmony A white boy's anger at his absent parents is redirected against his classmates and against blacks in this example of displacement.

Sleeping Beauty Jealousy tortures the queen so badly that she is willing to risk everything to destroy Snow White.

The Treasure of the Sierra Madre Dobbs projects his greed and aggression onto his partners.

LOSS

"Give sorrow words; the grief that does not speak whispers the o'er
fraught heart, and bids it break."
—WILLIAM SHAKESPEARE

As parents, we are so anxious to protect our precious children from
loss that we sometimes make the mistake of making them think that
we do not recognize or permit those feelings, minimizing the pain they feel
at the loss of a favorite toy or beloved pet. However, as Judith Viorst points
out in her book *Necessary Losses*, each of us must lose precious connections
and beliefs in order to grow. Parents cannot prevent loss, but we can teach
children important lessons about how to respond to it.

Viorst also wrote a sensitive children's book, *The Tenth Good Thing About
Barney*, about a child coping with the death of a cat. The mourning child's
family respects his feelings and helps him to focus on the good things that
Barney brought and will continue to bring to those who loved him.

If at all possible, it is much better to watch these movies before a child
is confronted with a devastating loss. Films like these can help families
begin to raise the subject in a general way, to help kids develop an emotional
vocabulary that will be in place if they (or anyone they know) must experience loss.

All the Way Home
1963, 103 min, NR, b&w, 12 and up
Dir: Alex Segal. Robert Preston, Jean Simmons, Pat Hingle

✳ **PLOT:** Set in Tennessee in 1815, this quiet, beautiful movie is a story
about Jay (Robert Preston) and Mary (Jean Simmons), who are deeply in
love, though she disapproves of his drinking, and he thinks she is too rigid
in her piety and primness about sex. They are loving parents to their little

boy, Rufus, give him comfort and guidance, and enjoy him very much. When Jay is killed in an accident, Mary and Rufus must try to make sense of the tragedy and find a way to go on.

✳ **DISCUSSION:** This movie is based on James Agee's novel *A Death in the Family* and its adaptation for the theater by Tad Mosel, both awarded the Pulitzer Prize. It is filled with memorable characters and moments of great insight and poignance. Jay is a warm and wise father. In the first scene, Jay and Rufus enjoy a Charlie Chaplin movie together. As they walk home together, we feel their closeness and the pleasure they feel in spending time with each other. When Rufus is shy in the presence of an elderly relative, Jay shows him that he can talk to her.

Mary is loving and devoted, but finds it very hard to talk about her feelings, and especially about sex. When Jay tells Mary it is time to let Rufus know that they are going to have another baby, all she can manage to say is that they are expecting a surprise from heaven. After Jay's death, Mary has to deal with Rufus's grief, as well as her own. And she has to find the best of Jay within herself, so she can give that to Rufus.

Kids may be especially disconcerted by Mary's reaction to the news of Jay's accident, before she learns that he has been killed. She goes through a variety of emotions while she waits with her aunt for news. She laughs over a story Jay had told her, nervously checks the teakettle to see if it has boiled yet, prepares a downstairs room in case he is well enough to be nursed at home, and prays for his life. Discuss with children and teens the way that the stress of uncertainty and the unwillingness to believe that her husband is dead produce this seemingly contradictory and even uncaring reaction.

PROFANITY: None.

NUDITY/SEXUAL REFERENCES: Although the references are so tame by today's standards, they would hardly qualify for a PG rating, one of the key issues in the movie is the contrast between Jay's openness and Mary's primness. After Jay's death, Mary realizes that she has to be able to be for Rufus what Jay would have been, and in the very last scene she puts his hand on her belly and tells him that is where the new baby is growing.

ALCOHOL/DRUG ABUSE: Jay and his brother drink. Mary disapproves, but after she gets the news of Jay's death, she takes a drink.

VIOLENCE/SCARINESS: No violence, but scary (off-screen) death of the father.

TOLERANCE/DIVERSITY ISSUES: Rufus tells Jay that the big boys teased him by telling him he has a "nigger name." Jay comforts him, and tells him never to use that word, because it is a hurtful word. The word he uses is "colored." Jay tells Rufus that "big boys don't cry."

✳ **QUESTIONS FOR KIDS:**
• What do Mary and Jay disagree on? How can you tell?

- Are those differences part of what makes them attractive to each other?
- Why does Rufus tell the minister and his uncle that they can't sit in his father's chair?
- How does Mary become more like Jay after his death? Why?

✳ **CONNECTIONS:** Robert Preston is the star of *The Music Man.* Jean Simmons appears as Estella in *Great Expectations* (and as Miss Havisham in a later production made for television), and as Sister Sarah in *Guys and Dolls.* Veteran character actor Pat Hingle played the father in *Splendor in the Grass,* and Commissioner Gordon in the Batman movies.

✳Houseboat

1958, 112 min, NR, 10 and up
Dir: Melville Shavelson. Cary Grant, Sophia Loren

✳ **PLOT:** Diplomat Tom Winston (Cary Grant) returns to Washington, D.C., following the death of his estranged wife. His three children, David, Robert, and Elizabeth, have been staying with his wife's sister, Caroline (Martha Hyer). They are hurt and resentful. He takes them to an outdoor orchestra concert, and Robert wanders off and meets Cinzia (Sophia Loren), the daughter of a visiting conductor. She has also wandered off, in search of adventure and companionship. When she brings Robert back, Tom sees that Robert likes her, and impulsively offers her a job as a housekeeper. She agrees, because traveling with her father has been boring and lonely.

David causes an accident that destroys their home, so the only place they can live is an old houseboat owned by Angelo, a handyman (Harry Guardino). They settle in there with Cinzia. It turns out she can neither cook nor do laundry, but the children adore her, and Tom warms to her, too. With her help, he reaches out to his children, and they reach out to him.

Caroline tells Tom that her marriage is ending, and that she has always loved him. On the way to a country club dance, a tipsy male friend of Caroline's swats Cinzia on her rear end, and she tosses wine in his face. Caroline, annoyed at Tom for sticking up for Cinzia (and jealous), leaves for the dance without him. Tom invites Cinzia to the dance, and she accepts, despite her promise to go fishing with David. At the dance, Tom proposes to Caroline, but then, as he dances with Cinzia, he realizes that she is the one he loves, and that she loves him, too.

At first, the children are terribly upset and feel betrayed by both of them. Cinzia, unwilling to make them unhappy, runs back to her father, apologizing, "I've learned many things, including how hard it is to be a father." Tom finds her there, but she refuses to go back with him. "Your children are your friends again, and that is the most important thing." He tells her that being their friend is not the most important thing; being their father is. They get married. And the children, at the last minute, join in.

❋ **DISCUSSION:** This is a warm, romantic comedy that is exceptionally perceptive and sensitive about the feelings of the children. It does a nice job of showing that David's truculence and petty theft are due to his feelings of vulnerability and loss. In one scene, Tom at first tries to show David how to fish, then, when David says that he feels incompetent, Tom asks him for advice, and they are able to talk for the first time about his mother's death. Tom shows David that nothing is ever really lost, and David is able to let Tom know that he fears losing Tom, too. After this talk, David feels safer, and confesses to Angelo that he took Angelo's knife. (Angelo is very understanding.) Robert's reaction to the loss of his mother is to withdraw, playing mournfully on his harmonica as his only means of expression. Elizabeth reacts by sleeping in her father's room every night, and becomes very upset when she learns that will not be possible after he and Cinzia get married.

This is also a rare movie that deals honestly with the issue of children's reaction to remarriage. Even though they love Cinzia, the children do not like sharing her with Tom, or sharing Tom with her. Children who have been in this situation will be grateful for the opportunity to see that they are not alone.

PROFANITY: None.
NUDITY/SEXUAL REFERENCES: References to adultery.
ALCOHOL/DRUG ABUSE: A friend drinks too much and behaves badly; jokes about falling off the wagon.
VIOLENCE/SCARINESS: None.
TOLERANCE/DIVERSITY ISSUES: Differences in class and culture.

❋ **QUESTIONS FOR KIDS:**
- How do each of the children show that they are hurt and sad? How do each of them show when they are beginning to feel better?
- What can you tell about Caroline's feelings when she gives the dress to Cinzia?
- Why does Cinzia tell Angelo the story about the necklace, and why does it make him leave without her?
- Was Cinzia wrong to leave for the dance when she had promised to go fishing with David?

❋ **CONNECTIONS:** This movie has two lovely songs, "Almost in Your Arms" (nominated for an Oscar) and "Bing Bang Boom."

❋ **ACTIVITIES:** Just about every child plays some kind of call and response game like the "Yes Sir, You Sir" game Tom plays with his children. There is one that begins "Who Took the Cookies from the Cookie Jar?" Another one is called "Concentration" and involves a series of claps accompanying the listing of items in selected categories. See if your children know any. If so, play one with them. If not, teach them one. Take them to an outdoor concert, like the one in the movie (the site of the concert in the movie is now the Kennedy Center in Washington, D.C.). Try playing the harmonica.

*My Life as a Dog

1987, 103 min, PG, 12 and up
Dir: Lasse Hallström. Anton Glanzelius
Swedish with subtitles

❋ **PLOT:** Ingemar is a twelve-year-old boy growing up in 1950s Sweden who goes to live with his aunt and uncle in Smaland while his mother is dying of tuberculosis. In the small town of Smaland he meets an assortment of eccentric and delightful characters who help him adjust to his new life without his mother, brother, and his beloved dog Sickan (he has never known his father).

He meets an athletic girl who loves to box but who also develops a crush on Ingemar. Berit, the most beautiful woman in town, befriends Ingemar and asks him to chaperon her while she models for the town artist. Ulla and Gunar, his aunt and uncle, adopt Ingemar and help him find family and normalcy during a traumatic period in his life.

❋ **DISCUSSION:** Told from the perspective of the child, this is an affecting and authentic portrayal of a young boy's attempt to understand the adult world. The director shows us Ingemar's world through a child's eyes, so that the smallest events and the largest are presented as equally important. He does not know enough to be able to distinguish ordinary behavior from eccentricity, or to fully understand why a nude model would want a young boy as a chaperon or why a dying man would be so interested in underwear catalogs. His acceptance of everyone he meets is part of his appeal.

Ingemar does not have enough experience of the world to be able to understand what his mother's symptoms mean, or to wonder if she will die. Because no one told him how ill she was, he blames himself for her death. He does not have the opportunity to express his grief, which adds to his feeling of disorientation and his identification with a dog who is circling the globe in a space capsule. The only comfort he (and the audience) have is the sense that his ability to form relationships with the new people in his life will be a source of strength and happiness to him in the future.

PROFANITY: None.

NUDITY/SEXUAL REFERENCES:: Brief, nonsexual nudity in an artist's studio; Ingemar's brother tells a bunch of kids how babies are born; girl laments the growth of her breasts, which will make it impossible for her to pass as a boy so that she can participate in sports.

ALCOHOL/DRUG ABUSE: None.

VIOLENCE/SCARINESS: There is some tension when Ingemar and his mother argue and she breaks down crying and tries to hit and push him away.

TOLERANCE/DIVERSITY ISSUES: A girl struggles with limits based on gender.

✳ **QUESTIONS FOR KIDS:**
- Why does Ingemar always say it's important to "compare"? Why do you think that Ingemar compares himself to Laika the space dog?
- Why does Ingemar tell us that he wishes he told his mom everything? Does he blame himself for not having told her everything?
- Why doesn't anyone tell Ingemar that Sickan is dead? Do you think that waiting to tell him made it easier or harder to deal with when he did learn the truth?

✳Old Yeller

1957, 83 min, G, 8 and up
Dir: Robert Stevenson. Dorothy McGuire, Fess Parker, Tommy Kirk, Kevin Corcoran

✳ **PLOT:** In 1869 Texas, Jim Coates (Fess Parker) says good-bye to his family as he leaves for three months to sell their cattle. He tells his older son, Travis (Tommy Kirk), to take care of his mother, Katie (Dorothy McGuire), and his younger brother, Arliss (Kevin Corcoran). Travis asks his father to bring him back a horse. His father says that what he needs is a dog, but Travis does not want one. "Not a dog in this world like old Belle was."

A stray dog comes to their farm and scares the horse, knocking over Travis and knocking down the fence. Travis throws rocks at the dog, saying, "That dog better not come around here while I got a gun." But the dog comes back, and Arliss "claims" him, over Travis's objections. Later, Old Yeller saves Arliss from a bear. Travis admits, "He's a heap more dog than I ever figured him for." Yeller turns out to be an outstanding dog for farming and hunting.

Old Yeller fights a wolf that was about to attack Katie. She insists he be tied up, because the wolf would not have attacked unless he had hydrophobia, and Yeller may have been infected. When Yeller becomes vicious, Travis knows he must shoot him.

Jim returns as Travis and his friend Elsbeth are burying Old Yeller. Jim tells him that the loss of Yeller is "not a thing you can forget. Maybe not a thing you want to forget . . . Now and then, for no good reason a man can figure out, life will just haul off and knock him flat. Slam him agin' the ground so hard, it seems like all his insides is busted. It's not all like that. A lot of it's mighty fine. You can't afford to waste the good part worrying about the bad. That makes it all bad . . . Sayin' it's one thing and feelin' it's another. I'll tell you a trick that's sometimes a big help. Start looking around for something good to take the place of the bad. As a general rule, you can find it." Jim has brought the horse Travis wanted, but says, "Reckon you ain't in no shape to take pleasure in him yet." Travis goes back to the house, where he sees Yeller's pup, and knows that he won't replace Old Yeller, but will be as good a friend as his father was.

✳ **DISCUSSION:** Jim's talk with Travis is a model of parental wisdom, understanding, and patience. He accepts and validates Travis's feelings completely, and does not try to minimize or talk him out of them. (Contrast that with Elsbeth, who tries to comfort Travis by encouraging him to "come to like the pup.") Instead of telling him what to do, he says, "I'll tell you a trick that's sometimes a big help," letting him decide for himself whether to take the advice and, if he does, letting him decide whether this is one of the times that it is a big help or not. By saying that Travis is not "in shape to take pleasure from the horse" yet, Jim is again letting him know that he respects his feelings of loss and sorrow, and that there will be time for him to feel happy about the horse later.

Travis is not just reluctant to adopt Old Yeller at first—he is downright hostile. The reason is his sense of loss over his first dog, Belle. His ability to accept Young Yeller more easily shows how much he has grown up.

This is one of the finest of the early Disney dramas. The fight scenes are exciting, and the family scenes are sensitive and evocative. It is a classic of loss, and an excellent way to begin a discussion of those issues.

PROFANITY: None.
NUDITY/SEXUAL REFERENCES: None.
ALCOHOL/DRUG ABUSE: None.
VIOLENCE/SCARINESS: Scary confrontations between Old Yeller and a bear, wild boars, and a wolf.
TOLERANCE/DIVERSITY ISSUES: None.

✳ **QUESTIONS FOR KIDS:**
- Why doesn't Travis want Old Yeller at first? Why doesn't he want the pup?
- How does he hurt Elsbeth's feelings?
- Why does Katie say, "No wonder they didn't want him on no cow drive," about Elsbeth's father?
- Why did Sanderson trade Old Yeller for the toad and a meal?
- Why did Sanderson say, "That's the way a man talks," when Travis told him that he was a little scared but would take Sanderson's advice? What made that "manly"?

✳ **CONNECTIONS:** McGuire, Kirk, and Corcoran appeared together in *Swiss Family Robinson.*

✳ **ACTIVITIES:** Kids who like animal stories may enjoy the book by Fred Gipson, who cowrote the screenplay.

The Three Lives of Thomasina

1964, 97 min, NR, 8 and up
Dir: Sir Don Chaffey. Patrick McGoohan, Susan Hampshire

✳ **PLOT:** The story takes place in Scotland in 1912. Mary MacDhui (Karen Dotrice) is a little girl whose mother has died. She loves her cat, Thomasina, more than anything in the world. Her father, Andrew (Patrick McGoohan), a veterinarian, is an ultrarational man who has trouble communicating and tends to see his animal patients in economic rather than emotional terms. He has a hard time showing Mary how much she means to him, or understanding how much Thomasina means to her. He is unable to cure Thomasina when she is hurt, so he puts her to sleep, a choice that is rational but insensitive.

Mary's friends help her plan a funeral with an enthusiastic chief mourner (He says with pride, "I can cry very loud!"). They reassure her that the whole town will understand the magnitude of the loss: "Everyone will say, 'There goes the poor widow McDhui a-burying her dear Thomasina, foully done to death, God rest her soul.'" The funeral is interrupted by Lori MacGregor (Susan Hampshire), a beautiful and mysterious woman who lives in the forest outside the town. She cures animals with herbs and affection and is thought to be a witch. Lori finds Thomasina, who is not dead; she has just used up one of her nine lives. In a fantasy scene set in Cat Heaven, Thomasina is reborn, with no memory of her previous life.

The people in the town begin to bring their sick animals to Lori, upset because Andrew put his daughter's cat to sleep. Mary, pining for Thomasina, glimpses her and runs after her, becoming drenched in a storm. She gets ill, and Andrew, desperate, goes to Lori for help. Lori tells him that his love is what Mary needs. Thomasina appears outside Mary's window, and Andrew brings her inside. Thomasina has brought them all together, and Andrew and Lori get married.

✳ **DISCUSSION:** Andrew represents the head, and Lori the heart. In the beginning of the story, both are isolated. Thomasina and Mary bring them together. Children may be interested in the way that the funeral arrangements are such a comfort to Mary. They also may want to know more about why Andrew had such a problem communicating his feelings. WARNING: Some children may be upset over the notion that a cat can die and come back; some who have lost a pet (or a family member) may be upset that theirs didn't come back.

PROFANITY: None.
NUDITY/SEXUAL REFERENCES: None.
ALCOHOL/DRUG ABUSE: None.
VIOLENCE/SCARINESS: None.
TOLERANCE/DIVERSITY ISSUES: None.

* **QUESTIONS FOR KIDS:**
  * What do you think about Mary's decision not to talk to her father? Was that a good way to solve the problem?
  * What was her father's reaction? Was that a good way to solve the problem?
  * Why is it harder for some people to talk about their feelings than others? Is it ever hard for you to talk about yours?

* **CONNECTIONS:** The children in this movie, Karen Dotrice and Matthew Garber, also appeared in **Mary Poppins,** released the same year, and *The Gnome-Mobile,* released in 1967.

The Yearling

1946, 129 min, NR, 8 and up
Dir: Clarence Brown. Gregory Peck, Jane Wyman, Claude Jarman, Jr.

* **PLOT:** This quiet, thoughtful, visually striking adaptation of the Pulitzer Prize–winning novel by Marjorie Kinnan Rawlings covers a year in the life of the Baxter family, post–Civil War settlers in remote Florida. The focus is on Jody (Claude Jarman, Jr.), age twelve, a dreamy boy who loves animals and wishes he could have a pet, "something for my own, something to follow me." Pa Baxter (Gregory Peck) is warm and understanding. Ma (Jane Wyman) seems harsh and rigid, but only because she has been so devastated by the loss of three children that she feels she has to contain her feelings, that if she allows herself to be vulnerable, she will not be able to stand the pain.

The only other boy Jody knows is a frail boy named Fodderwing, who lives nearby. Jody loves to visit him, to hear his imaginative tales and play with his pets. Over Ma's objections, Pa insists that Jody be allowed to have a young deer as a pet, and Jody goes to Fodderwing to ask him to name the deer. Fodderwing has died, but his father tells Jody he once said that if he had a deer, he would name it Flag, and that is the name Jody chooses. Jody loves Flag, and does everything he can to keep him, even building a high fence to keep Flag out of the corn crop, which is essential to the family's livelihood. But Flag cannot stop eating the crop and has to be destroyed. Ma shoots him, and then Jody has to put him out of his misery.

Jody runs away, but returns. His father notes approvingly that Jody "takes [the loss] for his share and goes on," and tells Ma, "He's done come back different. He's taken the punishment. He ain't a yearling no more."

* **DISCUSSION:** This is a classic story of loss, not just of a beloved pet but of the innocence and freedom of childhood that Flag symbolizes. Pa says to Jody: "Every man wants life to be a fine thing, and easy. Well, it's fine, son, powerful fine. But it ain't easy. I want life to be easier for you than it was for me. . . . A man's heart aches seeing his young 'uns face the

world knowing that they got to have their insides tore out the way his was tore." All parents want to protect their children this way. And yet, all parents realize that having one's "insides tore out" is a necessary part of growing up, that no one ever learns how to make responsible choices without these painful experiences. Pa tells Jody that life is "gettin', losin', gettin', losin'."

In the last moment of the film, as in the book, the boy and the deer run off together in Jody's imagination. In part, this means that Jody's innocence is gone with the deer. But it also means that a precious part of his spirit, the part that loved the deer so deeply, will be with him always, and will be a part of everything that he does.

PROFANITY: None.

NUDITY/SEXUAL REFERENCES: None.

ALCOHOL/DRUG ABUSE: None.

VIOLENCE/SCARINESS: Bear and dog fight; fistfights; Pa bitten by a snake; deer shot (off-screen).

TOLERANCE/DIVERSITY ISSUES: None.

✳ **QUESTIONS FOR KIDS:**
- Who is "the yearling"?
- What do you think of Pa's strategy for trading his dog for a gun? What did he mean when he later said that his words were straight but his intentions were crooked?
- What do Jody's friends Fodderwing and Oliver tell you about him?
- Why was it hard for Ma to show affection? How can you tell?
- How was Jody different when he came back home?

✳ **CONNECTIONS:** Mature teenagers may be interested in *Cross Creek,* a fictionalized account of Rawlings's life, including the writing of *The Yearling* and *Gal Young 'Un,* a film based on one of her short stories about an exploitive husband, his wife, and his girlfriend.

✳ **ACTIVITIES:** Middle-school kids will enjoy the book.

✳ TRULY, MADLY, DEEPLY

1991, 107 min, NR, 12 and up
Dir: Anthony Minghella. Juliet Stevenson, Alan Rickman

Nina (Juliet Stevenson) is a loving and kind young woman who teaches English as a second language. Her lover, Jamie (Alan Rickman), a musician, has just died, and she is utterly devastated. She is unable to let go of her devotion to him.

One day he reappears, explaining that he did not "die properly." She is overjoyed and happily puts up with the quirks of living with a ghost: staying in the apartment as much as possible, ignoring her job and her friends, keeping the apartment stifling hot (since Jamie is perpetually cold), and putting up with Jamie's ghost friends, who want to stay up all night to watch videos.

Nina meets an engaging teacher named Mark (Michael Maloney) and, despite misgivings, agrees to see him again. She is still committed to Jamie. Ultimately, however, she must make a choice between living in the past and going on into the future.

This lovely movie allows itself to be ambiguous about whether Jamie actually appears as a ghost to help Nina accept his death or whether it is just a metaphor for Nina's progress through the stages of grief. All of the performances are beguilingly natural, and Stevenson (who inspired the script) is luminously vulnerable, well worth coming back from the dead for.

✳ **CONNECTIONS:** Minghella went on to make the Oscar-winning *The English Patient*. Rickman appears in *Sense and Sensibility*.

SEE ALSO:

Fly Away Home A young girl becomes withdrawn after her mother dies, until she becomes responsible for a group of goslings.

Permanent Record A group of high school kids must come to grips with the suicide of a seemingly happy and successful friend.

Unstrung Heroes A young boy copes with his mother's illness by moving in with two loving but emotionally ill uncles.

Where the Lilies Bloom Fourteen-year-old Mary Call Luther cares for her sisters and brother after their parents die, and learns that may mean breaking a promise to her father.

Where the Red Fern Grows A boy copes with the loss of his beloved dogs.

WOMEN WORTH
WATCHING

I long to speak out the intense inspiration that comes from the lives of strong women.

—RUTH BENEDICT

Reviving *Ophelia*, the best-seller by clinical psychologist Mary Pipher, describes how girls often lose confidence as they enter adolescence, based in part on the messages they receive from the media. Certainly, there is a long tradition in the movies (as in the books and folktales that preceded them) of women who achieve success through good grooming and accessorizing, while the males in their lives are saving the world by swashbuckling with dragons, pirates, and each other.

There is no shortage of tough, smart heroines in movies and books about girls under twelve, like Pippi Longstocking, Brave Irene, Amazing Grace, Laura Ingalls Wilder, and Anne of Green Gables. But teenage and adult heroines in books and movies are most often passively good, like Cinderella, whose patient obedience is rewarded when she is given new clothes, and Sleeping Beauty, who literally sleeps while the prince fights the dragon. There are some welcome recent exceptions in books, like *Tatterhood,* edited by Ethel Johnston Phelps; *The King's Equal,* by Katherine Patterson; and *The Outspoken Princess and the Gentle Knight,* edited by Jack Zipes.

Still, little girls and bigger ones see a lot of what I call "makeover movies": In a crucial scene Our Heroine gets a new dress and hairstyle (or just takes off her glasses) and her life changes. Sometimes she transforms herself, as Ella does in **Bells are Ringing,** causing her to have enormous conflicts and self-doubt. More often, she is transformed by someone else. Cinderella's fairy godmother changes her sooty rags to a glamorous gown so that she can go to the ball and dazzle the prince. Her modern counterparts are Eliza Doolittle, who, like Cinderella, goes to a ball in borrowed finery (and accent) and dazzles everyone there in **My Fair Lady,** and *Gigi,* who is actually groomed by her grandmother and great-aunt to be a very elegant prostitute, trained almost like a geisha in manners and skills for pleasing a man. Over and over, we see the heroines rewarded for being lovely and passive pleasers.

The villains in family movies are equal opportunity, however, and Disney films in particular feature very powerful women as the bad guys. But it is hard to find a woman in movies who is both powerful and successful and one of the good guys.

Even more damaging are the constant messages to girls that they should be sexually provocative and available. One of the most popular movies among young girls on video is *Grease,* in which a "hopelessly devoted" young woman is able to realize her ultimate goal of getting her boyfriend's attention by dressing and acting like a biker chick. Most troubling, contemporary movies give teenagers no sense that there is any hierarchy of sexual contact. The overpowering message is that if you like a guy (or want him to like you), you have sex with him. Young women are not portrayed as though they are entitled to establish limits on physical intimacy; there is no sense that they have the right to decide that a kiss good night is sufficient. Female lead characters in an astonishing number of successful films are prostitutes or strippers. No wonder Ophelia has to be revived!

Girls and boys should watch the classic films because those stories are an important part of our cultural heritage and because they have themes with enduring appeal that we can both enjoy and teach our children to try to understand. The challenge is to watch them with a sense of heightened awareness, to learn to decode the hidden messages and to be explicit in our responses to them.

Fortunately, we also have some alternatives to help young women recognize that the important satisfactions come from self-respect, love based on trust and respect, and work that makes a contribution. The films of the 1930s gave us a lot of heroines who were strong, smart, independent, and accomplished. Think of the roles played by Katharine Hepburn, Bette Davis, and Rosalind Russell. For some reason, in the 1940s and especially in the 1950s, most female leads in movies could have stepped out of a "ring around the collar" ad. But even then, we had Doris Day. In the midst of the fluffiest sex comedies she was almost always shown as independent and superbly competent in her work. These days, some movies still sink into sexist stereotypes, but when they do, they are often criticized for it, as was the case with *True Lies,* which prompted not only reviews but editorials criticizing its misogyny.

We still have a long way to go. A recent guide to "nonviolent, nonsexist" videos included 800 videos, but only 100 of them feature girls or women in central roles, and even those usually have a male character as the lead.

It can help kids to understand these issues if you ask children and teens to compare Cinderella and Sleeping Beauty to more recent heroines of Disney animation. Today's female characters are much more active, curious, independent and intelligent: Look at Ariel in **The Little Mermaid**, Belle in **Beauty and** *the Beast,* Nala in *The Lion King*—though she was better qualified to lead the lions than Simba, Pocahontas, Mulan, and Meg in *Hercules.* They may still look like Barbie dolls, but they are not singing to the birds about "Someday My Prince Will Come"; they are taking care of themselves and pursuing what they want. And in 1998's *Ever After,* Drew Barrymore plays a Cinderella who makes her own magic, and even saves the prince.

Make sure that boys and girls see some of the movies that give us female characters who want more than a new outfit and hairdo, and who are respected for their abilities and accomplishments. And make sure they see movies with men and women who share a "marriage of true minds," couples united in the kind of love that is only possible between people who respect, admire, and trust one another.

Funny Girl
1968, 155 min, G, 8 and up
Dir: William Wyler. Barbra Streisand, Omar Sharif, Walter Pidgeon

✳ **PLOT:** Based on the real life of Ziegfeld comedy star Fanny Brice (Barbra Streisand), this is the story both of her triumphs as a performer and of her unhappy marriage to gambler Nicky Arnstein (Omar Sharif).

As the movie opens, Fanny is a teenager, passionately committed to becoming a performer. Despite the warnings of her mother's friends that she is not pretty enough to be successful, she believes in herself and her talent and refuses to take no for an answer. She is fired during rehearsal in a small vaudeville house but, promising she knows how to roller-skate, is hired again for a dance number on skates. She creates chaos out of the number, but sings a song and is a huge success. That night she meets Arnstein and is fascinated by his sophistication, charm, and good looks.

Soon afterward, she is hired by Florenz Ziegfeld, the greatest producer of the era, to be featured in his new show. They clash when he wants her to sing a song about a bride that has her describing herself as beautiful. At the last minute, on opening night, she decides to turn it into a comic number by making herself appear pregnant. Ziegfeld is furious but concedes that it was successful.

Arnstein reappears from time to time without warning, and she falls deeply in love with him, finally leaving the show to join him on an ocean liner to Europe. He makes enough in a poker game to marry her. She is thrilled to be a "Sadie, Sadie, Married Lady" and adores their daughter, Frances. But when his winning streak ends, he is upset that she is supporting him. Desperate, he tries to make money in a crooked bond deal, but he is discovered and is sent to prison. Fanny remains devoted to him, but when he is released he tells her that he cannot stay with her, and they divorce.

✳ **DISCUSSION:** Barbra Streisand won an Oscar for this, her movie debut (she also starred in the original Broadway production). Her mixture of bravado

("I'm the greatest star/I am by far/but no one knows it") and vulnerability shielded by humor ("You don't have to use leading lady lines on me; I'm a comedian"), both as Brice the performer and as Brice the woman, is captivating.

Contrary to the traditions of the "makeover movie," Brice achieves her dreams without a fairy godmother to give her glamour or teach her how to behave. She stays very much herself, insisting on her right to select her own material and create her own persona onstage. But she is not successful in her romantic relationship, at least in part due to the same ability to take care of herself, even when part of her wants to be taken care of.

The problem is as much his insecurity as hers. He cannot feel comfortable living on her earnings and in her shadow. His self-esteem depends on being able to take care of her, a real problem for a man who makes his living as a gambler. It doesn't matter to him that she does not care about his ability to provide for them, and that all she is looking for is his love and devotion. Nick and Fanny love each other but cannot stay together. This may be reassuring to children whose parents are apart, because it shows that they care about each other, and that the problems are between them, and not about their child.

PROFANITY: None.

NUDITY/SEXUAL REFERENCES: Despite the G rating, there is a PG-level seduction scene, and mild references to nonmarital sex; Fanny appears onstage as a pregnant bride (played for comedy).

ALCOHOL/DRUG ABUSE: Social drinking.

VIOLENCE/SCARINESS: Sad, but not scary.

TOLERANCE/DIVERSITY ISSUES: Acceptance of differences (Fanny refers to herself as "a bagel on a plate of onion rolls").

✲ QUESTIONS FOR KIDS:
- Why is Fanny so sure of herself as a performer, and so unsure of herself in other parts of her life?
- Was she right to lie to Eddie about being able to roller-skate?
- She promised to do whatever Mr. Ziegfeld told her—why didn't she?
- Why did Fanny care so much for someone who could not be as devoted to her as she was to him?
- Why was it hard for Nick to accept help from her?

✲ CONNECTIONS: *Funny Lady* is a sequel, which is not nearly as good, covering Brice's marriage to impresario Billy Rose, which broke up when he fell in love with a performer in one of his shows. In that movie, she must still deal with her love for Nick Arnstein. Kids who enjoy this movie might like to see the real Fanny Brice perform in a skit in *The Ziegfeld Follies of 1946,* a Hollywood version of a Ziegfeld-style revue. That movie also has other treats, including the only dance number ever filmed with both Fred Astaire and Gene Kelly. Kids might also like to see Willam Powell's appearance as "The Great Ziegfeld." And "Ziegfeld Girl" is a glossy and

enjoyable backstage soap opera starring Judy Garland, Hedy Lamarr, Jimmy Stewart, and Lana Turner.

✳Pat and Mike

1952, 95 min, NR, b&w, 8 and up
Dir: George Cukor. Katharine Hepburn, Spencer Tracy, Aldo Ray

✳ **PLOT:** Pat Pemberton (Katharine Hepburn), a physical education teacher at a small California college, is a superb athlete who is a bit insecure. A widow engaged to Collier Weld, a hearty faculty colleague (William Ching), Pat enjoys competing but fails whenever her fiancé is watching. Mike Conovan (Spencer Tracy), a fast-talking and slightly shady sports promoter, sees her at an amateur golf tournament, asks her to take a bribe to throw the game and, when she refuses, tells her that she can make a lot of money by competing professionally.

At first she says no, but later she comes back to him and asks for more information. When he finds out she is not only a superb golfer but an outstanding tennis player and even an expert with a rifle, he takes her on, in addition to his other "properties," a racehorse and Davie Hucko, a punchy boxer (Aldo Ray). She does very well, except when her fiancé is there. As she and Mike get closer, and she becomes more successful, Davie gets jealous. Mike's financial backers want Pat to lose an important golf match. He reminds them that he told them from the beginning that she was on the level. They take him out to rough him up, but Pat rescues him, using judo. Mike is embarrassed. But she finds a way for him to regain his sense of himself as her protector, and they agree to become a romantic team as well as a professional one.

✳ **DISCUSSION:** This is a delightful and witty love story, and a lot of fun to watch. And there are some thoughtful and insightful moments that make it especially worthwhile. In a very real sense, Pat is looking for a sense of herself and her own worth when she goes to Mike. At some level, she knows that the relationship with Collier is not working. Children, who so need their parents to root for them at soccer games or other kinds of competitions, will be interested to see that Pat unravels whenever Collier is near. He seems supportive and enthusiastic, but somehow he really sees her as incompetent, and that is what she becomes while he is there.

Mike's first observation of Pat is one of the most famous lines in the film—-with relish, he says, with his best Brooklyn twist, "Not much meat on her, but what there is, is 'cherse.' " He likes it that she wants to compete honestly. He sees and appreciates her strength.

And yet, he likes to be the one in charge; he likes to take care of her. He likes to tell her what to eat and to massage her muscle cramps. He is dismayed when she protects him from the thugs who are trying to muscle him into having her intentionally lose the match. A superficial viewing would suggest that her finding a way for him to save his face by protecting her later is a betrayal of any notion of equality. But what matters is the "five-oh, five-oh" definition of their relationship in the movie's last lines, where she turns the table by asking him his "three questions": "Who made you?" "You did." "Who owns the biggest piece of you?" "You do." "Where will you go if I dump you?" "Down the drain." "And?" "And drag you down with me!"

PROFANITY: None.

NUDITY/SEXUAL REFERENCES: Pat's fiancé is suspicious when he sees Pat and Mike together in an entirely innocent but mildly suggestive situation.

ALCOHOL/DRUG ABUSE: None.

VIOLENCE/SCARINESS: Pat uses judo to subdue three thugs.

TOLERANCE/DIVERSITY ISSUES: The issue of gender equality is implicit throughout the movie.

✳ QUESTIONS FOR KIDS:
- Why couldn't Pat play well while Collier was there? How does that show that she should not marry him? Why didn't she have the same problem with Mike?
- What does "five-oh, five-oh" mean, and why is it important to Pat and Mike?
- Why didn't Hucko like Pat? What did she do to make him like her?
- How did Mike feel when Pat stopped the men who were trying to beat him up? Why?
- Why did the men want Pat to lose on purpose? Why didn't she want to?

✳ CONNECTIONS:
Tracy and Hepburn made nine movies together. The best are *Adam's Rib*, *Woman of the Year*, *Without Love*, and *Desk Set*. This one allows Katharine Hepburn to show off her real-life athletic ability.

If an actor in this movie listed as "Charles Bushowski" looks familiar, that may be because you recognize him from his appearances under another name—Charles Bronson. Look also for Chuck (*The Rifleman*) Connors as a policeman, and Carl "Alfalfa" Sweitzer of The Little Rascals as a busboy. And note that several of the greatest athletes of the era appear as themselves, including Pancho Gonzales and Babe Didrikson Zaharias.

✳ The Rainmaker
1956, 121 min, NR, 10 and up
Dir: Joseph Anthony. Katharine Hepburn, Burt Lancaster, Lloyd Bridges, Earl Holliman

✳ PLOT:
Starbuck (Burt Lancaster) is a traveling salesman with enormous charisma. As the movie opens, he is selling tornado rods, to prevent damage

from tornados, but when he is called a con man, he quickly escapes. In the next town, he watches quietly from the shadows and sees Jimmy (Earl Holliman) awkwardly making overtures to Snookie (Yvonne Lime) at a dance to raise money for damage from a long drought.

Jimmy's sister, Lizzie (Katharine Hepburn), comes home from a visit to her cousins in search of a husband. She didn't find one; at first she hid in her room, and when she came down she made the mistake of letting them know she knew facts like where Madagascar was. Her father and brothers love her, and they say she's just afraid of being beautiful. Lizzie replies, "I'm afraid to think I am when I'm not." She says she wants "to make someone happy . . . I want him to tell me who he is, and to tell me who I am because I sure don't know." She says that this man she dreams of "never has to say thank you because thank you is our whole life together."

Lizzie's father, H. C., her stern, practical brother Noah (Lloyd Bridges), and Jimmy ask File, the new deputy sheriff (Wendell Corey), to dinner, but he refuses, saying, "I don't want to get married." H. C. tells him the town knows he is not a widower but a divorced man whose wife deserted him, and that he "needs mending."

Lizzie is at first ashamed to have her family so obviously trying to marry her off, but she is also terribly disappointed that File turned them down. Starbuck arrives, asking them to hire him to bring rain. Noah is opposed, but Jimmy wants to try it, and H. C. wants to know more about it. Starbuck tells them that "once in your life, you gotta take a chance on a con man."

File arrives. At first he and Lizzie talk, but then, remembering her brother's advice not to "talk too serious," she tries to flirt with him and he gets disgusted with her silly behavior and leaves. Noah tells Lizzie to give up and accept her fate as an old maid. "The sooner you accept it, the sooner you'll stop breaking your heart."

But Starbuck does not see her that way. He sees her as "Melisande" and tells her, "Don't let Noah be your looking glass." He kisses her, "because when you said you were pretty, it was true." File comes back, looking for Starbuck. Lizzie and her family persuade File to let him go. Starbuck asks Lizzie to go with him—"Go with me and you'll be so beautiful, you'll light the world!" File asks Lizzie to stay. She knows that her dream is the life she could have with File. Starbuck gives back the money they gave him, and rides away. But when the rain begins, he goes back to get the money, saying to Lizzie, "So long, Beautiful!"

✳ **DISCUSSION:** This is an excellent counterpoint to the "makeover movie" messages about achieving success in life and love through improvements in appearance and manners. Lizzie has to find herself, her dream, and her own beauty, and only then is able to accept that others find her beautiful. Ironically, it is Starbuck, a professional liar, who tells her the truth: that she has to know her own beauty, and that when she finds it for herself, it will be there for others as well. Starbuck gives her the gift of the truth about himself, about his real name, and how he picked the name he wanted to become.

Noah and Jimmy tell Lizzie to behave more like other girls to "get" a man, and she says, "If that is the way a man gets got, I don't want any." She wants to be wanted for who she is, by someone who will be proud that she knows where Madagascar is.

Noah is cerebral, practical, even cynical. He tries to persuade Jimmy not to get involved with Snookie and seems to think that everything that is not a prudent financial investment is a waste of time. Jimmy is impetuous and emotional. While Noah accuses him of being dumb, his father is closer to the truth when he says that Jimmy "always says the smart thing at the dumb time."

Starbuck is full of dreams; he cons himself as much as he cons anyone else, yet he is affected by Lizzie. He even returns the money, until it rains, and he can take credit for it. The rain can be seen as a symbol of the vitality he has brought to Lizzie, and the small piece of integrity she has brought out in him.

File won't let himself dream, because he has been hurt. Yet he has also been a con man in a way, telling the community he is a widower because he does not want them to know the truth. He says, "There's one thing I learned. Be independent! If you don't ask for things—if you don't let on you need things—pretty soon you don't need 'em." But he listens when Lizzie says he should not have let his pride keep him from asking his wife to stay, and he proves that by letting her know that he needs her.

PROFANITY: None.

NUDITY/SEXUAL REFERENCES: Very oblique references.

ALCOHOL/DRUG ABUSE: None.

VIOLENCE/SCARINESS: None.

TOLERANCE/DIVERSITY ISSUES: Issue of whether a woman can attract a man by being intelligent and telling the truth.

✳ **QUESTIONS FOR KIDS:**
- What do the family's different reactions to Starbuck show us about them?
- Noah tells Jimmy he is dumb, and tells Lizzie she is unattractive and destined to be an old maid. Why? What impact does it have on them?
- Why does Lizzie have to know she is beautiful before she can be beautiful to Starbuck or File?
- What do the draught and rain symbolize?
- Lizzie tells Starbuck that "it's no good to live in your dreams," and he replies "It's no good to live outside of them." What does that mean? Which one is right?

✳ **CONNECTIONS:** The importance of dreams is a theme of many enduring stories. Some, like **The Glass Menagerie** and *The Iceman Cometh,* focus on the destructive impact of using dreams to hide reality. But others show the way that dreams illuminate our lives (**Miracle on 34th Street**) and help us to understand reality, even to improve it (***Rocky, Field of Dreams, Lilies of the Field, Rudy, Holiday, Hello, Dolly***). In *Don Quixote,* both aspects of dreams are explored.

Teenagers might like to find out about the use of divining rods or about people like Starbuck who traveled the country selling all kinds of phony cures and spells. Compare this story to **The Music Man.** Starbuck and Professor Harold Hill are similar in many ways, but the movies have very different conclusions. Curiously, the name Starbuck gives Lizzie, "Melisande," is also the name Ella picks for her fictional self in **Bells Are Ringing.** Note: Do not confuse this with the 1997 John Grisham movie of the same name.

Mulan
1998, 88 min, G, 6 and up
Dir: Tony Bancroft, Barry Cook. Voices of Miguel Ferrar, Eddie Murphy, Soon-Tek Oh, Donny Osmond, Ming-Na Wen, B.D. Wong

✳ **PLOT:** This Disney animated feature is based upon the legend of Mulan, a Chinese girl who helps the Chinese army defeat the Mongols. After the Mongols invade, led by Shan-Yu (voice of Miguel Ferrar) every family is called upon to send one man to the army. Although Mulan's father, Fa Zhou (voice of Soon-Tek Oh) must use a crutch to walk, he is willing to fight for the honor of his family. Mulan (voice of Ming-Na Wen) disguises herself as a man so that her father will not have to risk his life. The ghosts of her ancestors order a powerful guardian dragon to protect her and bring her home. Instead, a tiny disgraced dragon named Mushu (voice of Eddie Murphy) joins her in the hope that he can help her achieve a triumph to bring honor to both of them.

Mulan finds pretending to be a man and meeting the standards of Shang, her tough captain (voice of B.D. Wong) tougher challenges than she imagined. But her determination earns her the respect of the others, and in the midst of battle her quick thinking and courage save the day—instead of shooting her hopelessly outnumbered battalion's last cannon at the enemy, she shoots at a snow-covered mountain, causing an avalanche that blankets them with snow. She then saves Shang from the avalanche.

Nevertheless, when her true gender is revealed, she is left behind. Instead of going home, Mulan and Mushu travel to warn the emperor that Shan-Yu is still alive, and again she saves the day when the Mongols attack.

✳ **DISCUSSION:** This is one of Disney's best, with gorgeous animation inspired by Chinese paintings, a hilarious performance by Eddie Murphy as Mushu, and a witty, intelligent script that transcends the usual formulas. In one nice twist, the macho soldiers who are certain that no "girl worth fighting for" would have a mind of her own end up having to dress as women to defeat the Mongols. And Captain Shang learns from the wise emperor that "the flower that blooms in adversity is the most rare and beautiful of all."

Families will have much to talk about—the notion of honor, the traditional Chinese view of the ancestors, and the importance of freedom from stereotypes.

PROFANITY: None.

NUDITY/SEXUAL REFERENCES: Soldiers bathing nude cause Mulan to flee (nothing shown).

ALCOHOL/DRUG ABUSE: None.

VIOLENCE/SCARINESS: Some scary war scenes, death of Shang's father in battle.

TOLERANCE/DIVERSITY ISSUES: A theme of the movie.

✳ **QUESTIONS FOR KIDS:**
- Why did Mulan's father want to join the army despite his bad leg?
- Why was it hard for Mulan to behave the way the matchmaker wanted her to?
- Why was it hard for Shang to accept Mulan's help? Why did he feel differently about her when he found out she was female?

✳ **CONNECTIONS:** Adults with sharp ears may recognize Donny Osmond singing Shang's songs and June Foray (of "Rocky and Bullwinkle") as Mulan's outspoken grandmother. Listen carefully when the grandmother sings, though—it's none other than Marni Nixon, who provided the bell-like singing voice for Natalie Wood in **West Side Story,** Deborah Kerr in **The King and I,** and Audrey Hepburn in **My Fair Lady.**

✳ THE BEST LITTLE GIRL IN THE WORLD
1981, 100 min, NR, 12 and up
Dir: Sam O'Steen. Jennifer Jason Leigh, Charles Durning, Eva Marie Saint

This "disease of the week" television movie about anorexia nervosa rises well above the average due to the performances of Jennifer Jason Leigh as the lead, Charles Durning and Eva Marie Saint as her parents, and Jason Miller as her therapist. Treatment of anorexia has made some progress since 1981, but the movie may still be a way of helping some girls recognize and understand eating disorders, which raise issues of a fear of growing up, of overwhelming images of the "perfect" body, and of a misplaced sense of control.

✳ A DOLL'S HOUSE
1973, 105 min, G, 12 and up
Dir: Patrick Garland. Claire Bloom, Anthony Hopkins

Nora is a "doll-wife," adored by her husband and children but treated like a cherished pet. She needs money to save her husband's life, and so in a shrewd and daring act, she commits forgery. Although she pays it back, her husband finds out about it. He cannot forgive her, not because she lied, but because she acted independently, and because she protected him. He is willing to go on as they were before, but she has found that she needs to be treated as a person, not a doll, and so she leaves, slamming the door.

✳ **CONNECTIONS:** Another movie version of this play was also released in 1973, directed by Joseph Losey, and starring Jane Fonda and David Warner. It is also rated G, but is most suitable for ages twelve and up.

Writer/director Nora Ephron (*Sleepless in Seattle, When Harry Met Sally*) was named after the leading character in this drama by her screenwriter parents.

✳ **ACTIVITIES:** Teens who enjoy this may like to read or see some of Ibsen's other plays, including *Hedda Gabler,* about a woman who destroys herself when she is not able to manipulate others to give her the power and control she desperately craves, and *Ghosts,* about the destructive power of secrets and overly restrictive social conventions.

✳ MY BRILLIANT CAREER

1979, 101 min, G, 10 and up
Dir: Gillian Armstrong. Judy Davis, Sam Neill

This movie is based on the autobiography of Miles Franklin, a girl from the Australian outback, who wrote the book when she was only sixteen. Judy Davis is brilliant as Franklin, whose independent spirit and sense of her own worth cannot be squelched by the suffocating conventions of the Victorian era. She is clearly attracted to handsome Harry Beecham (Sam Neill), but when he finally proposes, clearly loving her for what she loves most about herself, she cannot accept. What she wants from life cannot be found in the life he offers.

✳ MY GIRL

1991, 102 min, PG, 12 and up
Dir: Howard Zieff. Anna Chlumsky, Dan Aykroyd, Jamie Lee Curtis

This uneven story about a young girl trying to understand loss stars the talented and appealing Anna Chlumsky as Vada, the sensitive daughter of a loving but distant mortician father (Dan Aykroyd). The loss of her mother just after she was born, her grandmother's fading memory, the embalming facilities in the basement, and the prospect of growing up all leave her anxious, even worried that she herself is going to die. She has to deal with some major changes, including a romance for her father, with kindhearted Shelly (Jamie Lee Curtis), her first period, and the death of her closest friend, played by *Home Alone*'s Macaulay Culkin. Vada finds strength in herself and in her ability as a writer.

✳ **CONNECTIONS:** A sequel, *My Girl 2,* features much of the same cast, as Vada goes to visit her uncle and searches for information about her late mother. Vada is not just sensitive; she is smart and brave. Both movies are set in the 1970s, which can give parents a chance to point out some of the cultural touchstones of that era. NOTE: Both movies have some mature material. Parents should screen the films before showing them to young teens.

✳ SMOOTH TALK

1985, 92 min, PG-13, mature high schoolers
Dir: Joyce Chopra. Laura Dern, Treat Williams

Based on a story by Joyce Carol Oates, this is an exceptionally vivid portrayal of the restlessness (and risks) of adolescence. Laura Dern is outstanding as Connie, caught up in the small rebellions and obsessions (especially self-obsession) of a fifteen-year-old, bickering with her mother, sniping at her sister and, daringly, experimenting with her sexual power as she cruises through the mall with her friends. But things get sickeningly out of control when the signals she has been sending out are received by a much older man, disturbingly named "A. Friend" (Treat Willams), and she has none of the sense of self necessary to send him away. NOTE: This movie may provide a good opportunity for discussing important issues, but it deals with sexuality in a way that may be upsetting for teenagers (and their parents), and should be viewed by parents before deciding whether to show it to teens.

✳ THE TAMING OF THE SHREW

1967, 126 min, NR, 10 and up
Dir: Franco Zeffirelli. Elizabeth Taylor, Richard Burton, Michael York

Shakespeare's play about the wild woman tamed by an even wilder man stars then-married wild couple Elizabeth Taylor and Richard Burton, enjoying themselves enormously. Burton plays Petruchio, who comes "to wive it wealthily in Padua," saying he will marry any woman as long as she brings a fortune. This is very convenient for his friends, both of whom want to marry the beautiful Bianca, because Bianca's wealthy father has said she may not marry until someone marries her sister Katherina, also known as "Kate the cursed" for her temper. Petruchio agrees to marry Kate for her fortune. Once he meets Kate, he sees that she is both beautiful and witty, and that her temper stems from feeling misunderstood and unloved. He marries her quickly, and then "tames" her by showing her an excess of attention. When Petruchio and Kate return for a visit, they amaze the community with her docility, both hugely enjoying the joke.

Though sometimes criticized as a feminist nightmare (the idea of "taming" connotes mastering an animal), it is perfectly possible to view this play as quite the contrary, and the range of interpretations are well worth family discussion. NOTE: In Shakespeare's play, the entire story is a "play within a play," put on as a part of a prank designed to confuse a homeless man into thinking he is a nobleman. What does this tell us about Shakespeare's view of the story?

✳ WILD HEARTS CAN'T BE BROKEN

1991, 88 min, G, 8 and up
Dir: Steve Miner. Gabrielle Anwar, Cliff Robertson, Michael Schoeffling

In the 1930s, one of the top tourist attractions in the country was a girl who dove on a horse, in Atlantic City. That girl was Sonora Webster, and what the audience did not know was that she was blind as the result of an accident in one of her first dives. This movie is based on the real story of Sonora (Gabrielle Anwar), a plucky teenager who leaves home during the Depression and shows independence, persistence, and courage in following her dream.

SEE ALSO:

Adam's Rib Katharine Hepburn plays a feminist lawyer married to a man who respects and admires her intelligence and courage, even when they are on opposite sides in the courtroom.

Annie Oakley Contrary to the popular conception, fueled by Irving Berlin's *Annie Get Your Gun,* this version of the story accurately shows that Oakley's husband, fellow sharpshooter Frank Butler, was her most enthusiastic supporter.

Born Yesterday Judy Holliday plays a woman who learns that she has a fine mind and an honest heart, and that she can get more satisfaction from relying on them than she did in relying on her looks and ability to attract men.

Cat Ballou Jane Fonda plays a young woman of courage and determination in the Old West. When her father is killed by crooks who want their land, she takes charge.

The Journey of Natty Gann A young girl travels across the country to join her father.

Julia Two strong, independent women, friends since childhood, demonstrate commitment and loyalty as one helps the other in her fight against the Nazis.

A League of Their Own Based on a true story, this movie about women baseball players shows their spirit, skill, and teamwork, and the pleasure it gave them to be able to use them.

The Nasty Girl The heroine of this real-life story will not be dissuaded from her search for the truth about her town's culpability for Nazi war crimes, no matter what the cost.

National Velvet Velvet disguises herself as a boy to enter the Grand National Steeplechase with her beloved horse, and together they give everything they have to win.

The Solid Gold Cadillac A woman finds that asking honest questions and insisting on honest answers leads to the overthrow of corrupt managers.

Where the Lilies Bloom A young girl keeps her family together after her father dies.

SCHOOL DAYS

"Have you learn'd lessons only of those who admired you, and were tender with you, and stood aside for you?

"Have you not learn'd great lessons from those who reject you, and brace themselves against you? or who treat you with contempt, or dispute the passage with you?"

—WALT WHITMAN

Schools, like the Old West, provide a basic point of reference for almost any kind of story. They are arenas where an infinite number of stories and characters reside, a natural setting for drama or comedy, even for a musical or a thriller. We all go to school and we all have many of our formative experiences there. In our first venture outside of our families, we enter school, learning not just reading and writing and arithmetic but equally important lessons about the larger world. We learn about rules, explicit (hang your coat in your cubby, raise your hand before you speak, take turns on the swings) and implicit (kids who bring peanut butter sandwiches never get anyone to trade with them, kids who can cross the monkeybars without falling are cooler than ones who can't, takeovers only for interference). We have our first confrontations with bureaucracy. We eat whatever that gloppy mess is that the ladies with the hair nets give us every Tuesday. Teachers wield enormous power over our lives. Sometimes they make us miserable. But if we are very, very lucky, over the course of our school years, we have some who inspire us so much that their words live inside us forever.

Movies throughout this book draw on school as a setting. Some movies use schools as a microcosm of society, with firmly established hierarchies that have their own highly individualized criteria for determining status and power. This can be played as comedy (as in **The Lawrenceville Stories**) or drama (**The Chocolate War**). Some use school simply as the setting for a coming-of-age story, focusing almost exclusively on the students, with very little time in the classroom and no adult major characters. But many school movies do focus on a teacher who changes the students' lives, whose life is changed by teaching, or both. Occasionally, we also see a teacher with a malevolent influence or horrible schools with cruel teachers. But books, plays, and movies are all written by writers, all of whom at some time in their lives fell in love with words, and all of whom have some teacher they want to thank (as in *The Corn Is Green* for example), and movies give us a chance to be inspired by those who inspired them the most.

*Almost Angels

1962, 93 min, NR, 8 and up
Dir: Steve Previn. Peter Weck, Hans Holt

✳ **PLOT:** Toni, a young Austrian boy, joins the famous Vienna Boys Choir, which has been performing for more than 500 years.

At his audition one stage mother is very anxious to see her boy succeed. Toni's mother, in contrast, is there because "he has real talent and I want him to develop it." Toni's father does not want him to join the choir: "I want him to go to a proper school and learn a proper trade." He worries that once Toni's voice changes, the choir will have no interest in him, and Toni will be left with nothing. When he is accepted, his father agrees to let him go for one month, and then he will decide whether to keep Toni there.

The Choir boys attend school, and Toni has a problem with math. While the principal tells him he must improve his math grades, another teacher comforts him by telling him that Franz Schubert's father was so upset with his son's poor grades that he almost pulled him out of the school.

An older boy, Peter, becomes jealous of Toni. He knows he is getting older, and that once his voice changes, he will not be able to sing in the choir any longer. Peter tries to get Toni in trouble by playing his (forbidden) radio in the dorm, which leads to the movie's most memorable scene, a huge pillow fight. Their teacher, Max, hears what is going on, and is careful to jiggle the doorknob to let them know he is there before he comes in to stop it. Peter also locks Toni up to keep him from a performance. But the boys become friends, and Toni and the other boys show their loyalty by trying to keep the fact that Peter's voice has broken from the teachers. Max says, "This isn't the end—it's the beginning. It's fun being a kid, but 'til now you've only been rehearsing." Max arranges for Peter to come along on the tour, as his assistant. In the last scene, on the tour, the boys are performing with Peter as the conductor.

✳ **DISCUSSION:** This slight story has, in addition to some lovely music and pretty location photography, some worthwhile issues about jealousy, loyalty, ambition (for oneself and for one's children), hard work, and growing up. Peter locks up Toni just as he tries to lock up his voice, and his childhood, to keep himself from growing up. His wish to stay with the choir as a soprano is a symbol of his reluctance to grow up. But Max is understanding and sympathetic, showing Peter that there are additional opportunities and responsibilities available to him as he matures.

Kids may also want to discuss the parents' perspective. The mother at the audition wants the reflected glory of a child in the choir. Toni's father has his own ideas about what Toni needs. But Toni's mother wants Toni to be able to use his gifts.

PROFANITY: None.

NUDITY/SEXUAL REFERENCES: None.

ALCOHOL/DRUG ABUSE: None.

VIOLENCE/SCARINESS: None (except the pillow fight!).

TOLERANCE/DIVERSITY ISSUES: The Choir boys are all white males. Some children may be surprised at the Choir boys' tradition of having boys play girls' roles (and wear dresses) in their performances.

❋ **QUESTIONS FOR KIDS:**
* Why do Toni's parents want different things for him?
* What made Toni's father change his mind?
* Why does Peter lock Toni up so that he cannot perform?

❋ **CONNECTIONS:** The lip-synch scene is reminiscent of the dubbing in *Singin' in the Rain.*

❋ **ACTIVITIES:** This might have special appeal to children who sing in a choir. After seeing this movie, children might like to hear some of the records made by the Vienna Boys Choir, or go to see a performance when they are on tour. They also might like to hear music by Franz Schubert, who, as noted in the movie, was once a Vienna Choir boy.

❋Dead Poets Society
1989, 128 min, PG, 12 and up
Dir: Peter Weir. Robin Williams, Ethan Hawke, Robert Sean Leonard
12 and up

❋ **PLOT:** Welton is an exclusive boys' prep school, dedicated to "Tradition, Discipline, Honor, and Excellence." The boys' parents, arriving for the new term, are equally demanding, reminding their boys of the importance of academic success and encouraging conformity.

A new teacher named Keating (Robin Williams) takes a different approach with his boys. He urges them to "seize the day," make the most of their youth and energy, and express themselves as individuals through poetry and language. When he attended Welton, Keating was a founder of the "Dead Poets Society," a group dedicated to Thoreau's aim to "suck the very marrow out of life."

The boys take Keating's lessons to heart. They reestablish the society and, breaking out of the mold the school has formed for them, commit themselves to goals that mean something more important to them than achieving good grades. Knox Overstreet (Josh Charles) writes poetry to a beautiful girl; Neil (Robert Sean Leonard) auditions for a play and, forging his father's signature on the permission slip, accepts a lead part. Keating's words also have an effect on a nervous Todd Anderson (Ethan Hawke), who lives in the twin shadows of a successful older brother and out-of-touch parents.

The school authorities try to stamp out the boys' self-expression. The headmaster seeks to root out the Dead Poets Society and find out who put the boys up to it. The boys break ranks and admit that it was Keating.

Neil, meanwhile, glories in a highly successful portrayal of Puck in *A Midsummer Night's Dream*. His father is furious and wants to remove his son from Welton, send him to a military school, and groom him for Harvard and medical school as planned. Neil, despairing that he will never be allowed to do what he wants, commits suicide.

The Welton authorities blame Keating and the Dead Poets Society. Keating is fired, but some of his students have learned to seize the day.

✳ **DISCUSSION:** Keating's challenge is subtler than that of the teachers in *Stand and Deliver* or *The Blackboard Jungle.* His students are at the other end of the economic spectrum, with more material goods than they know what to do with. But, like the barrio and ghetto students, they have a kind of complacency that Keating must overcome. His challenge is to get them to accept the responsibility of thinking for themselves.

Despite Williams's magnetic and inspiring performance, the weakness of this plot makes this a hard movie for many grown-ups to take. But it is a popular and moving film for teenagers and provides a good opportunity for discussing important issues.

Keating challenges the boys to think for themselves instead of blindly accepting the system and values presented to them by the school and their parents. He asks why poetry was invented and brushes aside the expected "blue book" answers for one that goes straight to the boys' hearts: "To woo women." This is meaningful because it it is refreshingly honest and direct, and because it connects them with the "dead poets," who they now understand had precisely the same feelings as the boys themselves.

Though awkwardly and melodramatically handled, the film raises the issue of conflict between a parent's goals and ideas about what is best for a child and the child's own dreams. When do parents cross the line between using their experience and judgment about what is in a child's best interests and losing sight of the child as an indiviudal with his own talents and goals? It is also a chance to talk about Neil's decision to commit suicide, and why he felt he had no other alternatives.

Keating makes learning exciting. He orders his boys to tear up an introduction to poetry in their textbook that seeks to explain the value of Shakespeare by resorting to a mathematical graph. Instead, he teaches them to explore the vitality of language. He teaches his students to become thinking human beings, not robots, to challenge assumptions, to ask questions.

Keating teaches that there is nothing wrong in being a doctor or a lawyer. But it is wrong for anyone to commit himself to any career without the music and passion of language in his soul.

At the end, Keating is fired, one boy whom he has inspired lies dead, and another is expelled. Yet Keating has left something of lasting value and that the boys have learned—in the words of Drummond in *Inherit the Wind*, to think about what they think about.

PROFANITY: Mild.

NUDITY/SEXUAL REFERENCES: Mild.

ALCOHOL/DRUG ABUSE: Drinking at a party; Knox gets drunk, boys smoke pipes.

VIOLENCE/SCARINESS: Boy punished by being paddled, Neil commits suicide (off-camera).

TOLERANCE/DIVERSITY ISSUES: Tolerance of individual differences is a theme of the movie. The student body is all white males.

✳ **QUESTIONS FOR KIDS:**
- What is the meaning of *carpe diem* and why does Keating tell the boys it is important?
- Why is Todd Anderson so nervous about coming to Welton? Why does he find it hard to join the Dead Poets Society? Why is he unable to complete the poetry assignment?
- How does Keating turn the boys into "free thinkers"?
- How is Knox eventually able to win over Chris?
- Why are some of the boys willing to accuse Keating of inciting them to misbehavior?

✳ **CONNECTIONS:** Weir is also the director of *Witness* and *The Year of Living Dangerously*.

✳ **ACTIVITIES:** Form a Dead Poets Society and spend an hour every month reading aloud, starting with some of the poetry from this movie. Have each member of the family bring a poem, and hold the meetings at different times and places—midnight in the attic, dawn in the kitchen.

✳The Getting of Wisdom

1980, 100 min, NR, high schoolers
Dir: Bruce Beresford. Susannah Fowle, Hilary Ryan

✳ **PLOT:** Laura Tweedle Rambotham (Susannah Fowle) is an imaginative and talented girl from rural Australia who is sent to an exclusive girls' school in Melbourne in the mid-1800s. The school is very strict, and the girls are cruel and snobbish, making fun of her name, her clothes, her family, of what she does know (she is far ahead of them in some subjects), and of what she doesn't know (French pronunciation). Her desperate ploys to gain the acceptance of the other girls include joining in with them when they insult a new girl from a poor family and making up an elaborate story about a romance with the Reverend Shepherd, a handsome clergyman.

They find out she has lied, and ostracize her. The awkward new girl, who adores her, is her only friend. She steals money to buy Laura a ring and is expelled. This brings Laura to the attention of Evelyn, the school's wealthiest and most respected student. Evelyn takes Laura in, inviting her to become her roommate. Laura is so glad to have a friend at last that she becomes deeply devoted to Evelyn and is hurt and jealous when she shows interest in a young man. Evelyn leaves, telling Laura she is suffocating her. Laura resists Evelyn's efforts to remain friends.

Laura has fallen behind in her studies. But she is able to graduate (after cheating on an exam) and wins a prestigious music scholarship. The girls and the teachers speak to her with fond pride as she leaves.

✳ **DISCUSSION:** Like many teenagers, Laura has trouble picking up on the signals communicated by others, which causes her great distress. She has a particularly hard time trying to adjust to the different world of the school, not so much the rules and the academic requirements as the criteria for social success. Direct and open herself, she does not catch the tone of disapproval or irony in others. Her first roommate, Lilith, pretends to have a hurt finger so she will not have to perform at a party, but Laura does not understand, and volunteers to accompany her, thinking she is helping out. When asked icily, "Perhaps you could play something of your own choosing," she happily sits down to play an elaborate version of "Home Sweet Home." She lies about her family and her clothes and her relationship with the Reverend Shepard in order to fit in, but does it so awkwardly that it backfires.

One interesting scene has Laura fighting with her sister while on vacation from school. She fights with her for several reasons, including displaced anger at the school (for making her think badly of her family), at her family (for not being what the girls consider impressive), and perhaps also at her sister (for not understanding what she is going through, for not having to go through it herself), all worth discussing with kids.

Parents should be aware that Laura's decision to cheat on the exam is portrayed neutrally. There are no adverse consequences (it is never discovered), and can be seen as worthwhile subversion of the school's overly rigid system for evaluating people. Parents should discuss Laura's cheating and lying and possible future consequences of this behavior.

PROFANITY: None.

NUDITY/SEXUAL REFERENCES: Very brief glimpse of nudity when Evelyn walks out of the bathroom; girls have some curiosity about sex. Girls have schoolgirl crushes on the clergyman, and on each other. Laura climbs into bed with Evelyn and they embrace, but there is no suggestion of any sexual involvement.

ALCOHOL/DRUG ABUSE: None.

VIOLENCE/SCARINESS: None.

TOLERANCE/DIVERSITY ISSUES: Class issues; one of the girls makes an anti-Semitic remark about a teacher.

✳ **QUESTIONS FOR KIDS:**
- The title comes from a biblical quote recited in the movie. Who does "get wisdom"? Who does "get understanding"? Is the title supposed to be ironic?
- Why are the girls so mean to each other?
- Why does Laura lie about the Reverend Shepard? Why does she lie about her dress?
- Why is Laura so important to the new girl, and why is Evelyn so important to Laura?
- How does Laura's behavior at home show how she is changing at school?

✳ **CONNECTIONS:** The movie is based on an autobiographical novel by a woman named Henry Handel Richardson. One of the girls recites the "Busy Bee" poem that Lewis Carroll parodies in *Alice in Wonderland;* this is what children of the Victorian era were expected to be able to do when they appeared before grown-ups.

One of the girls is played by Sigrid Thornton, who later appeared in **The Man from Snowy River** and its sequel. Bruce Beresford later directed *Driving Miss Daisy.*

✳ **ACTIVITIES:** Mature teens who like this movie may enjoy *The Road from Coorain,* by Jill Ker Conway, the first volume of the autobiography of a woman who grew up in the Australian outback and became the president of Smith College.

✳The King and I

1956, 133 min, NR, 8 and up
Dir: Walter Lang. Yul Brynner, Deborah Kerr, Rita Moreno

✳ **PLOT:** British Anna Leonowens (Deborah Kerr) and her son, Louis, arrive in Siam in the mid 1800s. She has accepted a position as teacher for the children of the king (Yul Brynner). She is frightened and unsure, far from home in a place that seems very exotic. She tells her son that whenever she feels afraid she "whistles a happy tune" so no one will suspect, and so that she fools herself into thinking she isn't afraid.

She meets the king and is upset to find that contrary to his promise in the letter offering the position, he does not plan to give her a house of her own but wants her to live at the palace. She is ready to leave, but when she meets the children, she is utterly charmed by them and agrees to stay.

Anna becomes friendly with the king's first wife, Lady Thiang (Terry Saunders), mother of the heir to the throne, Prince Chulalongkorn. And she enjoys "getting to know" the children and their mothers, from the king's vast harem. Anna and the king find each other's cultures "a puzzlement," but grow to respect each other. She finds a special friend in Tuptim, who was delivered to the king as a "gift" and longs to be with the man she loves.

The king is devoted to the traditions of his country, but is also passionately interested in bringing the best of the modern Western world to his people. When British diplomats arrive, Anna helps the king show them that Siam need not be colonized. But Tuptim, who organized the entertainment, puts on a production of *Uncle Tom's Cabin* to make the point that the king should not have slaves. The king is furious, even more so when he finds that she has run away with her lover. He starts to whip her. But the traditions and modern concepts of "civilization" battle within him until he is stricken. He dies, Anna by his side, as the prince decrees the changes he will make for the country's future.

✳ **DISCUSSION:** The king is eager to embrace scientific advances, but has a hard time defining himself and his role in a manner consistent with the cultural traditions of his country. Those traditions place a huge burden on him by making him—at least in the eyes of his subjects—infallible. When confronted with too much conflict between his heart and his mind, he cannot bear it, and dies almost literally of a broken heart.

But there is also the more personal issue of pride. As Anna points out, when Tuptim runs away, his pride is hurt, not his heart. This provides a chance to talk about the difference between the kind of pride that means that you feel good about what you have accomplished and who you are and the kind of pride that makes you worry too much about how you appear to others.

In the letter he writes to Anna as he is dying, the king says that he thinks most often of those who insisted that he be his best self.

Talk to kids about the way the music helps to tell the story. See what they can tell about each of the children as they come in to greet their father, and what they learn from the way he greets them.

PROFANITY: None.

NUDITY/SEXUAL REFERENCES: The king has a harem, including slaves like Tuptim. Wives wear hoop skirts for the dinner with the British, but when they bow, Anna sees (off-camera) that they are not wearing underwear.

ALCOHOL/DRUG ABUSE: None.

VIOLENCE/SCARINESS: Tuptim is brought back to be beaten; the king's illness and death.

TOLERANCE/DIVERSITY ISSUES: A theme of the movie.

* **QUESTIONS FOR KIDS:**
  * Why does "whistling a happy tune" make Anna feel less afraid? What do you do when you need to feel less afraid?
  * In what ways does the king want to keep his traditions? In what ways does he want to change? What kinds of changes are the hardest?
  * Why does the king think that Lincoln is doing the right thing in freeing the slaves, while being unable to connect Lincoln's actions to the situation in his own country?
  * What can you tell about the king and Anna by the way she keeps her head no lower than his?
  * How is Chulalongkorn different from his father?

* **CONNECTIONS:** A nonmusical film of the story, *Anna and the King of Siam,* is also very good. Anna is played by Irene Dunne, and the king is played by Rex Harrison, a long way from his roles as Henry Higgins in **My Fair Lady** and as **Dr. Doolittle.** Children are not likely to enjoy Harriet Beecher Stowe's *Uncle Tom's Cabin,* but they may like to know more about Stowe's life, and about the story of her book and the role it played in educating Americans about the tragedy of slavery. Discuss the way that Tuptim adapted this very American story to Siamese traditions of storytelling.

  Yul Brynner won an Oscar for his performance as the king, the role for which he is best remembered. You can also see him in **The Magnificent Seven.** Deborah Kerr appeared in many outstanding films, playing a governess in **The Chalk Garden** and *The Innocents,* and appearing as the wife of a teacher in **Tea and Sympathy.** Rita Moreno, who plays Tuptim, appeared as Anita in **West Side Story.**

* **ACTIVITIES:** Look up Siam (now Thailand) on a map and read about it, and about the reigns of Mongkut and Chulalongkorn in an encyclopedia. You may be able to find instructions for making Thai shadow-puppets, a terrific craft for kids.

*My Bodyguard

1980, 97 min, PG, 10 and up
Dir: Tony Bill. Ruth Gordon, Martin Mull, Chris Makepeace, Adam Baldwin, Joan Cusack

* **PLOT:** Fifteen-year-old Cliff (Chris Makepeace) lives in Chicago's elegant Ambassador East Hotel with his kind but harried father, the hotel manager (Martin Mull), and his loving but dotty grandmother (Ruth Gordon). On Cliff's first day in a new high school, he offends the school bully, Moody (Matt Dillon). When Cliff refuses to pay protection money, Moody and his friends harass him relentlessly.

  Cliff has another classmate—huge, silent, and mysterious Ricky Linderman (Adam Baldwin); there are rumors that Ricky killed a kid and raped a teacher. Cliff asks Ricky to be his bodyguard. At first he refuses. Ricky is clearly someone who does not want to have any kind of relationship with anyone. But when he finds Cliff stuck in a locker, he agrees, and there is a supremely satisfying scene where Cliff springs his new bodyguard on Moody, to the cheers of his new friends.

Cliff, exulting, wants to make friends with Ricky, but Ricky refuses. Cliff asks a sympathetic teacher for advice, and learns that Ricky's brother accidentally killed himself with a gun, and that Ricky was the one who found him. Cliff follows Ricky, and gradually earns his trust. Together they find the missing piece of the motorbike Ricky is rebuilding. But Moody returns, with his own bodyguard, and Cliff and Ricky must both find a way to fight back.

✳ **DISCUSSION:** Just as life becomes the most confusing, as everyone around us seems to be at a different stage of development, and we seem to be at several different stages ourselves, we are confronted with problems our parents can't solve for us. This movie beautifully catches that moment. Without telling Cliff, his well-meaning father calls the school principal after Moody chases him on the first day of school. But Cliff already knows that this is not the answer, and sure enough, the next day, the principal calls them both in, tells Moody not to make jokes like that again, and tells Cliff not to be so quick to "cry wolf." Cliff is nervous about talking to Ricky, but he knows that he would rather pay to hire someone than pay extortion, so he approaches him. Cliff correctly sees that the problem is not the risk of physical injury as much as the risk of losing his self-respect. At the end of the movie, when Ricky has vanquished Moody's "bodyguard," Ricky insists that Cliff fight Moody himself; he understands the real problem, too.

Also well-handled is the way that Cliff gains Ricky's confidence, and the way that this allows Ricky to tell the truth about the accident that killed his brother, which in turn allows him to begin to heal at last. When Ricky pulls away from Cliff's grandmother's efforts to read his future in his palm to hide the scars on his wrist, she says to him quietly, "Open up, Ricky. You're among friends." The subplot at the hotel, about an ambitious employee who plots to get the manager's job, does not work as well as the rest of the movie, but it does provide a nice counterpoint; the employee is a menace in Cliff's father's life as Moody is in Cliff's.

PROFANITY: Mild.

NUDITY/SEXUAL REFERENCES: Cliff and his father use a telescope to gaze at women in lingerie. Cliff's grandmother flirts (sometimes outrageously) with just about everyone and is referred to as always "picking up men." Cliff's father has a conversation with some mild innuendo with a woman guest leaving the hotel.

ALCOHOL/DRUG ABUSE: Ricky smokes (but not after he makes friends with Cliff). The grandmother has a drinking problem and gets tipsy.

VIOLENCE/SCARINESS: The bullies engage in menacing behavior, but there is little violence until the fistfights at the end.

TOLERANCE/DIVERSITY ISSUES: All of the main characters are white. Gender roles are fairly standard—female teacher, male principal, etc.

☀ QUESTIONS FOR KIDS:
- How does Cliff know that he does not have to be scared of Ricky?
- Why are there untrue rumors about Ricky?
- What makes people act like bullies?
- Do some of the kids admire Moody for his behavior? How can you tell?

☀ **CONNECTIONS:** Veteran actress Ruth Gordon, an Oscar-winner for *Rosemary's Baby,* was also an accomplished screenwriter and playwright and, with her husband, Garson Kanin, wrote Tracy and Hepburn classics **Adam's Rib** and **Pat and Mike.** Fans of television's *Fernwood 2-Night* and *Roseanne* will recognize Martin Mull. Joan Cusack plays Cliff's friend Shelley.

☀The Prime of Miss Jean Brodie
1969, 116 min, PG, high schoolers
Dir: Ronald Neame. Maggie Smith, Pamela Franklin

☀ **PLOT:** Miss Jean Brodie (Maggie Smith) is a strong-willed and unconventional teacher at the Marcia Blaine School for Girls in Scotland in 1932. She tells her students, "I am in the business of putting old heads on young shoulders, and all of my students are the crème de la crème. Give me a girl of an impressionable age, and she is mine for life." She tells them, too, that she is giving them her "prime," that they are her life's work.

She teaches a small group of "impressionable" students whom she has selected to be her special followers, who must do big and important things. The girls, dazzled by her vibrance and independent spirit, are in thrall to her. Miss Brodie encourages foolish Mary McGregor to run away to fight on the side of the fascists in the Spanish Civil War, and she is killed when her train is blown up by rebel troops. Miss Brodie has determined that Jenny will be the romantic beauty and plans to make this happen by having her be seduced by Miss Brodie's own former lover, art teacher Teddy Lloyd. Sandy (Pamela Franklin), the brightest of the girls, decides to "put a stop to" her. Sandy deliberately has an affair with Teddy Lloyd both to spite Miss Brodie's plans and to compete with her, and she is hurt badly when she sees, in Teddy's portrait of her, that it is still Jean Brodie whom he cares for. Sandy "puts a stop" to her at last by giving the headmistress the ammunition she needs to fire Miss Brodie.

☀ **DISCUSSION:** Maggie Smith won an Oscar for her performance as Jean Brodie, brilliantly showing the fascinating as well as the foolish aspects of the character. As children begin to look beyond their parents for inspiration and validation, it is worthwhile for them to think about how easily they can be manipulated or simply misdirected. Some of Miss Brodie's students loved her because she was the only one who thought they were special. Mary McGregor died trying to live up to that image. Sandy knows that Mary was special, but not for the reasons Miss Brodie thought.

Miss Brodie projected herself—and her dreams—onto her students. Even Sandy was a victim. She did not develop or pursue her own dreams (any more than Teddy pursued her instead of Jean Brodie); everything she did was more about Miss Brodie than it was about herself.

PROFANITY: None.

NUDITY/SEXUAL REFERENCES: The girls compose a letter as they imagine Miss Brodie would to her beau, including, "allow me, in conclusion, to congratulate you warmly on your sexual intercourse as well as your singing." Miss Brodie hopes that Jenny will have a number of interesting lovers, and all but acts as a procurer to arrange (unsuccessfully) for Teddy to be her first. There is a brief nude scene when Teddy paints Sandy's picture.

ALCOHOL/DRUG ABUSE: None.

VIOLENCE/SCARINESS: None (Mary is killed off-screen).

TOLERANCE/DIVERSITY ISSUES: None.

✳ **QUESTIONS FOR KIDS:**
- In what ways is Miss Brodie good for her students? In what ways is she bad for them?
- What about her makes it possible for her to be such a strong influence on them? What about each of them makes this possible?
- How does Miss Brodie try to have her students live the lives she cannot or will not?
- How does Sandy "put a stop" to her? Why is she the only one who can do it?

✳ **CONNECTIONS:** The novel by Muriel Spark is well worth reading. Maggie Smith also appears in *A Room With a View,* playing a very different character. Fans of public television's *Upstairs, Downstairs* may recognize Gordon Jenkins as Hudson, the butler.

✳ **ACTIVITIES:** Teenagers may want to learn something about the Spanish Civil War to understand why Sandy objected to Miss Brodie's support of the fascists (in a small way, she was something of a fascist herself, which may explain her enthusiasm for them). *To Die in Madrid* is a documentary about the conflict. Another documentary, *The Good Fight,* focuses on the Americans who fought the fascists.

✳ **THE BELLES OF ST. TRINIAN'S**
1954, 90 min, NR, b&w, 8 and up
Dir: Frank Launder. Alistair Sim, Joyce Grenfell

Cartoonist and illustrator Ronald Searle created a fictional girls' boarding school called St. Trinian's, populated by students and faculty that were like a cross between *Dennis the Menace* and *The Addams Family*. This movie, based on his cartoons, has Alistair Sim playing both the redoubtable head-mistress and her disreputable brother. Joyce Grenfell is unforgettable as the policewoman who goes undercover at the school.

❋ **CONNECTIONS:** There are three moderately enjoyable sequels: *Blue Murder at St. Trinian's, Pure Hell of St. Trinian's,* and *The Great St. Trinian's Train Robbery.*

❋ THE BLACKBOARD JUNGLE
1955, 101 min, NR, b&w, 12 and up
Dir: Richard Brooks. Glenn Ford, Vic Morrow, Sidney Poitier
This movie shocked audiences when it came out, but audiences were more shockable back then. Just to put things in perspective, it was consid-ered shocking that the musical score included rock and roll (*Rock Around the Clock*), the first Hollywood release to do so. Glenn Ford plays the teacher who is confronted with a group of tough juvenile delinquents, including Vic Morrow and Sidney Poitier. The movie ends a little more positively than the book, but does not pretend to suggest that a teacher can reach more than a few of these kids.

❋ BRIGHT ROAD
1953, 69 min, NR, b&w, 10 and up
Dir: Gerald Mayer. Dorothy Dandridge
This very rare story of a black teacher in a pre–*Brown* decision segregated school gets sugary at times, but is still very worthwhile as a time capsule and for a chance to see the exquisite Dorothy Dandridge (whose career was destroyed by racism). She plays an elementary school teacher who tries to solve her students' problems and find a way to provide them with some dignity and sense of opportunity.

❋ THE BROWNING VERSION
1951, 90 min, NR, b&w, mature high schoolers
Dir: Anthony Asquith. Michael Redgrave
As a British prep school classics professor (Michael Redgrave) is forced to retire due to ill health, he is overcome by his failure to achieve any connection—to his bitter, unfaithful wife or to his bored students. He is able to gather the courage to acknowledge his failure and establish some sense of dignity and accountability following two unexpected expressions of support—from a student he has been tutoring and from his wife's lover. Redgrave is heartbreaking.

❋ **CONNECTIONS:** The 1994 remake (rated R for language and sexual references) is uneven, but Albert Finney is superb.

✳ CONRACK

1974, 107 min, PG, 12 and up
Dir: Martin Ritt. Jon Voight, Paul Winfield, Hume Cronyn

Before he wrote the books that became *The Prince of Tides* and *The Great Santini*, Pat Conroy spent a year teaching the children on an island off the coast of South Carolina. This movie is based on his memoir of that year (*Conrack* is what the kids called him). Jon Voight plays Conrack, who is horrified at the indifference and racism of the local school authorities and who, with more energy than strategy, does his best to help the children learn. Paul Winfield is terrific as a recluse who becomes his friend, and Hume Cronyn is smoothly wicked as a bigoted school administrator.

✳ GOODBYE, MR. CHIPS

1939, 118 min, NR, b&w, 10 and up
Dir: Sam Wood. Robert Donat, Greer Garson

The story of a shy schoolmaster, based on the sentimental novella by James Hilton (**Lost Horizon**) stars Oscar-winner Robert Donat. At first, he is so worried about losing control of the students that he is overly strict and humorless. But when he falls in love with the warm and understanding Katherine (Greer Garson, in her film debut), she encourages him to allow his compassion and affection for the boys to show. After her death in childbirth, he devotes his life to the boys, coming back from retirement when the younger teachers leave to fight in World War I, and staying on into his eighties, to provide tea and tutoring to "his boys."

✳ THE HAPPIEST DAYS OF YOUR LIFE

1950, 84 min, NR, b&w, 8 and up
Dir: Frank Launder. Alistair Sim, Margaret Rutherford, Joyce Grenfell

Through a clerical error, a British girls' boarding school is moved in with a boys' school, and before it can be sorted out, the school is simultaneously visited by three sets of girls' parents and the trustees who are evaluating the headmaster of the boys' school for a prestigious new position. The humor may be a bit understated for some kids, but others will love the contrast between the all-out farce of the plot with the dry humor of the performers. The three greatest British comic character actors of all time appear together, with Alistair Sim as the doleful but valiant headmaster of Nutbourne, Margaret Rutherford as the resolutely efficient and doughty headmistress of St. Swithin's, and Joyce Grenfell as the horsily enthusiastic games mistress, Miss Gossage ("Call me Sausage!").

✳ THE LAWRENCEVILLE STORIES

1988, 3 hour-long episodes, NR, 8 and up
Dir: Allan A. Goldstein. Zach Galligan, Nicholas Rowe, Stephen Baldwin, Dave Foley

Owen Johnson's classic stories of life at a turn-of-the-century boys' school have been turned into a completely delightful three-part miniseries produced for the Disney Channel and now available on video. Zach Galligan and Nicholas Rowe are superb as the two boys competing for status according to rules that are arcane and inexplicable but somehow completely understood and accepted by every boy and teacher, with the possible exception of one boy from a wealthy family dubbed, in the school's tradition of evocative nicknames, "The Uncooked Beefsteak." Highlights include "Hungry" Smeed's great pancake record, and the headmaster's sublime plan for letting the punishment fit the crime after an especially outrageous prank. The production values are gorgeous, with sumptuous period detail.

✳ **CONNECTIONS:** Future stars Stephen Baldwin (*The Usual Suspects*) and Dave Foley (television's *Kids in the Hall* and *NewsRadio*) appear as two of the students, known as "Gutter Pup" and "Old Ironsides." The headmaster is played by Edward Hermann (*Ri¢hie Ri¢h*).

✳ **ACTIVITIES:** The books were also filmed as *The Happy Years*, with Dean Stockwell, and are still delightful to read (or read aloud). Author Johnson insisted that all of the details were based on actual experience, even the nicknames.

✳ STAND AND DELIVER

1987, 105 min, PG, 12 and up
Dir: Ramon Menendez. Edward James Olmos, Andy Garcia

Edward James Olmos was nominated for an Oscar for his performance as Jaime Escalante, a real-life businessman who got a group of east Los Angeles barrio students so excited about calculus that every one of them passed a brutally difficult college-level exam. He does such a good job of showing the students that any dream is possible for them if they work hard and respect themselves that everyone who watches will begin to wonder whether there isn't something they should be studying instead of watching a movie. NOTE: Harsh language.

✳ **CONNECTIONS:** There is an entire genre of movies about idealistic teachers reaching out to cynical students despite being mired down in bureaucracy: *The Principal, Teachers, Lean on Me, Dangerous Minds,* among others. The genre is spoofed in the intermittently funny *High School High*.

❋ TEA AND SYMPATHY

1956, 122 min, NR, high schoolers
Dir: Vincente Minnelli. Deborah Kerr, John Kerr

It is dated now, but this story of a boy unsure of his masculinity who is given "tea and sympathy" by the understanding wife of his housemaster still provides a good opportunity for a discussion of growing up. John Kerr plays a sensitive teenager who becomes something of a Rorschach test for the fears others project onto him. He is not gay (and the movie completely shies away from what would happen if he were), but he is different in a way that makes the other boys—and the hearty housemaster—uncomfortable. He tries to prove his manhood by visiting a prostitute, but when he is unable to go through with it, it only makes him feel more humiliated and inadequate. Deborah Kerr (no relation) plays the housemaster's wife, who gives him a loving introduction to adult sexuality, asking only that "in the future, when you talk about this—and you will—be kind."

She also understands that her husband's revulsion masks his fears about himself. Like the boys he leads, he has retreated within limited notions of masculinity to give himself a safe place to operate from, a place that no one can question. Most teenagers go through this stage while they are learning about what it means to be a man or a woman. The movie can give parents a chance to talk to teens about the temptation to prove one's adulthood or sexuality (or, for girls in particular, to show sympathy) by having sex.

❋ **CONNECTIONS:** John Kerr appears as Lieutenant Cable in *South Pacific,* and Deborah Kerr stars in *The King and I, King Solomon's Mines,* and *The Chalk Garden.*

❋ THE TROUBLE WITH ANGELS

1964, 112 min, NR, 8 and up
Dir: Ida Lupino. Hayley Mills, Rosalind Russell

Based on *My Life with Mother Superior,* the memoirs of advertising executive Jane Trahey, this is the story of two rebellious girls at a Catholic boarding school. Hayley Mills is the one who always has some "scathingly brilliant idea" that gets both of them into trouble. Rosalind Russell is the wise Mother Superior who hasn't forgotten what it was like to be a teenager. The touching conclusion will leave you wanting to know more about what happened to the characters, but don't try to find it in the silly sequel, *Where Angels Go, Trouble Follows.*

❋ UP THE DOWN STAIRCASE

1967, 124 min, NR, mature high schoolers
Dir: Robert Mulligan. Sandy Dennis, Jean Stapleton

This Alice In Wonderland-like saga is based on the best-seller by Bel Kaufman. Sandy Dennis plays the idealistic teacher assigned to an inner-city school. She dreams of conducting classes on Chaucer but finds herself mired in a swamp of absurd administrative minutiae and overwhelmed by the needs of her students. The director of *To Kill a Mockingbird,* the playwright of *All the Way Home,* and a group of untrained teenage actors give the movie an authentic feeling, and Dennis conveys the sensitivity and humor that enable her to touch the students and, far more difficult, allow them to touch her. NOTE: This movie has frank language and discussions of unwed pregnancy and suicide.

✳ **CONNECTIONS:** See also *To Sir, With Love,* released the same year. Kaufman was the granddaughter of Sholem Aleichem, author of the stories that were the basis for *Fiddler on the Roof.*

SEE ALSO:

The Chocolate War A struggle for power between an ambitious teacher and a manipulative student focuses on the school's annual chocolate sale.

Educating Rita A tired, bored university professor is inspired by the enthusiasm for learning and the lively mind of his student.

Lucas A bright and sensitive kid with a crush on an older girl tries desperately to be the person he thinks she is looking for.

School Ties A poor Jewish student enters a stuffy WASP-y prep school on an athletic scholarship and encounters prejudice and dishonesty, but also loyalty and friendship.

To Sir, With Love A teacher assigned to a rowdy and rebellious group of students teaches them about respect for each other and themselves, and learns a great deal in the process about himself.

RECENT RELEASES—PARENTAL CONCERNS

Several movies about high school kids pose some real problems for parents. While they are interesting, engaging films with good performances and an appealing authenticity, and they raise issues well worth exploring with teenagers, they also include behavior that is presented without any kind of consequences, which will give parents some real problems. I strongly encourage parents who are considering these movies to watch them without the kids first, and then, if they decide the movies are appropriate, to watch them with the kids—not to provide the kind of running commentary that will have kids running from the room, but to watch their reactions and to make yourself available for discussion.

✳ THE BREAKFAST CLUB

1985, 97 min, R, high schoolers
Dir: John Hughes. Molly Ringwald, Anthony Michael Hall, Judd Nelson, Emilio Estevez, Ally Sheedy

Five very different kids are stuck in an all-day detention (called "the breakfast club"). They start the day ranging from indifference to hostility, but end up turning the day into something like group therapy. Adults will find no surprises, but teens will find it moving and true to their own experience. NOTE: The R rating is for strong language. Some parents will wince at the "makeover moment" in which a sullen girl is transformed with a little makeup.

✳ CLUELESS

1995, 97 min, PG-13, mature high schoolers
Dir: Amy Heckerling. Alicia Silverstone, Paul Rudd

A smash success, this very funny satire loosely based on Jane Austen's *Emma* is hugely popular with kids. Alicia Silverstone plays a pampered teen who tries to run other people's lives, only to discover that she first needs to work on her own. NOTE: Silverstone's sensational performance, the exceptionally funny script, and the core values all make it worth watching, but parents should be warned that substance abuse and sex are both treated casually to the point of nihilism. Parents, particularly of kids under fifteen, should watch it before making a decision whether to permit their kids to see it.

✳ FAME

1980, 134 min, R, mature high schoolers
Dir: Alan Parker. Irene Cara, Anne Meara, Barry Miller

Students at New York City's High School for Performing Arts go through adolescent drama and melodrama, but they do it while they are singing and dancing to an Oscar-winning score. Teens will relate to the anxiety and identity crises of the attractive and talented leads as they reconcile their dreams of fame with the reality of hard work, rejection, and growing up. NOTE: The R rating is for rough language, an out-of-wedlock pregnancy, brief nudity as a girl takes off her shirt for a man who promised to help her in show business, and a gay character.

✳ PRETTY IN PINK

1986, 96 min, PG-13, mature high schoolers
Dir: Howard Deutch. Molly Ringwald, Andrew McCarthy, James Spader, Annie Potts, Harry Dean Stanton

This time, Molly Ringwald plays Andie, a creative and self-sufficient girl from the wrong side of the tracks who falls for Blane, a rich kid played by

Andrew McCarthy, in this John Hughes production that has some sensitive moments and authentic insights. McCarthy's character is very attracted to Andie but breaks a date with her due to pressure from his bored and snobbish best friend (James Spader), who is bitter over being rejected by Andie. Andie also has a best friend, the quirky but funny and loyal Ducky (Jon Cryer), who is trying to figure out a way to let her know he loves her. (In the original script, they ended up together, but test audiences wanted Andie to end up with Blane so it was changed.)

✳ SIXTEEN CANDLES
1984, 93 min, PG (but probably a PG-13 by today's standards), high schoolers
Dir: John Hughes. Molly Ringwald, Anthony Michael Hall

Molly Ringwald is sensational as Samantha, whose sixteenth birthday is forgotten by her family in the flurry of preparations over her sister's wedding. Worse than that, the gorgeous senior she adores (Michael Schoeffling) never notices her, and a geeky freshman (Anthony Michael Hall) asks for her underpants.

This movie includes some exceptionally insightful material about being a teenager, but my recommendation has some serious reservations. Among my concerns: insensitivity to the point of racism in the portrayal of an Asian character (his name, Long Duk Dong, gives some idea of the level of humor), insensitive portrayals of the grandparents and the sister's fiancé, and extremely irresponsible treatment of alcohol, drugs, and sex (for example, the Geek not only sells peeks at Samantha's underpants to his friends, but also has sex with the senior's dreamboat girlfriend when they are both so blitzed they don't know what they are doing—and her only reaction afterward is that it was sweet).

✳ SOME KIND OF WONDERFUL
1987, 93 min, PG-13, mature high schoolers
Dir: Howard Deutch. Mary Stuart Masterson, Eric Stoltz, Lea Thompson

Kind of a gender-reverse of *Pretty in Pink,* this one has Mary Stuart Masterson as Watts, the tomboy who knows she is better for her friend Keith Nelson (Eric Stoltz) than Amanda Jones (Lea Thompson), the glamour girl he dreams of. There is some nice interaction between Keith and his father (John Ashton), who doesn't want anything to get in the way of his son's college education, and between close and supportive friends Keith and Watts.

IT'S TOUGH TO BE A TEENAGER

"The day the child realizes that all adults are imperfect, he becomes an adolescent; the day he forgives them, he becomes an adult; the day he forgives himself, he becomes wise."
—ALDEN NOWLAN

Poor teens. Their hormones go into overdrive, and their bodies start to change so fast that they feel like strangers to themselves. They realize their parents really do not have all the answers, and even if they do, it will destroy the teen's fragile but terribly important sense of independence to ask their parents for help. In a way, the teen years are a replay of the terrible twos. Toddlers show breathtaking courage and resilience in learning to stand, pulling themselves up, crashing down, then, astonishingly, starting over again and again, and putting everything they have into it in a way no adult could ever think of trying. Teens do the same on an emotional level, experiencing mood swings, rejection, and humiliation far past what any adult could tolerate, and yet they still pick themselves up and go on. Just as an infant can withstand a body temperature that would kill an adult, teenagers experience a range of feelings on a daily basis that might be considered evidence of psychosis in an adult.

Their poor parents. Just as our precious darlings confront the really scary issues, the ones with possibly permanent consequences, they don't want to listen anymore. At least not to us. They want to get their answers from their friends, of course, but for those really sensitive issues that are too painful to talk about, they read magazines and books, they listen to music, and they watch movies. And sometimes, if parents and teens watch together, they can find a way to talk about the issues faced by the characters that is a lot easier than talking about them in more personal terms.

Many parents find themselves withdrawing from their kids at this stage because it is so difficult to deal with them, rationalizing that that is what the teens want. Teens do not want less attention, they just want different attention. They want your time and interest, but they want a lot less of your telling them what to do. They need your support more than they need your advice.

The important thing is for parents not to take teenage angst personally, and not to give up. Remember that they do need your support. They barely know themselves anymore, and they need you to reflect back to them what you see as strong and positive. Somewhere inside that moody, self-centered person who won't get out of the shower is your precious baby (the one who always said he/she loved you the most in the world forever and ever). Even more amazing, somewhere in there is the fine, responsible, and loving adult who will be your greatest joy.

The discoveries, the changes, and the miseries of the teen years make such a powerful impression that there are many fine films with sensitive portrayals of this part of life. They can help convey to kids that the uncertainty and pain they experience is not just normal; it is universal, and it is all for a purpose. And they can help remind parents how real the pain of these years can be, in fact, must be, to enable them to achieve maturity.

One of the most important struggles for teens is the attempt to define what it means to be a man or a woman. Movies, of course, establish the icons of manhood and womanhood; if you ask anyone to define those terms, it is almost inevitable that within thirty seconds there will be a reference to John Wayne or Marilyn Monroe. These two icons come to mind because they represent extremes, of course, and that is why it is important for families to discuss their own views on this very complex issue. John Wayne often played men who kept all of their emotions inside. His characters demonstrated manhood through physical courage and power. Marilyn Monroe often played women who were softhearted and not very bright. Her power was achieved through her beauty, vulnerability, and sexuality. It is worthwhile making sure that teens and preteens see some of the exceptions: movie heroes and heroines who show some emotional vulnerability along with physical and intellectual power.

Even watching movies about teenagers can feel overwhelming to an adult, as we see teens struggle with the excruciating mortifications of that stage of life. But for kids it can seem validating, whether the characters are struggling with problems like a jealous boyfriend, a crush, leaving for college, a school bully, death of a sibling, suicide of a friend, racism, establishing independence, or handling sexual feelings and values. Many movies about teens deal with the passionate need for acceptance. Occasionally we see a teenager who confronts worldwide problems like the threat of nuclear war. Other important themes and conflicts faced by teenagers are explored in the movies discussed in the School and Women Worth Watching chapters.

One theme present in nearly every movie about teens is parents who do not understand or support them. *Rebel Without a Cause* is one classic example, and *Romeo and Juliet* is an even more classic example. This feeling of being misunderstood reflects one of the most conflicted but important aspects of the developmental stage of adolescence. As much as teens long to be understood, the importance of separating from their parents makes them prefer, on another level, to be if not misunderstood, then at least un-understood a little, to give them the breathing room they need to decide who they are and what they want. These movies can help families recognize and understand this process, and maybe talk about it.

*Alice Adams

1935, 99 min, NR, b&w, 12 and up
Dir: George Stevens. Katharine Hepburn, Fred MacMurray

✳ PLOT: Alice Adams (Katharine Hepburn) is desperate to be upper class, or at least to have everyone think that she is. She tells the florist that she can't have orchids for a corsage because she had one at the last party, when the truth is that she cannot afford one. Enormously excited about attending an elegant party, she picks violets to make a corsage for herself, and adds new flounces to her old dress. Her brother is a reluctant escort and deserts her to play craps with the servants. She meets Arthur Russell (Fred MacMurray), a handsome and genuinely nice young man. They dance together and they begin to spend a lot of time together.

Alice's mother continuously berates her father for being a failure. She persuades him to leave Mr. Lamb, the employer who has been very kind to him (keeping him on salary during a long illness), to start a factory to manufacture the glue formula he developed. Alice invites Arthur to dinner and persuades her family to do everything they can to make it the kind of dinner party that they believe wealthy people have. But it is a very hot night, and the hot, heavy, rich food is a mistake. Everyone is uncomfortable. Alice, always overanxious and pretentious, becomes tense and brittle and tells Arthur she knows he won't see her again.

Alice's brother, who still works for Mr. Lamb, confesses that he stole some money and is about to be discovered. Mr. Lamb comes to the house feeling angry and betrayed and tells Mr. Adams and Walter he will destroy them. Alice takes the responsibility for them both and persuades Mr. Lamb not to blame them. She goes outside, and Arthur is waiting, to tell her that he loves her.

✳ DISCUSSION: Teenagers will identify with Alice's excruciating adventures as she tries to create an image of herself as confident and popular. She works so hard to find a way to impress and imitate the socially promi-nent people in the community that she never takes the time to think about whether they deserve the effort. When the girls at the party insult her dress, she assumes that they are right, and will not allow herself to see that they are rude and snobbish. She admits to Arthur, "I should never dare to be myself when I am with you," and yet even then she is not being honest, because she goes on to say, "and yet here I am, being myself." She is not even honest with herself about what she needs for happiness. Finally, she tells her mother, "Things feel pretty beautiful to me, in spite of everything I've done to spoil them." She admires Arthur's honesty and wishes she could be equally honest. Nevertheless, she goes ahead with the dinner party, trying frantically to keep up the illusion, almost as agonizing for us to watch as it is for Alice to live through.

In the book (and the original silent movie version), Alice and Arthur do not end up together. Katharine Hepburn does such a good job of showing us Alice's vulnerability and genuine sweetness, her pretentiousness caused by insecurity, that it is almost possible to believe that Arthur sees her that way, too.

PROFANITY: None.

NUDITY/SEXUAL REFERENCES: None.

ALCOHOL/DRUG ABUSE: None.

VIOLENCE/SCARINESS: None.

TOLERANCE/DIVERSITY ISSUES: Though not intentionally racist, the movie reflects the era in which it was made in its depiction of the view of the white characters toward the black characters. Alice is afraid her brother's friendliness with black musicians shows that he is low-class; she tries to cover by saying that he enjoys amusing "darkie stories." Alice's mother promises to get a "colored woman" to wait on them when Arthur comes to dinner. The woman, played by Hattie McDaniel, is unimpressed with their pretensions and correctly warns them that it is too hot for soup.

✳ **QUESTIONS FOR KIDS:**
- Listen to the way that Alice describes Mildred to Arthur. She appears to be saying nice things about Mildred; why don't they sound complimentary?
- Why does Alice try so hard to be something she isn't? Is she honest with anyone?
- Where do you think she got her ideas about what is important?

✳ **CONNECTIONS:** The book, by Booth Tarkington (author of *Penrod* and *Seventeen*), won a Pulitzer Prize. MacMurray starred in a variety of roles in films and television, including the inventor of Flubber in **The Absent Minded Professor,** the amoral executive in **The Apartment,** and the father in television's *My Three Sons.*

✳ American Graffiti

1973, 110 min, PG, 12 and up
Dir: George Lucas. Richard Dreyfus, Ron Howard, Paul Le Mat, Charles Martin Smith

✳ **PLOT:** The movie takes place on a single night in 1962, immediately before two good friends, Curt (Richard Dreyfus) and Steve (Ron Howard), are about to leave for college. Curt and Steve are facing enormous changes and they are both scared and excited. Although the film is nostalgic in tone (based on the memories of director George Lucas), it is clear that the country is on the brink of enormous (and tumultuous) changes, too.

Most of the episodic plot centers on kids driving around and interacting with each other. Curt and Steve stop by the high school dance. Curt's sister, Laurie, is Steve's girlfriend, and is very concerned about losing him when he goes away.

Steve tells his friend Terry "the Toad" (Charles Martin Smith) that he can use Steve's car when he goes to college, and Terry spends the night driving around, feeling powerful and exciting. He meets Debbie (Candy Clark), a pretty, if slightly dim, girl, and is thrilled when she agrees to ride with him. But the car gets stolen, and he has a frantic time getting it back.

The boys have another friend, John Milner (Paul Le Mat), who is a hot-rod champion. When he tries to get some pretty girls to ride with him, they send a bratty thirteen-year-old (Mackenzie Phillips) to get in his car instead. John gets challenged by a tough guy named Bob (Harrison Ford). Laurie, angry with Steve, agrees to ride with Bob in the race.

Curt spends the night in search of a mysterious blonde (Suzanne Somers), who whispered "I love you" to him from her car. He finally goes to see Wolfman Jack, the DJ all the kids listen to, to ask for help.

John wins the race, but Bob's car crashes. Steve realizes he cannot leave Laurie, and promises to stay and attend the community college. Curt finally leaves, his radio on his lap as the plane takes off. He listens until the sound disappears in static.

✳ **DISCUSSION:** This brilliant and highly influential film (almost everyone connected with it became a star) provides a good opportunity for talking about some of the feelings teenagers have as they move into adulthood. Curt is deeply conflicted between his big dreams and his fear of leaving home. But it is Steve who finds that he is not ready to leave. Although he tries to break his ties to home by telling Laurie that he plans to date other people and giving his car to Terry, when Laurie is almost killed in the drag race he sees how much he cares for her. Thoughtful older kids may like to speculate about the symbolism of the mysterious blonde in the white Thunderbird, and the guidance from Wolfman Jack.

PROFANITY: Some.

NUDITY/SEXUAL REFERENCES: Some.

ALCOHOL/DRUG ABUSE: Some alcohol (Terry gets an adult to buy liquor for him to drink with Debbie).

VIOLENCE/SCARINESS: Hot-rod race; car thieves.

TOLERANCE/DIVERSITY ISSUES: Carol says she is not allowed to listen to Wolfman Jack because he is black (he isn't).

✳ **QUESTIONS FOR KIDS:**
• Why is Curt so ambivalent about leaving?

- What does Curt's ex-girlfriend's teasing tell you about him?
- Why is Laurie afraid to let Steve go?
- Why does Laurie ride with Bob? Who is she hurting?
- Why does the movie end by telling you what happens to those characters in the future?

✳ **CONNECTIONS:** Don't waste time on the sequel, *More American Graffiti*, with a different director, which is not nearly as good. This movie is a good place to find many future stars in small roles, including Harrison Ford, who went on to star in the director's next movie, **Star Wars**.

✳ **ACTIVITIES:** The sound track includes some of the greatest hits of the era. Listen to some other music by some of the artists, and see if teens can trace the influence of those artists on some of their favorite performers.

✳Breaking Away
1979, 100 min, PG, 12 and up
Dir: Peter Yates. Dennis Quaid, Dennis Christopher, Daniel Stern, Paul Dooley

✳ **PLOT:** Four friends just out of high school are enjoying the summer and thinking about their future. They live in Bloomington, Indiana, home of Indiana University, and consider themselves "cutters," the name the college students gave to the town kids a generation before, when most of the local men worked for the local quarry. Dave (Dennis Christopher) has tested well enough to go to college, but spends all his time racing his bicycle and trying to emulate his heroes, the Italian bicycle racing team, about to arrive in Bloomington on tour. Mike (Dennis Quaid) believes that his year as quarterback of the high school football team will be the highlight of his life, and is bitter and resentful of the college students. Cyril (Daniel Stern), lanky and sardonic, says that his father is always grateful when Cyril fails, so that he can show how understanding he is. Moocher (Jackie Earl Haley) is the only one with adult responsibilities and a steady girlfriend.

Dave's mother is sympathetic about his obsessions with Italy and bicycles, but his father is embarrassed and impatient. Dave tells a pretty coed named Katherine (Robyn Douglass) that he is an Italian exchange student, and she is charmed by him. When the university for the first time invites local teams to participate in their annual "Little 500" bicycle race, Dave's friends want to enter. Although it is supposed to be a relay race, they figure that Dave can ride the entire fifty miles and still beat the college teams. At first Dave refuses because he does not want Katherine to find out the truth about him. But when he is disillusioned by a race with his Italian idols and by his father's used-car lot sales policies, he tells Katherine the truth and agrees to race.

Dave is hurt in the race, all four of the friends end up participating, and Dave is able to lead them to finish in first place. He has developed enough of a sense of who he is to move on, and he starts college, where he meets a pretty exchange student—from France.

✳ **DISCUSSION:** This is a movie about friendship, about establishing identity, and about growing up. The friends stick together and support each other as they struggle in different ways with adulthood. Just out of high school, they feel that their youth is ending, while each fall a new generation of students begins at the university. Mike says, "These college kids out here, they're never going to get old. There'll always be new ones coming along." And each spring, they see a new generation leave to go on to better things while they stay behind. "At sixteen, they call it sweet sixteen. At eighteen, you get to drink, to vote, to see dirty movies. What the hell do you get to do when you are nineteen?" He hates to feel that "maybe they are better than us."

Dave, on the other hand, is thrilled by the thought that his heroes are "better than us." His heart is broken when the Italians cheat in a race, pushing him off the track. When he then finds that his father won't return a dissatisfied customer's money, he cries, "Everybody cheats. I just didn't know." Yet, somehow finding this out helps him to tell Katherine the truth, and to accept himself the way he is. And that is what enables him to take the risk of moving on, going to college, and becoming more than a "cutter."

PROFANITY: Some.
NUDITY/SEXUAL REFERENCES: Mild. Dave's mother becomes pregnant.
ALCOHOL/DRUG ABUSE: Some alcohol use and smoking.
VIOLENCE/SCARINESS: Cyril is beat up by Katherine's boyfriend. Moment of scariness when one of the boys tricks the others by pretending to be trapped under water.
TOLERANCE/DIVERSITY ISSUES: Class issues.

✳ **QUESTIONS FOR KIDS:**
- Why would the kids in a college town feel the way these kids do about the students? Why would the students feel the way they do about the town kids?
- What does Cyril mean when he says that his failure is like a gift for his father? Does that relate to his saying that he "lost all interest in life"?
- Why does Dave's father say, "You're not a cutter. I'm a cutter"? What does that tell Dave?
- What do you think of Dave's father's refusal to return the money to the dissatisfied customer? Do you agree that "everybody cheats"? How did Dave react? Why?
- How does what Dave sees lead him to tell Katherine the truth and take the chance on going to college?
- Why is Dave's mother's passport so important to her?

✳ **CONNECTIONS:** This movie won an Oscar for Best Screenplay. The most poignant town-gown confrontation in the movies is the scene in the fast-food place in Spike Lee's *School Daze*. This is most definitely not for children (and not for some adults), but the movie, which Lee says is based on his own college experience, is an important and insightful look at issues of identity for all races.

✳ **ACTIVITIES:** This may inspire you to go on a family bike ride. It may also inspire you to watch a bicycle race or read up on some of the famous teams that Dave admires. If you can, visit a quarry to learn more about how stone is cut to be used in buildings. If that is not convenient, you can take the kids for a walk to look at the materials used in some of the buildings near your house, and talk about where they come from, and what the advantages and disadvantages are of each kind of material.

Parents might also want to take their children for a walk through a local university campus, and even attend an event there. Talking about how Dave pursues his interest in bicycle racing and Italy may give kids some ideas on how to expand their own interest in a particular subject.

✳Bye Bye Birdie
1961, 112 min, NR 8 and up
Dir: George Sidney. Dick Van Dyke, Janet Leigh, Ann-Margret, Maureen Stapleton, Paul Lynde.

✳ **PLOT:** In this musical satire of 1950s popular culture and suburban life, America's most popular rock singer, Conrad Birdie (Jesse Pearson), like Elvis, has been drafted. Albert Peterson (Dick Van Dyke) is unable to tell his mother that he wants to be a biochemist and not a songwriter. His longtime fiancée, Rosie DeLeon (Janet Leigh), arranges for Birdie to sing Albert's song "One Last Kiss" on *The Ed Sullivan Show* before he leaves for boot camp. He will sing it to a member of his fan club, picked at random. This will give Albert the success he needs in order to please his mother, enabling him to quit songwriting.

The fan picked at random is Kim McAfee (Ann-Margret), a teenager who has just agreed to go steady with Hugo (Bobby Rydell). Everyone ends up at the McAfee home, including Albert's overbearing mother. As Albert obtains the cooperation of Kim's father (Paul Lynde) and others by promising them they will be on *The Ed Sullivan Show*, Hugo becomes more and more jealous, Rosie becomes frustrated and impatient, Kim dyes her hair, and Albert's invention, a pill that makes animals (and people) speed up their activity, comes in very handy when Birdie's number is bumped to make time for a Soviet ballet.

✳ **DISCUSSION:** It is fun for kids to get this glimpse (even though idealized and exaggerated) of how teenagers in the past behaved, how they felt about big issues like rock stars, going steady, and growing up. Like *Grease*, this musical starts with a song that amusingly illustrates the different reactions of the boys and girls to the news of a romance—here, the development that Kim and Hugo are going steady. Kids may be interested in why their reactions were different, and whether the same distinctions are made today.

Kim sings about how lovely it is to be a woman (as she dresses in sloppy old clothes) and airily informs her parents that she is going to start calling them by their first names. The call from Rosie about her selection as the girl to be kissed good-bye by Conrad Birdie has her calling for "Mommy" again. Albert has a huge problem in declaring independence from his mother. Children will react differently to this, based on their own development; younger children may be reassured that he still behaves with the obedience of a child, but teenagers will think that he should have established his own identity long before. Fortunately, this is a musical comedy, and when that moment comes, Albert's mother is as ready for it as he is.

In the song "Kids" Kim's father and Albert's mother sing about "what's the matter with kids today." It is possible to draw some parallels to the way parents think about kids now, and the conflicts you had with your own parents, and the conflicts they had with theirs.

It may be worth discussing what Kim and Rosie do when they are upset with the men in their lives. Both react by going off with other men (for some extraordinary dance numbers). Whether out of impatience or an attempt to make Hugo and Albert jealous, it is risky and manipulative behavior. (This is even more true in the original play.)

PROFANITY: None.

NUDITY/SEXUAL REFERENCES: Rosie and Kim admit to each other that they are both "good girls." Rosie appears in a bra.

ALCOHOL/DRUG ABUSE: Birdie drinks beer. Rosie and Albert go to a roadhouse. The speed-up pill, although a whimsical idea, is less charming in light of current issues of drug abuse.

VIOLENCE/SCARINESS: None.

TOLERANCE/DIVERSITY ISSUES: Rosie is Hispanic without any ethnic characteristics; everyone else is white and Anglo.

✳ **QUESTIONS FOR KIDS:**
- One of the interesting things about this movie is the way that so many people end up agreeing to do things they don't want to. Why does Hugo agree to let Kim kiss Conrad? Why does her father agree?
- Why does Kim call her mother "Doris"? Why does she change back to "Mommy"?
- What do you think of the song "Kids"? Is it as relevant today as it was when the movie was made?
- Why do Kim and Rosie decide to go off to dance with people other than their boyfriends? Does it accomplish what they intended?
- Does Albert pay too much attention to his mother? What makes you think so? What would you do if you were Albert?

✳ **CONNECTIONS:** This plot is reminiscent of *The Man Who Came to Dinner*, the Kaufman and Hart comedy about the ruin brought on to a 1940s family when a media celebrity stays at their home. Janet Leigh, who appears here in a black wig, is perhaps most famous for her shower scene in *Psycho*. Dick Van Dyke, repeating his role in the Broadway production, also appears in *Mary Poppins*.

✳ **ACTIVITIES:** Kids might like to listen to some of Elvis Presley's hit records or look at some of the publicity about his induction into the army, and talk about which star might have that kind of impact today.

The Flamingo Kid
1984, 98 min, PG-13, high schoolers
Dir: Garry Marshall. Matt Dillon, Richard Crenna

✳ **PLOT:** On a hot early summer day in Brooklyn in 1963, Jeffrey (Matt Dillon) is talking to his friends when some old friends who have moved out of the neighborhood come by to invite him to play cards at their country club on Long Island. The El Flamingo Club is a dazzling contrast to hot, sweaty Brooklyn, everything sleek and spotless. Jeffrey is self-conscious, but impressed. His friends are delighted when he helps them win their gin game. And he is delighted when he is offered a job parking cars at the club.

His father, Arthur (Hector Elizondo), however, is not delighted. He had arranged for Jeffrey to work as an office boy in an engineering firm. He finally agrees to let Jeffrey work at the El Flamingo.

At the club, Jeffrey sees Phil Brody (Richard Crenna), a car dealer and the champion player in the high-stakes gin game. Invited to dinner by Carla (Janet Jones), Brody's niece from California, Jeffrey is awkward but in awe of Phil, who treats him with easy charm and arranges for him to be promoted to cabana boy.

Jeffrey admires Phil, and Phil enjoys being admired. He gives Jeffrey advice on everything from playing gin to what to wear to what Jeffrey should do for a career. Phil has an answer for everything, and all of the answers appeal to Jeffrey. "The salesmen of the world make the money." "God put certain people on this earth to give you money, and your responsibility in life is to go out there and—get it."

Jeffrey goes home, repeating Phil's views, and his father is furious, especially when Jeffrey says that "college is overrated," and that he may not attend. When Arthur responds by saying he is the boss, Jeffrey says he has decided not to go to college. Jeffrey and his friends go to a racetrack, and his friend Fortune loses his college money. Afterward, they go to a restaurant and get into a fight with some other kids. They are arrested, and Arthur has to bail them out. "In Brooklyn, you go to school. In Long Island, you go to jail. From now on, you stay in Brooklyn." Jeffrey argues that his friends know how to have a good time, and that their family could live on Long Island if Arthur was willing to spend the money instead of saving every penny. Arthur hits Jeffrey. Later, he apologizes. "Something you ought to know about your father, Jeffrey. Fast things bother him," he explains. But Jeffrey likes fast things, and he moves out.

When he tells Phil he is ready for the job he promised at the car dealership, Phil offers him a job as a stock boy. On the last day of the season, Jeffrey realizes that Phil has been cheating at gin. When one of the opposing team members is hurt, Jeffrey offers to play against Phil. The game goes so long, it overlaps with the Labor Day dance. They double the stakes, and Jeffrey wins. Phil is a bad loser. When he realizes that Jeffrey knows the truth, Phil offers Jeffrey a sales job. Jeffrey responds by telling Phil's friends that Phil cheated. Jeffrey gives the money he won to his friend Fortune, to replace his losses at the racetrack. Then he joins his family for dinner at their favorite restaurant.

✳ **DISCUSSION:** While there are a number of caveats, due to language and other concerns, this movie raises some valuable issues for family discussion. At the club, Jeffrey sees a different way of life for the first time. At first, he is impressed by Phil, by his house, his car, his clothes, his smoothness, his view that "money is the name of the game, and if you can make it easy, make it easy." He is ready to put aside the values he learned from his father. But he finds out not just that Phil is dishonest, but that he is dishonest with his friends, and even with himself. Phil assumes everyone is either like him or stupid.

On Jeffrey's last night with Carla, he tells her how ships going out to sea sail back and forth between two lights to "box" (set) their compasses, before venturing into the ocean. This is a lovely metaphor for what Jeffrey does in this movie, as he sets his own moral compass by comparing Phil and his father.

PROFANITY: About a dozen four-letter words, including all of the most popular ones.

NUDITY/SEXUAL REFERENCES: There are some PG shots of Jeffrey and Carla spending the night together (bare backs and legs). One of the country club members asks if she can put his tip in Jeffrey's pocket, and he agrees. When he says, "You missed my pocket again, Mrs. Unger," she replies, "I like to miss it." She compliments him on his "behind." Reference to "jacking off."

ALCOHOL/DRUG ABUSE: Some alcohol.

VIOLENCE/SCARINESS: Fight in a restaurant. Arthur hits Jeffrey.

TOLERANCE/DIVERSITY ISSUES: Jeffrey's friend Fortune is black. No issue is made of this in any way (unless you consider it's sterotypical to have him going to college on a basketball scholarship). There are antihomosexual references, not to anyone in particular, just as general insults. The movie also raises class issues. Phil's wife is a snob.

✳ **QUESTIONS FOR KIDS:**
- Why does Jeffrey like Phil at first? What is it about Phil that he likes? How can you tell that Jeffrey likes Phil?

- What makes Jeffrey change his mind?
- Why does Carla like Jeffrey?
- What does Arthur mean when he says he is afraid of fast things?
- What is the importance of the explanation about boxing the compass?

✳ **CONNECTIONS:** Watch carefully as Richard Crenna tries out his new remote control and you will see him click by a quick glimpse of his younger self as Luke on television's *The Real McCoys*. Before that, he appeared as Walter Denton on the radio and television versions of *Our Miss Brooks*. Athlete Janet Jones, who plays Carla, is the real-life wife of hockey legend Wayne Gretsky. Bronson Pinchot, who appears in a small part, became well-known for his appearances in the *Beverly Hills Cop* movies, and played Balki on the television show *Perfect Strangers*.

The movie includes some of the finest songs of the era, well-used to comment on the story and characters, including, "Walk Right In," "Stand By Me," "Money (It's What I Want)," "South Street," "He's So Fine," and "It's All Right."

✳ **ACTIVITIES:** Teach the kids to play gin or poker. Take them to a swim club, and let them compare it to the El Flamingo Club.

Jezebel

1938, 103 min, NR, b&w, 10 and up
Dir: William Wyler. Bette Davis, Henry Fonda

✳ **PLOT:** Julie Marsden (Bette Davis) is a spoiled Southern belle in pre–Civil War New Orleans. She does not hesitate to pull Preston Dillard, her fiancé (Henry Fonda), out of a business meeting to consult on a clothing purchase, and uses sulking and petulance to get her way. She decides to punish Pres for failure to devote his complete attention to her by doing something shocking—wearing a scarlet dress to the Olympus Ball, where by tradition unmarried ladies always wear white.

When she gets to the ball, however, she is embarrassed and asks to leave. Pres insists on dancing with her. The two of them waltz around the empty dance floor, watched by everyone there, and then he takes her home. He breaks off their engagement and moves North. She insists that he will come back to her. Three years later, he returns, and she puts on a white dress to greet him with an apology, but he is married to Amy, a Northern lady. Devastated, Julie manages to get Buck Cantrell (George Brent), another suitor, to challenge Pres to a duel, and, when Pres's brother takes his place, Buck is killed.

Julie's guardian refuses to have anything to do with her anymore, comparing Julie to Jezebel in the Bible. Pres gets yellow fever in an epidemic, and the patients are evacuated. Julie persuades Amy to let her go nurse him, to redeem herself, risking her own life by exposure to the disease. She promises that if he gets well, she will bring him back to Amy.

✳ **DISCUSSION:** This is a great movie for teenagers because it is an entertaining depiction of the kind of immature behavior people engage in when they are just trying out the complications of adult relationships, particularly romantic ones. Julie's spoiled and selfish actions have nothing to do with intimacy; on the contrary, they are all about power, and power in a very superficial sense at that. She wants Pres completely within her control. She could have that from Buck, but is not interested, because he is not enough of a challenge. Julie is only attracted to men she cannot control, yet she cannot be happy unless she is in control—a collision course with disaster.

It is important to recognize that Julie makes decisions that seem as though they will make her feel better, but they never do. She backs herself into a corner with the red dress, leaving herself no graceful way out. When she gets to the ball, she finds that she really did not want to shock people as much as she'd thought she did. And of course the ultimate consequence of her decision is losing Pres for good.

Compare Julie to Scarlett O'Hara in **Gone With the Wind** (some people consider this film a consolation prize to Bette Davis for not being cast as Scarlett). Both manipulate men rather than attempt genuine intimacy, and both end up losing the men they really want.

Teens may be interested in considering how much of Julie's frustration and manipulation might stem from the highly restricted forms of power women had in both the era depicted and the era in which the movie was made. If Julie could have attended her own business meetings, would she have wanted to make Pres leave his? It is also worth looking at the way Bette Davis resolved some of the problems she faced in her career, challenging the studio system's control of actors. Ultimately, the issues she raised ended up in the Supreme Court, resulting in a decision that gave actors much more freedom to choose their own projects.

PROFANITY: None.
NUDITY/SEXUAL REFERENCES: None.
ALCOHOL/DRUG ABUSE: None.
VIOLENCE/SCARINESS: None.
TOLERANCE/DIVERSITY ISSUES: Depiction of blacks typical of the era.

✳ **QUESTIONS FOR KIDS:**
• Why was Julie so spoiled? Do you think she was a "Jezebel"?
• What should Pres have done about the red dress?
• Could Julie and Pres have ever been happy together?

✳ **CONNECTIONS:** Both Bette Davis and Fay Bainter won Oscars for their performances. The "red" dress used in the movie was, in reality, a deep rust color, for a more effective contrast on black-and-white film. A movie with an even more jealous, insecure, and destructive heroine is *Leave Her to Heaven*.

✳ **ACTIVITIES:** Look up Jezebel in the Bible to see why Julie's aunt made the comparison. Read "Here We Are" and "The Sexes," by Dorothy Parker, for exquisite renditions of similarly manipulative women who are—at least temporarily—more successful; read some of her other short stories for what happens after the men in the lives of women like this get frustrated or bored by that treatment. And read a famous short poem called "The Glove and the Lions," by Leigh Hunt, about a lady who drops her glove among the lions at a sporting event, knowing that the count who loves her will risk his life to get it back for her. He gets it back, then throws it in her face, while the king notes approvingly, " 'No love,' quoth he, 'but vanity, sets love a task like that.' "

✳The Learning Tree
1969, 107 min, PG, high schoolers
Dir: Gordon Parks. Kyle Johnson, Dana Elcar, Estelle Evans

✳ **PLOT:** Photographer-filmmaker Gordon Parks produced, wrote, directed, and even scored this movie, based on his autobiographical novel about coming of age in a black family in 1920s rural Kansas. Like *The Wizard of Oz*, that other great novel of Kansas, it begins with a twister that causes great disruption. And like that other great American autobiographical novel, *Tom Sawyer*, this is the story of two boys—one from a loving family, the other the son of an abusive alcoholic father—and of a murder that involves them both.

Fourteen-year-old Newt Winger comes from a family that is comfortable, respected, and principled. When Newt and his friends steal some apples, the owner, Mr. Kiner, comes after them with a whip. He catches up to Marcus (Alex Clarke), who beats Kiner badly. Newt and his mother, Sarah (Estelle Evans), visit Kiner in the hospital, and Newt promises to work for no pay to make up for what happened. Marcus is charged and sent to a reformatory, where he is cruelly beaten, and becomes even more hostile, especially toward Newt.

Newt, in the meantime, has his first girlfriend, Arcella Jefferson (Mira Waters). Chauncey Cavenaugh, son of the judge for whom Sarah keeps house, sees Newt and Arcella and invites them for a Coke. But the waiter refuses to serve them, insisting they take the Cokes and leave. Later, Newt sees Arcella get in Chauncey's car. She will not see Newt anymore and won't tell him what the problem is. She is pregnant; Chauncey is the father. She and her family leave town.

Marcus is released from the reformatory. He fights Newt at a fair, but Newt wins. Newt sees Marcus's father, Booker, kill Kiner. A white man named Silas is charged. Newt is afraid to tell the truth because he fears reprisals against the black community. But he cannot see Silas convicted, and he testifies about what he saw. When the crowd in the courtroom shouts, "Kill the nigger," Booker runs out of the room and kills himself. Marcus comes after Newt with a gun. Newt subdues him, and he runs. The sheriff shoots him. He offers Newt a ride home, and Newt says, "I can make it by myself."

✳ **DISCUSSION:** In addition to the classic coming-of-age themes of confronting death and losing innocence, this movie adds issues of racism and tolerance—by both blacks and whites. By some standards, there is much in the town that is very progressive, despite segregation. Sarah does not hesitate to tell the (racist) white sheriff to watch his tongue when he tells her (correctly) that her son is in trouble. She speaks very openly and directly to the judge, and even more directly to his son. The black Wingers and the white Kiners are mutually respectful and genuinely friendly. The same is true of their relationship with the white doctor. The judge tells the crowd in the courtroom that they executed Booker by their reaction to Newt's testimony, and it was Newt's fear of just this kind of racist reaction that made him hesitate about telling the truth.

This makes the racism that does exist stand out more sharply. As the principal admits, black students are not allowed on the school teams or at the dances. When Newt complains to his teacher about his grade, she says it is a waste of time for black students to go to college. He argues, and she takes him to the principal's office. The principal sides with Newt but asks Newt to remember that the teacher is a victim, too, and that he can't change all the rules he would like to. He will speak to the teacher, but Newt must always treat her with "the highest respect."

When Newt asks his uncle Rob why white people "do so many awful things," Rob explains that, since he is blind, he just looks at people as individuals. "I don't figure his color into it; I figure his deed." This ties in with Sarah's advice to Newt that their community is like a tree, with some of the fruit good and some bad. (This should be a "learning tree" for him.) The movie is evenhanded in its portrayal of both good and bad in blacks and whites. Most important, it is a fine portrait of a fine family.

Note that the way people express themselves indicates something about what they think and about their relationships. It is revealing to notice who gets to use first names, for example. It is also worthwhile discussing what the community's responsibility should have been to Marcus. Sarah tells the judge that it is not Marcus's fault that he behaves so badly, and the judge says, "I can't send the father to the reformatory for something the son did."

PROFANITY: Reference to "I hear you ain't got no cherry no more" after (off-screen) sexual encounter; racial epithets.

NUDITY/SEXUAL REFERENCES: Nudity at a swimming hole; out-of-wedlock pregnancy; nude couple in bed; scenes in a whorehouse.

ALCOHOL/DRUG ABUSE: Booker abuses alcohol.

VIOLENCE/SCARINESS: Fights; one character is beaten to death; two are shot; one commits suicide (off-camera); scary nightmare of bringing dead body up from under the water; death of Newt's mother.

TOLERANCE/DIVERSITY ISSUES: One of the themes of the movie.

* **QUESTIONS FOR KIDS:**
  * What do you think about the scene in the restaurant? If you were Chauncy, what would you do? If you were Newt or Arcella, what would you do?
  * Why didn't Arcella want to be with Newt anymore? Why did her family leave town?
  * What do you think about what the judge said about Arcella to Sarah?
  * Why does Newt say, after Sarah's death, that he is not afraid anymore?
  * How does Newt's brother help him?

* **CONNECTIONS:** *The Learning Tree* was among the first twenty-five films included in the Library of Congress's National Film Registry as "culturally, historically, or esthetically significant." Parks's background as one of *Life* magazine's greatest photographers is evident in this film's exceptional visual flair. Parks's later movies were the "blaxploitation" hits *Shaft* and its sequel, *Shaft's Big Score*, featuring a powerful black hero who battles racist cops and criminals and romances many women along the way.

Lucas

1986, 100 min, PG-13, high schoolers
Dir: David Seltzer. Corey Haim, Kerri Green, Charlie Sheen, Winona Ryder

* **PLOT:** Lucas (Corey Haim) is a very bright fourteen-year-old, in high school with older kids. He is confident enough to approach Maggie (Kerri Green), a pretty girl who is new in town and vulnerable because of her parents' recent divorce. They become close friends. On the first day of school, Lucas is humiliatingly carried up onstage by a football player named Bruno during a rally. He manages to turn it to his advantage by making fun of the coach, but he is embarrassed. That night, at a movie with Maggie, Bruno harasses him again, but the captain of the team, Cappie (Charlie Sheen), intervenes. Cappie likes Lucas and owes him a lot because Lucas helped Cappie with his schoolwork when he was sick.

Lucas is heartbroken when Cappie and Maggie are attracted to each other. He is barely aware of Rina (Winona Ryder), who likes him very much. He decides to go out for the football team, even though he had always been contemptuous of the "superficiality" of football, and even though he is about one-third the size of the other players. When the coach refuses to let him play, he threatens a lawsuit. In the locker room, Cappie is not able to save him, when, responding to taunts about his masculinity, Lucas bravely lashes back. The other players rub deep-heating ointment on his genitals, then throw him outside wearing nothing but a towel. Even though Maggie is there, all he can do is run for the drinking fountain and jump in.

The principal forbids him to play. But at a big game, when the team is losing badly, he persuades the coach to put him in. He is hurt, and Cappie, Maggie, and Rina go to the hospital with him. Rina tells the others that Lucas does not live in the mansion he told Maggie was his home. That is where he works as a gardener's assistant. He lives in a trailer park, with an alcoholic father.

Lucas returns to school, not sure how he will be received. Bruno is standing near his locker, waiting for him. So are Rina, Cappie, and Maggie. He opens his locker to find a football jacket with his name on it. As he tries it on, the students applaud.

✳ **DISCUSSION:** This is an exceptionally intelligent and sensitive movie about an exceptionally intelligent and sensitive kid (based in part on the memories of writer-director David Seltzer). It evokes the emotions of high school: terror, exhilaration, the breathtaking swings from confidence to self-doubt.

Lucas is fascinated by insects, especially the locusts who take seventeen years to mature and emerge from their cocoons. He is impatient to emerge from his cocoon, to grow into the feelings he has for Maggie, to be seen by others the way he sees himself inside. His lies about his parents, and his devastation when Maggie and Cappie become involved show that despite his ability to handle Bruno's harassment and his courage in confronting the coach and insisting on playing football, he is very vulnerable.

Departing from the usual formulas, this movie has the intelligence to make Cappie a thoughtful, funny, caring person (very well-portrayed by Charlie Sheen), and the courage not to have Lucas win the football game. Kids who see this may want to talk about why Lucas is attracted to Maggie and why he does not see that Rina is attracted to him. Older kids may be interested in talking about the way that some big, tough, physically mature boys like Bruno are threatened by small, brainy kids like Lucas because of their developing and uncertain notions of masculinity and sexual power.

PROFANITY: Strong language, especially in the locker-room scene, is the reason for the PG-13 rating.

NUDITY/SEXUAL REFERENCES: Typical adolescent talk about who has "done it"; behavior is comparatively circumspect, however.

ALCOHOL/DRUG ABUSE: None.

VIOLENCE/SCARINESS: Lucas is assaulted with deep-heating ointment in the locker room and injured when he is tackled on the football field.

TOLERANCE/DIVERSITY ISSUES: Tolerance of individual differences is a theme of the movie.

✳ **QUESTIONS FOR KIDS:**
- Why does Lucas describe his parents the way he does?
- What does it show when Maggie is honest about her parents and their problems?
- How does Lucas turn the situation to his own advantage when he is pulled up onstage?

- Should Maggie not have gone out with Cappie? What are the obligations of friends like Maggie and Cappie in this situation?
- What kind of grown-up do you think Lucas will become?

✳ **CONNECTIONS:** This was the first movie for gifted actress Winona Ryder, who went on to play sensitive teenagers in a number of films, including *Beetlejuice*, *Mermaids*, and **Little Women.**

✳Rebel Without a Cause

1955, 110 min, NR, 12 and up
Dir: Nicholas Ray. James Dean, Natalie Wood, Sal Mineo, Jim Backus

✳ **PLOT:** Teenager Jim Stark (James Dean), new in town, is picked up by the police for being drunk. At the police station, he sees two other teens, Judy (Natalie Wood), who has been walking around miserably, feeling rejected by her father, and Plato (Sal Mineo), neglected by his parents, brought in for killing some puppies. Jim's parents and grandmother come to pick him up, but they are too caught up in their own bickering to listen to him. Judy's mother comes for her, and Plato is picked up by his housekeeper. Only Ray, the understanding policeman, listens, and he encourages Jim to come talk to him at any time.

The next morning is Jim's first day at his new high school. He tries to talk to Judy, but she rejects him harshly and goes off with Buzz, her tough boyfriend, and his punk cronies. At a field trip to the local planetarium, Buzz challenges Jim to a knife fight. Jim wins, and Buzz challenges him to a "chickie run" with stolen cars that night at eight o'clock. Jim tries to get advice from his father, asking what he should do when something very dangerous is "a matter of honor"? His father's response is patronizing and ineffectual. Jim is disappointed: "I want answers now. I'm not interested in what I'll understand ten years from now."

At the "chickie run," Jim asks, "Why do we do this?" and Buzz answers, "We gotta do something." Jim jumps out of the car just before it goes off the cliff, but Buzz's sleeve gets caught, and he cannot get out in time. He is killed. Jim goes home and asks his parents for help. His mother wants to move, as she always does when there is any trouble. They tell Jim not to go to the police, to stay out of it. Jim is desperate. He asks his father to stand up for him, wanting him to show some kind of support. When he sees none, Jim is disgusted and shoves his father aside.

He goes to the police station alone. Buzz's friends, brought in for questioning, see him and want to stop him from telling what happened. When Jim finds that Ray is not there, he leaves, and sees Judy. Together, they go to an abandoned mansion near the planetarium and have some happy moments, pretending they are safe and grown up, in their own home, away from all their troubles. Plato arrives with a gun. He wants to protect them.

For a moment, they make up a family, Jim and Judy as the parents, Plato as the child they cover tenderly when he falls asleep. Judy and Jim realize they care deeply for each other. She is happy to have found "a man who can be gentle and sweet . . . and someone who doesn't run away when you want him."

Buzz's friends arrive. Plato panics when he wakes up and doesn't see Jim and Judy, and feels abandoned again. When the police arrive, he shoots one of the policemen and runs to the planetarium. Jim and Judy go in after him, and Jim calms him down and takes the bullets from his gun. But the police think Plato is going to fire the gun again, so they shoot him and he is killed. Jim sobs in his father's arms as his father assures him, "You did everything a man could," and promises, "I'll try to be as strong as you want me to be." Jim and Judy reach out for each other as the movie ends, just twenty-four hours after it began.

✳ **DISCUSSION:** This is the ultimate classic of teenage angst, and an excellent movie for families to watch together to talk about some of the feelings parents and kids have during these years.

A generation later, James Dean is still the teenage icon, partly because he died a few months after this film was released, and so remains frozen in time, but partly because his performance in this film had—and has— such resonance for teenagers and for everyone else who feels unsure and angry, and unsure of why they feel angry. The title says it all: Jim is a rebel without the ability to put into words what he is rebelling against. Even teenagers like those in the 1960s, who found causes for their rebellions, identify with Jim's feelings of frustration and loneliness as they begin to establish their own identities and take responsibility for their own choices.

As Judy's mother says, this is "that age when nothing seems to fit." Judy feels rejected by her father. He, in turn, feels rejected by her simply because she is growing up. He is uncomfortable with her as she becomes a woman, and has no way to relate to her except to call her a tramp when she wears makeup or slap her away when she tries to kiss him.

Jim, like most teenagers, looks for extremes of gender definition and identification while he is sorting out what it all really means. He is humiliated by his father's submission to his mother's insults and even says he wishes his father would hit her. He hates to see his father wearing an apron and bringing up dinner on a tray for his wife. This seems unmasculine to him. Perhaps one reason he feels such a need to prove his courage and "honor" is his conflict about his own feelings of tenderness and vulnerability. In the very first scene, drunk and lying on the ground, he gently covers a little mechanical bear as though it were a child. At the police station, he asks if he can keep the toy. He is gentle with Plato, offering him his jacket in the police station and at the planetarium, and Judy tells him how important that is to her. He is everything to Plato that he wishes his father could be for him, "standing up" for him with the police, promising to take care of everything.

But he cannot take care of everything, and Plato is killed. He learns, tragically, a little of what it is like to be a parent, and has to give up the idea forever (as all teenagers must) that parents are all-powerful. But his father learns something, too: that he can draw on his strength, as his son did; that they can be strong for each other.

It is interesting that the sympathetic policeman is named Ray, like the director, underscoring that character's representation of the director's perspective. Note that Jim asks both Ray and his father to put limits on him, and parents should talk with their kids about why Jim is afraid he cannot limit himself—but most importantly, they should talk about why the parents and kids in this movie find it so hard to communicate.

PROFANITY: None.

NUDITY/SEXUAL REFERENCES: None.

ALCOHOL/DRUG ABUSE: Teens smoke and drink.

VIOLENCE/SCARINESS: Characters are in peril; Buzz is killed in "chickie run"; Plato shoots at two people and is himself shot and killed.

TOLERANCE/DIVERSITY ISSUES: None.

✳ **QUESTIONS FOR KIDS:**
- What does the title mean?
- Judy says, "You shouldn't believe what I say when I'm with the rest of the kids." What does that mean? Why does she say things with the others that she is uncomfortable about?
- What do we learn from Buzz's "we gotta do something" answer about why they do the "chickie run"?
- What does Judy discover when she says that "All the time I've been looking for someone to love me, and now I love somebody"?
- What does it show that Jim wears a jacket and tie in some scenes and a T-shirt and windbreaker in others?

✳ **CONNECTIONS:** Dean starred in only two other movies, and he is riveting in both: *Giant,* an epic saga of Texas oil and cattlemen, and *East of Eden*, from the John Steinbeck novel of two brothers who are rivals for their father's affections. Goon is played by Dennis Hopper, who starred in *Easy Rider* and played memorable villains in *Blue Velvet* (for adults only) and *Waterworld*. Jim's father is played by Jim Backus, best known for his more humorous television appearances, as Mr. Howell on *Gilligan's Island* and as the voice of Mr. Magoo. Ed Platt, who plays Ray, the sympathetic cop, also played the Chief, Maxwell Smart's choleric boss on television's *Get Smart*. Judy's father is played by William Hopper (son of Hedda Hopper), who was Paul Drake on television's *Perry Mason*.

*Say Anything

1989, 100 min, PG-13, high schoolers
Dir: Cameron Crowe. *John Cusack, Ione Skye, John Mahoney*

✱ **PLOT:** Lloyd Dobler (John Cusack) is an engagingly aimless high school graduate who likes junk food and kick-boxing. Courageously, he sets his heart on Diane Court (Ione Skye), the most beautiful and brilliant girl in school, described as a brain "trapped inside the body of a game show hostess." Lloyd has no conventional "smooth" talk, but his free-association "say anything" style, good humor, and obvious genuineness make her laugh. She agrees to let him take her to a graduation party, and they have a good time together.

Diane and her father, James (John Mahoney), are very close, and he assures her that they can always "say anything" to each other. When Diane wins a prestigious fellowship to study in England, he tells her that it is everything they have ever worked for. One problem is Diane's fear of flying. The other problem is her growing attachment to Lloyd.

Though she tries not to become too involved, Diane becomes closer to Lloyd. Her father feels that she is drifting away from him. Diane and Lloyd make love—a gentle, intimate experience—and she immediately tells her father about it. Finally, James forces Diane to choose, and she chooses her father over Lloyd. She tells Lloyd she just wants to be friends.

But her father's love, which has always bordered on the obsessive, has also developed into the criminal. His nursing home is investigated for tax fraud. James has been taking money from the residents to spend on Diane. Diane is shattered. She returns to Lloyd for support. She cannot bring herself to visit her father in jail, so she sends Lloyd to see him with a letter. In an exceptionally sweet final scene, Lloyd and a terrified Diane are on the plane to England.

✱ **DISCUSSION:** In this movie, the guy who appears to be aimless and incapable of achieving anything turns out to have a stronger moral code than James and to be more in control of his life than Diane. Diane may have an outstanding record, but she has missed out on making friends. Lloyd has excellent relationships with his sister and her son and with a number of friends. He is the one reliable enough to be the "key master" to make sure that no one leaves the party too drunk to drive. When he wavers about taking a stand with Diane, his friend reminds him not to be "a guy," but to be "a man." He is even willing to mediate the relationship between Diane and her father.

Lloyd waits for his future to come to him. As he says, "I don't want to sell anything, buy anything, or process anything as a career. I don't want to sell anything bought or processed, or buy anything sold or processed, or process anything sold, bought, or processed, or repair anything sold, bought, or processed. You know, as a career, I don't want to do that." But he knows that he wants to be with Diane, and he is willing to do whatever it takes to make that possible. Lloyd is ready to make his own choices and make his own mistakes. Diane, by contrast, has always had all her choices made for her.

The strength of Lloyd's relationship with Diane is also contrasted with the disastrous teenage relationships of his friends, especially Cory's broken heart over Joe. In a memorable scene, Lloyd's buddies offer him (terrible) advice on how to treat women, and he responds, "I got a question. If you guys know so much about women, how come you're here at, like, the Gas 'n' Sip on a Saturday night completely alone drinking beers with no women anywhere?" "Conscious choice, man" is their funny but unconvincing reply.

Diane's father, desperate for her to succeed, is too overprotective and too involved with her. He has made her dependent. She is only able to flourish in Lloyd's company. She appreciates Lloyd's thoughtfulness in guiding her around some broken glass and his willingness to help her become more independent by teaching her to drive. Yet, she is still not ready to be on her own. She needs Lloyd to deliver her message to her father, and to comfort her as the plane takes off for England.

PROFANITY: Mild expletives.

NUDITY/SEXUAL REFERENCES: Diane and Lloyd make love in the back of a car, an overwhelming and intimate experience for both of them. She goes home afterward and tells her father about it, pleased that she can "say anything" to him.

ALCOHOL/DRUG ABUSE: Liberal drinking at high school party with a couple of students actively drunk. Lloyd is responsible for making sure everyone gets home safely.

VIOLENCE/SCARINESS: None.

TOLERANCE/DIVERSITY ISSUES: None.

✳ QUESTIONS FOR KIDS:
- Why would a girl as successful and ambitious as Diane like Lloyd?
- If all James does is try to do what is best for his daughter, how does this go wrong?
- Lloyd has a lot of friends—what makes him so likable?
- What will happen to Lloyd and Diane? Why do you think so?

✳ CONNECTIONS:
Ione Skye (the daughter of 1960s pop star Donovan) appeared in another story about a young man who flounders through his attraction to her, *The Rachel Papers* (deservedly rated R), based on the novel by Martin Amis. Cusack stars in **The Sure Thing** and **The Journey of Natty Gann**, and provides the voice of Dimitri in **Anastasia**. Mahoney appears on television's *Frasier*.

Splendor in the Grass

1961, 124 min, NR, high schoolers
Dir: Elia Kazan. Warren Beatty, Natalie Wood, Pat Hingle

✳ **PLOT:** In this classic of repressed teenage sexuality, set in the 1920s, Bud (Warren Beatty) and Deanie (Natalie Wood) are high school students who are newly in love and breathless with desire, physical and emotional. Deanie's parents are unable to give her any guidance. They make her feel ashamed of her feelings. Her mother says, "Your father never laid a hand on me until we were married and then I just gave in because a wife has to. A woman doesn't enjoy these things the way a man does. She just lets her husband come near her in order to have children." Bud's father, Ace (Pat Hingle), tells Bud that there are two kinds of girls, "good" and "bad," and the "bad" ones are fair game. This apparently applies to Bud's sister, whose reputation has been "ruined" by having sex and has come home from college in disgrace. At a party, she drinks too much and has sex with a group of men.

Deanie will not have sex with Bud, and they break up. Both suffer breakdowns. His is moral; he has sex with another girl, known to be "easy." Hers is emotional; overcome with despair and self-loathing, Deanie has a breakdown and becomes a patient at a mental hospital. Ace will not permit Bud to go to agricultural college and insists that he go to Yale. But when the stock market crashes, Ace is wiped out and kills himself. Bud leaves college.

When Deanie comes home from the hospital, her mother does not want her to see Bud. Deanie's father tells her how to find him, and, with some friends, Deanie drives out to the shack where Bud lives with his wife. Deanie and Bud speak, briefly, achieving some resolution, enabling them to go on, if not as they had once hoped, at least grateful for what they have had. Deanie remembers the words of the Wordsworth poem she learned in school: "Though nothing can bring back the hour/Of splendor in the grass, of glory in the flower;/We will grieve not, rather find/Strength in what remains behind."

✳ **DISCUSSION:** This Oscar-winning screenplay by William Inge was immensely controversial when the film was made. (A brief glimpse of nudity as Deanie ran from the bathtub was cut from the final print.) Most teenagers face a different set of issues today, but they are presented with no less hypocrisy or more reassurance than the messages to kids like Bud and Deanie. Instead of being told that sexual feelings are nonexistent or evidence of being "bad," today's teenagers often get the message that they are "bad" or lacking if they do not feel ready to engage in sexual activity freely almost as soon as they enter high school. The issues of honesty in communicating about sexuality and the overwhelming confusion of teenage passion remain important and valid, and this movie can provide a good opening for a talk about what has changed and how teenagers feel about the decisions and the consequences Bud and Deanie face in this movie.

PROFANITY: Mild.
NUDITY/SEXUAL REFERENCES: Sexuality is a theme of the movie.

ALCOHOL/DRUG ABUSE: Bud's sister gets drunk.

VIOLENCE/SCARINESS: Bud's sister is sexually assaulted.

TOLERANCE/DIVERSITY ISSUES: Some class issues.

✳ **QUESTIONS FOR KIDS:**
- Why does Ace make a distinction between "good" and "bad" girls? Do people make that distinction today? What makes a girl "bad"?
- Is anyone honest with Bud and Deanie?
- What do Bud and Deanie mean when they say that they don't think about happiness anymore?
- Why did Deanie refuse to have sex with Bud? Why did Bud refuse to have sex with Deanie? What should two people think about before they make the decision to have sex?

✳ **CONNECTIONS:** In another classic movie of teenage sexual repression, *A Summer Place*, Sandra Dee and Troy Donahue do have sex, and she becomes pregnant. Dee's mother is repressed to the point of hysteria, but her father, who has left his wife to be reunited with the woman he loved when they were teenagers, is sympathetic and supportive, all to lush and unforgettable theme music by Max Steiner.

William Inge (who appears as the minister) won an Oscar for Best Screenplay. He also wrote *Picnic*, **Bus Stop** and *The Dark at the Top of the Stairs*, all about vulnerable people who must struggle to find intimacy and happiness—especially appealing to sensitive teens.

✳The World of Henry Orient

1964, 104 min, NR, 12 and up
Dir: George Roy Hill. Peter Sellers, Tippi Walker, Merrie Spaeth, Angela Lansbury, Tom Bosley, Phyllis Thaxter, Paula Prentiss

✳ **PLOT:** Valerie Boyd (Tippi Walker) and Marian "Gil" Gilbert (Merrie Spaeth) become good friends after they meet at a posh New York prep school for girls. Valerie is the child of wealthy parents who travel most of the time and send her gifts like a mink coat. Gil lives with her mother (Phyllis Thaxter) and her mother's friend "Boothy" (Bibi Osterwald) in a modest home.

The girls see pianist Henry Orient (Peter Sellers) with Stella (Paula Prentiss), a married lady friend, in Central Park. Stella is attracted to Henry but panicked about being discovered by her husband. Val develops a huge adolescent crush on Henry, and the girls begin following him around, researching his career and establishing elaborate silly rituals for pledging their devotion. Stella is close to hysterics, thinking they are employed by her husband to report on her.

Val's parents, Isabel (Angela Lansbury) and Frank (Tom Bosley), return to New York. Isabel is annoyed to hear of Val's escapades. When she meets

Henry herself, though, she is attracted to him, and they sleep together. Frank can no longer ignore Isabel's infidelities and, more importantly, her neglect of Val. He leaves Isabel, taking Val with him to Europe. When she comes back for a visit with Gil, they excitedly talk about boys.

❊ **DISCUSSION:** This is an appealing and believable story of two girls who are at that stage where they are not quite ready to enter into real relationships with real boys, so they "practice" the emotions of romance by fixating on an unattainable object. The two girls who play Val and Gil are wonderfully natural, and the film makes New York City look as invitingly enchanting as the land of Oz.

Even though Gil's parents are not together, she has a warm and loving family with her mother and Boothy. Val's more extravagent behavior reflects a neediness and self-doubt that stems from the neglect by her parents.

PROFANITY: None.
NUDITY/SEXUAL REFERENCES: Henry's prolonged attempt to seduce Stella; Henry and Isabel have a one-night stand; in the last scene, Val brags about kissing a boy whose name she didn't know.
ALCOHOL/DRUG ABUSE: Social drinking.
VIOLENCE/SCARINESS: None.
TOLERANCE/DIVERSITY ISSUES: None.

❊ **QUESTIONS FOR KIDS:**
- Why does Val pick Henry Orient to have a crush on?
- What do Stella and Isabel see in him?
- What makes Frank decide to leave Isabel? How did his talk with Gil's mother play a role?
- Does the movie do a good job of showing how friends behave? What parts seemed real to you and what parts didn't?

❊ **CONNECTIONS:** This movie was written by longtime screenwriter Nunnally Johnson (*The Grapes of Wrath*), based on a semiautobiographical novel written by his daughter. Famed society band leader Peter Duchin plays Joe Byrd. The score, by legendary composer Elmer Bernstein (*The Magnificent Seven*) and Ken Lauber, is superb.

❊ THE CHALK GARDEN

1964, 104 min, NR, 14 and up
Dir: Ronald Neame. Hayley Mills, Deborah Kerr

Hayley Mills plays Laurel, a troubled teenager who lives with her eccentric grandmother, Mrs. St. Maugham (Dame Edith Evans). Miss Madrigal (Deborah Kerr), a mysterious woman with no references, is hired to be Laurel's governess. While Mrs. St. Maugham encourages Laurel's wild and manipulative behavior, Miss Madrigal realizes that Laurel is acting out because she is desperately unhappy, and that if she does not find a home with someone who loves her enough to impose limits, it will be like planting flowers in a chalk garden. She must confront her own tragic experiences to make it possible for Laurel to return to her mother. The sensitive portrayal of a girl's reaction to her feelings of hurt and abandonment and the performances by all of the actors are exceptional.

✳ **CONNECTIONS:** Maitland the butler is played by John Mills (*Swiss Family Robinson*), Hayley's real-life father. The movie is based on a play by Enid Bagnold, who also wrote *National Velvet*.

✳ GIDGET

1959, 95 min, NR, 10 and up
Dir: Paul Wendkos. Sandra Dee, Cliff Robertson, James Darren

The original movie in the series about the surfing teenager is dated in the details, but the themes are eternal. Francie Lawrence (Sandra Dee) wants to please her loving but overprotective parents, but she also wants to grow up. She wants to be a part of the group of boys she admires on the beach, who dub her "Gidget" for "girl midget." Moondoggie (James Darren), already a part of the group, is also struggling to find himself. His parents want him to go to college, but he is drawn to the life of the Big Kahuna (Cliff Robertson), who has given up his career as a pilot to become a surfer bum.

In this gentle romantic comedy, Gidget and Moondoggie try to find themselves and learn some lessons about how much to compromise and about the consequences of choices. Even the Big Kahuna learns something about the importance of self-respect.

Kids might like to know that the original novel about Gidget was based on the real-life experiences of the author's daughter. The sequels (with other actresses in the title role) are moderately entertaining, but more superficial and sitcomlike.

✳ GOOD WILL HUNTING

1997, 126 min, R, mature high schoolers
Dir: Gus Van Sant. Matt Damon, Robin Williams, Ben Affleck, Minnie Driver

Mature teens will appreciate this story, written by its appealing young stars, about a brilliant young man with a troubled past. Will (Matt Damon), who grew up as an abused foster child in tough South Boston, works as a janitor at MIT. When he solves advanced math problems that stump the students, a professor searches for him, only to find that he is in jail for having hit a policeman. The professor promises that he will work with Will and will get him some psychiatric help. Will manages to scare off a string of therapists, so the math professor seeks out his estranged college friend, Sean (Robin Williams), a therapist. Like Will, the survivor of a tough Southie upbringing, and, like Will, still struggling with his own loss, Sean is able to help Will realize that he is not betraying his friends by using his gifts to enlarge his world. Will falls in love with Harvard premed student Skylar

(Minnie Driver). She and Sean teach him that the walls he has built to protect himself from pain are no longer needed, and are getting in his way. NOTE: Very strong all-but-incessant profanity and very explicit sexual references.

✳ GREGORY'S GIRL
1981, 91 min, PG, 12 and up
Dir: Bill Forsyth. Gordon John Sinclair, Dee Hepburn

Gregory (Gordon John Sinclair) is a gangling but amiable Scottish teenager who is mildly befuddled by just about everything, especially Dorothy (Dee Hepburn), who takes his place on the soccer team. In contrast, the girls he knows, including his ten-year-old sister, seem to understand everything in this sweet, endearing comedy with a great deal of insight and affection for its characters.

✳ THE MANHATTAN PROJECT
1986, 117 min, PG-13, 12 and up
Dir: Marshall Brickman. Christopher Collett, Cynthia Nixon

Paul Stephens (Christopher Collett) is a very bright kid with an exceptional talent for science. His mother (Jill Eikenberry) begins to date a scientist from a nearby research lab (John Lithgow), and Paul grows suspicious about what the lab is researching. He decides that he can make his point about the ethical dilemma posed by nuclear weapons (and, not incidentally, prove something to all of the people who underestimated him) by stealing plutonium from the lab to make a nuclear weapon for his science fair project, with the help of a friend from school who wants to be a journalist (Cynthia Nixon). This is a rare movie that does a convincing job of portraying smart people. The characters and performances are exceptional.

✳ **CONNECTIONS:** Writer-director Marshall Brickman has been a collaborator with Woody Allen, and shared an Oscar for the screenplay of *Annie Hall*. Television viewers will recognize John Mahoney from *Frasier*, John Lithgow from *Third Rock from the Sun*, and Jill Eikenberry from *L.A. Law*.

✳ PERMANENT RECORD
1988, 91 min, PG-13, high schoolers
Dir: Marisa Silver. Keanu Reeves, Kathy Baker

A high school senior who seems to have everything commits suicide, leaving his friends groping for clues about what was really going on inside him, and how they can put their own lives back together. Keanu Reeves plays his best friend, an underachiever who must learn that in some important way he has achieved more than his friend ever can simply by being willing to continue to face whatever challenges life holds. The reactions of the school administration will be of special interest to kids. The understanding principal knows that the students need to have a ceremony to pay some tribute to their friend, but his supervisor forbids it, saying that it will somehow make suicide seem more glamorous. And kids may also want to discuss the way that the friend who seems to be far less accomplished in reality has a core of loyalty and strength that even he had not suspected. NOTE: Rough language, alcohol and drug use by teenagers, mature themes. The boy who commits suicide has a passionless sexual relationship with a girl, with the agreement that they never ask questions of each other or share their feelings.

✳ POWDER

1995, 111 min, PG-13, high schoolers
Dir: Victor Salva. Sean Patrick Flanery, Mary Steenburgen, Jeff Goldblum

Powder (Sean Patrick Flanery) was born when his mother was struck by lightning. He was abandoned by his father as a freak because he had no skin pigmentation or hair. He stayed on his grandparents' farm, having no contact with the outside world, until their deaths, when a kind social worker (Mary Steenburgen) finds him. She discovers that he has extraordinary intellectual gifts and has memorized hundreds of books. She puts him in an institute for kids in trouble, where he astounds the bullies with his ability to give objects a powerful electric charge.

The rest of the film consists of a number of scenes in which Powder astonishes everyone with his extraordinary gifts, which include telepathy and telekinesis. While most of the locals resent and fear him, a few (including Jeff Goldblum as a science teacher) are awestruck. Ultimately, even these friends cannot protect Powder, but he finds a way to unite his energy with the powerful forces all around us.

This movie has much more appeal for teens, who will identify with the sensitive hero's inability to find a place for himself in an insensitive world, than it has for parents, who will find the plot too pedestrian for an allegory and too awkwardly constructed to garner much sympathy.

WARNING: Parents should know that one reason this film did not succeed in theatrical release was the controversy over its director-screenwriter, who served time in prison for molesting a young boy who appeared in one of his earlier films. Viewed through that lens, parts of the movie seem a bit creepy, and teens who have heard of this issue may want to discuss the life of the artist in interpreting a work of art and whether it is appropriate to boycott the film.

✳ **CONNECTIONS:** Characters with special perception abilities who feel misunderstood by those around them are particularly appealing to teenagers, because they identify most with characters who feel isolated and unappreciated. Other films with this theme include *Phenomenon* and *Charly*, films about gifted and lonely people who make those around them feel both inspired and threatened. Mature teens might also want to compare these films to *Being There* (PG, but some strong sexual references), the story of a retarded man, isolated all his life, who is perceived by politicians as brilliant when he states what he thinks in the simplest terms.

✳ ROMEO AND JULIET

1968, 138 min, PG, 12 and up
Dir: Franco Zeffirelli. Olivia Hussey, Leonard Whiting

Shakespeare's play about the "star-crossed lovers" is the ultimate tale of misunderstood teenagers. In this lush and romantic version, with the memorable Nino Rota score, the title characters are played by real teens Olivia Hussey and Leonard Whiting, only fifteen and seventeen when the movie was made.

✳ **CONNECTIONS:** *William Shakespeare's Romeo & Juliet,"* released in 1996, is a dazzling television-style staging of the play, retaining much of the original dialogue but setting it in contemporary Venice, California. Leonardo DiCaprio and Clare Danes play the lead roles, and John Leguizamo is an electrifying Tybalt.

✳ STAND BY ME

1986, 87 min, PG, 10 and up
Dir: Rob Reiner. River Phoenix, Wil Wheaton, Corey Feldman, Jerry O'Connell, Richard Dreyfus, Kiefer Sutherland

Four twelve-year-old boys hear of a dead body out in the woods and they agree to go on an overnight hike to find it so they can be on the news. They come back having learned a lot about themselves and about what it takes to be independent and brave. The friends are tough Chris Chambers (River Phoenix), sensitive Gordon LaChance (Wil Wheaton), Teddy Du-Champ (Corey Feldman), and Vern Tessio (Jerry O'Connell). The plot focuses on the relationship between Chris and Gordon, who are very different but support and learn from each other.

The movie follows the boys as they leave their small town in Oregon for an overnight hike along the tracks to where the dead body is said to be. The movie sets up the inevitable confrontation at the train tracks where the body is located between the young friends, and their older brothers who originally knew the location of the body. The confrontation proves to be nonviolent but tense.

✳ **DISCUSSION:** This movie is based on a novella by Stephen King called *The Body*, but it is by no means a horror movie. It is an especially well-crafted "road picture," with four friends learning about life and each other as they travel together. Each of the characters is appealing, but most appealing of all is the loyalty and trust they share.

PROFANITY: Schoolyard language.
NUDITY/SEXUAL REFERENCES: Minor.
ALCOHOL/DRUG ABUSE: The older brothers of the boys abuse alcohol, drink and drive, and smoke.
VIOLENCE/SCARINESS: Characters in peril; a dead body; some fistfights.
TOLERANCE/DIVERSITY ISSUES: Class issues.

※ QUESTIONS:
- Why does Chris cry when he tells the milk money story even if he did take it? Do you think it is fair for him to feel disappointed by the teacher, and by what other people expect of him?
- Why do you think Gordon's dad is so uncaring toward him?
- How are Gordon and Chris alike?
- Why is Teddy destined for failure?
- Do you think you will look back at your friends when you are grown up the way the narrator does in this story?

※ WHERE THE BOYS ARE

1960, 99 min, NR, 12 and up
Dir: Henry Levin. Paula Prentiss, Jim Hutton

Four young women leave their snow-covered college for spring vacation in Florida's Fort Lauderdale, because that's "where the boys are." This movie is very dated in its treatment of women (Paula Prentiss famously declares that all she wants is to become a "walking, talking, baby machine," and at least three of the women seem to believe that finding a husband is all that matters), but its treatment of the pressures women feel to have sex holds up surprisingly well.

Intellectually, Dolores Hart believes that it is not wrong to have sex before marriage, but she refuses handsome (and very rich) George Hamilton, and he respects her for it. Yvette Mimieux falls for a line from a boy who uses her and then passes her on to a friend. When she is the victim of what today would be called date-rape, she is so devastated that she walks out onto the highway in a daze and is hit by a car. Far more damaging is her loss of self-respect. Families with teenagers, especially teenage girls, can watch this together to talk about what has changed—and what hasn't.

※ **CONNECTIONS:** Ignore the 1984 remake, which is dreadful.

SEE ALSO:

Mask In this true story, a teenager with a severe facial disfigurement finds acceptance and a way to make a contribution to those he loves.

My Bodyguard A teenager facing a bully at school must find a way to keep both his self-respect and his lunch money.

The Sure Thing A college student who is promised a "sure thing" (a beautiful girl guaranteed to have sex with him) finds that his developing relationship with a prickly classmate becomes even more important to him.

Tex A high school student being cared for by his older brother learns to take care of himself.

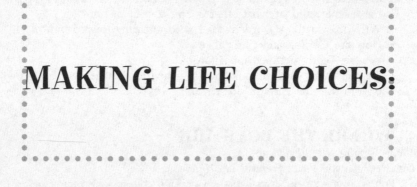

MAKING LIFE CHOICES:

"Be neither chided nor flattered out of your position of perpetual inquiry. Neither dogmatize nor accept another's dogmatism. Why should you renounce your right to traverse the star-lit deserts of truth for the premature comforts of an acre, house and barn? Truth also has its roof, bed and board."

—RALPH WALDO EMERSON

Movies provide a wonderful opportunity to talk about choices—how they are presented, how to make them. Even very young children can appreciate Robert Frost's "The Road Not Taken" and talk about how the characters in movies think about which road to take, what they consider and how much weight they give to each factor.

Sigmund Freud said that the most important elements of a healthy life are "love and work." The movies in this chapter feature characters who must make important choices about the direction of both aspects of their lives, especially about evaluating their priorities and their tolerance for risk. Over and over we see people examining their options, often discovering that what they want is not what they thought they wanted. As La Rochefoucauld said, "Before we set our hearts too much on anything, let us examine how happy are those who already possess it."

In some movies, characters have explicitly devoted their lives to a goal they must reconsider once they are close to attaining it. Usually, for men, the goal is money (and sometimes power); for women, this goal is usually represented through marriage (often to a wealthy and powerful man), the choice of husband the defining choice. In **7 Faces of Dr. Lao**, a greedy and unethical man is close to realizing his dream of economic domination of a community. In **Local Hero**, a man who measures his success by his job title and his possessions is about to succeed in an important business deal. In *I Love You Again* and in *The Music Man* a con man is about to close a successful swindle. But something makes them change direction. In *I Know Where I'm Going!* a determined young woman is close to achieving her life's dream of marriage to a wealthy and powerful man, just as in *Ball of Fire* a showgirl is about to marry a wealthy and powerful gangster. In *His Girl Friday* a woman reporter is about to leave journalism to marry a man who sells insurance. In *The Philadelphia Story* a wealthy, upper-class woman is about to marry a man who worked for her family's business. In *A Room With a View* a young woman is about to marry a rather prim but wealthy gentleman. In all of these films, the women chose men who love them for what is important to them about themselves instead. We do see men being kept by wealthy women in *An Affair to Remember*, *An American in Paris* and *Breakfast at Tiffany's*, but they are all artistic (and one of them is Cary Grant), which somehow seems to make them less dishonorable. A young woman makes an important choice about her professional life, with no romantic context, in *Up the Down Staircase*. She decides to stay with the inner-city students who need her most instead of leaving for the rarefied environment of a private school. A male teacher makes a similar choice in *To Sir, With Love*, giving up his earlier plans to be an engineer. Preston Sturges, who loved to turn convention on its head, gave us a completely different approach in *Sullivan's Travels*, in which a wealthy and successful Hollywood director tries hard to do something more "meaningful" only to discover that he was already making an important contribution.

Each of these characters is confronted with a situation or with some knowledge (particularly self-knowledge) that leads them to a different choice. In most of these movies, the character realizes that money and power are less important than love, and they want to be loved by someone who sees in them what they want seen, whether it is a side of them they have been reluctant to show or a kind of emotional honesty they have not been aware of themselves. In some, they end up alone, but happier.

These movies often provide early indications of the main character's dissatisfaction with the choices he or she has made that establish a foundation for the satisfying conclusion of changing direction. This is worth discussion in the family, for two reasons. The first is to help understand motivation, foreshadowing, and narrative structure, and develop interpretive skills and an understanding of context, all crucial in understanding literature (and in getting through high school English). The second is to develop sensitivity to indicators of motivation in ourselves and those around us. The only way to make sense of the plot of *I Love You Again* is to understand that at some level in his days as a con man, Larry really wanted a middle-class existence, and could find no other way to get there but to develop amnesia (this kind of emotional truth is one reason this is among the best of all screwball comedies). This same idea is explicit in *The Music Man*, when Harold Hill confides that he wishes he could really lead a band. And in *Lili*, we see an even clearer example, as Paul expresses his tender and vulnerable side only through the puppets.

Some movies show us characters who do not appear to have thought much about their choices. In *Awakenings*, Dr. Sayer's research position is discontinued, and he is thrust into a job treating patients. For that very reason, he brings a freshness of perspective to the chronic ward that the other doctors do not. His exposure to the patients on that ward causes him to rethink the choices that have left him isolated. Another movie with Robin Williams, **Dead Poets Society** shows us a teacher who inspires his entire class to rethink their complacent resignation about the direction of their lives and seize the day.

Movies also show us the consequences of choices, sometimes difficult or even wrong ones. Movies can show us how people make choices, and what the consequences of those choices are, but they can also remind us that we can learn from our mistakes, and go on to do better.

*Awakenings

1991, 121 min, PG-13, 10 and up
Dir: Penny Marshall. Robin Williams, Robert De Niro, Penelope Ann Miller, Julie Kavner

✳ **PLOT:** Malcolm Sayer, a shy neurologist (Robin Williams), is assigned to work with patients for the first time after his research funding is cut off. His patients, all but catatonic, are in a ward called "the garden" because their only treatment consists of "watering and feeding." Ever since an epidemic of encephalitis ("sleeping sickness") decades before, they have not spoken or appeared to understand anything that was going on around them. Everyone else has given up hope, but Sayer, approaching them as a researcher, notices that they are capable of reflex reactions, and believes that new medication used for patients with Parkinson's disease may help these patients, too. Over the objections of the doctors in charge, he gets permission to try it on one patient, Leonard Lowe (Robert De Niro).

At first, there is no reaction, but soon Leonard "awakens." His transformation is so thrilling that Malcolm is easily able to get permission and funding to treat the other patients. They, too, awaken, some more fully than others. A onetime musician does not speak, but plays the piano. Some of them are horrified at the time they have lost. But most are giddy with the pleasures of being alive. Malcolm takes Leonard outside, and Leonard's embrace of everything around him contrasts sharply with the inhibitions of Malcolm, who hesitates to try anything but his work and cannot even bring himself to have a cup of coffee with a friendly nurse (Julie Kavner).

Leonard becomes impatient to experience more. He develops a warm friendship with the daughter of another patient in the hospital (Penelope

Ann Miller). He asks for permission to leave the hospital on his own. But he becomes hyperactive, angry, and ridden with tics. The medication's side effects begin to overwhelm him. Malcolm sees that he is losing Leonard, and the other patients know that it must soon happen to them, too.

Soon, all of them are returned to their previous state of catatonia, the only evidence of their brief awakening the greater respect and affection they receive from the staff, and their impact on Malcolm, who heeds Leonard's call to life by reaching out to the nurse.

✳ **DISCUSSION:** This movie is based on the book of the same name by neurologist Oliver Sacks, who was the basis for the character Malcolm Sayer. It is a powerful and moving story, brilliantly acted and directed. Like Malcolm, we can all use a reminder to appreciate the pleasures of being alive, including the pleasures that require us to take risks.

PROFANITY: A few expletives.

NUDITY/SEXUAL REFERENCES: None.

ALCOHOL/DRUG ABUSE: None.

VIOLENCE/SCARINESS: Sad, but not scary.

TOLERANCE/DIVERSITY ISSUES: Theme of respecting the humanity of those who are different.

✳ **QUESTIONS FOR KIDS:**
- What does the neurologist mean when he says, "Because the implications of that would be unthinkable"? Why would he prefer to believe that the patients are not aware of what is going on?
- Were you surprised by the way any of the patients reacted to being "awakened"? Which reaction was most like the way you think you might feel?
- Why is it hard for Malcolm to interact with other people?
- How does Leonard change the way Malcolm behaves?
- Why does the staff treat the patients differently after the awakening, even when they go back to the way they were?

✳ **CONNECTIONS:** Compare this movie to Thornton Wilder's play *Our Town*, especially Emily's speech after her death, about what she misses and what she wants the living to be aware of.

Scriptwriter Steven Zaillian also wrote the screenplay for ***Schindler's List*** and wrote and directed ***Searching for Bobby Fischer***.

✳ **ACTIVITIES:** Teens will enjoy reading the Sacks book, and some of his others, especially *The Man Who Mistook His Wife for a Hat* and *An Anthropologist on Mars*, with astonishing and compassionate descriptions of some of his neurology patients.

Breakfast at Tiffany's

1961, 119 min, NR, 12 and up
Dir: Blake Edwards. Audrey Hepburn, George Peppard, Mickey Rooney

* **PLOT:** Paul Varjack (George Peppard), a writer who is being supported by a wealthy woman (Patricia Neal), is intrigued by his upstairs neighbor, Holly Golightly (Audrey Hepburn). Holly is an enchanting combination of breathtaking elegance, glossy Manhattan sophistication, and an engaging willingness to confide in Paul because she says he reminds her of her brother Fred. Still, she doesn't really tell him anything about herself except that she likes to go to Tiffany's when she has "the mean reds" and needs to be surrounded by something comforting. She has a very active social life, but no particular job, and she picks up money in a number of odd ways from men, the oddest being getting paid to visit an elderly mob figure in Sing Sing prison once a month.

A man seems to be following Paul, but when Paul confronts him it turns out he was following Holly. He explains he was once Holly's husband, and that he took care of Holly and Fred when their parents died and married her when she was fifteen. He has come to take her back home to rural Texas. But she tells him that she is a "wild thing" and cannot be kept in a cage, and sends him home alone.

Holly's plan is to marry a wealthy man so she can take care of Fred when he gets out of the army. She is almost successful in becoming engaged to a millionaire, but he is scared off when it turns out that she has unknowingly been carrying messages back and forth in her visits to Sing Sing. Paul comforts her when her brother is killed, and he realizes he has fallen in love with her. She will not admit to loving him, and he accuses her of being afraid to let herself become too close to anyone, even her cat. She realizes that she wants to be with someone she can really love and runs after him and the cat in the pouring rain.

* **DISCUSSION:** Holly says, "I can't think of anything I've never done," and, "I'm used to being top banana in the shock department." This might sound tawdry from most people, but she manages to make it seem as though she found it all a delicious adventure. She tries hard to protect herself from her feelings, categorizing all the men she considers possible partners for her as "rats and super rats," planning to marry a man she does not love, refusing to give Cat a real name, trying to create a world for herself that is a perpetual Tiffany's, where "nothing bad could happen to you," but it does not work. Holly's carelessness about forgetting her keys and imposing on others to get in, about her apartment decor and about Cat, and about her means of support all hide a core of pragmatic resolve, as we see in Doc Golightly's story about her, and by her devotion to Fred. They also hide her vulnerability, as though she feels that if she does not float above her emotions she will give way entirely. She does give way entirely when Fred is killed, an outpouring of real emotion that scares away the man she is cultivating.

Paul sees this because it parallels his own experience. He once cared about writing, but as the movie opens he has given up any notion of personal or artistic integrity to allow himself to be kept by a wealthy woman. Her grotesque overdecoration of his apartment makes him just another ornament for her collection. His relationship with her is his way of protecting himself from taking the risk of feeling deeply, as an artist or as a man. Paul and Holly understand each other, and that understanding makes them ashamed of the hypocrisy of their lives.

Holly describes "the mean reds" as "suddenly you're afraid, and you don't know what you're afraid of." Everyone has this feeling from time to time, but it resonates particularly with teenagers, who experience more volatile and complex emotions than any they have known before, and who tend to conclude that since these emotions are new to them, they have never been felt before. This movie provides a good opportunity to talk about those feelings and about strategies for handling them.

Parents should note that on their day in New York City together, Paul and Holly steal two masks from a dime store for fun. Although it is probably not a good idea to make heavy-handed references to this as a moral failure, in discussions with teenagers, parents may want to voice their concerns.

PROFANITY: None.

NUDITY/SEXUAL REFERENCES: Very subtle references to the fact that Holly is practically a paid escort.

ALCOHOL/DRUG ABUSE: Drinking and smoking; characters get drunk.

VIOLENCE/SCARINESS: Some mild suspense; Holly's hysteria when she receives the telegram about her brother may be scary.

TOLERANCE/DIVERSITY ISSUES: Mickey Rooney plays a Japanese man in an exaggerated style that is very insensitive by today's standards.

❋ **QUESTIONS FOR KIDS:**
- Have you ever felt "the mean reds"? Why does Tiffany's make Holly feel better when she feels that way? What makes you feel better?
- Why did Holly marry Doc? Why did she leave him?
- What makes Paul decide to break up with the woman he refers to as "2-E"?
- What did Holly's friend mean when he called Holly a "real phony"?

❋ **CONNECTIONS:** The young boys in *To Kill a Mockingbird* and *A Christmas Memory* are based on the childhood of author Truman Capote. "Moon River," one of the most memorable songs in the history of the movies, was written around Hepburn's sweet, but limited, range and won the Oscar for Best Song.

Blake Edwards enjoyed making the party scene in this movie so much that he went on to make an entire movie about a crazy party called, not surprisingly, *The Party*. It is not as good as some of his other movies, including this one, *The Great Race*, *The Pink Panther*, and (for mature teenagers only) *Days of Wine and Roses*, and *Victor/Victoria*.

❋ **ACTIVITIES:** Visit Tiffany's. The novella, by Truman Capote, is worth reading for mature teenagers, but his Paul is gay, his Holly does not have the elegance and class that Hepburn brought to the role, and his Holly does not have the Hollywood happy ending of the movie.

✳ I Know Where I'm Going!

1945, 91 min, NR, b&w, 10 and up
Dir: Michael Powell and Emeric Pressburger. Wendy Hiller, Roger Livesey

✳ **PLOT:** As a baby, as a five-year-old, as a schoolgirl, and as a young woman, Joan Webster (Wendy Hiller) always knows exactly what she wants. And whether it is "real silk stockings" instead of synthetic ones, or dinner in an elegant restaurant instead of an evening at the movies, she insists on getting it. As the movie begins, she tells her father she is about to marry one of the richest men in England, and that she is leaving that night for his island off the coast of Scotland. At each step of the trip, one of her fiancé's employees is there to make sure things go smoothly, but once she gets to Scotland the fog is so thick, she cannot take the boat to the island. That night she wishes for a wind to blow away the fog, and the next morning she finds that she has been too successful—the wind is so strong that no boats can get to the island. Stuck where she is, she meets some of the people from the community, including Torquil MacNeil (Roger Livesey), a naval officer home on leave.

"People are very poor around here," she comments to Catriona, a local woman who is a close friend of Torquil's. "Not poor, they just haven't got any money." "Same thing." "No, it isn't." While waiting for the wind to die down, Joan has a chance to see something of the life she would have as the wife of Sir Robert Bellinger. She meets his bridge-playing friends and hears of his plans to install a swimming pool on the Kiloran estate he is renting. (It turns out that he is renting it from Torquil, who is the Laird of Kiloran.) She visits a castle where Torquil's ancestors lived, and where it is said that any Laird of Kiloran who goes inside will be cursed. She goes to the sixtieth wedding anniversary party of a local couple, still very much in love.

Even though it is still not safe to take the boats out, she is desperate to leave, telling Torquil, "I'm not safe here . . . I'm on the brink of losing everything I've ever wanted since I could want anything." She pays a young man to take her out in the boat, and Torquil goes along. The boat almost sinks, and she loses the bridal gown she had planned to be married in. When it is finally safe to go, Joan and Torquil say good-bye. He asks her to have the bagpipes play for him someday, and she asks him for a kiss. They part, but she returns with three bagpipe players and joins him in the castle, where it turns out the curse provides that any Laird of Kiloran who enters will never leave it a free man. "He shall be chained to a woman until the end of his days and he shall die in his chains."

❋ **DISCUSSION:** Like *I Love You Again*, this movie falls into the category of "the life I didn't know I wanted." Joan thinks she knows what she wants and where she is going, but she is given the gift of a chance to see the alternatives. She learns that, while the people from the community miss having money, there are other things they care about more. And she learns that she can fall in love with someone who is is going in a very different direction from her ideas of "where I'm going."

This movie provides a good starting point for a discussion of how we make decisions about what we want out of life, how we pursue those goals, and what we do when we are presented either with obstacles or with new information. And it is a good starting point for a discussion of what is important, and how we determine what is important to us.

PROFANITY: None.

NUDITY/SEXUAL REFERENCES: None.

ALCOHOL/DRUG ABUSE: Drinking at a party.

VIOLENCE/SCARINESS: Reference to curse; stories of women whose infidelity leads to disaster; near shipwreck.

TOLERANCE/DIVERSITY ISSUES: None.

❋ **QUESTIONS FOR KIDS:**
- The title of this movie is taken from a famous old folk song. Why did the filmmakers choose it? Why did they insist on an exclamation point at the end of the title?
- *Does* Joan know where she is going? When does she know? Where is she going?
- What makes Joan change her mind? What do you think her life will be like?
- What is the meaning of the "terrible curse"?

❋ **CONNECTIONS:** The little girl who seems so much more mature than her parents is played by then-child actress Petula Clark, who became a pop star in the 1960s ("Downtown") and appeared in the musical version of ***Goodbye, Mr. Chips.***

❋ **ACTIVITIES:** The bagpipe plays an important role in this movie. Children might enjoy hearing more bagpipe music, especially if they can see it performed live. Look up the Hebrides, where this movie takes place, in an atlas or encyclopedia. Find out if your area has any legends like the ones described in the movie.

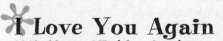

❋ I Love You Again

1940, 99 min, NR, b&w, 8 and up
Dir: W. S. Van Dyke. William Powell, Myrna Loy

❋ **PLOT:** Prissy, stingy Larry Wilson (William Powell) bores everyone aboard ship on his way back to the United States from a business trip.

When Ryan, a fellow passenger, falls overboard, Larry is accidentally knocked overboard trying to save him. Hit on the head, he comes to as George Carey, a smooth con man whose last memory is of a train ride nine years before, when someone stole the money he was taking to bet on a fight. He has no recollection of his life as Larry, in a small town called Habersville. When he finds "Larry's" bankbook with a substantial balance, he and Ryan decide to visit Habersville to get as much of it as they can.

At the dock, they are met by Larry's wife, Kay (Myrna Loy). Carey is smitten with her, but she has come to get him to agree to a divorce. They go back to Habersville together, where Carey and Ryan plan an elaborate swindle, with the help of Carey's former partner, Duke. Constantly confronted with people and questions he cannot remember, Carey manages to fake his way through, even on a hilarious hike with a Scout-like troop of boys. Kay begins to warm to him and, when she finds out the truth from Ryan, she remains loyal. Carey tries to call off the swindle and, when that does not work, resolves everything with his last con job, happily looking forward to staying in Habersville with Kay.

⁂ **DISCUSSION:** Powell and Loy appeared in more films together than any screen couple since the silents, and this delightful romantic comedy is one of their best films. Carey's horror as he finds out more and more about his life as "Larry" is balanced by Powell with smooth maneuvering to keep everyone from finding out that he can't remember anything about his life in Habersville. Loy is, as always, "the perfect wife," witty, wise and loyal— she sees the essence of the truth and is adorably charmed by it.

Amnesia of this kind occurs only in the movies and in soap operas. Even though it makes no sense medically, it does make sense dramatically. When Carey was hit on the head in a robbery nine years before, he became Larry, the boring businessman. It had to be because, on some level, a part of him wanted a "respectable life." At the end, he is neither Carey nor Larry, but a synthesis of both, ready to stay in Habersville with Kay and live happily ever after. Kay's motives are also justified. She married a bore like Larry because, as she says, she saw something exciting behind his eyes. She was the only one who glimpsed Carey inside of the stiff and proper Larry. And she also sees Carey at his best. When she says he is noble and honest, she turns out to be right.

PROFANITY: None.

NUDITY/SEXUAL REFERENCES: None

ALCOHOL/DRUG ABUSE: Carey drinks (before he gets hit on the head, his refusal to drink is a signal of his prissiness); Kay gets tipsy.

VIOLENCE/SCARINESS: A couple of punches.

TOLERANCE/DIVERSITY ISSUES: None.

⁂ **QUESTIONS FOR KIDS:**
- What does Carey do to convince everyone that he is Larry, and that he remembers his life in Habersville?

- When he is closest to being found out, how does he handle it?
- How does he con Duke into letting him out of the swindle?
- What do you think will happen after Duke leaves with the money?
- Will Carey be at all like Larry in the future? How?

✳ **CONNECTIONS:** As in *The Music Man*, this is a story about a con man who comes to a small town and is redeemed by love. Another movie with a funny scene involving a counterfeit Scout leader is *It's a Wonderful World*, with Jimmy Stewart and Claudette Colbert, and also directed by W. S. Van Dyke. A romantic drama about amnesia is *Random Harvest* in which Greer Garson marries Ronald Colman, who has forgotten his past, and loses him when he remembers it.

Any of the Powell and Loy movies are a pleasure to watch, especially *The Thin Man* series and *Libeled Lady*. Harkspur, Jr., is played by Carl "Alfalfa" Switzer of *Our Gang*.

✳ Lili

1953, 87 min, G, 6 and up
Dir: Charles Walters. Leslie Caron, Mel Ferrar, Jean Pierre Aumont, Kurt Kaszner, Zsa Zsa Gabor

✳ **PLOT:** Lili (Leslie Caron), a French orphan, is dazzled by a handsome carnival magician named Marcus (Jean Pierre Aumont) when he is friendly to her, and she follows him back to the carnival. She gets a job as a waitress there, but is fired for spending too much time watching his act. Lonely and sad, she thinks of suicide, but a puppet called Carrot Top calls out to her kindly, and she starts to talk to him and the other puppets: Golo, the simple giant who is shy with girls; Marguerite, the vain beauty; and Renaldo, the sly, crafty fox.

Paul (Mel Ferrar), the puppeteer, a bitter, angry man, offers her a job in the act. His assistant, Yacov (Kurt Kaszner), explains that he had once been a great dancer but was wounded in the war. Paul, drunk, refers to himself as "half man, half mountebank."

Audiences love Lili's conversations with the puppets because she is so sincere, and the show is very successful. She spends the money she makes on foolish games and knickknacks, and Paul angrily asks if there isn't something she really wants. At the show, the puppets gently ask the same thing, and we see Paul's face as he has the puppets tell Lili that what she wants is to be loved, and that he cares for her.

Marcus gets an offer from a hotel and leaves the carnival. It turns out he was secretly married to his assistant (Zsa Zsa Gabor). When Lili runs after Marcus to give him the ring he dropped in her trailer, Paul thinks she is running after him because she loves him, and he slaps her.

Paul is offered a wonderful opportunity to take his act to Paris. Asked by the producers if Lili is a superb actress or if he is a Svengali, he says, "She's like a little bell that gives off a pure sound no matter how you strike it, because she is in herself so good and true and pure." When he finds that they did not know he had been crippled, he is deeply moved. He has succeeded in transcending his disability and no longer sees himself as less than a complete man.

But Lili has decided to leave. She tells Marcus, "I've been living in a dream like a little girl, not seeing what I didn't want to see," and that sometimes a person outgrows dreams like a girl outgrows her dresses.

As she leaves, Carrot Top calls her back again, and asks to go with her. As each of the puppets tells her how much they care, we see Paul speaking through them. At first very touched, she thrusts back the curtain to see Paul. All he can do is speak harshly to her about the new offer, and she thinks he has been pretending to be nice to her just to get her to stay with the show.

He tells her that the puppets are the parts of him he cannot show any other way. But she runs away. On the road, she dreams of dancing with the puppets, each one transforming itself into Paul. Understanding that all of the characters she loves are really him, she runs back to him.

✳ **DISCUSSION:** This is a charming story with a lovely theme song, simply told but with a great deal of psychological insight. Lili believes what she sees on the surface. She believes the shopkeeper who offers her a job, but it turns out that he is just making a pass at her. She believes Marcus's easy charm and small tricks. She believes Paul is unfeeling. But that same naïveté is what makes her interaction with the puppets so endearingly believable. As she says, she always forgets that they are not real. Just as Paul can only open up through them, she only opens up to them.

Paul is attracted to Lili because she is such a contrast to him—she is direct, completely clear about her feelings. His leg is not as crippled as his heart. He has closed himself off, and yet his spirit needs to express itself; he needs to relate to people. So he does it through the puppets, and through them he has a freedom he could not otherwise have. When the act becomes successful, he can for the first time since his injury begin to develop the self-confidence he needs to be able to open himself up to a relationship without going through the puppets as his intermediaries.

PROFANITY: None.
NUDITY/SEXUAL REFERENCES: G-rated references to infidelity, seduction.
ALCOHOL/DRUG ABUSE: Paul gets drunk.
VIOLENCE/SCARINESS: Paul slaps Lili.
TOLERANCE/DIVERSITY ISSUES: Coming to terms with disability.

✳ **QUESTIONS FOR KIDS:**
- Why is it easier for Paul to say what he is thinking through the puppets?
- What does he mean when he says, "I am the puppets"?

- What does Lili mean when she says that people outgrow dreams?
- Why is it so important to Paul that the men who made him the offer didn't know he had a limp?

✳ **CONNECTIONS:** The story for this movie was by Paul Gallico, who was inspired by Burr Tillstrom and his television show *Kukla, Fran and Ollie*. Gallico was a prolific writer who enjoyed writing in a variety of genres, and films made from his work include, *Pride of the Yankees*, *The Three Lives of Thomasina*, and *The Poseidon Adventure*.

✳ **ACTIVITIES:** Put on a puppet show. Let the kids try to make puppets that express different parts of themselves or behave in ways they cannot.

✳Local Hero

1983, 111 min, PG, 12 and up
Dir: Bill Forsyth. Peter Riegert, Burt Lancaster

✳ **PLOT:** McIntyre (Peter Riegert) is an ambitious executive with Knox Oil & Gas, based in Houston, Texas. He is dispatched by Happer (Burt Lancaster), the company's eccentric billionaire chief executive, to a remote corner of Scotland to acquire a fishing village named Ferness and the land surrounding it for an oil refinery and storage facility.

McIntyre, all business, arrives in Ferness with Danny Oldsen (Peter Capaldi), a Knox employee from Scotland. At first, McIntyre finds it hard to adjust to the pace of Ferness. Gordon Urquhart (Denis Lawson), the local innkeeper and resident accountant, tells him to enjoy the area for a couple of days before they open negotiations. Gordon tells the villagers about the offer from Knox. They are delighted at the prospect of being bought out and begin to debate the relative merits of a Rolls-Royce over a Maserati. The only hitch to finalizing the deal is Ben, a reclusive beachcomber who lives in a shack by the shore. He owns several miles of beach and refuses to sell.

Meanwhile, McIntyre sheds his hurried Houston style and comes to enjoy the tranquil rhythms of the village. In a whiskey-induced moment, he tells Urquhart that he wants them to swap jobs. Following Happer's order to "watch the sky," he is dazzled by the aurora borealis, the northern lights, and calls Happer to report.

Happer arrives from Houston. He establishes an instant rapport with Ben and decides that instead of the refinery, he will create an observatory and marine laboratory—the Happer Institute. McIntyre is sent back to Texas to organize the changes. McIntyre returns to Houston, deeply missing the charm and character of his brief Highland life.

✳ **DISCUSSION:** McIntyre's life in Houston is cluttered but empty. He resorts to phoning colleagues seated ten yards away to see if they are free for lunch. He cares a great deal about material things. In Ferness, his expensive watch falls into the water, and he doesn't miss it. He learns to enjoy collecting shells and examining the night sky.

In a poignant final shot we see McIntyre calling the village's pay phone. It rings and rings, but no one answers. The suggestion is that while the village has invaded McIntyre's soul, he has not had a similar impact in return. McIntyre represented a fleeting interest in lives that run to slower rhythms.

The film is to be noted less for its messages or themes than its magnificent cast of quirky, delightfully observed characters and gorgeous location photography. There is a touch of magic in the story, with a marine biologist who seems to be part mermaid, and a deus ex machina happy ending for most of the characters.

NOTE: This movie has the feel of a fairy tale, but there are some odd moments that may bother some kids. Happer hires a "therapist" for a bizarre "abuse therapy." Danny saves a rabbit that is then cooked and served to Danny and McIntyre by Gordon. And the very un-Hollywood resolution, with McIntyre back in Texas by himself, should prompt some discussion of what kids think may happen to him.

PROFANITY: Mild.

NUDITY/SEXUAL REFERENCES: Gordon and his wife have frequent (offscreen) sex; McIntyre uses a mild epithet when he is angry at his former girlfriend.

ALCOHOL/DRUG ABUSE: A great deal of social drinking; McIntyre gets drunk.

VIOLENCE/SCARINESS: None.

TOLERANCE/DIVERSITY ISSUES: Tolerance of individual differences.

✳ **QUESTIONS FOR KIDS:**
- What does McIntyre list as the requirements for an excellent life in Houston? Do the villagers agree with him, since all but Ben are anxious to sell?
- Why does the girl with the punk outfit say that she likes McIntyre?
- Why didn't Ben want to sell?
- Why, when McIntyre calls the village pay phone at the end of the film, does no one answer?

✳ **CONNECTIONS:** Forsyth is also the director of the wonderful *Gregory's Girl*.

✳ **ACTIVITIES:** Find Scotland on a map. Visit a marine study facility like the one they plan to build in Ferness.

The Music Man

1962, 151 min, NR, 6 and up
Dir: Morton Da Costa. Robert Preston, Shirley Jones, Buddy Hackett, Ronny
Howard, Hermione Gingold, Paul Ford

✳ **PLOT:** "Professor" Harold Hill (Robert Preston) is a con man posing as a salesman of band instruments and uniforms. He happens upon River City, a small town in Iowa. As the citizens explain in song, Iowa is a place of stubborn people who keep to themselves unless someone needs help. But Hill happens upon an old friend, Marcellus Washburn (Buddy Hackett), and is ready to run his favorite scam. He plans to sell the town on the idea of a boys' band, with himself as leader, get them to order instruments and uniforms, and skip town with the money. Marcellus tells him a bit about the town and its people, and especially about the town librarian and music teacher, Marian Paroo (Shirley Jones).

Marian lives with her mother (Pert Kelton) and her little brother, Winthrop (Ronny Howard), a shy boy with a lisp, who deeply mourns his late father. In her own way, Marian, like Winthrop, is still grieving, and finds it hard to allow herself to become close to anyone. This is especially difficult because she is the subject of some gossip in the town. She has the job as librarian because an elderly man, a friend of her father's, bequeathed the library building to the town, but left the books to her, to ensure that she would have permanent employment. This has caused some speculation about their relationship. And the ladies in the town also think the books she recommends (including the *Rubaiyat of Omar Khayyam* and Balzac) are improper. Despite her mother's attempts to encourage her to be friendlier, Marian is very skeptical about Harold's motives and his credentials. He is able to dazzle the town (with the famous patter song "Trouble," offering the band as an alternative to the decadence of the town's new pool parlor), but she vows to check his credentials.

The town gets caught up in the notion of the band. Harold's charm and smooth promises enrapture everyone from the town council (he transforms them from four squabbling politicians into a harmonizing barbershop quartet) to the teenage boy all the others look up to (Harold challenges him to invent an apparatus for holding the music so that the piccolo player can read it and encourages his romance with the mayor's daughter). Harold even charms Winthrop, who is at last excited and happy about something. Harold tells all the parents that their children are wonderfully gifted and that the band will make them stars. Meanwhile, Harold's attention to Marian is becoming more than just a way to help him get the money. And, despite evidence that he does not have the credentials he claims, and her certainty that he is not what he pretends to be, she finds herself softening toward him and protecting him.

Because of her, he stays too long, and he is arrested. As he says, "For the first time, I got my foot caught in the door." But somehow, the boys force a few sounds out of the instruments, enough for their proud parents.

And Harold stays on—it turns out that all along, deep inside, what he really wanted was to lead a band.

✳ **DISCUSSION:** Robert Preston brought his award-winning performance as Harold Hill on Broadway to the screen in this impeccable production, perfect in every detail. In addition to the glorious production, with some of the most gorgeous music and dancing ever filmed, there is a fine story with appealing characters. Marian learns about the importance of dreams from Harold, and he learns about the importance of responsibility from her.

Harold has made a life out of other people's dreams, creating them and then spoiling them. He gives people an image of themselves as important and creative, and it is clear that this is what he loves about what he does, not stealing the money from them. Marian has faith in Harold. It is not the blind faith of the rest of the town, the people who see the seventy-six trombones he sings about. She sees what is good inside him, the real way that he affects people like Winthrop, the way he affects her. (She sings, "There were bells on the hills, but I never heard them ringing, oh, I never heard them at all, 'til there was you.") When Marian sees Harold and is willing to love him in spite of his past, he is for the first time able to move on from the notion of himself as a thief and a liar. Each finds the core of the other, allowing both of them to heal and take the risk necessary to make their dreams come true. For him, the risk is prison and disgrace. For her, the risk is the kind of hurt she felt when her father died, the risk we all take in loving someone. And because this is a musical, they live happily ever after.

PROFANITY: None.

NUDITY/SEXUAL REFERENCES: Very oblique speculation by the "Pick a Little, Talk a Little" ladies and by Harold and Marcellus about why the elderly gentleman donated the library building to the city but left the books to Marian; also, criticism of the raciness of the books she recommends; Harold's song about the "Sadder But Wiser Girl for Me" describes (in G-rated terms) his preference for women with some sexual experience.

ALCOHOL/DRUG ABUSE: None.

VIOLENCE/SCARINESS: None.

TOLERANCE/DIVERSITY ISSUES: None.

✳ **QUESTIONS FOR KIDS:**
- Why is Winthrop so shy? What makes him change?
- How does Harold change people's minds? Is that good or bad?
- How does the music help to tell the story? Listen to the songs "Seventy-six Trombones" and "Good Night, My Someone" again. They are very much alike, as you can tell when they are sung together. What did the composer want that to tell you about the people who sing them?

- Why were the parents worried about their children playing pool? What do parents worry about today?
- How is Marian's library like yours? Do you know your librarian? Do people in your town ever argue about what books should be in the library?

✳ **CONNECTIONS:** This movie shows some of the most talented people of their time at the top of their form. Shirley Jones appeared in many musicals, including *Oklahoma!* and *Carousel*, always exquisitely lovely in voice and appearance. She also won an Oscar for her dramatic role as a prostitute in *Elmer Gantry*. And of course she was the mother in television's musical comedy series, *The Partridge Family*.

Robert Preston had more luck in theater than in movies finding roles that gave him a chance to show all he could do. But every one of his film appearances is worth watching, including *The Last Starfighter* and *All the Way Home*. Choreographer Oona White also did the sensational dance numbers in *Bye Bye Birdie*. Composer Meredith Wilson never again came close to the glorious score for *The Music Man*, but he produced some nice songs for *The Unsinkable Molly Brown*.

Ninotchka

1939, 101 min, NR, b&w, 10 and up
Dir: Ernst Lubitsch. Greta Garbo, Melvyn Douglas

✳ **PLOT:** Three Soviet bureaucrats arrive in Paris to sell some jewels so they can buy tractors. But the former Grand Duchess Swana (Ina Claire), who lives in Paris, is outraged because they were her jewels confiscated during the Russian Revolution. Her beau, Count Leon (Melvyn Douglas), goes to court on her behalf, seeking return of the jewels. More importantly, he goes to the three Russians and plies them with wine, food, and fun to distract them from their mission.

The Soviets respond by sending a stern and severe senior official, Lena Yakushova (Greta Garbo), to straighten things out. Leon, who calls her by the nickname "Ninotchka," is unsuccessful in persuading her to enjoy the pleasures of Paris. Finally, he just tries to make her laugh. She is unmoved by even his best jokes, but when he falls over in his chair, she laughs uproariously. From then on, she warms to the pleasures of Paris and the charms of Leon. She dons an elegant little hat and a glamorous gown. She drinks champagne until she is tipsy.

Swana gets the jewels from a hotel employee sympathetic to the exiled Russian nobility. She tells Ninotchka she will give them back if Ninotchka will leave Paris (and Leon) immediately. Given her duty to the Soviet Union, Ninotchka has no choice. But soon, based on the success of their mission, the same three men are dispatched to Constantinople to sell furs, and soon

Leon has corrupted them again and Ninotchka is sent to straighten things out. This time Leon is waiting for her, so they can stay together forever.

❊ **DISCUSSION:** Kids will need some introduction to the issues behind this enchanting romantic comedy. A few words about the state of the Soviet Union following the Revolution and the different ideas of the Communists and the capitalists will prepare them. The movie is really not about politics; it is about romance, and being open to the pleasures of life. Leon learns as much about this as Ninotchka does. Before she arrives, he is in what looks more like a business partnership than a love affair with Swana. He does not introduce the Soviets to food, drink, and girls in order to teach them about having a good time, but in a calculated attempt to profit. Ninotchka makes an emotionally honest man out of him as he makes an emotionally honest woman out of her. And note that as much as Ninotchka loves Leon, she will not compromise on her duty to her country. She completes her mission, even though she knows it may mean she will never see him again.

In a way, the story is the obverse of **Born Yesterday** and **My Fair Lady**. The women in those stories grow by using their intellect; Ninotchka grows by using her emotions.

Ernst Lubitsch was the master of the sophisticated romantic comedy. Close observers of his films notice that he often uses doors to tell the story. An example in this film is the way the count's successful corruption of the Soviet emissaries is shown through a succession of delightful treats being delivered to them through the doors of their hotel suite.

PROFANITY: None.
NUDITY/SEXUAL REFERENCES: None, though an intimate relationship between Swana and Leon is implied.
ALCOHOL/DRUG ABUSE: Festive drinking; Ninotchka gets tipsy on champagne.
VIOLENCE/SCARINESS: None.
TOLERANCE/DIVERSITY ISSUES: Ninotchka is a high-ranking and highly respected official.

❊ **QUESTIONS FOR KIDS:**
• If they had gone to court, who would have won the jewels? What is the best argument for each side?
• What does Swana try to do when she sees Ninotchka at the nightclub?
• What would you say the "moral" of this little romantic comedy is?

❊ **CONNECTIONS:** This movie had one of the most famous ad slogans of all time: "Garbo Laughs." The mysterious dramatic actress had not made a comedy before. Director Ernst Lubitsch reported that when he was considering her for the part, he asked her if she could laugh, and she said she would let him know, and then came back the next day to say she could, and to show him. **Silk Stockings** is a musical version of this story, with songs by Cole Porter. An odd update made in 1956 with Katharine Hepburn and Bob Hope(!) is called *The Iron Petticoat*.

Compare this movie to **Ball of Fire** by the same screenwriting team, another story of an intellectual who is taught to appreciate the more frivolous pleasures of life.

❋ **ACTIVITIES:** Older kids may want to read more about this era in Soviet history, or find out about the fall of the U.S.S.R. and the current efforts of the former Soviet states at capitalism and democracy.

❋The Quiet Man
1952, 129 min, NR, 8 and up
Dir: John Ford. John Wayne, Maureen O'Hara, Barry Fitzgerald

❋ **PLOT:** Tall American Sean Thornton (John Wayne) arrives in Innisfree, a small, beautiful Irish village, and meets Michaeleen Flynn (Barry Fitzgerald), who drives him into town. Something of a busybody, Michaeleen is very curious and is delighted to find that Sean was born in Innisfree, and that he has come back to buy back his family home and settle there. Over the objections of "Squire" Will Danaher (Victor McLaglen), a huge fiery man, Sean buys the cottage, called White O'Morning, from the Widow Tillane (Mildred Natwick), a wealthy woman who owns the adjoining property, and settles in.

Sean sees Will's sister, Mary Kate Danaher (Maureen O'Hara), out in a field and is immediately struck by her. Sean finds her in his cottage, "being neighborly" by cleaning it for him, and he grabs her and kisses her. He sees her again at church. He approaches her as he would approach an American girl, but finds that the customs are different in Ireland, and that if he wants to court Mary Kate, he must do it according to quaint, old-fashioned rules, with the permission of her brother. Will's objections to their courtship are overcome by Father Lonergan (Ward Bond) and others, who persuade Will that he must allow Mary Kate to marry in order to be able himself to marry the Widow Tillane. He grudgingly consents, and allows them to proceed under the eye of a chaperon, none other than Michaeleen, who reminds them, "The proprieties must be observed." They drive off with Michaeleen, sitting on opposite sides of a wagon, but they get off the wagon and run away together, and as they are drenched by a sudden rainstorm, they cannot wait for "the proprieties" any longer, and they kiss.

At the wedding, Will finds that he has been tricked, and that the Widow Tillane does not want her acquiescence to marry him taken for granted. He is furious. He refuses to give Mary Kate her dowry or the fine furniture she inherited from her mother. Sean does not care, and cannot understand why it is important to Mary Kate. All he wants is her. But far from being reassured by this, Mary Kate is hurt. She feels that her things and her dowry are part of who she is and part of what she brings to the marriage, and that if Sean cared about her he would fight for them. They sleep apart.

The next morning, their friends arrive with the furniture. They have "persuaded" Will to give it to her. But he still won't give her the dowry. Although they love each other deeply, Sean and Mary Kate cannot resolve that problem. Mary Kate is ashamed of herself and ashamed of Sean, and goes to the train station, planning to leave him. He follows her and drags her back to a confrontation with Will, telling Will that if he will not pay the dowry, he must take her back. Will gives them the money, and together, they burn it. Mary Kate smiles with delight and tells Sean she will go home and prepare supper for him.

Will and Sean then enter into an epic fistfight, which takes them all the way through the town as crowds gather to watch, cheer, and bet on the outcome. Finally, bruised, drunk, and happy, they arrive at White O'Morning for supper, Will bawling happily, "Bless all in this house."

✳ **DISCUSSION:** Some critics have claimed that this is an antifeminist movie, but that is a very superficial perspective. The furniture and money are important to Mary Kate because she wants to enter the relationship as an equal. She believes that without them she will be to Sean what she was in Will's house, just someone to do the work. She says, "Until I've got my dowry safe about me, I'm no married woman. I'm the servant I've always been, without anything of my own!" But it is just as important to Sean to let her know that what he cares about is his love for her, and that alone is enough to make her an equal partner. For this reason, burning the money, which might otherwise seem foolishly wasteful, was a way for them to each win a victory.

Sean also has to conquer his fear of fighting, which requires him to open up emotionally. As "Trouper Thorn," a professional boxer in the United States, he accidentally killed an opponent in the ring. This left him afraid to let go. In the fights with Will and Mary Kate he learns that he can let go physically and emotionally and strengthen his relationships. Notice how Sean and Mary Kate seem to affect even the weather as they fall in love. Gusty winds and torrential rain reflect the emotions they are feeling for each other.

PROFANITY: None.

NUDITY/SEXUAL REFERENCES: References (fairly subtle) to the fact that Mary Kate and Sean do not sleep together following their wedding. Seeing a broken bed frame following the wedding night, Michaeleen, says, "Impetuous! Homeric!"

ALCOHOL/DRUG ABUSE: A lot of drinking in pubs; references to Michaeleen's "terrible thirst"; drunkenness.

VIOLENCE/SCARINESS: Fistfight. (Flashback to Sean's professional boxing career, in which he accidentally killed another boxer, which is the reason he is reluctant to fight in Ireland.) References to ability of married couples to hit each other.

TOLERANCE/DIVERSITY ISSUES: Some prejudice against Sean as an American and an outsider. Very nice depiction of religious tolerance, as the Catholic priest tells his parishioners to pretend they are congregants of the Protestant minister, so he can impress his bishop with how many members he has in his congregation. Brief references to a (nonviolent) IRA.

By today's standards, the scene where Sean drags Mary Kate quite forcibly from the train to her brother's house (and where a woman from the village hands him a stick to "beat the lovely lady with") and Michaeleen tells Mary Kate not to hit Sean until they are married, when he will be entitled to hit her back, are quite sexist, but the essence of the story shows that Mary Kate and Sean are equals in the marriage.

✳ **QUESTIONS FOR KIDS:**
- Sean and Mary Kate loved each other very much, but had a hard time understanding each other. Why was Mary Kate's dowry so important to her? How did Sean show he understood that?
- Why did they burn the money? Was that a good way to solve the problem of the dowry for both of them?
- How did Sean's friends persuade Mary Kate's brother to let Sean marry her? Was that fair?
- Why did Sean and Will like each other better after fighting each other?

✳ **CONNECTIONS:** One of the highlights of *E.T.* is the scene in which E. T. is in Eliot's house alone, watching *The Quiet Man* on television. We see his connection to Eliot; E. T. sees Sean kiss Mary Kate as the wind rushes through the cottage, and Eliot, at school, grabs a classmate and gives her a kiss.

Maureen O'Hara, born in Ireland, was never more ravishing than here on her home ground, shot in magnificent technicolor. She and Wayne made four other films together, including *Rio Grande*, also directed by Ford. She also plays the mother in **Miracle on 34th Street** and **The Parent Trap.**

This was quite a family affair. The Reverend Cyril Playfair is played by character actor Arthur Shields, in real life the brother of Barry Fitzgerald (Michaeleen). Francis Ford, who plays the man who gets off his deathbed to watch the fight, is the older brother of director John Ford. Wayne's four children and two of O'Hara's brothers also appear in the movie.

Ford won an Oscar for Best Director.

A Room With a View

1985, 115 min, NR, 10 and up
Dir: James Ivory. Helena Bonham Carter, Maggie Smith, Julian Sands, Daniel Day-Lewis

✳ PLOT: Lucy Honeychurch (Helena Bonham Carter) arrives in Italy with her straitlaced aunt Charlotte (Maggie Smith). Disappointed at not getting the room with a view they had been promised when making their reservations at the inn, they are not sure whether it is proper to accept the offer of Mr. Emerson (Denholm Elliot) and his son George (Julian Sands), staying at the same inn, to switch rooms so they may have a view after all. Reassured by the clergyman, Mr. Beebe (Simon Callow), they agree.

Later, out in the countryside, George impetuously kisses Lucy, and her aunt, horrified, whisks her back to England. There, Lucy is engaged to Cecil, a prissy man who likes Lucy's "freshness" and "subtlety" and kisses her lightly only after asking her permission. Mr. Beebe says, "If Miss Honeychurch ever takes to live as she plays (the piano), it will be very exciting—both for us and for her." He clearly does not think the engagement to Cecil is evidence that she has.

The Emersons move into a cottage near the Honeychurch family, invited by Cecil, who does not realize that Lucy knows them. Lucy is distressed, partly because she wanted two elderly ladies she met in Italy to live there, and partly because having George so near is disturbing to her. She does her best to resist her attraction to him and to the passionate reality that he offers, but ultimately breaks the engagement to Cecil, marries George, and returns with him to the room with a view.

✳ DISCUSSION: Lush natural settings have a powerful affect on fictional characters, especially those in love or wanting to fall in love. In Shakespeare, lovers go to the woods to straighten things out. In the British literature of the nineteenth and early twentieth century, they often go to Italy, which represents freedom from repression, with *Enchanted April* and this film as prime examples. The wheat field where George kisses Lucy is in sharp contrast to the manicured lawns of the Honeychurch home, as the precise and cerebral Cecil is in contrast to the passionate George.

This is a movie about having the courage to face one's feelings, and to risk intimacy, fully knowing and being known by another person. George never hesitates to take that risk. Cecil, sensitively played by Daniel Day-Lewis as a full character and not a caricature of a fop, has feelings but will never be able to "take to live as (he) plays." Clearly, he does care deeply for Lucy, but he does not have the passionate nature to respond to hers fully, as George does. As George says, Cecil "is the sort who can't know anyone intimately, least of all a woman." Cecil wants Lucy as an ornament, perhaps to enjoy her passionate nature by proxy, not realizing that his own proximity is likely to stifle it. George wants Lucy "to have ideas and thoughts and feelings, even when I hold you in my arms."

PROFANITY: None.

NUDITY/SEXUAL REFERENCES: Brief nude scenes as the men go swimming (and as they run when the women approach); overall theme of the importance of sensuality.

ALCOHOL/DRUG ABUSE: None.

VIOLENCE/SCARINESS: None.

TOLERANCE/DIVERSITY ISSUES: None.

✳ QUESTIONS FOR KIDS:
- Mr. Emerson refers to a "Yes! And a Yes! And a Yes" at the "side of the Everlasting Why." What does this mean?
- What leads Lucy to break her engagement to Cecil? What leads her to accept her feelings for George?
- What is the meaning of the title?

✳ CONNECTIONS: Some of the themes of this movie are reminiscent of movies like *I Know Where I'm Going!, Born Yesterday, Sabrina, Breakfast at Tiffany's, It Happened One Night,* and others in which the leading lady ends up marrying someone other than the man she'd planned to marry, choosing true love and intimacy over comfort and a relationship that seemed safer.

✳ ACTIVITIES: Teenagers might enjoy the book by E. M. Forster, and some of his other books, including *Howards End.*

✳The Sound of Music

1965, 174 min, NR, 6 and up
Dir: Robert Wise. Julie Andrews, Christopher Plummer

✳ PLOT: This beloved musical is the fictionalized story of Maria von Trapp (Julie Andrews). It is an outstanding family film, filled with glorious music ("Do Re Mi", "My Favorite Things", "Edelweiss", "So Long, Farewell"), a real-life love story right out of *Jane Eyre*, a courageous moral choice, and a heart-stopping escape.

As a postulant, Maria is "not a credit to the Abbey." While she means well, she is constantly in trouble. The wise Mother Abbess sends her away to be the governess for the seven children of a stern widower, Captain von Trapp. Obedient to their disciplinarian father, the children are uncooperative with Maria until she wins them over with her own high spirits, as well as her kindness. She also shares her love of music and her joy in the beauty around them, and they become devoted to one another.

The captain's friend Max (Richard Hadyn) hears the children sing and wants them to perform at the local festival. But the captain refuses, thinking it is foolish and inappropriate. Meanwhile, the captain is considering marriage to a titled and wealthy woman, and his oldest daughter, Leisel, is beginning a romance with Rolfe. And as the Nazis threaten control of Austria, the captain knows that his military skill and experience will lead them to him. He knows that they will ask him to join them, and that they will not accept a negative answer.

Maria, realizing that she has fallen in love with the captain, runs back to the Abbey. But the Mother Abbess counsels her to follow her heart, and she returns to the children. The captain realizes that he loves Maria, and they are married in the Abbey. They return from their honeymoon to find that an invitation to join the Nazi Navy is waiting.

Max has put the children on the festival program, hoping the captain would relent. He forbids them to participate and makes plans to escape. But when the Nazis arrive to stop him, he explains that they are just on their way to perform at the festival. The Nazis escort them to the festival, where they win first prize and use their encore number to camouflage their escape. On their way out of Austria, they are betrayed by Rolfe, now a Nazi, but they are protected by the nuns in the Abbey, and they leave for Switzerland, over Maria's beloved mountains.

✻ **DISCUSSION:** A number of people in this movie must make important choices when they face challenges that are completely unexpected. Maria and the captain both thought they had established what their lives would be like. Maria planned to be a nun and live in the Abbey all her life. Maria's unexpected challenge comes from within herself. She is lucky to have the wise Mother Abbess help her examine her heart to learn that she is better suited for a life outside the Abbey. The Captain expected to continue with the life he had, a loving but stern father to his children and a respected aristocrat and military leader. His family had always lived in Austria, and he expected his children and grandchildren would live there, too.

The captain is used to being in control. It may be that his regimental approach to the children is as much prompted by a need to feel in greater control following the loss of his wife as it is by his military training. His original inclination to marry the baroness seems to be led by his head rather than his heart; it feels more like an alliance than a romance. But he finds that he cannot resist Maria's warm and loving heart.

Just as all of this is happening, every aspect of the life they had known in Austria is challenged by the Nazis. Unlike his friends, the captain does not have the option of making a slight accommodation to the Nazis. He must fight for them if he wants to keep his home. He gives up every material possession he has to get away, preserving freedom for himself and his family.

Everyone in Austria has to make a choice when the Nazis arrive. Rolfe becomes so committed to the Nazis that he is willing to betray the young woman he cared for. Even the nuns in the Abbey must make a choice. They decide to protect the Von Trapps and impede the Nazis, risking their own freedom. Children, especially young children, will need some background to understand what these choices involved and what the risks were. It is also worthwhile to discuss with them the sweet song that the captain sings to Maria, telling her that he must have done something good in his past to deserve her love and the happiness she has given him.

PROFANITY: None.

NUDITY/SEXUAL REFERENCES: None.

ALCOHOL/DRUG ABUSE: None.

VIOLENCE/SCARINESS: Tension as the family escapes.

TOLERANCE/DIVERSITY ISSUES: None.

✳ QUESTIONS FOR KIDS:
- Why does Maria have a problem fitting in at the Abbey?
- What does the captain learn from Maria?
- The same people wrote the song about "My Favorite Things" in "Sound of Music" and "Whistle a Happy Tune" in *The King and I.* How are they alike? (Think about when it is that Maria sings the song.) If you were going to write the song, what would be on your list of favorite things?
- What is the difference in the way the captain, Max, and Rolfe each react to the Nazis?
- What does the song "Climb Every Mountain" mean?

✳ CONNECTIONS: Sister Sophia is played by Marni Nixon, a rare on-screen appearance by the off-screen singing voice from *My Fair Lady, West Side Story, and The King and I.*

✳ ACTIVITIES: Kids who enjoy this movie can read more about the real-life family in one of the books written by Maria von Trapp, and can visit the family's lodge in Stowe, Vermont. Find Austria, Germany, and Switzerland on a map but do not try to trace the family's escape route. If they had climbed over the mountains they took in the movie, they would have ended up in Germany.

✳ AN AFFAIR TO REMEMBER

1957, 115 min, NR, 10 and up

Dir: Leo McCarey. Cary Grant, Deborah Kerr

This schmaltzy classic, immortalized in *Sleepless in Seattle,* is about two people (Cary Grant and Deborah Kerr), both more or less "kept" by wealthy lovers, who meet on an ocean voyage and fall deeply in love. In order to prove themselves worthy of these feelings, they make a commitment to separate for six months, to support themselves through their work to see if they are both really willing to live that way together. When she is seriously injured on her way to meet him (at the top of the Empire State Building), he believes she has decided that she is not willing. He is deeply hurt, but his feelings for her have made it impossible for him to return to his old life. Fast-forward through the part with the singing kids and linger over the classic weepy ending, when he discovers the real reason she was not there to meet him.

✳ **CONNECTIONS:** The original version, *Love Affair*, by the same director, stars Irene Dunne and Charles Boyer, and is just as good. But stay away from the 1994 remake with Warren Beatty and Annette Bening.

✳ SENSE AND SENSIBILITY
1995, 135 min, PG, 10 and up
Dir: Ang Lee. Emma Thompson, Kate Winslet, Hugh Grant, Alan Rickman

Based on Jane Austen's first published novel, this is the story of two sisters, one representing "sense" (rationality) and one "sensibility" (emotion). Each falls in love, and each must struggle with the limitations of trying to conduct herself exclusively according to one of those extremes. One (Emma Thompson, who also wrote the Oscar-winning screenplay) almost loses her chance at happiness from an excess of prudence, and the other (Kate Winslet) almost loses her reputation and self-respect from an excess of romantic ardor. When the man she thinks she loves turns out to be unworthy of her admiration, she is shattered. But she finds that, contrary to her "sensibility," it is possible to love again, and that the heart and the head can work together to achieve love.

SEE ALSO:

His Girl Friday A reporter, recently divorced from her editor, decides to marry an insurance salesman and live a quiet life, until the editor finds a way to remind her how much she loves her work—and how much she loves him.

Holiday All three leading characters are faced with a choice between a life of comfort and status and a life of adventure and meaning.

Pat and Mike A superb—but insecure—athlete finds that she wants something more than a quiet life in a college town with a fiancé who does not have confidence in her.

The Philadelphia Story An heiress about to marry a "man of the people" discovers that spirit, intelligence, and understanding can be found in the upper classes as well as the lower.

Sullivan's Travels A successful movie director wants to make serious films, until he finds out that it is comedies that provide the greatest benefit to those in need.

Part 3

Just for Fun

Action and Adventure

"We triumph without glory when we conquer without danger."
—CORNEILLE

Action and adventure movies allow us to identify with brave heroes (and a few brave heroines) who go places and take on challenges we can only dream of. Some seek knowledge, some protect themselves or others, and some decide to right a wrong, but all display courage, quick thinking, and imagination. As we watch, we have the pleasure of feeling that they are in terrible peril and the satisfaction of seeing them get out of it.

As with mysteries, some kids may be overwhelmed by the tension of these movies, even if they are reassured that it will all be okay in the end. Many of the films present good examples of problem-solving and show us characters making moral choices or dealing with consequences of choices already made. They also give us a chance to think about the nature of heroism. But most of all, these movies are fun, and especially fun to watch together, to cheer on the good guys and boo at the bad guys.

King Solomon's Mines
1950, 103 min, NR, 8 and up
Dir: Compton Bennett and Andrew Marton. Stewart Granger, Deborah Kerr

PLOT: Elizabeth Curtis (Deborah Kerr) hires the best "white hunter" in Africa (Stewart Granger as dashing Allan Quartermain) to help her find her husband, who was lost searching for the legendary King Solomon's diamond mines. At first, he refuses, saying that women have no place on safari. When she offers twenty times his usual fee, he accepts but he remains skeptical about her motives and about her ability to survive the trip. In the traditional "road movie" fashion, they develop respect and affection through their adventures.

DISCUSSION: This is the best of the many versions of the classic adventure novel by H. Rider Haggard. The story (and the performances) are a bit creaky, but it is an old-fashioned Technicolor spectacular, with breathtaking Oscar-winning cinematography. Filmed on location in Kenya, and the then-Tanganyika and Belgian Congo, the outtakes from this movie were used in several other movies, including the otherwise poor 1977 remake. The footage of the landscapes and of the animals is strikingly clear and vivid, especially an unforgettable shot of a just-uncurling brand-new baby alligator and the scenes of the Watusi dancing. NOTE: Some children may be disturbed by the violence, and others may be upset by the scene in which Elizabeth Curtis admits that she did not love her husband and that she is seeking him out of guilt rather than devotion.

PROFANITY: None.
NUDITY/SEXUAL REFERENCES: None.
ALCOHOL/DRUG ABUSE: The bad (white) guy drinks brandy.
VIOLENCE/SCARINESS: Some, including fights to the death with various weapons.
TOLERANCE/DIVERSITY ISSUES: This movie is based on a late nineteenth-century novel of the colonialist era and reflects its views and assumptions. The African natives are treated respectfully (that is, they are treated as individuals with a right to their own way of doing things), but the main characters are the white English people. Umbopa (played by Watusi actor Siriaque), who joins the expedition as a bearer but turns out to be the rightful Watusi chief, has such presence and power that he lends some balance to the story.

✳ **QUESTIONS FOR KIDS:**
- How did Elizabeth Curtis and Allan Quartermain learn to trust each other? How could you tell?
- Would you have liked to go on that safari? Which part was the scariest?
- What would you do if you found the diamonds?

✳ **CONNECTIONS:** *King Solomon's Mines*, by H. Rider Haggard, remains an exciting adventure novel (without the romance added by the screenplay). The 1937 version includes Paul Robeson (football star, opera singer, lawyer, and radical) as Umbopa.

✳ THE ANDROMEDA STRAIN
1971, 131 min, G, 10 and up
Dir: Robert Wise. Arthur Hill, David Wayne, Kate Reid

A group of top scientists must track down a mysterious virus that has wiped out an entire town with only two exceptions: an alcoholic old man and a baby with colic. This is a tense and absorbing drama, based on the book by Michael Crichton (*Jurassic Park*). Particularly worth discussion are the processes the scientists use to analyze the problem, the mistakes they make and the way they respond to them. The movie is ambiguous at best about whether the efforts of the humans caused more problems than they solved. NOTE: It would probably be rated PG today; not for younger children.

✳ AROUND THE WORLD IN 80 DAYS
1956, 167 min, NR, 8 and up
Dir: Michael Anderson. David Niven, Shirley MacLaine

Phileas Fogg (David Niven) bets his fellow club members that he can go around the world in eighty days in this exciting and colorful Best Picture Oscar–winner, based on the book by Jules Verne. The voyage, set in 1872, includes boats, trains, an elephant, and all kinds of adventures and characters along the way, most memorably Shirley MacLaine as a young Indian widow rescued from a funeral pyre (kids may need to be reassured that this custom was outlawed in 1829).

✳ **ACTIVITIES:** Examine a map of the world to trace Fogg's path and look at the time zones to find the international date line.

✳ CAPTAIN BLOOD
1935, 119 min, NR, b&w, 7 and up
Dir: Michael Curtiz. Errol Flynn, Olivia de Havilland

This classic swashbuckler made Errol Flynn a star. He plays a doctor who becomes a pirate when he is sentenced to slavery for treating a wounded rebel. His view is that his loyalty lies with his fellow man, not with the king. He escapes and becomes captain of a pirate ship, but ends up helping England against the French.

✳ **CONNECTIONS:** This was the first of the many films Flynn and de Havilland made together (including *The Adventures of Robin Hood,* with the same director). Fans of this movie will also enjoy *Against All Flags,* another Flynn swashbuckler, with Maureen O'Hara.

✳ THE CRIMSON PIRATE
1952, 104 min, NR, 8 and up
Dir: Robert Siodmak. Burt Lancaster, Eva Bartok

Burt Lancaster has so much vitality that he almost bursts off the screen in this exuberant swashbuckler about the pirates of the late nineteenth-century Caribbean. Before the credits have a chance to roll, he swings to the top of the mast, looks right into the eyes of the viewer, and warns us to believe only half of what we are to see. We're in for action and adventure done with energy, panache, and dazzling acrobatics, featuring former acrobat Lancaster (as pirate leader Vallo) and his partner from his circus days, Nick Cravat (as his silent comrade Ojo). And there is a (highly anachronistic) scientist who befriends Vallo and his lady love Consuela, bringing the technology of explosives and hot-air balloons to save the day.

NOTE: Lots of action, some violence. Murphy is killed with a knife. Consuelo sees her father being whipped. Part of the fantasy is that the pirates are amoral. One of them boasts, "It is my opinion that no one is fit to fly a pirate's colors unless he is willing to sell his friend, his brother, or his sweetheart." They have no loyalty to anyone or any ideal. Ultimately, Vallo falls in love with Consuelo, daughter of the rebel leader, and helps the rebels for her sake. But unlike Robin Hood, he has no underlying sense of justice or commitment. And unlike *Captain Blood* (or even *Pirates of Penzance)*, there is no growth or redemption. Vallo steals more than worldly goods—in an early scene he grabs an elegant lady and kisses her. In true movie fashion she melts, dazed, into his arms. He asks Consuelo why she locked her cabin door, and she replies, "If you know it was locked, you tried it. And if you tried it, you know why it was locked."

✳ FANTASTIC VOYAGE
1966, 100 min, NR, 8 and up
Dir: Richard Fleischer. Edmond O'Brien, Donald Pleasence, Stephen Boyd, Raquel Welch

A crew and their submarine are shrunk to microscopic size so they can be injected into the bloodstream of an injured spy. The passengers include a volatile surgeon, his beautiful but serious assistant (Raquel Welch), and several others, one of whom may be trying to sabotage the effort. The crew has just one hour to complete the mission before they begin to grow back to normal size, which will trigger attacks by the patient's antibodies. If at all possible, try to see it in a theater, for maximum appreciation of the still-stunning special effects.

✳ **CONNECTIONS:** Stephen Boyd appeared as Messala in *Ben-Hur*.

✳ THE HUNT FOR RED OCTOBER
1990, 135 min, PG, 10 and up
Dir: John McTiernan. Alec Baldwin, Sean Connery, Scott Glenn, James Earl Jones, Richard Jordan

Jack Ryan (Alec Baldwin), a bookish analyst for the CIA, becomes convinced that a distinguished Soviet general named Ramius (Sean Connery) is planning to defect with the super-secret nuclear submarine that he commands. He must persuade his superiors, the White House, and the military to give him a chance to find out whether that is the case before they attack the submarine. The strategies and maneuvers of the various characters are clever, and there are some very tense and scary moments (and some violent ones) before it gets resolved.

✳ **CONNECTIONS:** Two sequels, *Patriot Games* (rated R) and *Clear and Present Danger* (rated PG-13), star Harrison Ford as Ryan. Both are exciting adventures, though more violent than the original.

✷ IVANHOE
1952, 106 min, NR, 6 and up
Dir: Richard Thorpe. Robert Taylor, Joan Fontaine, Elizabeth Taylor

This exciting story is set in the same era as *The Adventures of Robin Hood* (one minor character is called Locksley), with Ivanhoe (Robert Taylor) returning from the Crusades to help raise the ransom for King Richard. His father is still angry that he left with the king instead of staying at home to fight the Normans, but Rowena, the woman he loves (Joan Fontaine), is loyal to him. Prince John, who wants Richard's throne, has Ivanhoe and his friends arrested. They are rescued by Locksley. Prince John then captures Rebecca (Elizabeth Taylor), the daughter of a Jewish man who is helping Ivanhoe raise money for Richard's ransom. Ivanhoe must joust with wicked Bois-Guilbert to save her. The movie is sometimes a bit staid, but the action scenes are exceptionally well-done, especially the jousting.

✷ **CONNECTIONS:** A nice made-for-television version starring Anthony Andrews and James Mason is also available in video.

✷ **ACTIVITIES:** Any child who likes this movie should read Edward Eager's classic novel, *Knight's Castle,* a hilarious story about some children who are able to enter the story of Ivanhoe and make some long-overdue changes. (Hint: In their version, Ivanhoe does not end up with Rowena.)

✷ JOURNEY TO THE CENTER OF THE EARTH
1959, 132 min, 6 and up
Dir: Henry Levin. James Mason, Arlene Dahl, Pat Boone

The title says it all—it is the story of an expedition to the center of the earth, in this movie based on the Jules Verne novel. Professor Lindenbrook (James Mason) and his student Alec (Pat Boone) lead Carla (Arlene Dahl), the widow of his rival, and a strong Icelander (Peter Ronson) with a pet goose down through a volcano. The movie was shot in the Carlsbad Caverns, which provide a suitably otherworldly (or, more properly, innerworldly) setting, and there are action-filled confrontations with prehistoric lizards and with yet another rival, Count Saknussemm.

The way that groups of people attempt to achieve justice when they are removed from the systems and structures developed by society is interestingly raised when a "court" convened by the professor sentences the count to death, yet, the other members of the party, each for his own reasons, refuse to carry out the sentence. NOTE: There is a certain amount of "women can't do that" talk, but Carla shows herself to be strong, determined, intelligent, resourceful, and capable.

✷ **CONNECTIONS:** In addition to inspiring kids to research the earth's inner layers and core, this movie may lead to discussions of the role of competition in scientific inquiry. Older kids will also enjoy *Mountains of the Moon,* about the real-life race between two explorers to find the source of the Nile.

✳ JURASSIC PARK

1993, 126 min, PG-13, 10 and up
Dir: Steven Spielberg. Sam Neill, Laura Dern, Jeff Goldblum

This record-breaking blockbuster about dinosaurs brought back to life for a modern-day theme park is more thrill ride than story, but the thrills are as thrilling as they come, even on video, and even though we are now used to the computer effects that were so astonishing when this film was first released. NOTE: In a movie theater, this is a solid PG-13, and the tension is overwhelming. At home, on a television, it may be manageable for younger kids who are not easily scared. Parents should be aware, though, that adults are killed (sometimes in grisly fashion), and children are in peril, though never hurt. This is one that young kids should watch only with parents, so that their reactions can be monitored.

✳ **CONNECTIONS:** Visit the local museum to see dinosaur fossils (and maybe some insects trapped in amber as well).

✳ THE MAN FROM SNOWY RIVER

1982, 118 min, PG, 8 and up
Dir: George Miller. Kirk Douglas, Sigrid Thornton

A young Australian man goes to work on a ranch owned by a wealthy and demanding man who has a spirited colt and a spirited daughter. He gains the trust of both in this exciting story set in the gorgeous Australian low country.

✳ **CONNECTIONS:** There is a sequel called *Return to Snowy River.*

✳ THE MAN WHO WOULD BE KING

1975, 129 min, PG, 10 and up
Dir: John Huston. Sean Connery, Michael Caine

In this throwback to the epics of the 1930s, two British soldiers (Michael Caine and Sean Connery) go in search of adventure, hoping to find a place where the natives will be so impressed by their guns and knowledge, they will make them kings. They ultimately do find such a place, and Connery is made a god, but things do not work out the way they'd planned. This is an old-fashioned adventure with, as the ads used to say, thrills, chills, and laughter. NOTE: This would probably get a PG-13 rating today. The violence and tragic ending may be too intense for some kids.

✳ **CONNECTIONS:** Director Huston originally planned to make this movie, based on a story by Rudyard Kipling, with Humphrey Bogart and Clark Gable, but shelved the project when Bogart died. Roxanne is played by Shakira Caine, wife of Michael Caine.

✳ THE MARK OF ZORRO

1940, 93 min, NR, b&w, 8 and up
Dir: Rouben Mamoulian. Tyrone Power, Basil Rathbone, Linda Darnell

Tyrone Power plays the champion swordsman who masquerades as a fop when he returns to California to find that his father, once the alcalde (appointed leader of the community), has been replaced by an evil and corrupt man. He creates a secret identify as a mysterious avenger named Zorro ("the Fox") to outsmart the new alcalde and his henchman (Basil Rathbone). This is one of the all-time great swashbuckling adventures, with a terrific score and electrifying swordsmanship.

✳ **CONNECTION:** The Disney television version, with Guy Williams, is terrific fun as well. And the 1998 version starring Antonio Banderas and Anthony Hopkins (rated PG-13 for violence) is great fun, with Disney TV series sensational stunts and a brave and capable heroine. *The Mask of Zorro*, released in 1998, features Antonio Banderas and Anthony Hopkins, sensational action, and the dazzling Catherine Zeta Jones as the brave and spirited heroine.

✳ THE PRINCESS BRIDE

1988, 98 min, PG, 8 and up
Dir: Rob Reiner. Cary Elwes, Robin Wright (Penn), Wallace Shawn, Mandy Patinkin, Christopher Guest

This witty modern fairy tale by William Goldman (screenwriter of **Butch Cassidy and the Sundance Kid** and **All the President's Men**) is resoundingly satisfying. The most beautiful woman in the world (Robin Wright) is engaged to the cruel prince (Chris Sarandon) but is kidnapped by a huge man with enormous strength (Andre the Giant), a master swordsman (Mandy Patinkin), and an evil genius (Wallace Shawn). She is rescued by a mysterious masked man who must defeat them all and then escape with her through the treacherous Fire Swamp. But then she is captured again by the prince, until honor, courage, and true love prevail.

✳ **CONNECTIONS:** The book by Goldman is even better, and lots of fun to read aloud, though I admit that when I read it to my children I skipped his asides, which are better appreciated by adults.

✳ RAIDERS OF THE LOST ARK

1981, 115 min, PG, 8 and up
Dir: Steven Spielberg. Harrison Ford, Karen Allen

A thundershakingly exciting movie, this is a supercharged salute to the old cliff-hanger matinee serials. Harrison Ford plays Indiana Jones, an archaeologist-adventurer in search of the lost ark containing the tablets with the Ten Commandments given to Moses. On his side is former girlfriend, Marion (Karen Allen), and on the other side are a devious French archaeologist and the Nazis.

✳ **CONNECTIONS:** The first sequel, *Indiana Jones and the Temple of Doom*, has some good moments but is just too shrill and much too grisly. (The PG-13 rating was developed in response to the kids—and parents—who got grossed out by this film.) The third installment, *Indiana Jones and the Last Crusade*, has some nice moments featuring Indiana's father, played by Sean Connery, and a search for the Holy Grail. The first one is still by far the best.

✳ THE ROCKETEER
1991, 108 min, PG, 8 and up
Dir: Joe Johnston. Bill Campbell, Timothy Dalton, Alan Arkin, Jennifer Connelly
    Based on a comic book that re-created the deco feel of the pre–WWII era, this Disney movie has a 1940s feel—with 1990s special effects. Cliff Secord (Bill Campbell) is a stunt flyer who discovers a contraption designed by Howard Hughes that, when strapped to his back and combined with a helmet for steering, allows him to fly. The equipment is being sought by the U.S. government and by thugs in the employ of sleek Neville Sinclair (Timothy Dalton), a swashbuckling movie star and Nazi sympathizer. This has exciting action in terrific locations, including a glamorous Hollywood nightclub and onboard a zeppelin, and very appealing lead characters. NOTE: The movie has some comic-book-style violence and some tense and scary moments. One of the bad guys has a misshapen face that may be upsetting to younger kids.

✳ THE SCARLET PIMPERNEL
1935, 95 min, NR, b&w, 10 and up
Dir: Harold Young. Leslie Howard, Merle Oberon, Raymond Massey
    Leslie Howard plays Sir Percy Blakenly, a British nobleman who rescues French aristocrats from the guillotine, disguised as the Scarlet Pimpernel. He pretends to be foolish and superficial so that no one will suspect that he is the daring hero. He even fools his wife, because he thinks (wrongly) that she has given the authorities information leading to the capture of some of the prisoners. The only person she is trying to help capture is the Pimpernel himself (not knowing it is her husband), to help save her imprisoned brother. Interestingly, the movie never makes us question our loyalties, despite the American tendency to side with the peasants in the French Revolution, and the mistrust of aristocracy (especially, as portrayed here, as inherently noble). Themes to discuss include trust and loyalty. Parents should point out that Sir Percy relies on his wits, not his sword.

✳ **CONNECTION:** A very good made-for-television version with Anthony Andrews is also available on video. The book, by Baroness Orczy, is worth reading, though it may be hard going for kids used to more contemporary storytelling. Kids who enjoy it will also enjoy classics like *The Count of Monte Cristo*, by Alexandre Dumas, and *Scaramouche*, by Rafael Sabatini.

✳ SINBAD THE SAILOR

1947, 117 min, NR, 8 and up
Dir: Richard Wallace. Douglas Fairbanks, Jr., Anthony Quinn, Maureen O'Hara
   Douglas Fairbanks, Jr. and Maureen O'Hara star in this witty and colorful adventure saga, reminiscient in tone and setting of **Aladdin** and **The Thief of Bagdad.** Anthony Quinn is the bad guy, but he and Sinbad have to work together because each has one half the clues necessary to find the treasure of Alexander the Great. Sinbad's unquenchable spirit and athletic grace are irresistible, and the issue of what constitutes real wealth is handled nicely.

✳ THE THREE MUSKETEERS

1974, 105 min, PG, 8 and up
Dir: Richard Lester. Michael York, Oliver Reed, Charlton Heston, Faye Dunaway, Raquel Welch, Richard Chamberlain, Geraldine Chaplin
   A rowdy and raucous retelling of the classic story by Alexandre Dumas: A country boy (Michael York) joins the title heroes to protect the honor of the queen from the scheming Cardinal Richelieu (Charlton Heston) and the cold-blooded Lady deWinter (Faye Dunaway). Raquel Welch has one of her best roles as the queen's loyal maid-in-waiting. The director (who also made the Beatles' films **A Hard Day's Night** and **Help!)** mixes anarchy and adventure to highly satisfying effect. NOTE: Violence; plot involves adulterous relationships.

✳ **CONNECTIONS:** There are many other versions of the story, including one with Gene Kelly as a very athletic D'Artagnan, and a 1993 version that has a lot of energy but no class.

SEE ALSO:

   The Adventures of Robin Hood In this thrilling classic with a sensational swordfight, a dashing nobleman robs from the rich to give to the poor and ransom the captured king.

   The Four Feathers A soldier whose friends give him feathers as an indictment of his cowardice proves his courage and loyalty to each of them.

   The Journey of Natty Gann During the Depression, a young girl crosses the country to find her father, with the help of a young man and a loyal wolf.

   The Prisoner of Zenda A vacationing Englishman is asked to impersonate his distant relative, the kidnapped king of a small European country, and must defeat a plot to overthrow him.

AMERICAN LIVES

There is no psychology; there is only biography and autobiography.
—THOMAS SZASZ

Much as we love the fantasy of films, there is something extra special about movies based on the lives of real people, whether famous or not. We feel that we are getting a privileged glimpse inside these lives, and the fact that the stories really happened is terrifically inspiring—if they did it, maybe we can, too. These movies can make history come alive for us, showing us the people behind great events and accomplishments as they grapple with hard choices, persevere after setbacks, and triumph over obstacles. These films can also lead kids to books, to find out more about the characters, how they got where they were, and what happened to them after the movie ended.

Edison The Man
1940, 107 min, NR, b&w, 10 and up
Dir: Clarence Brown. Spencer Tracy, Charles Coburn

❋ **PLOT:** The movie begins with a dinner in 1929 honoring the "Golden Jubilee of Light," the anniversary of the invention of the electric lightbulb. But the guest of honor has not yet left home. He is being interviewed by two high school students, telling them that success is 99 percent perspiration and 1 percent inspiration, and that the most valuable thing in the world is time, because all the money in the world won't buy one minute of it.

At the dinner, he is spoken of as a man who created with the light "a new declaration of independence, a freedom of the mind." The movie flashes back to Edison's arrival in New York as a young man. His first invention, a vote recorder, failed, not because it didn't work, but because no one wanted to buy it, and he swears not to make that mistake again. He invents a stock ticker, expecting to get no more than $2,000 for it. Taking the advice of his girlfriend, he waits to get an offer, and ends up selling it for $40,000, which he uses to set up the first industrial research laboratory in the United States.

He almost loses everything with his failure to create the electric light, which scientists have proclaimed impossible. Noticing the properties of one of the pieces of equipment in the lab, he invents the phonograph, which is enormously successful, and the lab is saved. He keeps working on the lightbulb, testing more than 9,000 substances as filaments. When one of his colleagues says, "We're as sorry as you are that you didn't get results," he replies, "Results? Man, I got a lot of results. I now know nine thousand things that won't work."

Finally, they find a filament that works. The science has been successful, but the next challenge is politics. The powers behind gas do not want electricity because they will lose money. They impose a seemingly impossible deadline, but Edison meets it, and New York City is electrified.

At the celebration in 1929, the speaker worries that man will destroy himself with technology. Edison responds that man's ingenuity and humanity must work together in balance. "What man's mind can conceive, man's character can control."

✳ **DISCUSSION:** Made just nine years after Edison's death, and on the brink of World War II, this movie is very much a reflection of the concerns of its time. It is a glossy MGM production, part history (Edison did save the day and come to the attention of financiers by fixing the broken stock ticker), and part fiction (the details of his personal life). In a world with too few heroes, it is good to let kids see a movie about an American who transformed the world with his mind, whose dream was not to make money but to make the world easier, more efficient, more comfortable, and safer. Explain to kids that one thing that made Edison special was that he never lost his overwhelming curiosity, something kids have naturally, and that was the major force behind his inventions. Remind them that they are always surrounded by his inventions, including the very process that was used to film and project this movie.

> PROFANITY: None.
> NUDITY/SEXUAL REFERENCES: None.
> ALCOHOL/DRUG ABUSE: None.
> VIOLENCE/SCARINESS: None.
> TOLERANCE/DIVERSITY ISSUES: None.

✳ **QUESTIONS FOR KIDS:**
  • What would life be like now if we didn't have electric lights? If we didn't have any of Edison's inventions?
  • What does it mean to say that success is 99 percent perspiration, and 1 percent inspiration? How do we see that in the movie?
  • If you could invent something, what would it be?

- What inventions since your parents were your age have made the biggest changes in our lives? What inventions do you think will change things for your children?

✳ **CONNECTIONS:** *Young Tom Edison,* starring Mickey Rooney, was made by MGM in the same year and is a lot of fun for kids. It is a very entertaining portrayal of Edison's curiosity and inventiveness—and his proclivity for getting into trouble. When his mother cannot have the operation she desperately needs because there will not be enough light until morning, kids can see how Edison improvises a temporary means to create more light, and how he decides that he must find a way to invent electric light.

Connoisseurs of character actors will recognize Gene Lockhart (of *A Christmas Carol,* and *Miracle on 34th Street)* behind a beard as Mr. Taggart, and Henry Travers, the angel Clarence in *It's a Wonderful Life,* as Ben Els. Rocky and Bullwinkle fans should look closely at the teenager interviewing Edison in the opening scene. It is Jay Ward, later the creative force behind Rocky, Bullwinkle, Fractured Fairy Tales, George of the Jungle, Dudley Do-Right, and their friends.

✳ **ACTIVITIES:** Kids will enjoy reading more about Thomas Edison and might like to know that he was thrown out of school after three months by a teacher who insisted he was "retarded" (possibly because of his hearing loss). Help kids look for Edison's inventions in the house and community, and ask them to draw a picture (or make a model) of something they'd like to invent.

✳The Miracle Worker
1962, 108 min, NR, b&w, 10 and up
Dir: Arthur Penn. Anne Bancroft, Patty Duke

✳ **PLOT:** Helen Keller, blind and deaf from an illness she had as a toddler, is treated more as a pet than as a child by her family. She has no knowledge or understanding, and just grabs whatever she wants and breaks whatever she doesn't want. Her parents hire Annie Sullivan, once blind herself, to be her teacher, though Helen's father and brother have no hope that Helen will ever learn anything, and her mother is too tenderhearted to support any attempt to impose any rules on Helen.

Sullivan begins by teaching Helen basics like insisting that she eat only from her own plate. She also teaches Helen finger spelling, using her hands to spell out the names of everything Helen touches. Helen learns to imitate the finger motions, but does not connect them to anything. "Obedience without understanding is a blindness, too—is that all I wished on her?" Sullivan asks. Before Helen can learn language, she must understand that there is such a thing as language.

Sullivan gets permission to take Helen to live in a small building on the Kellers' property so she can uphold consistent standards without being undermined by the family. They have some fierce battles, but make enough progress to move back into the house. Once home again, Helen reverts to her wild ways. After one chaotic meal, Sullivan grabs her and forces her to the pump, to fill the pitcher of water she knocked over. As Helen feels the water rush over one hand, Sullivan finger spells "water" into the other. Suddenly, Helen understands. A word she heard as a baby comes back to her, and she knows that "w-a-t-e-r" spells water. She runs all over, asking for the names of everything. As the movie ends, it is clear that Sullivan has opened the world to her.

✳ **DISCUSSION:** This outstanding movie is based on the true story of two of the great figures of American history, Helen Keller and Anne Sullivan Macy. Keep in mind that the title refers to Sullivan; when the playwright-screenwriter William Gibson is asked about "the movie about Helen Keller," he says, "If it were about her, it would be called 'The Miracle Work-ee.'" Helen Keller was a woman of astonishing achievement, but all of it was made possible by her teacher.

Talk to kids about how people learn, about the importance of language and the challenges of teaching children with disabilities. Discuss the different ways that the main characters felt about Helen and how that affected their ability to teach her.

PROFANITY: None.
NUDITY/SEXUAL REFERENCES: None.
ALCOHOL/DRUG ABUSE: None.
VIOLENCE/SCARINESS: Helen's tantrums.
TOLERANCE/DIVERSITY ISSUES: A theme of the movie, as applied to the disabled.

✳ **QUESTIONS FOR KIDS:**
- Why did Helen's father and brother think that she could not learn? Why did Annie Sullivan think that she could?
- Why was it hard for Helen's mother to help her?
- Why is it important to be taught by someone who believes in you?

✳ **CONNECTIONS:** The movie was remade for television, with Duke playing Annie Sullivan.

✳ **ACTIVITIES:** Kids can read one of the many biographies of Helen Keller, and *The Story of My Life,* her autobiography. Most dictionaries include a diagram of finger spelling. Children can have a lot of fun learning to finger spell and sending messages to each other. Let them experiment walking around the house blindfolded, watching television with the sound off, or trying to understand someone speaking a language they don't know, to give them an idea of the challenges faced by people with disabilities.

Sunrise at Campobello

1960, 143 min, NR, 10 and up
Dir: Vincent J. Donehue. Ralph Bellamy, Greer Garson, Hume Cronyn

❊ **PLOT:** This is the story of President Franklin Delano Roosevelt (Ralph Bellamy), from the time he became disabled by polio to his comeback into mainstream politics, as he introduced candidate Al Smith to the Democratic convention of 1928.

❊ **DISCUSSION:** Franklin, a man of unquenchable vigor, was forced to reconsider his future when his legs became paralyzed. His close friend and political adviser, Louis Howe (Hume Cronyn), tells him he has two choices: to become a "country squire" and write books, or to get up and get back into politics. His mother urges him not to overdo: "I don't want to see you hurt."

He must learn patience. "When you're forced to sit a lot—and watch others move about—you feel apart, lonely, because you can't get up and pace around. I find myself irritated when people come in here and parade all over the place. I have to keep exercising self-control to prevent myself from screaming at them to sit down—quiet down—stand still." His compassion for others is deepened by his experience as well. He tells his wife, Eleanor (Greer Garson), "I turned to my faith, Babs—for strength to endure. I feel I have to go through the fire for some reason. Eleanor, it's a hard way to learn humility—but I've learned it by crawling. I know what is meant—you must learn to crawl before you can walk." Eleanor herself must learn, too. She has to overcome her shyness to become his eyes and ears, giving speeches and meeting people.

This is an exceptional and inspiring story, all the more so because it really happened. It also raises some important questions about public service, what it means and how the public interest is best determined and best served. Franklin's mother tells him that those who are privileged owe a duty to the rest, but Franklin argues that this noblesse oblige notion of public service is "an excuse for indifference," and avoids the real issues of equality and opportunity. Eleanor says, "I have the naive view that you should pursue principles without calculating the consequences," to be advised dryly by Louis that "You're no politician."

The meeting between Al Smith, Franklin, and Louis is a model of indirect communication, and it can be fun to watch how each one manages to get information from the others and get his own messages across (from Smith that he wants Franklin to give the nomination speech and from Franklin that he wants to do it and can do it standing) without ever being explicit about it. Smith comments on just this issue when he leaves, saying, "You were both too surprised to be surprised"—in other words, he could tell that they knew what he wanted and were prepared to answer his questions in a way they knew would satisfy him before he ever got there.

PROFANITY: None.
NUDITY/SEXUAL REFERENCES: None.

ALCOHOL/DRUG ABUSE: None.

VIOLENCE/SCARINESS: Tense, but not scary.

TOLERANCE/DIVERSITY ISSUES: Class issues; issue of treatment of the disabled; character expresses concerns about a Catholic running for the presidency.

❋ **QUESTIONS FOR KIDS:**
- What does Mrs. Roosevelt mean when she tells Franklin that "your stubbornness is not only your strength but your weakness"?
- What is the difference between Mrs. Roosevelt's views about public service and Franklin's?
- Why was it so important that Roosevelt stand to give the speech? Would that be as important today?
- How did Franklin and Eleanor change as a result of his paralysis?

❋ **CONNECTIONS:** The exceptionally literate screenplay is based on the award-winning play, both written by longtime MGM chief of production Dore Schary. Jean Hagan, who plays Roosevelt's secretary, Missy LeHand, is better known for her unforgettable performance as Lola Lamont in *Singin' in the Rain.* *Eleanor and Franklin,* an outstanding television miniseries about the Roosevelts, starring Edward Hermann and Jane Alexander, is available on video. Another made-for-television movie, *Eleanor, First Lady of the World,* starring Jean Stapleton, is also available.

❋ ABE LINCOLN IN ILLINOIS
1940, 110 min, NR, b&w, 8 and up
Dir: John Cromwell

Raymond Massey beautifully portrays this icon of American history in this version covering thirty years of his career, from shopkeeper to lawyer, through the debates with Stephen Douglas, and ending with his election to the presidency. Ruth Gordon is an acerbic Mary Todd, and Gene Lockhart plays his rival in romance and politics, Stephen Douglas.

❋ **CONNECTIONS:** *Young Mr. Lincoln,* directed by John Ford and starring Henry Fonda, is an appealing look at his early law practice and his tragic romance with Ann Rutledge. Particularly exciting and moving are the scenes in the courtroom as Lincoln defends two brothers charged with murder. Both have refused to talk about what happened, each thinking he is protecting the other, and Lincoln finds a way to prove their innocence.

❋ BIRDMAN OF ALCATRAZ
1962, 143 min, NR, b&w, 10 and up
Dir: John Frankenheimer. Burt Lancaster, Telly Savalas, Karl Malden

After Robert Stroud (Burt Lancaster), already in prison for murder, kills a prison guard, he is sentenced to a life term in prison with no possibility of parole. In solitary confinement, his only contact with another living creature is when a sick bird flies into his cell. He concocts a cure and then becomes fascinated with birds, reading and experimenting, finally publishing articles about cures for bird diseases and achieving recognition as a worldwide authority. His redemption through learning and through work that benefits living creatures is well-portrayed.

✳ COAL MINER'S DAUGHTER
1980, 125 min, PG, 12 and up
Dir: Michael Apted. Sissy Spacek, Tommy Lee Jones, Beverly D'Angelo

Loretta Lynn grew up in the coalfields of Kentucky. She was married at thirteen, a mother at fourteen, and a country music superstar in her twenties. Spacek won a well-deserved Oscar for her portrayal of the shy but stubborn Lynn. Jones is also outstanding as her husband "Mooney," who may cheat on her and ignore her, but who also gets her a pawnshop guitar and an opportunity to perform at a local bar, takes her first publicity pictures, and drives her to radio station interviews. They both have a great deal to learn, but the deep commitment they have to one another keeps them going through personal and professional crises.

NOTE: Frank (but not graphic) depiction of the wedding night; references to extramarital affairs; abuse of pills, drinking, smoking.

✳ FEAR STRIKES OUT
1957, 100 min, NR, b&w, 10 and up
Dir: Robert Mulligan. Anthony Perkins, Karl Malden

Anthony Perkins plays Jimmy Piersall, a gifted baseball player who had an emotional breakdown. A bit outdated in its simplistic approach to explaining and resolving Piersall's problems, it is still a moving story with sensitive performances by Perkins and by Karl Malden as Piersall's domineering father.

✳ THE FIVE PENNIES
1959, 117 min, NR, 8 and up
Dir: Melville Shavelson. Danny Kaye, Barbara Bel Geddes

Danny Kaye plays pioneering jazz trumpeter Red Nichols, who gave up music when his daughter (Tuesday Weld) needed him to help her recover from polio. Some bright musical numbers help keep this very sentimental (and highly fictionalized) story from getting too soggy.

✳ THE GIRL WHO SPELLED FREEDOM
1986, 100 min, NR, 8 and up
Dir: Simon Wincer. Wayne Rogers, Mary Kay Place, Kieu Chinh

This Disney made-for-television movie is about a young Cambodian refugee who arrived in the United States with her family in 1979, speaking no English, and who, four years later, became the national spelling champion. It is also the story about the American family who sponsored them, who are presented as heroic but also as very human.

✳ THE GREAT WHITE HOPE
1970, 104 min, PG, 10 and up
Dir: Martin Ritt. James Earl Jones, Jane Alexander
James Earl Jones plays Jack Johnson (here called Jack Jefferson), the black heavyweight champion (1908–15) whose ability to beat all of the white fighters was such a humiliation in that racist era that promoters begged for a "great white hope" who could win the title from him. Jones and Jane Alexander appear in the roles they played in the Pulitzer Prize–winning play by Howard Sackler. NOTE: Some sexual references and racist epithets.

✳ HEART LIKE A WHEEL
1983, 118 min, PG, 12 and up
Dir: Jonathan Kaplan. Bonnie Bedelia, Beau Bridges, Anthony Edwards
Bonnie Bedelia **(The Boy Who Could Fly)** is terrific as Shirley Muldowney, who fought to become the first woman champion auto racer. NOTE: Scary car crashes and extramarital sex.

✳ HOUDINI
1953, 106 min, NR, 10 and up
Dir: George Marshall. Tony Curtis, Janet Leigh
Tony Curtis plays the greatest of all magicians and escape artists, and his then-wife, Janet Leigh, plays his wife, Bess. The tricks, especially his bet that he can escape from an "escape-proof" British prison, are great fun to watch, and Houdini's devotion to his wife and his mother is very touching.

✳ THE JACKIE ROBINSON STORY
1950, 76 min, NR, b&w, 8 and up
Dir: Alfred E. Green. Jackie Robinson, Ruby Dee
The primary appeal of this movie is that Robinson plays himself (with Ruby Dee as his wife). It is forthright about the racial issues, but inevitably appears somewhat naive by today's standards.

✳ **CONNECTIONS:** Dee appears as Robinson's mother in a worthwhile made-for-television movie called *The Court-Martial of Jackie Robinson*.

✳ PRIDE OF THE YANKEES

1942, 127 min, NR, b&w, 8 and up
Dir: Sam Wood. Gary Cooper, Teresa Wright

This classic baseball movie stars Gary Cooper as Lou Gehrig, whose talent and spirit made him a hero for all Americans, and made all Americans Yankee fans. Teresa Wright is luminous as Eleanor Gehrig.

Gehrig begins playing baseball to get money for his mother's operation and earns the nickname "Iron Man" for a record of consecutive games that would not be broken for more than half a century (by Cal Ripkin). When Gehrig became ill with amyotrophic lateral sclerosis (now known as "Lou Gehrig's disease"), he made a famous farewell appearance in Yankee Stadium, telling the fans, "Some people say I've had a bad break, but I consider myself to be the luckiest man on the face of the earth." This is more a love story than a sports story, with little footage on the field and the emphasis on Gehrig's modesty, integrity, and devotion to his family.

✳ **CONNECTIONS:** Watch for Babe Ruth playing himself, along with real-life players Bill Dickey, Robert W. Meusel, and Mark Koenig. The footage of Cooper playing was reversed to make it look like he was a lefty.

✳ THE RIGHT STUFF

1983, 193 min, PG, 12 and up
Dir: Philip Kaufman. Dennis Quaid, Ed Harris, Scott Glenn, Fred Ward

This outstanding movie about the early days of the space program is brilliant in every detail, from the art direction to the script to the performances by a range of future stars, including Dennis Quaid, Ed Harris, Scott Glenn, and Fred Ward. It is not just a thrilling story about one of America's most exciting (and successful) adventures, it is also a thoughtful commentary on the American spirit and the meaning of "the right stuff." It begins with one American archetype—a cowboy—looking at his counterpart, the plane that would break the sound barrier. And it ends with another telling juxtaposition: the astronauts celebrated at a huge dinner (entertained by another archetype, fan dancer Sally Rand), as the man who broke the sound barrier, the modern cowboy, continues on alone, as cowboys always do.

Topics for discussion include loyalty (especially as John Glenn sticks up for his wife, despite pressure from Vice President Johnson, and his fellow astronauts stick up for him), maintaining integrity under commercial and political pressure, problem solving (they considered a range of backgrounds for the first astronauts, including acrobat), and what "the right stuff" really is. NOTE: Some references to infidelity; locker-room humor.

✳ SERGEANT YORK

1941, 134 min, NR, b&w, 8 and up
Dir: Howard Hawks. Gary Cooper, Walter Brennan, June Lockhart

Gary Cooper won an Oscar for his performance as WWI hero Alvin York, the pacifist from the hills of Tennessee who carried out one of the most extraordinary missions in military history. He captured 132 men by himself, still the most men ever captured by a single soldier. In addition to the exciting story of his war record, this is also the thoughtful story of a man's spiritual journey. He remains opposed to fighting of any kind, but thinks of what he is doing as saving lives, making his extraordinary achievements even more meaningful.

✳ THE SPIRIT OF ST. LOUIS

1957, 138 min, NR, b&w, 8 and up
Dir: Billy Wilder. Jimmy Stewart

Jimmy Stewart plays Charles Lindbergh in this respectful story about the brave and determined twenty-five-year-old who made the first solo flight across the Atlantic and became a worldwide hero. As he flies, he fights fatigue and boredom by remembering his days of learning to fly, barnstorming, and delivering mail. He has to navigate by the stars when his compass fails, and he nearly crashes when the wings get iced over, but he arrives to great acclaim and returns home in triumph.

✳ **CONNECTIONS:** Stewart, at forty-eight, was a bit old to play the young pilot, but his own love for flying shines through. Playwright Marc Connelly plays Father Hussman.

✳ **ACTIVITIES:** There are some good books for children about this historic flight, and kids who visit Washington, D.C., can see the plane he flew at the Air and Space Museum. Kids may also enjoy the books by the late Anne Lindbergh, the daughter of the famous aviator. Teens may want to know more about Lindbergh's life after the famous flight, including the tragic kidnapping and murder of his young son (featured in two made-for-television movies) and his naive support of the Nazis before World War II.

✳ THE STORY OF ALEXANDER GRAHAM BELL

1939, 97 min, NR, b&w, 8 and up
Dir: Irving Cummings. Don Ameche, Henry Fonda, Loretta Young

This is a classic biopic (more dramatic than historically accurate) about the inventor of the telephone. Don Ameche plays Bell (note that in **Ball of Fire,** Sugarpuss calls the telephone the "Ameche"), and Henry Fonda is the recipient of the first telephonic message, "Watson, come here—I need you." Bell was trying to invent a device to help his deaf wife—a lovely performance by Loretta Young (with her real-life sisters playing her sisters)—and never suspected that his invention would transform communication throughout the world.

✻ TO HELL AND BACK

1955, 106 min, NR, 10 and up
Dir: Jesse Hibbs. Audie Murphy, Denver Pyle

Audie Murphy, the most decorated American soldier of WWII, plays himself in this movie, based on his autobiography. His youthful demeanor and cheery modesty make a nice contrast to his breathtaking daring. It is worthwhile to let kids see what a real hero looks like in contrast to the Schwarzeneggers and Stallones of the movies.

✻ WILSON

1944, 144 min, NR, 12 and up
Dir: Henry King. Alexander Knox, Thomas Mitchell, Eddie Foy, Jr.

Alexander Knox makes an appealing Wilson in this thoughtful biopic about the president who tried to prevent future wars by establishing the League of Nations.

SEE ALSO:

All the President's Men Two young reporters unravel the information leading from the break-in at the Democratic headquarters to Richard Nixon's reelection campaign.

Annie Oakley A young woman becomes America's foremost sharpshooter.

Apollo 13 Three astronauts on a mission to the moon must find a way to get back home after an explosion cripples their spacecraft.

Brian's Song Two players for the Chicago Bears support and inspire each other.

The Buddy Holly Story A young man from Lubbock, Texas, revolutionizes rock and roll.

Cheaper by the Dozen and **Belles on Their Toes** The pioneers of "motion study" (efficiency) and their twelve children apply its principles at home.

Funny Girl Ziegfeld comedian Fanny Brice strives for stardom.

Hoop Dreams Two young black boys from the inner city of Chicago try to use basketball as a bridge to better lives for themselves and their families in this riveting documentary.

King: A Filmed Record . . . Montgomery to Memphis

This documentary about the life of the civil rights leader includes news footage and commentary.

Malcolm X Denzel Washington is mesmerizing as the leader who was always learning and growing.

Norma Rae A young woman changes the life of everyone in the community by bringing the union into the local mill.

1776 The events leading to the Declaration of Independence are depicted in a rousing musical rendition.

Stand and Deliver A gifted teacher shows inner-city kids that they can conquer calculus.

Animals

No philosophers so thoroughly comprehend us as dogs and horses.
—HERMAN MELVILLE

Kid and animal stories have only one or at most two basic structures, very similar to the classic "boy meets girl/boy loses girl/boy gets girl" formula. In these movies, a kid is influenced by his or her friendship with an exceptional animal. Some bad force wants to take the animal away or mistreat it. It gets resolved, either happily (as in **Lassie Come Home)** or unhappily (as in **The Yearling)**, and the child learns an important lesson. In the movies of the 1930s–60s, the child is usually just dealing with issues of growing up, but in movies of the 1970s and later, the child is more likely to be shy or sullen or recovering from a bad family situation and is then rescued by the relationship with the animal: Compare the original **Lassie Come Home** with the 1994 version, or **National Velvet** with **Free Willy.**

That is not to suggest that these movies are not worthwhile; on the contrary. The formula endures, like its romantic counterpart, because it is so reliably satisfying. But the sameness of the plots does mean that the details really matter. There is all the difference in the world between **Lassie Come Home,** with its classic themes of loyalty and devotion, and *Beethoven,* with its slapstick and misogyny.

A theme worth discussing that often arises in these movies is responsibility, as many of them concern a child's or teen's first experience being responsible for another living creature.

CATS

✳ RHUBARB
1955, 91 min, NR, b&w, 8 and up
Dir: Arthur Lubin. Ray Milland, Gene Lockhart, Jan Sterling

An eccentric millionaire leaves his baseball team to his cat with very funny consequences.

✳ **CONNECTIONS:** Watch for a pre–Mr. Spock Leonard Nimoy.

✳ THAT DARN CAT

1965, 116 min, NR, 8 and up
Dir: Robert Stevenson. Hayley Mills, Dean Jones, Dorothy Provine

This is a cute Disney suspense comedy about a cat named D.C. (for "Darn Cat") who helps solve a mystery when he returns home with a scribbled note asking for help. It turns out to have been written by Margaret Miller (Grayson Hall), a bank teller who has been kidnapped by robbers. Dean Jones plays FBI agent Zeke Kelso, who (despite being allergic to cats) has to trail D.C. to see if he will lead them back to Margaret. An assortment of characters interferes in one way or another, including D.C.'s owners, Patti and Ingrid Randall (Hayley Mills, Dorothy Provine), their boyfriends, and their neighbors. Character actors Elsa Lanchester, William Demerest, Ed Wynn, and Frank Gorshin add a lot of color.

✳ **CONNECTIONS:** The movie was remade in 1996 by Disney with Christina Ricci.

SEE ALSO:

The Three Lives of Thomasina

DINOSAURS

Children often feel anxious because they are small and dependent on the adults who loom so large in their lives. Learning about dinosaurs helps children to resolve their fears, giving them hundreds of facts to store and sort about enormous creatures who really lived but who have been extinct for millions of years. The combination of the dinosaurs' extraordinary power and their being safely extinct, along with the feeling of power and control over the information the children absorb, can be a great source of comfort to them.

✳ BABY . . . SECRET OF THE LOST LEGEND

1985, 95 min, PG, 8 and up
Dir: B. W. L. Norton. William Katt, Sean Young

A sort of *Jurassic Park*–lite, this movie is about two Peace Corps volunteers who discover a baby dinosaur and try to protect it from evil scientists in this uneven (but very popular) fantasy. NOTE: Some violence; somewhat racist depiction of African natives.

✳ WE'RE BACK: A DINOSAUR'S STORY

1993, 72 min, G, 5 and up
Dir: Dick Zondag. Ralph Zondag, Phil Nibbelink, Simon Wells

The same year he released **Jurassic Park,** Steven Spielberg produced this unexceptional but pleasant animated story of dinosaurs who are brought to New York (and smartened up with magic pills) by a friendly alien with the voice of Walter Cronkite. Listen for the voices of some other unexpected stars, such as Jay Leno and Julia Child.

SEE ALSO:

Fantasia (Stravinsky sequence)

Jurassic Park

The Land Before Time

DOGS

✳ LASSIE COME HOME

1943, 88 min, NR, b&w, 6 and up
Dir: Fred M. Wilcox. Roddy MacDowell, Elizabeth Taylor

This is the classic boy and dog story. The boy is Joe (Roddy MacDowell), his friend is Priscilla (a very young Elizabeth Taylor), and the dog, of course, is Lassie. Lassie is devoted to her young master, and waits for him every day in the schoolyard to walk him home. But when the boy's father loses his job, he sells Lassie to a duke. Lassie escapes twice, and then is sent to Scotland. But she comes home again, with many adventures along the way, for a joyous reunion with the boy she loves.

✳ **CONNECTIONS:** There are at least ten films featuring Lassie, including *Son of Lassie,* in which she helps to win WWII, and *The Magic of Lassie,* in which she costars with Jimmy Stewart.

SEE ALSO:

Old Yeller

The Shaggy Dog

FARM ANIMALS

✳ ADVENTURES OF MILO AND OTIS

1989, 76 min, G, 4 and up
Dir: Masanori Hata. Dudley Moore (narrator)

A charming film for the whole family, this is the story of Milo the cat and Otis the dog, best friends who live on a farm until Milo is swept down a stream and Otis goes to rescue him. They have many adventures, both funny and exciting, as they try to find their way home. Dudley Moore provides the witty narration. Themes for discussion include cooperation, loyalty, and growing up.

✳ SO DEAR TO MY HEART
1948, 84 min, NR, 5 and up
Dir: Harold Schuster. Burl Ives, Bobby Driscoll

This gentle Disney musical is about a boy (Bobby Driscoll) who wants to enter Danny, his beloved black sheep, in the state fair. Along with nicely handled themes of believing in yourself (and those you love) and the importance of persistence, there are some classic musical numbers, including Burl Ives singing "Lavender Blue (Dilly Dilly)."

SEE ALSO:

Babe

Charlotte's Web

GEESE

✳ FLY AWAY HOME
1996, 107 minutes, PG, 8 and up
Dir: Carroll Ballard. Anna Paquin, Jeff Daniels, Dana Delaney

Amy, a thirteen-year-old girl from New Zealand (Anna Paquin), wakes up in a hospital bed after an automobile accident to see her father, Tom (Jeff Daniels), whom she barely knows. Her mother was killed in the crash, and she must go back with Tom to his remote farm in Canada. He is an eccentric sculptor and inventor, preoccupied with his work and unsure of how to try to comfort her. Amy does not want to be comforted, and wanders silently through the marshes. When developers illegally mowing down the marsh kill a goose, Amy finds the eggs she left behind, and begins to resolve her loss by mothering the goslings. Since she is the first thing they see when they hatch, they think of her as their mother, following her everywhere, even into the shower. The local authorities insist that their wings be clipped, since without their mother they cannot learn to migrate and will cause problems for the community when they try to fly. But Amy and her father will not allow the geese to be harmed.

Tom devises a way for Amy to play the role of "Mother Goose" in teaching the geese to migrate, by learning to fly herself, in an ultralight plane, and leading them south. With Tom's brother (Terry Kinney) and girlfriend (Dana Delany), they plot a course to a wetland preserve that is scheduled to be developed unless geese arrive by November 1. As they work together, Amy finds a way to begin to heal her loss of her mother and her relationship with Tom.

This is a thrilling adventure, exquisitely told, by the same director and photographer who made **The Black Stallion**. Ballard has the patience to let the story tell itself, and the quiet moments are breathtakingly beautiful and heartbreakingly touching. NOTE: There is one profanity in the movie, demanded by the studio, who insisted that the movie must have a PG rating so that it would not scare off school-age kids. Of more concern to many parents will be Amy's nose ring, which Tom permits and even appears to encourage.

HORSES

The Black Stallion

1979, 118 min, G, 8 and up
Dir: Carroll Ballard. Kelly Reno, Mickey Rooney, Hoyt Axton

PLOT: A young boy named Alec Ramsey (Kelly Reno) is on a ship with his father. Everything seems mysterious to him, the exotic passengers, the high-stakes poker game his father is playing, the wild and beautiful black horse he comforts with sugar cubes. Then the ship is destroyed in a storm, and only Alec and the horse survive. Alec patiently and persistently tames the horse. They are rescued and return to Alec's home. When the horse runs to a farm, Alec meets Henry (Mickey Rooney), a former trainer. They enter the horse in a race against two champions, and he and Alec triumph.

DISCUSSION: Walter Farley's novel was adapted by director Ballard and Francis Ford Coppola's studio into one of the most breathtakingly beautiful and genuinely magical movies ever made. Part of the magic is that the movie has the courage to be quiet. There is very little dialogue, and long stretches without a single word. It allows its images to do the work, and the cinematography, by Caleb Deschanel (**The Right Stuff**, *The Natural*), is a joy for the eye and for the spirit, creating exactly the right atmosphere for what Pauline Kael said "may be the greatest children's movie ever made."

There are some good themes to discuss here, including Henry's views about being a trainer: "It was a lot of work, but it was worth it," and the way that Alec's relationship with the horse (and with Henry) help him deal with the loss of his father.

PROFANITY: None.
NUDITY/SEXUAL REFERENCES: None.
ALCOHOL/DRUG ABUSE: None.
VIOLENCE/SCARINESS:Although the movie is rated G, the shipwreck is very scary, and Alec's father (Hoyt Axton) is killed.
TOLERANCE/DIVERSITY ISSUES: None.

✳ **QUESTIONS FOR KIDS:**
- What is the importance of the story Alec's father tells about Alexander the Great and his horse?
- Why does the horse trust Alec?
- Why is it important for Alec to win the race?
- What is the most important lesson Alec learns from Henry?

✳ **CONNECTIONS:** There is a sequel called *The Black Stallion Returns,* which is enjoyable, but not nearly as good.

Misty

1961, 92 min, NR, 6 and up
Dir: James B. Clark. Arthur O'Connell, David Ladd

✳ **PLOT:** This is a faithful adaptation of the classic (and fact-based) children's book *Misty of Chincoteague,* by Marguerite Henry, about two children who fall in love with a wild horse, descended from the Spanish ponies who escaped from a sinking ship and swam to Assateague, an island off the coast of Virginia. The children are Paul and Maureen, who live with their grandparents on Chincoteague, a neighboring island. Once a year, the residents of Chincoteague go to Assateague to capture ponies.

✳ **DISCUSSION:** There is a very nice presentation of the challenge of teaching the foal independence, how hard it is for her, but how much love it shows. Paul learns this when he has to let the Phantom go back to Assateague. He tells Misty, her foal, to go, too, but Misty stays and runs after them. Her home is with them now. This movie provides a good opportunity to talk about showing love by letting go. The brother and sister have a very good, supportive relationship. And their grandfather (Arthur O'Connell) is strict and proud but understanding, as shown by his reaction when Paul goes off to Assateague alone.

PROFANITY: None.
NUDITY/SEXUAL REFERENCES: None.
ALCOHOL/DRUG ABUSE: None.
VIOLENCE/SCARINESS: None.
TOLERANCE/DIVERSITY ISSUES: There is no thought that girls or women can go on the pony roundup, and Maureen helps with the cooking while Paul brushes the horse. In other areas they are very much equal partners, and Maureen reminds him that "I know just as much about it as you do" when they are training for the race. Contrast this movie's "Never had a girl rider before, but there's no rule against it" with *National Velvet,* where having a girl rider disqualifies the winning horse.

✳ **QUESTIONS FOR KIDS:**
- Why is it important for Misty to learn to be independent? What is a good way to teach her?

- Does Misty know that her mother loves her even though she is trying to teach her to do things for herself?
- Why does Misty want to stay with the children? Why doesn't the Phantom want to stay?
- How does Paul know?

❉ **CONNECTIONS:** David Ladd is the son of 1940s star Alan Ladd (*Shane*).

❉ **ACTIVITIES:** Children will enjoy *Misty of Chincoteague* and its sequels. See if they can find the island of Chincoteague on a map, and send away to the Virginia Tourism Office for information about it. Take the kids to a pony ride, or to a place where they can feed and pet some horses.

❉ MY FRIEND FLICKA
1943, 89 min, NR, 6 and up
Dir: Harold Schuster. Roddy MacDowell

Roddy MacDowell (*Lassie Come Home*) plays a sensitive boy who loves a rebellious horse. He and the horse bring out the best in each other.

❉ **CONNECTIONS:** There are two pleasant sequels, *Thunderhead, Son of Flicka*, and *The Green Grass of Wyoming*.

SEE ALSO:

National Velvet

JUNGLE ANIMALS

❉ BORN FREE
1966, 96 min, NR, 6 and up
Dir: James Hill. Bill Travers, Virginia McKenna

This is the true story of George and Joy Adamson (Bill Travers and Virginia McKenna), and the lion they adopted while George was serving as game warden in Kenya. George brings home three tiny cubs after he had to kill their mother, who charged at him, thinking he was going to attack her children. Joy babies them and gives them the run of the house, and gets especially close to the smallest, named Elsa. The other two go to a zoo, but Joy keeps Elsa as a pet.

When Elsa accidentally causes an elephant stampede, they are ordered to send her to a zoo, but Joy resolves that instead they will undo the effects of their domestication, and teach Elsa how to live in the wild. It is a struggle, as Elsa has never had to catch her own food, and has not lived with other lions since she was a baby. But they are able to teach her what she needs to be able to take care of herself and join the other lions in the wild. Kids may like to talk about the way that parents have to prepare their children for life "in the wild" and how difficult that is when their inclination is to protect them. NOTE: In the subtext of the movie there is a subtle but arrogant colonialism.

✻ **CONNECTIONS:** Older kids will enjoy Adamson's books, the basis for this movie, the sequel, and a short-lived television series. The score and theme song both won Oscars. The sequel, *Living Free,* about Elsa's cubs, stars Susan Hampshire (*The Three Lives of Thomasina*). Travers and McKenna, married in real life, often appeared together. Their films include the remake of **The Barretts of Wimpole Street** and **The First Olympics.**

✻ HATARI
1962, 159 min, NR, 8 and up
Dir: Howard Hawks. John Wayne, Red Buttons

This leisurely adventure-comedy about trappers in Africa stars John Wayne and includes an irresistible score by Henry Mancini, featuring the "Baby Elephant Walk." Wayne and his colleagues trap animals for circuses and zoos. A beautiful journalist arrives to write a story about them and adopts three baby elephants who follow her around. The movie has a lot of typical John Wayne macho byplay, but it includes a surprisingly nice discussion of why people sometimes have a hard time treating those they like nicely.

NOTE: Even by the standards of that era this movie has a lot of smoking, and a good bit of drinking, including casual drunkenness. While a group of trappers from a variety of backgrounds and cultures work well together, the natives are treated like servants and referred to as "boys." Even though the characters are trappers, not hunters, the movie reflects, by today's standards, a lack of sensitivity to environmental and preservationist concerns.

SEE ALSO:

The Jungle Book

King Solomon's Mines

MARINE ANIMALS

✻Andre
1994, 94 min, PG, 6 and up
Dir: George Miller. Keith Carradine, Tina Majorino, Chelsea Field

✻ **PLOT:** A shy little girl from Maine makes friends with a seal in this fact-based story about a seal that swam from Boston to Maine every summer for twenty-four years. Toni (Tina Majorino) is more comfortable with animals than with kids. Her father, Harry (Keith Carradine), is not very responsible, but he has a real gift for animals, and his wife manages to cope with the chaos and be "the only grown-up in the house."

Andre the seal is a delightful playmate, a sensational participant in "show-and-tell" at school, and a courageous lifesaver, warning Harry away from a sunken mine when he is scuba diving and rescuing Toni in a storm. The local fishermen blame the seals for their unusually low catches. One of them, a bitter man who hates Harry and his family, calls the Fish and Wildlife Administration. They send an inspector, who insists that Andre must go. Finally, Andre goes to a Boston aquarium. But, set free every summer, he comes back to be with his family.

✳ **DISCUSSION:** Kids will enjoy this movie, with its adorable, raspberry-blowing, television-loving seal (portrayed by a sea lion). Parents will enjoy the sound track, filled with 60s oldies.

To the extent that it feels a bit messy, due to its episodic structure, that seems consistent with its portrayal of the chaotic life of the Whitney family, though the mother is impossibly understanding and the problems are all resolved a bit too neatly at the end. Andre gets to be in an aquarium and be with the family. And the motivations all seem much too simplistic. It turns out that Billy's bitterness is because he envies Harry's family and his job, and that he believes (correctly) that he would be a better harbormaster. So, he gets that job (and, one presumes, then becomes a nice guy), and Harry gets to work for the government on marine protection.

Toni's older sister Paula has the thankless task of appearing petty and jealous; she's furious because Harry misses her appearance in a Fourth of July pageant, and even more furious when he tells her boyfriend, Mark (Billy's son), that he can't see her anymore after Andre alerts him to their smoking. So Paula helps Mark take Andre out into the ocean, until she sees he plans to shoot the seal—and then she stops him. This could be the basis for a worthwhile talk about displaced anger.

PROFANITY: Very mild.
NUDITY/SEXUAL REFERENCES: None.
ALCOHOL/DRUG ABUSE: Teenagers caught smoking; Billy gets drunk.
VIOLENCE/SCARINESS: Toni in peril; Andre in peril; fistfight.
TOLERANCE/DIVERSITY ISSUES: Tolerance of people who are different.

✳ **QUESTIONS FOR KIDS:**
- How did Andre make Toni's life different?
- Why was Paula so angry with her father?
- Why did Toni think her father was "magic" with animals?
- What does it mean to say, "sometimes if you really love someone, you have to let them go"?

✳ **CONNECTIONS:** Read *A Seal Called Andre,* by Harry Goodridge and Lew Dietz. And watch for some home movies of the real Andre at the end of the movie.

✳ FLIPPER

1996, 95 min, PG, 8 and up
Dir: Alan Shapiro. Paul Hogan, Elijah Wood

For anyone who has seen **Free Willy** (or even **Lassie Comes Home,** or any other kid and animal movie ever made), there are no surprises here. Aside from that, it is a perfectly pleasant family movie, with not too much scary stuff, first-rate actors (Elijah Wood as the teenager and Paul (*Crocodile Dundee*) Hogan as his aging hippie uncle), an exceptionally endearing dolphin (portrayed by three different dolphins and a mechanical replica), beautiful photography, and a satisfyingly loathsome bad guy (not only does he have a shiny, fancy boat, but he shoots dolphins, dumps toxic waste into the water, and is willing to kill a kid). Wood is the sullen teen, dumped on his uncle while his mother copes with a divorce. When he makes friends with Flipper (and with a pretty local girl), he begins to feel less sorry for himself and become more responsible. Hogan, whose idea of hospitality is bread toasted with a butane flame, begins to think about whether his commitment-free lifestyle could use some improvement. His girlfriend, a marine biologist, has a mechanical genius son who won't talk, until he is finally willing to say, "Flipper." Kids may want to talk about the way Sandy feels about being sent to stay with his uncle, and about how to help the dolphins and prevent pollution (there is a toll-free number at the end of the movie for people who want to help).

✳ FREE WILLY

1993, 112 min, PG, 10 and up
Dir: Simon Wincer. Jason James Richter, Lori Petty, Michael Madsen

Jason James Richter plays Jesse, a bitter street kid abandoned by his parents, who is picked up by the authorities when he vandalizes the underwater observation area of an amusement park. Placed with foster parents and assigned to clean up the mess, he can think of nothing but running away until he sees Willy the whale through the observation area windows. The two lonely and uncooperative creatures find a bond, and their response to each other transforms both of them. The boy learns responsibility and self-respect and begins to allow himself to make connections with humans as well: a Native American handyman (Michael Ironside) and an animal trainer (Lori Petty) who work at the park. When he finds out that the evil park owner has decided to kill Willy for the insurance money, the boy must figure out a way to rescue his friend, which means learning to ask for help and trust others.

✳ **CONNECTIONS:** The social worker is played by Mykelti Williamson, who appeared as Bubba in *Forrest Gump.* The 1995 sequel, in which Jesse meets his half brother and has to protect Willy and his family from some nasty polluters, is very watchable, but by the third in the series the formula is getting tired.

MONKEYS AND CHIMPS

✳ MONKEY TROUBLE
1994, 95 min, PG, 6 and up
Dir: Franco Amurri. Thora Birch, Harvey Keitel, Mimi Rogers
　　Thora Birch is very winning as Eva, a little girl who has to learn a lot about unselfishness and responsibility when she secretly adopts a capuchin monkey, not knowing that it had been trained as a thief by its former owner Azro (Harvey Keitel). Eva has to keep the monkey a secret from her mother (who thinks she is not responsible enough to have a pet) and stepfather (who is allergic). She does not know that the monkey is a pickpocket, which leads to even more trouble. Meanwhile, Azro is trying to get the monkey back, because he had promised some tough bad guys that he would let them use the monkey for a heist. NOTE: Unfortunate stereotyping by Keitel as a Gypsy.

✳ TOBY TYLER
1960, 96 min, NR, 6 and up
Dir: Charles Barton. Kevin Corcoran,
　　This Disney classic about the boy (Kevin Corcoran) who runs away to join the circus is a lot of fun. Toby runs to the circus, thinking that his aunt and uncle do not want him. At the circus, Toby learns to be a bareback rider, and befriends the mischievous chimp Mr. Stubbs before being reunited with his family.

SEE ALSO:

Bedtime for Bonzo

WOLVES

✳ THE JOURNEY OF NATTY GANN
1985, 101 min, PG, 10 and up
Dir: Jeremy Kagan. Meredith Salenger, John Cusack
　　Natty Gann (Meredith Salenger) is a tough young girl who lives with her father in Chicago during the Depression. He leaves her with his landlady when he has to go to Seattle for a job, and Natty runs away to find him. She rides the rails and meets some young drifters who take care of her but insist that she join them in stealing. She is caught and sent to an orphanage but escapes. She is befriended by a beautiful wolf and finally finds a friend (John Cusack) among the homeless people as well. Everyone tells Natty that her father does not want her, and everyone tells her father that Natty has been killed, but neither one of them gives up, and they are reunited. NOTE: This is a Disney movie, but parents should be aware that Natty uses some

rough language, there are some fistfights and scary moments, and a man who gives her a ride makes sexual advances.

✳ WHITE FANG

1991, 107 min, PG, 10 and up
Dir: Randal Kleiser. Ethan Hawke, Klaus Maria Brandauer

Jack London's story of a wolf has been adapted by Disney into a story of a boy and a wolf. Jack (Ethan Hawke) goes to the Yukon to work his father's claim and meets the wolf (who is part dog), originally owned by Indians, and then by men who trained him for dog fights. White Fang befriends Jack, saves him from a bear and from claim jumpers, and teaches him some important lessons. NOTE: Some violence and characters in peril.

✳ **ACTIVITIES:** Some kids will enjoy the book. The Alaskan scenery should inspire kids to find out more about that environment.

ZOO ANIMALS

✳ ZEBRA IN THE KITCHEN

1965, 83 min, NR, 5 and up
Dir: Ivan Tors. Jay North, Martin Milner

This is by no means a great movie, but animal-loving kids will get a kick out of the silly consequences when the animals escape from the zoo, and its casual episodic style is easy for even small children to follow. They will also appreciate the importance of respecting the animals.

✳ **CONNECTIONS:** Fans of 1960s television will recognize Jay North as Dennis the Menace and Martin Milner from *Adam-12*.

ANIMATED CLASSICS

"Animation can explain whatever the mind of man can conceive."
—WALT DISNEY

Animation is the expression of pure imagination, utterly free from the reality of time, place, and the laws of nature. When Wile E. Coyote runs off a cliff, he stays suspended for a moment just to give us the pleasure of seeing the expression on his face as he realizes he is going to drop like an anvil before we have the pleasure of watching him do it. Reassuringly, in the next scene he is back opening up the latest package from Acme, perhaps with one bandage around his tail, still boundlessly optimistic that this time he will catch the Road Runner. Sleeping Beauty and her prince waltz off into the sky, barely noticing they've left the ground; hippos dance a ballet with ostriches; Monstro the whale sneezes Pinocchio and Gepetto out into the churning waves; Dumbo clutches the white feather in his nose and flies, and we believe it.

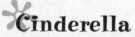
Cinderella

1950, 74 min, NR, 5 and up
Dir: Wilfred Jackson, Hamilton Luske, Clyde Geronimi, Ilene Woods, Eleanor Audley, Verna Felton

✻ **PLOT:** The classic fairy tale by Charles Perrault is lovingly and imaginatively brought to life. Cinderella, a sweet, docile, and beautiful girl forced to act as a servant for her mean stepmother and stepsisters, goes to the ball with the help of her fairy godmother. But her godmother warns that the beautiful coach and gown will last only until midnight. Cinderella meets the prince at the ball, and they share a romantic dance. But when the clock begins to strike midnight, she runs away, leaving behind one of her glass slippers. The prince declares he will marry the girl whose foot fits that slipper. He finds her, and they live happily ever after.

✳ **DISCUSSION:** Disney expanded the simple story with vivid and endearing characters and some of its most memorable songs. The animation is gorgeously detailed and inventive. In one musical number, as the stepsisters squawk their way through their singing lesson in another room, Cinderella sings sweetly as she scrubs the floor, reflected in dozens of soap bubbles. When Cinderella asks if she can go to the ball, her stepmother tells her she can if she can make an appropriate dress. She then keeps Cinderella much too busy to have time to make the dress. But Cinderella's friends, the mice and birds, make one for her in another delightful musical number. As the fairy godmother sings "Bibbidi Bobbidi Boo," she transforms a pumpkin into a coach, the mice into horses, the horse into a coachman, and finally, Cinderella's rags into a magnificent ballgown. The scene when the duke comes looking for the girl whose foot will fit the glass slipper is very suspenseful and highly satisfying.

While the story has enduring appeal, many people are troubled by the passive heroine who meekly accepts her abusive situation and waits to be rescued, first by her godmother and then by the prince. It is worth discussing, with both boys and girls, what some of her alternatives could have been ("If you were Cinderella, would you do what that mean lady told you?"), and making sure they have some exposure to stories with heroines who save themselves. A superb book called *Ella, Enchanted,* by Gail Carson Levine, has an ingenious explanation for the heroine's obedience. The 1998 release *Ever After* stars Drew Barrymore as a Cinderella who triumphs without a fairy godmother.

In today's world of blended families, it might also be worth discussing that not all stepparents and siblings are mean. Even children who are living with intact families of origin may need to hear this so that they will not worry about their friends.

PROFANITY: None.

NUDITY/SEXUAL REFERENCES: None.

ALCOHOL/DRUG ABUSE: None.

VIOLENCE/SCARINESS: None, though very small children are sometimes scared when the mean stepsisters tear Cinderella's dress apart. Some are also scared by the stepsister's cat, Lucifer.

TOLERANCE/DIVERSITY ISSUES: As noted above.

✳ **QUESTIONS FOR KIDS:**
- Why does Cinderella do what her stepmother says? What could she have done instead?
- Why is the king so worried about whether the prince will get married?
- If you had a fairy godmother, what would you like her to do for you?
- Or would you like to be a fairy godmother? Whose wish would you grant?

✳ **CONNECTIONS:** This story has been told many times, including *Cinderfella*, with Jerry Lewis as the title character and Ed Wynn as his fairy godfather. The made-for-television musical version starring Leslie Ann Warren, with songs by Rodgers and Hammerstein, and the remake with Whitney Houston and Brandy, are available on video and well worth watching.

Children might be amused to hear that Cinderella's most famous accessory is the result of a mistake. In the original French story, her slipper was made of fur. But a mistranslation in the first English version described it as glass, and it has stayed that way ever since.

Dumbo
1941, 64 min, NR, 5 and up
Dir: Ben Sharpsteen. Edward Brophy, Verna Felton, Cliff Edwards

✳ **PLOT:** The stork delivers babies to the circus animals, including Mrs. Jumbo's baby, an elephant with enormous ears. The other elephants laugh at him and call him Dumbo, but Mrs. Jumbo loves him very much. When Dumbo is mistreated, she is furious and raises such a fuss that she is locked up. Dumbo is made part of the clown act, which embarrasses him very much. He is a big hit and, celebrating his good fortune, accidentally drinks champagne and becomes tipsy. The next morning, he wakes up in a tree, with no idea how he got there. It turns out that he flew! He becomes the star of the circus, with his proud mother beside him.

✳ **DISCUSSION:** The themes in this movie include tolerance of differences and the importance of believing in yourself. It also provides a good opportunity to encourage empathy by asking kids how they would feel if everyone laughed at them the way the animals laugh at Dumbo, and how important it is to Dumbo to have a friend like Timothy.

PROFANITY: None.

NUDITY/SEXUAL REFERENCES: None.

ALCOHOL/DRUG ABUSE: Dumbo and his friend Timothy accidentally become drunk and have "Pink Elephants on Parade" hallucinations.

VIOLENCE/SCARINESS: Younger children may be scared when Mrs. Jumbo is locked up, or when Dumbo has to jump in the clown act.

TOLERANCE/DIVERSITY ISSUES: Respecting individual differences is a theme of the movie. The crows who sing "When I See an Elephant Fly" would be considered racist by today's standards (one of them is named "Jim Crow," and they speak with "Amos 'n' Andy"–style accents), but clearly are not intended to be insulting.

✳ **QUESTIONS FOR KIDS:**
- Why does Timothy tell Dumbo he needs the feather to fly?
- How does he learn that he does not need it?

- Why do the other elephants laugh at Dumbo's ears? How does that make him feel?

✳ **CONNECTIONS:** The circus train, Casey, Jr., puffs, "I think I can" as it goes up the hill, just like in *The Little Engine That Could.* Compare this story to *How the Elephant Got Its Trunk,* by Rudyard Kipling (read by Jack Nicholson in the Rabbit Ears production), in which another elephant finds his larger-than-expected feature first ridiculed and then envied by the other elephants. Kids may also enjoy comparing this to *Rudolph the Red-Nosed Reindeer, The Ugly Duckling,* and other stories about differences that make characters special.

✳Lady and the Tramp

1955, 75 min, NR, 4 and up
Dir: Hamilton Luske. Clyde Geronimi, Wilfred Jackson, Peggy Lee, Stan Freberg

✳ **PLOT:** Lady is the pampered cocker spaniel of a couple she knows as "Jim Dear" and "Darling." Her best friends are Jock (a Scottie) and Trusty (a basset hound who has no sense of smell). They ignore a stray named Tramp. When Darling has a baby, Lady is apprehensive, but Jim Dear and Darling assure her that she is still important to them. The couple has to go away, though, and Aunt Sarah arrives, with her nasty Siamese cats, to care for the baby. The cats make a mess of the living room, and Lady gets the blame. Aunt Sarah puts Lady in a muzzle, and Lady, hurt and humiliated, runs away.

She meets Tramp, who finds a way to get the muzzle off with the help of an obliging beaver (Stan Freberg). Then Tramp takes Lady out on the town, ending with a romantic spaghetti dinner at Tony's restaurant. The next morning, on her way home, she is captured by the dogcatcher. At the pound, she hears from Peg (Peggy Lee) that Tramp is a rogue with many lady friends, and she is disillusioned.

Aunt Sarah gets Lady and takes her home, banishing her to the dog-house. But with Tramp's help, Lady gets inside to save the baby from a rat. The crib is knocked over, and Aunt Sarah blames Tramp. She calls the dogcatcher to take him away. Just in time, Jim Dear and Darling return, and understand what has happened. With the help of Jock and Trusty, they get Tramp back. Trusty is hurt, but not badly, and he and Jock go to visit on Christmas to see Lady and Tramp and meet their new puppies.

✳ **DISCUSSION:** This is one of Disney's best animated films, with an appealing story and memorable music by Peggy Lee and Sonny Burke. Kids with new (or expected) siblings may like to talk about Lady's concerns about the new baby. The way the story is told from the dogs' perspective may be of interest to younger kids, who are just learning that not everyone sees the same things exactly the same way. And many kids will identify with Lady's sense of frustration when the adored Siamese cats frame her for destroying the living room.

> PROFANITY: None.
> NUDITY/SEXUAL REFERENCES: None.
> ALCOHOL/DRUG ABUSE: None.
> VIOLENCE/SCARINESS: Lady is unfairly blamed, captured by the dog-catcher; a scene with a rat.
> TOLERANCE/DIVERSITY ISSUES: Class issues.

✳ **QUESTIONS FOR KIDS:**
- Why does Lady think her owners' names are "Jim Dear" and "Darling"?
- Why was Lady worried about what would happen when the baby came?
- How did Lady feel when Aunt Sarah blamed her for what the cats did?
- Why didn't Lady like Tramp at first? What made her change her mind?

✳ **ACTIVITIES:** Make up a story about what might happen with the puppies after the movie ends. And have a spaghetti dinner!

✳ Peter Pan

1953, 77 min, NR, 4 and up
Dir: Hamilton Luske, Clyde Geronimi, Wilfred Jackson. Hans Conreid, Bobby Driscoll, Kathryn Beaumont

✳ **PLOT:** This is the Disney version of the Victorian classic about the boy who would never grow up. Wendy, Michael, and John Darling, three London children, meet Peter Pan, a boy who can fly. He has been drawn to their warm, comfortable home, and to Wendy's stories. He sprinkles them with fairy dust, and they fly off past the "second star to the right," where he lives in a magical place called Neverland. There they rescue an Indian princess and fight pirates led by Captain Hook before returning home to wave good-bye as Peter returns to Neverland without them.

✳ **DISCUSSION:** The animation in this movie is as lively as its energetic hero. The scenes set in Victorian London are beautiful, and the shift in perspective as the children round Big Ben and fly off to Neverland is sublimely vertiginous.

Most children see Peter as that wonderful ideal, a child with the power to do whatever he pleases for as long as he pleases. The story does have moments that are whimsical but also very odd: The nanny is a dog; the crocodile that ate Captain Hook's hand keeps following him for another taste; Peter loses his shadow; the Lost Boys have no parents and, unlike Peter, no special powers, fairy guardian, or unquenchable brio. Some children find this engaging, but a few find it troublesome, or worry about what happened to Peter's parents and whether he will be all right without them. They may also be sad that the story ends with Peter bringing the Darling children home and then going back to Neverland without them.

PROFANITY: None.

NUDITY/SEXUAL REFERENCES: None.

ALCOHOL/DRUG ABUSE: None.

VIOLENCE/SCARINESS: Sword fight.

TOLERANCE/DIVERSITY ISSUES: The "What Makes the Red Man Red" song is embarrassingly racist and sexist. There is also a sexist overlay to the entire story, with Peter rapturously adored by all the females and at best indifferent in return. A best-selling pop psychology book of some years ago played off of this notion, theorizing that some men suffer from "the Peter Pan Syndrome" (fear of commitment), dividing women into two categories: mother-figure "Wendys" and playmate "Tinkerbells." Tinkerbell, who is, of course, a fairy, is the only female in the story who is capable of much action other than nurturing, and she is petty and spiteful (though ultimately loyal). When he first meets Wendy, Peter says, "Girls talk too much," which one boy who watched with me thought was rapturously funny.

✳ **QUESTIONS FOR KIDS:**
- Have you ever thought that you didn't want to grow up?
- Have you ever thought that you'd like to be a grown-up right now? What would you do?
- Would you like to visit Neverland?

✳ **CONNECTIONS:** The animated version of this popular story is the first to feature a real boy (instead of a woman) in the title role. The Mary Martin version for television that parents of today's kids may remember from their own childhoods is also available on video, with Cyril Ritchard impeccable as Mr. Darling/Captain Hook, and a terrific score that includes "I'm Flying" and "Tender Shepherd."

Don't waste your time on Steven Spielberg's 1991 sequel, *Hook,* with Robin Williams as a grown-up Peter Pan who must go back to rescue his children from Dustin Hoffman as Captain Hook with the help of Julia Roberts as Tinkerbell. The stars, the production design, and some spectacular special effects cannot make up for the incoherent joylessness of the script and genuinely disturbing moments like the death of one of the Lost Boys.

✳ Sleeping Beauty

1959, 75 min, NR, 5 and up
Dir: Clyde Geronimi. Mary Costa, Eleanor Audley

✳ **PLOT:** The king and queen happily celebrate the birth of their daughter, Princess Aurora. The young prince who is betrothed to the baby and three good fairies, Flora, Fauna, and Merryweather, join the celebration. But wicked Maleficent, a bad fairy, is enraged when she is not included. She arrives at the party to cast a spell on the baby princess. When she turns sixteen, she will prick her finger on the spindle of a spinning wheel and die.

The good fairies cannot remove the spell, but they change it from death to a deep sleep from which Aurora can be awakened only by love's first kiss. The king and queen try to protect the princess by sending her off with the good fairies to live in a tiny cottage in the woods until her sixteenth birthday is over. They cannot use their magic powers because it would lead Maleficent to the princess. Aurora (called Briar Rose) grows up. Out in the woods, she meets the prince, and they fall in love, not knowing they are already engaged. But the fairies prepare for her birthday party and argue about whether the dress they are making for Aurora should be pink or blue, and cannot resist using their magic. Maleficent discovers where they are and is able to make Aurora prick her finger and fall into a deep sleep. Maleficent also captures the prince to make sure he cannot break the spell. After the fairies help him escape, Maleficent turns herself into a dragon to stop him. He kills the dragon and wakes Aurora with a kiss. At her birthday party, they dance, not even noticing that her dress turns from blue to pink as the fairies continue to argue about the color.

✳ **DISCUSSION:** In this classic story, as in *Snow White,* a sleeping princess can only be awakened by a kiss from the prince. Psychiatrist Bruno Bettelheim and others have written extensively about the meaning of these stories, and the ways in which they symbolize the transition to adulthood and sexual awakening. Bettelheim's theory was that such fairy tales begin to prepare children for developments they are not ready to assimilate consciously.

There is no reason to discuss this interpretation with children, of course. But it is worthwhile to talk with them about Maleficent, one of Disney's most terrifying villains, and why her bitter jealousy makes her so obsessed with vengeance. Is that what she really wants? Isn't she doing exactly the opposite of what is required to achieve her real goal, acceptance? Children also enjoy the little squabbles of the three good fairies, which may remind them of arguments with their siblings.

PROFANITY: None.
NUDITY/SEXUAL REFERENCES: None.
ALCOHOL/DRUG ABUSE: None.
VIOLENCE/SCARINESS: Very scary battle with the dragon.
TOLERANCE/DIVERSITY ISSUES: None.

✳ **QUESTIONS FOR KIDS:**
• Why is Maleficent so angry?
• Why does she think that hurting Aurora and her family will make her feel better?
• Why do the good fairies argue with each other?

❋ **CONNECTIONS:** Watch the Faerie Tale Theatre version of this story and compare them.

❋ **ACTIVITIES:** The score in this movie is based on Tchaikovsky's *Sleeping Beauty* ballet. Play that music and see if your family can hear the melody used in "Once Upon a Dream." Read some of the other versions of the story.

Snow White and the Seven Dwarfs

1937, 83 min, NR, 5 and up
Dir: Ben Sharpsteen. Adriana Caselotti, Lucille LaVerne

❋ **PLOT:** Snow White (Adriana Caselotti) is a sweet girl whose stepmother, the queen (Lucille LaVerne), is vain and cruel. Snow White dreams of a prince to love, and meets the prince of her dreams when she is fetching water for the castle. Meanwhile, each night, the queen looks into a magic mirror and asks who is the fairest one of all. The mirror tells her that it is she, and she is satisfied. But one night, the mirror tells her that Snow White has become more fair, and the queen, consumed with jealousy, tells her huntsman to take Snow White to the forest and kill her. The tenderhearted huntsman cannot kill her and instead tells her to run away. Racing through the forest terrified, Snow White collapses in tears. But she makes friends with the animals who live in the woods, and they lead her to a small cottage. Once inside, she cleans up the mess, singing, "Whistle While You Work." She sees the small beds and thinks that children live in the house, but it turns out that it is the home of seven dwarfs, who work each day digging jewels from a mine. When they come home, they are surprised to find her stretched out across their beds, sound asleep. But they soon make friends with her and are delighted to have her stay and take care of them.

Eventually, the queen discovers that Snow White is still alive. The queen makes a poisoned apple and turns herself into an old hag so she can deliver it to her. Snow White at first follows the dwarfs's advice not to speak to strangers, but finally she takes a bite of the apple and collapses. The queen runs away and falls into a steep ravine.

The dwarfs are heartbroken and create a beautiful crystal bier for Snow White to lie on. The prince discovers her there and gives her a kiss, which awakens her, whereupon he carries her off to live happily ever after.

❋ **DISCUSSION:** Children used to today's Disney stories may be surprised by a more passive heroine and by a score more classical than pop. But in addition to its historical value as the first animated feature, it is still a delight, with memorable songs and characters. It is hard to remember that before Disney the dwarfs in the Snow White story had no names and no individual characters. Sneezy, Sleepy, Grumpy, Dopey, Doc, Happy, and

Bashful are all vivid characters, and their dance number with Snow White is a highlight.

This movie provides a good opportunity to discuss jealousy, and how to handle it. And, of course, it raises issues about women and beauty, about women's role in the home, and about finding happiness only through dreams of "Someday My Prince Will Come." Blended families are often sensitive about the traditional fairy-tale villain being the "wicked step-mother," and some children will need reassurance.

Talk to kids about how characters like Snow White might be different if they were created today, and make sure that they see a range of alternative role models.

PROFANITY: None.

NUDITY/SEXUAL REFERENCES:None.

ALCOHOL/DRUG ABUSE: None.

VIOLENCE/SCARINESS: Scary when Snow White is running through the forest (though reassuring when the animals turn out to be friendly) and when she bites the apple; the queen is scary, especially when she turns into the old hag.

TOLERANCE/DIVERSITY ISSUES: By today's standards, Dopey might well be considered an insensitive stereotype of a developmentally disabled person.

✳ QUESTIONS FOR KIDS:
- Why is the queen jealous of Snow White? Why is being beautiful so important to her?
- Why did Snow White stay at the castle?
- Why did the huntsman disobey the queen's orders?
- Why did the dwarfs love Snow White so much?

✳ CONNECTIONS: Watch some of the other versions of the Snow White story, including the Faerie Tale Theatre production with Elizabeth McGovern.

✳ ALADDIN

1992, 90 min, G, 4 and up

Dir: John Musker and Ron Clements. Robin Williams, Gilbert Gottfried

One of the best of the contemporary Disney releases, this classic tale of the magic lamp benefits tremendously from the energy and humor of Robin Williams as the genie. Only the Disney animators could find a way to keep up with Williams's pop culture Cuisinart of a brain, and the big blue genie is a marvel of rapid-fire images and associations, deliciously irreverent, a nice surprise in a Disney film.

Aladdin, a "street rat," meets the beautiful Princess Jasmine when she sneaks out to wander through the city. Jasmine refuses all of the men who want to marry her to get the throne and wants to find out more about the world outside the castle walls. Evil Jafar, the trusted adviser to the Caliph, sends Aladdin to get the magic lamp. The genie appears and offers Aladdin three wishes. Aladdin promises he will use the third wish to free the genie, and then wishes to be a prince so he can court Jasmine.

But Jafar, too, wants Jasmine, and the kingdom she will inherit. Aladdin has to find a way to free the king from Jafar's control using his own powers. And he has to find a way to feel comfortable enough about himself to allow Jasmine to know who he really is.

The songs by Alan Menken and Howard Ashman, are tuneful, sparkling, and exceptionally clever. After Ashman's death, lyrics for three songs were written by Tim Rice of **The Lion King** and *Jesus Christ, Superstar,* including those for the Oscar-winning song "A Whole New World."

✳ **CONNECTIONS:** Disney issued two made-for-video sequels, *The Return of Jafar* and *Aladdin and the King of Thieves* (only the second one featuring Williams), both very entertaining. Note that in the second, while Aladdin behaves in an honorable and accountable fashion, there is a fairly happy resolution of the relationship between Aladdin and his father, and Kaseem acknowledges that the relationship with his son is "the ultimate treasure," parents may still have concerns about some aspects of the story. Kaseem's original desertion of Aladdin and his mother and his failure to care for Aladdin after his mother's death are never really justified or apologized for; nor does he ever address or repent for his lifelong career as a thief. Kaseem seems unconcerned when the outlaws insist that Aladdin pass the test for becoming one of them, a fight to the death, and almost casually approves. He leaves the outlaws to drown when their ship sinks. And at the end, he rides off with Iago the parrot (again, voiced by the wickedly funny Gilbert Gottfried), apparently to return to a life of thievery. Parents should be prepared for questions, and may want to initiate discussion of how Aladdin might feel about his father and why he has decided to make different choices in his own life.

✳ AN AMERICAN TAIL
1986, 80 min, G, 5 and up
Dir: Don Bluth. Dom DeLuise, Christopher Plummer

Fievel Mousekewitz is a little Russian mouse who emigrates to the United States with his family after they are told that "there are no cats in America and the streets are paved with cheese." He becomes separated from his parents and sister, and is forced to work in a sweatshop by the evil Warren T. Rat (a cat in disguise). Fievel is resilient and courageous, and finds friends (including a kind cat) who help him until he finds his family. The score features the hit song "Somewhere Out There."

✳ **CONNECTIONS:** The sequel, *An American Tail: Fievel Goes West,* features the voice of Jimmy Stewart as the slow-talking Sheriff Wylie Burp.

✳ ANASTASIA
1997, 94 min, G, 5 and up
Dir: Don Bluth, Gary Goldman. Meg Ryan, John Cusack, Angela Lansbury

A sumptuous (if completely inaccurate) animated retelling of the legend of the Tsar's lost daughter, this movie will captivate kids and their families. In this version, the little Anastasia and her adored grandmother (voice of Angela Lansbury) are separated after escaping the execution of the royal family. Years later, "Anna" (Meg Ryan), who remembers nothing of her early years, leaves the orphanage where she has been raised and goes off in search of her family. She is discovered by a couple of con men who have been searching for a young woman they can pass off as Anastasia to get a reward from the dowager grandmother, who now lives in Paris. They persuade her that they are just trying to help her find out whether she is in fact the missing Anastasia, never suspecting that she really is. Trying to stop her is the evil specter Rasputin, who becomes so angry that pieces of his face and body fall off and have to be reapplied.

The animators learned their craft at Disney, and it shows. Other than the mostly forgettable score, the production is first-class, with an appealing heroine, exciting action, glamorous settings, and a tender love story. Anna is smart, brave, and loyal. She is also a rare leading lady who vanquishes the bad guy on her own.

NOTE: Kids may be concerned that, having found her grandmother, Anastasia leaves again, not wanting the life of an expatriate princess. Younger kids may be upset by the (off-screen) execution of the Tsar's family and the scary villain.

✳ **CONNECTIONS:** Older kids will want to know more about the real story. They may like seeing a live-action (but also fictionalized) version also called *Anastasia*, starring Ingrid Bergman (who won an Oscar), Helen Hayes, and Yul Brynner, or a later version made for television starring Amy Irving.

✳ THE ARISTOCATS
1970, 78 min, G, 4 and up
Dir: Wolfgang Reitherman. Eva Gabor, Phil Harris

Not one of Disney's best, but this is a nice animated story of an elegant cat (Eva Gabor) who must find her way back home with her kittens to protect their inheritance from an evil butler. The plot is sort of **Lady and the Tramp** crossed with **101 Dalmations,** with less memorable characters and songs. The highlight is the jazzy "Everybody Wants to Be a Cat" number, with Phil Harris as Thomas O'Malley "The Alley" Cat singing the lead. NOTE: There is a very odd, but brief, drunken scene when a goose drinks the wine that was supposed to be used to marinate him.

✳ BALTO
1995, 77 min, G, 5 and up
Dir: Simon Wells. Kevin Bacon, Bridget Fonda, Bob Hoskins

This is the true story of the brave dog who saved the lives of Alaskan children with diphtheria when he brought medicine to them through the snow. Kevin Bacon provides the voice for the heroic canine, half wolf/half dog, who is not accepted by either species. A jealous rival frames Balto for theft so that he will be selected to lead the rescue mission. But when they get lost, Balto steps in to save the day, with the help of his friends, a Russian goose (Bob Hoskins) and two polar bears (both pop star Phil Collins).

✳ **ACTIVITIES:** Children who visit Central Park in New York City can see a statue of Balto.

✳ BEAUTY AND THE BEAST
1991, 85 min, G, 4 and up
Dir: Gary Trousdale and Kirk Wise. Robby Benson, Jerry Orbach, Angela Lansbury

Belle is the book-loving daughter of an absent-minded inventor. She wants "more than this provincial life" and the boorish hunter Gaston, who hopes to marry her.

Lost in the woods, Belle's father stumbles into what appears to be a deserted castle. But the castle is inhabited by the Beast, once a prince, now under a spell that will last forever unless he finds love before he turns twenty-one, who locks Belle's father in the dungeon. Belle comes after her father and offers to stay in his place. At first antagonistic, she begins to find the Beast appealingly gentle and kind, wounded in spirit rather than cruel. Gaston tries to get Belle's father committed, saying that his talk of the Beast shows he is delusional. When Belle proves that the Beast exists, the townspeople form a mob to kill him, and she cannot stop them. In a fight with Gaston, the Beast is badly wounded. Belle tells him she loves him, which ends the spell. He becomes once again the handsome prince, and they live happily ever after.

✳ **CONNECTIONS:** This film became the first animated film ever to be nominated for a Best Picture Oscar. One of the most lyrically beautiful of all films ever made is Jean Cocteau's version of this story, *Belle et Bete*. The Faerie Tale Theatre version stars Susan Sarandon and Klaus Kinski, and is very well done.

✳ THE BRAVE LITTLE TOASTER
1987, 90 min, NR, 6 and up
Dir: Jerry Rees. Jon Lovitz, Phil Hartman

A group of household appliances in a summer cottage, worried about their young master, leave home to go find him, encountering many challenges and adventures along the way. Exciting and fun, with a thrilling climax and delightful voice characterizations by *Saturday Night Live* stars Phil Hartman and Jon Lovitz. NOTE: Some very tense moments, with characters in peril.

❊ **CONNECTIONS:** The story is by science-fiction author Thomas M. Disch. A straight-to-video sequel was released in 1998.

❊ THE COSMIC EYE
1985, 76 min, NR
Dir: John and Faith Hubley. Maureen Stapleton, Dizzy Gillespie
John and Faith Hubley pioneered an award-winning impressionistic, watercolor-style animation, and some of their best short pieces are included in this collection of musings on the state of the world, especially the world of children. They feature improvised dialogue by an eclectic group of professionals and amateurs, with one highlight a dialogue between two opposing soldiers guarding a border after one's hat blows over to the other one's side.

❊ FERNGULLY: THE LAST RAINFOREST
1992, 76 min, G, 6 and up
Dir: Bill Kroyer. Robin Williams, Samantha Mathis, Christian Slater, Tim Curry, Ton Loc
An evil and destructive spirit named Hexxus (voice of Tim Curry) is imprisoned in a tree by Magi, the leader of the fairies, who believes that all humans have been destroyed. Many years later, as Magi is teaching Crysta, her apprentice (voice of Samantha Mathis), they find that the humans have returned, and are cutting down all the trees. Crysta shrinks one of the humans, a young man named Zak, to save him from being hit by a falling tree, and teaches him about the importance of preserving the forest. Highlights include Robin Williams as the aptly named "Batty Koda," and gravel-voiced rapper Ton Loc as a Goanna lizard singing "If I'm Gonna Eat Somebody, It Might as Well Be You." There are some very scary moments, and the magic characters may distract kids from the lesson about environmental conservation, but it does provide a good opportunity for discussions that may help in increasing sensitivity to environmental concerns.

❊ HERCULES
1997, 93 min, G, 6 and up
Dir: John Musker, Ron Clements. James Woods, Danny DeVito, Tate Donovan
According to Disney, Hercules was the adored son of gods Zeus and Hera, stolen by Hades, ruler of the underworld, and made mortal. He must become a true hero to become a god again, so he can live with his parents on Mount Olympus. To do this, he seeks out a grouchy satyr (voice of

Danny DeVito), who trains him in fighting techniques and strategy. When he saves some children (so he thinks) and defeats the hydra (its many heads masterfully provided by computer animation), he becomes an instant celebrity, with action figures and "Air Hercules" sandals. He goes on to his other labors, but finds that is not enough to be a real hero—that comes from the heart, not the muscles.

Kids will need some preparation for this movie. What little exposition there is is provided by Spice Girl–style "muses" as a sort of gospel Greek chorus that's fun to watch but hard to follow. The role of the three fates, who share one eye between them and cut a thread when a human's life is ended, is particularly confusing.

The love interest in this movie is Meg, who sold her soul to Hades to save the life of her boyfriend, and must now try to find Hercules's weakness so that Hades can take over Olympus. She is tougher and braver than the traditional DID (as "damsels in distress" are referred to in the movie), but still very much on the sidelines in the big moments. Parents may want to talk to both boys and girls about her choices. They may also want to talk about the absence of people of color (other than the muses). The movie's other weakness is its lackluster score.

As in *Aladdin,* this movie's white-bread "aw, shucks" teenage protagonist is utterly outshone by a star turn of astonishing verve—this time, James Woods as bad guy Hades, who joins Cruella de Vil in the pantheon of unforgettable villains. Sidekicks Pain and Panic (Bobcat Goldthwait and Matt (*Max Headroom*) Frewer) are wickedly funny as well.

This provides a good opportunity to talk to kids about who the real heroes are, and how society treats its heroes. Why do we buy products endorsed by athletes (or movie tie-ins)? It is also worth talking with them about Hercules's motivation: Is wanting to be a god a good reason to want to be a hero? Do we see any evidence that he (or anyone else in the movie) has much concern for the well-being of the community?

NOTE: While the tone of the movie is lighthearted, parts of it may be too scary and intense for smaller children. Some may also be confused or even upset about the underworld and what happens when people die.

✳ THE LAND BEFORE TIME
1988, 69 min, G, 5 and up
Dir: Don Bluth

Littlefoot, a young orphan Apatosaurus, must find his way to the Golden Valley, the last place with the food he needs to survive, where his grandparents are waiting. He meets up with Cera (a Triceratops), Ducky (a Hadrosaur), and Petrie (a Pteradactyl), and they learn to respect, protect, and rely on each other. NOTE: Scary scene when Littlefoot's mother is killed; other scenes with characters in peril.

✳ **CONNECTIONS:** There are several made-for-video sequels.

✳ THE LION KING
1994, 88 min, G, 5 and up
Dir: Roger Allers and Rob Minkoff. James Earl Jones, Jeremy Irons, Matthew Broderick, Moira Kelly

Sort of a cross between *Richard III* and *Hamlet,* this is the story of Simba (Jonathan Taylor Thomas as a child, Matthew Broderick as an adult), the cub of Mufasa (James Earl Jones), the king of the jungle. Simba "just can't wait to be king." But his evil Uncle Scar (Jeremy Irons), bitterly jealous of Mufasa, wants to be king, so he arranges for Mufasa to be killed in a stampede and to have Simba think he is responsible.

Simba runs away and finds friends in Pumbaa the warthog (Ernie Sabella) and Timon the meerkat (Nathan Lane), who advise him that the best philosophy is "hakuna matata" (no worries). Simba grows up thinking he has escaped from his past, but his childhood friend Nala finds him and tells him that under Scar's leadership, the tribe has suffered badly. She persuades him to return to take on his responsibilities as King of the Pridelands. He learns that it was Scar who caused Mufasa's death, and he vanquishes Scar to become king.

NOTE: The death of Mufasa is genuinely scary. More troubling is the arrogance of the "Circle of Life" explanation, which is mighty reassuring as long as you are the one on top of the food chain. And worse than that is the whole "hakuna matata" idea, which is genuinely irresponsible. Make sure that kids realize that even Simba finds out that he cannot run away from his problems.

✳ **CONNECTIONS:** Not just a movie, but a marketing phenomenon, this blockbuster was one of the highest grossing films of the year. Amazingly, it made even more money in merchandise than it did at the box office, a fact for which audiences have been paying ever since, as each subsequent Disney animated movie seems to be designed primarily as a commercial for T-shirts, lunch boxes, and action figures. The score, and the song "Circle of Life," with authentic African rhythms and instruments, won Oscars for Elton John and Tim Rice, and the movie later became a Broadway blockbuster.

✳ THE LITTLE MERMAID
1989, 82 min, G, 5 and up
Dir: John Musker and Ron Clemente. Pat Carroll, Buddy Hackett

After some lackluster years, Disney came back into the top rank of animated features with this superbly entertaining musical, based loosely on the fairy tale by Hans Christian Andersen (but with a happier ending). Ariel was the first in a series of refreshingly plucky Disney heroines. Instead of dreaming about the day her prince will come, or waiting for a fairy godmother or a prince's kiss, Ariel is a spirited and curious mermaid who is willing to take action in order to meet Prince Eric, the man of her dreams, though she is gullible and impetuous in agreeing to the terms demanded by the seawitch in exchange for making it possible for her to go on land. She goes to the seawitch (Pat Carroll, who is first rate as Ursula the octopus) to ask her to turn her tail into legs. But Ursula has two conditions. Ariel has to give up her voice. And if Eric does not kiss her within three days, Ariel will become Ursula's slave forever. She agrees, and has to find a way to persuade Eric to fall in love with her without using her voice, despite Ursula's crafty plans to prevent it. NOTE: In addition to the "normal" scariness of the seawitch, some children may find the casual bloodthirstiness of the French chef upsetting, especially in the musical number in which he tries to turn Sebastian into crabmeat.

✳ **CONNECTIONS:** The wonderful voice characterizations in this film include Buddy Hackett (*The Music Man*) as Scuttle the scavanging seagull, and Samuel E. Wright as Sebastian, the calypso-singing crab. The first-class musical score by Alan Menken and Howard Ashman (who worked together on the Off-Broadway hit *Little Shop of Horrors*) ranks with the best of Broadway and won Oscars for Best Score and Best Song (for "Under the Sea").

✳ LITTLE NEMO: ADVENTURES IN SLUMBERLAND

1990, 85 min, G, 5 and up
Dir: Misami Hata and William T. Hurtz. Mickey Rooney

The brilliant comic strip series by Winsor McCay was adapted for this colorful film about a boy who must save King Morpheus of Slumberland from the King of Nightmares after he disobeys orders and opens the forbidden door. NOTE: Some scary scenes can get too intense for very young children.

✳ **CONNECTIONS:** The songs are by Richard M. and Robert B. Sherman (*Mary Poppins*).

✳ OLIVER & COMPANY

1988, 72 min, G, 5 and up
Dir: George Scribner. Billy Joel, Bette Midler, Dom DeLuise

Loosely based on Dickens's *Oliver Twist,* this animated Disney release is the story of an orphaned cat named Oliver who is befriended by vagabond dogs led by the dashing rapscallion, Dodger. Oliver is adopted by lonely rich girl Jenny, whose prize-winning poodle Georgette (Bette Midler) has a world-class case of jealousy. First Oliver and then Jenny are kidnapped for ransom, but are saved from wicked Sikes by the clever animals.

While not up there with the Disney classics, this movie has real pleasures, especially Dodger's "Why Should I Worry" musical number (written and sung by Billy Joel) with Dodger leaping and dancing through Manhattan traffic. There are also some scary moments, but kids will appreciate the way that Oliver takes care of himself, and the way that the dogs take care of him, of each other, and of their human friend, the hapless Fagin (Dom DeLuise).

❄ **CONNECTIONS:** Watch the Academy Award–winning musical version of *Oliver!* or the David Lean drama *Oliver Twist* to see a more authentic presentation of Dickens's story.

❄ ONE HUNDRED AND ONE DALMATIONS
1961, 79 min, G, 5 and up
Dir: Wolfgang Reitherman, Hamilton Luske, and Clyde Geronimi. Rod Taylor, J. Pat O'Malley

Like **Lady and the Tramp,** this story is told from the perspective of dogs, this time two dalmations, Pongo and Perdita, the cherished pets of Roger and Anita. Anita's old friend, one of the most notorious villains in movie history, is the aptly named Cruella de Vil. Her henchmen kidnap Perdita's puppies and eighty-four others so she can make them into a dalmation fur coat. Pongo and Perdita, with the help of their animal friends, undertake a daring rescue. The puppies are adorable, and the movie is exciting, funny (with a sly poke at television and the kids who watch it), and fun.

❄ **CONNECTION:** *Movieline* magazine once asked actresses to name the most memorable female villain in the history of the movies, and Cruella was at the top of the list. A live-action version was released in 1997, with Glenn Close as Cruella. Close is wonderful, but the movie relies too much on slapstick, and the real dogs do not have the personality and range of expression of their animated predecessors.

❄ THE RESCUERS
1977, 76 min, G, 5 and up
Dir: Wolfgang Reitherman, John Lounsbery, and Art Stevens. Eva Gabor, Bob Newhart, Geraldine Page

Margery Sharp's beloved books about the tiny but brave mice of the Rescue Aid Society are the basis for this story about elegant Miss Bianca (Eva Gabor) and cautious but valiant Bernard (Bob Newhart), who rescue an orphan girl kidnapped by wicked Madame Medusa (Geraldine Page).

❄ **CONNECTION:** The sequel, *The Rescuers Down Under,* sends them to Australia.

❄ THE SWAN PRINCESS
1994, 90 min, G, 5 and up

Dir: Richard Rich. Jack Palance, John Cleese, Stephen Wright

This animated fairy tale never got the audience it deserved, possibly because the title led some kids to think it was just for girls. But it is an exciting story, based on the classic ballet about a princess turned into a swan by an evil sorcerer. Not only is the heroine braver than Disney's *Pocahontas,* but the movie has more imaginative artwork, funnier animal sidekicks, and better music, and is lots more fun.

✳ THE THIEF AND THE COBBLER
1995, 72 min, G, 5 and up
Dir: Richard Williams. Jennifer Beals, Matthew Broderick, Jonathan Winters, Vincent Price

This neglected but absolutely delightful animated musical (theatrically released as *Arabian Knight*) is a must for family viewing. A shy cobbler and a plucky princess save ancient Baghdad in this fairy tale, produced by the Oscar-winning animator from *Who Framed Roger Rabbit.* It is one of the most visually inventive animated movies ever made, with dazzling optical illusions and shifts in perspective. Jennifer *(Flashdance)* Beals and Matthew *(Ferris Bueller's Day Off)* Broderick provide the voices for the leads, and Vincent Price provides silky menace as the voice of the evil sorcerer. Jonathan Winters provides the voice for the hilarious thief. The musical numbers are pleasant, with one sensational showstopper when the desert brigands explain that if you don't go to school, you'll turn out like them. Unlike the recent Disney movies, this was not designed to sell merchandise, just to tell a story, which it does very, very well. It is suitable for everyone except maybe the smallest children, who might be frightened by the hulking bad guys.

✳ TOY STORY
1995, 80 min, G, 5 and up
Dir: John Lasseter. Tom Hanks, Tim Allen

This Disney release is the first feature film animated entirely by computer. Although the dazzling technology is especially well-suited to a story in which the major characters are made out of plastic, it is the unpretentious imagination and energy of the people behind the story and the outstanding vocal performances that make the movie an instant classic.

The story is about the toys belonging to a boy named Andy. His favorite is a sheriff from the Old West named Woody (Tom Hanks). He acts as the leader of the rest of Andy's toys, including a Tyrannosaurus rex (Wallace Shawn) and Mr. Potatohead (Don Rickles). All is going well until Andy receives for his birthday an astronaut named Buzz Lightyear (Tim Allen of television's *Home Improvement*). Woody becomes jealous, and in an effort to keep Andy from taking Buzz with him on an excursion, Andy accidentally knocks Buzz out the window. Woody follows, and the rest of the movie consists of their efforts to return home before the family moves away.

Children may relate to the idea of the sibling rivalry between Woody and Buzz, and the movie may provide a good starting point for a discussion of jealous feelings. It may also be fun for parents to point out some favorites from their own childhoods, including Mr. (and Mrs.) Potatohead, Etch-A-Sketch, Slinky Dog, and Barrel Of Monkeys.

NOTE: This movie may be too scary for very young children. The three-year-old with me insisted on leaving less than halfway through, and it got scarier after that. Andy's next-door neighbor is a vicious and destructive boy named Sid, who mutilates and tortures toys. His room is filled with genuinely grotesque creations made from bits and pieces of toys—sort of Geppeto's workshop as seen by Stephen King. Sid gets a relatively mild comeuppance as the toys "break the rules" to scare him into being kind to all toys in the future. Children may also be troubled by the notion that the toys are "real" whenever the humans are out of the room. This is even more confusing because one of the cleverest aspects of the movie's plot is that Buzz does not know he is a toy, and thinks he really is a space explorer on his way "to infinity and beyond."

Note also that Andy does not have a father, although it is presented so subtly that most kids will miss it. The two toys have special appeal not only for Andy to use to imagine himself as the fantasy male archetypes of cowboy and astronaut, but also perhaps as father substitutes. Meanwhile, there are no strong female toys, only a simpering Bo Peep, who flirts with Woody.

✳ YELLOW SUBMARINE
1968, 84 min, G, 4 and up
Dir: George Dunning. The Beatles

All is peace, love, and music in gentle Pepperland until the wicked Blue Meanies take over. The Beatles come to the rescue via the title vessel, meeting all kinds of strange and interesting characters along the way. This movie is a pleasure for the eye, ear, and heart, featuring spectacular animation, gorgeous music (including the title song, "When I'm 64," "Lucy in the Sky with Diamonds," "All Together Now," and the lovely "Sea of Time," (written by longtime Beatle collaborator George Martin), witty wordplay (lots of puns and some sly political satire), and a sweet story with a nonviolent happy ending.

NOTE: Although rumors suggest that songs like "Lucy in the Sky with Diamonds" are veiled references to drugs, and the animation sometimes has a psychedelic look, there is nothing that remotely approaches drug or alcohol use of any kind. The violence is extremely mild, especially by cartoon standards. The Meanies take over by "bonking" people with green apples.

✳ **CONNECTIONS:** Actors provide the voices of the animated Beatle characters, but the Beatles themselves appear in the last few minutes of the movie exhorting the audience to keep Blue Meanies away from "this theater" by singing along. Note that one of the scriptwriters was then-obscure classics professor Erich Segal, who would go on shortly afterward to write the book and screenplay for *Love Story*.

SEE ALSO:

Alice in Wonderland

Charlotte's Web

Fantasia

The Great Mouse Detective

Gulliver's Travels

The Phantom Tollbooth

Pinocchio

The Point

The Sword in the Stone

BOOKS ON THE SCREEN

Fiction reveals truth which reality obscures.
—JESSAMYN WEST

One of the greatest of family pleasures is reading a book aloud and then watching the movie together. The following movies are based on books that are exceptionally good for family reading. Many are classic books for children to read on their own, as well. Although it usually works best to read the book first so that your ability to visualize the story is not hampered by the movie, in some cases a movie can lead a child to the book, especially in the case of a reluctant reader. It can also be fun to set up a parent-child reading group with a few other families, to read and discuss a book and then watch the movie together. The Rabbit Ears series, all based on outstanding books for children, and episodes of the great PBS series, "Reading Rainbow," "Ghostwriter," and "Wishbone" (all available on video) are well worth watching to expand a child's interest in books and reading.

Alice in Wonderland
1951, 75 min, NR, 4 and up
Dir: Clyde Geronimi, Hamilton Luske, Wilfred Jackson. Kathryn Beaumont, Ed Wynn, Richard Hadyn, Sterling Holloway

* **PLOT:** The children's classic by Lewis Carroll about the girl who falls down a rabbit hole is presented by Disney in this lively and tuneful version. Alice is reading with her sister when she sees a white rabbit, fully dressed, muttering about being late. She follows him down a rabbit hole to Wonderland, where she grows bigger and smaller, meets the Cheshire Cat, attends a mad tea party, talks to a caterpillar who puffs on a hookah, and triumphs over the Queen of Hearts, before finding that it was all a dream.

* **DISCUSSION:** Like another perennial favorite, *The Wizard of Oz,* this is the story of a girl who thinks she wants to go somewhere exciting but,

once she gets there, spends the entire time trying to find her way home. Wonderland may be different and exciting, but its inhabitants are often rude and unfriendly, even hostile. It is worth noting that Alice does just about everything we tell our children not to do, including going off with strangers and eating and drinking things that may be dangerous. She acknowledges her mistakes, which children will relate to, singing "I give myself very good advice (but I very seldom follow it)." Children may enjoy silly characters like the Mad Hatter and March Hare (they love the celebration of "unbirthdays"), and the tantrums of the despotic Queen of Hearts, who constantly screams, "Off with their heads!"

PROFANITY: None.

NUDITY/SEXUAL REFERENCES: None.

ALCOHOL/DRUG ABUSE: During the psychedelic 60s, the scene with the caterpillar puffing on a hookah was popularly considered to be a reference to opium or hashish, possibly because the movie, like the book, has such a surreal and dreamlike quality, but there is nothing in the movie (or the book) to suggest that connection.

ALCOHOL/DRUG ABUSE: None.

VIOLENCE/SCARINESS: None.

TOLERANCE/DIVERSITY ISSUES: None.

✳ **QUESTIONS FOR KIDS:**
- Would you like to go to Wonderland? Who would you like to see there? Who would you like to *be* there?
- Who is the silliest person in Wonderland? Why?
- Alice sings "I give myself very good advice (but I very seldom follow it)." Do you ever feel that way? Why is it sometimes hard to follow your own advice?

✳ **CONNECTIONS:** Some of the voices may sound familiar. Old-time radio stars Ed Wynn (the Mad Hatter), Richard Haydn (the Caterpillar), and Jerry Colonna (March Hare) appear, as does the inimitable Sterling Holloway (Cheshire Cat), best known to children as the voice of Winnie the Pooh.

✳ **ACTIVITIES:** All children should read (or have read aloud to them) the book by Carroll, as well as its sequel, *Through the Looking Glass.* They may not appreciate the arcane references to Victorian conventions and mathematical concepts that Oxford mathematician Charles Dodgson included in the story, but they will enjoy the book's delightful language and more detailed descriptions and adventures. Middle schoolers and high schoolers will appreciate the wonderful *Annotated Alice,* by Martin Gardner, which explains most of the allusions and brain teasers.

Have an unbirthday party—or a mad tea party!

Bedknobs and Broomsticks

1971, 112 min, G, 6 and up
Dir: Robert Stevenson. Angela Lansbury, David Tomlinson, Roddy McDowall

PLOT: Based on the book by Mary Norton (also the author of *The Borrowers*) this is the story of three Cockney children evacuated from London during WWII, who are placed with Miss Eglantine Price (Angela Lansbury), though she is reluctant to take them and insists it can only be temporary. Miss Price is completing a correspondence course in witchcraft and has reached the level of "apprentice witch," permitting her to fly on a broomstick. When she takes it out for a spin, the children see her and, threatening to expose her, persuade her to let them into the magic. She then enchants the bedknob so that when it is twisted, it will take them wherever they want to go. When she receives word that the correspondence course has been canceled, she and the children go off together in search of the teacher, Professor Brown (David Tomlinson). He joins them as they travel on the bed, first undersea and then to an island in another dimension, where the inhabitants are talking animals. On the island, they find the necklace containing the secret magic words they need for a spell to make inanimate objects behave as though they were alive. Home again, they use that spell to fight off Nazi invaders. Afterward, Miss Price retires from witchcraft and Professor Brown joins the army, but it is clear they have become a family.

DISCUSSION: Many of the people behind *Mary Poppins* worked on this movie. While it does not have the same magic as *Mary Poppins,* there are some delightful moments, especially as Miss Price struggles to master basic witchcraft skills. The animated scenes on the island are done with a great deal of verve and imagination, especially the fast-moving slapstick of a soccer game featuring animal athletes, including an ostrich who sticks his head into the field whenever trouble approaches. The movie is long and episodic, so it lends itself well to viewing in shorter segments for restless younger children.

PROFANITY: None.
NUDITY/SEXUAL REFERENCES: None.
ALCOHOL/DRUG ABUSE: None.
VIOLENCE/SCARINESS: Battle between the enchanted suits of armor and the Nazis.
TOLERANCE/DIVERSITY ISSUES: A couple of "women can't do that" remarks.

QUESTIONS FOR KIDS:
- Listen to the song about "The Age of Not Believing." What is that about?
- Why can small children believe in magic more easily than older ones?
- Look at the way two of the characters on the island react when they are upset: The ostrich buries his head, and the king (a lion) screams and acts like a bully. How well do those ways work? Why?

✳ **CONNECTIONS:** Children might recognize a grown-up Roddy McDowall as the boy from *Lassie, Come Home* and *My Friend Flicka,* and Angela Lansbury from *National Velvet* and television's *Murder, She Wrote.* Tomlinson played the father in *Mary Poppins.*

✳The Jungle Book
1942, 109 min, NR, 8 and up
Dir: Zoltan Korda. Sabu

✳ **PLOT:** Based on Rudyard Kipling's book about a boy raised by wolves, this version concentrates on Mowgli's return to his family's village and the challenges he faces as he tries to adjust to "civilized" life. When Mowgli's father is killed by Shere Kahn (the tiger), the toddler wanders off into the jungle and is raised by wolves. He finds the village again when he is about fourteen (played by Sabu). His mother, who does not recognize him at first, teaches him how to speak their language and how people in the village behave.

Mowgli wants to buy a "tooth" (knife) to kill Shere Kahn. He buys one from Buldeo (Joseph Calleia), a hunter who hunts for reasons of pride instead of need. Though Buldeo tells his daughter Mahala not to talk to Mowgli, she goes with him into the jungle, where he shows her an abandoned palace filled with gold and jewels. In the palace, a cobra warns them that the jewels are deadly, especially a ruby-embedded ax. Mowgli allows Mahala to take one coin. When her father finds it, he wants Mowgli to show him how to get more. He accidentally drops the coin so that a barber and his customer see it, and they want to find the palace, too. They all find the palace, but fight over the treasure. When the barber and his customer are killed, Buldeo lights a fire in the jungle. Mowgli saves his mother and goes back to live in the jungle.

✳ **DISCUSSION:** Visually lush and striking (produced by some of the same people who made *The Thief of Bagdad*), this version is in sharp contrast with the Disney animated movie, and has a real sense of the dangers in the jungle and the different kinds of dangers in the "civilized" village.

Like other "fish out of water" stories, this movie provides an opportunity to deconstruct "civilization" a bit by looking at it from the perspective of an outsider. Mowgli compares the values of the "wolf-pack" and the "man-pack" and finds it hard to understand why someone would take something of no inherent value (money) in exchange for something of value (a "tooth" to help him kill Shere Kahn), or why someone would kill an animal to display its hide. Children will enjoy Mowgli's ability to talk to animals, and the way he treats them with respect and affection. He is clearly more at home with the animals than he is with the humans.

PROFANITY: None.

NUDITY/SEXUAL REFERENCES: None.

ALCOHOL/DRUG ABUSE: None.

VIOLENCE/SCARINESS: Mowgli's father is killed by a tiger (off-screen); Mowgli subdues a cobra and kills a tiger with a knife; hunter kills a cobra; a fire in the forest; bad guys kill each other; person is eaten by a crocodile (not explicit).

TOLERANCE/DIVERSITY ISSUES: Native parts played by Caucasian actors, except for Sabu.

✳ QUESTIONS FOR KIDS:

- What things are difficult for Mowgli when he comes back to the village?
- What does he think is better in the jungle?
- Why doesn't Mowgli think the treasure in the palace has value?
- Why does the barber's customer think that Mowgli can change into animals?
- What is the difference between Mowgli's ideas about hunting and Buldeo's ideas?
- Why does Mowgli's mother let him go back into the jungle?

✳ **CONNECTIONS:** The author is Rudyard Kipling, also the author of *Kim* and the *Just So Stories*. The animated Disney ***The Jungle Book*** focuses on Mowgli's years in the jungle, ending as he approaches the village for the first time. Disney also made a good live-action version in 1995 (released as *Rudyard Kipling's Jungle Book*). It may be more accessible to kids used to modern styles of moviemaking, but despite an appealing performance by Jason Scott Lee as Mowgli, it does not have the atmosphere and resonance of this earlier version.

✳ **ACTIVITIES:** Take the kids to the zoo to see the panther, tiger, and cobra.

Kim

1950, 113 min, G, 8 and up
Dir: Victor Saville. Errol Flynn, Dean Stockwell, Paul Lukas, Cecil Calloway

✳ **PLOT:** Kim (Dean Stockwell) is a street kid who lives by his wits in Victorian India. The orphaned son of white English parents, he disguises himself as a native, because "missionaries take white boys to school" and he wants his freedom. He lives by petty theft and by running small errands for people like Red Beard (Errol Flynn), also a white man who dresses and lives as a native.

On his way to deliver a message for Red Beard, Kim meets a mysterious holy man (Paul Lukas), who is searching for a mythical holy river that will cleanse sins. Kim accompanies the holy man as an apprentice to make it easier for him to reach the place where he must deliver Red Beard's message. He becomes fascinated with the holy man and stays on with him until he is discovered by British officers who realize that he is the son of a former colleague and send him to a military orphanage, promising him they will "make a white boy of you." Unhappy at the orphanage, he is sent to a posh private school, St. Xavier's, where he has trouble fitting in. He lags far behind the other boys in schoolwork, and is constantly told that what he is used to doing is "not done at St. Xavier's." On his way back to the military orphanage for school break, he runs away and returns to native garb. Red Beard's friend trains him in "the great game," espionage, and, reunited with the holy man, he gives crucial aid to the British in the battles along the Afghanistan border. The holy man dies, and Kim and Red Beard ride off together.

✳ **DISCUSSION:** This is a colorful and exciting story based on the book by Rudyard Kipling. As in **Oliver!, Huckleberry Finn, Aladdin,** and *Home Alone,* it is the story of a boy who must take care of himself in the adult world, and Kim does a reassuringly good job. He even takes good care of the holy man. One theme of interest in the movie is the way that he is able to move back and forth between two different worlds, each apparently requiring different clothes. In one scene, he is able to make himself almost invisible by dyeing his skin and putting on a turban; even his schoolmate does not recognize him when he asks for alms. Only one character can tell that he is a fraud: the "fat man," who sees that his beads and belt are wrong.

Topics for discussion include the various petty thefts and subterfuges Kim uses and whether they are justified, as well as the larger issues of colonialism and the author's point of view.

PROFANITY: None.

NUDITY/SEXUAL REFERENCES: None.

ALCOHOL/DRUG ABUSE: None.

VIOLENCE/SCARINESS: Battle scenes; holy man dies; Kim kills an enemy; Kim in peril.

TOLERANCE/DIVERSITY ISSUES: Issues of caste and race are an implicit theme, though from the perspective of the colonists.

✳ **QUESTIONS FOR KIDS:**
- Why didn't Kim want to be with people like his parents?
- Kim lied and stole—was this right?
- How did Kim know which was the right side in the battle between the British and the Russians?
- Kim lived in several different environments—what were the advantages and disadvantages of each one?
- What do you think Kim will do next?

✳ **CONNECTIONS:** Other movies of this era include the charming *Wee Willie Winkie,* with Shirley Temple (directed by John Ford), and the adventure classic *Gunga Din,* with Cary Grant, Victor McLaglen, and Douglas Fairbanks, Jr. Older children and teenagers may like to see colonialism from the other side in *Gandhi.*

Dean Stockwell has had a long and varied career, including *Compulsion* (based on the Leopold and Loeb murder case) and *Married to the Mob,* along with television's *Quantum Leap.*

✳ **ACTIVITIES:** Kim tests his memory with a game, in which he has to memorize the objects on a tray. It might be fun to test the family the same way—or by looking at several items on a tray and then trying to guess which ones have been removed.

✳Little Lord Fauntleroy

1936, 98 min, b&w, NR, 6 and up
Dir: John Cromwell. Freddie Bartholomew, C. Aubrey Smith, Mickey Rooney

✳ **PLOT:** Cedric (Freddie Bartholomew), who lives in New York with his widowed mother, finds out that he is the grandson of a British earl and is to go to England to live in his castle. After marrying an American, Cedric's father was estranged from the earl, but now that both of the earl's sons have died, Cedric is the only heir. He says good-bye to his best friends, Mr. Hobbs (Guy Kibbee) and Dick (Mickey Rooney), and leaves for England, not knowing that the earl has forbidden his mother to set foot in the castle.

The earl is a rigid and somewhat pompous man, but, encouraged by his mother, Cedric sees everything the earl does as wonderfully generous and kind. The old man is utterly charmed by Cedric, as are all who meet him, and he tries to live up to Cedric's image of him. They grow to love each other. There is a crisis when they are told that the earl's older son was married and had a son of his own before he died, and that boy is the rightful heir. With the help of Dick, they prove the new heir a fraud, the earl realizes that Cedric's mother is a fine woman, and they all live happily ever after.

✳ **DISCUSSION:** This is basically a male version of **Pollyanna.** Like Pollyanna, Cedric goes to live with a wealthy but crusty and snobbish relative, insists on seeing the best in everyone (even when it isn't there), and wins the hearts of all who know him. Not quite as sugary as its reputation, it may still put off kids who think Cedric is too perfect. But his colorful friends, his maturity under stress, and the fun of the idea of his being brought from poverty to an Earldom make it hold up surprisingly well.

PROFANITY: None.
NUDITY/SEXUAL REFERENCES: None.
ALCOHOL/DRUG ABUSE: None.
VIOLENCE/SCARINESS: None.
TOLERANCE/DIVERSITY ISSUES: Class issues.

✳ QUESTIONS FOR KIDS:
- Why do Cedric and his friends in New York get along so well?
- Why doesn't he notice that his grandfather doesn't like his mother?
- Why doesn't his mother want him to know that his grandfather will not talk to her?
- What is hardest for Cedric? What is hardest for his grandfather?
- Why does Mr. Hobbs not like earls? Why does the earl not like Cedric's mother? Who is more prejudiced? Why do they change their minds?

✳ **CONNECTIONS:** Kids will enjoy the book, by Frances Hodgson Burnett, the author of *The Secret Garden* and *The Little Princess*. A made for television remake in 1980 starred Ricky Schroder and Alec Guinness.

✳ A Little Princess
1995, 97 min, G, 6 and up
Dir: Alfonso Cuaron. Liesel Matthews, Eleanor Bron

✳ **PLOT:** Sara Crewe is brought to Miss Minchin's boarding school by her adored father, and promises to be "a good soldier" and be brave about staying there without him. She is the brightest girl in the school, with exquisite manners, but her odd fancies and her father's lavish provisions for her make the other girls uncomfortable or jealous. Her only friend in the school is Ermengarde, a pudgy girl who has trouble with her lessons and is very grateful for Sara's attentions. Sara also befriends Becky, a scullery maid.

Captain Crewe is missing in action. Miss Minchin takes everything from Sara and has her stay on at the school as a servant, living in an attic next to Becky. She continues to think of herself as "a good soldier," and tries to imagine she is a princess undergoing a trial to keep her spirits up despite deprivation and abuse. One night, while she is sleeping, her little attic is transformed into a comfortable bower with delicious food. She shares it with her friends. It comes from the gentleman across the street. It turns out that he has been befriending her father, not knowing that he was a close friend of his late son. Sara goes to thank him, and her father, seeing her, regains his memory. Sara leaves the school, taking Becky with her.

✳ **DISCUSSION:** Unlike Cedric in **Little Lord Fauntleroy**, Sara Crewe cannot be accused of being perfect, though she is not as deliciously unlikable as Mary in **A Secret Garden**. It takes her a long time to lose her temper and snap at Ermengarde, but she does, and she almost gives up hope. Her imagination is an important source of solace for her, and in a sense she is a stand-in for the author herself when she uses it to create stories for her friends.

This is also a wonderful movie to use for a discussion of empathy and compassion. Although Sara is desperately hungry, she gives almost all her food to a beggar child who is even hungrier. Note the way that her compassion inspires others: The baker who watches her give the buns to the beggar child is so moved that she gives the child a home.

PROFANITY: None.

NUDITY/SEXUAL REFERENCES: None.

ALCOHOL/DRUG ABUSE: None.

VIOLENCE/SCARINESS: None.

TOLERANCE/DIVERSITY ISSUES: Tolerance of individual differences.

✳ **QUESTIONS FOR KIDS:**
- Why do many of the girls in the school dislike Sara?
- Why was she ashamed when the little boy gave her a coin?
- Why did she decide to give the buns to the beggar girl? What impact did that have on the baker?
- Why was Miss Minchin so mean? What should she have done when she got the news that Sara's father was missing?

✳ **CONNECTIONS:** There are three filmed versions of this story. This version is sumptuously filmed, with gorgeous images. The time and location were changed to WWI–era New York, and the plot is changed to keep Sara's father alive. To make the story more acceptable for contemporary children, Becky, who is black, leaves with Sara, not to be her maid, as in the book, but to be her adopted sister. And Sara democratically says that all girls are princesses.

The version that is most faithful to the book is the BBC miniseries, which is available on video and is my own favorite. There is also a version with Shirley Temple, in which, she spends much of the movie looking through veterans' hospitals for her father, wounded in WWI, finally finding him.

✳ Mary Poppins
1964, 140 min, G, 6 and up
Dir: Robert Stevenson. Julie Andrews, Dick Van Dyke, Glynis Johns

✳ **PLOT:** In the London of 1910, the Banks family has a loving, if rather chaotic, household. A nanny has just stormed out, fed up with the "incorrigible" children, Jane and Michael. Mr. Banks (David Tomlinson) writes an ad for a new nanny, and the children compose their own, which he tears up and throws into the fireplace. The pieces fly up the chimney, where they reassemble for Mary Poppins (Julie Andrews), who is sitting on a cloud. The next day, a great wind blows away all of the nannies waiting to be interviewed, as Mary floats down.

She takes the measure of the children and her own ("practically perfect in every way") and slides up the banister. She directs them to clean up the nursery and shows them how to make it into a game. Once it is clean, they go out for a walk and they meet Bert (Dick Van Dyke) drawing chalk pictures on the sidewalk. They hop into the picture and have a lovely time. Mary takes them to see her uncle Arthur (Ed Wynn), who floats up to the ceiling when he laughs, and they find this delightful condition is catching. Later, their father takes them to the bank where he works, and Michael embarrasses him by refusing to deposit his tuppence because he wants to use it to buy crumbs to feed the birds. There is a misunderstanding, and this starts a run on the bank with everyone taking out their money, and Mr. Banks is fired.

Mr. Banks realizes that he has been too rigid and demanding. He invites the children to fly a kite with him. Mrs. Banks realizes that in working for the vote for women, she had neglected the children. Her work done, Mary Poppins says good-bye and floats away.

✳ **DISCUSSION:** This sumptuous production deserved its many awards (including Oscars for Andrews and for "Chim Chim Cher-ee" as Best Song) and its enormous box office. It is fresh and imaginative, and the performances are outstanding. (Watch the credits carefully to see that Van Dyke also plays the rubber-limbed Mr. Dawes.) The "jolly holiday" sequence, featuring the live-action characters interacting with animated ones, is superb, especially Van Dyke's dance with the penguin waiters.

Although the story's resolution may grate a bit on today's families that have two working parents, the real lesson is that parents should take time to enjoy their children—but not that they should forego all other interests to spend all of their time with them.

PROFANITY: None.
NUDITY/SEXUAL REFERENCES: None.
ALCOHOL/DRUG ABUSE: None.
VIOLENCE/SCARINESS: None.
TOLERANCE/DIVERSITY ISSUES: The cause of votes for women is presented as unimportant, even daffy; subtext that parents should spend time with their children instead of working.

✳ **QUESTIONS FOR KIDS:**
• Which of the children's adventures would you like best?
• What do you think of the list of qualifications the children prepare? Why is it different from the one prepared by Mr. Banks?
• How can you make "a spoonful of sugar [to] help the medicine go down" at home?

✳ **CONNECTIONS:** Julie Andrews starred in another family favorite, *The Sound of Music*. Dick Van Dyke starred in *Bye Bye Birdie*.

✳ **ACTIVITIES:** Read the four books about Mary Poppins by P. L. Travers, which include many more adventures. Then feed the birds or go fly a kite!

Pollyanna

1960, 134 min, NR, 6 and up
Dir: David Swift. Hayley Mills, Jane Wyman, Agnes Moorehead, Adolphe Menjou,
Karl Malden, Richard Egan

❋ **PLOT:** Pollyanna (Hayley Mills) arrives in Harrington to live with her wealthy aunt, Polly Harrington (Jane Wyman), after the death of Pollyanna's missionary parents. Polly is generous with money, buying Pollyanna lots of beautiful clothes, but is reserved and joyless. She uses her influence to run all aspects of the town, even telling the Reverend Ford (Karl Malden) what to preach on Sundays. His fire-and-brimstone sermons make the congregation miserable. Pollyanna's friendliness and her expectation that everyone else will be friendly, too, endear her to everyone from Polly's servants and the Reverend Ford to a cranky invalid (Agnes Moorehead as Mrs. Snow) and the town recluse (Adolphe Menjou as Mr. Pendergast). She teaches her friends "the glad game," finding something to be glad about in any situation.

When the people in the town decide that instead of accepting Polly's charity they will give a bazaar to raise money for a new orphanage, Polly forbids Pollyanna to go. She sneaks out by climbing down a tree and has a wonderful time, but falls on the way back in and is badly hurt. She no longer wants to try to play the glad game, until the whole town shows up to tell her how much she means to them. She leaves for an operation, confident that she will soon be well.

❋ **DISCUSSION:** This is Disney at its finest, a lavish and gorgeous fantasy of an idyllic American past. Using first-rate actors (including two former Oscar-winners) and sumptuous period detail, this movie is a delight for the eyes as well as the spirit.

Pollyanna is best remembered for "the glad game," in which the challenge is to find something to be glad about, no matter how bleak the situation. But what really makes her special is the way that she expects the best from everyone, and the transforming effect it has on each person she meets. Pollyanna wears on a chain a quote from Abraham Lincoln: "When you look for the bad in men, expecting to find it, you surely will." She thanks Aunt Polly for her generosity, and the clothes become a gift instead of a duty or a way of establishing position. (Cedric has the same effect on others in **Little Lord Fauntleroy**.) Pollyanna expects Mrs. Snow and Mr. Pendergast to want to participate in the bazaar, and they do. She quotes her father to the Reverend Ford. He told her that with 826 "happy texts" in the Bible, God must have wanted people to be happy. Pollyanna helps Ford find again not just his own joy in preaching, but also his integrity in preaching what is in his heart and not what Polly Harrington tells him to say. At his next sermon, he tells everyone to enjoy the beautiful day (and to come to the bazaar), and admits, "I should have been looking for the good in you, and I failed, and I apologize."

Many of the mistakes people make in this movie come from trying to protect themselves from hurt. Polly, hurt by her estrangement from Dr. Chilton, relies on her sense of duty. Mrs. Snow, worried about illness and dependence, tries to blame others and achieves some sense of control (and some attention) with her contrariness. Mr. Pendergast just avoids any contact at all. Pollyanna shows them how to make sure that fear of pain and loss do not prevent opportunities for joy.

Pollyanna, like George Bailey in *It's a Wonderful Life,* gets a rare opportunity to have all she has done recognized and acknowledged by the community. Ask kids who in their community has had a beneficial impact, and how it could be acknowledged.

PROFANITY: None.

NUDITY/SEXUAL REFERENCES: None.

ALCOHOL/DRUG ABUSE: None.

VIOLENCE/SCARINESS: Scary fall from tree.

TOLERANCE/DIVERSITY ISSUES: None.

✴ **QUESTIONS FOR KIDS:**
- Can you play "the glad game"?
- Why do people change when they meet Pollyanna? Who changes the most? How can you tell?
- Why does Mrs. Snow spend so much time thinking about illness and dying? Why does she seem determined not to like anything?
- Why do the people in the town want to raise the money for the orphanage themselves, instead of having Polly give it to them?
- Why does the Reverend apologize?

✴ **CONNECTIONS:** Hayley Mills received a special Oscar for her appearance in this film, and went on to star in many other Disney movies that have been loved by generations of kids, especially *The Parent Trap* and *The Moon-Spinners.* Her father, distinguished actor John Mills, appeared as the father in *Swiss Family Robinson,* and they appeared together in *The Chalk Garden.* Agnes Moorehead appeared in *Citizen Kane* and is familiar to Nick-at-Nite fans as Endora on *Betwitched.* This was the last film appearance of Adolphe Menjou (Mr. Pendergast), a rare departure from his usual dapper and impeccably attired roles.

✴ **ACTIVITIES:** Pollyanna and Jimmy are enchanted by the way that sunlight through prisms makes rainbows on the walls. Try hanging a few prisms on some of the windows in your house, and watching which times of day make the best rainbows. Read the encyclopedia together to learn why the prisms split the light beam into separate colors. Children may also enjoy the Pollyanna series of books by Eleanor H. Porter, which follow Pollyanna into adulthood.

The Secret Garden

1993, 101 min, G, 8 and up
Dir: Agnieszka Holland. Maggie Smith, Kate Maberly

✳ **PLOT:** Mary Lennox is a sour and selfish girl, spoiled by an Indian nanny and neglected by her parents. When Mary's parents are killed, she is sent back to England to live with her uncle, Archibald Craven, a mysterious and lonely man. He rarely returns to his home in Yorkshire, and leaves Mary to the care of Mrs. Medlock, the housekeeper, and Martha, the maid. Both are busy, and Mary has nothing to do but wander around the moors.

One day, Mary finds the key to a secret garden, once the favorite place for her uncle and his wife, whom he adored. After she died, he locked it up and swore no one would go in there again. Mary is determined to find it.

Following the sound of crying she often hears in the night, she finds that there is another child living in the house. It is her uncle's son, Colin. He has been confined to bed all his life and is spoiled and demanding to the point of hysteria. Mary soothes him by telling him about the garden. Later, when he has a tantrum, she is the first person ever to impose limits on his behavior. He tells her that he is afraid he will have a hunched back like his father, and she tells him his back is fine.

Mary finds the garden, and she and Colin and Martha's brother, Dickon, work to bring it back to life. As they do, Mary and Colin get stronger in body and in spirit. When Archibald returns, he meets them in the garden. They run to him, and it is clear that the garden will heal him, too.

✳ **DISCUSSION:** Every child should read this book and see at least one of the filmed versions. Children respond to Mary Lennox because (at least in the beginning) she is so unlikable, a relief from all the Pollyannas and Cinderellas who are rewarded for their relentlessly sunny characters and good deeds. And then there is the pleasure of meeting Colin, who is even worse, a "young rajah" who has had his every wish granted instantly and is surrounded only by those who live in terror of his hysteria. Mary and Colin are a perfect match for each other, and the scene in which she responds to his tantrum with fury is one of the most satisfying in any children's book—indeed, in any book, as is the scene in which they enter the garden together, a wonderful metaphor for all that is going on inside their spirits.

PROFANITY: None.

NUDITY/SEXUAL REFERENCES: None.

ALCOHOL/DRUG ABUSE: None.

VIOLENCE/SCARINESS: None. (In the 1984 version, we see what happens to the characters and learn that Dickon has been killed in WWI.)

TOLERANCE/DIVERSITY ISSUES: None. (In the BBC version, the domestics are less subservient than they are in the book.)

✳ **QUESTIONS FOR KIDS:**
• How does making friends with the robin change Mary? Why?

- How is her relationship with Ben different from her relationship with Martha? Why is Mary the only one who refuses to do whatever Colin asks? What effect does that have on him?
- How are Mary and Colin alike, and how are they different?
- What do you think will happen after the book ends?

✽ **CONNECTIONS:** This classic story by Frances Hodgson Burnett has been beautifully filmed four times, and any and all of them are well worth watching. The first, filmed in 1949, stars Margaret O'Brien and Dean Stockwell. Like *The Wizard of Oz,* the early part of the film is in black and white, and then, when they enter the garden, it turns to color. The 1984 version, made for British television is (unsurprisingly) the most authentic, and the Yorkshire accents are a delight. The 1987 version, made for American television, is fine, with Derek Jacobi as Archibald Craven. The 1993 theatrical release has some exquisitely beautiful images, but the first one is the strongest dramatically.

✽ **ACTIVITIES:** Look up Yorkshire in an atlas or get some travel brochures to see pictures of the moors. Encourage your children to start a garden, even if it consists only of a flowerpot near the kitchen window.

✽ The Wizard of Oz

1939, 101 min, NR, 6 and up
Dir: Victor Fleming. Judy Garland, Ray Bolger, Bert Lahr, Frank Morgan, Jack Haley, Margaret Hamilton

✽ **PLOT:** Dorothy Gale (Judy Garland) lives in Kansas with her aunt and uncle and her dog, Toto. Mean Miss Gulch (Margaret Hamilton) swears she will have Toto taken away. Auntie Em and Uncle Henry support Dorothy, but they are too distracted by the coming tornado to pay much attention to her. Dorothy dreams of a place "over the rainbow" where everything is beautiful, "troubles melt like lemon drops," and "the dreams that you dare to dream really do come true." She starts to run away to protect Toto, but is sent back home by the kindly Professor Marvel (Frank Morgan), a traveling fortune-teller.

When the tornado arrives, Dorothy is outside the shelter. She goes to her room, where she is hit on the head by a piece of wood torn loose by the wind. The whole house rises, and is carried away by the tornado.

The house lands with a crash, and when Dorothy opens the door, she finds she has landed in the colorful world of Oz (the movie, black and white up to this point, becomes Technicolor). Her house has landed on the Wicked Witch of the East, killing her, and the tiny Munchkins celebrate Dorothy as a great heroine. Their friend Glinda the good witch (Billie Burke) arrives and gives her the Wicked Witch's magic ruby slippers, just as the Wicked Witch of the West (Margaret Hamilton) arrives to take them. The

Wicked Witch of the East was her sister. Furious, she swears revenge. Dorothy wants to go home and is told to seek out the Wizard of Oz, who lives in the Emerald City, for help.

On the way to the Emerald City, Dorothy meets a talking Scarecrow (Ray Bolger) who wants a brain, a Tin Woodsman (Jack Haley) who longs for a heart, and a cowardly Lion (Bert Lahr) who wants courage. They all join her to seek the help of the Wizard. At the Emerald City, the Wizard at first refuses to see them, then finally tells them they must earn their wishes by bringing him the broom of the Wicked Witch of the West. They are captured by the witch's flying monkeys, and just as she is about to kill them, Dorothy douses her with water, trying to protect the Scarecrow from fire, and the witch melts.

They return to the Emerald City only to find that the Wizard cannot help them. He is a fraud, just "the man behind the curtain," whose terrifying displays of smoke and light hide a "humbug" who has no magical powers at all. But he is able to show the Scarecrow, Tin Woodsman, and Lion that all along they really did have what they've been seeking, and he promises to take Dorothy back to Kansas in his hot-air balloon.

Toto jumps out of the balloon's basket. Dorothy runs after him and misses the balloon launch. But, just as Dorothy despairs of ever going home, Glinda arrives and shows Dorothy that she, too, all along had the means of getting home. Back in Kansas, Dorothy wakes up to find her aunt and uncle, the farmhands, and Professor Marvel (who strongly resemble the Scarecrow, Tin Woodsman, Lion, and Wizard), and tells them that "there's no place like home."

❋ **DISCUSSION:** This movie is an ideal family film, superb in every aspect, with outstanding art direction, music, and performances. It is still as fresh and engrossing as it was in 1939, and improves with every viewing. If you ever have a chance to see it on a big screen, in a theater with a good sound system, you will enjoy it even more.

It is hard to imagine what it would have been like with the original intended cast, including Shirley Temple as Dorothy and Buddy Ebsen as the Tin Woodsman. But 20th Century Fox would not lend its top star, and Ebsen was hospitalized when he inhaled the aluminum dust in the Tin Woodsman's makeup. Judy Garland is a perfect Dorothy—vulnerable, sensitive, completely believable. On the brink of leaving childhood, her dreams of a place "over the rainbow" are in part a yearning to escape the concerns of adulthood.

There is something especially satisfying about the way that the main characters find what they need within themselves. Talk with children about the way that the Scarecrow demonstrates his intelligence, the Tin Woodsman demonstrates his heart, and the Lion demonstrates his courage. Even the humbug Wizard finds that he had the means to go home all the time. Dorothy, who in the first part of the movie runs away from home to try to solve her problems, spends the rest of the movie trying to get back. Even if the story is just a dream (in the book, it is a real adventure), this makes a great deal of emotional sense, a way of working through her inner conflicts.

It is also worth talking about the scene in which Dorothy and her friends disregard the Wizard's plea to "pay no attention to the man behind the curtain" and discover that he is really just an ordinary man. This can be a touchstone or metaphor for many kinds of challenges children face. It can help them recognize that the overpowering figures in their lives (parents, teachers, adults, sports figures) are just imperfect human beings. And it can also help them recognize attempts, by themselves as well as by others, to distract people in hopes of hiding our imperfection and vulnerability.

NOTE: There are a number of different scenes in this movie that may be scary for children. Many adults still remember being scared by the flying monkeys or Dorothy looking into the crystal ball and seeing her aunt turn into the witch. Parents should talk to children about the story before seeing the movie, and watch with them to gauge their reactions.

PROFANITY: None.

NUDITY/SEXUAL REFERENCES: None.

ALCOHOL/DRUG ABUSE: None.

VIOLENCE/SCARINESS: Lead characters in peril. Many young children are especially scared by the flying monkeys who guard the Wicked Witch.

TOLERANCE/DIVERSITY ISSUES: Tolerance of individual differences and frailties.

✳ **QUESTIONS FOR KIDS:**
- Why does the Scarecrow think he doesn't have a brain? What does he want to be able to do? Why does the Tin Woodsman think he doesn't have a heart? Why does the Lion think he doesn't have courage?
- How can you see that they do have these things? How does the Wizard show them that they do?
- If Oz is the land "over the rainbow" that Dorothy dreamed of, why does she want to go home?
- Why does the Wizard pretend to have more powers than he really does?
- What does the Wizard mean when he says, "Hearts will never be made practical until they can be made unbreakable"?

✳ **CONNECTIONS:** Some editions of the video include a fascinating documentary about the making of the film, showing some scenes that were cut, including a musical number called "The Jitterbug."

The fourteen Oz books by L. Frank Baum are still loved not only by children but also by adult fans so committed that there is a flourishing Oz society; children who love this movie and read the books may enjoy getting on its mailing list.

Children will enjoy picking out the actors who have double roles in the movie: Margaret Hamilton as Miss Gulch and the Wicked Witch; Ray Bolger as the Scarecrow and Hank; Jack Haley as the Tin Woodsman and Hickory; and Bert Lahr as the Cowardly Lion and Zeke. Watch closely and you will see Frank Morgan in four roles: not just Professor Marvel and the Wizard, but also the guard at the gate of the Emerald City and the guard at the castle.

You can see the astonishingly limber Ray Bolger in *The Harvey Girls* (again with Judy Garland) and *Babes in Toyland,* and Jack Haley with Shirley Temple in *Poor Little Rich Girl* and *Rebecca of Sunnybrook Farm.* Composer Harold Arlen, who also wrote standards like "Stormy Weather," "That Old Black Magic," and "Accentuate the Positive," was nominated for eleven Academy Awards, but won only once, for "Over the Rainbow."

The Wiz is a black urban version of the same story and contrasting the different interpretations of the material is very interesting for kids.

THE WORLD OF ROALD DAHL

This popular author wrote books that kids adore, but parents are often troubled by the exaggerated and grotesque behavior of his adult characters who are often abusive toward children. Parents and children will probably enjoy these movies most (or know whether or not they will enjoy them) if they are familiar with the books before they watch.

❄ JAMES AND THE GIANT PEACH
1996, 80 min, PG, 6 and up
Dir: Henry Selick. Susan Sarandon, Simon Callow

James has a blissful life with loving parents until they are both killed by a rhinoceros. He then goes to live with his horribly mean aunts, until a mysterious stranger brings him a bag of magical crocodile tongues. James trips and spills them on the ground near a tree that then grows a giant peach as large as a house. When James climbs inside, he meets a collection of human-sized insects, including the lovely Polish-accented spider (voice of Susan Sarandon) and violin-playing grasshopper (voice of Simon Callow). The peach takes off and, tethered to 300 seagulls, flies to New York. Claymation, computer animation, and special effects combine to create real movie magic.

❄ MATILDA
1996, 93 min, PG, 8 and up
Dir: Danny DeVito. Mara Wilson, Danny DeVito, Embeth Davidtz

Danny DeVito directed and stars in this story of a wise little girl (Mara Wilson) who triumphs over dreadful adults. Matilda's hilariously tacky parents (DeVito and his real-life wife, Rhea Perlman) can barely remember Matilda's name and age. They alternately ignore and insult her, insisting she put down her beloved books and watch television, and refuse to allow her to go to school. When they finally do send her to school, the principal,

Miss Trunchbull, hates children and enjoys tossing them over the fence like the shot-putter she once was. Matilda discovers she has "powers" (telekinesis) and, with the support of sweet Miss Honey, her teacher, finds a way to live happily ever after.

Parents (and some kids) may be concerned by the comic treatment of abusive behavior. As in *James and the Giant Peach* and some of Dahl's other books, most of the grown-ups are stupid, dishonest, and cruel, genuinely relishing their power over children. Some kids may get upset. But, as with *Home Alone,* many kids find the comic exaggeration reassuring, especially when the child proves less vulnerable than the grown-ups expected. Kids who will enjoy this movie most are those who liked the book—those who are unfamiliar with it should be prepared by parents for what to expect.

DeVito and Perlman made this movie because it was their daughter's favorite book. And Dahl's lesson that children can solve their problems by reading and by finding good, trustworthy friends to help them is very worthwhile.

✳ **CONNECTIONS:** Miss Honey is played by Embeth Davidtz, who appears in *Schindler's List* as the Jewish concentration camp prisoner who fascinates the Nazi commandant.

✳ WILLIE WONKA AND THE CHOCOLATE FACTORY

1971, 91 min, G, 6 and up
Dir: Mel Stuart. Gene Wilder, Jack Albertson

Dahl's beloved *Charlie and the Chocolate Factory* is transformed into a lavish and colorful musical with Gene Wilder in the title role as the world's most successful (and eccentric) candy-maker. Charlie is the poor but honest boy who wins one of five golden tickets for a tour of the chocolate factory and brings his beloved grandfather along. The other four winners are obnoxious and spoiled children: a gum-chewer, a television-addict, a glutton, and a selfish rich girl. Each of them is felled by some imaginative catastrophe, leaving Charlie to win the biggest prize of all.

✳ **CONNECTIONS:** Rock band Veruca Salt is named after one of the characters in this story. Kids who enjoy the movie will want to read Dahl's sequel, *Charlie and the Great Glass Elevator.*

✳ **ACTIVITIES:** Make some candy from scratch.

 **The Witches**

1990, 91 min, PG, 8 and up
Dir: Nicolas Roeg. Anjelica Huston, Mai Zetterling, Rowan Atkinson

✳ **PLOT:** Luke hears about witches from his grandmother (Mai Zetterling). She says they have to wear gloves to hide their clawlike hands and shoes that fit their square feet without toes, and that they are bald and scratch under their wigs. They have a purple gleam in their eyes. They are evil and they steal children, who are never seen again.

Luke's parents are killed, and his grandmother takes him to England. When she is diagnosed with mild diabetes, the doctor advises a vacation, so they go to Cornwall. As it happens, a convention of all the witches in England is staying in the same hotel, posing as the Royal Society for the Prevention of Cruelty to Children. Their leader is slinky, black-clad Eva Ernst (Anjelica Huston). Luke overhears her telling the witches to wipe out all the children in England by turning them into mice, and he watches as she demonstrates by giving a potion to a greedy child named Bruno, transforming him into a mouse. The witches find Luke and, after a chase, capture him and turn him into a mouse. With the help of his grandmother, he steals some of the potion and puts it into the soup to be served to the witches, who are all turned to mice except for Eva's assistant. Luke manages to get Eva's trunkful of money, along with her notebook listing the addresses of all the witches in America, and he and his grandmother plan to go after them.

✳ **DISCUSSION:** This story has a genuinely twisted flavor that some children will love and others will find disturbing. Luke is exceptionally brave and enjoys being a mouse (in the movie, he is changed back, but in the book, he stays a mouse). Children may be upset not only by the witches, but by the death (off-screen) of Luke's parents, and by his seeming indifference to it.

> PROFANITY: None.
> NUDITY/SEXUAL REFERENCES: None.
> ALCOHOL/DRUG ABUSE: None.
> VIOLENCE/SCARINESS: Scary witches; children in peril, including a baby in a carriage pushed down a hill (and rescued); Luke's parents are killed in an (off-screen) accident, which does not seem to bother him too much.
> TOLERANCE/DIVERSITY ISSUES: None.

✳ **QUESTIONS FOR KIDS:**
- Do you believe in witches?
- Can you think of other witches in stories or movies? How are they the same? How are they different?
- Is it good for adults to tell children scary stories?
- Why do you think Eva's assistant turns out to be a good witch? Were there any clues that you missed?

✳ **CONNECTIONS:** Roald Dahl was married to actress Patricia Neal (**The Day the Earth Stood Still**). Huston is the daughter of director John Huston (**The Maltese Falcon**) and the grandaughter of actor Walter Huston (**The Treasure of the Sierra Madre**). Rowan Atkinson is better known as "Mr. Bean." This was the last film worked on by Muppeteer Jim Henson, and his mouse puppets are a marvel.

OTHER CLASSICS

✳ ANNE OF GREEN GABLES
1985, 195 min, NR, 6 and up
Dir: Kevin Sullivan. Colleen Dewhurst, Megan Fallows

L. M. Montgomery's book about the red-haired orphan who found a home on Canada's Prince Edward Island comes to life in this made-for-television production (originally shown in two parts, and followed by sequels), a sheer delight, exceptional in every detail. Colleen Dewhurst is ideally cast as Marilla, the stern farm woman who decides to adopt a boy to help with the chores and ends up with Anne Shirley, a talkative and fanciful girl who is desperate for love. Richard Farnsworth is every bit as good as Marilla's shy brother, Matthew. And Megan Fallows is just right as Anne.

✳ **CONNECTIONS:** An earlier movie, made in 1934, is also very good (though it takes some liberties with the plot). The actress who starred in the title role liked it so much, she changed her name to Anne Shirley.

✳ THE BABY-SITTER'S CLUB
1995, 85 min, PG, 8 and up
Dir: Melanie Mayron. Schuyler Fisk, Ellen Burstyn, Brooke Adams

Based on the best-selling series of books by Ann Martin, this is a well-produced story of friendship, responsibility, and growing up. As the baby-sitters decide to run a summer camp together, they each face challenges, including the reappearance of a long-absent father, a crush on an older boy, and a difficult science test, and they have to learn something about honesty, commitment, and loyalty.

✳ **CONNECTIONS:** Schuyler Fisk, outstanding in a leading role, is the daughter of Sissy Spacek. Director Melanie Mayron and featured actor Peter Horton appeared together on television's *Thirtysomething*.

✳ THE BORROWERS
1997, 85 min, PG, 8 and up
Dir: Peter Hewitt. John Goodman, Jim Broadbent, Flora Newbigin, Hugh Laurie

Mary Norton's charming fantasy about the tiny people who live beneath the floorboards is delicious fun. What a reassuring explanation for the disappearance of household items—it turns out that they are "borrowed" to make clothes, furniture, and food for the little Clock family who shares the house happily with the well-named Lender family. But Ocious P. Potter (John Goodman), a wicked lawyer, steals the will leaving the house to the Lenders, and he hopes to have the house torn down so that he can put up an apartment building. Arrietty Clock, the Borrowers' daughter, curious about the world of the "Beans" (human beings), violates the first rule of borrowing by letting herself be seen by the Lender's son Pete. They form a friendship that saves the day as Pete and the Borrowers show courage and resourcefulness to stop Mr. Potter. The art direction is outstanding, a perfect blend of wit and whimsy, and the performances are captivating. This is lots of fun for the entire family—the PG rating is for characters in peril and some potty humor.

❋ BRIDGE TO TERABITHIA
1985, 58 min, NR, 10 and up
Part of the **Wonderworks** series, this is the story of a lonely boy's special friendship with a warm-hearted and imaginative girl, based on the book by Katherine Patterson. NOTE: There is a very sad death.

❋ CHARLOTTE'S WEB
1973, 85 min, G, 6 and up
Dir: Charles A. Nichols and Iwao Takamoto. Debbie Reynolds, Paul Lynde, Henry Gibson, Agnes Moorehead
The E. B. White incomparable tale of friendship and loyalty (an outstanding book to read aloud to kids) is respectfully treated in this handsome animated musical. Charlotte the spider (voice of Debbie Reynolds) is the "great friend and great writer" who finds a way to save Wilbur the pig (voice of Henry Gibson) from the butcher. Paul Lynde (**Bye Bye Birdie**) gives his deliciously snarly voice to Templeton the Rat.

Like **Babe**, the film acknowledges where bacon and sausages come from, which may upset some children. Pleasant songs by the Sherman brothers (who wrote the score for **Mary Poppins**) and first-class performances help compensate for animation that is not up to the Disney level, but no movie could do full justice to White's wonderful storytelling.

❋ **CONNECTIONS:** White made a superb audiotape recording of the book.

❋ DOCTOR DOOLITTLE
1967, 144 min, NR, 4 and up
Dir: Richard Fleischer. Rex Harrison, Anthony Newley
This slow-moving version of the classic book by Hugh Lofting is about the adventures of the doctor who could "talk to the animals." It has some nice songs, Oscar-winning special effects, and a good performance by Rex Harrison in the title role.

❋ **CONNECTIONS:** Skip the 1998 version with Eddie Murphy, rated PG-13 for potty humor and sexual references.

❋ FROM THE MIXED-UP FILES OF MRS. BASIL E. FRANKWEILER

1973, 105 min, G, 8 and up
Dir: Fielder Cook. Ingrid Bergman

E. L. Konigsburg's novel is about a girl who wants to run away from home and has to include her brother in her plans. She doesn't get along with him particularly well, but he has the money she needs to finance the trip. They hide out in New York City's Metropolitan Museum of Art, where they begin to develop more respect for each other and discover the key to identifying the artist of a beautiful statue of an angel. This takes them to the mansion of the statue's owner, the eccentric Mrs. Frankweiler (Ingrid Bergman), for the final clue.

❋ **CONNECTIONS:** This movie is also known as *The Hideaways*. Kids should read the book as well as Konigsburg's other novels, especially *Jennifer, Hecate, Macbeth, William McKinley, and Me, Elizabeth*, and *The View From Saturday*. The movie was remade for television starring Lauren Bacall.

❋ HARRIET THE SPY

1996, 101 min, PG, 8 and up
Dir: Bronwen Hughes. Rosie O'Donnell

Harriet is a sixth grader who thinks of herself as a spy because she observes the world around her closely and writes everything down in her notebook. When the notebook is discovered and read aloud, her classmates are hurt and angered by her frank criticism, and even her closest friends, Janie and Sport, join the others in forming a "Spy-Catcher's Club" to ostracize her. Harriet is devastated but decides she would rather be a spy without friends than have friends without being a spy. She makes a list of the kids who have shunned her and extracts revenge on each of them. Instead of making her feel better, it leaves her isolated and miserable.

Her former nanny, the wise and understanding Ole Golly (Rosie O'Donnell), tells her she must do two things—"apologize and lie"—explaining that while she is lucky to be perceptive and original, these qualities will make people uncomfortable, and she has to find a balance that will enable her to preserve her friendships and pursue her writing. Telling the truth has hurt people (Harriet tells the kids that a girl whose popularity and reputation mean everything to her has been lying about her close relationship with her father, and that in fact he has not seen her for three years). Harriet learns that the truth is more complex than she thought, and that she can accept responsibility for what she has done and reconnect to her friends.

The first movie produced by kids' television network Nickelodeon, this gets a bit MTV-ish at times, but is well-produced and faithful to the book, a longtime favorite. NOTE: Some harsh schoolyard language.

✳ HEIDI

1937, 88 min, NR, b&w, 6 and up
Dir: Alan Dwan. Shirley Temple, Arthur Treacher

Shirley Temple had one of her best roles as the Swiss orphan who is left with her hermitlike grandfather (Jean Hersholt), who lives in the mountains. Heidi and her grandfather develop a warm and loving relationship. But her aunt comes to take her away. She has accepted a position in the home of a wealthy man, on condition that she bring a companion for his frail daughter, Clara (Marcia Mae Jones). Heidi is heartbroken, and misses her grandfather terribly. But she and Clara become good friends, and she encourages Clara to learn to walk again. Clara wants Heidi to stay with her forever, but finally, Heidi does get to go home to her grandfather.

✳ **CONNECTIONS:** If you ever wonder, as you watch the Oscars, who the Jean Hersholt Humanitarian Award is named for, you can find out by watching this movie, where he appears as the grandfather. Hersholt served as the President of the Academy in its early days, and was a strong advocate for actors.

There are at least four other worthwhile versions of the story available on video, especially the 1993 Disney version, with Jason Robards as the grandfather, but avoid the aminated version and *The New Adventures of Heidi,* which takes place in New York.

✳ THE INDIAN IN THE CUPBOARD

1995, 96 min, PG, 8 and up
Dir: Frank Oz. Hal Scardino, Litefoot, Lindsay Crouse

The well-loved children's book by Lynn Reid Banks is about a boy named Omri who finds that when he locks his small plastic Indian in a cupboard with a magic key, the Indian comes to life. What makes this story especially touching is that Omri learns about the responsibility as well as the delights of caring for someone very small. When Omri and his friend bring other toys to life, including a cowboy who does not like Indians, they confront real issues of life, death, and the importance of freedom.

✳ JANE EYRE

1944, 96 min, NR, b&w, 12 and up
Dir: Robert Stevenson. Joan Fontaine, Orson Welles

This is the best version of the classic gothic romance by Charlotte Bronte about the shy governess and her brooding and mysterious employer. Jane is an unloved child sent to a brutal school. When she grows up, she is employed as the governess for the ward of Mr. Rochester, with whom she falls deeply in love, though she does not expect him to notice her. But he proposes, and they marry. She discovers his terrible secret and runs away, but ultimately, after he pays for his mistakes, they are reunited. It is perfectly cast, with Joan Fontaine and Orson Welles as Jane and Mr. Rochester. Peggy Ann Garner as young Jane and Elizabeth Taylor as her only friend are also excellent, but Margaret O'Brien gives a rare weak performance as Jane's pupil.

❋ THE MANY ADVENTURES OF WINNIE THE POOH

The Milne classic (and its illustrations by Shepard) are lovingly brought to life by Disney. Pooh, Piglet, Tigger, Owl, Kanga, Roo, and Christopher Robin have many adventures, indeed, including Pooh's impersonation of a little black raincloud. NOTE: Be careful—Disney also produced some Pooh videos not based on the Milne stories, which are not nearly as good. Stick to the "Storybook Classics" series and stay away from *The Search for Christopher Robin,* but due to repackaging, it is a good idea to double check the credits on the box to make sure.

❋ MUPPET TREASURE ISLAND

1996, 100 min, G, 8 and up
Dir: Brian Henson. Tim Curry

The Robert Louis Stevenson classic of pirate treasure is presented with the Muppets' special blend of irreverent wit and impeccable production values. Human and Muppet actors blend as seamlessly as the combination of adventure and humor. NOTE: Younger children may find it a bit hard to follow, because of the accents and the anachronistic asides thrown in to keep the grown-ups amused. There are some sword fights that will thrill some kids, but others will hide their eyes. Parents of younger kids should tell children something about the story before they see it. Parents of older kids may want to talk about some of the issues it raises: Why did Jim decide not to tell the others when Long John Silver stole the treasure? Who did the treasure really belong to?

❋ THE PHANTOM TOLLBOOTH

1969, 90 min, G, 6 and up
Dir: Chuck Jones, Abe Levitow (animation), and David Monahan (live-action).
Hans Conreid, Mel Blanc, June Foray

A bored kid named Milo finds a mysterious tollbooth in his bedroom. He gets into his toy car, pays the toll, and drives off to a magic land in which two kings battle over which is more important: words or numbers. With the help of a watchdog named Tock and a man called the Humbug, he goes on a quest to find Rhyme and Reason (two wise and gentle princesses, who have been banished). While not up to the standard of the book by Norton Juster, which is one of the best ever for any age, this animated version (directed by the man who brought us Bugs Bunny) is worth watching.

✳ SARAH, PLAIN AND TALL
1991, 100 min, NR, 8 and up
Dir: Glenn Jordan. Glenn Close, Christopher Walken
    Glenn Close plays the title character in this story by Patricia MacLachlan of a woman from Maine who travels to the prairies of Kansas in 1910 to care for the family of a widower (Christopher Walken). As in the book, there are nicely handled themes of recovery from loss and adjusting to different circumstances and people.

✳ TREASURE ISLAND
1950, 96 min, NR, 8 and up
Dir: Byron Haskin. Robert Newton, Bobby Driscoll
    There are four movies of this classic adventure story; this is the Disney version, in which Robert Newton is unforgettable as Long John Silver. Young Jim Hawkins (Bobby Driscoll) goes after buried treasure with Doctor Livesey and Squire Trelawny, only to discover that the mysterious ship's cook is a pirate, planning to mutiny and claim the treasure for himself. Jim faces a number of interesting choices in his dealings with Silver because they are both friends and antagonists.

✳ TUCK EVERLASTING
1981, 100 min, NR, 10 and up
Dir: Frederick King Keller. Margaret Chamberlain, Paul Flessa
    Natalie Babbitt's award-winning novel of the family invulnerable to pain, injury, or aging is lovingly brought to life in this film. A young girl meets the family and, when they offer to make her one of them, she must make a very difficult decision.

✳ WHERE THE LILIES BLOOM
1974, 96 min, G, 10 and up
Dir: William A. Graham. Julie Gholson, Jan Smithers, Harry Dean Stanton
    Mary Call Luther, a young girl from the hills of North Carolina, promises her dying father that she will keep the family together, take pride in the family name, and never take charity, and that she will never allow her older sister to marry the man who bought their property by paying back taxes. After he dies, she finds a way for them to support themselves through "wildcrafting," harvesting herbs and wildflowers. They keep his death a secret, so that the state will not take the children away. Ultimately, she has to break one of her promises, and she learns that "you can love someone

even though they fail you." Based on the book by Vera Cleaver and Bill Cleaver, this is a touching story of commitment and courage.

✳ **CONNECTIONS:** The script is by Earl Hamner, Jr., who based his television series, *The Waltons,* on his own family.

✳ WHERE THE RED FERN GROWS
1974, 90 min, G, 8 and up
Dir: Norman Tokar. James Whitmore, Beverly Garland

Based on the book by Wilson Rawls, this is the story of Billy Coleman, a young boy in Oklahoma who works hard to realize his dream of buying two hunting dogs. When his grandfather (James Whitmore) tells him he will have to meet God halfway, Billy understands that this means "my share was to do the work and God's share was to give me the heart, courage, and determination."

Billy works tirelessly at any odd job he can find to earn the money for the dogs. Although he knows the family could use the money to buy a mule, he wants them so badly, he decides to buy them, using the money left over to buy gifts for the family. Billy patiently trains them, and is very proud when they do well. He brings more coon skins than any other hunter does into his grandfather's store to be sold.

His grandfather, proud of Billy and the dogs, makes a bet with two arrogant boys that Billy's dogs can tree the "ghost coon" that has eluded them. The dogs are sucessful, but Billy refuses to kill the coon, out of respect for its record of escaping capture. He fights with the boys, and one of them is accidentally killed. Billy blames himself and says he will never hunt again.

His grandfather urges him to enter the dogs in the State Championship Coon Hunt, and he agrees. But during the final round, his grandfather gets separated from the others and is hurt. Billy forfeits the competition to use the dogs to search for his grandfather. The man who wins the contest gives Billy the prize, anyway, knowing he deserves it. When they get home, one of the dogs is killed while protecting Billy from a mountain lion, and the other dies of grief. Billy must learn to keep what he loved most about the dogs and their time together inside himself, as the prize money the dogs won makes it possible for the family to move away from the mountains.

SEE ALSO:

The Black Stallion

Cheaper by the Dozen

The Diary of Anne Frank

Ferdinand the Bull

I Remember Mama
Johnny Tremain
Little Women
Misty
National Velvet
The NeverEnding Story
The "Ramona" series
To Kill a Mockingbird
Shane
Swiss Family Robinson
A Tree Grows in Brooklyn
20,000 Leagues Under the Sea
White Fang
The Yearling

COMEDY

"Even the gods love their jokes."
—PLATO

There is no activity that brings a family closer together than sharing laughter, and I believe that the importance of laughter is one of the most essential family values. Sharing a movie comedy is great fun, and favorite moments often become a part of the family's own set of in-jokes. As *Sullivan's Travels* reminds us, "There's a lot to be said for making people laugh . . . It isn't much, but it's better than nothing in this cock-eyed caravan." And as Sullivan himself realizes, those who laugh are not disrespectful of real problems; it is in some cases the kindest and wisest response to them. Laughter provides essential perspective. One of the sweetest family moments on screen is the end of *A Christmas Story,* when the family's reaction to their hilariously bizarre Christmas dinner is not disappointment or blame, but laughter. Genuine humor is the highest level of emotional and mental functioning—if you can get the joke, especially when it is on you, you can handle anything.

For some reason, people are much more sensitive about their sense of humor than any other attribute. We don't take it personally if someone likes chocolate when we like vanilla, but for some reason we do take it personally when we like the Marx Brothers and someone else likes the Three Stooges. Try to avoid these kinds of debates within the family. Instead, talk more generally, especially with older kids, about what makes something funny. There is a very fine line between comedy and tragedy, with both encompassing the same kinds of events: mistakes, misunderstandings, near misses, and embarrassing mishaps. The difference between comedy and tragedy is that in comedy the characters get a second chance. In a tragedy, Romeo doesn't get the message and, thinking Juliet is dead, he kills himself. In a romantic comedy, he would get the message just in time. In a screwball comedy, she would not have gotten the message that she was supposed to take the potion in the first place, and would be racing around trying to find him. In a fantasy comedy, she would have taken the wrong potion and turned into a purple monkey with feathers. In a slapstick comedy, she would have taken the wrong potion, and it would have made her sneeze every time someone sat down. But it all would work out all right in the end.

One of the reasons we love comedy is its reassuring sense that no matter how many times Moe bonks Curly, no matter how many times Baby the leopard escapes, no matter how many people squeeze into Groucho's stateroom, everything will turn out all right. A fall that hurts someone isn't funny, but a fall that doesn't hurt is. The bombastic Clarence Day of *Life With Father* is funny, but the tyrannical father in *The Barretts of Wimpole Street* is not. The cowardly milquetoast in *Fancy Pants* is funny, but the cowardly milquetoasts in *High Noon* are not. The greed is comic in *It's a Mad Mad Mad Mad World;* it is tragic in *The Treasure of the Sierra Madre.* The direst circumstances often inspire the wildest comedy, as we see in movies like *The Great Dictator, Arsenic and Old Lace,* and *Dr. Strangelove.* See if your family can figure out what makes the difference; how the director, screenwriter, actors, and composer set the mood for laughter instead of tension or tears.

Another reason we love comedy is that it is inherently subversive, questioning our assumptions, our standards, and our sacred cows. Movies like *The Great Dictator* and *To Be or Not to Be* took on Hitler much more aggressively than any pre–WWII dramas did. Humor allows a movie like *Some Like It Hot* to make humorous references to transvestism and impotence long before they were considered appropriate subjects for serious movies. Two movies addressing the perils of the Cold War arms race were made in 1964. It was the comedy (*Dr. Strangelove*) that had the greatest impact and the most enduring appeal, not the drama (*Fail-safe*).

Talk to the family about what makes something funny. Humorist Christopher Cerf has identified what he calls the "joke-oid," often found on television sitcoms. They have the rhythm of a joke (often the classic three-count), and the language of a joke (as Walter Matthau explains, courtesy of Neil Simon, in *The Sunshine Boys,* words with a letter "k" are funnier than words without), they have the element of surprise, and there is laughter on the sound track, but they are not actually funny. In real humor, the element of surprise usually comes from making you see something from an angle you hadn't considered, whether it is, "What's black and white and red all over?" or a sophisticated political cartoon. Often in "joke-oids" this element comes not from an insightful surprise but from mere incongruities, like insults or precocious comments about sex from small children, elderly people, or someone otherwise relatively powerless. Getting kids to recognize this distinction is a step in the right direction, because they will learn about critical listening, and because they will then begin to insist on better.

They should watch critically as well. Many comic actors and comedians (the classic vaudeville distinction is that "A comic does funny things; a comedian does things funny") have exceptional physical grace and timing that is an essential part of their humor. Bob Hope was a boxer. Buster

Keaton and Cary Grant were acrobats. W. C. Fields began as a juggler. When Fields saw *The Great Dictator,* he announced with jealous fury that Chaplin was "a ballet dancer." Today, Steve Martin and Jim Carrey are extraordinary physical comedians. In comedy, even more than in drama, precise timing is essential, and this is never more clear than when we watch Stan Laurel, Buster Keaton, Charlie Chaplin, or Jacques Tati.

It is a great joy to watch the development of humor in your children as they grow. There is the low humor of the potty-training period, and the laughter at the misfortunes of others. Then there is this wonderful moment when they are around seven, when they first really understand that a word can have more than one meaning, and they spend a year asking you riddles. By then, some of them will begin to think up wisecracks, not to be rude or sarcastic, or even cynical, just to show that they don't take themselves or the world too seriously. Others will need a bit more time. Others may need a lot more time. Maybe those are the ones who need these movies the most.

Bringing Up Baby

1938, 103 min, b&w, NR, 6 and up
Dir: Howard Hawks. Cary Grant, Katharine Hepburn

PLOT: Shy paleontologist David Huxley (Cary Grant) is hoping for three things: a rare dinosaur bone fossil, a million-dollar research grant, and his marriage to colleague Miss Swallow. Madcap heiress Susan Vance (Katharine Hepburn), instantly smitten with David when he objects to her playing his golf ball and driving off in his car, manages to disrupt his life completely when she asks him to help her transport a leopard named "Baby" to her aunt's estate in Connecticut. Complications include Susan's dog, George, taking the irreplaceable bone fossil to bury somewhere, serenading the leopard to get him down from a neighbor's roof, being thrown in jail, confusing Baby with a vicious circus leopard, and the destruction of an entire dinosaur skeleton. David does not ultimately get the million dollars (it turns out that Susan's aunt was the prospective donor), but Susan does, so everyone lives happily ever after, including Baby.

DISCUSSION: *Bringing Up Baby* is generally considered to be the ultimate example of the screwball comedy, which reached its apex in the 1930s. These movies featured outlandish plots (most often featuring wealthy people subjected to utter chaos) carried out at breakneck speed with a lot of witty repartee and romantic tension.

PROFANITY: None.
NUDITY/SEXUAL REFERENCES: When asked by Aunt Elizabeth what he is doing in a feathery negligee, David explodes, "I just went *gay* all of a

sudden!" which is likely to be interpreted differently by today's audiences than it was when the film was released.

ALCOHOL/DRUG ABUSE: None.

VIOLENCE/SCARINESS: None.

TOLERANCE/DIVERSITY ISSUES: None.

✳ **QUESTIONS FOR KIDS:**
- What is it that Susan likes so much about David?
- Why, ultimately, does he like her?
- Would you like to meet someone like Susan?

✳ **CONNECTIONS:** Grant and Hepburn made three other films together. Two are also classic: **The Philadelphia Story** and **Holiday**. The third, *Sylvia Scarlett,* is an odd little movie (though with an enthusiastic cult following) about a group of performers that has Hepburn dressed as a boy through most of it. Other classic screwball comedies include **My Man Godfrey,** *Nothing Sacred,* **It Happened One Night,** The Palm Beach Story, and Peter Bogdanovich's attempted update, **What's Up, Doc?** For very thoughtful and serious essays on *Bringing Up Baby* and some of the other screwball classics, see *The Pursuit of Happiness,* by Stanley Cavell.

✳ **ACTIVITIES:** Kids who enjoy this kind of comedy might enjoy some of the stories by P. G. Wodehouse, like "Uncle Fred Flits By," which portray the same kind of deliriously joyful anarchy. And this movie may inspire them to take a look at dinosaur skeletons in a museum, though there is no such thing as an "intercostal clavicle."

✳The Court Jester

1951, 101 min, NR, 6 and up
Dir: Norman Panama and Melvin Frank. Danny Kaye, Glynis Johns, Basil Rathbone, Angela Lansbury

✳ **PLOT:** Hawkins (Danny Kaye) is a follower of the Black Fox, a Robin Hood–style rebel who hopes to put the royal heir on the throne in place of the usurper. Hawkins wishes for more exciting assignments, but is assigned to entertain the troops and care for the heir, a baby with the royal birthmark on his rear. He is in love with Jean (Glynis Johns), a smart, courageous, and tough captain of the rebel forces.

Hawkins disguises himself as Giacomo, the king's new jester, to get access to the palace. He finds himself in the midst of intrigue, hypnotized into wooing the princess (Angela Lansbury) by her lady-in-waiting (Mildred Natwick), and hired by Sir Ravenhurst (Basil Rathbone) to kill those who stand between him and the throne. Jean is captured by the king's soldiers, who have been told to round up the prettiest "wenches" in the kingdom. And Hawkins has to do battle with a huge knight named Sir Griswold. Although he has trouble remembering that the pellet with the poison is in the pestle with the vessel, the good guys triumph, and "life could not better be."

✳ **DISCUSSION:** Pure joy. This is Danny Kaye's best movie, and one of the funniest comedies ever, with a plot that is both exciting and hilarious. The "pestle with the vessel" scene is a classic, but just as good are the scenes in which a snap of the fingers puts Hawkins in and out of his hypnotic state. Terrific family fun.

It is worth pointing out the scene in which Jean and Hawkins confess their love for one another. He asks shyly if she could love a man who was not a fighter, and she explains that tenderness and kindess are important to her. They are each proud of the other the way they are, almost revolutionary for a movie of that era.

PROFANITY: None.
NUDITY/SEXUAL REFERENCES: None.
ALCOHOL/DRUG ABUSE: None.
VIOLENCE/SCARINESS: Comic battles, jousting match, and sword fights.
TOLERANCE/DIVERSITY ISSUES: Exceptionally active and competent heroine, and a hero who respects her for it.

✳ **QUESTIONS FOR KIDS:**
- How is this movie like *The Adventures of Robin Hood* and *Ivanhoe?* How is it different?
- Why did the soldiers cheat on Hawkins's tests for becoming a knight?
- Why did courts have jesters? Whose job is most like that today?

✳ **CONNECTIONS:** Kids who enjoy this movie will also enjoy some of Danny Kaye's other comedies, especially *The Inspector General* and *Knock on Wood.* Kaye also played the title role in *Hans Christian Andersen.* They might also enjoy seeing him perform with Bing Crosby in *White Christmas* and play the more dramatic role of coronet player Red Nichols in *The Five Pennies.*

Basil Rathbone's performance here, especially in the sword fight, is reminiscent of his appearances in *The Adventures of Robin Hood* and *The Mark of Zorro.* Glynis Johns played Mrs. Banks, the mother, in *Mary Poppins.* Angela Lansbury played Velvet's older sister in *National Velvet* and Mrs. Price in *Bedknobs and Broomsticks,* as well as Jessica Fletcher in television's *Murder, She Wrote.*

Dr. Strangelove or: How I Learned to Stop Worrying and Love the Bomb
1964, 93 min, b&w, NR, high schoolers
Dir: Stanley Kubrick. Peter Sellers, George C. Scott, Sterling Hayden

✳ **PLOT:** In this blackest of black comedies, a *Duck Soup* for the Cold War era, a rogue American general named Jack D. Ripper (Sterling Hayden) goes mad and sends planes to drop nuclear bombs on the Soviet Union. He cuts off all communication to the base, and only he knows the three-letter code to cancel the attack.

The mild-mannered president of the United States (Peter Sellers) and Captain Mandrake, a highly civilized British officer (Sellers again), are no match for the bloodthirsty General Buck Turgidson (George C. Scott) and the demented Dr. Strangelove (Sellers again!), a former Nazi expert on nuclear weapons whose prosthetic arm gets out of control, giving a "Heil, Hitler" salute and even trying to choke him. Turgidson's view is that America should take advantage of the accidental initiation of war to fight to the finish and establish American supremacy. Mandrake is unable to trick Ripper into revealing the code, but after Ripper commits suicide, following his explanation that flouridation is a Communist plot, Mandrake figures it out. He is almost prevented from revealing it, however, when the suspicious Colonel "Bat" Guano (Keenan Wynn) arrives in search of Ripper, and then when it turns out that no one has change for the pay phone. At the last minute, the correct code is sent, but an enterprising American pilot insists on carrying out the mission. The Americans spend their last moments designing a postnuclear world, where the few remaining people live in mine shafts, with ten women (selected for their fertility and appeal) for every man. The Soviet ambassador thinks this is an outstanding idea, but Turgidson still worries that the Soviets might have more mine shafts than the Americans.

✳ **DISCUSSION:** Teens who view this movie may need some background to understand the sense of helpless peril of the Cold War years. More importantly, they may need some preparation to understand the nature of black comedy, and some may find it very disturbing, particularly the unconventional ending, in which the world is annihilated. This can be a good way to initiate discussions about the nature of war and peace (begin with Ripper's quote from Clemenceau about war's being too important to be left to the generals), and about the best ways of ensuring an enduring peace.

PROFANITY: None.

NUDITY/SEXUAL REFERENCES: Many references, mostly euphemistic, beginning with a suggestive opening shot of one plane refueling another. The imagery (and to a lesser extent, the dialogue) create a link between men's sexual impulse and their interest in war. Buck and his secretary (who is wearing a bikini) are clearly having an affair, and the men are delighted with the idea that in a postnuclear world they will be obligated to impregnate many women.

ALCOHOL/DRUG ABUSE: Soviet leader reported to be drunk.

VIOLENCE/SCARINESS: It is a comedy about nuclear war—in addition to the mushroom clouds and reports of planes being shot down, there is an off-camera suicide.

TOLERANCE/DIVERSITY ISSUES: All the people in power are white males; women are sex objects (part of the satire).

* **QUESTIONS FOR KIDS:**
  - What do you think of making fun of issues like madness and nuclear destruction? Does it make you feel more or less comfortable about the possibility of nuclear war?
  - If the movie were to be made today, what details would be changed? Who would the nuclear threat come from?
  - Who should decide when to initiate nuclear warfare?

* **CONNECTIONS:** The same issues are addressed in a serious dramatic context in *Fail-Safe,* released the same year. Some of the same issues of control of the war machinery are raised by *WarGames* and even by *Independence Day* (which has an explicit reference to this movie in Randy Quaid's attack on the alien spaceship).

* **ACTIVITIES:** Teens should see if they can find out what the current state of nuclear disarmamant is and what the current issues are.

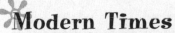

Modern Times

1936, 89 min, NR, b&w, 6 and up
Dir: Charlie Chaplin. Charlie Chaplin, Paulette Goddard

* **PLOT:** This Chaplin classic (he produced, wrote, directed, starred, and composed the music) is about two people struggling with the isolation of the industrial era. Chaplin (simply called "A worker" in the credits) is tightening bolts on an assembly line. He does it so intently that his arms continue to twitch as though he is still tightening when he takes his break. On a break, he smokes in the men's room until the big boss appears on a television screen to tell him to quit stalling and get back to work.

The boss watches a demonstration of a new machine, designed to feed employees while they work, to reduce breaks. Chaplin is selected to try it out. Everything goes wrong in the most deliriously slapstick fashion. He eventually becomes trapped in the huge factory machine itself, stuck in the gears. He comes out a little crazed, tightening everything resembling bolts. He loses his job. A doctor tells him to take it easy and avoid excitement.

Nevertheless, he almost immediately finds excitement by accidentally leading a Communist parade while just trying to return the red flag to the man who dropped it. He is arrested. The prison is not unlike the factory in its regimentation. At lunch, the guards come in "searching for smuggled nose powder." The prisoner who has smuggled it puts it in a salt shaker. When he is taken away, Chaplin sprinkles it on his food and becomes a bit delirious. When he comes upon an attempted escape, he captures the prisoners and releases the guards.

Meanwhile, we have met "a gamine," Paulette Goddard, stealing food for herself and other children. Her unemployed father is killed in a street fight, and she and her siblings are taken into state custody, to be sent to an orphanage. Goddard escapes as Chaplin remains "happy in his comfortable cell." However, he is pardoned because of his heroism in the attempted escape, and is given a letter of recommendation to get a job.

After another job disaster, he is "determined to go back to jail," where he was safe and warm. He sees Goddard captured for stealing bread and confesses that it was he who stole it. But a witness identifies Goddard. He orders a large meal, eats it, then turns himself in as being unable to pay, and happily settles into the police truck on the way back to jail. When Goddard is put in the same truck, they escape together. He takes a job as night watchman in a department store, and they enjoy having the store to themselves. But robbers break in—Chaplin's former colleague at the factory. And the next morning, Chaplin is arrested again.

Goddard is waiting for him when he gets out of the police station. Goddard gets a job as a dancer in a nightclub and arranges a job for him as a singing waiter. He is a huge hit (even though he forgets the words to the song and has to make them up). But the police come after Goddard, to take her back into the custody of the state. They escape once more, and walk off into the sunset together.

✳ **DISCUSSION:** We have to remind ourselves how prescient this movie was. To us, it may not be surprising that the boss watches the workers on a screen, but this was before the invention of television—and more than a decade before the publication of Orwell's *1984*. Interestingly, it was several years after the invention of the talkies. But Chaplin wanted to make a silent movie, and silent this one is, except for a few words, some sound effects, and a gibberish song. Children will adore the slapstick in this movie, especially the scenes where Chaplin tries out the feeding machine and when he experiments with roller skates at the department store. Grown-ups who watch with younger children can read them the title cards and help them follow the story. They can tell older children something about the Depression and the concerns about the dehumanizing effect of technology that are a part of this movie. Point out the use of sheep at the beginning, and then their human equivalents, the crowds of people on their way to work.

PROFANITY: None.

NUDITY/SEXUAL REFERENCES: None.

ALCOHOL/DRUG ABUSE: Cocaine ("nose powder") accidentally ingested by Chaplin.

VIOLENCE/SCARINESS: None.

TOLERANCE/DIVERSITY ISSUES: Use of the term "darkie" in a song.

✳ **QUESTIONS FOR KIDS:**
- Why did the boss want Chaplin to try the feeding machine? What would Frank Gilbreth of *Cheaper By the Dozen* think of the machine?
- Why did Chaplin want to go back to jail? Why didn't Goddard want to go to jail?

- Did Chaplin want you to think that prison was like the factory? Better? How can you tell?
- How did Chaplin and Goddard differ in their reactions to their troubles?
- For high school age: Why was Chaplin arrested for leading the Communist parade? Does that violate the freedom of speech guaranteed by the First Amendment?

✳ **CONNECTIONS:** Some of the Chaplin shorter movies, like *The Rink* and *The Gold Rush,* are delightful for kids. *City Lights* is a wonderful movie with a darker tone and a more ambiguous ending.

✳ A Night at the Opera

1935, 96 min, NR, b&w, 8 and up
Dir: Sam Wood. The Marx brothers, Kitty Carlisle, Allan Jones, Margaret Dumont

✳ **PLOT:** Harpo, Chico, and Groucho Marx bring their sublime brand of anarchy to perhaps its most fitting setting in this comic masterpiece. Groucho is (as ever) a fast-talking fortune hunter (this time called Otis P. Driftwood), chasing (as ever) dim dowager Margaret Dumont (this time called Mrs. Claypool).

Mrs. Claypool brings two Italian opera stars to the United States (Kitty Carlisle as sweet Rosa and Walter Woolf King as cruel Rodolfo Laspari) onboard an ocean liner. Talented tenor Riccardo (Allan Jones), who loves Rosa, his manager Fiorello (Chico Marx), and Tomasso (Harpo Marx), Rodolfo's abused dresser, stow away in Driftwood's steamer trunk. They manage to get off the boat disguised as bearded Russian aviators, but are discovered and chased by a New York detective. When Rosa refuses Rodolfo's romantic advances, she is fired. But Tomasso and Fiorello wreak havoc on the opera's performance of *Il Trovatore,* until Rosa and Riccardo come in and save the show.

✳ **DISCUSSION:** Many of the Marx brothers' best-loved routines are here, including the wildly funny contract negotiation, as Groucho and Chico try to con each other ("That's what we call a sanity clause." "Oh no, you can't fool me. There ain't no Sanity Clause!"), and the famous stateroom scene, as person after person enters Groucho's closet-sized room on the ship while Harpo manages to stay asleep (and draped over as many women as possible) and Groucho stays philosophical (when the manicurist asks if he wants his nails long or short, he says, "You'd better make them short; it's getting pretty crowded in here."). The movie veers happily from the wildest slapstick (the Marx brothers replace the music for *Il Trovatore* with *Take Me Out to the Ballgame*) to the cleverest wordplay (by George S. Kaufman and Morrie Ryskind), punctuated by musical numbers that range from pleasant to innocuous. Children studying piano may especially enjoy Chico's specialty—playing the piano while his fingers do acrobatics. And all children will enjoy learning that the stars were real-life brothers, who performed together for most of their lives.

PROFANITY: None.

NUDITY/SEXUAL REFERENCES: None.

ALCOHOL/DRUG ABUSE: None.

VIOLENCE/SCARINESS: None.

TOLERANCE/DIVERSITY ISSUES: None.

✳ **QUESTIONS FOR KIDS:**
- Why won't Rodolfo sing to the people who came to say good-bye to him?
- The Marx brothers play people who are not very nice in this movie—they steal, they cheat, they lie, and they cause havoc. How does the movie make you like them, anyway?

✳ **CONNECTIONS:** This was the most commercially successful of the Marx brothers movies, in part because of the very sections that seem most tedious to us now—the serious musical numbers and the romance. Children will enjoy the other Marx brothers movies as well, especially *A Day at the Races* (NOTE: That movie contains some material that seems racist by today's standards, particularly a rather minstrel show-ish musical number), *Duck Soup,* *Horse Feathers,* and *Monkey Business.* Fans of the many movie references in *The Freshman,* with Matthew Broderick and Marlon Brando, may notice that Broderick's fake passport is in the name of Rodolfo Laspari.

✳Some Like It Hot

1959, 119 min, NR, b&w, 10 and up
Dir: Billy Wilder. Marilyn Monroe, Tony Curtis, Jack Lemmon, Joe E. Brown, George Raft

✳ **PLOT:** In the first moments of the movie, what appears to be a hearse turns out to be carrying bootleg liquor, and we are prepared for a movie in which nothing will be what it seems and nothing will be treated very seriously. It is the 1920s, during Prohibition, and Joe (Tony Curtis) and Jerry (Jack Lemmon) are two musicians who play in a speakeasy. When they accidentally witness the Saint Valentine's Day massacre of a group of bootleggers by Spats Columbo (George Raft) and his mob, they have to hide out. So they accept a job with a band on its way to Florida—an all-girl band—and they dress as women, calling themselves "Josephine" and "Daphne."

On the train, they meet the rest of the band, including lead singer Sugar Kane (Marilyn Monroe). Both men are very attracted to her. She quickly becomes friends with "Daphne," and they have a late-night pajama party. But when they get to Florida, Joe adopts yet another disguise, this time as a wealthy bachelor. Meanwhile, Osgood (Joe E. Brown), a really wealthy bachelor, is interested in "Daphne." Joe gets "Daphne" to distract Osgood so he can use Osgood's yacht for a date with Sugar.

Meanwhile, Spats and his gang arrive at the hotel for a conference with other gang leaders that results in even more bloodshed. Joe realizes that he does not want to mislead Sugar anymore and sends her a diamond bracelet (from Osgood) and a farewell note. But, seeing her sadness, he is overcome and kisses her, forgetting that he is dressed as Josephine. She runs after them, and joins Joe, Jerry, and Osgood as they escape on Osgood's boat.

✳ **DISCUSSION:** This is one of the wildest farces ever filmed, but it has a lot of heart as well, with brilliant performances by all three stars. Monroe is heartbreakingly vulnerable as Sugar, explaining that she always gets "the fuzzy end of the lollypop." Joe must become someone else in order to learn the truth about Sugar (who would never have confided in a man) and about himself (as he sees the consequences of his exploitive behavior and feels what it is like to have men try to force their attentions on him). Jerry, hilariously, turns out to be as suggestible as a woman as he was as a man. As himself, he ends up going along with whatever Joe tells him. In women's clothes, he starts to think of himself as a woman. The scene where he tells Joe that he and Osgood are engaged is a classic.

PROFANITY: None.
NUDITY/SEXUAL REFERENCES: Oblique and lighthearted references to everything from transvestism to impotence.
ALCOHOL/DRUG ABUSE: Sugar drinks when she is unhappy.
VIOLENCE/SCARINESS: Off-screen gangland slaying; characters in peril.
TOLERANCE/DIVERSITY ISSUES: A theme of the movie.

✳ **QUESTIONS FOR KIDS:**
- How does Joe change, and what makes him change?
- What does he learn from being dressed as a woman?
- How do Joe and Jerry react differently to dressing as women?
- How does Sugar behave differently with "Junior" and "Josephine"?

✳ **CONNECTIONS:** Other movies with male characters disguising themselves as women include the venerable *Charlie's Aunt*, filmed seven times, including a musical version with Ray Bolger, and *Tootsie*, with Dustin Hoffman (rated PG, but with mature themes). Curtis and Lemmon also appeared together in **The Great Race**. George Raft engagingly spoofs his tough-guy performances in 1930s gangster movies, even repeating his coin-flipping habit from *Scarface*.

What's Up, Doc?

1972, 94 min, PG, 6 and up
Dir: Peter Bogdanovich. Barbra Streisand, Ryan O'Neal

✳ **PLOT:** "Once upon a time there was a plaid overnight bag," this movie begins. But actually there are four, identical on the outside, but with very different contents. One contains a set of rare rocks on their way to being presented at a conference of musicologists. One contains a very valuable collection of jewelry. One contains top-secret government documents. The last one contains nothing more than a change of clothes. All four bags converge in a large hotel to provide the framework for an affectionate valentine to the classic screwball comedies of the 1930s. Like **Bringing Up Baby,** this centers on a madcap young woman (Barbra Streisand), Judy Maxwell, who decides to show her appreciation for a shy professor in spectacles (Ryan O'Neal), Howard Bannister, by disrupting his life as much as is humanly possible and then some. The attempts by a spy to steal the bag with the documents and a thief to steal the bag with the jewels help to make things a bit more complicated.

Professor Bannister is at the hotel to present his findings about the musical qualities of rocks used by ancient societies as primitive instruments. He is accompanied by his stuffy and overbearing fiancée, Eunice (Madeline Kahn). He hopes to get a research grant from wealthy Mr. Larabee, who will be attending the conference. Judy, who came to the hotel to cadge a free meal, is drawn to Howard, and stays on to be near him. She impersonates Eunice at the opening dinner, utterly captivating Larabee. She then proceeds, as Howard says, to "bring havoc and chaos to everyone," including the destruction of a hotel room (and Howard's engagement), and a wildly funny car chase through the streets of San Francisco, before it all gets straightened out.

✳ **DISCUSSION:** This movie is a lot of fun, but it does not come close to meeting the standards of the movies it is trying to emulate. The main flaw is that Judy and Howard (and the actors who portray them) are simply not as appealing as their prototypes in classics like **Bringing Up Baby.** For example, as we meet Judy, she is stealing a meal from a hotel, something which may have had more appeal in the "antiestablishment" early 1970s, but which now seems less than charming. The big laugh line at the end of the movie, a poke at O'Neal's overwhelmingly successful previous movie, *Love Story,* will not mean anything to today's kids.

> **PROFANITY:** None.
> **NUDITY/SEXUAL REFERENCES:** One mild joke as Eunice tells the judge, "They tried to molest me," and he replies, "That's . . . unbelievable."
> **ALCOHOL/DRUG ABUSE:** None.
> **VIOLENCE/SCARINESS:** None.
> **TOLERANCE/DIVERSITY ISSUES:** None.

✳ **QUESTIONS FOR KIDS:**
- What do you think about the way Judy behaved? Did she ever think ahead, or did she just do what seemed right at the moment?

- Eunice tells Howard that she does not want romance because she wants something stronger—trust. What is the point of view of the movie about that? How can you tell?
- Which is the funniest part of the movie? Were there any parts that were supposed to be funny that you did not think were funny? Why?

✳ **CONNECTIONS:** See *Bringing Up Baby* and compare it. Some of the other classic screwball comedies are *My Man Godfrey* and *The Lady Eve*.

✳ BEDTIME FOR BONZO

1951, 83 min, b&w, NR, 6 and up
Dir: Frederick de Cordova. Ronald Reagan, Diana Lynn

Even if it didn't star future President Ronald Reagan at close to the bottom of his film career, this film would still be worth watching as a cute comedy about a nature/nurture experiment that has a professor bringing home a chimp to be treated like a human baby. It may even lead to a discussion of the nature/nurture debate, as you ask children and teens whether they think they were more influenced by their genes or their environment.

✳ **CONNECTIONS:** Kids may get a kick out of knowing that the actor in this movie went on to become president. He also appears briefly in *Dark Victory,* and memorably in *Knute Rockne, All American* as "the Gipper."

✳ **ACTIVITIES:** Kids who enjoy the movie will enjoy learning about Koko and Washoe, primates who were taught sign language by scientists.

✳ A BIG HAND FOR THE LITTLE LADY

1966, 95 min, 10 and up
Dir: Fielder Cook. Henry Fonda, Jason Robards, Joanne Woodward

This neglected film has not only a first-rate cast but also a marvelously clever plot. It all begins when a poor farmer (Henry Fonda) agrees to sit in on a big-stakes poker game with a high roller (Jason Robards), over the protests of his devoted wife (Joanne Woodward), and to tell any more would be to spoil the surprises.

✳ DUCK SOUP

1933, 70 min, NR, b&w, 6 and up
Dir: Leo McCarey. Marx brothers, Margaret Dumont

For purists, this is the best of the Marx brothers movies, a joyously anarchistic satire about a silly war between two little countries. This features the classic sequence (later re-created in television's *I Love Lucy*) of Harpo pretending to be Groucho's reflection in a mirror.

✳ **CONNECTIONS:** In a way, this movie's portrayal of war as a silly and pointless game played by foolish politicians and egotistical madmen is the precursor to **Dr. Strangelove.** Sophisticated teens might want to try viewing them together to compare them.

✳ FANCY PANTS
1950, 92 min, NR, 6 and up
Dir: George Marshall. Bob Hope, Lucille Ball
A nouveau riche woman and her rambunctious daughter Agatha (Lucille Ball) bring Humphrey, a British valet (Bob Hope), back to their home in 1905 New Mexico, then still a territory. When the community gets the mistaken impression that he is an earl, Agatha and her mother persuade him to pretend to be one, to help them impress their friends. They do not know that in reality he is not a valet and not even British—he is an American actor. Underneath the slapstick and the musical numbers is a story worth discussing about a woman who wants to change her family to be more like her idea of the way that upper-class people behave. Impressing her neighbors is so important to her that she is willing to lie to them.

✳ **CONNECTIONS:** A quieter, drier, and more pointed earlier version of this story is *Ruggles of Red Gap,* in which a rough cowboy wins a butler in a card game. It is well worth watching. A similar theme is in *The Admirable Crichton,* by James M. Barrie, author of **Peter Pan,** about a "gentleman's gentleman" who shows himself much more capable than his master when they are shipwrecked. Curiously, Hope, who plays an American pretending to be British, was himself born in England.

✳ FOUR CLOWNS
1970, 97 min, G, b&w, 4 and up
Dir: Robert Youngson. Laurel and Hardy, Buster Keaton, Charley Chase
This is a terrific introduction to four of the greats of the silent era: Laurel and Hardy, Buster Keaton, and Charley Chase, sheer delight for any age.

✳ THE GENERAL
1927, 74 min, NR, b&w, 6 and up .
Dir: Buster Keaton. Buster Keaton
Based on a true story, Keaton plays a Southerner in the Civil War era who loves two things: his train (called "The General") and a girl named Anabelle Lee (Marion Mack). He ends up having to rescue them both from the Union army in a mission as thrilling as it is hilarious. NOTE: Many kids have trouble adjusting to a silent film—try to get a version with a musical sound track if possible.

✳ **CONNECTIONS:** Keaton's other classics include *Steamboat Bill, Jr.* and *The Navigator.*

✳ HELP!
1965, 90 min, NR, 6 and up
Dir: Richard Lester. The Beatles, Leo McKern

The Beatles' second film is a wild chase about a ruby ring, worn by the sacrificial victims of an obscure Eastern religion, sent to Ringo by an adoring fan. That is just the excuse for sublime silliness (if they couldn't sing, the Beatles could have been the modern-day Marx brothers) and, of course, a sensational score, featuring "Ticket to Ride," "Another Girl," "You've Got to Hide Your Love Away," and the title tune, plus *Beethoven's Ninth.*

✳ **CONNECTIONS:** Watch for Leo McKern (television's Rumpole) as Clang.

✳ HIS GIRL FRIDAY
1940, 92 min, NR, b&w, 10 and up
Dir: Howard Hawks. Cary Grant, Rosalind Russell

The Front Page, by Ben Hecht and Charles MacArthur, is a raucous romp based on the authors' experiences as reporters in the days when major cities had a dozen different newspapers competing with each other. There are a couple of good movies by that name, but in this version there is a crucial difference—the star reporter, Hildy Johnson, is played by a woman (Rosalind Russell), and the editor, Walter Burns (Cary Grant), is her ex-husband. So, his interest in keeping her at the newspaper is romantic as well as professional. When Hildy tells Walter she is about to be married again (to a mild-mannered insurance salesman, played by Ralph Bellamy), and that she plans to move to Albany with him, Burns does everything he can to obstruct their departure. Director Hawks said he wanted to make this movie the fastest ever, and the dialogue spills all over itself as all of the characters talk at the same time. Walter persuades Hildy to cover one last story, the execution of Earl Williams, a mild-mannered man who accidentally killed a policeman. When Earl escapes, Hildy wants to make sure her paper gets the exclusive. This is a fast and funny movie, with some barbed portrayals of reporters and government officials. NOTE: A reference to the political difficulty of the murder of a "colored" policeman is insensitive by today's standards.

✳ **CONNECTIONS:** Watch for Grant's reference to "Archie Leach" (his real name).

✳ HONEY, I SHRUNK THE KIDS
1989, 93 min, PG, 6 and up
Dir: Joe Johnston. Rick Moranis, Matt Frewer, Marcia Strassman

Another "absentminded professor" style movie from Disney, this one has scientist Rick Moranis inventing a ray that shrinks things. When his children and their friends are accidentally shrunk, they have to find their way back across the yard, now a terrifying jungle of sky-high blades of grass and monstrous insects. Exciting and fun (though with an absolutely unnecessary concluding joke about French kissing that will be lost on most of the intended audience).

✷ **CONNECTIONS:** The 1992 sequel, *Honey, I Blew Up the Kid,* has Moranis's toddler stomping through Las Vegas like Godzilla. A 1997 straight-to-video release, *Honey, We Shrunk Ourselves,* has Moranis's character shrinking himself, his brother, and their wives, so that their children think they are alone in the house. The plot and dialogue are weak, but sensational special effects make up most of the brief (seventy-five-minute) video, especially a roller coaster of a ride in a Hot Wheels car, floating in soap bubbles, and close encounters with a cockroach and a daddy longlegs. And there is time for everyone to learn a lesson about the importance of trust and respect for each other, and about what family members really need from one another. Parents will want to talk to kids about what happens when the children, thinking they are alone in the house, have a party that gets out of hand, and when one of the kids decides to rebel by not taking his medicine. There is a nice scene in which a teenage girl tells a boy in no uncertain terms that he may not kiss her without her permission.

✷ THE IMPORTANCE OF BEING EARNEST
1952, 95 min, b&w, NR, 10 and up
Dir: Anthony Asquith. Michael Redgrave, Joan Greenwood, Dame Edith Evans
Oscar Wilde's delicious comedy of manners is impeccably presented by an ideal British cast, including Michael Redgrave, Joan Greenwood, Dame Edith Evans, and, as the absentminded governess who left her book in the baby carriage and the baby in a handbag, Margaret Rutherford. Wilde's epigrammatic dialogue is delivered as though it all made perfect sense, and the settings are so thoroughly civilized that it only makes the satire even more deliciously subversive. Absolutely the top of the genre.

✷ THE INSPECTOR GENERAL
1949, 102 min, NR, 6 and up
Dir: Henry Koster. Danny Kaye, Walter Slezak
Danny Kaye stars as the illiterate assistant to a charlatan (Walter Slezak) who is mistaken for the Inspector General by the corrupt officials of a small town. As the various kinds of dishonesty play out in various slapstick encounters, there are a few worthwhile thoughts about honesty and its rewards (very material ones, in this case).

❊ IT'S A MAD MAD MAD MAD WORLD

1963, 155 min, NR, 6 and up
Dir: Stanley Kramer. Spencer Tracy, Sid Caesar, Mickey Rooney, Ethel Merman

Every television, movie, and vaudeville comedian in Hollywood and every conceivable slapstick stunt appear in this epic comedy about a disparate group of characters racing each other and the police to find a stolen $250,000. Jimmy Durante is the thief on his way to collect his loot when his car runs off the highway and he "kicks the bucket," telling the drivers who stopped to help him only that it is buried under "a big W." They try to cooperate, but when they cannot agree on how to split the money, it is every man (and woman) for himself, and the race is on, picking up more greedy treasure seekers along the way. Spencer Tracy is the long-suffering police chief on the trail of the money and the people who are after it. It might be simpler to list the comic actors who do not appear in this movie than to list the ones who do, so suffice it to say that the cast includes: Mickey Rooney, Phil Silvers, Ethel Merman, Dorothy Provine, Jonathan Winters, Terry-Thomas, Arnold Stang, the Three Stooges, and Jerry Lewis. Themes worth discussing include greed, loyalty, integrity, and the importance of laughter.

❊ **CONNECTIONS:** A movie with similar themes is Mel Brooks's *The Twelve Chairs.*

❊ MR. HULOT'S HOLIDAY

1954, 83 min, NR, b&w, 6 and up
Dir: Jacques Tati. Jacques Tati

This is just a gentle slapstick comedy about a man's vacation at the beach. There is no plot to speak of. In a series of elaborate episodes, he creates complete chaos wherever he goes.

This movie requires a bit of patience from viewers who are used to slam-bang, nonstop action, even in comedies. But its charms are worth it. Tati, who directed, cowrote, and stars, is a master of (almost) silent comedy, especially intricate physical comedy. Themes to discuss with kids include their thoughts on Mr. Hulot's reactions when things go wrong, comparing them to other comic actors and fictional characters, from Donald Duck (the ultimate in apoplectic hysteria) to Buster Keaton (the ultimate in Spartan emotionlessness). What makes these reactions funny?

NOTE: It is a French movie, but the opening titles and most of the (very little) dialogue is in English.

❊ MONKEY BUSINESS

1952, 97 min, NR, b&w, 6 and up
Dir: Howard Hawks. Cary Grant, Ginger Rogers, Marilyn Monroe

Not to be confused with the Marx brothers comedy of the same title, this is an *Absent-minded Professor*–style farce, this time with Cary Grant as the professor who accidentally creates a youth serum, or one that makes people act young, anyway. The next thing you know, he and his wife, Ginger Rogers, are acting like teenagers, and then like children. As an added treat, this movie includes an early appearance by Marilyn Monroe as a secretary who enjoys modeling one of the company's products—nylon stockings—for Grant.

✳ THE MOUSE THAT ROARED

1959, 83 min, NR, 6 and up
Dir: Jack Arnold. Peter Sellers, Jean Seberg

Some of the humor is dated, and some of the jokes a bit subtle for kids, but there is still plenty to enjoy in this farce about the smallest country in the world, which decides to declare war on the United States so that it can lose quickly and receive foreign aid. (This was a more pointed joke in the post–WWII era, as the wartorn United Kingdom watched the United States give money to rebuild its former enemies.) Peter Sellers plays three roles: the Prime Minister, the Grand Duchess (whose late husband was from the then-esoteric Bosnia-Herzegovina), and the leader of the tiny band of invaders. When the Fenwickians arrive in New York, dressed in medieval chain mail, they discover that everyone is underground for an air-raid drill, so they capture the inventor of the latest atomic weapon (and his beautiful daughter, played by Jean Seberg) and declare victory, taking the bomb (and the general, the scientist, and his daughter) back home with them so that the superpowers must come to them to negotiate.

✳ MY MAN GODFREY

1936, 95 min, NR, b&w, 8 and up
Dir: Gregory La Cava. Carole Lombard, William Powell, Mischa Auer

In this Depression-era screwball comedy, Carole Lombard plays Irene Bullock, a flighty girl from a wealthy family who meets "Godfrey" (William Powell) when she and her haughty sister Cornelia (Gail Patrick) must provide a "forgotten man" for a party scavenger hunt. Godfrey is living with other homeless men in shacks near the river. He refuses to go with Cornelia, but Irene persuades him that he will be able to help her win the game and beat her sister if he returns to the party with her. He does help her win (and lectures the frivolous party guests), and Irene invites him to become her family's new butler. Godfrey is really an educated man from a wealthy family who lost interest in life after an unhappy love affair. But he cannot resist the challenge of Lombard's crazy family, including her silly mother and her outrageous "protégé" (Mischa Auer). Godfrey teaches the family a few lessons about respect, honesty, and caring for one another, saves them from financial disaster, and finds a way to help his friends from his homeless days. He finds a purpose for his life, a sense of respect for himself—and, in spite of his best efforts, true love with Irene.

This may provide an opportunity to talk about why Cornelia's behavior was so insensitive and rude, why Irene insisted on announcing her "engagement" when she did, why the family had grown so far apart, and about homelessness, and Godfrey's efforts to help his friends.

✳ **CONNECTIONS:** Lombard and Powell were happily divorced in real life, but enjoyed working together. Lombard was one of the screen's loveliest comediennes, and families who enjoy this movie will also enjoy *Nothing Sacred* and *To Be or Not to Be*. Gail Patrick, also the sleek menace in *Stage Door*, went on to become a successful producer of television shows like *Perry Mason*.

✳ **ACTIVITIES:** The kids might enjoy a scavenger hunt (presumably for items, not people).

✳ THE PARENT TRAP

1961, 124 min, NR, 6 and up
Dir: David Swift. Hayley Mills, Brian Keith, Maureen O'Hara

Hayley Mills plays identical twins, separated at birth when their parents divorced, who do not even know of each other's existence. They first discover each other's identity when they meet at summer camp. Initially hostile, they become good friends when they discover they are sisters. They decide to switch places, each going "home" to the parent she hasn't seen. When the parents (Brian Keith and Maureen O'Hara) discover what has happened, they meet to straighten things out, and the girls get them back together, despite the inconvenience of Keith's recent engagement to the social-climbing Joanna Barnes. NOTE: This might be painful for kids who are dealing with divorce. It also suggests that playing pranks on a prospective stepmother is the way to get parents back together.

✳ **CONNECTIONS:** The 1998 remake stars Lindsay Lohan who is adorable. Watch for Joanna Barnes, the icky fiancée in the original, as the mother of the icky fiancée in the remake.

✳ THE ROAD TO BALI

1952, 90 min, NR, 6 and up
Dir: Hal Walker. Bob Hope, Bing Crosby

Bob Hope and Bing Crosby were the only comedy team to feature two stars who reached the top of their careers independently. Yet in the seven "Road" movies they made together and in many other joint appearances they work so well together it is easy to forget they ever worked apart. Hope and Crosby play drifters, Hope an unabashed coward and Crosby an unabashed con man who rarely cons anyone but Hope. In between ad libs and outlandish gags (some of the jokes are quite dated), they seek fortune and the affections of sarong-girl Dorothy Lamour.

✳ **CONNECTIONS:** All of the "Road" movies are fun, but I'm especially fond of this one (the only one filmed in color). Kids who enjoy this should see *The Road to Morocco* (with the unforgettable title song, concluding: "Like Webster's Dictionary, we're Morocco-bound") and *The Road to Rio* (Crosby and Hope, dressed as South American women, sing the sublimely silly "Ah Ya Ya" song).

✳ THE SOLID GOLD CADILLAC

1956, 99 min, NR, b&w, 10 and up
Dir: Richard Quine. Judy Holliday, Paul Douglas

At the annual shareholders meeting of a company led by corrupt managers and directors, a young woman (Judy Holliday) gets up to ask a few questions, starting with what the executives do to earn their enormous salaries. The executives decide to neutralize her by giving her a job. They tell her to communicate with the small shareholders, and they think they'll never hear from her again. But then she goes to Washington to tell the honest former chief executive (Paul Douglas), now a Defense Department official, about her concerns, and they get caught up in a scandal. Meanwhile, the company's management is so incompetent, it drives one of its own divisions out of business. If you added a couple of zeros to the numbers, this story could have come from today's business section. Funny and romantic, with terrific performances from Holliday and Douglas, this comedy reminds us of the power of asking questions and seeking the truth. The co-author of the play was George S. Kaufman, but the ending feels more like Frank Capra.

✳ **CONNECTIONS:** That's George Burns doing the narration.

✳ WHO'S MINDING THE MINT?

1967, 97 min, NR, 8 and up
Dir: Howard Morris. Jim Hutton, Milton Berle, Walter Brennan

A money checker at the U.S. Mint (Jim Hutton) accidentally destroys $50,000 and has to arrange an elaborate scheme to print enough extra to replace it (with more to pay off everyone he needs to help him). To carry it out, he calls on an assortment of eccentrics, played by top character actors including Milton Berle, Walter Brennan, Bob ("Gilligan") Denver, and Jack Gilford, as well as pretty colleague Dorothy Provine (***It's a Mad Mad Mad Mad World*** and ***The Great Race***). The caper itself is deliciously chaotic, with one hilarious mishap after another. Themes to discuss include greed and loyalty. NOTE: There's a quick joke about a "sex party"; one part of the plot involves having a male member of the team distract a possible female witness with a romantic evening; Hutton explains that he will not date Provine because she is interested in "dinner" and he likes girls who want "din-din," and he is even more exploitive in other aspects of his life, living far above his income by taking expensive items on approval.

✳ **CONNECTIONS:** Kids who enjoy this movie may also enjoy a sweet little comedy called *Mister 880*. Based on a true story, it is about a gentle old man (Edmund Gwenn, Santa in *Miracle on 34th Street*) who happens to be an incompetent but highly successful counterfeiter. Burt Lancaster plays the Treasury Department investigator who tracks him down with the help of Dorothy McGuire.

✳ **ACTIVITIES:** This movie should interest kids in finding out more about how currency is made, and could be a prelude to a trip to the Bureau of Engraving and Printing.

NOT FOR ALL TASTES

A sense of humor is very personal, and all comedies are a matter of taste. But those in this category require special warning. Some people consider them the funniest movies ever made because they have no compunctions about bad taste or propriety, but those who do not think they're funny may be offended by them. As George Eliot said, "A different taste in jokes is a great strain on the affections." With that caveat in mind:

✳ JERRY LEWIS

Jerry Lewis will do *anything* to make you laugh. If he could, he'd climb out of the screen and grab you. This makes some people uncomfortable, but others (legendarily, the French) adore him. Some of his best films include *The Bellboy, The Disorderly Orderly,* and *The Nutty Professor*.

✳ MEL BROOKS

The same thing goes for Mel Brooks, whose best movies, like *Young Frankenstein, High Anxiety, Silent Movie,* and *Blazing Saddles* (rated R) have a lot of toilet and sexual humor. The worst ones have little else (there is an extended chastity belt joke in *Robin Hood: Men in Tights*). In *Young Frankenstein* (rated PG), a woman who is forced to have sex with the monster is so thrilled by the experience that she breaks into song: "Ah, Sweet Mystery of Life at Last I Found Thee." In *Silent Movie*, a group of men are sitting around a table and when they see a sexy picture of a woman, the table levitates, apparently balanced on their erections. Again, these movies can be very funny, but parents should screen them before allowing their children to watch them, and you may want to try to find one of their rare broadcast appearances, when some of the most obviously problematic material will probably be cut.

✳ THE THREE STOOGES

More than 200 two-reel short comedies featuring Moe, Larry, and Curly (or Shemp, or Joe Besser, or Curly Joe) were made between 1938 and 1954. A sort of "Dumb, Dumber, and Dumbest," their humor consisted mostly of punching, gouging, and tweaking each other, while creating happy chaos all around them. A compilation of their best films, called *Stop! Look! and Listen!* was released in 1960 and is available on video.

✳ ZUCKER, ABRAHAMS, ZUCKER AND THEIR IMITATORS

With *Airplane!* and the *Naked Gun* series, these producers and those who tried to repeat their success created a brand of comedy harking back to the tradition of *Hellzapoppin'* and television's *Laugh-In* that can only be described as "anything goes, and if it doesn't, it doesn't matter, because by the time you figure it out, twenty more jokes will have gone by, and at least one of them will work." The movies are undeniably hilarious (there are so many different kinds of jokes that anyone will find something to laugh at), but beware—some of these jokes are not appropriate for kids. *Airplane!* for example, has Peter Graves asking a young boy if he's ever seen a grown man naked, has a visual depiction of the expression referring to what hits the fan, and has a woman blowing up the "automatic pilot" in a suggestive fashion. Recent movies like *There's Something About Mary* and *Baseketball* have gone even further, with jokes about every possible body part and bodily fluid. Screen these movies before watching with kids to determine your comfort level, and watch with them to determine theirs.

SEE ALSO:

Arsenic and Old Lace

The Great Race

The Ladykillers

Sullivan's Travels

What a Way to Go!

FANTASY AND
SCIENCE FICTION

Fantasies are more than substitutes for unpleasant reality; they are also dress rehearsals, plans. All acts performed in the world begin in the imagination.

—BARBARA GRIZZUTI HARRISON

Movies take us to other worlds. Some of the most memorable and exciting are those that exist only in the imagination, yet once we go there in a movie they are as much a part of our lives as our own neighborhoods. One reason is that no matter how fantastic and strange they seem, all of these worlds are built from our own reality. Everything we can conceive of is in some way based on what we already know. Fantasy and science fiction are often used as a device to help us see our own world in sharper relief.

Take, for example, the various movies about aliens from other planets. In some movies, aliens are portrayed as evil and mindlessly predatory (*Independence Day*). In others, they are super-intelligent and peaceful (*E.T.* and *The Day the Earth Stood Still*). In *Forbidden Planet,* the evil force turns out to be a manifestation of a human's hostility and jealousy. In fact, virtually all movies about aliens serve as something of a Rorschach test by which we project our notions of ourselves, and of the way outsiders might see us.

The same is true of movies that explore the future, like *2001: A Space Odyssey,* which links the future to the prehistoric past. In *The Time Machine* Jules Verne imagines a future after civilization has been all but eliminated by war. In both movies, the writer and director want us to think differently about the present by projecting our current choices and behavior into the future. Characters from mythology can also be seen in Jungian terms as illustrating our internal struggles.

It is interesting that most characters who are transported to other worlds, like Dorothy in *The Wizard of Oz,* Milo in *The Phantom Tollbooth,* and Alice in *Alice in Wonderland* spend the entire movie trying to get back home. All three of them begin by wishing for something different, and all three find, as soon as they get it, that they can't wait to get back to what they had. Movies are just such a round-trip ticket to a place of imagination, with a reminder (as shown in **The NeverEnding Story**) to use our own.

Use these films to talk to kids about their own fantasies. Which movie is the most appealing to them. Which of these characters would they like to visit? Which are scariest, and why? If they could make a time machine, where would they go, forward or back? Who would they want to meet? What will the world be like when they are grown up? What movies will their children like to watch?

The Boy Who Could Fly

1986, 108 min, PG, 8 and up
Dir: Nick Castle. Lucy Deakins, Jay Underwood, Bonnie Bedelia, Fred Savage, Fred Gwynne, Colleen Dewhurst, Louise Fletcher

❋ **PLOT:** Milly (Lucy Deakins), her mother, Charlene (Bonnie Bedelia), and her brother, Louis (Fred Savage), move into a new home, still feeling bereft over the loss of the father of the family. Milly sees a mysterious boy (Jay Underwood) on the roof next door. She finds out that his name is Eric, and that he is autistic. He has never spoken, and ever since his parents were killed in a plane crash when he was five, he has apparently thought he was a plane. He lives with his alcoholic uncle, who confides to Milly that Eric really can fly.

Adjustment to the new environment is difficult. Charlene is overwhelmed by the computers at her new job. Louis is terrorized by neighborhood bullies who won't let him ride around the block. Even the dog, Max, is vanquished by the neighborhood Doberman.

At school, Milly befriends Eric, and when an understanding teacher (Colleen Dewhurst) sees that he responds to Milly, she asks her to work with him as a project for school, telling her that he doesn't need a doctor as much as he needs a friend. Milly spends a lot of time with Eric, reading him stories and trying to teach him to understand and not just imitate. He does not speak, but when a ball is thrown at Milly's head, he protects her by catching it.

Milly falls off a bridge on a class trip, and insists that Eric saved her by flying. A psychiatrist (Louise Fletcher) tells her that her mind played tricks, and gently gets her to admit that her father killed himself when he found he had cancer.

Eric is sent to an institution. He somehow escapes, and he and Milly run away from the guards sent to retrieve him. They are chased up to the roof of the high school, where we discover that he really can fly. Eric and Milly float off together, to the astonishment of the entire community. Eric speaks at last, telling Milly he loves her, and flying away forever. She realizes why he had to leave when the scientists and journalists arrive the next day. Eric's influence continues. Charlene masters the computer. Louis triumphs over the bullies. Max even scares away the Doberman. "He made us believe in ourselves again . . . We're all special. We're all a little like Eric. Maybe we can't soar off into the clouds. But somewhere, deep inside, we can all fly."

✳ **DISCUSSION:** This is a charming fantasy with a lot of heart and outstanding performances by three terrific kids who keep up with some of the finest adult actors in movies. Eric and Milly heal each other by responding to each other. For him, she provides the first reason he has ever had to try to make contact with another person. For her, he provides a reason to feel, and to give to another person, especially important after the loss of her father.

> PROFANITY: Mild schoolyard terms.
> NUDITY/SEXUAL REFERENCES: None.
> ALCOHOL/DRUG ABUSE: Milly and her friend Geneva experiment with liquor. Milly has a bad hangover. Eric's uncle is an alcoholic.
> VIOLENCE/SCARINESS: No violence, but some mildly scary moments.
> TOLERANCE/DIVERSITY ISSUES: Tolerance of individual differences is a theme of the movie.

✳ **QUESTIONS FOR KIDS:**
- Why was Eric so important to Milly? Why was she so important to him?
- What did Eric teach Milly's family?
- Where do you think he will go next?
- Why did Louis get so upset about his action figures being out in the rain?

✳ **CONNECTIONS:** Writer-director Nick Castle also directed **The Last Starfighter**. Bonnie Bedelia, who starred in **Heart Like a Wheel,** is the aunt of former child star Macaulay Culkin. Many of the other performers are better known for television appearances. This was the first movie appearance for Fred Savage, who went on to star in television's The Wonder Years and appeared in **The Princess Bride.** Fred Gwynne will be familiar to old-time television fans as Herman Munster, and as Officer Muldoon of Car 54, Where are You? Mindy Cohn starred for many years in The Facts of Life. And if you pay close attention, you will catch a glimpse of future 90210 superstar Jason Priestley as Gary.

✳ **ACTIVITIES:** This is a fantasy, and is in no way intended to be an accurate portrayal of autism. But kids who want to know more about this mysterious disease may want to read books like An Anthropologist on Mars, by Oliver Sacks (of **Awakenings**). David and Lisa has a more dramatic portrayal of two disturbed teenagers reaching out to help each other. Teenagers will appreciate Dustin Hoffman's Oscar-winning portrayal of an autistic savant in **Rain Man.**

Clash of the Titans

1981, 118 min, PG, 8 and up
Dir: Desmond Davis. Laurence Olivier, Maggie Smith, Claire Bloom, Harry Hamlin, Ursula Andress

✳ **PLOT:** This is the story of Perseus (Harry Hamlin), the son of Zeus (Laurence Olivier), king of the gods, and Danaë, a mortal princess. As half god and half mortal, Perseus is the subject of great interest from Mount Olympus. Zeus is so angry when Danaë and Perseus are thrown into the sea by King Acrisius, Danaë's father, that he orders Poseidon to destroy Acrisius's kingdom. When Perseus grows up, Zeus sends him a divine sword, shield, and helmet. A face speaks to Perseus from the shield and tells him to fulfill his destiny. When he sees Princess Andromeda (Judi Bowker), he says, "I have found my destiny." He helps Andromeda break a curse, and they are married. But she is cursed again when her mother says that Andromeda is more beautiful than the goddess Thetis. In thirty days she must be sacrificed to a monster called the Kraken. Perseus must go to see the three blind witches (who share one eye by passing it between them) to ask how to defeat the Kraken. The witches tell Perseus that the only way to defeat the Kraken is with Medusa, the monster who turns to stone anyone who looks at her, and whose blood is poison—"a titan against a titan." Perseus fights Medusa by watching her from the reflection in his shield.

The thirty days are almost up. Perseus has to find Pegasus to get back in time. Perseus arrives just as Andromeda is chained to the rock, with the Kraken approaching. Perseus holds Medusa's head before the Kraken, the Kraken is turned to stone, and the curse is over. "My son has triumphed," says Zeus. "Fortune is ally to the brave."

✳ **DISCUSSION:** There are many interesting issues here, as in the myths themselves, about destiny and free will. As the gods plot, they pick up small clay figures of the people they are influencing. Zeus may be the leader of the gods, but even he is not all-powerful, which is what makes Perseus's triumph meaningful to him.

The gods claim Perseus's good qualities as their legacy. "What if one day courage and imagination become everyday mortal qualities? What would become of us?" one asks. "We don't have to worry about that," replies Zeus. "There is sufficient cowardice, sloth, and mendacity on earth to last forever." He notes, however, that "Even if the gods are abandoned or forgotten, the stars will never fade, never. They will burn until the end of time." Children may enjoy thinking about why it was that the ancient Greeks thought all good qualities came from the gods, and how the gods were as dependent on people as the people were on the gods.

PROFANITY: None.
NUDITY/SEXUAL REFERENCES: There is a brief nude shot of Andromeda

getting out of the bath. According to the curse, Andromeda must be "untouched by man" for the sacrifice.

ALCOHOL/DRUG ABUSE: None.

VIOLENCE/SCARINESS: Bloody combat with swords; scary monsters. The soldiers who accompany Perseus are killed.

TOLERANCE/DIVERSITY ISSUES: Andromeda is rather spirited, insisting on accompanying Perseus for part of the quest, but she is still pretty much an old-fashioned damsel in distress.

✳ QUESTIONS FOR KIDS:

- When do the gods intervene in the lives of the humans in this story? How much power do they have? How can you tell?
- Why must Perseus lose each of his divine gifts?
- What does Ammon mean when he asks, "When will they ever learn?"
- Why was Thetis angry when Cassiopeia said her daughter was more beautiful? Does that remind you of any other stories?
- What does it mean when Perseus says, "I have found my destiny"? What do you think "destiny" means? How will you know your own destiny? To what extent do we make our own destiny?

✳ CONNECTIONS:
The Medusa character also appears in *7 Faces of Dr. Lao*. There are also about a dozen movies about Hercules, but unfortunately most of them range from poor to dreadful, like *Hercules in New York,* featuring a very young Arnold Schwarzenegger, whose dialogue is dubbed by someone else.

The special effects in this movie are the best example of the fine work done by Ray Harryhausen. Before the days of computerized special effects, he led the field. In this movie alone he used many different techniques, including miniatures, animation, and optical effects. Some other examples of his work are *Mighty Joe Young, The Golden Voyage of Sinbad,* and *Earth vs. the Flying Saucers.* Another one of his best is ***Jason and the Argonauts,*** also based on the Greek myths, which raises similar themes about free will.

This movie features many of the finest British actors, including Laurence Olivier (*Wuthering Heights, Hamlet, Pride and Prejudice, A Little Romance*) and Maggie Smith (***The Pride of Miss Jean Brodie***). Fans of television's *L.A. Law* will recognize Harry Hamlin as handsome attorney Michael Kuzak.

✳ ACTIVITIES:
Most children study the Greek and Roman myths in school, and those who have will especially enjoy this movie. As pointed out at the end of the movie, there are constellations named after Perseus, Andromeda, Pegasus, and Cassiopeia. Children might like to read a book on the constellations or visit a planetarium to try to find them. There are a number of excellent books about mythology for children, and children always enjoy writing their own myths.

Close Encounters of the Third Kind

1977, 134 min, PG, 8 and up
Dir: Steven Spielberg. Richard Dreyfuss, Melinda Dillon

PLOT: When Roy Neary (Richard Dreyfuss) and Jillian Guiler (Melinda Dillon) "encounter" a UFO, they are compelled to travel to its landing site, Devil's Tower, Wyoming. Jillian is seeking her son, who disappeared with the alien ship, but Roy is strangely drawn to go in a way that is incomprehensible to him. Obsessed with re-creating the monolithic Devil's Tower out of shaving cream, the mashed potatoes on his dinner plate and, finally, out of mud, in a massive sculpture that takes over the living room, Roy drives his family away.

Roy meets Jillian, also drawn to the Devil's Tower in Wyoming. They find that they are not the only ones who feel they have been called there. French scientist Claude Lacombe (François Truffaut), a top-secret U.S. government team, and others feeling the same compulsion are there to meet the enormous spacecraft, which returns dozens of humans taken over decades (including Jillian's son). Then the aliens leave the ship, and Roy joins the group boarding the ship in an intergalactic exchange program. In the reissue, which added some new scenes, we get a glimpse of the inside of the spacecraft.

DISCUSSION: This is a thrilling adventure story and a brilliant example of the art and craft of moviemaking. The craft is in the way the story is told. It unfolds with extraordinary power, involving us as much in Roy's inexplicable compulsion as in Jillian's search for her son. The art is in the story itself, the idea not just that "something" is out there, but that it is something wonderful. Watch how Spielberg lets us know that the aliens are friendly. In one of several tributes to Disney, the interplay between the large and small spaceships has a fond, protective, almost maternal quality. This is a device Disney uses over and over, perhaps most memorably with the dancing mushrooms in **Fantasia**. And there is something very believable and compelling about the way the aliens use music to communicate, and to teach the people on Earth. They use art as well—Roy's sculptures and Jillian's drawings help the message to reach their conscious minds. Spielberg creates a sense of wonder not just in Jillian's son Barry (Cary Guffey), but in the adult characters and in the viewers, making them children again, with the aliens as the "adults," who reassuringly look and behave like gentle children, giving us a sense of comfort.

PROFANITY: Some.
NUDITY/SEXUAL REFERENCES: None.
ALCOHOL/DRUG ABUSE: None.
VIOLENCE/SCARINESS: The arrival of the spaceships is suspenseful and can be scary. There are tense moments as Roy and Jillian approach Devil's Tower. Smaller children may be scared when Barry is taken by the

aliens, and by his mother's distress. Older children may be upset when Roy's family leaves him.

TOLERANCE/DIVERSITY ISSUES: Tolerance on an interplanetary level.

✳ QUESTIONS FOR KIDS:
- Why was music a good way for the aliens to communicate with the people on Earth?
- What did the scientist mean when he said it was the first day of school?
- What movie did Roy want his family to see? What does that tell you about him? How does that movie relate to this one? (Hint—listen for a familiar song.)
- Do you think aliens will come to Earth? What will they be like?
- What do you think would happen in a sequel to this movie?

✳ **CONNECTIONS:** François Truffaut was a distinguished French film critic and director (*The 400 Blows*, **Small Change**).

✳ **ACTIVITIES:** Kids can draw a picture of what they think the aliens' planet looks like. Do they live in cities? What kinds of inventions do they have that we don't have? Make a model or draw a picture of the planets in our solar system. Go to the library or a museum to get information about space travel. Check out NASA on the World Wide Web at http://www.nasa. gov to get information about the next space mission. Or write to the SETI Institute, 2035 Landings Drive, Mountain View, CA 94043 for the latest research on UFOs and extraterrestrials.

✳Dragonslayer
1981, 108 min, PG, 10 and up
Dir: Matthew Robbins. Sir Ralph Richardson, Peter MacNichol, Albert Salmi

✳ **PLOT:** Set in medieval times, the story begins as villagers with torches approach the home of a famous sorcerer (Sir Ralph Richardson). They need his help to fight a dragon. If they do not sacrifice a virgin twice a year, he will destroy their community. The sorcerer agrees, but he is killed when a warrior with the group insists on a test. The sorcerer's apprentice, Galen (Peter MacNichol), goes in his place, telling them, "I am the sorcerer you seek."

On the way to the village, Galen discovers that Valerian, the boy who spoke for the group, is in fact a girl brought up as a boy to protect her from the lottery used twice a year to select a female virgin for sacrifice. They reach the dragon's lair, and Galen casts a spell that causes an avalanche. Sure that the dragon is killed, they celebrate, and Valerian appears in a dress. The king is worried, telling Galen, "You came here to toy with a monster? Who are you to risk these people's lives?" It was he who agreed to sacrifice the girls, after his brother was killed by the dragon. He throws Galen in the dungeon.

Galen is freed by the princess, who is horrified when Galen tells her that she has not been included in the lottery. She had been assured that she ran the same risk as everyone else, and she feels betrayed and ashamed. It turns out that the dragon has not been killed, and it is time for another sacrifice. The princess puts her name on all of the lots, to make up for the risks she avoided over the years. The king, heartbroken, begs Galen to fight the dragon. But the warrior tries to stop him, believing that the sacrifice is the only way to keep the rest of the village safe. As they fight, the princess is killed and eaten by the just-hatched baby dragons.

Galen fights the dragon with a shield made of dragon scales by Valerian and a sword made by her father. He is defeated and starts to leave, when he realizes that the sorcerer can still help him. He uses his magic to bring back the sorcerer, who fights the dragon until they destroy each other. It is not just the end of the two of them, but the end of that era, as Christianity replaces sorcery.

✳ **DISCUSSION:** When the community is at risk, how do you decide what to do? History is filled with problems created by people who made the wrong choices. Many people criticize those who tried to compromise with Hitler. Many criticize those who decided Americans should fight in Vietnam. The king here makes the decision to compromise after his brother is killed. He negotiated a terrible deal with the dragon, but it was better for his people than the uncertainty they had before. In contrast, Galen wants to risk his own destruction and the town's by fighting. When he loses, he leaves until he figures out a way to defeat the dragon.

And what about the king's compromise, the lottery itself, and its fairness in theory and as practiced? The way we evaluate risks and benefits in making our choices (sometimes emotionally rather than analytically) is demonstrated here. Note the king's change of heart when his own daughter is at risk.

Like the other famous sorcerer's apprentice (memorably portrayed by Mickey Mouse in **Fantasia**), Galen doesn't know what he doesn't know. He thinks because he knows a few tricks, he has enough magic to defeat the dragon. But he is wrong, and the princess dies because of his mistake. He doesn't know what he does know, either—it takes him a while to figure out why the sorcerer allowed himself to be "killed" before starting on the journey. But when the time comes, and he has to know the right moment to destroy the amulet, he is able to trust himself, and he gets it right.

Sorcerers and dragons cannot exist without each other. Valerian's father says approvingly that magic is dying out. Particularly well-handled here is the notion that religion replaced magic.

PROFANITY: None.

NUDITY/SEXUAL REFERENCES: Very brief flash of nudity as Galen discovers Valerian is a girl; a virgin sacrifice theme.

ALCOHOL/DRUG ABUSE: None.

VIOLENCE/SCARINESS: Some graphic violence, and the dragon is genuinely scary. The baby dragons gnaw on the princess's disembodied limbs.

TOLERANCE/DIVERSITY ISSUES: Valerian is successful in both "boy" and "girl" terms; brave, resourceful, faithful. She says, "I'm not afraid—I was a man, remember?"

✳ **QUESTIONS FOR KIDS:**
- What do you need to know in deciding whether to fight, compromise, or run? How have you seen those questions presented?
- What adjustments might be difficult for Valerian after the way she grew up?
- What was the point of having both the king and the priest claim credit for defeating the dragon?
- What do you think about the princess's decision? Why did she say that putting her name on all of the tiles "certified" the lottery?

✳ **CONNECTIONS:** Other "sword and sorcery" movies include *Labyrinth* and *Ladyhawke*.

✳ **ACTIVITIES:** Read Shirley Jackson's famous story, "The Lottery," about a small town that uses a lottery to determine which of its citizens will be sacrificed.

✳Forbidden Planet

1956, 98 min, NR, 6 and up
Dir: Fred McLeod Wilcox. Walter Pidgeon, Anne Francis, Leslie Nielson

✳ **PLOT:** It is the year 2200, and Commander Adams (Leslie Nielson) directs his spaceship to an Earthlike planet called Altair-4 in search of a former Earth colony, out of contact for many years. They receive a transmission from Dr. Morbius, telling them to go away, but they insist on landing. When they arrive, a huge robot named Robby greets them and brings Adams and two crew members to the home of Dr. Morbius (Walter Pidgeon). Morbius shows off Robby's many accomplishments and tells them that, with the exception of Morbius and his wife, everyone else in the colony perished violently, killed by an unseen force, which has not bothered him since. His wife now dead, he lives there with his daughter, Alta (Anne Francis), and Robby. Curious about the men, Alta introduces herself. She has never seen any human other than her father, and her only friends are the animals, descendants of those brought from Earth years before

Morbius explains that a great race once lived on the planet, and he has studied their artifacts. In an attempt to use their minds and spirits to create something, he inadvertently created a creature made up of their fears and anger. It is called the Id. It reappeared when the colonists arrived, out of their subconscious urges. And, with the arrival of the crew from Earth, it has come back again. The invisible being damages the spacecraft and kills three of the men before Morbius, realizing that the Id came from within him, renounces that part of himself, destroying both of them. Adams and Alta escape with the crew before the planet explodes.

✳ **DISCUSSION:** This was the first big-budget science-fiction movie, and the only one for over a decade. It is loosely based on Shakespeare's *The Tempest,* the story of Prospero the Sorcerer and his daughter Miranda, who are alone on an island until a storm brings their former countrymen to them. Robby the Robot is the obedient Ariel. And the Id is the powerful and angry Caliban. The gadgets and special effects seem almost quaint to us now, but the movie is still fun to watch for younger children and it still raises some important questions for older ones.

The Id, of course, is named for Freud's famous concept of the id, the instincts and impulses of the unconscious mind. Morbius says that he and his wife survived because they were the only ones who loved the planet and wanted to stay, that the monster was created from the fears and jealousies of the other colonists. The implication (more explicit in portions cut from the film), is that it is the jealousy Morbius feels when Alta falls in love with Adams that brings the Id's destructiveness out again. In a way, this movie is more a way of exploring unconscious feelings we all harbor than it is speculation about life in the future or on other planets.

PROFANITY: None.
NUDITY/SEXUAL REFERENCES: Farron "teaches" Alta about kissing, and there is some discussion of its stimulating qualities. She feels nothing, though, until she kisses Adams.
ALCOHOL/DRUG ABUSE: Cook tells Robby to make liquor and gets drunk (parallel to scene with Trinculo in *The Tempest*).
VIOLENCE/SCARINESS: Characters in peril and some killed by Id monster.
TOLERANCE/DIVERSITY ISSUES: These filmmakers viewed the future as peopled primarily by white males. As with most other science-fiction stories, the assumption is that in the future, attire for women will be very scanty.

✳ **QUESTIONS FOR KIDS:**
- This story shows the way people more than forty years ago thought about the future. What things might make people's ideas about the future different now?
- It is interesting that the threat in this movie comes not from some kind of space alien or "bug-eyed monster" but from within the humans themselves. If your feelings could create a creature like the Id, what would it look like when you are mad? When you are sad? When you are lonely? When you are happy?
- Do you think we will ever have robots like Robby? What would be the best thing about having one? Would there be any disadvantages?
- Is the rule making it impossible for Robby to harm any rational beings

a good one, even though it makes it impossible for him to protect them from the Id? Can you think of a better rule?

❋ **CONNECTIONS:** Robby inspired, among others, the robot in "Lost in Space" and possibly the "Droids" in *Star Wars* as well. Anne Francis also appeared in *Bad Day at Black Rock* (again, as the only woman in the story). Leslie Nielson is now best known for his work in wild comedies like the *The Naked Gun* series.

❋ **ACTIVITIES:** Read or see a production of *The Tempest* and compare it to this story. (Mature high schoolers might enjoy a modern interpretation in a movie called *Tempest,* directed by John Cassavetes.) The idea of robots is a fairly recent one, dating back to a play called *R.U.R.,* by Karl Capek. Teenagers should read *R.U.R.* and *I, Robot,* by Isaac Asimov, and become familiar with Asimov's "rules" for fictional robots, including the one forbidding robots to harm living things.

High schoolers might appreciate some exposure to Freud's ideas about the id, the ego, and the superego, which were very current in public consciousness at the time of this move. His book *An Introduction to Psychoanalysis* is a good place to start.

❋Return to Oz
1985, 110 min, PG, 8 and up
Dir: Walter Murch. Nichol Williamson, Jean Marsh, Piper Laurie, Fairuza Balk

❋ **PLOT:** Six months after her return to Kansas, Dorothy can't forget Oz. Just as in Oz she longed for home, once home she longs for Oz. Her pet chicken Bellina finds a key marked "Oz." Aunt Em, worried about Dorothy, takes her to an ominously mysterious experimental sanitarium, and Dorothy brings the key. Just as she is about to be "treated" with the doctor's electrical machine, a huge thunderstorm destroys the sanitarium and brings her back to Oz. The yellow brick road has been broken, and the Munchkins are all gone. The Emerald City is destroyed, and its people turned to stone, including the Cowardly Lion and the Tin Woodsman.

The only living creatures she finds are the Wheelers, scary-looking and aggressive creatures who zoom around on wheels instead of hands and feet. Dorothy meets Tik-Tock, a robot whose works have run down. She uses the Oz key to wind him up again. He says he has been waiting for her to bring the key, and that "the Scarecrow must have sent it to you somehow." Tik-Tock fights the Wheelers and gets them to explain what happened. They tell her that only Mombi can tell them what happened to the Scarecrow.

Princess Mombi can change heads at will. She wants Dorothy's head for her collection, and when Dorothy refuses, Mombi locks her in the tower. There Dorothy meets Jack Pumpkinhead, and together they create a flying animal out of a moose head, palm fronds, a soda, and some life-powder, and escape. They find the home of the Nome King, rescue the Scarecrow, and break Mombi's spell on Ozma, the rightful ruler of Oz. Dorothy returns home, this time able to stay in touch with Oz through her mirror, knowing she can go back again someday.

✻ **DISCUSSION:** As long as you don't expect this much darker movie to be anywhere near the unforgettable Judy Garland original, you can enjoy its own pleasures, including exciting adventures, outstanding special effects (especially those by Claymation superstar Will Vinton), and a brave and resourceful heroine. As in the original, the same actors appear in both the Kansas and Oz portions of the story: Nicol Williamson as both the doctor and the Nome King, Jean Marsh as the nurse and Mombi, and Emma Ridley as the girl who befriends Dorothy in the sanitarium and as Ozma. Some children may be frightened by Dorothy's all-but-mad scenes in the early part of the movie, and Aunt Em's refusal to believe in Oz.

> PROFANITY: None.
> NUDITY/SEXUAL REFERENCES: None.
> ALCOHOL/DRUG ABUSE: None.
> VIOLENCE/SCARINESS: Lead characters in peril.
> TOLERANCE/DIVERSITY ISSUES: None.

✻ **QUESTIONS FOR KIDS:**
- Why did Dorothy want to go back to Oz so badly?
- Would you like to have a lot of different heads, like Mombi? What are some of the faces you would like to try?

✻ **CONNECTIONS:** Children will enjoy the entire Oz book series, especially those books written by L. Frank Baum. And of course every child should see *The Wizard of Oz*.

✻7 Faces of Dr. Lao

1964, 101 min, NR, 6 and up
Dir: George Pal. Barbara Eden, Arthur O'Connell, Tony Randall

✻ **PLOT:** Along a dusty western trail, an elderly Chinese man on a donkey stops beside a rough wooden sign that says "Abalone" to light his pipe—with his thumb, which spouts fire like a lighter. He is Dr. Lao and he says he has a traveling circus, though all anyone can see is his donkey and a small fish in a bowl.

Lao arrives just as a wealthy man named Stark (Arthur O'Connell) is trying to buy the whole town. He warns the citizens in a town meeting that the water supply is at risk and that they must sell quickly or risk losing everything. Most are inclined to go along with him, except for Ed Cunningham, the newspaper editor (John Ericson), and Angela Benedict, the town librarian (Barbara Eden). Only Stark knows that the town will become more valuable soon when the railroad is built nearby.

Just as the town is debating Stark's offer, the circus opens. The "performers" (all played by Randall) are Merlin the Magician, Medusa, Pan, the Abominable Snowman, and the blind fortuneteller, Apollonius. Each has a lesson for someone in the town. Ultimately, the circus teaches them all the importance of staying in Abalone, and Lao goes on to his next performance.

✳ **DISCUSSION:** The classic characters are all here: the idealistic newspaper editor, the lovely widowed librarian who thinks she cannot love again, the foolish middle-aged flirt, the overbearing loudmouth, and of course the avaricious villain, who brags that he bets on weakness and never loses. That works well in this story, which mixes myth and fantasy. The loudmouth is turned to stone by looking at Medusa (and when turned back by Merlin, her personality is sweetened). The librarian's heart is awakened by Pan, who changes to resemble the editor who loves her. Stark has a delightful conversation with a rattlesnake whose resemblance to him is more than physical. The low-key approach lets the children notice for themselves that Dr. Lao really is all of the characters himself. Other issues: The librarian's son begs to go with Dr. Lao, and some children may be upset when he cries at the end because Dr. Lao has left without him (even though he has left him a gift).

> PROFANITY: None.
>
> NUDITY/SEXUAL REFERENCES: In a very mild scene, Pan's music and dancing excite the librarian, who loosens up considerably.
>
> ALCOHOL/DRUG ABUSE: Lao smokes a pipe, Stark smokes a cigar, and there is a stereotypical "town drunk."
>
> VIOLENCE/SCARINESS: Very mild. Thugs smash the newspaper office; they are later vanquished by the Loch Ness monster.
>
> TOLERANCE/DIVERSITY ISSUES: Today the casting of Caucasian Tony Randall as an Asian would probably cause controversy. It is not inconsistent, though, with the character's ability to transform himself into many shapes and personas. As one of the characters notices, even when he is appearing as Dr. Lao, his English shifts from fluent to pidgin depending on the circumstances.

✳ **QUESTIONS FOR KIDS:**
- What does it mean when Dr. Lao tells Mike that "All the world's a circus"?
- If you went to that circus, what would you want to see?
- If it came to your town, who would you want to learn something from it?

✳ **CONNECTIONS:** Pal was a pioneer of special effects, before the days of computers. His other films include **tom thumb** and *When Worlds Collide*.

The Thief of Bagdad

1940, 106 min, NR, 8 and up
Dir: Ludwig Berger, Tim Whelen, Michael Powell. Conrad Veidt, Sabu, Rex
Ingram, John Justin, June Duprez

✳ **PLOT:** A blind beggar and his dog are really a king and his street-urchin friend, enchanted by the evil Grand Vizier, Jaffar. The king, Ahman (John Justin), once had 50 palaces and 365 wives, but "no past, no aim, no purpose." He says, "With every desire satisfied, I grew empty of desire." He left the decisions to Jaffar, and made only a mild objection when Jaffar told him he had a man executed "for thinking." Jaffar warns him that men are filled with evil and hatred, and that the only things they respect are, "the lash that descends, the yoke that breaks, and the sword that slays."

Jaffar encourages Ahmad to go in disguise among his subjects to see for himself that men are bad. While out in the marketplace, Ahmad hears for the first time that he is seen as a tyrant by his people. But it is a trap. Jaffar orders him arrested, to be executed the next morning.

In prison, Ahmad meets Abu (Sabu), an irrepressible street thief, who has stolen the jailer's keys. They escape together. Ahmad tells Abu who he is. They go by boat to the city of Basra, where the local sultan cares only for his collection of mechanical toys. No one is allowed to look at the princess. As her procession goes through the town, Ahmad glimpses her and falls deeply in love. He visits her in her garden, and she falls in love with him.

Jaffar arrives in Basra to bring the Sultan the most magical toy of all, a life-size flying mechanical horse. The Sultan says he will give anything to have it. Jaffar says that he wants the princess. The princess runs away, and Ahmad is caught. Jaffar blinds him with a magic spell and transforms Abu into a dog. The spell will last until the princess is in Jaffar's arms.

Jaffar captures the princess, but she is in a deep sleep and cannot awaken until Ahmad is with her. Jaffar arranges for him to see her, then takes her away, telling her he will take her to a doctor who can cure Ahmad. On his boat, he tells her of the spell, and she allows him to embrace her so that the spell will be broken. Ahmad and Abu follow, but Jaffar sinks their boat. Abu, washed ashore, finds a bottle and opens it. A huge Djinni (genie) comes out swearing he will kill whomever opened the bottle. But Abu tricks the Djinni into giving him three wishes. They steal "the all-seeing eye" to find Ahmad. Meanwhile, Jaffar has made the princess lose her memory, and has almost persuaded her that she is in love with him when Ahmad appears. Jaffar, furious, sentences both the princess and Ahmad to death.

Abu, riding a flying carpet, arrives just in time to save them, just as prophesied. Ahmad promises to send Abu to school and make him his Grand Vizier, but Abu takes the carpet and flies off in search of fun and adventure.

✳ **DISCUSSION:** After more than half a century, this remains one of the most lush and gorgeous movies of all time. It won well-deserved Oscars for art direction, special effects, and color cinematography. The Maxfield Parrish–style settings bring the Arabian Nights to life, and the colors, from the bright orange sails on Jaffar's boat in the first scene to the carpet flying off in the sky in the last, glow like jewels on velvet. Amazingly, at least six different directors worked on this movie. But it is very much the vision of one man: producer Alexander Korda (brothers Zoltan and Vincent also contributed, the first as one of the directors and the second as the production designer). I am not as big a fan of the performances as some critics, and find Sabu especially hard going, but it is a genuine pleasure for the eye and spirit.

PROFANITY: None.

NUDITY/SEXUAL REFERENCES: None.

ALCOHOL/DRUG ABUSE: None.

VIOLENCE/SCARINESS: Sword fights.

TOLERANCE/DIVERSITY ISSUES: In the classic fairy tale tradition, this princess (who does not even have a name) resolves her problem by going to sleep and refusing to wake up. She tells Ahmad that her purpose is to please him. The Djinni is played by black American actor Rex Ingram.

✳ **QUESTIONS FOR KIDS:**
- What did Ahmad mean when he said, "Richest among my subjects, I was the poorest of the poor?"
- What does he mean when he says, "I've had everything but freedom?"
- Jaffar says that people are evil. Why does he say that? Do you think people start out good, bad, or both? What makes them do good or bad things?
- Why does the Sultan say he likes the toys better than people?
- Why does the Djinni say that for the first 1,000 years he was in the bottle, he swore to enrich whomever opened the bottle, but for the second 1,000 years, he swore to kill whomever opened the bottle? At whom was he really angry? Would killing whomever opened the bottle solve anything? How does Abu trick him back into the bottle?

✳ **CONNECTIONS:** This move is reminiscent of Disney's *Aladdin,* even down to some of the names of the characters. Sabu also appeared with John Justin look-alike Jon Hall in the 1942 *Arabian Nights*. The dazzling and delightful animated movie **The Thief and the Cobbler** is a pleasure for all ages.

✳ 2001: A Space Odyssey
1968, 139 min, G, 10 and up
Dir: Stanley Kubrick. Keir Dullea, Gary Lockwood

✳ **PLOT:** In this science-fiction masterpiece, Stanley Kubrick tracks the odyssey of mankind, from the dawn of man 4 million years ago to the exploration of deep space. The film begins with a desolate time when our apelike predecessors led frightened and brutal lives, scrounging for food and huddling against the cold night while wild animals howled in the distance. In a few short minutes, Kubrick has spanned the epochs, depicting the origins of tribes and the miraculous morning when apes awoke and learned how to use tools. With this ability, mankind was launched on its journey to the stars. On Kubrick's time line, it is just a small next step to the exploration of the moon. And from the moon, mankind heads off to Jupiter. But what is triggering these immense changes? Why are humans evolving, and what is their destiny? At transforming moments along this odyssey, a mysterious black monolith appears, drawing humans ever forward. But toward what? The surprise ending to this film is legendary, and has probably inspired more late-night discussions in college dorms than any other movie.

✳ **DISCUSSION:** For children twelve or older, *2001* can be a mind-boggling experience. In a series of dramatic vignettes, it introduces children to cosmic mysteries and gives them an opportunity and an incentive to grapple with issues that span the millennia, rather than dwell on their last argument over a toy. Younger children may be impressed by the drama, the special effects, and the beautiful music, but may have a hard time following the plot. In addition, they will lose patience with some of the longer segments dealing with space exploration. (The special effects used by Kubrick were revolutionary in their day, but will seem commonplace to children raised on **Star Wars** and *Star Trek: The Next Generation*). Even twelve-year-olds may not appreciate the subtle references to political rivalries and intrigue on Earth, the cover-up of mysterious developments on the moon, or the more ironic aspects of the clash between man and machine (HAL the computer plaintively crying that he is afraid and that he can feel his mind going is a poignant example). In fact, the cryptic ending of the movie is famous for stumping even adults.

Most teenagers cannot help but be swept up in this film, which stretches their minds and gives them mysteries and uncertainty instead of endings where everything is neatly tied up with a bow. As children strive to deal with the uncertainty of the ending, and fill in its gaps and illuminate its gray areas by drawing upon their own personality and sense of the world, they are on their way to appreciating greater and more mature forms of art.

PROFANITY: None.

NUDITY/SEXUAL REFERENCES: None.

ALCOHOL/DRUG ABUSE: None.

VIOLENCE/SCARINESS: Characters in peril; some are killed.

TOLERANCE/DIVERSITY ISSUES: None.

✳ **QUESTIONS FOR KIDS:**
- Why is the moment the apes use tools a turning point?
- What does the monolith represent?

- HAL says he was made in 1992—now that we have passed that date, how many of the film's ideas about the future seem to be accurate?
- HAL says he can "feel"—what does "he" mean?
- What happens to Dave at the end? Why?

✳ **CONNECTIONS:** A sequel, *2010*, was made in 1984, with author Arthur Clarke appearing briefly on a park bench. It answers many of the questions raised in *2001*, at least in a literal sense, but is not as satisfying as the more open-ended original. Kids who like this movie should read some of Arthur C. Clarke's science-fiction books, especially *Childhood's End*, and Isaac Asimov's *Foundation* trilogy.

✳ **ACTIVITIES:** Teens may want to use the Internet to learn more about artificial intelligence and space travel.

✳Who Framed Roger Rabbit?

1989, 109 min, PG, 6 and up
Dir: Robert Zemekis. Bob Hoskins, Christopher Lloyd, Stubby Kaye

✳ **PLOT:** In this technical marvel of a movie, human and animated actors interact seamlessly. It begins with a cartoon, lovable Roger Rabbit taking care of adorable Baby Herman, despite every kind of slapstick disaster. Then, as birdies are swimming around Roger's head after a refrigerator crashes down on him, a live-action director steps in to complain that the script called for stars, and we are in a 1947 Hollywood where "Toons" are real.

A private detective named Eddie (Bob Hoskins) is hired by the head of Roger's studio to get evidence that Roger's gorgeous wife, Jessica, is seeing another man. Eddie does not want the assignment. Once a friend to the Toons, he hates them since one of them killed his brother. But he needs the money badly, so Eddie goes to the Ink and Paint nightclub, where Jessica performs, and he takes photos of her playing "patty-cake" (literally) with Marvin Acme (Stubby Kaye), maker of novelties and gags. Roger is distraught when he sees the photographs. But it turns out that Jessica is completely faithful to Roger, and that she is caught up in a complex plot to close down Toon Town and Los Angeles's excellent public transportation system to build freeways. Eddie's efforts lead him to Toon Town and then to a warehouse where the real villain is revealed.

✳ **DISCUSSION:** Children will be delighted with the Toon characters, and with the interaction of the cartoons with the human actors and with the physical world. Eddie's venture into Toon Town is almost as good. The story is fast-paced and exciting, and the slapstick is outstanding. But the human and cartoon characters mix more smoothly than the combination of slapstick and film noir references in this movie. The plot includes murder, corruption, and suspected adultery. The premise that the only possible explanation for the traffic system in Los Angeles is that it was the vision of a sinister madman is funnier for adults than it is for kids. Eddie is not an especially attractive leading character. Still reeling from his brother's murder, he drinks too much and is surly to his clients, to his girlfriend, and to Roger.

> PROFANITY: Some mild language (i.e., "wiseass"; "kick you in the—" (balls); "booby" trap; "Is that a rabbit in your pocket . . .")
>
> NUDITY/SEXUAL REFERENCES: Alleged affair between Jessica and Acme; Jessica is an exaggerated sex symbol.
>
> ALCOHOL/DRUG ABUSE: Eddie has a drinking problem; several scenes in a bar. When Roger drinks alcohol, he has a cartoon-y reaction, turning colors and bouncing around the room.
>
> VIOLENCE/SCARINESS: Some fighting. One Toon killed; one human killed; main characters in peril
>
> TOLERANCE/DIVERSITY ISSUES: The Toons conjure up thoughts of the history of racial discrimination, with the Ink and Paint club reminiscent of nightclubs with white audiences and black performers, and the segregated Toon Town and "otherness" of the Toon characters.

✳ QUESTIONS FOR KIDS:
- Why does Eddie blame all the Toons for his brother's death?
- Why is it so hard for him to be nice to anyone?
- Why don't the humans and Toons get along better?
- Would you like to visit Toon Town? What would you do there?

✳ **CONNECTIONS:** This was a one-time opportunity for cartoon characters from all the studios to join forces, and it is one of the great pleasures in movie history to see them all together. Donald Duck and Daffy Duck perform a hilarious duet at the Ink and Paint club. On his way out the door at Maroon Studios, Eddie brushes by several members from the "cast" of *Fantasia*. The penguin waiters from Mary Poppins show up in another scene, as do Pinocchio, Mickey Mouse, and Woody Woodpecker. The mix of characters and styles works extremely well, and kids will enjoy seeing some of their favorite characters in a different context. Kathleen Turner provided the sultry speaking voice of Jessica Rabbit, but her singing voice was provided by Amy Irving.

✳ **ACTIVITIES:** A key element of the plot concerns invisible ink. Kids will enjoy making their own or using some from a magic store to write secret messages. Kids lucky enough to go to Walt Disney World or Disneyland will enjoy the Roger Rabbit attractions.

Willow

1988, 130 min, PG, 8 and up
Dir: Ron Howard. Val Kilmer, Jean Marsh, Warwick Davis

✳ **PLOT:** This "sword and sorcery" epic has a somewhat biblical theme, as wicked Queen Bavmorda (Jean Marsh) receives a prophesy that a child about to be born will overthrow her. She orders all pregnant women captured. But the baby of the prophesy is born, with the special birthmark to show she is the true ruler of the land. Her mother places her in a raft in the rushes, where she is found by a group of gentle dwarves called Nelwyns. Willow, a young father (Warwick Davis), becomes attached to the baby, and takes on the task of bringing her to her people. On the road, he is joined by Madmartigan, a brash, irresponsible warrior (Val Kilmer), an enchanted sorceress (who is transformed into increasingly higher levels of animals as the enchantment is lessened), two tiny quarrelsome Brownies, and ultimately the daughter of Bavmorda (Joanne Whalley).

✳ **DISCUSSION:** While the story is long and sometimes hard to follow (it doesn't help that you can barely understand the brownies, who squabble all the time without the underlying affection of counterparts like R2D2 and C3PO), the themes of dealing with the responsibilities that destiny brings to you and the importance of believing in yourself are nicely handled, and the battles are exciting and inventive. Furthermore, there is a good depiction of the folly of bigotry, as the Brownies, dwarves, and other humans are shown as prejudiced against each other, each group with its own derisive terms for the others.

> PROFANITY: None.
> NUDITY/SEXUAL REFERENCES: Madmartigan is something of a ladies' man.
> ALCOHOL/DRUG ABUSE: None.
> VIOLENCE/SCARINESS: Sword fights.
> TOLERANCE/DIVERSITY ISSUES: As noted above, each of the three groups has to overcome prejudice toward the other two.

✳ **QUESTIONS FOR KIDS:**
> • What did Willow think about when he was trying to decide whether to take the baby to her people?
> • Why did Bavmorda's daughter help Willow?
> • Did Madmartigan learn anything? Did he change?

✳ **CONNECTIONS:** If this movie has something of a *Star Wars* feeling, it is because the story was written by George Lucas, the creator of *Star Wars*. Director Ron Howard is the former child start of *The Music Man* and the director of *Splash, Far and Away, Backdraft,* and *Apollo 13.* Val Kilmer, a versatile and underrated performer, is the star of the third *Batman* movie.

✳ THE ABSENT MINDED PROFESSOR

1961, 97 min, b&w, 4 and up
Dir: Robert Stevenson. Fred MacMurray

Fred MacMurray is the title character, who is so absentminded that he has missed his own wedding twice due to preoccupation with his experiments. He develops a substance he calls "Flubber" (for flying rubber). He puts it on his Model-T car, and it flies. He puts it on the shoes of the school basketball team, and they all but float into the air to win the big game. Bad guy Keenan Wynn tries to get the Flubber for himself, but MacMurray and his (finally) bride (Nancy Olson) fly off to Washington to deliver it to the government.

Parents may want to discuss whether the use of Flubber to win a basketball game is cheating.

✳ **CONNECTIONS:** In a sequel, *Son of Flubber,* Flubbergas is used to win a football game, while another invention, "dry rain," produces an artificial rain cloud.

A 1997 remake, *Flubber,* features Robin Williams as the professor. Despite spectacular special effects, it loses some of the sweetness and heart of the original. As the title suggests, the star of this version is not the professor, but his creation. And the presence of producer-coscreenwriter John (*Home Alone*) Hughes means that the bad guys will get banged on the head many, many times. In this version, the professor has a delightful and highly anthropomorphic floating robot companion named Weebo, reminiscent of Tinkerbell. "Her" sweet voice is provided by Jodi Benson (also the voice of Ariel in **The Little Mermaid**), and her commentary is spiked with a kaleidoscope of video clips. Weebo's jealousy of Brainard's fiancée may need some explaining, and her "death" may be upsetting for some children.

✳ BACK TO THE FUTURE

1985, 116 min, PG, 8 and up
Dir: Robert Zemeckis. Michael J. Fox, Christopher Lloyd, Lea Thompson

Teenager Marty McFly (Michael J. Fox) goes back in time and meets his parents when they were teenagers. When he accidentally interferes in their first meeting, he has to find a way to get them together or risk never being born. The Oedipal situation (Marty's teenage mother develops a crush on him) is played for comedy, as is the comparison of life in the 1950s with life in the 1980s. Exciting, funny, and heartwarming, the movie prompted two sequels, which are not in the same league but are clever and very watchable.

✳ THE DARK CRYSTAL

1983, 84 min, PG, 8 and up
Dr: Jim Henson and Frank Oz

This dark medieval fantasy with some gruesome and grotesque images, may be produced by the Muppets, but it is a long way from *Sesame Street*. Older kids who enjoy Tolkienesque stories will enjoy this inventive saga of the little Gelfling who must find the crystal to save the world from being ruled by evil.

✳ DRAGONWORLD

1994, 84 min, PG, 4 and up
Dir: Ted Nicolaou. Sam Mackenzie, Brittney Powell

After his parents are killed, Johnny McGowan, five years old, goes to live in his grandfather's castle in Scotland. When he wishes for a friend on a wishing tree, a baby dragon appears from the mist, and after a chase they get acquainted and become good friends. Fifteen years later, John and Yowler the dragon are grown up, and John's grandfather has died. When Yowler is discovered by a television producer and his daughter, Beth, John reluctantly agrees to allow Yowler to be put on display for a limited time, to raise the money he needs to pay the taxes on the castle. But the business-man who made the deal is unscrupulous, and mistreats Yowler. Yowler conveniently grows into his flying and fire-breathing powers just in time to fly home. Knowing that Yowler can never enjoy peace and privacy at the castle, John sends him away. John marries Beth, and when their first child is born, Yowler returns.

NOTE: Some younger children may be scared by the dragon, and some may lose interest when Johnny grows up, or be concerned about the death of his parents and grandfather.

✳ E. T. THE EXTRA-TERRESTRIAL

1982, 115 min, PG, 6 and up
Dir: Steven Spielberg. Henry Thomas, Drew Barrymore

A young boy named Elliott (Henry Thomas) finds an extraterrestrial who has been left behind when his expedition of alien botanists had to depart quickly to avoid detection. He brings E. T. home, finding in their connection a way to begin to heal his sense of loss at his father's absence. E. T. loves Elliott, but begins to weaken in earth's atmosphere and needs to go home. With the help of Elliott and the neighborhood children, he sends a message to his friends. But before they can come for him, he is captured by govern-ment scientists. E. T.'s connection with Elliott is so strong, Elliott becomes very ill, too. But both recover, and the children return E. T. to the spaceship, after E. T. reminds Elliott that they will always be together.

This is an outstanding family movie, with themes of loyalty, friendship, trust, and caring. Talk to kids about the way that the adults and the kids see things differently, and have a hard time understanding each other's perspective—one reason is that they don't try to share their feelings with each other). NOTE: Strong language used by kids. This film was justifiably criticized for its almost complete absence of nonwhite characters.

✳ FANTASIA

1940, 120 min, NR, 4 and up
Dir: Ben Sharpsteen.

Considered a failure when it was originally released, this eight-part combination of images and music is now indisputably a classic. Musicologist Deems Taylor explains that there are three kinds of music: music that paints a picture, music that tells a story, and "absolute music," or music for music's sake, and then shows us all three. Highlights include Mickey Mouse as the Sorcerer's Apprentice, whose plan to save himself from a little work by enchanting a broom to carry the buckets of water gets out of control; the *Nutcracker* Suite's forest moving from fall into winter (with the mushrooms dancing to the Chinese Dance); Beethoven's *Pastoral* Symphony, with characters from Greek mythology celebrating at a festival and seeking shelter from a storm; and the *Dance of the Hours,* with ostrich and hippo ballerinas dancing with gallant (if overburdened) crocodiles.

✳ **CONNECTIONS:** Play classical and other kinds of music for kids and have them draw their own pictures to illustrate the sounds. Kids might like to read more about the Greek mythological characters.

✳ THE 5,000 FINGERS OF DR. T

1953, 88 min, NR, b&w, 6 and up
Dir: Roy Rowland. Hans Conried, Tommy Rettig

This is the only movie written by Dr. Seuss, and it is a wild fantasy nightmare. A boy hates his piano lessons and his scary teacher Mr. Terwilliker (Hans Conried). He has a nightmare that Mr. Terwilliker is the evil Dr. T, who has 500 children playing his masterpiece on an enormous two-story piano. As in **The Wizard of Oz,** the people in the boy's real life show up in the dream as wild caricatures of his fears. His widowed mother appears as Dr. T's secretary, and his friend the plumber shows up in the nightmare, too, advising him that "People should always believe in kids. They should even believe their lies." Though some of the nightmare images are scary, the emphasis on the importance of a child's perspective is reassuring.

✳ THE INCREDIBLE SHRINKING MAN

1957, 81 min, NR, b&w, 8 and up
Dir: Jack Arnold. Grant Williams

A man exposed to a mysterious cloud begins to shrink, giving him a very different perspective on the world (as he lives in a dollhouse and fights with the cat) and on his role in the universe.

✳ **CONNECTIONS:** *The Incredible Shrinking Woman* is a satiric comedy starring Lily Tomlin as a woman whose exposure to household products causes her to shrink.

✳ INDEPENDENCE DAY
1996, 143 min, PG-13, 10 and up
Dir: Roland Emmerich. Will Smith, Jeff Goldblum, Bill Pullman, Margaret Colin

In this heart-thumping, slam-bang action extravaganza, aliens arrive and blow up the world's major cities. The president (Bill Pullman) and fighter pilots (led by Will Smith) must find a way to fight back. Some kids will find this too intense and scary, but others will want to see it over and over (and over) again. Themes to discuss include behavior in a crisis, honesty, the dilemma faced by the president in making the choice to use nuclear weapons, and, for film fanatics, finding all of the references to other classic films, from **Dr. Strangelove** to **2001**.

NOTE: The movie was justifiably accused of being sexist. One of the female leads is a stripper. We see her perform, though she remains covered. Her lover resists marrying her because it would hurt his career. Another couple divorced because she was too committed to her career. In addition, parents may be concerned about an unmarried couple that is clearly intimate, and by the tension as the characters are in peril, as well as a massive number of deaths, including two of the main characters.

✳ JASON AND THE ARGONAUTS
1963, 104 min, G, 6 and up
Dir: Don Chaggey. Todd Armstrong, Honor Blackman

Ray Harryhausen's precomputer-era special effects are the highlight of this movie, based on the myth of Jason's search for the golden fleece. The Argonauts must battle a huge bronze statue, a horde of harpies, and sword-wielding skeletons to get the golden fleece that will help Jason win his kingdom back from the evil Pelias. Like **Clash of the Titans,** it raises questions about free will and destiny, as Zeus and Hera move people like chess pieces, and yet, like chess players, must do so within strict rules. When evil Pelias murders Jason's sister, he asks, "Why did Zeus drive me to kill this girl?" and Hera answers, "Zeus cannot drive men to do what you have done. Men drive themselves to do such things that the gods may know them, and that men may understand themselves." NOTE: More violence than the rating suggests.

✳ **CONNECTION:** Hera is played by Honor Blackman, who appeared in *Goldfinger.*

✳ LABYRINTH
1988, 101 min, PG, 10 and up
Dir: Jim Henson. Jennifer Connelly, David Bowie

An imaginative teenager named Sarah (Jennifer Connelly) impulsively wishes that her fretful baby brother would be taken away by goblins. When her wish comes true, she must go through the labyrinth to the castle of the King of the Goblins (David Bowie) to rescue him.

This is an entertaining adventure, with a clever script and exceptionally imaginative art direction. Like Alice in Wonderland and Dorothy in Oz, Sarah finds the power to solve the problem within herself.

✳ **CONNECTIONS:** This movie was produced by George Lucas (of **Star Wars** and **Raiders of the Lost Ark)**, written by Terry Jones (of Monty Python), and directed by Jim Henson (of the Muppets).

✳ **ACTIVITIES:** Kids who like this movie will enjoy looking at the pictures of artist and optical illusionist M. C. Escher, who inspired the set for the final confrontation. You can glimpse one of his posters in Sarah's bedroom.

✳ LADYHAWKE

1985, 123 min, PG-13, 10 and up
Dir: Richard Donner. Matthew Broderick, Rutger Hauer, Michelle Pfeiffer

Matthew Broderick plays Philippe "the Mouse," a medieval pickpocket, who meets up with an enchanted couple, a knight named Navarre (Rutger Hauer) and his lady love, Isabeau (Michelle Pfeiffer). An evil and jealous bishop has called upon the devil to help him cast a spell on them. Each sunset, Navarre becomes a wolf, and each sunrise, Isabeau becomes a hawk. They travel, "always together, eternally apart," able to glimpse each other for just a brief moment as the sun rises and sets.

Hauer and Pfeiffer are outstanding as the lovers, and (except for some jarring rock music) the period detail is exceptionally well-handled. Mouse, who has always relied on his wits and his ability to lie and steal, learns about honor (though he does not reform entirely). NOTE: The PG-13 rating is for violence, mostly sword fights.

✳ THE MASK

1994, 100 min, PG-13, 10 and up
Dir: Charles Russell. Jim Carrey, Cameron Diaz, Peter Riegert, Amy Yasbeck

A sweet, mild-mannered bank clerk named Stanley Ipkiss (Jim Carrey) finds a mysterious mask. When he puts it on, he is transformed into a real-life version of a cartoon character, who acts out Stanley's wildest impulses, going after a spectacularly beautiful nightclub singer, standing up to the bad guys, and exacting revenge from an uncooperative car repair shop. NOTE: The movie has a couple of mildly raunchy jokes and some bathroom humor.

✳ **CONNECTIONS:** The filmmakers were inspired by the cartoons of Tex Avery, and kids may enjoy watching them on video to see if they can find the similarities.

✳ MEN IN BLACK
1997, 98 min, PG-13, 10 and up
Dir: Barry Sonnenfeld. Will Smith, Tommy Lee Jones, Linda Fiorentino, Vincent D'Onofrio

In this fast and funny science-fiction comedy, the premise is that everything in the tabloids is true, and that a mysterious government organization called the Men In Black is responsible for monitoring resident and visiting aliens from outer space. K (Tommy Lee Jones) recruits policeman J (Will Smith) after a hilarious series of tests, and they go off on adventures that include saving a missing galaxy and delivering an alien baby. NOTE: Some mild profanity and cartoon-style violence, some of it gross.

✳ THE NEVERENDING STORY
1984, 92 min, PG, 6 and up
Dir: Wolfgang Peterson. Noah Hathaway, Barret Oliver, Moses Gunn

Bastian is a boy who runs into a musty old bookstore when he is chased by bullies. He begins to read a huge and ancient book, and is astounded to find that he is part of the story: The beautiful princess of Fantasia is asking for Bastian to give her a name, so her kingdom can be saved. The hero of the story is Atreyu, who must complete a quest to save the kingdom. But his courage and power is less important than Bastian's belief and imagination. The characters and effects are wonderfully imaginative and, interestingly, the force they must fight is not a bad guy but Nothingness, a sort of mindlessness and apathy.

✳ **CONNECTIONS:** There are two sequels (the last one straight-to-video), but they are not nearly as good.

✳ THE RED BALLOON
1956, 35 min, NR, 3 and up
Dir: Albert Lamorisse

In this short, wordless movie, a red balloon befriends a little boy, following him and playing with him. When the other children become jealous and burst the balloon, he is rescued by a cloud of multicolored balloons, which lift him up into the sky. (Sometimes included on the same video as *White Mane*, another fantasy, about a French boy who loves a mysterious horse and escapes with him to an island where children and horses can be friends forever.)

✳ THE SECRET OF ROAN INISH
1994, 103 min, PG, 8 and up
Dir: John Sayles. Jenni Courtney, Eileen Colgan

A little Irish girl named Fiona goes to stay with her grandparents and becomes convinced that her baby brother, whose cradle was carried off to sea years before, is alive and being cared for by Selkies, seals who can transform themselves into humans. This is a quiet film, filled with lovely images that convey the magic surrounding anyone who believes in it. It explores themes of loyalty and commitment to family and following your heart.

✳ THE SHAGGY DOG

1959, 104 min, G, b&w, 4 and up
Dir: Charles Barton. Fred MacMurray, Jean Hagan, Tommy Kirk, Annette Funicello
     A ring falls into the cuff of a pair of pants worn by teenager Wilby Daniels (Tommy Kirk) while he is visiting a museum, and, not noticing, he carries it home with him. The ring's ancient spell turns him into a huge shaggy dog, identical to the one owned by his pretty new neighbor, Franceska (Roberta Shore). Wilby's father (Fred MacMurray) is allergic to dogs, so Wilby hides out in Franceska's house, where he overhears Franceska's father plotting to steal secret missile plans. Still a dog, Wilby has to figure out a way to foil the spies and save Franceska. This low-key fantasy/comedy is a longtime family favorite, and children love to see the dog driving the car and wearing pajamas.

✳ **CONNECTIONS:** The 1976 sequel, "The Shaggy D.A.," was followed by two more made-for-television sequels starring Harry Anderson.

✳ SUPERMAN

1978, 143 min, PG, 4 and up
Dir: Richard Donner. Christopher Reeve, Margot Kidder, Gene Hackman
     The greatest of all superheroes is brought thrillingly to life by Christopher Reeve. His escape from the planet Krypton just before it explodes, his childhood in Smallville with the Kents and his discovery of his superpowers, his work as Clark Kent for the *Daily Planet*, his romance with star reporter Lois Lane, and his battles with Lex Luthor are all handled with wit and brio.

✳ **CONNECTIONS:** The first sequel, directed by *Hard Day's Night* director Richard Lester, is also great fun, but numbers III and IV are not nearly as good.

✳ TIME BANDITS

1981, 110 min, PG, 8 and up
Dir: Terry Gilliam. Sean Connery, David Warner
     One of the most wildly imaginative and visually entertaining films ever made, this is the story of an English boy whisked through time by six dwarfs who have stolen a map showing the holes in creation. Their plan is to use the holes to go back in time to steal treasure. They visit Agamemnon (Sean Connery), Napoleon (Ian Holm), the *Titanic,* and Robin Hood (John Cleese), chased by the Supreme Being (God) and by the Evil Genius (the devil). NOTE: The individual episodes are uneven. The director and coscriptwriter are graduates of Monty Python, and like some of their other work,

it lurches from inspired lunacy to lame misfires. The most serious of the latter is the very end, in which the little boy is left alone after his foolish parents are incinerated. This may upset younger children, but those who can handle fairy-tale (or Roald Dahl)-style gore will enjoy it.

✳ THE TIME MACHINE

1960, 103 min, NR, 8 and up
Dir: George Pal. Rod Taylor, Yvette Mimieux

In this Jules Verne fantasy, Rod Taylor plays a man who invents a time machine and uses it to travel to the future, where he finds a postapocalyptic world of gentle Eloi and monstrous Morlocks. It is an exciting adventure, and well worth discussing. Ask kids why Verne thought that this was where the future would lead and what he would predict if he set the story 100 years from now.

✳ tom thumb

1958, 98 min, NR, 6 and up
Dir: George Pal. Russ Tamblyn, Alan Young

The fairy tale about the boy no bigger than a thumb is brought to life with former gymnast Russ Tamblyn as the title character. Tom is as irresistibly charming as his "Very Own Song," one of several bright musical numbers. Fiendish villains Terry Thomas and Peter Sellers try to get the tiny boy to steal for them, but watching over tom is a good fairy. And watching over the good fairy is the handsome woodsman (Alan Young), whose kiss can turn her into a mortal.

✳ **CONNECTIONS:** Tamblyn also appears in *West Side Story* and *Seven Brides for Seven Brothers*. Young is best known as the owner of television's "Mr. Ed."

✳ THE WONDERFUL WORLD OF THE BROTHERS GRIMM

1962, 129 min, NR, 6 and up
Dir: Henry Levin and George Pal. Laurence Harvey, Claire Bloom, Barbara Eden, Russ Tamblyn

This is the colorful, if fictionalized, story of the brothers who collected and published the folktales that are now known to almost every child in the Western world. The brothers must struggle to support their families by doing a genealogy of an egotistical nobleman. They argue with one another over how much time to devote to the fairy tales. The highlight of the movie is the depictions of four of the brothers' stories, including "The Dancing Princesses" and "The Cobbler and the Elves." But Wilhelm's love for the stories of princesses, ogres, and enchantments and his devotion to finding and telling the stories of the common people are well worth discussing.

SEE ALSO:

Alice in Wonderland

The Canterville Ghost

The Day the Earth Stood Still

Faerie Tale Theater series

Freaky Friday

Here Comes Mr. Jordan

Invasion of the Body Snatchers

The Phantom Tollbooth

Star Wars

The Wizard of Oz

MUSICALS

A well-placed dissonant chord can stop an audience cold in the middle of a sentimental scene, or a calculated woodwind passage can turn what appears to be a solemn moment into a belly laugh.
—AARON COPLAND

These films could just as easily be classified as fantasies, because they are all set in a wonderful fantasy world in which people just break into song and dance (perfectly in tune and step with each other) whenever they feel like it. In some movies, the songs tell us about the character or move the plot forward. In some, they are there for pure pleasure. And they deliver—musicals are wonderful family films because, like comedies, the best of them have something for every age.

ASTAIRE AND ROGERS

Fred Astaire and Ginger Rogers were the most successful dance team in the history of the movies. While they each did well as solo performers and as partners with others, their ten films together are masterpieces of ecstatic grace and, to quote one of the songs they performed together, of "la belle, la perfectly swell romance."

All their movies are terrific for family viewing, with some of the loveliest music ever written (by Cole Porter, Irving Berlin, George and Ira Gershwin, and Jerome Kern, among others) and some of the most sublime dances ever performed, all strung together with gossamer story lines (far too insubstantial to be dignified with the term "plot"). In one memorable example, the entire plot revolves around Astaire's friends persuading him that he cannot appear at his wedding without cuffs on his striped trousers. Older children may be interested in thinking about the appeal of these glossy fantasies during the Depression, and contrasting the music and dance styles of the first seven with the last three, as fashions in music and dance changed. Many of the stories depend on silly misunderstandings, which can provide an opportunity for families to talk about the importance of making sure you don't jump to conclusions. But first and foremost, these movies are to sit back and luxuriate in.

There are no issues of concern regarding violence, or substance abuse. There are a few regarding sexual content, so mild by today's standards that they may not even be noticed. For example, the plot of **The Gay Divorcee** concerns Rogers's need to hire a "professional correspondent" to gather the documentation for a trumped-up adultery case she needs to get a divorce from her husband. (The correspondent's slogan is a memorable one: "Your wife is safe with Tonetti. He prefers spaghetti.") The very title of **The Gay Divorcee** may need some explanation for today's kids. In **Shall We Dance,** a (faked) photo of the two of them together in a bedroom wearing pajamas is considered conclusive proof that they must be married.

Virtually everyone in the movies is white. **Flying Down to Rio** features multiethnic performers, but the lovely Etta Moten (star of the original Broadway cast of *Porgy and Bess*) is listed in the credits only as "colored singer." Astaire does a blackface number in **Swing Time.** Although it is intended to be a tribute to dancer Bill Robinson, it is clearly insensitive by today's standards.

The movies also include several of the all-time great character actors, especially wry Alice Broderick (mother of actor Broderick Crawford), Edward Everett Horton (the fussy, silly man), and Eric Blore (the very proper British servant). Viewers with sharp ears will recognize the last two as voices from the *Rocky and Bullwinkle* cartoons.

✳ THE BARKLEYS OF BROADWAY

1949, 109 min, NR, 8 and up
Dir: Charles Walters

When Judy Garland could not appear in this movie, intended to be a sequel to the Garland-Astaire **Easter Parade,** Rogers stepped in to rejoin her former partner, ten years after their previous film, and their only color movie together. They play a married couple who have performed successfully together in musicals. Now Rogers wants to be seen as a serious actess (not unlike their real-life situation). Rogers succeeds as a dramatic actress, and then concludes that she wants to go back to dancing with Fred Astaire— a decision that is easy to understand! Be sure to watch this one from the beginning, as the dance number under the title sequence is one of the highlights of the film. Note the reprise of "They Can't Take That Away From Me" from **Swing Time.** Another highlight is the "Shoes with Wings On" number, in which Astaire is a shoe repair man whose shoes begin dancing by themselves, in a sort of "Sorcerer's Apprentice" theme.

✳ CAREFREE

1938, 83 min, NR, b&w, 6 and up
Dir: Mark Sandrich

After seven films in four year, Astaire and Rogers performed with other partners in a few movies before getting back together in this one, with another Irving Berlin score. Their reunion film has a different feeling, more of a slapstick comedy with a few dance numbers than a dance movie with romance. Rogers plays the lead comic role. This time Astaire is a psychiatrist(!) treating Rogers, who keeps backing out of marriage at the last minute. Astaire orders her to eat bizarre foods so that she will have interesting dreams, to reveal the source of the problem. The problem seems to be that she is in love with him. So he hypnotizes her into hating him and loving her original fiancé (the inevitably dumped Ralph Bellamy). Various slapstick consequences ensue before he asks her to "Change Partners (And Dance with Me)." The lively "Yam" song was later used during WWII as "Any Bonds Today?"

✳ FLYING DOWN TO RIO

1933, 89 min, NR, b&w, 6 and up
Dir: Thornton Freeland

The ostensible stars of this movie are Dolores del Rio and Gene Raymond, and Astaire and Rogers are relegated to only one dance number together, but it was immediately clear to audiences and studio executives that they were the highlight of the movie. Raymond and Astaire are in a band, and they want to put on a show at a Brazilian hotel, and end up having the dancers perform on airplanes while they sing the title song. Astaire and Rogers dance "The Carioca" ("It's not a fox trot or a polka . . ."), and Rogers sings a cute song called "Music Makes Me."

✳ FOLLOW THE FLEET

1936, 110 min, NR, b&w, 6 and up
Dir: Mark Sandrich

Astaire is a sailor, and Rogers his former vaudeville partner, now singing in a dance hall. Her serious sister is played by Harriet Hilliard. Look carefully and you will also see Lucille Ball as a wisecracking showgirl, and Betty Grable singing backup. Harriet has a glamour makeover to attract Astaire's shipmate Randolph Scott. Astaire accidentally gets Rogers fired, and then, trying to help her by sabotaging her competition for another job, accidentally ruins her audition. A few other silly complications lead to the necessity of putting on a show, ending the movie with the magnificently romantic "Let's Face the Music and Dance." This movie also includes the delightfully slapstick "I'm Putting All My Eggs in One Basket" and the energetic challenge dance (featuring real-life amateur dance contest winners), "Let Yourself Go," "I'd Rather Lead a Band," and "Let's Face the Music and Dance," all composed by Irving Berlin. Harriet sings "Get Thee Behind Me Satan," in which she asks for help in resisting temptation.

✳ **CONNECTIONS:** Harriet Hilliard later became Harriet Nelson, wife of Ozzie and mother of Dave and Ricky.

✳ THE GAY DIVORCEE
1934, 107 min, NR, b&w, 6 and up
Dir: Mark Sandrich

Rogers and her aunt meet Astaire on their way to a resort, where Rogers is scheduled to have a phony tryst with a hired "correspondent" to provide grounds for her divorce. Rogers mistakes Astaire for the correspondent, and Astaire, a bit taken aback by her businesslike approach but eager to pursue her, goes along. This movie had the first of their trademark dance sequences showing us, more eloquently than words, Astaire and Rogers falling in love. She tries to resist, but is overcome by the movement and the music, the Cole Porter song "Night and Day." This movie also features up-and-coming Betty Grable in a silly number with Edward Everett Horton called "Let's K-nock K-nees."

✳ ROBERTA
1935, 105 min, NR, b&w, 8 and up
Dir: William A. Seiter

Astaire and Rogers are still the second leads in this movie set in a Paris fashion salon. Astaire is a musician, and Rogers his childhood friend, now masquerading as a Russian countess. The leading roles are played by Irene Dunne and Randolph Scott. It has a Jerome Kern score and some of the duo's best numbers, including, "I'll Be Hard to Handle" and "Smoke Gets in Your Eyes." Those interested in the fashions of the period will enjoy the "Lovely to Look At" fashion show. NOTE: An elderly character dies peacefully.

✳ SHALL WE DANCE
1937, 108 min, NR, b&w, 6 and up
Dir: Mark Sandrich

Astaire is a tap-dancing ballet artist named Pete Peters, but performing under the name of Petrov. He tells a friend that he has never met Rogers, but now that he has seen her dance, he'd "kinda like to marry her." He has a tiny flip-book, a souvenir from her show, and he flips the pages to watch the way she moves. She does not like him at first, but when rumor gets out that they are married (as noted above, the faked photo of them in the bedroom together is presumed to be definitive), they find that they have to get married in order to be able to get divorced and go on with their lives. But in the course of doing so, through some of the most delightful musical numbers ever filmed, they realize they are in love. In "They All Laughed," they celebrate what they have in common, and in "Let's Call the Whole

Thing Off" ("You say eeether, and I say eiiither . . .") they celebrate their differences (with a tap dance on roller skates!). Children will enjoy the way that Astaire turns an ocean liner's boiler room into an array of percussion instruments (like today's musical group Stomp).

✲ THE STORY OF VERNON AND IRENE CASTLE

1939, 90 min, NR, b&w, 8 and up
Dir: H. C. Potter

Vernon and Irene Castle were the Astaire and Rogers of the pre–WWI era, so it was only fitting that Astaire and Rogers should make this movie. It never attempts to consider the Castles' influence in setting a social and stylistic standard for early twentieth-century America. Instead, it is a simple (and tragic) love story of two dancers. All of the songs in the movie are from that period (including "By the Light of the Silvery Moon" and "Waiting for the Robert E. Lee"), except for "Only When You're in My Arms." Astaire and Rogers re-create the Castles' dances, including one on a turbulent ocean liner. The movie covers the time from their first meeting through their success in Paris, their triumphant return to America, and his death in WWI. Astaire and Rogers touchingly convey the deep commitment and true partnership of these performers.

✲ **CONNECTIONS:** Vaudevillian Lew Fields plays himself.

✲ SWING TIME

1936, 105 min, NR, b&w, 6 and up
Dir: George Stevens

The score is again by Irving Berlin, but Astaire is not a dancer or a musician in this movie—he's a gambler who happens to dance. And Rogers is a dance instructor who, in a delightful scene, has to teach Astaire to dance. This is the one where Astaire's friends convince him that he cannot marry his sweetheart because he does not have cuffs on his pants. Having left her at the altar, he now has to earn enough money to persuade her father to let him marry her. Astaire and Rogers perform together so he can earn enough money to marry his fiancée, but of course they fall in love, and believe it or not the cuff routine has to be called on again in order for everything to turn out all right. Some of the highlights include "Pick Yourself Up," "The Way You Look Tonight" (sung to Rogers with shampoo in her hair), "A Fine Romance," and "Never Gonna Dance." NOTE: This also includes a blackface number, Astaire's tribute to Bill Robinson, "Bojangles of Harlem."

✲ **CONNECTIONS:** Astaire's fiancée is played by Betty Furness, later a *Today* show correspondent.

✳ TOP HAT
1935, 101 min, NR, b&w, 6 and up
Dir: Mark Sandrich

Many people consider this the zenith of the series, with Astaire and Rogers finally taking center stage, lots of dance numbers, an Irving Berlin score, and the unforgettable "Cheek to Cheek" dance number. This time, Astaire is a dancer who meets Rogers when she complains that his tapping is keeping her awake. She is even more annoyed by him when he substitutes for the driver to take her to the stables. But when she stops for shelter from a storm, he shows off by dancing to "Isn't This a Lovely Day (To Be Caught in the Rain)?" When she joins in, showing him she can match him step for step, they are in love. There is something of a complication when she believes he is her friend's new husband, but following the ravishing "Cheek to Cheek" number, with her gown divinely feathered, everything gets straightened out. This movie also includes Astaire's trademark "Top Hat, White Tie, and Tails."

ASTAIRE AND OTHERS

Fred Astaire never had another partner like Ginger Rogers, and never made more than two movies with anyone else, but many of his other movies—and all his dance numbers—are well worth watching. Some of the best include:

✳ THE BAND WAGON
1953, 111 min, NR, 6 and up
Dir: Vincente Minnelli. Fred Astaire, Cyd Charisse, Oscar Levant, Nanette Fabray

Astaire plays a onetime movie dancing star, now almost forgotten, who is asked to perform in a new musical play. The script is by old friends played by Nanette Fabray and Oscar Levant (and based on the screenwriters Betty Comden and Adolph Green). The problems are the stunningly pretentious director (Jack Buchanan, in a performance based on the movie's director, Vincente Minnelli) and the costar, a ballerina (Cyd Charisse). The play is a huge flop, but Astaire and his friends rework it into a revue (an excuse for a bunch of delightful but completely unrelated musical numbers), and everyone lives happily ever after. Today's children will probably not appreciate the satire, but the music and the comedy are as fresh as ever, and they will love the silly "Triplets" number. Other highlights include "Shine on Your Shoes" and "Dancing in the Dark."

✳ DADDY LONG LEGS
1955, 126 min, NR, 8 and up
Dir: Jean Negulesco. Fred Astaire, Leslie Caron

The classic children's book by Jean Webster about the orphan befriended by a mysterious man she calls "Daddy Long Legs" (because she saw only his elongated afternoon shadow) is loosely adapted for this musical version with Astaire and Leslie Caron. The big surprise in the book about the identity of the benefactor is clear to everyone but the orphan from the beginning, but it provides an excuse for a dance fantasy as she imagines him as a Texas oilman, a continental playboy, or a guardian angel. The sparkling Johnny Mercer score also includes the magnetically romantic ballad "Something's Got to Give."

✳ EASTER PARADE

1948, 103 min, NR, 6 and up
Dir: Charles Walters. Fred Astaire, Judy Garland, Ann Miller

Astaire plays one half of a successful vaudeville team. The day before Easter, his partner, played by Ann Miller, leaves for a solo career. Astaire swears he can teach any other girl to take her place. He happens upon Judy Garland, dancing in a chorus line, and picks her as the replacement, promising that in one year, at the next Easter Parade, all eyes will be on her instead of on the elegant Miller. After months of trying to make her into another Miller, Astaire finally realizes that Garland has her own style, very warm and appealing, and he realizes that he is in love with her. The terrific songs by Irving Berlin include the title tune, "I Love a Piano," "Shaking' the Blues Away," "Steppin' Out With My Baby," and the hobo-costumed "A Couple of Swells." Themes to discuss include the importance of being yourself instead of imitating someone else.

✳ FINIAN'S RAINBOW

1968, 145 min, G, 6 and up
Dir: Francis Ford Coppola. Fred Astaire, Petula Clark, Tommy Steele

Astaire is an Irishman who comes to America because he believes that the pot of gold he stole from a leprechaun (Tommy Steele) will grow if he buries it near Fort Knox. The leprechaun's three wishes end up including one that turns a bigoted white senator into a black man. The songs by E. Y. Harburg and Burton Lane are lovely (including "How Are Things in Glocca Morra?" and "When I'm Not Near the Girl I Love"), and Astaire is never less than magnificent (even though Coppola managed to shoot the dance numbers so that you can't see his feet in some shots).

This is not a great movie by any standards. It was dated by the time it was made (twenty years after the play opened on Broadway), and is even more so now. Still, it is worth watching because in addition to the music, it is a rare movie that addresses the issue of racial prejudice. Indeed, even though it is a fantasy, it addresses that issue more directly and effectively than a movie like *South Pacific.*

✳ FUNNY FACE

1957, 103 min, NR, 8 and up
Dir: Stanley Donen. Fred Astaire, Audrey Hepburn

Astaire is a fashion photographer, and Audrey Hepburn is a Greenwich Village intellectual who agrees to be a model as a way of getting a trip to Paris to meet her idol, a professor of philosophy. Spectacular Gershwin songs (including "How Long Has This Been Going On?" "'S' Wonderful," and the title number), breathtaking photography (inspired by the photographs of Richard Avedon), and the luminous Hepburn make this movie unforgettable. The magazine editor is played by Kay Thompson (spoofing *Vogue*'s Diana Vreeland). NOTE: It is worth talking about the imperiousness of the fashion magazines in imposing "taste" standards, and the 1950s perspective on relationships between the sexes: Astaire reassures Hepburn, after her idol makes a pass at her, that "He's no more interested in your mind than I am!"

✳ **CONNECTIONS:** Kay Thompson was the author of *Eloise*, the deliciously wicked book about the little girl who lives in the Plaza Hotel.

✳ HOLIDAY INN
1942, 100 min, NR, b&w, 6 and up
Dir: Mark Sandrich. Fred Astaire, Bing Crosby

For some reason, the only two movies Astaire made in which he did not get the girl were the two he made with Bing Crosby. *The Sky's the Limit* has some good numbers, and this one, which introduced "White Christmas," is better, though the story is less than satisfying. Astaire, Crosby, and Marjorie Reynolds are a successful team until Crosby quits to live on a farm. Astaire and Reynolds continue together for a short time, but then Reynolds goes to work for Crosby at his new hotel, which will be open only on holidays. Most of the numbers relate to the holidays, including a spectacular Fourth of July number with Astaire tapping on firecrackers. NOTE: The Lincoln's Birthday number (with Crosby in blackface) is embarrassingly racist by today's standards.

✳ ROYAL WEDDING
1951, 93 min, NR, 6 and up
Dir: Stanley Donen. Fred Astaire, Jane Powell, Peter Lawford, Sarah Churchill

This lively musical is really nothing more than an excuse to put some song-and-dance numbers around footage of the wedding of Princess Elizabeth and Prince Philip (very exciting in a world before satellite television). Loosely based on the real-life story of Fred Astaire's performances with his sister, before she retired to marry an Englishman, this is a lightweight and even silly saga of a brother-and-sister act who go to England and each fall in love. Jane Powell plays the sister, who falls for Lord John Brindale (Peter Lawford). Astaire falls for an engaged dancer played by Sarah Churchill. Keenan Wynn plays twin theatrical agents who somehow speak completely different forms of English. This film includes some of Astaire's most memorable numbers, like "You're All the World to Me" (where he, astoundingly but believably dances on the walls and ceiling), "Sunday Jumps" (where he dances with a hat rack and makes it look as graceful as a ballerina), and the hilarious "How Could You Believe Me When I Said I Love You When You Know I've Been a Liar All My Life?"

✳ **CONNECTIONS:** The songs are by "My Fair Lady" lyricist Alan Jay Lerner and his "On a Clear Day You Can See Forever" partner, Burton Lane. Sarah Churchill was the daughter of former Prime Minister Winston Churchill.

✳ SILK STOCKINGS
1957, 117 min, NR, 8 and up
Dir: Rouben Mamoulian. Fred Astaire, Cyd Charisse

A musical version of **Ninotchka** with songs by Cole Porter, this is the story of a Soviet emissary who is happily "corrupted" by Paris and by falling in love with Astaire, who plays a Hollywood producer and contented capitalist. Children may need some background to understand what the conflict was about, and some explanation of the terms (like "imperialistic" and "capitalistic"), which serve as some of Porter's cleverest rhymes. Three Soviet officials go to Paris to bring home a Soviet composer, who is working on a movie score for Astaire's character. The people from Hollywood co-opt the Russians completely, and their beautiful but very strict supervisor (Cyd Charisse) comes after them. She, too, is won by the atmosphere ("We have the ideals, but they have the climate") and by Astaire's charm. The movie also has some pointed satire about the Hollywood of that era, with Janis Paige terrific as a movie star based on swimmer Esther Williams. It's possible to use this movie for a discussion of the real differences between Communism and capitalism, but more likely you'll all just sit back and enjoy it. NOTE: 1950s-era scene in which Paige dances in her underwear to get the composer to agree to her plans for changing the movie.

GENE KELLY

Gene Kelly made dancing look like something that a regular guy could do. In fact, he made dancing look like the most fun a guy could have. Kelly didn't need elegant clothes or glamorous settings; his grace was more athletic and energetic than balletic. But the grace was always there, whether he was splashing in puddles, performing a pas de deux with Jerry the (animated) mouse, or tap-dancing with garbage can lids on his feet.

✳ AN AMERICAN IN PARIS
1951, 115 min, NR, 8 and up
Dir: Vincente Minnelli. Gene Kelly, Leslie Caron

This winner of seven Academy Awards (including for Best Picture) does not hold up as well as **Singin' in the Rain** or even **On the Town,** but it is still a delight for the eye and ear, especially for viewers who love dance. Its center-piece is an eighteen-minute ballet, inspired by the paintings of French artists, to the title music by George Gershwin. The other dance numbers, including the casual "I've Got Rhythm" and the radiant "Our Love Is Here to Stay," are marvelous. What doesn't work so well is the story, which has expatriate Kelly in love with Leslie Caron, but impeded by their previous entanglements, each with older, wealthier people on whom they have been dependent.

✳ ANCHORS AWEIGH
1945, 140 min, NR, 6 and up
Dir: George Sidney. Gene Kelly, Frank Sinatra
Kelly and Sinatra are sailors who befriend a singer—Kathryn Grayson—with an adorable little nephew—Dean Stockwell. But this deserves a mention (and a viewing) if for no other reason than the spectacular dance number with Kelly and Jerry the cartoon mouse. If computerized special effects and **Roger Rabbit** have you feeling jaded, take a look at this and remind yourself that people painstakingly painted every animation cell, twenty-four per second, and then did them all over when they realized they had forgotten to paint in Jerry's reflection in the shiny floor.

✳ BRIGADOON
1954, 108 min, NR, 8 and up
Dir: Vincente Minnelli. Gene Kelly, Van Johnson, Cyd Charisse
Two Americans (Kelly and Van Johnson) hunting in the Scottish High-lands come across an enchanted village that comes alive only one day every hundred years. Kelly falls in love with a girl from the village (Cyd Charisse), leaves her to go back to his life in modern Manhattan, and then triumphs over time and space to find her again. Gorgeous music by Alan Jay Lerner and Frederick Loewe (before **My Fair Lady** and **Gigi**) includes "The Heather on the Hill," "Go Home With Bonnie Jean," and "Almost Like Being in Love." Themes worth discussing include the reasons the village wanted to be isolated, even protected, from the outside world; the reasons Kelly might want to leave the world he knows for Brigadoon; the reason that Harry, one of the residents of Brigadoon, would risk his life to leave; the ethical dilemma he faced in leaving, exposing everyone else to the risk of losing their enchanted protection; the ethical dilemma the rest of the villagers had in responding to him; how to reconcile conflicting views of happiness. NOTE: A character is accidentally killed by one of the Americans.

✳ **CONNECTIONS:** Compare this to **Lost Horizon,** another movie about an isolated utopia with someone from the outside wanting to get in and someone from the inside willing to risk everything to leave.

✳ IT'S ALWAYS FAIR WEATHER
1955, 102 min, NR, 8 and up
Dir: Gene Kelly and Stanley Donen. Gene Kelly, Michael Kidd, Dan Dailey

At the end of WWII, three army buddies (Kelly, Dan Dailey, and, in a rare appearance before the camera, choreographer Michael Kidd) promise to meet in ten years to catch up with each other. Ten years later, none of them has done what he'd dreamed of. Kelly is a two-bit hustler whose only asset is the management contract of a boxer he won in a card game. Dailey, who'd dreamed of being an artist, is a dyspeptic advertising executive. Kidd, who'd dreamed of having an elegant restaurant, has a burger joint. At first, they can barely remember their friendship. But they team up to defend Kelly from some crooked fight promoters, and each finds something to be proud of in himself and the others. If at all possible, see this one in a theater or in a Letter-Box format, as it makes sensational use of the wide screen, especially in the number where they dance with garbage can lids on their feet. There is also a spectacular number with Kelly on roller skates. And Cyd Charisse, as the brilliant and beautiful executive, sings a song with the names of all of the heavyweight champions! Screenwriters Betty Comden and Adolph Green put some real bite into the script, especially in dealing with television, then the movies' greatest nemesis. Themes for discussion include friendship and loyalty, the role of advertising, finding self-respect.

✳ ON THE TOWN
1949, 98 min, NR, 8 and up
Dir: Gene Kelly and Stanley Donen. Gene Kelly, Frank Sinatra, Vera-Ellen, Betty Garrett, Ann Miller

Three sailors with "just one day" to see New York manage to cram a lot of romance and adventure and some spectacular musical numbers into their twenty-four hours. Kelly, Frank Sinatra, and Jule Munshin are the three sailors, who begin with a musical argument about how to spend their time (sight-seeing or picking up girls), and end up doing a bit of both when Kelly sees a poster of "Miss Turnstiles" and falls instantly in love. Sinatra pairs up with brash cabbie Betty Garrett, and Munshin with an anthropologist (Ann Miller) who says he is a ringer for her "prehistoric man." Kelly finds Miss Turnstiles (Vera-Ellen), loses her (when her mean dance teacher forces her to go to Coney Island to do a "cooch dance"), and finds her again, making it back to the ship just in time, as three new sailors depart for their day in New York. This was the first musical shot on location, and it makes great use of the city. NOTE: The story (based on a ballet) has a slightly raw feel—the "cooch dance," the insulting treatment of Garrett's unattractive roommate, the aggressiveness of Garrett and Miller—but the exuberance of the musical numbers, the vitality of the locations, and the singing and dancing by Sinatra and Kelly are spectacular.

SEE ALSO:

Singin' in the Rain

JUDY GARLAND

The greatest female star of movie musicals began performing in vaudeville when she was three years old. Her big, gorgeous voice, as sensitive as it was spirited, is always thrilling to experience.

✳ GIRL CRAZY
1943, 99 min, NR, b&w, 8 and up
Dir: Norman Taurog

Mickey Rooney and Garland put on a show in almost every one of their movies; in this one, they put on a show to save their school. The movie includes some great Gershwin classics, like "Embraceable You," "I Got Rhythm," "But Not for Me," and "Bidin' My Time."

✳ THE HARVEY GIRLS
1946, 101 min, NR, 8 and up
Dir: George Sidney. Judy Garland, Angela Lansbury, Ray Bolger

Garland is reunited with Ray Bolger (the Scarecrow from **The Wizard of Oz**,) in this highly fictionalized story about waitresses in the early days of the railroad. The theme song, "On the Atcheson, Topeka, and the Santa Fe," won an Oscar. Garland arrives as a mail-order bride, but after meeting the prospective groom decides to join the waitresses and ends up fighting with locals Angela Lansbury and John Hodiak before finally falling in love with him and living happily ever after.

✳ **CONNECTIONS:** Watch for a brief early appearance by Cyd Charisse as Deborah.

✳ IN THE GOOD OLD SUMMERTIME
1949, 102 min, NR, 8 and up
Dir: Robert Z. Leonard. Judy Garland, Van Johnson

This musical version of **The Shop Around the Corner** is the story of two people (Judy Garland and Van Johnson) who work together, thinking they can't stand each other, not knowing that they are "dear friends" through a pen-pal correspondence. Themes for discussion include judging people for superficial reasons and the importance of being open-minded about finding good in others.

✳ **CONNECTIONS:** Look quickly in the last scene and you will see Garland holding her real-life daughter, Liza Minnelli.

✳ SUMMER STOCK
1950, 109 min, NR, 8 and up
Dir: Charles Walters. Judy Garland, Gene Kelly, Phil Silvers

Farmer Judy Garland has a sister (Gloria De Haven) who wants to be in show business. When she returns to the farm with her show business friends (including Gene Kelly and Phil Silvers), it seems like a good idea to use the barn to put on a show. In Garland's last movie for her longtime studio, MGM, she and Kelly have some very nice numbers together, especially "You Wonderful You." Kelly does an impossible but seemingly effortless dance on a piece of newspaper, and Garland ends the movie with one of her all-time best numbers, "Get Happy."

SEE ALSO:

Easter Parade
Meet Me in St. Louis
The Wizard of Oz

RODGERS AND HAMMERSTEIN

Many of the classic Broadway musicals were written by Rodgers and Hammerstein. Movies based on their plays (and one musical they wrote directly for the screen and one for television) rank among the most beloved of all musicals. Be aware, however, that they are often dated and insensitive on issues of race and gender by today's standards, and kids may need some explanation or context.

✳ CAROUSEL
1956, 128 min, NR, 10 and up
Dir: Henry King. Shirley Jones, Gordon MacRae

A sweet young girl (Shirley Jones) falls in love with a tough carnival barker (Gordon MacRae). When he marries her, he loses his job, and when she becomes pregnant, he is desperate to make money. He agrees to help a friend with a robbery. But it goes wrong, and he is killed. Up in heaven, he sees his daughter growing up lonely and unhappy, and he returns to Earth to try to help her. Songs include "If I Loved You," "June Is Busting Out All Over," "You'll Never Walk Alone," and the famous "Soliloquy," in which he dreams of the fun he will have with his son, and then soberly realizes that "you've gotta be a father to a girl." Kids (and adults) may have a tough time with the sexism in that song, and with the idea that a slap from someone who loves you can be like a kiss, but the theme of love transcending everything else is still worthwhile. Themes for discussion include having trouble expressing your feelings, and the choice Billy faced when he felt desperate for a way to support his family.

✳ CINDERELLA

1967, 83 min, NR, 4 and up
Dir: Charles S. Dubin. Lesley Anne Warren, Celeste Holme

Lesley Anne Warren is delightful as Cinderella in this tuneful and amusing retelling of the story.

✳ **CONNECTIONS:** This was remade for television in 1997, a lavish and colorful production starring Whitney Houston as the fairy godmother and Brandy as Cinderella.

✳ FLOWER DRUM SONG

1961, 133 min, NR, 6 and up
Dir: Henry Koster. Nancy Kwan, Miyoshi Umeki

Set in San Francisco's Chinatown, this story about a mail-order bride is very dated, but the issues of tradition versus assimilation and the struggle for independence from parents are still important ones, even for those who are not immigrants. Songs include "I Enjoy Being a Girl" and "I Am Going to Like It Here."

✳ OKLAHOMA!

1955, 145 min, NR, 8 and up
Dir: Fred Zinnemann. Shirley Jones, Gordon MacRae, Eddie Albert, Rod Steiger

Rodgers and Hammerstein transformed the Broadway theater when they wrote a musical about a cowboy and used the songs to help tell the story. The music is glorious (including the title number, "People Will Say We're in Love," "Oh, What a Beautiful Mornin,'" and "The Surrey with the Fringe on Top"), but the plot is hard to take—including the death of one character and the humorous portrayal of the "girl who can't say no." Kids often find it confusing that substitutes for the characters perform a dance number.

✳ SOUTH PACIFIC

1958, 151 min, NR, 8 and up
Dir: Joshua Logan. Mitzi Gaynor, John Kerr, Rossano Brazzi, Ray Walston

In the midst of the WWII battles in the South Pacific, an army nurse and an officer must search their hearts before they can allow themselves to admit that they have each fallen in love with someone of another race or culture. John Kerr plays Lieutenant Cable, who meets Liat, a beautiful Tonganese girl (France Nuyen), and Mitzi Gaynor is Nellie Forbush, whose "wonderful guy" is a French planter with two half-Tonganese children by his late wife. Songs include "Nothing Like a Dame," "I'm Gonna Wash That Man Right Outta My Hair," and "Some Enchanted Evening." NOTE: The movie tries to take a stand against racism, with a song explaining that "you have to be carefully taught" to be prejudiced. But by today's standards, its attempts to deal with prejudice are badly dated. Kids today may have trouble understanding why Nellie hesitates at all over Emile's children. More troubling, Liat's mother, "Bloody Mary," plays an unsavory procurer role in presenting Liat to Cable, whose passionate love for her is based on a swim and a song.

✻ STATE FAIR
1945, 100 min, NR, 8 and up
Dir: Walter Lang. Jeanne Crain, Dana Andrews, Vivian Blaine

The only Rodgers and Hammerstein musical written directly for the screen, this is the second of three movies about the adventures of a farm family at the state fair, each seeking something different. The two grown children each find romance at the fair, though only one ends happily. Songs include "It Might as Well Be Spring" (which won an Oscar) and the title number.

✻ **CONNECTIONS:** The 1933 nonmusical version with Will Rogers is still a pleasure to watch, but skip the boring 1962 version with Pat Boone and Ann-Margret.

✻ **ACTIVITIES:** Take the kids to a county fair or a state fair, or have them put on a backyard fair with the neighborhood pets and homemade cookies.

SEE ALSO:
The King and I
The Sound of Music

OTHERS

✻Hello, Dolly!
1969, 146 min, G, 6 and up
Dir: Gene Kelly. Barbra Streisand, Walter Matthau, Michael Crawford, Tommy Tune

✻ **Plot:** Dolly Levi (Barbra Streisand) is a matchmaker in turn-of-the-century Yonkers, outside of New York. She is hired by Horace Vandergelder (Walter Matthau) to find him a wife. He also hires her to take his niece Ermengarde (Joyce Ames) to New York City, to encourage her to forget about marrying her artist beau, Ambrose (long-legged Tommy Tune). Instead, Dolly makes matches for his two clerks (Michael Crawford and Danny Lockin), advises them on how to get promotions from Horace, and helps Ermengarde get permission to marry Ambrose. Finally, after a series of intricate maneuvers, Dolly makes a match for herself, with Horace.

✻ **DISCUSSION:** This is one of the last of the big-time, old-fashioned musicals, with lavish production values and a dozen hummable tunes. The very slight story is bolstered by terrific singing and dancing—staged by two masters of the genre: Gene Kelly, who directed, and Michael Kidd, who choreographed. The elaborate sets, costumes, and musical numbers make this movie a treat for the eyes and ears.

Dolly is almost a magical figure, with business cards for every purpose. When she tells Ermengarde and Ambrose they can earn the money they need by winning the dance contest at Harmonia Gardens, she produces one that says ARTISTS TAUGHT TO DANCE. With all the confidence it takes to transform the lives of everyone around her, she still hesitates when it comes to herself. She still mourns her late husband, Ephraim, but she wants more out of life "Before the Parade Passes By." Yet when Horace finally proposes, she waits for a sign of Ephraim's approval. What she gets is a sign that Horace has the qualities she is looking for: that, as she suspected all along, his gruff exterior conceals a warm heart and a wish to help others.

PROFANITY: None.

NUDITY/SEXUAL REFERENCES: None.

ALCOHOL/DRUG ABUSE: None.

VIOLENCE/SCARINESS: None.

TOLERANCE/DIVERSITY ISSUES: None.

✳ QUESTIONS FOR KIDS:
- Why doesn't Dolly just tell Horace the truth about what she thinks is right for him and for Ermengarde?
- How does she help the people in the movie to think differently about themselves, and how does that help them change?
- What does Dolly mean when she sings "Before the Parade Passes By"?
- When the young couples sing "We've Got Elegance," do they really think they are fancy?
- What would you do if you were Barnaby and Cornelius at the Harmonia Gardens?
- What is the difference between Dolly's view of money and Horace's view?

✳ **CONNECTIONS:** Michael Crawford went on from male ingenue parts (*A Funny Thing Happened on the Way to the Forum*) to star in the title role of *Phantom of the Opera*. This story, originally a German play, has been produced in a number of forms, including *The Matchmaker*, a nonmusical play written by Thornton Wilder (of *Our Town*), filmed with Shirley Booth, and most recently redone by avant-garde playwright Tom Stoppard, from the perspective of the two clerks, as *On the Razzle*.

✳ **ACTIVITIES:** Take the kids to a parade, preferably one where they can march along. They might also enjoy making some hats inspired by the spectacular creations in the movie.

Oliver!

1968, 153 min, G, 8 and up
Dir: Carol Reed. Mark Lester, Ron Moody, Oliver Reed

✳ **PLOT:** This glorious musical (and Oscar-winner for Best Picture) is based on Charles Dickens's *Oliver Twist*. Oliver is an orphan who so outrages the staff at the orphanage by asking for a second bowl of gruel that he is sold to an undertaker as an apprentice. He runs away from the abuse and is taken in by a group of child pickpockets, led by Fagin (Ron Moody). He is arrested for picking the pocket of a wealthy man, who becomes interested in him, and takes him home. Bill Sikes (Oliver Reed), a murderous thief who works with Fagin, kidnaps Oliver to prevent him from giving away the details of their enterprise. Bill kills his girlfriend, Nancy, when she tries to help Oliver escape. Bill himself is killed, and Oliver is returned to his friend, who turns out to be his uncle.

✳ **DISCUSSION:** Dickens wanted his readers to contrast the harshness of the approved establishments, the orphanage and apprentice system, with the friendly welcome of the street people's demimonde. Fagin and the boys give Oliver his first sense of family, singing warmly to him that he is to "consider yourself one of us!" They are the first to see him as an individual instead of as a troublesome animal, and the first to give him any affection.

Note how some of the characters calibrate their moral choices. Bill Sikes seems entirely amoral, willing to do anything to further his own interests. Mr. Bumble and Mr. Sowerberry, both considered by themselves and those around them to be sterling, law-abiding citizens, are not much better. Like Bill, they have no compunctions about putting their own interests first, no matter what the cost is to others. But Nancy and Fagin have limits. They will engage in small crimes, but have some sense of fundamental integrity.

Parents may want to talk to older kids about Nancy's relationship with Bill, and about the mistakes people often make when they think that loving someone can change them, or that someone who abuses others will not ultimately abuse them as well.

PROFANITY: None.
NUDITY/SEXUAL REFERENCES: None.
ALCOHOL/DRUG ABUSE: A lot of drinking.
VIOLENCE/SCARINESS: Bill kills Nancy and is himself killed; Oliver is in peril.
TOLERANCE/DIVERSITY ISSUES: Class issues.

✳ **QUESTIONS FOR KIDS:**
- Why does Mr. Sowerberry insult Oliver?
- Oliver wants someone to "buy" his happy moment and save it for him. If you could pick a day to have saved that way, what day would you choose?
- Why did Nancy stay with Bill?
- Why does Mr. Brownlow think that he can trust Oliver? How does that trust make Oliver feel?

- What would Mr. Brownlow have done if he had not turned out to be related to Oliver?

✻ **CONNECTIONS:** David Lean's superb *Oliver Twist* (with a long-delayed release in the United States for what was considered an anti-Semitic depiction of Fagin) is an outstanding version of this story, which was also adapted by Disney as **Oliver & Company.** Oliver Reed (nephew of director Carol Reed) played Athos in **The Three Musketeers.**

✻ Seven Brides for Seven Brothers

1954, 103 min, NR, 6 and up
Dir: Stanley Donen. Howard Keel, Jane Powell, Russ Tamblyn

✻ **PLOT:** Handsome backwoodsman Adam Pontabee (Howard Keel) strides into town, singing "Bless Your Beautiful Hide" to his future wife "whoever she may be." He has given himself one day to find a wife to take back to his ranch. He meets Milly (Jane Powell), a spirited waitress, proposes, and she accepts. He neglects to tell her that back at the ranch are his six brothers, and that he is bringing her back to cook and clean for all of them.

When she finds out, she is hurt, feeling that he wanted a housekeeper more than a wife, and she is horrified when she meets the brothers, who are boorish slobs. The next morning, she informs the brothers that they must learn to behave. They come to love her for her courage and values, and begin to long for wives of their own. She brings them to a barn raising, where they each fall in love. Back at the ranch, they long for their girls. Adam tells them they should go into town and steal them, just as in the story of the "Sobbin' Women" (the ancient Roman tale of the Sabine women). They do, but the women are furious, and won't have anything to do with the brothers, even though they are snowed in at the ranch until the spring thaw. Milly is so angry with Adam for telling the brothers to kidnap the girls that he leaves to spend the rest of the winter in a hunting cabin, not knowing that Milly is pregnant. The girls soften toward the brothers, and by spring are ready to marry them, in one big ceremony. And Adam returns, realizing how much Milly means to him.

✻ **DISCUSSION:** This movie includes some of the most thrillingly energetic dances ever put on film, including the classic barn-raising number (which unfortunately suffers on the small screen). Based on a short story by Stephen Vincent Benét, it is almost an icon of America as it saw itself in the 1950s—brash, energetic, adventuresome, and cocky. Some critics have complained that the movie all but promotes rape, but that is unfair. Even though the girls are very attracted to the brothers, they are very angry at being kidnapped, and the brothers are banished to the barn. They must earn their way back into the girls' affections by treating them with courtesy and respect, and ultimately it is very much the girls' own decision to stay and marry them.

With the help of youngest brother Gideon, Milly teaches Adam that even though she accepted his proposal quickly, she is still worth earning.

PROFANITY: None.

NUDITY/SEXUAL REFERENCES: Reference to Adam's having to sleep outside. At the end, when the fathers arrive, they hear Milly's baby cry. In order to make sure that their fathers allow them to marry the Pontabee brothers, the girls all say the baby is "mine!"

ALCOHOL/DRUG ABUSE: None.

VIOLENCE/SCARINESS: Fistfight.

TOLERANCE/DIVERSITY ISSUES: The movie deals with the role of women (in a musical-comedy context). Milly wants to be seen as a partner who has opinions and value, not a servant without wages. The girls want to be asked, not kidnapped.

❋ **QUESTIONS FOR KIDS:**
- How does the barn-raising dance number help to tell the story?
- Milly and Adam get married very quickly without talking about what they want. How does that create problems?
- How does Milly show how important family is to her?
- Why is it hard for Adam to realize how important Milly is to him?

❋ **CONNECTIONS:** Handsome baritone Howard Keel starred in a number of movie musical classics, including *Kiss Me Kate, Show Boat,* and *Annie Get Your Gun.* Jane Powell starred in *Royal Wedding* and a number of lesser musicals. Russ Tamblyn appeared in *West Side Story* and *tom thumb.* Ephraim is played by ballet superstar Jacques D'Amboise, whose work with kids was later featured in the Academy Award–winning documentary *He Makes Me Feel Like Dancing.* Dorcas is played by Julie Newmar (then called Newmeyer), whose autographed photo provided the title for the 1995 release *To Wong Foo, Thanks for Everything, Julie Newmar.*

❋ ANNIE
1982, 128 min, PG, 6 and up
Dir: John Huston. Albert Finney, Ann Reinking, Carol Burnett, Tim Curry, Aileen Quinn

A great cast, great songs, and one of the all-time great directors can't quite make this the success it should have been. But kids will enjoy the adventures of Annie, the spunky orphan, and her dog Sandy. Carol Burnett is mean Miss Hannigan, head of the orphanage, and Albert Finney plays Daddy Warbucks, the zillionaire with everything but a little girl to love.

❋ BABES IN TOYLAND
1961, 105 min, 6 and up
Dir: Jack Donohue. Annette Funicello, Tommy Sands, Ray Bolger, Ed Wynn

The Victor Herbert operetta about the nursery rhyme characters is produced by Disney, starring Mouseketeer queen Annette as Mary Quite Contrary. She is engaged to Tom the Piper's Son (Tommy Sands), but wicked Barnaby (Ray Bolger) is jealous, and kidnaps Tom so he can have Mary for himself. Mary's brothers and sisters wander off into the Forest of No Return and have to be rescued. Barnaby manages to shrink Tom, but Tom leads the toy soldiers in battle and manages to get back to normal size and marry Mary. Look for Barnaby's henchmen, Henry Calvin and Gene Sheldon (both of Disney's "Zorro"), imitating Laurel and Hardy, who starred in an earlier version.

✳ BILLY ROSE'S JUMBO

1962, 125 min, NR, 6 and up
Dir: Charles Walters. Doris Day, Jimmy Durante, Martha Raye
Doris Day, Jimmy Durante, Jumbo the elephant, and some Rodgers and Hart standards star in this affectionate tribute to the big top. Songs include "The Most Beautiful Girl in the World" and "This Can't Be Love."

✳ CABIN IN THE SKY

1943, 100 min, NR, b&w, 8 and up
Dir: Vincente Minnelli. Ethel Waters, Lena Horne
Minnelli's first directing assignment was this all-black musical starring Ethel Waters, Lena Horne, and Eddie "Rochester" Anderson. The plot is racist by today's standards, but the performances and musical numbers are still outstanding, especially Horne's "Happiness Is Just a Thing Called Joe" and Waters's "Taking a Chance on Love." This is a rare opportunity to see some of the finest performers of the era, barred by prejudice from "mainstream" films. Duke Ellington and Louis Armstrong play, Horne and Waters sing, and John "Bubbles" Sublett dances.

✳ **CONNECTIONS:** The devil is played by Rex Ingram of *The Thief of Bagdad.*

✳ GENTLEMEN PREFER BLONDES

1953, 91 min, NR, 6 and up
Dir: Howard Hawks. Marilyn Monroe, Jane Russell, Charles Coburn
Marilyn Monroe is the showgirl who thinks that "diamonds are a girl's best friend," and Jane Russell is her wisecracking best friend in this delightful (if retro) musical about two showgirls and their impact on men of all nationalities.

✳ GOOD NEWS

1947, 95 min, NR, 6 and up
Dir: Charles Walters. Peter Lawford, June Allyson
Movie critic Dale Thomajan had not only the wit to create a category called

"Best MGM Musical Not to Involve Fred Astaire, Judy Garland, Gene Kelly, or Vincente Minnelli," but also the wisdom to select *Good News* as the winner. Peter Lawford is the football star the school needs to win the big game, and June Allyson is the brainy girl who tutors him in French to make sure he'll be able to play. It's so far past dated that it is a period piece, and not even a child would think it bears any relation to today's college life. Some great old numbers, like the very un-PC "Pass That Peace-Pipe" and "The Varsity Drag" and "The Best Things in Life Are Free," will leave you wishing that it did. The cast also includes Mel Tormé and the very funny Joan McCracken.

✳ HANS CHRISTIAN ANDERSEN
1952, 120 min, NR, 6 and up
Dir: Charles Vidor. Danny Kaye

Danny Kaye and songs like "Thumbelina," "Wonderful, Wonderful Copenhagen," and "Inchworm," by Frank Loesser (composer of *Guys and Dolls*) are the highlights of this uneven, episodic (and completely fabricated) story of the author of some of the world's most beloved fairy tales. Children will respond as Kaye sings "The Ugly Duckling" to comfort a little boy who has lost his hair and is taunted by the other children. NOTE: Kids may be disturbed by the last part of the movie, a pointless and disturbing subplot about Andersen's crush on a ballerina and his mistaken hope that she will allow him to rescue her from a husband he perceives as abusive.

✳ A HARD DAY'S NIGHT
1964, 85 min, NR, b&w, 8 and up
Dir: Richard Lester. The Beatles

The documentary style of this movie masks its tight construction, clever script, and sublime anarchy second only to the Marx brothers. A surrealistic day in the life of the most overwhelmingly popular rock group of all time, it portrays the Beatles sympathetically. Like the heroine of *It Happened One Night*, they are constantly told what to do and are smothered by all they have, while Paul's "clean" grandfather causes most of the trouble. Musical numbers include "Can't Buy Me Love" and "Should Have Known Better." Themes for discussion include the nature of fads and the problems created by success.

✳ **CONNECTIONS:** See also *Help!* (more like a comedy with music, while this is more like a musical with comedy). Kids twelve and up might enjoy *I Wanna Hold Your Hand*, about teens overcome by Beatlemania, or *That Thing You Do*, written and directed by Tom Hanks, the story of a 1960s Erie, Pennsylvania, rock group that has an unexpected hit song.

✳ HIGH SOCIETY

1956, 107 min, NR, 6 and up
Dir: Charles Walters. Grace Kelly, Bing Crosby, Frank Sinatra, Celeste Holm
    This musical version of **The Philadelphia Story** misses the lustre of the original, but offers its own pleasures, with Grace Kelly, Bing Crosby, and Frank Sinatra (in the Hepburn, Grant, and Stewart roles), some nice songs by Cole Porter (including the hit "True Love"), a Crosby-Sinatra duet performance of "Did You Evah" and Louis Armstrong performing "Now You Has Jazz."

✳ KISS ME KATE

1953, 109 min, NR, 6 and up
Dir: George Sidney. Howard Keel, Kathryn Grayson, Ann Miller
    A musical version of **The Taming of the Shrew** stars two formerly married actors in this witty and energetic musical featuring the songs of Cole Porter. Howard Keel and Katherine Grayson are at their very best as the immature (but highly tuneful) couple, and Ann Miller is sensational as the brassy tap-dancer cast as Bianca. James Whitmore and Keenan Wynn play small-time hoods who advise Keel to "Brush Up Your Shakespeare," and Carol Haney and Bob Fosse are on hand for some sensational dancing.

✳ **CONNECTIONS:** The movie was originally filmed in 3-D, which is why the characters keep throwing things at the screen!

✳ LI'L ABNER

1959, 113 min, NR, 6 and up
Dir: Melvin Frank. Peter Palmer, Leslie Parrish, Stubby Kaye, Julie Newmar
    This low-budget but lively version of the Broadway play about the characters in the Al Capp comic strip makes cheerful fun of just about everyone and everything, especially politicians, industrialists, and male-female relationships. Daisy Mae wants to catch Abner in the annual Sadie Hawkins race so she can marry him. Obstacles include Abner's not wanting to be caught, interference by the government (which has designated the town the least valuable place in the country so it can be used to store atomic weapons), and General Bullmoose (who wants the secret of Mammy Yokum's tonic).

✳ **CONNECTIONS:** Watch for Jerry Lewis in a cameo appearance. The tradition of a girl-ask-boy "Sadie Hawkins" dance was inspired by Capp's characters.

✳ ON A CLEAR DAY YOU CAN SEE FOREVER

1970, 129 min, G, 8 and up
Dir: Vincente Minnelli. Barbra Streisand, Yves Montand
    In this musical about extrasensory perception and reincarnation, by Alan Jay Lerner (**My Fair Lady**), Barbra Streisand plays an insecure and clumsy

young woman who asks a psychiatrist (Yves Montand) to help her quit smoking to please her fiancé. Under hypnosis, she reveals a past life in nineteenth-century England as a poor but daring woman who uses her extrasensory perception to achieve fortune and position for herself and the man she loves. The psychiatrist, skeptical at first, is fascinated and ultimately enchanted by this earlier personality and is frustrated when he cannot find those qualities in the awkward person before him. She finds acceptance of the person she is now with her former stepbrother (Jack Nicholson). The psychiatrist finds some solace in the prospect of finding the magnetic woman he loved in a future lifetime.

✳ ROBIN AND THE SEVEN HOODS

1964, 103 min, NR, 8 and up
Dir: Gordon Douglas. Frank Sinatra, Dean Martin, Sammy Davis, Jr., Barbara Rush
    Frank Sinatra, Dean Martin, and Sammy Davis, Jr., star in this easygoing Rat Pack update of the story of Robin Hood, transplanted to gangster-era Chicago. The highlight is when Bing Crosby drops by to sing a number with fellow crooners Sinatra and Martin.

✳ SHOW BOAT

1951, 107 min, NR, 10 and up
Dir: George Sidney. Howard Keel, Kathryn Grayson, Ava Gardner
    Edna Ferber's novel and Jerome Kern's music are the stars of this colorful story of a young woman named Magnolia (Kathryn Grayson), who falls in love with handsome Gaylord Ravenal (Howard Keel) on her family's show boat, a sort of traveling vaudeville show. Magnolia's best friend is Julie (Ava Gardner), whose mixed race causes problems when the police arrive to arrest her husband for miscegenation. He outsmarts them, but they leave the showboat and the stress breaks up their marriage. Colorful characters, gorgeous music, and a tragic love story intertwined with one that ends happily make this epic musical a classic.

✳ **CONNECTIONS:** A 1936 version featured Irene Dunne, Helen Morgan, and Paul Robeson.

✳ STORMY WEATHER

1943, 77 min, NR, b&w, 10 and up
Dir: Andrew L. Stone. Bill Robinson, Lena Horne
    A highly fictionalized account of the life of Bill "Bojangles" Robinson is just an excuse to let Robinson and a huge cast of other greats do their stuff, including: Fats Waller (singing "Ain't Misbehavin' "), Lena Horne, Cab Calloway, Dooley Wilson (of *Casablanca*), Katherine Dunham and her dancers, the Nicholas Brothers, Eddie "Rochester" Anderson, and Benny Carter.

✳ SUMMER MAGIC

1963, 100 min, 6 and up
Dir: James Neilson. Dorothy McGuire, Hayley Mills

A great cast and some good musical numbers make up for a creaky plot (based on *Mother Carey's Chickens*, by Kate Douglas Wiggin). After the father dies, Mrs. Carey (Dorothy McGuire) moves her family to a broken-down house in Maine, given to her for no rent by the local postmaster (Burl Ives), who neglects to tell her that he does not have permission from the owner, who is traveling in Europe. Furthermore, the family's snooty cousin Julia (Deborah Walley) comes to visit, which is especially hard on down-to-earth Nancy (Hayley Mills). The owner comes home unexpectedly, but since he is an attractive young man, all works out well. "The Ugly Bug Ball" is sung by Ives to some cute footage of insects. NOTE: The ode to "Femininity" might seem grating to today's kids. Or, it could seem like a humorous artifact. After all, the movie is set nearly 100 years ago.

✳ THAT'S ENTERTAINMENT!

(Parts 1 (1974), 2 (1976), and 3 (1994), 6 and up

These compilations of the best of the MGM vaults are filled with delight from classic musicals. Watch with pen in hand to take notes on which movies you want to see in full.

✳ **CONNECTIONS:** The first one is directed by Jack Hayley, Jr., the son of the man who played the Tin Woodsman in **The Wizard of Oz**. The second one is directed by Gene Kelly.

SEE ALSO:

Bells Are Ringing

Bye Bye Birdie

Damn Yankees

Fiddler on the Roof

Funny Girl

The Pajama Game

The Pirate

The Pirate of Penzance

MYSTERY AND SUSPENSE

To surround anything, however monstrous or ridiculous, with an air of mystery is to invest it with a secret charm, and power of attraction which to the crowd is irresistible.
—CHARLES DICKENS

It's much harder to suggest age-meaningful ranges when it comes to mysteries, thrillers, and suspense movies. One reason is the highly personal tolerance each viewer has for scary material, which bears little relationship to chronological age or even emotional maturity. Some kids can watch *Psycho* without blinking, while some adults still can't take a shower without worrying about Norman Bates. Part of it is tolerance for suspense, more a factor of temperament than maturity.

Equally important, kids differ greatly in the ability to follow complex stories about not very nice people and really dreadful deeds, often filled with false clues and murky motives. Some very young kids enjoy these movies as puzzles and are not bothered at all by the fact that many of them focus on murders or other unpleasant behavior. But others really can't handle them until they are well into their teens, because they find the betrayals, the cruelty, the greed, the violence, and the willingness to disregard the rules genuinely upsetting. These kids should not be pushed or made to feel that their lack of appreciation for these films is "babyish." After all, some adults still cover their eyes when it gets too scary.

Mysteries often raise important issues of trust that can be a good starting point for discussions with the family. In some of them, a sympathetic soul trusts someone, in spite of the evidence that he or she shouldn't. In others, the character insists on some proof that the hero/heroine is trustworthy before lending support. In some stories people trust the wrong characters. In **Night of the Hunter,** the adults make the mistake of trusting Robert Mitchum (the "preacher" with LOVE and HATE tattooed on his knuckles), but the children know better.

These films are excellent examples of problem solving. Whether we are rooting for the cops or the robbers, we get to see our heroes work through complex puzzles with imagination and persistence. In movies like **The Sting** and **Topkapi,** we see how the most precise and careful plans have to be amended quickly when circumstances change, a good example of the importance of a "plan B" and of being able to think and adapt quickly without getting flustered.

Another good topic for discussion relates to the point of view of the movie. We can happily root for the cops in one movie, the private detective (whose goals may conflict with those of the cops) in another, and the clever jewel thieves or con men in another. Talk with older kids and teenagers about how the screenwriter and director earn our sympathies for the characters they want us to identify with. Note that one way to get the audience to sympathize with the criminals is to have them steal from someone even worse. Another is to have them steal for a selfless reason. There is a time-honored third way, but I can't reveal it without giving away too much of the plots of some of these movies. And it is only fair that this chapter have a little mystery of its own for families to solve together.

ALFRED HITCHCOCK

The greatest director of mystery and suspense in the history of the movies, Hitchcock's best films rank among the finest ever made. Hitchcock was a master of psychology, not only of his characters, but of his audience. To watch his films is to get, in addition to the thrilling suspense, an education in storytelling, in which every shot, every word, every image, and every sound contributes to the overall effect.

One of Hitchcock's trademarks was a brief appearance by the director in each of his movies. If you want to try to spot him on your own, don't peek at the upside-down notes at the end of each write-up.

✳ THE LADY VANISHES
1938, 97 min, NR, b&w, 10 and up
Dir: Alfred Hitchcock. Margaret Lockwood, Michael Redgrave

Iris Henderson (Margaret Lockwood) is a young English woman taking a train home from her vacation. She meets a lovely elderly lady, Miss Froy (Dame May Whitty), who mysteriously vanishes. To make things even more mysterious, everyone on the train denies that she ever existed. Henderson is about to give up when she meets Gilbert Redman (Michael Redgrave), a musician who is sympathetic but skeptical until he finds evidence that persuades him Miss Froy is really missing. He joins with Henderson to find the missing lady. This movie also raises issues of trust that are worth discussing.

✳ **CONNECTIONS:** Movies with similar themes include *Gaslight, So Long at the Fair,* in which Jean Simmons's brother disappears from a hotel, and all evidence of his ever having been there is gone as well, and (for grown-ups) *Bunny Lake Is Missing,* about a missing child.

Watch the scene with the doped drink carefully. It was shot through two giant-sized glasses. In the 1980s there was a PBS series based on the two Cricket fans in this movie called *Charters and Caldicott*.

Hitchcock appearance: At the train station

✳ LIFEBOAT
1944, 96 min, NR, b&W, 10 and up
Dir: Alfred Hitchcock. Tallulah Bankhead, William Bendix, Hume Cronyn

The survivors of a shipwreck must find a way to stay alive until they can be rescued in this taut drama. Families may want to discuss the way the characters change and reevaluate their priorities, as exemplified when the spoiled journalist uses her prized diamond bracelet as bait.

✳ **CONNECTIONS:** Canada Lee, who also appears in *Body and Soul,* plays the pickpocket. Coscreenwriter John Steinbeck wrote the original story for the movie.

Hitchcock appearance: This was Hitchcock's greatest challenge. The entire movie takes place in the cramped confines of the lifeboat. He didn't want to play the part of one of the survivors. He had just lost a great deal of weight and was proud of his slimmer silhouette. So he put "before and after" pictures of himself in a phony ad for a diet product called "Reduco," which can be seen when one of the characters picks up a newspaper.

✳ NORTH BY NORTHWEST
1959, 136 min, NR, 10 and up
Dir: Alfred Hitchcock. Cary Grant, Eva Marie Saint, James Mason

In this classic of the everyday-man-thrust-into-terror-and-intrigue genre, Cary Grant plays Roger Thornhill, an advertising executive who is mistaken for a spy by the bad guys (spies for an unidentified enemy) and mistaken for a murderer by the good guys (the local police). Fleeing from both on a cross-country train, he meets Eve Kendall (Eva Marie Saint), who helps him hide, until both are back in the hands of the bad guys again. Romantic, witty, clever, and thrilling, this movie includes two of the all-time great movie scenes: the crop-duster plane coming after Grant out in the cornfield, and the chase on Mount Rushmore.

NOTE: Saint and Grant share a cabin on the train, and there is an oblique suggestion (by today's standards) that they have sex.

✳ **CONNECTIONS:** The title refers to a quote from "Hamlet:" "I am but mad north-north-west." Jessie Royce Landis, who plays Grant's mother, was exactly Grant's age. She is more suitably cast as Grace Kelly's mother in *To Catch a*

Thief. Fans of vintage television spy shows may recognize Martin Landau from *Mission: Impossible,* and Leo G. Carroll from *The Man from U.N.C.L.E.*

Hitchcock appearance: Running to catch a bus under the opening credits

✳ NOTORIOUS
1946, 101 min, NR, b&w, 10 and up
Dir: Alfred Hitchcock. Ingrid Bergman, Cary Grant, Claude Rains

Ingrid Bergman plays Alicia, the daughter of a man who has been convicted of spying for the Nazis. She is so humiliated and angry that she spends all her time drinking and going to parties. Cary Grant is Devlin, an American spy, who determines that she is loyal to the United States, and then enlists her to infiltrate a group led by one of her father's former colleagues (Claude Rains), who lives in Rio de Janeiro with his mother.

Talk to kids about the conflict Alicia and Devlin face between their emotions and their duty, and how they each misinterpret the other's silence on the subject as evidence of lack of love and respect. Talk to older kids about making moral choices in desperate circumstances, for example, Bergman's decision to marry Rains, and how some moral compromises may be justified by the greater good.

✳ **CONNECTIONS:** Hitchcock and his producer wanted the secret uncovered by Alicia to be believable but not so realistic that it would reveal any information about what was really going on in the U.S. war effort. They accidentally got too close to reality with the uranium, and Hitchcock was trailed by federal agents for a few months, who sought to find out where he got his information.

Hitchcock appearance: as a party guest, drinking champagne

✳ REAR WINDOW
1954, 112 min, NR, 8 and up
Dir: Alfred Hitchcock. Jimmy Stewart, Grace Kelly

Jeff Jeffries (Jimmy Stewart) is a photographer who is confined with a broken leg to a wheelchair. He becomes fascinated with the people he observes across the courtyard from his window. Finally, he and his girlfriend, Lisa (Grace Kelly), become convinced that a man in one of the apartments has murdered his wife.

Watch how Hitchcock tells you everything you need to know about Jeff and how he broke his leg with just one tracking shot at the start of the film, and how Jeff uses the tool of his trade, his camera, to get clues and to defend himself. Talk to younger kids about how Jeff uses evidence to draw conclusions about the people across the courtyard (and possibly about the dangers of spying on people's private moments). Older kids may be more interested in the ways Jeff distances himself—from his girlfriend, from the events he photographs, the people he watches, and the way that all the stories behind the windows, including the story of Jeff himself, are about romantic love in every possible form.

✳ **CONNECTIONS:** Lars Thorwald is played by Raymond Burr, later television's Perry Mason. The songwriter is played by Ross Bagdasarian, who as Dave Seville created Alvin and the Chipmunks.

Hitchcock appearance: Butler in songwriter's apartment

✳ SHADOW OF A DOUBT

1943, 108 min, NR, b&w, 10 and up
Dir: Alfred Hitchcock. Teresa Wright, Joseph Cotton

Teresa Wright plays "Charlie," a young woman who is devoted to her Uncle Charlie, played by Joseph Cotton. When he comes to visit, she begins to suspect that he is the notorious "Merry Widow" serial killer, who marries wealthy widows and then murders them. Topics for discussion include the way that the uncle justifies his actions to himself, and the issue faced by the family of whether to tell the police what they have learned.

✳ **CONNECTIONS:** This is widely believed to be Hitchcock's favorite among his movies, though he demurred in his interview with Truffaut. The screenplay is credited to three writers: Thornton Wilder, who wrote the play *Our Town,* Sally Benson, author of the book that became the movie *Meet Me in St. Louis,* and Alma Reville, Hitchcock's wife and frequent collaborator.

Hitchcock appearance: Playing bridge on the train

✳ THE 39 STEPS

1935, 87 min, NR, b&w, 10 and up
Dir: Alfred Hitchcock. Robert Donat, Madeleine Carroll

Robert Donat plays Richard Hannay, a man who becomes swept up in intrigue when he goes to see a performer called Mr. Memory. At the theater, he meets a young woman who tells him she is a spy and asks for his help. When she is killed, he becomes a suspect, and he flees to escape arrest and to find the secrets she was seeking. He meets Pamela (Madeleine Carroll), who tries to turn him over to the police twice, but, when she, too, is taken away, she discovers that he has been telling the truth, and together they find the missing secrets.

This is good movie to use for a discussion of trust, because people make all kinds of good and bad judgments about whom to trust throughout the movie, from the farmer's mistrust of his wife to Donat's trust of his genial host.

✳ **CONNECTIONS:** The 1959 remake is fun, but not as good as the original. The 1978 version is not worth watching.

✳ **ACTIVITIES:** Teenagers will enjoy the book by Robert Buchan, as well as his others, which are equally exciting.

Hitchcock appearance: Passing on the street as Hannay leaves the theater.

✳ TO CATCH A THIEF
1955, 106 min, NR, 8 and up
Dir: Alfred Hitchcock. Cary Grant, Grace Kelly
　　Cary Grant plays John Robie, a retired jewel thief, once known as "The Cat" for his ability to navigate tricky roofs to enter the homes of wealthy people. When a series of robberies using his methods is committed, he is placed under suspicion. As he tries to find the real thief, he meets Frances Stevens (Grace Kelly), a beautiful heiress.

✳ **CONNECTIONS:** Costume designer Edith Head, who won more Oscars than any other individual, said that her favorite people to design clothes for were Grant and Kelly. In this movie, she got to design for them both, and the results are spectacular, especially at the costume ball.

Hitchcock appearance: On a bus, next to Grant.

DONEN DOES HITCHCOCK

Stanley Donen (director of **Seven Brides for Seven Brothers,** and **Two for the Road**) paid loving tribute to Alfred Hitchcock with two glossy, sophisticated, romantic mysteries, featuring two of Hitchcock's favorite male stars.

✳ ARABESQUE
1966, 105 min, NR, 12 and up
Dir: Stanley Donen. Gregory Peck, Sophia Loren
　　Gregory Peck stars as David Pollack, a professor at a British school, hired by a mysterious man in London to translate a hieroglyphic code. There he meets Yasmin Azir (Sophia Loren). The script is a bit on the silly side, and there are a few moments that can be described as genuinely kinky—one where David hides in the shower stall while Yasmin is taking a shower, and one (often cut for television) where Loren models exotic footwear for wicked Beshraavi (Alan Badel). But the stars are at their best (it doesn't get any better than that), and the film is a lot of fun.

✳ **CONNECTIONS:** Watch for George Coulouris, who played Thatcher in **Citizen Kane,** as Ragheeb.

❋ CHARADE
1963, 113 min, NR, 12 and up
Dir: Stanley Donen. Cary Grant, Audrey Hepburn

Audrey Hepburn and Cary Grant star in this thoroughly entertaining blend of romance and intrigue, set in Paris. When her estranged husband is murdered, Reggie (Hepburn) finds out that he had absconded with the loot from a WWII heist, and his erstwhile comrades are back to get their share. Aided by charming Cary Grant, whose various aliases cast some doubt on his trustworthiness, she races to keep ahead of the crooks.

❋ **CONNECTIONS:** The score, by Henry Mancini, is as suspenseful and romantic as the witty script by Peter Stone (*Skin Game, 1776*).

ORSON WELLES

The director of *Citizen Kane* and *The Magnificent Ambersons* made two stunningly atmospheric thrillers.

❋ THE LADY FROM SHANGHAI
1948, 87 min, NR, b&w, 12 and up
Dir: Orson Welles. Orson Welles, Rita Hayworth

Welles and his then-wife Rita Hayworth, star in this story of an Irish sailor named Michael O'Hara who accepts a position on the yacht of a disabled lawyer named Arthur Bannister (Everett Sloane) and his young and beautiful wife, only to be drawn into a complex web of betrayal. The lawyer's associate is murdered, and O'Hara is accused. Bannister defends him, and it is clear that he intends to lose. He runs away, but is captured and brought to an abandoned amusement park, where he meets up again with the Bannisters and finds out what really happened.

❋ **CONNECTIONS:** See Woody Allen's *Manhattan Murder Mystery* (for mature high schoolers and adults) for an affectionate homage to this movie's riveting climax, a shoot-out that takes place in a hall of mirrors.

❋ TOUCH OF EVIL
1958, 93 min, NR, b&w, 12 and up
Dir: Orson Welles. Charlton Heston, Janet Leigh, Marlene Dietrich, Orson Welles

Charlton Heston is "Mike" Vargas, a Mexican police detective, newly married to Susan (Janet Leigh), an American. When a car explodes on the border of the United States and Mexico, both countries' authorities are involved, and Heston must work with the enormous, and enormously corrupt American detective, Hank Quinlan, played by Welles. Especially unforgettable are the astonishing three-minute tracking shot that opens the film, the mesmerizing scene in which Welles takes the eggs from a bird's nest, and Marlene Dietrich's performance as a cynical madam.

✳ **CONNECTIONS:** Adults who see *Ed Wood* will enjoy a brief conversation between the title character, the world's worst director, and Orson Welles (superbly played by Vincent D'Onofrio), where they discuss this movie. A 1998 re-release used a memoranda by Welles to recut it according to his plan.

OTHER THRILLERS

✳ LAURA

1944, 85 min, NR, b&w, 10 and up
Dir: Otto Preminger. Dana Andrews, Gene Tierney, Clifton Webb

Mark McPherson (Dana Andrews) is a police detective investigating the murder of Laura Hunt (Gene Tierney), an advertising executive. As he learns about her life, talks with her friends, and gazes at her portrait, he begins to fall in love with her. The haunting theme song, the Oscar-winning cinematography, the unpredictable twists of the plot, Tierney's timeless beauty, and Clifton Webb's brilliant performance as acid-tongued Waldo Lyedecker combine to make this a film noir classic.

✳ **CONNECTIONS:** Horror movie legend Vincent Price plays Laura's silky fiancé, and distinguished actress Dame Judith Anderson (***Cat on a Hot Tin Roof***) plays his wealthy protector.

✳ NIGHT OF THE HUNTER

1955, 93 min, 12 and up
Dir: Charles Laughton. Robert Mitchum, Shelley Winters, Lillian Gish

Robert Mitchum is "Preacher" Harry Powell, an ex-convict posing as an itinerant preacher (with LOVE and HATE tattooed on his knuckles). His prison cellmate confided that he hid stolen money, and then died. Powell seeks out the cellmate's widow, Willa Harper (Shelly Winters), and marries her, hoping to find the money. Powell murders her and goes after her children, but Rachel (Lillian Gish), a strong, religious, older woman, takes them in. Powell follows them there, but finds that Rachel will not let them go. Throughout the movie, the children see more clearly than the adults do, which adds to the suspenseful and mystical atmosphere.

✳ **CONNECTIONS:** This is the only movie directed by actor Charles Laughton (***The Canterville Ghost, Witness for the Prosecution***), and he imbued it with a rich and very scary creepiness that few full-time directors ever achieved. Lillian Gish was one of the very first movie stars, and with her sister Dorothy appeared in many silent films directed by D. W. Griffith. Mitchum's cellmate is Peter Graves, of ***Stalag 17*** and television's *Mission: Impossible*. The screenwriter was James Agee (***All the Way Home***).

ROOTING FOR THE GOOD GUYS: SHERLOCK HOLMES, PHILIP MARLOWE, HERCULE POIROT, MISS MARPLE, AND NICK AND NORA CHARLES

Sherlock Holmes has appeared in more movies than any other fictional character. He has been portrayed by everyone from John Barrymore (in silent movies) to Michael Caine. Even Steven Spielberg produced *Young Sherlock Holmes* (directed by Barry Levinson), a moderately entertaining—if overly gory—fantasy about Holmes's school days that has special appeal for anyone familiar enough with the stories by Arthur Conan Doyle to appreciate all the references. In addition to the excellent PBS series featuring Jeremy Brett, some of Holmes's best appearances are:

✳ THE BIG SLEEP
1946, 114 min, NR, b&w, 12 and up
Dir: Howard Hawks. Humphrey Bogart, Lauren Bacall
   Humphrey Bogart plays Raymond Chandler's detective hero, Philip Marlowe, in this exciting (if murky) film noir classic. He is hired by a wealthy old man, frail after years of dissipation, to look into the disappearance of his friend and employee. Bogart gets involved in a plot that involves drugs, nymphomania, blackmail, and murder. Don't try to figure it all out—the director and even Chandler himself admitted they had no idea who did one of the murders. Just enjoy the sensational script (cowritten by William Faulkner), where almost everything has a double meaning (the conversation between Bogart and Lauren Bacall, one of the old man's daughters, about racehorses and their jockeys is a notorious example), and the dark atmosphere, as lonely as Edward Hopper's *Nighthawks* painting.

   ✳ **CONNECTIONS:** In addition to being imitated by just about every private detective in any movie, Chandler's character Marlowe was portrayed by many different actors, including Robert Mitchum (*Farewell My Lovely* and a remake of *The Big Sleep*), Elliot Gould (*The Long Goodbye*), Dick Powell (*Murder, My Sweet*), James Garner (*Marlowe*), and Robert Montgomery (*The Lady in the Lake*). *The Lady in the Lake* is of some interest as the only Hollywood film to be filmed entirely from a subjective viewpoint. Everything in the movie is seen through Marlowe's eyes, and the only glimpses we get of him are when Montgomery (who also directed) looks into a mirror.

✳ THE GREAT MOUSE DETECTIVE
1986, 80 min, G, 6 and up
Dir: John Musker, Ron Clements, Dave Michener, Burny Mattinson. Voices of Vincent Price, Alan Young, Melissa Manchester
   This animated film from the Disney studios is based on *Basil of Baker Street*, by Eve Titus. Basil is a Holmes-ish mouse who lives beneath Holmes's

apartment on Baker Street. Basil Rathbone, who played Holmes in the best-known series of films, lends his voice to a brief appearance as the animated Holmes, and the villain (named Ratigan) is performed by suitably sinister Vincent Price. It isn't one of Disney's classics, but it is enjoyable.

✳ THE HOUND OF THE BASKERVILLES
1939, 80 min, NR, b&w, 8 and up
Dir: Sidney Lanfield. Basil Rathbone, Nigel Bruce

This version of one of Conan Doyle's most popular stories (there are four others) is the first of the series featuring Basil Rathbone (**The Adventures of Robin Hood**) as Holmes, with Nigel Bruce as Dr. Watson. Another especially good one is *The Adventures of Sherlock Holmes,* and most of the rest of the movies in this series are very watchable, especially for Holmes fans.

✳ MURDER MOST FOUL
1960, 90 min, NR, b&w, 10 and up
Dir: George Pollack. Margaret Rutherford, Ron Moody, Francesca Annis

Deliciously dotty Margaret Rutherford was perfectly cast in four films as Agatha Christie's Miss Marple. In this one, based on *Mrs. McGinty's Dead,* she is the only member of a jury to believe in the innocence of the accused, and sets out to find the real killer. Others in the series are *Murder She Said* (based on *4:50 from Paddington*), *Murder at the Gallop* (based on *After the Funeral*), and *Murder Ahoy,* (an original script).

✳ **CONNECTIONS:** Angela Lansbury plays a pre–Jessica Fletcher version of Miss Marple in *The Mirror Crack'd,* which features dueling divas Elizabeth Taylor and Kim Novak. *Murder She Said* features an appearance by Joan Hickson, the future television Miss Marple.

✳ MURDER ON THE ORIENT EXPRESS
1974, 127 min, PG, 10 and up
Dir: Sidney Lumet. Albert Finney, Ingrid Bergman, Sean Connery

A gorgeously produced version of the famous novel by Agatha Christie, with a world-class all-star cast that includes Albert Finney as Belgian detective Hercule Poirot, Wendy Hiller, Sir John Gielgud, Ingrid Bergman (who won an Oscar), Sean Connery, Anthony Perkins, and Richard Widmark. A notorious criminal is murdered on the train, and Poirot must find the killer before they reach their destination.

✳ **CONNECTIONS:** Peter Ustinov played Poirot in three showy but slow-moving adaptations from other Christie novels. Hiller starred twenty-nine years earlier in **I Know Where I'm Going!** Director Sidney Lumet discusses this film in his book *Making Movies.*

✳ THE SEVEN-PER-CENT SOLUTION

1976, 113 min, PG, 12 and up
Dir: Herbert Ross. Nicol Williamson, Alan Arkin, Robert Duvall

It is beguiling to wonder how Holmes would have interacted with some of the real-life figures of his day. Two movies speculate about how he would have tracked down Jack the Ripper. This one asks how he would have done as a patient of Sigmund Freud (Alan Arkin), and how they would have handled an investigation together. Holmes is played by Nicol Williamson, and Robert Duvall plays Dr. Watson. The script by Nicholas Meyer is based on his best-seller. NOTE: This movie would probably get a PG-13 rating today, due to violence, prostitution, and Holmes's drug use.

✳ THE THIN MAN

1934, 93 min, NR, b&w, 10 and up
Dir: W. S. Van Dyke, II. William Powell, Myrna Loy, Maureen O'Sullivan

Once and for all, William Powell was not the thin man. The thin man was Clyde Wynant, a key to solving the mystery in the first of the films, but the pairing of Powell and Myrna Loy as the sublimely elegant and witty Nick and Nora Charles was so resoundingly successful that they kept the name through five sequels. Created by Dashiell Hammett (*The Maltese Falcon*) and adapted for the screen by Frances Goodrich (*It's a Wonderful Life* and *Easter Parade*), Nick and Nora presented American viewers with a married couple who got a huge kick out of each other but didn't take marriage, murder, or themselves too seriously. Their easy banter set the standard for hundreds of movies that followed, from screwball comedies to the darkest film noir.

NOTE: Parents should be warned that drinking, including drinking to excess, is humorously presented as glamorous and sophisticated.

✳ **CONNECTIONS:** Watch for Maureen O'Sullivan (Jane in the *Tarzan* series and Mia Farrow's mother). A very young Jimmy Stewart appears in *After the Thin Man*.

SEE ALSO:

The Maltese Falcon

ROOTING FOR THE BAD GUYS: DASHING THIEVES AND CHARMING CON ARTISTS

✳ THE GREAT TRAIN ROBBERY

1979, 111 min, PG, 10 and up
Dir: Michael Crichton. Sean Connery, Donald Sutherland

This glossy period piece is based on a real 1855 robbery that became a legend for its brilliance and daring. Sean Connery, Donald Sutherland, and Lesley-Anne Down are the robbers who can't resist the gold bullion being shipped to pay the soldiers fighting in the Crimean War.

✳ **CONNECTIONS:** Director Crichton wrote the screenplay, based on his novel. He is also the author of **The Andromeda Strain,** *Westworld,* and **Jurassic Park.** A silent movie with this title made in 1903 by Edwin S. Porter is considered by film historians to be the first movie to tell a story.

✳ HOW TO STEAL A MILLION
1966, 127 min, NR, 8 and up
Dir: William Wyler. Audrey Hepburn, Peter O'Toole, Eli Wallach

Audrey Hepburn plays Nicole Bonnet, the daughter of a French art collector (Hugh Griffith), whose secret is that many of the items in the collection are forgeries, including the "Van Gogh" and the "Cellini Venus" about to be lent to the local museum. The forgeries were made by Bonnet and his father. Peter O'Toole plays Simon Dermott, a specialist in art authentication. Nicole mistakes him for a thief, and then asks him to help her steal the Venus, to protect her father from being discovered. The romance is delicious, and the heist is sheer delight.

✳ THE LADYKILLERS
1955, 90 min, NR, 10 and up
Dir: Alexander Mackendrick. Alec Guinness, Peter Sellers

This is the blackest of comedies about five hilariously dastardly bad guys who are completely thwarted by their greed, their incompetence, and especially by their dotty old landlady. Alec Guinness and Peter Sellers head the cast, but Katie Johnson (seventy-seven years old at the time the movie was made) stole the show (and won the British Academy Award). She plays Mrs. Wilberforce, a dear soul whose suspicions of criminal behavior in the neighborhood are genially tolerated by the local police. She has no suspicions, however, of strange-looking Professor Marcus (Guinness), who rents a room from her, telling her he is a music teacher, and by the time she does figure out that he and the other "musicians" are really robbers, the police assume it is just another of her fantasies. The gang decides she must be killed, but it is she who (inadvertently) gets rid of each of them.

✳ **CONNECTIONS:** Two of the most chameleonlike actors who ever put on makeup appear in this film: Alec Guinness (**Star Wars** and **Great Expectations**), almost unrecognizable behind those teeth, and Peter Sellers, who played multiple parts in both **Dr. Strangelove** and **The Mouse That Roared.** You can see Guinness as all eight victims of a ruthlessly ambitious social climber in another classic black comedy, *Kind Hearts and Coronets.*

✳ THE LAVENDER HILL MOB
1951, 82 min, NR, b&w, 8 and up
Dir: Charles Crichton. Alec Guinness, Stanley Holloway

Henry Holland (Alec Guinness) is a mild-mannered bank clerk with an impeccable record who decides to steal the gold bullion he has been so honorably transporting through the years. His plan for getting it out of the country is brilliant (and very funny), until one small problem develops. . . .

✳ **CONNECTIONS:** Watch quickly for a very young Audrey Hepburn getting some money from Guinness just as the movie opens.

✳ THE STING
1973, 129 min, PG, 10 and up
Dir: George Roy Hill. Paul Newman, Robert Redford, Robert Shaw

This story of an elaborate con game reunited Paul Newman and Robert Redford with their **Butch Cassidy and the Sundance Kid** director and won seven Oscars, including Best Picture, Director, Screenplay, and Musical Score. In 1936, a small-time con man named Johnny Hooker (Redford) makes the mistake of conning an employee of big-time hoodlum Doyle Lonnegan (Robert Shaw). Lonnegan retaliates by killing Hooker's partner. With Lonnegan's men and a corrupt sheriff chasing after him, Hooker escapes to Chicago to find Henry Gondorff, a legendary "grifter" con man. Hooker asks for his help in avenging his partner's death, which requires a deliciously elaborate series of scams to get Lonnegan's money and keep Hooker safe. NOTE: Redford spends the night with a woman he has just met; violence.

✳ TOPKAPI
1964, 120 min, NR, 10 and up
Dir: Jules Dassin. Melina Mercouri, Maximilian Schell

Elizabeth Lipp (Melina Mercouri) and William Walter (Maximilian Schell) plot to steal a priceless jeweled dagger from a museum in Istanbul called Topkapi. They decide to work with "amateurs," people who have no criminal records, and they assemble a team that includes a strong man, an eccentric inventor, and an inept con artist (Oscar-winning Peter Ustinov). They have to find a way to surmount the extraordinary museum security, which includes a floor alarm sensitive to the slightest pressure.

✳ **CONNECTIONS:** The 1996 film *Mission: Impossible* borrowed the central heist sequence from this movie, which in turn (and in keeping with the ethos of its hero thieves), stole parts of it from the famous *Rififi*. Since Dassin directed both *Rififi* and *Topkapi*, however, perhaps we can just call it his style.

SEE ALSO:
The Fallen Idol

Witness for the Prosecution

ROMANCE

And what's romance? Usually a nice little tale where you have every-thing As You Like It, where rain never wets your jacket and gnats never bite your nose and it's always daisy-time.
—D. H. Lawrence

We get our first lessons in romance from the movies. Whether comedy, drama, adventure, fantasy, or musical, we never tire of seeing the boy meet the girl, lose the girl, and get the girl. For kids, in addition to learning about the way people fall in love, they also learn from these movies the way that people learn to trust, communicate, resolve differences, and get close to each other.

Frequently, in movie romances, the conflict comes from a secret—or a lie—that one at first does not want the other to know, and then, once they are close to one another, cannot figure out a way to reveal. We also often see someone transformed by love, with a new sense of confidence, trust, and optimism. These stories symbolize the issues of intimacy and the conflicts each of us feel in giving our trust and allowing ourselves to be known.

Look at the myth of Cupid and Psyche as one source of these stories. Cupid, the essence of love, will stay with Psyche only so long as she refrains from looking at him. When she lifts the lamp to see him, she burns him with the oil, and he flies away forever. Psyche's name became the source of the word we use for the study of our emotions.

A story like **Beauty and the Beast** or **Lili** gives us a variation on that theme, with a hero who hides his tender side from the woman he loves. In **The Shop Around the Corner** (remade as a musical, **In the Good Old Summertime,** and adapted for the age of the modem as *You've Got Mail*), a young man and woman who are antagonists find that they are each other's secret pen pal, and that they are really deeply in love. And in many other movies the lovers are changed profoundly through their love for one another.

NOTE: Children's interest in (and tolerance for) romantic movies vary widely. Some are fascinated by them at age eight; others have no interest until well into their teens. So the age recommendations that follow should be revised according to your own child's preferences.

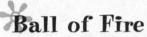Ball of Fire
1941, 111 min, NR, b&w, 8 and up
Dir: Howard Hawks. Gary Cooper, Barbara Stanwyck, Dana Andrews

✳ **PLOT:** In this modern version of *Snow White and the Seven Dwarfs*, eight professors are writing an encyclopedia, funded by a bequest. They all live together, cared for by a grumpy housekeeper, and work together in one large room. As the movie opens, they have been working for seven years and have only reached the letter "S." All are unmarried (one is a widower) and all are elderly, except for Professor Bertram Potts (Gary Cooper), a scholar of English literature and language. When the garbage man comes by to ask for help in answering a radio quiz, Potts listens to his speech and is appalled to find that his article on slang, based on scholarly papers, is years out of date. So, for the first time in seven years, he ventures out into the world, taking notes on everything he hears, and inviting the most colorful speakers he meets back to the house for further study.

Among his subjects is the dazzling Sugarpuss O'Shea (Barbara Stanwyck), whom he spots performing in a nightclub and invites back to the house. She turns him down. But then she has to lay low while her mobster boyfriend, Joe Lilac (Dana Andrews), is under investigation, and she decides the professor will provide the perfect hideout. She shows up on his doorstep and insists on moving in.

She brings chaos to the professors, but also fun and music. Potts falls in love with her and proposes. Lilac proposes, too (via his henchmen), as a handy way of making sure she won't be able to testify against him. Pretending that she is taking him to meet her family, she gets the professors to drive her to Lilac. But when she changes her mind and refuses to marry Lilac, the professors are taken hostage and must escape and rescue her, using their expertise in almost every subject, including physics, anatomy, geography, and psychology.

✳ **DISCUSSION:** This movie is sheer delight, with one of the wittiest scripts ever, cowritten by Billy Wilder, the screenwriter-director of *Some Like It Hot* and *Sunset Boulevard*. It is astonishing to think that a movie so knowing about American English was written by Wilder, who first came to the United States as an adult to escape the Nazis. The movie includes my all-time favorite line of dialogue: When told her sore throat shows "a slight rosiness," Sugarpuss answers, "It's as red as *The Daily Worker,* and just as sore!" It must be watched more than once to get all of the jokes and references.

Kids will enjoy the way Sugarpuss disrupts the lives of the professors, and the way that the professors use their expertise (and a book on boxing) to rescue Sugarpuss. Older kids might be interested in the disagreement between Potts and Oddly about the best way to show love for a woman, and by the psychological validity of Magenbruch's conclusion that Sugarpuss didn't want to marry Lilac because she sent back the wrong ring.

PROFANITY: None.

NUDITY/SEXUAL REFERENCES: None.

ALCOHOL/DRUG ABUSE: None.

VIOLENCE/SCARINESS: Characters in peril, but nothing scary.

TOLERANCE/DIVERSITY ISSUES: None.

✻ QUESTIONS FOR KIDS:
- Why do people use slang? Where does slang come from?
- What slang words do you like best?
- What can you tell about someone by what kind of slang words he or she uses?

✻ CONNECTIONS: The professors are played by some of Hollywood's finest character actors, including S. Z. "Cuddles" Sakall and Henry Travers (Clarence the angel in *It's a Wonderful Life*). Drummer Gene Krupa makes a memorable appearance playing "Matchstick Boogie."

The movie was remade by the same director as *A Song Is Born*, a musical starring Danny Kaye and Virginia Mayo.

✻ ACTIVITIES: Of course the slang is very outdated today, dating back half a century. Ask kids to imagine what would catch Potts's ear if he went out today. Where would he go? Compare Potts to Professor Higgins in *My Fair Lady*, who could locate someone by hearing their speech. Note that Potts listened to many different groups of people to get examples of different kinds of slang.

Professor Potts would be delighted to see the *Random House Dictionary of American Slang*, by J. E. Lightner. Lightner's schedule would also delight Potts; at this writing, only the dictionary's first two volumes have been published (four years apart), listing slang words through the letter "O."

✻The Enchanted Cottage
1945, 92 min, b&w, 10 and up
Dir: John Cromwell. Dorothy McGuire, Robert Young, Mildred Natwick, Herbert Marshall

✻ PLOT: Mrs. Minnett (Mildred Natwick), a widow, owns a small cottage that she rents out to honeymooning couples. Some people believe there is a magic about the house that keeps the couples safe and happy. Laura (Dorothy McGuire) is a plain girl who comes to work in the house because she responds to its special feeling. Oliver (Robert Young), rich and careless, comes to see the house and reserves it for his honeymoon. But before he can be married, he is called off to war and seriously injured. He comes to the cottage alone and bitter, to retreat from the world. Wanting to shield himself from his family and his former fianceé, he impulsively proposes to Laura, who accepts but does not tell him that she loves him. He is so self-absorbed that he does not even wonder why she agrees.

After the wedding, they go back to the cottage, embarrassed and uncomfortable. But the cottage works its enchantment, and they realize that they have become beautiful and whole, and deeply in love. They live in blissful happiness, confiding only in Mrs. Minnett and their blind friend. But when Oliver's family arrives, they cannot see the transformation. Oliver and Laura are crushed, until they realize that the enchantment was love, and that it would always make them beautiful to one another.

✻ **DISCUSSION:** Like the magic in the story, this movie is only for believers, but there are many cynics who have a special affection for what can only be called its enchantment. As Antoine de Saint-Exupéry says in *The Little Prince,* "It is only with the heart that one can see rightly; what is essential is invisible to the eye." Many children will not have the patience for this story, but others will find it one of their favorite films.

PROFANITY: None.

NUDITY/SEXUAL REFERENCES: None.

ALCOHOL/DRUG ABUSE: None.

VIOLENCE/SCARINESS: None.

TOLERANCE/DIVERSITY ISSUES: Blind character is treated very respectfully; overall issue of tolerance of differences of appearance, ability, and class.

✻ **QUESTIONS FOR KIDS:**
- How do the writer and director help the viewer believe in the magic that Oliver and Laura feel?
- Why doesn't Oliver want to see his family?
- Do people in love see each other differently than others see them? Can you think of other movies or books where this happens?

✻ **CONNECTIONS:** Dorothy McGuire, who is highly unsuccessful in her attempt to appear unattractive in this movie, was Kathy in *Gentleman's Agreement* and played the mothers in *Swiss Family Robinson* and *A Summer Place.* Following a successful career as a leading man in the movies, Robert Young turned to television as the star of *Father Knows Best* and *Marcus Welby, M.D.*

✻It Happened One Night

1934, 105 min, NR, b&w, 8 and up
Dir: Frank Capra. Clark Gable, Claudette Colbert

✻ **PLOT:** Ellie Andrews (Claudette Colbert), a sheltered heiress, is furious with her industrialist father (Walter Connelly). She impetuously married an aviator named King Westley, and her father brought her home and carried her off on his yacht. She jumps overboard, swims ashore, and gets a bus ticket to get back to Westley.

On that bus is Peter Warne (Clark Gable), a hard-boiled reporter who has just been fired for drinking on the job. They annoy each other immediately. He discovers who she is and knows he has the story of a lifetime. Without letting her know that he has guessed her identity, he resolves to stay with her so he can write about whatever she does.

A storm makes the road impassable. Without much money, Peter and Ellie are forced to share a cabin at an "auto camp" (predecessor to motels in the days before interstate highways). He hangs a blanket between their sides of the room, calling it "the wall of Jericho," assuring her that "I have no trumpet." The next morning, detectives come to the cabin looking for Ellie, and Peter is charmed by her quick thinking and imagination as she pretends to be his squabbling wife. She is not the spoiled brat he imagined, just rebelling against an overprotected life.

When one of the other bus riders recognizes Ellie, they realize they will have to leave. Peter tries to teach her to hitchhike, but Ellie has her own method, which works even better. They fall in love. Through a misunderstanding, each thinks the other has left. So she goes back home, and her chastened father promises her a real wedding to Westley. The day of the wedding, Peter shows up to get reimbursed for the $39.60 he spent on Ellie. Andrews, realizing that Ellie and Peter really love each other, escorts her down the aisle at the wedding, urging her to make a break and run off with Peter. In the last scene, Ellie and Peter are back at the auto camp, and the walls of Jericho are tumbling down.

✱ **DISCUSSION:** This is an exemplar of the "road picture," in which two people who don't like each other much have to get someplace together and through their adventures develop respect (and usually fall in love). In Capra's autobiography he notes that he and the screenwriter made a crucial change to the story (which originally appeared in a magazine as "Night Bus"). In that story, the rich girl was spoiled. Capra knew that the audience and Peter both had to sympathize with her, so they made her someone whose zest for life and adventure was so strong, she felt smothered by her wealth. The scene in which she explains that she had never been allowed to do anything for herself does away with any feeling of envy or resentment the audience (or Peter) might feel.

PROFANITY: None.

NUDITY/SEXUAL REFERENCES: Mild spiciness of "wall of Jericho"; in the famous hitchhiking scene, Ellie gets a car to stop by raising her skirt to show off her pretty calf, which would send an entirely unacceptable message today.

ALCOHOL/DRUG ABUSE: Peter is fired for drunkenness.

VIOLENCE/SCARINESS: None.

TOLERANCE/DIVERSITY ISSUES: Class issues (prejudice against the upper class).

❋ **QUESTIONS FOR KIDS:**
- What makes Peter and Ellie change their minds about each other?
- If it happened today, what would be different?
- Why did Ellie and her father have a hard time communicating with each other?

❋ **CONNECTIONS:** Neither of the stars was enthusiastic about this film. Clark Gable was lent to Columbia as punishment for lack of cooperation, and assigned to do this movie. Several top female stars turned down the script, and Claudette Colbert said she would appear only if they doubled her usual salary. But it went on to become the first movie to win all five top Academy Awards: Best Picture, Director, Actress, Actor, and Screenplay (the only others so honored were *The Silence of the Lambs* and *One Flew Over the Cuckoo's Nest*). This movie established a standard for "screwball comedy," which has been imitated constantly but seldom matched. A crisis ensued in the underwear industry when Gable removed his shirt and audiences saw that he wasn't wearing an undershirt. Millions of men abandoned theirs in imitation. A book called *The Runaway Bride* uses the image of Ellie's change of heart as she walks down the aisle as the symbol of one of the most enduring themes in movies.

❋ SABRINA
1954, 113 min, NR, b&w, 10 and up
Dir: Billy Wilder. Audrey Hepburn, Humphrey Bogart, William Holden
Audrey Hepburn is incandescent in this story of the dreamy, impractical chauffeur's daughter who falls in love with the playboy son of a millionaire (William Holden). Sent to Paris to get over him, she returns more in love than ever, but now so soigné that he is utterly dazzled by her. When his businessman older brother (Humphrey Bogart) tries to distract her, he finds that he is the one becoming distracted.

❋ **CONNECTIONS:** Avoid the 1995 remake.

❋ SHADOWLANDS
1993, 130 min, PG, high schoolers
Dir: Richard Attenborough. Anthony Hopkins, Deborah Winger
Anthony Hopkins plays author C. S. Lewis (whom teens may know best from the Narnia series), a man very sure of his faith and of his life alone until he meets Joy Gresham (Debra Winger), an American poet. He cannot allow himself to admit his feelings for her until it is almost too late; she is diagnosed with terminal cancer. Through his love for her, he finds a deeper

faith and understanding of himself. It is through his own experience of love that he begins to achieve a more profound understanding of God.

✳ **CONNECTIONS:** An excellent earlier version of this story, made for the BBC with Joss Ackland and Claire Bloom, is also available on video.

✳ THE SHOP AROUND THE CORNER

1940, 97 min, NR, b&w, 10 and up
Dir: Ernst Lubitsch. Jimmy Stewart, Margaret Sullavan

   The employees in a Budapest leather goods shop run by Hugo (Frank Morgan) work closely together and get along well, albeit a few rough spots. Alfred (Jimmy Stewart) is used to being Hugo's favorite, and he is disconcerted when Hugo hires Klara (Margaret Sullavan). Alfred and Klara dislike each other, not realizing that each is the other's secret pen pal. As pen pals, they share their feelings and fall deeply in love. As coworkers, it takes more time for them to appreciate each other. NOTE: Hugo finds that his wife is having an affair with one of his clerks, and tries to kill himself.

✳ **CONNECTIONS:** The musical remake starring Judy Garland is *In the Good Old Summertime*. There was also a Broadway musical called *She Loves Me*, and *You've Got Mail*, with Tom Hanks and Meg Ryan courting via e-mail. Hugo is played by Frank Morgan, who plays the title role in *The Wizard of Oz*.

SEE ALSO:

Bus Stop

Born Yesterday

Gregory's Girl

I Know Where I'm Going!

Ninotchka

Romeo and Juliet

Say Anything

SPORTS

Sports do not build character. They reveal it.
—Heywood Hale Broun

Like movies about kids and animals, movies about sports tend to follow one formula. Roger Ebert puts it this way:

> The recipe for such movies is set in stone. . . . We begin with underdogs, coached by a loser with a scandal in his past and a lot to prove. We linger for a scene or two over the personalities on the team. We show practice sessions in which the team is absolutely without talent. We show despair. Then, just when things look their bleakest, the guys decide not to give up, and somehow they start to get better.

He then goes on to delineate the "obligatory setback," followed by the Big Event, at which at first it appears everything will go wrong, but then, finally, the heroes triumph.

Certainly, at least some of these elements are found in just about any movie about sports. And there is a whole subcategory of dreadful movies about kids' teams made up of losers and rejects who somehow pull together to beat the rich, snobby kids. Movies like *The Mighty Ducks, The Bad News Bears, The Big Green,* and *Little Giants* are all but interchangeable, and almost completely devoid of any intelligence or sincerity.

But sports are, in addition to being fun to watch, great repositories of passion and commitment, and wonderful metaphors for triumph and redemption. For that reason, there are many terrific family movies set in the world of sports.

BASEBALL

For some reason I have never been able to figure out, there are more great sports movies about baseball than about all other sports combined. And virtually every sports fantasy movie is about baseball, like **Field of Dreams,**

Angels in the Outfield, It Happens Every Spring, Damn Yankees, Rookie of the Year. Perhaps it is because baseball is a slow game, played outdoors in warm weather, which lends itself well to the cadences of movies and dreams.

❋ BASEBALL

1994, 9 60-minute episodes, NR, 8 and up
Dir: Ken Burns

The PBS series may have seemed overwhelming when it was broadcast, but watching the videos one at a time (there are nine, of course, one for each inning of a game) is very enjoyable for fans of baseball and of Americana. The episode about Jackie Robinson and Branch Rickey is especially moving.

❋ EIGHT MEN OUT

1988, 119 min, PG, 10 and up
Dir: John Sayles. D. B. Sweeney, John Cusack, David Straithairn, Bill Irwin, John Mahoney

In 1919, members of the Chicago White Sox agreed to throw the World Series. Known forever after as the notorious "Black Sox," they included "Shoeless" Joe Jackson (D. B. Sweeney), possibly the most talented player ever. This sympathetic treatment by writer-director John Sayles (who also appears as sportswriter Ring Lardner) puts the blame on the owners, who exploited the players, virtually cheating them out of their money. Jackson, who could not read or even write his name, in particular is shown to be an unfair victim.

❋ **CONNECTIONS:** Jackson is played by Ray Liotta in *Field of Dreams*. It will help kids to have some familiarity with the story before they see this film. The PBS *Baseball* series describes what happened in detail.

❋ ROOKIE OF THE YEAR

1993, 103 min, PG, 6 and up
Dir: Daniel Stern. Thomas Ian Nicholas, Gary Busey, Eddie Bracken

Henry Rowengartner (Thomas Ian Nicholas) is a twelve-year-old whose broken shoulder healed just a little too tightly, giving him an extraordinary fastball. The next thing he knows, he is the starting pitcher for the Chicago Cubs. This is a very pleasant little film, with a nice relationship between Henry and his single mother (who of course has to be saved from her icky boyfriend, who wants to "manage" Henry's career but is otherwise a sensible and capable woman). The impact on Henry's friends—and on his own ability to be a kid—is particularly well-handled.

❋ **CONNECTIONS:** Director Daniel Stern is the actor who appeared in *Breaking Away* as Cyril, and in *Home Alone* as Marv. In this film, he plays the clumsy pitching coach.

✳ THE SANDLOT

1993, 101 min, PG, 6 and up
Dir: David Mickey Evans. Dennis Leary, Karen Allen, James Earl Jones

In the 1960s, a boy whose mother has just remarried moves to a new town and begins to make friends when he joins in a sandlot baseball game. The boy's challenges include developing some baseball skills, trying to achieve a comfortable relationship with his new stepfather (Dennis Leary), and finding a way to triumph over "The Beast" (a junkyard dog) and the bigger, tougher kids who challenge his friends to a game. All are well-handled in this exceptionally perceptive story of growing up. NOTE: Some gross-out moments (which most kids will enjoy). One of the boys pretends to be drowning to get a kiss from a beautiful lifeguard.

BASKETBALL

✳ HOOP DREAMS

1994, 169 min, PG-13, 14 and up
Dir: Steve James.

Over four years, a dedicated documentary team followed the lives of two promising inner-city high school basketball players and their families. Arthur Agee and William Gates were initially given athletic scholarships to a prestigious private school, the one once attended by NBA star Isiah Thomas, but Agee's scholarship is cut off when his skills (and his height) do not meet the coach's expectations. The boys and their families dream of using their basketball skills to get to college, and then to the NBA. Where they are, even that .00005 percent chance seems a better bet than any of their alternatives for making it out of the inner city. This extraordinary film is one of the most perceptive and involving portraits of America ever made. Its portrayal of these families and its messages about race, class, and American notions of success are unforgettable. There is heartbreak and triumph on and off the basketball court. At the end, one of Gates's friends asks, "If you get to the NBA, will you remember me?" and Gates responds, "If I don't, will you remember me?" NOTE: Mature language and themes; out-of-wedlock pregnancies; drug use.

✳ HOOSIERS

1986, 114 min, PG, 10 and up
Dir: David Anspaugh. Gene Hackman, Dennis Hopper, Barbara Hershey

In small towns, high school sports can assume transcendent importance. In this story set in the 1950s, a tiny farm community's basketball team becomes the state champion, led by a coach (Gene Hackman) thrown out of college basketball for failure to control his temper. His redemption, and that of his alcoholic assistant (Dennis Hopper), father of one of the players, parallels the effort and triumph of the team. This is an exceptionally moving film, with outstanding performances, and very evocative of the place and time.

SEE ALSO:

The Absent Minded Professor

BOBSLEDDING

✳ COOL RUNNINGS
1993, 97 min, PG, 8 and up
Dir: Jon Turtletaub. John Candy, Doug E. Doug

At the 1988 Olympics, one of the star attractions was the Jamaican bobsled team. There had never been a bobsled team from Jamaica before, possibly because Jamaica has no snow. This Disney feature takes a lot of liberties with the real story, making it much more formulaic. This unfortunately adds an (unintentional) colonist-racist overtone, as the American white coach with a reputation to clear (John Candy) is the one who shows the black natives what to do. However, as underdog movies go, this one is fairly lively, with appealing characters. NOTE: Mild expletives; some alcohol use.

BOXING

✳ BODY AND SOUL
1947, 104 min, NR, b&w, 8 and up
Dir: Robert Rossen. John Garfield, Lili Palmer, Anne Revere

In this classic parable of corruption and redemption, John Garfield plays Charlie Davis, who becomes a boxer to get money for his mother but is seduced by the world of money, glamour, and power. All of the performances, especially Garfield's, Anne Revere's, as his mother, Lili Palmer's, as his girlfriend, and Canada Lee's, as a former champion, are superb. NOTE: This is a rare film made before the 1960s that treats a black character (albeit a tragic one) with dignity.

✳ HERE COMES MR. JORDAN
1941, 93 min, NR, b&w, 8 and up
Dir: Alexander Hall.

In this fantasy-romance, Robert Montgomery plays a boxer who is killed in a plane crash. But when he gets to heaven, he finds there has been a mistake. He was not scheduled to die for many years. So the apprentice angel assigned to him (Edward Everett Horton) must take him to find a new body to live out the rest of the years allotted to him. He agrees to try the body of a wealthy man named Farnsworth, who is about to be killed by his wife and his assistant, and he finds himself straightening out Farnsworth's life before he can get on with his own. NOTE: Parents should use caution in deciding whether to let young children see this movie, especially if they may take too literally its notions about the afterlife.

✳ **CONNECTIONS:** This story was remade as *Heaven Can Wait* in 1978, with Warren Beatty, in this version a quarterback who falls in love with an environmentalist, played by Julie Christie.

KARATE

✳ THE KARATE KID
1984, 126 min, R, 14 and up
Dir: Jon Avildsen. Ralph Macchio, Pat Morita, Elisabeth Shue

The director of *Rocky* brings us essentially the same story, only this time the protagonist is a teenager and the sport is karate. Daniel (Ralph Macchio) and his mother, new in Los Angeles, meet Mr. Miyagi (Pat Morita), a janitor, who turns out to be a karate master. NOTE: The R rating is for language and violence; parents might want to preview the film before showing it to kids.

✳ **CONNECTIONS:** There are three sequels (rated PG) that are not very good.

✳ SIDEKICKS
1993, 102 min, PG, 10 and up
Dir: Aaron Norris. Chuck Norris, Joe Piscopo, Beau Bridges

Real-life karate kids (and those who would like to be) will enjoy this fantasy about Barry (Jonathan Brandis), an asthmatic boy who dreams of having Chuck Norris as his friend. His dreams become reality when he studies karate with Mr. Lee, a cook (their team is called "The Frying Dragons"), and Chuck Norris shows up at the big meet and decides to join them when they need another teammate. Joe Piscopo plays the evil leader of the opposing team. The movie is formulaic, but still enjoyable.

SEE ALSO
Baseball
Angels in the Outfield
The Bingo Long Traveling All-Stars & Motor Kings
Damn Yankees
Field of Dreams
It Happens Every Spring
The Jackie Robinson Story
A League of Their Own
Pride of the Yankees
Boxing
Rocky
Football
Brian's Song
Track
Chariots of Fire

WESTERNS

The national hero is not a prince, not a king, not a rich man—but a cowboy.

—*Frank Tannenbaum*

The very first film to tell a story was a Western made in 1903, *The Great Train Robbery*, and movies ever since have reflected and expanded the American notion of the West as the location for some of our deepest mythology. The endless vistas and blue skies, the courage and independence of the heroes, the battles between law and lawlessness, between farmers and ranchers, between Indians and settlers, the issues raised by the encroachment of "civilization" in the form of railroads and bureaucracy—all these themes play out in literally hundreds of movies, many of them enduring classics. Stories of cowboys and gunfighters are our culture's equivalent to medieval stories of knights and chivalry. Like the knights, our heroes ride off in search of treasure, adventure, and honor, relying only on their spirit and their skill. The risk is total; this is not about whether a business deal falls through or whose car crosses the finish line first. Every confrontation can lead to death. Every decision could influence the foundation of what would become modern America. Westerns encompass every genre: gentle romance, action/adventure, drama, comedy, even musical. Watching the endless variations, we can try to understand the endless appeal of the Western and its heroes (and rare heroines), and what it tells us about the way we see our country and ourselves.

Red River

1948, 125 min, NR, b&w, 12 and up
Dir: Howard Hawks. John Wayne, Montgomery Clift, Walter Brennan, Joanne Dru

✳ **PLOT:** Tom Dunson (John Wayne) and his friend Groot (Walter Brennan) leave a wagon train to find some ranchland in Texas. The woman Tom loves begs to stay with him, but he says he never changes his mind, so he tells her to go on and he will send for her later. Indians burn the wagon train, and everyone on it is killed except for one boy, who comes over to Tom and Walter, shell-shocked and almost delirious, leading a cow. His name is Matthew Garth, and he is the only survivor. Tom smacks him, tells him it's all right, and then takes the boy's gun away, telling him, "Don't ever trust anybody 'til you know 'em." The boy replies, "I won't, after this. Thanks for telling me."

The boy with the cow and the man with the bull go on together, Groot following, until they reach the Red River, where Tom claims the land for his ranch. He draws his brand in the dirt—the river and his initial. Matthew wants his initial in the brand, too. Tom says there'll be one when he earns it, and Matthew agrees. The landowner's henchmen come to tell them to leave. Tom shoots one and sends the other one back with the message that this is his land now. He buries the man he killed, conducting a full burial service.

Fourteen years later, the ranch is filled with cattle, but they have no cash. They have to take the cattle to a city where they can be sold. Matt (now played by Montgomery Clift, in his first movie role), has just come home. Tom tells his men that it is their choice whether they want to go along; he knows it will be a long and dangerous trip. And it is. A man named Kelly starts a stampede by knocking some metal plates together while he is stealing a taste of sugar. Another man is killed by the cattle. Tom tells Kelly he will whip him. Kelly apologizes, but refuses to be whipped and draws on Tom. Tom and Matt both draw back, but Matt is faster, and shoots Kelly before Tom can kill him.

Later, when some of the men quit, Tom has them brought back and orders them hanged. Matt takes over, leaves Tom behind, and takes the cattle through the new Chisholm Trail, even though he is not sure there is a railroad on the other side. Tom comes after him, swearing to kill him. Matt sells the cattle successfully. When Tom catches up, Matt at first refuses to fight, until finally he punches back. Tess Millay (Joanne Dru) shoots at them both to stop them, telling them they love each other. Tom agrees to stop telling everyone what to do, and tells Matt he has earned the right to have his initial on the brand.

✷ **DISCUSSION:** This movie raises issues of loyalty and Oedipal conflicts, as Matt must decide between his loyalty to Tom and fairness to the men. Earlier, he acknowledges that he does not always agree with Tom, but will support him, as when he allows Tom to put his brand on cattle from other herds, and when he kills the men who threaten to quit. Matt says, "I'll take your orders about work, but not about what to think." But Tom becomes harder—and harder to reach. One of the quitters brought back by Cherry (John Ireland) says, "I signed a pledge, sure, but you ain't the man I signed it with." For the good of the men, for the good of the cattle, and for his own sense of justice, Matt has to take over.

PROFANITY: None.

NUDITY/SEXUAL REFERENCES: None.

ALCOHOL/DRUG ABUSE: None.

VIOLENCE/SCARINESS: Stampede, gunfights, and fistfights.

TOLERANCE/DIVERSITY ISSUES: Typical movie Indian, but at least played by an Indian actor and shown as smart and tough. The women are smart and tough, too—Tess keeps talking tough with an arrow in her shoulder!

✳ QUESTIONS FOR KIDS:
- When does Matt disagree with Tom?
- When does Matt decide to take over? Why does he decide then?
- Why doesn't Matt fight back at first, when Tom comes after him?
- How does Tess try to stop Tom?
- Tom is both good and bad in this movie—can you think of examples of both?

✳ **CONNECTIONS:** This is the first Western directed by Howard Hawks, who went on to make many others, including *El Dorado, Rio Brave,* and *Rio Lobo,* all with John Wayne. He was one of the primary auteurs of the movie mythology of the West, and his hallmarks are all here: men who are macho icons of cool, independent but committed to their own sense of honor; women who are tough and smart; and action excitingly filmed as though the viewer is right in the middle of it.

Compare this story to other stories about rebellions, like **Mutiny on the Bounty, The Adventures of Robin Hood, The Caine Mutiny,** and *Crimson Tide.* Compare it also to *A Few Good Men,* where the soldiers were judged guilty because they did what they were told.

If the ending of this movie seems a bit artificial, it may be because it is not what the author wrote. In the original version, Tom does come after Matt, Cherry shoots him, and they bring him back to die by the Red River.

✳Shane
1953, 118 min, NR, 8 and up
Dir: George Stevens. Alan Ladd, Van Heflin, Jean Arthur, Jack Palance, Brandon de Wilde

✳ **PLOT:** *Shane* is an old-fashioned Western about a battle of wills between homesteaders trying to plant crops and cattle ranchers trying to graze cattle on the open range. Shane (Alan Ladd), a reformed gunfighter trying to escape his past, rides into town and immediately gets caught up in the dispute. The homesteaders initially mistake Shane for one of the hired guns of the Stryker family, who dominate the cattle ranchers. But Shane soon bonds with a farmer named Joe (Van Heflin) and becomes a protector for the whole beleaguered community of homesteaders.

Stryker first tries to buy out the stubborn farmers but when that doesn't work, he tries to drive them away by force. He increases the pressure, finally bringing in a hired killer named Wilson (Jack Palance). Joe feels it is his responsibility to go to town for the final confrontation with Stryker, but Shane recognizes that this is not a job for a farmer—it is a job for a man with Shane's skills, a professional. Shane knocks Joe unconscious so that "nobody can blame him for not keeping that date," then deliberately walks into the trap set for Joe. Shane vanquishes the bad guys, then leaves town for good, acknowledging that he can't settle down: "There's no going back for me."

✳ **DISCUSSION:** By today's standards, Shane seemed riddled with clichés. This is the movie where the hero walks into a bar and orders "soda pop," only to be heckled by the grimy, bearded bad guys; this is the movie where the womenfolk wail, "We'd all be better off if there were no guns in this valley," while their menfolk go off to fight battles of honor; this is the movie where the homesteader gives an impassioned speech about how he won't be driven off his land because "our roots are here"; this is the movie where villains in black hats gang up on the hero in a fistfight, or shoot in the back. This movie may not have invented these archetypes, but it helped define them.

Yet these wooden and obvious stereotypes help frame the issues in ways that make them more accessible. how do people behave when "the law is a three-day ride from here"? What is true strength and what is weakness? When is violence justified? Joe's son, Little Joey, provides a child's-eye view of frontier justice as he observes how different men behave. He is proud of his father, but dazzled by Shane. He asks his father, "Can you whip Shane?" "Can Shane shoot better than you?" Little Joey emulates Shane, and asks for shooting lessons. He begins to define masculinity in Shane's terms and is disappointed when Shane does not fight the men who make fun of him for ordering a soda. Joe's wife, Marion (Jean Arthur), is not immune to his appeal. Joe understands this, telling Marion, "I been slow, but I see things. . . . I know if anything happened to me, you'd be taken care of— better than I could myself."

Shane, of course, remains heroic but remote, feeling deeply but recognizing that "there is no living with a killing—it's a brand that sticks." And Stryker's position is portrayed with some sympathy, as he explains how he came to this spot many years ago, facing death to tame it and make it safe, only to be followed by "squatters" who dam up all the rivers and fence in the grazing land. The movie has enough complexity so that children can recognize that there are genuine tensions to be resolved and hard decisions to be made, but ultimately it makes no secret about what is right and what is wrong.

Like ranchers and farmers, the community builders and the outsiders both serve different but necessary functions that coexist uncomfortably at best. It is very rare that anyone can become an insider after living successfully as an outsider—Dana Andrews as Fred in *The Best Years of Our Lives* learns that just as the bomber planes he used to fly in can be made into homes, he can learn peacetime skills. More often, we see people like Shane, or Johnny Ringo in *The Gunfighter,* trapped by the choices they have made. It is worth talking about how people make choices that put them in one category or the other, and the consequences that follow.

PROFANITY: None.

NUDITY/SEXUAL REFERENCES: Ryker suggests that Shane stays on at Joe's ranch because he has designs on Marion.

ALCOHOL/DRUG ABUSE: Drinking as a sign of manliness.

VIOLENCE/SCARINESS: Gunfights; characters in peril.

TOLERANCE/DIVERSITY ISSUES: Tensions between farmers and ranchers.

✳ QUESTIONS FOR KIDS:
- Why did Shane leave at the end? Why didn't he settle down and become a farmer?
- What makes Joey admire Shane? When does he change his mind? How will he feel about Shane when he grows up?
- Why did Stryker resort to violence? Was there another way to resolve the conflict between the farmers and the ranchers?
- Who is right? The farmers, the cattle ranchers, or Shane? Can you find ways that each of them is right and each is wrong?
- What disputes about land use are going on in your community? How are they resolved?
- What will Shane do next?

✳ CONNECTIONS:
This movie explores many of the classic themes presented in Westerns (and also found in stories about knights, war movies, and crime dramas), particularly the irony of the community's need for an outsider who can by definition never be a part of them, and the longing of each for what the other has. Like Johnny Ringo in *The Gunfighter* (though for a different reason), Shane finds he cannot hang up his guns and become like Joe. Like Destry in *Destry Rides Again,* and Will in *High Noon,* Shane finds that there are some problems that can only be resolved with guns.

Shane was the only Western directed by George Stevens, and it is interesting to compare it with some of the classic Westerns by veteran directors John Ford and Howard Hawks. Stevens was attracted to stories about outsiders, and he does a superb job of evoking the longing of the outsider for the society he helps make possible in this film, creating a sense of connection between Shane and the Starretts, but always showing that he can never be a part of what they are building.

Palance, who has only twelve lines in this film, became something of an icon of Western menace, a role that he parodied with great enthusiasm and affection in *City Slickers,* which brought him an Oscar. Warren Beatty says that the sound of the shots in this movie was so far superior to those in any other that he used the same technique in *Bonnie and Clyde.* Though the movie was nominated for several Oscars, including Best Picture, it won only for Cinematography, which is ironic because the footage was converted to wide-screen after it was shot, and lost some of its original composition and color.

Watch for Nancy Kulp (Miss Hathaway on television's *The Beverly Hillbillies*) as Mrs. Howell.

✳ **ACTIVITIES:** Kids will enjoy the classic book by Jack Shaefer, as well as some of his others like *Old Ramon*, a Newberry Honor book.

✳ MY DARLING CLEMENTINE
1946, 97 min, NR, b&w, 8 and up
Dir: John Ford. Henry Fonda, Victor Mature

Henry Fonda plays Wyatt Earp in the story of the shootout at the O.K. Corral. He and Doc Holliday (Victor Mature) represent law and justice. Walter Brennan as Old Man Clanton represents lawlessness and the abuse of power. This is one of Ford's best; like its hero, it has a quiet power.

✳ **CONNECTIONS:** There are at least half a dozen other movies about this famous confrontation, including two made in 1995, but this one is still by far the best.

✳ THE SEARCHERS
1956, 119 min, NR, 12 and up
Dir: John Ford. John Wayne, Jeffrey Hunter, Natalie Wood

In this influential drama, Ethan Edwards (John Wayne) and Martin Pawley (Jeffrey Hunter) spend years searching for Ethan's niece Debbie, captured by Indians who massacred her family. At first, all Ethan wants is to get her back. Later, as time passes and she is old enough to become romantically involved with an Indian, he becomes obsessed with the idea that he must kill her to prevent her being further sullied by contact with another race. When they find her, she tells them to leave her there; she has been with the Indians so long (and has been treated so well by them) that she feels the Indians are her family now. But Ethan will not give up, and they need to take her before the cavalry attacks the Indians. The corrosive effect of prejudice and the healing power of love are thoughtfully raised. Ultimately, when Ethan holds Debbie (Natalie Wood) in his arms, he can only say, "Let's go home."

✳ **CONNECTIONS:** One of the many legends about this movie is that Ethan's frequent phrase "That'll be the day" inspired the song of that name by Buddy Holly.

✳ SILVERADO
1985, 132 min, PG-13, 12 and up
Dir: Lawrence Kasdan. Kevin Kline, Kevin Costner, Scott Glenn, Danny Glover, Linda Hunt, Brian Dennehy

This affectionate contemporary re-creation of the classic Western is thoroughly enjoyable. Four men unite to oppose the corrupt forces running the town, and all of the classic characters of American mythology are there: the lovable gambler, the impetuous but big-hearted young gunslinger, the quiet but honorable cowboy, the beautiful woman on the wagon train who knows the real beauty is her land, the wise woman who runs the local saloon, the man who has been cheated and the man who cheated him.

✳ STAGECOACH
1939, 96 min, NR, b&w, 10 and up
Dir: John Ford. John Wayne, John Carradine, Thomas Mitchell

The stagecoach holds a variety of passengers whose lives are all dramatically affected by the journey: a doctor with a drinking problem (Thomas Mitchell in an Oscar-winning performance), a lady of easy virtue (Claire Trevor), a gambler (John Carradine) escorting the pregnant wife of a cavalryman, a banker traveling with his wife and a valise he won't let out of his sight, and a traveling salesman. They meet up with the Ringo Kid (John Wayne), who is arrested by the sheriff, and find themselves in the midst of a battle between the Indians and the cavalry and then in the midst of a gunfight between the Ringo Kid and the men who killed his father and brother. If much of it seems familiar, that is because this director, and especially this movie, established the conventions of the classic Western.

SEE ALSO:

Cat Ballou

Destry Rides Again

The Gunfighter

High Noon

The Magnificent Seven

Part 4

Special Occasions, Special Kids

A CALENDAR
OF MOVIES

Holidays are about the stories we think are important enough to pass on to future generations. In the midst of the fun of travel and vacation from school and trips to the mall, movies can remind us about the people and the struggles that led us to set these days aside and help us tell those stories to our children. Furthermore, children's interest in festivities or seasonal activities can help some of these classics capture their attention.

NEW YEAR'S DAY

❋ HOLIDAY

Set before and after a New Year's Eve party that becomes an engagement party, this story of setting priorities is a nice way to start the year.

MARTIN LUTHER KING DAY

❋ THE AUTOBIOGRAPHY OF MISS JANE PITTMAN

1974, 110 min, NR, 8 and up
Dir: John Korty. Cecily Tyson

Cecily Tyson is brilliant as a woman born into slavery who lives through Reconstruction, Jim Crow, and the early days of the civil rights movement. At the age of 110, she walks slowly and deliberately over to a "whites only" drinking fountain to taste the water. This is a rare movie that succeeds both as drama and as social history. NOTE: There is a good deal of bigotry and some violence.

❋ KING: A FILMED RECORD . . . MONTGOMERY TO MEMPHIS
1970, 153 min, NR, 8 and up
Dir: Joseph L. Mankiewicz. Sidney Lumet.

This excellent documentary features news footage of Dr. King's life and career from 1955 to his death in 1968. There is a ninety-minute version as well.

SEE ALSO:

The Long Walk Home The story of the Montgomery bus boycott is told through the eyes of a young white girl.

BLACK HISTORY MONTH

In addition to the preceding movies listed for Martin Luther King Day, families may want to watch the miniseries *Roots* and both parts of the PBS documentary miniseries *Eyes on the Prize,* both available on video.

GROUNDHOG DAY

❋ GROUNDHOG DAY
1993, 103 min, PG, mature high schoolers
Dir: Harold Ramis. Bill Murray, Andie MacDowell

An arrogant and self-centered television weatherman (Bill Murray) discovers to his horror that he has somehow gotten stuck in a time warp and must repeat February 2 over and over, apparently for all eternity—or at least until he gets it right. NOTE: This very funny comedy deserves a PG-13 for sexual references and behavior (he uses the knowledge he gains by repeating the days to sexually exploit a young woman and then tries to do the same with his producer, played by Andie MacDowell). But it can also be used to illustrate values like responsibility, empathy, and making every minute count.

VALENTINE'S DAY

I am not a fan of the perennial Charlie Brown Valentine special, which is too downbeat. It seems to me that even Charlie Brown should get the Valentine he dreams of. But it may be useful for underscoring to grade school kids how easy it is to hurt someone's feelings, and reminding them that no matter how they feel, if their school celebrates Valentine's Day, they should send one to every child in the class.

Older kids may enjoy some of the classic romances for Valentine's Day, including *The Enchanted Cottage* and *The Barretts of Wimpole Street, Romeo and Juliet,* or stories of teenage romances like *Say Anything, The Sure Thing,* or *Gregory's Girl.*

PRESIDENTS' DAY

For some reason, there are at least three good movies about Abraham Lincoln, and not one about George Washington, though he appears as a minor or off-screen character in movies like *1776*, the unremarkable *The Howards of Virginia*, the miserable *Revolution*, and even Bob Hope's *Monsieur Beaucaire*. Here's hoping someone in Hollywood realizes what an opportunity has been missed. In the meantime, though, we can concentrate only on Lincoln.

✻ ABE LINCOLN IN ILLINOIS
Raymond Massey plays Lincoln as a would-be politician, courting Mary Todd and debating Stephen Douglas.

✻ YOUNG MR. LINCOLN
1939, 100 min, NR, b&w, 8 and up
Dir: John Ford. Henry Fonda
Henry Fonda plays Lincoln as a young lawyer mourning his first love and defending his first clients.

SAINT PATRICK'S DAY

✻ DARBY O'GILL AND THE LITTLE PEOPLE
1959, 93 min, NR, 8 and up (but see note)
Dir: Robert Stevenson. Sean Connery, Janet Munro, Albert Sharpe
A pre–James Bond Sean Connery stars in this Disney fantasy about an Irishman (Albert Sharpe) who loves to tell stories about his adventures with the "little people," leprechauns, and learns a few lessons when the stories come true. Sharpe's daughter (and Connery's love interest) is played by the pretty and spirited Janet Munro. NOTE: Some children may be upset by a few genuinely scary scenes in this movie, especially those with the ghostly coach who comes to take away the souls of those who have died.

SEE ALSO:

The Quiet Man A love letter to Ireland by John Ford, John Wayne, and Maureen O'Hara.

EASTER

In addition to the classics that follow, other films relating to Easter include the allegorical *Strange Cargo,* with Ian Hunter leading a group of prisoners escaping from Devil's Island, and *He Who Must Die* (in French) about the performers in a Passion Play who begin to assume the roles of their characters. Jesus' life is portrayed in *The Greatest Story Ever Told, Godspell,* and *Jesus Christ, Superstar.*

✳ BEN-HUR
1959, 212 min, NR, 10 and up
Dir: William Wyler. Charlton Heston, Stephen Boyd

This exciting epic broke the record for the most Oscars, winning eleven of them, including Best Picture, Actor, Supporting Actor, and Director. Charlton Heston is Ben-Hur, a wealthy prince sent to become a slave by the jealous Messala (Stephen Boyd), a childhood friend, now angry because Ben-Hur opposes the Roman tyrants. Working as a slave, Ben-Hur collapses from dehydration, and is given a drink by Jesus. Later, returning to Rome as the adopted son of a consul, he seeks his mother and sister, but Messala tells him they are dead. He and Messala compete in a thrilling chariot race and Messala is killed, but not before telling Ben-Hur that his mother and sister are worse than dead—they are living in a leper colony. He finds them and takes them in search of the great healer, not knowing it is the same man who gave him the water when he was a slave. When they arrive in Jerusalem, they find Jesus has been condemned to death. Ben-Hur recognizes Jesus and tries to give him water, but the soldiers push him away. After the Crucifixion, his mother and sister are healed.

✳ THE GOSPEL ACCORDING TO ST. MATTHEW
1966, 135 min, NR, b&w, 8 and up (in Italian with subtitles)
Dir: Pier Paolo Passolini

This quiet, almost documentary-style portrayal of the life of Christ, as described by St. Matthew, was acted entirely by amateurs, including the director's mother, and remarkably, directed by an atheist and Marxist. Nevertheless, as its dedication to Pope John XXIII indicates, it is a dignified and moving presentation of the story.

❋ THE ROBE
1953, 135 min, NR, 10 and up
Dir: Henry Koster. Richard Burton, Jean Simmons, Victor Mature
Richard Burton plays a Roman centurion who presides over the Crucifixion and must find a way to redeem his soul.

PASSOVER

❋ MOSES IN EGYPT
Rabbit Ears, 6 and up
Danny Glover reads the story of how Moses was summoned by God to deliver the Israelites from slavery.

❋ MOSES THE LAWGIVER
Rabbit Ears, 6 and up
Ben Kingsley reads the story of the exodus and the delivery of the Ten Commandments.

❋ THE TEN COMMANDMENTS
1956, 220 min, NR, 8 and up
Dir: Cecil B. DeMille. Charlton Heston, Anne Baxter, Yul Brynner
Charlton Heston plays Moses in this powerful and epic story of the exodus of the Jews from Egypt, which includes the burning bush, the plagues, the parting of the Red Sea, and the gift of the Ten Commandments.

❋ THE PRINCE OF EGYPT
1998, 97 min, PG, 8 and up
Dir: Brenda Chapman, Steve Hickner. Val Kilmer, Ralph Fiennes
This animated version of the book of Exodus shows Moses as he grows from a fun-loving prince to a forceful and devoted leader.

MOTHER'S DAY

❋ I REMEMBER MAMA
1948, 138 min, NR, b&w, 6 and up
Dir: George Stevens. Irene Dunne, Barbara Bel Geddes
Kathryn Forbes's memoirs of her Norwegian immigrant family are lovingly brought to life in this classic, often found on television on Mother's Day. Mama is played by the luminous Irene Dunne, far from the sophisticated comedies and glossy romances she appeared in with Cary Grant, Charles Boyer, and Spencer Tracy. She presides over a large extended family with wisdom and good humor and, in the best possible sense of the term,

family values. A daughter's adored cat who is injured, a roomer who skips out on the rent, a shy sister who wants to marry her timid gentleman friend, a gruff uncle who is not going gently into that good night, another daughter who wants to write—she handles them all so smoothly that it isn't until the writer daughter sits down to tell her story that they see what she has done for all of them.

NOTE: This movie provides a good opportunity for a discussion of honesty. Mama bends the rules more than once. She pretends to be a washerwoman at the hospital when she is told that her daughter cannot have visitors. She gently blackmails two of her sisters so that they won't tease the third about her fiancé. She doesn't tell Dagmar the truth about her cat. And she lies to her children about the bank account so that they will feel secure. Yet she has an essential honesty, and all of her actions are grounded in her devotion to her family and her strong sense of values, lovingly communicated to her children.

Other Memorable Movie Mothers Include:

Distinguished actress Anne Revere appeared as strong, wise mothers in several movies, including **National Velvet** (for which she won an Academy Award), **Gentleman's Agreement,** and **Body and Soul.** Spring Byington was a warm and tender mother in **Little Women,** and a loving if dotty mother in **You Can't Take it With You.** Mothers who sacrificed for their children include *Stella Dallas* (who gave up custody of her beloved daughter so that she would have greater opportunities) and *Mildred Pierce* (who sacrificed everything for a spoiled and selfish daughter who still wanted more). Doris Day was a mother who seemed to actually enjoy coping with the chaos of four sons in *Please Don't Eat the Daisies.* Myrna Loy was often referred to as "the perfect wife," but she was also the perfect mother in **Cheaper By the Dozen** and *Belles on Their Toes.* Indomitable real-life mothers were played by Sally Field in her Oscar-winning performance in *Places in the Heart,* Susan Sarandon in **Lorenzo's Oil,** and Kathy Bates in *A Home of Our Own.* The most manipulative and selfish movie mothers include those in **Now, Voyager** and *The Silver Cord,* plus all those wicked fairy-tale stepmothers. But there have been understanding and loving stepmothers in the movies, too, including Lucille Ball in **Yours, Mine, and Ours,** and Julie Andrews in **The Sound of Music,** as well as future stepmother Shirley Jones in **The Courtship of Eddie's Father.**

✳ **CONNECTIONS:** Director Ron Howard cast his mother as the mother of astronaut Jim Lovell in **Apollo 13.** Director Rob Reiner gave his mother the best line in the movie (in the delicatessen scene) in his (not for kids) *When Harry Met Sally.* You can catch a glimpse of Ginger Rogers's mother, Lela, playing the mother of Ginger's character in *The Major and the Minor.* In the last scene of **In the Good Old Summertime,** the little girl playing Judy Garland's daughter in the last shot is her real-life daughter, Liza Minnelli. Catherine Scorsese appeared in several movies directed by her son, Martin, including *King of Comedy* and *Goodfellas*.

BASEBALL SEASON

✳ ANGELS IN THE OUTFIELD
1952, 101 min, NR, b&w, 6 and up
Dir: Clarence Brown. Paul Douglas, Janet Leigh

The Pittsburgh Pirates cannot seem to win until their tempermental baseball manager, Guffy McGovern (Paul Douglas), meets an orphan girl (Donna Corcoran) who sees angels in the outfield. Guffy must learn to control his temper—and his language—if the angels are to help the team. Janet Leigh plays the pretty journalist who helps both Guffy and the little girl live happily ever after.

✳ **CONNECTIONS:** The movie was remade in 1994 with Danny Glover as the manager and Tony Danza as a washed-up player. It isn't bad, but the original is better.

✳ DAMN YANKEES
1958, 110 min, NR, 10 and up
Dir: George Abbott and Stanley Donen. Tab Hunter, Gwen Verdon, Ray Walston

A middle-aged fan of the Washington Senators rashly trades his soul to the devil (Ray Walston) to help them beat the Yankees. The devil transforms him into a young and handsome star player (Tab Hunter) and then tries to make it impossible for him to exercise the "escape clause," using femme fatale Lola (Gwen Verdon) as his bait. The film is not entirely successful, but it has some sensational musical numbers, including "You Gotta Have Heart" and "Whatever Lola Wants."

✳ IT HAPPENS EVERY SPRING
1949, 87 min, NR, b&w, 6 and up
Dir: Lloyd Bacon. Ray Milland

In this delightful fantasy-comedy, a baseball-loving professor (Ray Milland) invents a chemical that repels wood. His dream of playing baseball comes true when he rubs the chemical on his mitt, so that when he pitches, the baseball jumps away from the bats.

✳ **CONNECTIONS:** The screenplay is by Valentine Davies, the author of **Miracle on 34th Street**.

✳ A LEAGUE OF THEIR OWN

1992, 128 min, PG, 12 and up
Dir: Penny Marshall. Geena Davis, Tom Hanks, Lori Petty, Madonna, Rosie O'Donnell

While the men were off fighting in WWII, the baseball owners sponsored a league of women baseball players, and this movie is a loving tribute to their skill and sportsmanship. Geena Davis is a superb pitcher who joins the team with her jealous younger sister (Lori Petty). Their teammates each find new self-respect, even the coach, a onetime star player (Tom Hanks), who is now an alcoholic. This is an exceptionally thoughtful, intelligent, and funny film with a lot of respect for its characters, and it makes its point about the impact the experience had on the women with sensitivity and skill. In one especially poignant scene, a black woman comes onto the field and throws a baseball to the players, showing that one important group is still excluded. NOTE: Some alcohol abuse and some sexual references; the character played by Madonna is referred to as "All the Way Mae."

SEE ALSO:

Field of Dreams An Iowa farmer builds a baseball field where his corn crop should be, and heavenly players return to play ball.

Pride of the Yankees The story of "the luckiest man in the world," Yankee Lou Gehrig.

FATHER'S DAY

✳ LIFE WITH FATHER

1949, 118 min, NR, 8 and up
Dir: Michael Curtiz. William Powell, Irene Dunne

William Powell plays the bombastic Clarence Day, in this movie version of the record-breaking Broadway hit, based on the memoirs of Clarence Day, Jr. Day, Sr. (Powell), is very much the head of a prosperous turn-of-the-century New York family, constantly trying to maintain his strict standards in a world that finds it hard to live up to them. His wife, Vinnie (Irene Dunne), is the heart of the family, and their deep love for each other gets them through their struggles over their different perspectives on religion and the management of their finances. The junior Day is well played by Jimmy Lydon, and his love interest is a ravishing teenage Elizabeth Taylor. Michael Curtiz (director of **The Adventures of Robin Hood** and **Casablanca**) keeps the various plot lines moving briskly.

SEE ALSO:

To Kill a Mockingbird Based on Harper Lee's memories of her own father, Atticus Finch is devoted, brave, wise, and deeply honorable.

Other Memorable Movie Fathers Include:
Paul Lynde in *Bye Bye Birdie* sings "What's the Matter With Kids Today," Christopher Plummer is the stern but loving captain in *The Sound of Music,* Clifton Webb is Frank Gilbreth, pioneer efficiency expert and father of twelve, in *Cheaper By the Dozen,* Paul Winfield is the decent man who will do anything for his family in *Sounder,* Cary Grant explains loss to his son in *Houseboat* and patiently opens his home and his heart to foster children in *Room for One More,* Laurence Fishburne is a father named Furious who insists on raising his son with strong values through troubled times in *Boyz N the Hood,* Yul Brynner is father to dozens in *The King and I,* and James Earl Jones is Mufasa, Simba's father, in *The Lion King.* Probably the meanest father in the movies was Edward Moulton Barrett, played by Charles Laughton, the tyrannical father of Elizabeth Barrett Browning in *The Barretts of Wimpole Street,* though Ralph Richardson in *The Heiress* comes close. Karl Malden played the demanding father of baseball player Jimmy Piersall in *Fear Strikes Out.* James Dunn was a charming alcoholic who adored his daughter in *A Tree Grows in Brooklyn,* as was Jackie Gleason in *Papa's Delicate Condition.* Grown-up sons have to take care of difficult fathers in *I Never Sang for My Father,* *Nothing in Common,* and *Memories of Me.*

❊ **CONNECTIONS:** Possibly the most accommodating Hollywood father was actor Walter Huston, who not only appeared briefly (without credit) in the first film directed by his son John Huston (*The Maltese Falcon*) but also agreed to take out his false teeth for a performance in another John Huston movie, *The Treasure of the Sierra Madre.* It paid off—Walter Huston won an Oscar, quite a Father's Day gift. John Huston did the same favor for another generation when he directed his daughter Angelica in her Oscar-winning performance in the (not for kids) *Prizzi's Honor.*

INDEPENDENCE DAY

❊ JOHNNY TREMAIN
1957, 83 min, NR, 8 and up
Dir: Robert Stevenson. Hal Stalmaster, Richard Beymer, Sebastian Cabot

From the book by Esther Forbes, this is the story of a boy who gets caught up in the early days of the Revolutionary War. He is befriended by Paul Revere and participates in the Boston Tea Party and the skirmish at Lexington. While not strictly accurate, the movie does a good job of exploring the reasons for the rebellion and, unlike many movies, makes it clear that no matter how just the cause, war is always a tragedy.

❊ 1776
1972, 141 min, G, 8 and up
Dir: Peter H. Hunt. Ken Howard, William Daniels

This rousing musical about the Declaration of Independence makes the Founding Fathers vivid, human, and interesting characters, and is so involving that you almost forget that you already know how it all turned out. William Daniels is the "obnoxious and disliked" John Adams, Ken Howard is Thomas Jefferson, who would rather be with his wife than work on the Declaration, and Howard da Silva is a wry and witty Benjamin Franklin. As they debate independence, we see the courage that went into the birth of the United States, and as they compromise with the South to permit slavery in the brand-new country, we see the tragedy. Outstanding family entertainment.

❋ **CONNECTIONS:** Kids will also enjoy the books by Jean Fritz, *Can't You Make Them Behave, King George?* and *Will You Sign Here, John Hancock?* and (also available in video) *Six Revolutionary War Figures* and *Shh! We're Writing the Constitution.*

❋ YANKEE DOODLE DANDY
1942, 126 min, NR, b&w, 8 and up
Dir: Michael Curtiz. James Cagney, Walter Huston, Eddie Foy, Jr.
The director of **The Adventures of Robin Hood** and **Casablanca** made this affectionate tribute to Broadway performer George M. Cohan, with James Cagney in an unforgettable (and Oscar-winning) performance as the brash but intensely patriotic singer-dancer-songwriter.

LABOR DAY

❋ THE PAJAMA GAME
1957, 101 min, NR, 8 and up
Dir: George Abbott and Stanley Donen. Doris Day, John Raitt
This musical about the romance between a representative of the union (Doris Day) and a representative of management (John Raitt) has the good sense to keep the plot out of the way of the wonderful songs (like "Hey There" and "Steam Heat") and the ebulliently energetic dance numbers (choreographed by Bob Fosse). But there is enough of a plot to provide an opportunity to discuss the ways in which workers and managers might feel differently about things, and how they work together to find the best solution for both of them. NOTE: There is a subplot about a man who is irrationally jealous and possessive, played for humor.

❋ **CONNECTIONS:** John Raitt, repeating his Broadway role, is the father of singer Bonnie Raitt. Vernon Hines is played by Eddie Foy, Jr., son of the vaudevillian portrayed by Bob Hope in *The Seven Little Foys.*

SEE ALSO:

Norma Rae A Southern textile worker helps a labor organizer bring the union to her factory.

BACK TO SCHOOL

See discussion of school movies.

JEWISH HIGH HOLY DAYS

✳ THE CREATION
Rabbit Ears, 6 and up
   Amy Grant reads the story of Genesis.

✳ JONAH AND THE WHALE
Rabbit Ears, 6 and up
   The story told each year on Yom Kippur is read by Jason Robards. Jonah tries to refuse God's command to warn the people of Ninevah, and is swallowed by a whale, a powerful reminder to do what he has been told, to help save the community of Ninevah.

HALLOWEEN

   Halloween is a magical time for children. It is the only holiday designed just for them. It gives them a chance to be the magical and powerful characters they hope to find inside themselves. It also gives them a chance to confront some of their fears in what we hope will be a safe and reasonably comfortable way. But children, even older children, are not as clear as adults on what is real and what is not. It is impossible to predict what will scare a child in a movie, which is why it is especially important for you to be there with your child for these movies. Some movies are simply too scary, though, and you should be extra careful to make sure that you are not going to be sending your trick-or-treater to bed with nightmares.
   There are three kinds of scary movie moments, though many movies feature all three techniques. First are surprises—something jumping out at you. Second is suspense—long anticipation of something jumping out at you. Third is horror—something really disgusting jumps out at you. Most young children can handle the first pretty well, but for some even that is overwhelming. Similarly, most middle-school kids enjoy the third (I'm not talking about slasher movies, just some oozing and scary faces), but some have no interest in it. Kids have a good idea of what they can handle. Don't push your child to watch anything that makes him or her uncomfortable. Halloween should be fun. And just because a child can repeat—and even explain—"it's only pretend" does not mean that he or she may be able to muster the distance and context necessary to enjoy a scary movie.
   Some Halloween movies raise troubling issues. *Hocus Pocus*, for example, marketed as a movie for children, has some inappropriate material—an

important element of the plot is that only a virgin can call back the witches by lighting the magic candle, for example. And the witches themselves, while comic in appearance, do genuinely dreadful things (like sucking the life out of children). Children familiar with **The Witches,** by Roald Dahl, may not be startled by the movie's portrayal of cruelty, but others may be. *The Nightmare Before Christmas,* in which the spirit of Halloween takes over Christmas celebrations, is inventive, even charming, but is genuinely disturbing. There is a scene where a child pulls a shrunken head out of a Christmas stocking, for example. It was not designed for kids and may upset them, especially those young enough to believe in Santa. Some parents have reported that *Casper* and other movies with ghosts raise questions that make kids uncomfortable about what happens when people die.

There are classic animated movies for this time of year, including the Peanuts cartoon *It's the Great Pumpkin, Charlie Brown,* Disney's *Ichabod and Mr. Toad,* and Rabbit Ears' **The Legend of Sleepy Hollow.** The first is fairly innocuous, especially for kids already familiar with Linus's odd belief that on Halloween a creature called "The Great Pumpkin" comes to the pumpkin patch. The magical movie musical **Meet Me In St. Louis** has a lovely episode about a turn-of-the-century Halloween celebration, very different from today's trick-or-treating. It shows the child's point of view, with the mixed feelings of excitement and terror, and the exaltation of being called "the most horrible" for being brave enough to "kill" the neighborhood grouch (throwing a handful of flour at him). A nice non-Halloween story about a little girl who befriends a ghost is **The Canterville Ghost** with Margaret O'Brien. Kids eleven and older who like scary movies might enjoy *Poltergeist, Beetlejuice* or *Ghostbusters* (all of which have the three types of scariness previously mentioned, though in the last two they are mostly played for laughs). And teenagers who are willing to forego *The House That Dripped Blood* or *Halloween IX* might enjoy the subtle and romantic scariness of *The Haunting, The Uninvited, The Ghost and Mrs. Muir, Bell, Book, and Candle, Dead of Night,* or *Pandora and the Flying Dutchman.*

ELECTION DAY

Movies about politics and elections are superb starting points for discussions of the challenges—and the obligations—of democracy. Many of these movies are morality plays of a kind, as people who seek power, even for the most altruistic of reasons, find themselves having to make compromises in pursuit of a greater good. Unfortunately, as they often realize too late, those very compromises often lead, insidiously but inexorably, to a corruption that makes it impossible for them to achieve their original goals. In *Alias Nick Beal,* that is presented explicitly through a literal bargain with the devil. In the other movies, it is presented allegorically, as the candidates must decide how far they can go without losing sight of what they originally wanted.

Preston Sturges, as always, gives us his own twist on the formula in **The Great McGinty.** The politician in question begins in happy corruption, and makes it all the way to the governor's chair before thinking about going straight.

Today's kids (and their parents) have a tendency to feel cynical and powerless as they are relentlessly bombarded with stories of scandal and abuse. These movies can help them think about the challenges, choices, and obstacles faced by people—including those of honor and integrity—who seek to gain or keep power, and our obligations as those who give it to them.

✳ ADVISE & CONSENT
1962, 139 min, NR, b&w, 12 and up
Dir: Otto Preminger. Henry Fonda, Don Murray, Charles Laughton

Henry Fonda plays a man whose nomination as Secretary of State is in jeopardy because of his past association with Communists. An honorable man, he has to struggle to decide whether to lie about his past in order to be able to accomplish goals that he believes will help make things better in the future. While dated in some respects, the "character question" and the wheeling and dealing (almost entirely regardless of the merits of the issues) are just as relevant today. NOTE: A Mormon senator commits suicide when he is blackmailed about a homosexual incident in his past, presented very obliquely by today's standards.

✳ **CONNECTIONS:** I cannot resist pointing out that the pretty secretary sitting behind Fonda in the confirmation hearing is my own mother, one of a number of real-life Washingtonians included to give the movie authenticity.

✳ THE BEST MAN
1964, 102 min, NR, b&w, 12 and up
Dir: Franklin J. Schaffner. Henry Fonda, Cliff Robertson

At the convention of an unidentified political party, two candidates vie for the nomination. One, played by Henry Fonda, is a thoughtful intellectual. The other, played by Cliff Robertson, is ruthlessly ambitious. Both use a range of tactics and face a range of ethical dilemmas. Fonda must decide whether to use some smarmy (and, as he finds out, untrue) rumors about Robertson—to beat him, or just to stop him.

Based on a play by Gore Vidal, one of the wittiest and most trenchant of writers and a close observer of politics (as a relative of the Gore family and of Jackie Kennedy), this is the best movie ever made about politics. It is worth discussing the difference in today's conventions, which are media events that merely ratify the nominees selected through the primaries, and discuss the advantages and disadvantages of each approach. NOTE: The rumors are allegations of homosexual activity while the Robertson character was in the service—it turns out that the Robertson character was instead involved in getting the homosexuals dismissed, for which he was commended.

✳ **CONNECTIONS:** Vidal appeared as an incumbent senator running for reelection in the R-rated 1992 political satire, *Bob Roberts.*

✳ THE CANDIDATE
1972, 109 min, PG, 12 and up
Dir: Michael Ritchie. Robert Redford, Peter Boyle, Melvyn Douglas
Eight years after *The Best Man,* this movie presented a very different kind of candidate—an idealistic (and telegenic) nonpolitician (Robert Redford) drafted (and manipulated) by professional "handlers." Originally assured that he can run a campaign with complete integrity (because there is no way he can win), things change quickly when he moves ahead in the polls. Listen carefully for the powerful last line.

✳ **CONNECTIONS:** Melvyn Douglas, elegant leading man turned character actor, saw a good deal of politics as the husband of Helen Gahagan Douglas, defeated by Richard Nixon in a notoriously vicious campaign for Congress.

✳ THE GREAT MCGINTY
1940, 81 min, NR, b&w, 12 and up
Dir: Preston Sturges. Brian Donlevy, Akim Tamiroff
Preston Sturges won an Oscar for the screenplay of this film, which was also his debut as a director. Brian Donlevy plays a bum who impresses the local Tammany Hall–style boss (Akim Tamiroff) by voting thirty-seven times in one day. He is rewarded with a political appointment and rises to become governor, always following Tamiroff's directions. But when he falls in love, he tries to go straight, and that proves fatal to his career as a politician. Sturges's characteristic clever dialogue and sharp satire make this memorable.

✳ **CONNECTIONS:** As a joke, Donlevy and Tamiroff briefly reprised their roles in a later Sturges classic, *The Miracle of Morgan's Creek.*

✳ STATE OF THE UNION
1948, 124 min, NR, b&w, 10 and up
Dir: Frank Capra. Spencer Tracy, Katharine Hepburn, Angela Lansbury
A popular industrialist (Spencer Tracy) is brought into politics by a wealthy and manipulative woman (Angela Lansbury) who thinks she can make him president. His estranged wife (Katharine Hepburn) must be at his side for appearances, so she is persuaded to come back to help him. He becomes more and more enmeshed in political intrigue and compromise until the final scene, which is so striking that life imitated art—Presidential

candidate Ronald Reagan borrowed Tracy's best line in a real primary debate and made front pages all across the country.

SEE ALSO:

All the President's Men The real-life story of the *Washington Post* reporters who would not give up on the story of the Watergate scandal.

Mr. Smith Goes to Washington An idealistic young man becomes a senator and fights for what he believes.

THANKSGIVING

It's a good thing that Thanksgiving has so many football games and the Macy's parade, because there aren't any great Thanksgiving movies. The Rabbit Ears video about Squanto is a good introduction to the origins of the holiday. Another related movie is *Plymouth Adventure,* with Spencer Tracy as the captain of the *Mayflower* and Oscar-winning special effects. In *Rugrats Thanksgiving,* the children befriend the live turkey Grandpa Lou won and manage to cause chaos for their mothers (who are trying to cook) and their fathers (who want to watch football).

HANUKKAH

❊ STORIES FROM THE JEWISH TRADITION
4 and up

One of a series of videotapes produced by Children's Circle, this tape features two folktales. *In the Month of Kislev* (narrated by Theodore Bikel), concerns a wealthy, arrogant merchant who sues the family of a poor peddler for enjoying the aroma of his wife's pancakes from outside their window, only to learn the true meaning of Hanukkah. In "Zlateh the Goat," written by Nobel Prize–winner Isaac Bashevis Singer, a poor family plans to sell their beloved goat to get what they need for the holidays, until their son has another idea.

CHRISTMAS

Christmas has inspired some of the most beloved family films of all time, and watching them together is a Christmas tradition for many families.

❊ A CHARLIE BROWN CHRISTMAS
1965, 30 min, NR, 3 and up
Dir: Bill Melendez

The first and best of the Charlie Brown animated television specials, this features the evocative Vince Guaraldi music and a gently funny story that reminds us of what is really special about the Christmas season.

✳ A CHRISTMAS MEMORY
1967, NR, 8 and up
Dir: Frank Perry. Geraldine Page
Originally made for television and now available on video, this story, based on Truman Capote's memoir of his lonely childhood, stars Geraldine Page as his one friend, an elderly woman relative with a young and generous heart. They make fruitcakes for everyone they know, find the best tree in the state, and make kites for each other to fly on Christmas. NOTE: Some kids may be upset about the boy's mean relatives, and by the (off-screen) death of his friend.

✳ **CONNECTIONS:** The 1997 made-for-television remake, starring Patty Duke, is also very good.

✳ HOW THE GRINCH STOLE CHRISTMAS
1992, 26 min, NR, 5 and up
Dir: Chuck Jones. Boris Karloff
The Dr. Seuss classic about mean Mr. Grinch is a great reminder of what matters most at Christmas.

✳ THE SANTA CLAUSE
1994, 97 min, PG, 8 and up
Dir: John Pasquin. Tim Allen, Wendy Crewson, Peter Boyle
Tim Allen plays Scott Calvin, a loving but bitter single father who invokes "the Santa Clause" when he goes outside to investigate a noise he hears on Christmas Eve and startles Santa, who falls off the roof. In Santa's pocket there is a card, directing whoever finds it to put on the suit, and explaining that "the reindeer know what to do." Calvin and his son end up delivering all the presents and returning to the North Pole, where Calvin is informed that he must now take over as Santa, and has eleven months to prepare. Calvin struggles to believe it was all a dream, even when he sprouts a white beard and puts on thirty pounds, but his son's belief never wavers. Calvin starts to become Santa from the inside as well as the outside, warming to children and categorizing people walking down the street as "naughty" or "nice." NOTE: Be careful about showing this to children who are dealing with the issue of whether Santa Claus is "real."

✳ THE SAVIOR IS BORN

Rabbit Ears, 5 and up

Morgan Freeman reads the story of the Nativity, with music by the Christ Church Cathedral Choir, Oxford.

✳ WHITE CHRISTMAS

1954, 120 min, NR, 4 and up
Dir: Michael Curtiz. Bing Crosby, Danny Kaye

Two ex-GIs put on a show to help a retired general, with the indispensable song sung by Bing Crosby. Danny Kaye, Rosemary Clooney, and Vera-Ellen are along to help out with other Irving Berlin standards, including "Sisters," "Snow," and "Counting My Blessings."

A CHRISTMAS CAROL

No story has been filmed more often, or more lovingly, than the Dickens tale of the selfish miser redeemed by the spirits of Christmas. And one of the Christmas season's most reliable pleasures is the chance to watch one or more of the movie versions of the story, perhaps while wrapping presents, filling stockings, or sipping the hot cocoa left for Santa. Every family should read the story aloud at least once. Here is a quick run-down of some of the best.

✳ A CHRISTMAS CAROL

1938, 69 min, NR, b&w, 6 and up
Dir: Edwin L. Marin. Reginald Owen, Gene Lockhart

This is a glorious example of the MGM studio at its best. Cratchit is played by Gene Lockhart, and Cratchit's wife and daughter are played by Lockhart's real-life family (yes, June Lockhart, in her movie debut, is the one who went on to television fame as Timmy's mother in *Lassie* and the astronaut mother in *Lost in Space*). Scrooge is Reginald Owen, and Andy Hardy's neighbor Anne Rutherford is a delectable Ghost of Christmas Past.

✳ A CHRISTMAS CAROL

1951, 86 min, NR, b&w, 6 and up
Dir: Brian Desmond-Hurst. Alistair Sim

This is the classic English version, with the magnificent Alistair Sim as Scrooge. No one does a better job with the giddiness of Christmas morning, sending the boy to buy the big turkey, than Sim. The scene at the end, when he shyly enters the home of his nephew to the song "Barbara Allen," is heartbreakingly touching.

❋ A CHRISTMAS CAROL
1984, 100 min, NR, 6 and up
Dir: Clive Donner. George C. Scott, Frank Finlay, Edward Woodward, Roger Rees
   George C. Scott plays Scrooge in an excellent made-for-television production, filmed on location in England.

❋ MR. MAGOO'S CHRISTMAS CAROL
   Don't laugh. This is a terrific animated movie, very faithful to the story, and with outstanding songs by the same team who wrote the music for *Funny Girl*. Watch for it, and set your VCR, as it is a genuine holiday classic.

❋ THE MUPPET CHRISTMAS CAROL
1992, 85 min, G, 6 and up
Dir: Brian Henson. Michael Caine
   Michael Caine plays Scrooge in this lively musical version, with Kermit the Frog as an adorable Bob Cratchit. This is probably the best version for small children, but there is plenty to amuse parents as well.

❋ SCROOGE
1970, 118 min, G, 6 and up
Dir: Ronald Neame. Albert Finney, Alec Guinness
   Albert Finney has the title role in a musical version, with gorgeous art direction, an excellent cast, but only one good song, "Thank You Very Much."

SEE ALSO:

   A Christmas Story A young boy wants a Red Ryder BB gun for Christmas in this delightful movie based on the memoirs of humorist Jean Shepherd.

   It's a Wonderful Life This Christmas classic about a man who finds out how many lives he has touched is superb family viewing.

   Miracle on 34th Street A little girl and her mother find out that Santa Claus is real after all.

HOMEBOUND

There is nothing like a movie on a day when you have to be indoors. Whether it is weather or illness that is keeping you home, a movie (or two) will allow your mind and spirit to leave it behind. So put on the popcorn, snuggle up on the sofa, sit back, and enjoy.

RAINY DAYS AND SNOW DAYS

Sometimes it is fun to watch movies that feature the weather that is keeping you indoors, like *Top Hat,* with the classic number "Isn't It a Lovely Day to Be Caught in the Rain?" or, *Singin' in the Rain* or, *The Rainmaker,* all of which put rain in the most positive light. *Thundercake* is the video version of the award-winning book about a cake that can only be made during a thunderstorm. A collection of short films called *Ida Fanfanny* includes a cartoon about thunder and lightning that is instructive and reassuring—and fun. The littlest kids will enjoy some of the videos about snow removal (like *Snowplows on Patrol* and *Snowplows at Work*) that will give them a sense of reassurance and power and provide some important safety tips as well.

The benefits of snow are the subject of two songs in *White Christmas* and the Pontabees use the snow on the mountain to help them capture their brides in *Seven Brides for Seven Brothers.* Snow comes to the rescue of Dorothy and her friends in *The Wizard of Oz* and *The Wiz.* The lovely, wordless short animated film *The Snowman* is a favorite of all ages. And

George Kennedy pulls an airplane out of a snowbank just in time in the original *Airport*.

Sometimes, though, the weather outside is so miserable that you feel like going far, far away. That's a good time for a nice, hot, dry movie like Disney's *The Living Desert* or, *Lawrence of Arabia,* or one of the silly but fun beach party movies with Annette Funicello and Frankie Avalon. Or, it may be time for a cheery musical like **The Music Man,** a rousing adventure like **The Adventures of Robin Hood,** or a zany comedy like **A Night at the Opera.**

GREAT DOUBLE FEATURES

Having to spend a lot of time inside is a great opportunity for a double feature. Sometimes the only thing better than a movie is two movies, and showing movies with related themes or other connections together can help us understand both of them better. All of these double features are recommended for kids who are high school age at least, with the exception of **The Scarlet Pimpernel/The Mark of Zorro/The Adventures of Robin Hood, Crisis at Central High/The Ernest Green Story,** and **The Wizard of Oz/ The Wiz,** which are appropriate for grade school kids and older.

✳ THE AFRICAN QUEEN/WHITE HUNTER, BLACK HEART
High schoolers

The first is a thrilling adventure-romance about a prim missionary and a rowdy boatman who transform his creaky riverboat into a missile to destroy a German gunboat. The second is a movie based on the real-life experience of what went on behind the scenes while *The African Queen* was filming. Clint Eastwood plays a director based on John Huston, who is more interested in killing an elephant than in making his movie.

✳ AIRPORT/AIRPLANE!
High schoolers

The first is a big movie with big stars (Burt Lancaster, Helen Hayes, Maureen Stapleton, Dean Martin) about life at a big airport during a big snowstorm—completely irresistible melodramatic fluff. Also irresistible was the chance to make fun of it in the most impertinent and subversive manner possible, and that is what *Airplane!* does, trashing not only *Airport* but also other airborne epics from *The High and the Mighty* to *Zero Hour*. There are a dozen jokes every minute, with at least one out of ten in highly questionable taste, so screen it carefully before allowing kids to watch.

✳ BECKET/THE LION IN WINTER
High schoolers

Peter O'Toole plays the same king, Henry II, at two very different stages of his career in these two movies. In the first, he is a young man who feels betrayed when his closest friend, with whom he has shared years of happy dissolution, takes his appointment as Archbishop of Canterbury seriously, and insists on remaining independent. In the second he is an old man trying to decide the future of the throne in the midst of the squabbles and power plays of his three sons, his estranged wife (Katharine Hepburn), and his mistress. One of his sons became King John, and the other (played by a young Anthony Hopkins) became King Richard the Lionhearted. Their story is told in **The Adventures of Robin Hood** and **Ivanhoe,** worth adding if you want a quadruple feature!

✳ BELL, BOOK AND CANDLE/VERTIGO
High schoolers

Jimmy Stewart and Kim Novak costarred in two movies, both romantic, but with utterly different tones. One is a comic romance about a witch who falls in love with a mortal, and the other is the darkest of Hitchcock thrillers. Watching them together gives you additional appreciation for the versatility of these two actors and for the range of mood and subject matter the movies provide.

✳ BORN YESTERDAY/NINOTCHKA
12 and up

All work and no play makes Jack a dull boy. Apparently all play and no work isn't much good, either. In *Born Yesterday,* a young woman who has never thought past her next mink coat finds that everything changes when she starts to read and ask questions. In *Ninotchka,* a Soviet official who does not believe in fun or frivolity finds that everything changes when she learns to laugh. Of course, both women also learn how to love in these two delightful comedies that are like mirror images of one another.

✳ CRISIS AT CENTRAL HIGH/THE ERNEST GREEN STORY
10 and up

The same true story—the integration of a Little Rock high school—is shown from two different perspectives, that of a white teacher and a black student. Both are well done, and *The Ernest Green Story* (produced by Disney) has a very good discussion of the strategy of nonviolence.

✳ DR. STRANGELOVE or: HOW I LEARNED TO STOP WORRYING AND LOVE THE BOMB/FAIL-SAFE

12 and up

In 1964, two very different movies with the same premise were released—both concern the consequences of a mistaken missile attack by the United States on the Soviet Union. *Fail-Safe* is a tense drama; *Dr. Strangelove* is the blackest comedy ever made. Both are very worthwhile viewing for a discussion of anything from arms limitations to ways of using art to comment on politics.

✳ FRANKENSTEIN/YOUNG FRANKENSTEIN

12 and up

The first is the classic film, based on the classic novel by Mary Shelley, about the scientist who wants to play God and brings a dead man back to life, only to see him destroy others. One possible double feature would be to combine it with its sequel, *Bride of Frankenstein,* or the more recent version, *Mary Shelley's Frankenstein,* starring Kenneth Branaugh and Robert DeNiro. But it might be more fun to watch it with the affectionate Mel Brooks parody instead, with Gene Wilder as the doctor, and Peter Boyle as the monster. Gene Hackman is terrific (though barely recognizable) as the blind man. NOTE: Some sexual references, including forced sex played as comedy.

✳ HENRY V/HENRY V

12 and up

Two brilliant but very different productions of Shakespeare's play about the coming of age of the dissolute Prince Hal provide us with an outstanding opportunity to evaluate the role of the director and the performer (in this case, both actors directed themselves) in establishing tone and perspective (and the validity of two very different approaches to the characters). The Laurence Olivier version, released during WWII, is patriotic to the point of jingoism. The Kenneth Branagh version is more naturalistic, less certain about the justification for battle. Both are riveting.

✳ KNUTE ROCKNE, ALL AMERICAN/RUDY

High schoolers

Two different movies tell true stories about football at Notre Dame and both are rousingly moving. The first has Pat O'Brien as the legendary coach and the story that inspired the most electrifyingly motivational locker room speech in history. (The dying player, George Gipp, is played by future President Ronald Reagan.) The second is the story of a kid who doesn't have talent or physical strength, but does have a big dream and the persistence to make it come true.

✳ THE RED SHOES/THE TURNING POINT
High schoolers

Two classic movies about the struggle to balance work and love are both set in the world of ballet, possibly because ballet is the most demanding art form in terms of physical effort and the commitment of time.

✳ ROMEO AND JULIET/WEST SIDE STORY
12 and up

Shakespeare's classic of the misunderstood teenage lovers from opposing sides was turned into the musical set in the slums of New York. For a triple feature, add *Shakespeare's Romeo + Juliet,* the 1997 MTV-style version, starring Claire Danes and Leonardo DiCaprio.

✳ THE SCARLET PIMPERNEL/THE ADVENTURES OF ROBIN HOOD/THE MARK OF ZORRO
10 and up

This is a triple feature of dashing heroes who have something else in common—all three of them have absolutely clear loyalty to people they believe are not being treated fairly by those in power. Robin Hood and Zorro oppose those of their own class. The Scarlet Pimpernel protects his fellow aristocrats from the bloodthirsty rebels. This can lead to an interesting discussion of how these heroes decide which side is right, and how they decide to carry out their opposition. Two of them use secret identities, and one does not. What are the advantages and disadvantages of each approach? Is it fair to say that the Scarlet Pimpernel would have been on the opposite side from Zorro and Robin Hood?

✳ SOME LIKE IT HOT/THE GREAT RACE
10 and up

Tony Curtis and Jack Lemmon star in both these classic—but very different—comedies. You could use this double feature to examine their abilities as actors and the way they adapt their characterizations and timing for different material, but I suggest you just sit back and enjoy two deliciously delightful films.

✳ THE TAMING OF THE SHREW/KISS ME KATE

10 and up

The Taming of the Shrew is one of Shakespeare's best comedies (and one of his best romances), the story of an angry "shrewish" young woman named Kate and the fortune hunter who marries her and tames her. Often misunderstood as antifeminist, it is in reality quite the contrary, as Kate and Petruchio each find their match—in both senses of the word. Cole Porter's delicious musical about battling ex-spouses who play opposite each other in a musical theater version of *The Taming of the Shrew* is colorful, tuneful, and very funny, with sensational dance numbers (featuring Ann Miller, Tommy Rall, Carol Haney, and Bob Fosse).

✳ THE WIZARD OF OZ/THE WIZ

8 and up

The all-black version of the classic story (and film) doesn't quite succeed, but the musical numbers (performed by Diana Ross, Michael Jackson, Mabel King, and Lena Horne) are magnificent, and it is a good exercise to see the story told from another perspective, both to see how a great story can thrive on many different interpretations and to examine how a different culture can bring its own feeling and experience to a story. NOTE: The screenwriter and director of *The Wiz* are white.

CHICKEN SOUP MOVIES

One of the best ways to watch movies is when you are sick in bed, propped up by pillows, with a box of tissues and a bowl of soup. But be careful in your choice of movie. Do not pick any of the following:

- Movies with complicated plots
- Movies with sad endings
- Movies that take place in a lot of snow or blistering heat
- Movies about sick people (except for *Ramona,* below)

You want movies that will cheer you up and make you feel good. Norman Cousins pioneered the study of helping your body heal through laughter after he recovered from a debilitating illness with the help of the Marx brothers and reruns of *Candid Camera.*

When you are sick, you need to watch:

- Movies with lots of singing and dancing
- Movies with silly (but not stupid) plots that do not require alertness

- Movies where everything ends happily

Ideal movies for kids (or parents) to watch when they are home sick:

❋ RAMONA: THE PATIENT

In this episode of the delightful Ramona series, based on Beverly Cleary's books, Ramona throws up at school and has to go home. It's very reassuring to kids who are embarrassed about getting sick or worried about the difficulties it creates.

ALSO GOOD FOR SICK DAYS:

Anything with Annette Funicello and Frankie Avalon

Anything with Bob Hope and Bing Crosby

Anything with Gene Kelly in a sailor suit

Anything with the Marx brothers

The Court Jester

It's a Mad Mad Mad Mad World

Maurice Sendak's Really Rosie (Especially the song about Chicken Soup with Rice)

The Russians Are Coming! The Russians Are Coming!

Singin' in the Rain

Yellow Submarine

THE BEST VIDEOS FOR KIDS FROM AGES 2–6

✳ ALEXANDER AND THE TERRIBLE, HORRIBLE, NO GOOD, VERY BAD DAY

30 min, 3 and up

All kids understand and sympathize with poor Alexander, who has a day in which everything goes wrong, from not getting a prize in his cereal to losing his marbles down the drain to having to watch kissing on television, and just generally being the littlest, with two big brothers. This musical adaptation of the popular book by Judith Viorst has music by Charles Strouse (*Annie*).

✳ **CONNECTIONS:** Children will enjoy the book, as well as the other books about Alexander and his brothers. There is also a live-action, nonmusical version of the book that may be available on video.

✳ ALL ABOUT HELICOPTERS and SNOWPLOWS AT WORK

30 min each, 2 and up

These two videos by Bill Aaron are techno-kid heaven. Narrated by children, each has exciting and informative footage, showing both men and women (but no minorities) operating the machinery. The helicopter video includes some terrific old footage of early "helos" and thrilling rescues by medical and military crews. The huge and powerful snowplows will delight kids the same way dinosaurs do. Both videos include information about the machines and the people who operate and maintain them, as well as important safety tips.

❋ THE BIG ADVENTURE SERIES

If anything can come close to answering all of a child's questions, it is this series of very comprehensive but accessible videos. Each about forty minutes long, these videos take kids on a tour of *The Big Aircraft Carrier, The Big Plane Trip, The Big Zoo, The Big Submarine,* and *The Big Space Shuttle.*

CHILDREN'S CIRCLE

The slogan of this wonderful company's videos is "Where books come alive!" They take outstanding books for children and put them on video, very simply, with superb narration and the books' illustrations. All are well worth watching.

❋ AMAZING GRACE AND OTHER STORIES
4 and up

Because she is black and a girl, no one thinks that Grace should play the part of Peter Pan. But she proves to herself and her classmates that she can be anything she wants to be. This tape also includes *Who's in Rabbit's House,* a Masai folktale narrated by James Earl Jones.

❋ THE DAY JIMMY'S BOA ATE THE WASH AND OTHER STORIES
3 and up

Four funny stories, including *Monty,* about an alligator who takes kids to school every day, until their nagging inspires him to take a vacation.

❋ DISNEY SING-ALONG SERIES
2 and up

Disney Studios has created music videos featuring songs from Disney movies, with compilations devoted to the circus, underwater scenes, flying, princesses, Christmas, friendship, the beach, and other subjects. Each video is thirty minutes long. They are lots of fun, and the lyrics on the bottom of the screen may help kids learn to pick out words and letters. They may also serve as a good introduction to the characters and stories for the littlest kids, preparing them for full-length features.

✳ HAPPY BIRTHDAY MOON AND OTHER STORIES
3 and up

In addition to the classics, *The Owl and the Pussycat* and *The Three Little Pigs,* this tape includes *Peter's Chair,* about a boy who wants to run away when he gets a new baby sister, and *The Napping House,* a lovely story about what happens when a wakeful flea on a slumbering mouse on a snoozing cat on a dozing dog on a dreaming child on a snoring grandma on a sagging bed has an itch. In the title story, a little bear thinks it is the moon's birthday, too, when he hears his own voice echoing back a birthday greeting.

✳ HAROLD AND THE PURPLE CRAYON
3 and up

Crockett Johnson's Harold has a magic purple crayon. Everything he draws with it comes to life. This video includes three stories about Harold and an interview with the animator, describing the challenge of bringing Harold to life on film.

✳ HOMER PRICE STORIES
4 and up

Two incidents from the life of Robert McCloskey's engaging hero are included on this video: the famous story of the doughnut machine that won't stop making doughnuts, and the adventure of going to meet superhero *Super-Duper* when he comes to town to promote his movie.

✳ KIDS FOR CHARACTER
2 and up

Tom Selleck and many of preschoolers' favorite television figures like Barney, Miss Frizzle of *The Magic Schoolbus,* the Puzzle Place kids, and Shari Lewis explain concepts like trustworthiness, fairness, caring, and citizenship in this entertaining and enlightening video. It comes with a workbook to help parents reinforce the ideas and serve as a starting point for discussions of values.

✳ KUKLA, FRAN, AND OLLIE
3 and up

Burr Tillstrom's Kuklapolitans starred in one of the most beloved children's programs in the early days of television. The puppets included the wide-eyed and optimistic Kukla, the mischievous dragon Ollie, operatic Madame Ogelpuss, Beulah Witch, and many others. Their unscripted conversations with the lovely Fran Allison inspired the story for the musical *Lili.* The video series is made up of selections from their 1969–71 series on PBS, and its gentle wit and imagination appeal to parents as well as children.

❈ LYLE, LYLE CROCODILE
25 min, 4 and up

The beloved book by Bernard Weber about the crocodile who lives on East 88th Street is beautifully brought to life in this delightful animated musical. The Primms, understandably a bit taken aback to find a crocodile living in the bathtub of their new house, quickly find out how lovable Lyle is, and soon can't imagine life without him. But Lyle's former owner, a performer, wants Lyle to rejoin his act. All ends happily, the songs (by Charles Strouse of *Annie*) are outstanding, and the narration, by Tony Randall, is superb.

❈ MAURICE SENDAK'S REALLY ROSIE (IN *THE MAURICE SENDAK LIBRARY*)
3 and up

The delightful books of poetry for children are put to the music of Carole King, who also sings them as *Rosie,* a girl who gets her friends to help her put on a show. *One Was Johnny* teaches numbers; *Alligators All Around* goes merrily through the alphabet; *Chicken Soup with Rice* teaches the months of the year; but the best of all is the story of *Pierre,* who always said, "I don't care" until he learned an important lesson.

❈ MAX'S CHOCOLATE CHICKEN AND OTHER STORIES FOR YOUNG CHILDREN
2 and up

Four stories include *The Circus Baby,* in which a baby elephant learns table manners and the importance of being himself, and *Each Peach Pear Plum,* in which children are invited to find hidden pictures.

❈ MIKE MULLIGAN AND HIS STEAM SHOVEL AND OTHER STORIES
3 and up

Mike loves his steam shovel, Mary Ann. But the new diesel machines are more powerful. Mike and Mary Ann prove themselves with one last job, which unexpectedly leads to a new home for both of them, with a way for them to keep being productive. In the other stories, *Moon Man* explores the earth, and *Burt Dow: Deep Water Man* explores the sea.

✳ THE ROBERT MCCLOSKEY LIBRARY
3 and up

This collection includes *Make Way for Ducklings,* about Mr. and Mrs. Mallard leading their babies through Boston to the Public Garden, and *Blueberries for Sal,* about two mothers—a bear and a human—who both take their children to pick blueberries, but absentmindedly each grab the wrong child when it is time to go home.

✳ SMILE FOR AUNTIE AND OTHER STORIES
3 and up

In the title story, poor Auntie does every silly thing she can think of to get the baby to smile. When the baby finally smiles, the kids in the audience are just as delighted. The tape also includes *Make Way for Ducklings* and the lullabye "Wynken, Blynken, and Nod."

✳ STORIES FROM THE BLACK TRADITION
4 and up

Folktales and fairy tales from Africa and one from the inner city demonstrate both the similarity and differences to traditional European stories. In addition to *A Story-A Story,* this tape includes *Why Mosquitoes Buzz in People's Ears* and *Mufaro's Beautiful Daughters.*

✳ STREGA NONNA AND OTHER STORIES
3 and up

Big Anthony gets himself into big trouble when he tries to use Strega Nonna's magic pasta pot, and finds that making it start is a lot easier than making it stop. This collection of classics also includes: *Tikki Tikki Tembo,* about the boy with the very long name; *The Foolish Frog,* sung by Pete Seeger; and *A Story-A Story,* about Ananse the Spider Man, who goes to buy some stories from the Sky God.

✳ **CONNECTIONS:** Compare what happens to Big Anthony to Mickey Mouse in *The Sorcerer's Apprentice* segment of **Fantasia.** Compare this story about Ananse to the Rabbit Ears version.

✳ THE UGLY DUCKLING AND OTHER CLASSIC FAIRY TALES
4 and up

In addition to the classic story of the ugly duckling who turns out to be a swan, this tape includes *The Stonecutter,* a fairy tale about a man whose wish for ultimate power teaches him an important lesson, and *The Swineherd,* about a prince in disguise and a spoiled princess.

✳ THE WILLIAM STEIG LIBRARY
4 and up

In these four beloved stories, characters must confront difficult problems with courage and inventiveness. In *Sylvester and the Magic Pebble,* a donkey who cleverly turns himself into a rock to escape a lion has quite a challenge changing himself back. In *Doctor DeSoto,* a mouse dentist must think quickly when a hungry fox shows up as a patient. *Brave Irene* must deliver a ballgown in a snowstorm for her seamstress mother. And Pearl the pig finds an amazing bone in a field of dandelions.

NATIONAL GEOGRAPHIC

4 and up

This series for kids is a terrific introduction to animals and nature.

✳ GEO KIDS: BEAR CUBS, BABY DUCKS, AND KOOKY KOOKABURRAS
How animals care for their young

✳ GEO KIDS: COOL CATS, RAINDROPS, AND THINGS THAT LIVE IN HOLES
Animal homes

✳ GEO KIDS: FLYING, TRYING, AND HONKING AROUND
Animals that fly

SCHOOLHOUSE ROCK

3 and up

The favorites of the 1970s are back and on video. Designed not by educators but by advertisers, they "sell" kids elementary math, grammar, and science concepts and facts with delightful songs and animation. The *American History* tape does very well with simpler issues, like how a bill becomes a law. But it suffers by having a subject that lends itself less well than arithmetic and grammar to the five-minute format. It suffers even more by the passage of time. For example, the representation of the pursuit of happiness as a man chasing a woman is insensitive by today's standards.

SESAME STREET

In addition to videos featuring highlights from the regular broadcasts, there are a number that deserve special mention.

✳ BIG BIRD IN CHINA and BIG BIRD IN JAPAN
4 and up
> Superb footage of faraway lands

✳ DON'T EAT THE PICTURES: *SESAME STREET* AT THE METROPOLITAN MUSEUM OF ART
4 and up
> A delightful introduction to art museums

✳ GETTING READY FOR SCHOOL
3 and up
> An encouraging and comforting video that makes it easier for kids to talk about concerns they may have

✳ I'M GLAD I'M ME
2 and up
> A reassuring self-esteem builder

✳ SHALOM SESAME
3 and up
> Several copies of the Israeli edition of Sesame Street are available on video.

SHARI LEWIS

Beloved entertainer-ventriloquist Lewis produced tapes that invite participation from kids, getting little couch potatoes off the couch.

✳ LAMB CHOP IN THE LAND OF NO MANNERS
44 min, 3 and up
> Shari and Lamb Chop visit a place where there are no rules and people

do not have to take turns—a very good opportunity to talk with children about why we have rules, and how we decide which rules to have.

✳ LAMB CHOP'S PLAY-ALONG
45 min, 3 and up
This tape includes Betchas, Tricks, and Silly Stunts, Jokes, Riddles, Knock-Knocks and Funny Poems, Action Songs, and Action Stories.

✳ 101 THINGS TO DO
45 min, 3 and up
Shari teaches kids all kinds of craft projects and games.

SPOT

✳ WHERE'S SPOT?, SPOT GOES TO THE FARM, and SPOT GOES TO A PARTY
Each 30 min, 2 and up
Eric Hill's books about the curious puppy are longtime favorites with the littlest children, because each page has a flap to turn back to find something fun. These videos bring Spot to life, and are excellent companions to the books.

THE BEST VIDEOS FOR KIDS FROM AGES 6–12

There is a terrific assortment of video series available for grade school-age children, many based on classic books and stories, others about subjects that will inspire their curiosity. Watching these videos can help encourage them to read.

RAMONA

Based on the classic series of books by Beverly Cleary, these stories are about Ramona, a third grader, her older sister, Beezus, and her family. She confronts many of the challenges of growing up with spirit and sensitivity, and everyone who has ever lived in a family will identify with these characters. Parents and children may want to read these books together first, or listen to them on the outstanding audiotapes, narrated by Stockard Channing.

✳ THE GREAT HAIR ARGUMENT
Beezus persuades her mother to let her get a new haircut for a special occasion but is not at all happy with the result.

✳ MYSTERY MEAL
When Beezus and Ramona criticize the dinner their mother makes, they are told to make dinner themselves.

✳ NEW PAJAMAS
Ramona experiences some embarrassments at school.

✳ PERFECT DAY/BAD DAY
Aunt Beatrice's wedding goes very well, but on another day, everything goes wrong. (Two half-hour episodes on one tape.)

✳ SIBLINGITIS
Ramona's parents are expecting a new baby, and Ramona has to sort out her feelings.

✳ SQUEAKERFOOT/GOODBYE, HELLO
In *Squeakerfoot,* Ramona has a problem at school and, misunderstanding what she hears her teacher say, thinks the teacher doesn't like her. It shows the importance of communication, as Ramona finds out that what she thought was a criticism was really just a misunderstanding. In *Goodbye, Hello,* Ramona and her sister put their squabbles in perspective when they must face together the loss of their cat. (Two half-hour episodes on one tape.)

WALLACE AND GROMIT

Oscar-winner Nick Parks created these Claymation masterpieces, which are thrilling, witty, and enormous fun for all ages. All three feature dim inventor Wallace and his silent but wise dog, Gromit. Kids may need a moment to get used to Wallace's English accent, but all family members will enjoy the fun. NOTE: Characters in peril and cartoon-style violence.

✳ A CLOSE SHAVE
Wallace and Gromit need money, so they start a window-washing business. One customer is the lovely Wendolene, the owner of a wool shop. Wallace builds a machine to clean and sheer the sheep for wool, but Wendolyne's dog turns out to have a diabolical plan to use the machine for something much more sinister.

✳ A GRAND DAY OUT
Wallace decides that he fancies some cheese for his tea, so he builds a rocket ship to the moon. The cheese on the moon is delicious, but there is a slight problem when they meet up with a robot who has his own ideas.

✳ THE WRONG TROUSERS

One of Wallace's inventions, mechanical trousers designed for walking Gromit, are rewired by a wicked penguin who turns out to be a master thief.

THE MUPPET MOVIES

Jim Henson's Muppets took to film with the same exuberant refusal to take themselves too seriously that they brought to television. All of their films are inventive, witty, and ideal family entertainment, featuring affectionate parodies of favorite movie genres and cameo appearances by a cavalcade of stars.

✳ THE GREAT MUPPET CAPER

1981, 95 min, G, 4 and up
Dir: Jim Henson. Charles Grodin, Diana Rigg

Kermit and Fozzie are reporters, and Miss Piggy is a would-be model. They must solve a missing jewel mystery in London. Although this is the series' weakest entry, it is still very watchable.

✳ THE MUPPET MOVIE

1979, 94 min, G, 4 and up
Dir: James Frawley. Charles Durning, Austin Pendleton

In this affectionate parody of every movie about a kid who dreams of becoming a star, Kermit sets out for Hollywood and manages to pick up most of the Muppets along the way (except for Big Bird, who appears just long enough to announce that he is on his way to public television). Miss Piggy, Dr. Teeth and the Electric Mayhem, Gonzo, Dr. Bunsen, and Beaker are joined by Mel Brooks, Steve Martin, Orson Welles, and Henson inspiration Edgar Bergen.

✳ THE MUPPETS TAKE MANHATTAN

1984, 94 min, G, 4 and up
Dir: Frank Oz. Dabney Coleman, Art Carney, Joan Rivers

Kermit and his friends arrive in New York City with hopes of producing their college variety show on Broadway. They are turned down by every producer they meet, and have to take jobs to support themselves. Finally, they get the chance to put on the show, but shortly before opening night, Kermit gets amnesia, and his friends can't find him until the very last minute.

SEE ALSO:

The Muppet Christmas Carol

Muppet Treasure Island

SHELLEY DUVALL'S FAERIE TALE THEATRE

Actress Shelley Duvall and her friends in Hollywood lovingly bring classic fairy tales to life in this series originally produced for the Showtime cable network. The casting is impeccable, with Elizabeth McGovern as Snow White, Bernadette Peters as Sleeping Beauty, Pam Dawber as the Little Mermaid, Liza Minnelli as the princess who feels the pea beneath all the mattresses, Billy Crystal as one of the Little Pigs, Jeff Goldblum as the Big Bad Wolf, James Earl Jones as the genie, Robin Williams as the Frog Prince, and Matthew Broderick, Christopher Reeve, and Tom Conti as various Charming Princes. The art direction, based on classic illustrations, makes up in imagination what it lacks in opulence, and the stories are told with wit and affection. A second series, of folk tales, is also very good.

✳ ALADDIN AND HIS WONDERFUL LAMP

Robert Carradine as Aladdin and James Earl Jones as the genie appear in a more traditional story than the Disney animated version.

✳ BEAUTY AND THE BEAST

Susan Sarandon and Klaus Kinski appear in this version of the tale about the beautiful woman who learns to love a beast.

✳ THE BOY WHO LEFT HOME TO FIND OUT ABOUT THE SHIVERS

A boy (Peter MacNichol) who has never felt fear seeks adventure that will show him what it is like.

✳ CINDERELLA

Jennifer Beals and Matthew Broderick play the girl who sleeps in the cinders and the prince she meets at the ball.

✳ THE DANCING PRINCESSES

Every morning, the seven princesses are exhausted, and their slippers are worn out, but they have no memory of where they have been until an enterprising young man (Peter Weller) follows them and helps them break the spell.

❊ THE EMPEROR'S NEW CLOTHES

Alan Arkin and Art Carney are the con men who find the perfect scheme—telling the king that their cloth is so special that it is invisible to those who are stupid or unfit for their jobs.

❊ GOLDILOCKS AND THE THREE BEARS

Tatum O'Neal is the inquisitive girl who tries the chairs, beds, and porridge of the three bears.

❊ HANSEL AND GRETEL

When a brother and sister are captured by the witch (glamorous Joan Collins under a lot of makeup), they show courage, loyalty, and teamwork in figuring out a way to escape.

❊ JACK AND THE BEANSTALK

Dennis Christopher (*Breaking Away*) plays Jack, who trades a cow for magic beans, leading him to a giant's treasure.

THE GREAT COMPOSERS

Devine Entertainment has produced a very nice series of videos depicting great composers in (fictional) encounters with children. In each story, a child helps the musician find the confidence, the courage, or the inspiration to create. The programs are very appealing, a terrific introduction to classical music, and a great starting point for listening to the pieces excerpted in the videos in full.

❊ BACH'S FIGHT FOR FREEDOM

Bach is a court organist who wants to be permitted to compose and perform. Frederick, the son of servants, wants to be a stonemason. Bach is jailed for insubordination, but both he and Frederick are able to realize their dreams.

✳ BIZET'S DREAM

As Bizet struggles to finish work on *Carmen,* he is befriended by his twelve-year-old piano student, who is worried about her father, fighting in Spain.

✳ HANDEL'S LAST CHANCE

James, a poor boy, is enrolled in an expensive school by his mother. He is treated as an outsider until he is selected for a solo in a performance of Handel's *Messiah.* He and Handel form a friendship, and Handel stands up for James when he is wrongly accused of stealing. James then helps to make the *Messiah* the success Handel hoped for.

✳ LISZT'S RHAPSODY

Liszt is a spectacular success as a performer, but wants the chance to compose. He meets Josy, a young boy who plays the violin in the streets, and arranges for Josy to live with him and receive formal training. Liszt, inspired by the folk tunes Josy plays, is able to compose successfully.

✳ ROSSINI'S GHOST

Reliana helps Rosalie, her grandmother, and Martina, her grandmother's friend, in the kitchen. As they argue about their past, Reliana is transported back to the time they are describing, just before the premiere of a new opera by Rossini. One problem after another plagues the production, but Reliana, as a ghost only Rossini can see, provides encouragement and learns something herself about art, persistence, and friendship.

✳ STRAUSS: THE KING OF THREE-QUARTER TIME

Nicholas, a stable boy afraid of his abusive stepfather, finds a friend in Strauss, a successful composer who fears the disapproval of his own father.

SHAKESPEARE ANIMATED TALES

These half-hour animated versions of Shakespeare's plays are a great introduction to the stories and the language of the classics. NOTE: The tragedies are very bloody and violent, as Shakespeare wrote them.

✳ HAMLET

Hamlet, a young Danish prince, is devastated to learn that his uncle had murdered his father and married his mother so that he could become king. As Hamlet agonizes about how he should respond, his behavior is so bitter and angry that everyone around him wonders if he has become ill. He has a traveling theatrical troupe reenact the murder to see his uncle's reaction and ultimately chooses to take action to punish those who deserve it.

✳ JULIUS CAESAR

After the wicked and ambitious Cassius persuades the honorable Brutus that Caesar's power is a threat to the freedom of Rome, Brutus assassinates Caesar, stabbing him on his way to the Senate. Antony hides his fury so that he can have the opportunity to speak at the funeral. His oration so inflames the people that they drive the assassins out of Rome.

✳ MACBETH

Macbeth, a victorious general, meets three witches who predict that he will become king of Scotland. He becomes consumed with ambition, and he and his wife plot to kill Duncan, the king, and seize the throne. Lady Macbeth is driven mad by her crime, Macbeth is killed, and Duncan's son becomes king.

✳ TWELFTH NIGHT

A young woman named Viola, washed ashore after a shipwreck, disguises herself as a man for protection, and goes to work for Orsino, a lord. They form a fast friendship, and he tells "Cesario" (the name she adopts) to visit Olivia, a nearby noblewoman, to persuade her to marry him. Olivia, instead of falling in love with Orsino, falls for Cesario. This is all complicated further when Viola's brother, Sebastian, washed up farther along the shore, and believing her to be dead, comes to the town and is mistaken for Cesario while Cesario is mistaken for him. As in the title of another Shakespeare comedy, "all's well that ends well."

GLOBAL STAGE

This company has a terrific idea—they seek out the best theatrical productions for children and put them on video, with introductions that help prepare kids for some of the issues raised in the story and backstage tours to demonstrate stagecraft. The videos available so far are:

✳ CYRANO

Cyrano, a brilliant poet/soldier, loves the beautiful Roxanne, but she is interested only in the handsome Christian. Cyrano writes love letters for his awkward friend, courting Roxanne on Christian's behalf. Three young actors play all the parts in this simple but very moving production.

✳ FRANKENSTEIN

This appealing production focuses more on the tragedy than the horror of the story, as a young man devastated by the loss of his mother tries to find a way for science to triumph over death. The introduction puts this into the context of current debates over the ethics of scientific experimentation.

✳ PINOCCHIO

The classic story of the wooden puppet brought to life shows how Pinocchio must work hard to deserve the privilege of becoming a human boy. Presented in a charming, commedia dell'arte production, this version provides insight into the nature of storytelling.

WONDERWORKS

Some of the shows from the PBS series called *Masterpiece Theatre* for Children are now available on video.

✳ THE CHRONICLES OF NARNIA

(3 *tapes*)

The classic fantasy by C. S. Lewis is brought to life.

✳ THE HOBOKEN CHICKEN EMERGENCY

This is a funny story about a 266-pound chicken named Henrietta.

✳ HOW TO BE A PERFECT PERSON IN JUST THREE DAYS

A twelve-year-old who feels that everything he does is wrong agrees to follow the advice of an eccentric man (Wallace Shawn) who promises him perfection. The requirement for the first day is to wear broccoli on a string around his neck, and it gets even wilder after that. This is a terrifically funny and insightful story.

✳ JACOB HAVE I LOVED

Louise (Bridget Fonda), growing up on an island during WWII, feels that her twin sister is everything she is not: talented, beautiful, admired. She loves her sister, but she is jealous and bitter. She longs to leave the island and help in the war effort. She meets a retired captain, who becomes her friend, but she is hurt when he uses a small legacy to pay for her sister's music school. He tells her that she is not ready to leave because she is still the captive of her jealousy, and has not learned enough about who she is. He tells her that she needs to "find the one gift that's yours because that's the sign of God in you." When she helps with the birth of another set of twins on the island, she begins to learn to leave behind her anger and resentment, accept unfairness, and make her own destiny.

✳ A LITTLE PRINCESS

(3 tapes)

This is the most authentic version of the classic book by Frances Hodgson Burnett, exceptionally well-produced, and a genuine delight.

RABBIT EARS

Rabbit Ears has produced genuine works of art for the whole family. These classic stories are read aloud by Meryl Streep, Jack Nicholson, Robin Williams, Denzel Washington, and other fine actors, accompanied by glorious original music and outstanding illustrations. They have been issued in several categories: Storybook Classics; We All Have Tales (world folklore); American Heroes and Legends (American folklore); The Greatest Stories Ever Told (Bible stories); and Holiday Classics. Available as audiotapes and videotapes, every one of them is a jewel.

American Heroes and Legends

These wild and comic tales of larger-than-life heroes tell us a lot about the way Americans like to see themselves. From Paul Bunyan to Pecos Bill to Stormalong, we like our heroes to be strong, confident, and courageous. And, with rare exceptions like John Henry, we like them to be able to triumph over any challenge. The sense of newness of our country is reflected in the many stories that purport to explain its traditions and even its terrain. Contrast the folk heroes with the real ones, like Annie Oakley, Squanto, and Sacajawea.

✳ ANNIE OAKLEY

Read by Keith Carradine; music by Los Lobos

This is a far more accurate depiction of the greatest sharpshooter in history than *Annie Get Your Gun* and far more interesting and moving as well. Keith Carradine, who portrayed Will Rogers on Broadway, re-creates that role as the narrator, a dear friend of Annie Oakley's.

✳ BRER RABBIT AND BOSS LION

Read by Danny Glover; music by Dr. John
    In this Uncle Remus tale, clever Brer Rabbit outsmarts Boss Lion.

✳ BRER RABBIT AND THE WONDERFUL TAR BABY

Read by Danny Glover; music by Taj Mahal
    This time Brer Rabbit is ultimately outsmarted himself.

✳ **CONNECTIONS:** See Disney's *Song of the South* for another version of the Brer Rabbit stories (and for "Zippity Doo Dah").

✳ DAVY CROCKETT

Read by Nicolas Cage; music by David Bromberg
    This is the "half-alligator and half-snapping turtle with a touch of earthquake thrown in" hero who could grin a bear down out of a tree.

✳ FOLLOW THE DRINKING GROUND—A STORY OF THE UNDERGROUND RAILROAD

Read by Morgan Freeman; music by Taj Mahal
    Runaway slaves used a song to pass on the information about the Underground Railroad. This touching story covers one family's flight toward freedom.

✳ JOHN HENRY

Read by Denzel Washington; music by B. B. King
    John Henry, the greatest of all steel-driving men, proves that no machine can beat him.

✳ JOHNNY APPLESEED

Read by Garrison Keillor; music by Mark O'Connor
    A gentle soul with a frying pan on this head roamed America planting apple trees, and is still fondly remembered.

❋ THE LEGEND OF SLEEPY HOLLOW
Read by Glenn Close; music by Tim Story
    Washington Irving's story of Ichabod Crane's meeting with the headless horseman is a Halloween perennial.

❋ **CONNECTIONS:** Compare this to the Disney version. In *Curse of the Cat People,* this legend is mentioned.

❋ MOSE THE FIREMAN
Read by Michael Keaton; music by John Beasley and Walter Becker
    Mose is the brave fireman in the New York of the 1800s. Discovered as a foundling by fire fighters in 1809, he grew up in the firehouse and became a hero, helping to create the subway system.

❋ PAUL BUNYAN
Read by Jonathan Winters; music by Leo Kottke with Duck Baker
    Paul Bunyan, big as a mountain and strong as a bear, was the greatest of all lumberjacks, with the help of Babe, the Blue Ox.

❋ PECOS BILL
Read by Robin Williams; music by Ry Cooder
    Pecos Bill is the cowboy who put the "Wild" in Wild West, rode hurricanes for fun, and is credited with inventing the lasso and the cattle drive.

❋ PRINCESS SCARGO & THE BIRTHDAY PUMPKIN
Read by Geena Davis; music by Michael Hedges
    An Indian girl gives up her birthday gift to save her village.

❋ RIP VAN WINKLE
Read by Anjelica Huston; music by Jay Ungar and Molly Mason
    Lazy Rip went to sleep one night, after playing ninepins with mysterious mountain men, to wake up twenty years later and find that America is no longer a British colony.

❋ THE SONG OF SACAJAWEA
Read by Laura Dern; music by David Lindley
    Lewis and Clark were guided on their famous expedition up the Missouri River and across the Rocky Mountains by a brave and strong seventeen-year-old Indian woman named Sacajawea.

✳ SQUANTO AND THE FIRST THANKSGIVING
Read by Graham Greene; music by Paul McCandless

The first English settlers in America would not have survived without the help of Squanto, an English-speaking Indian who had been captured by the Spanish and sold into slavery. Years later, after his return to America, he was instrumental in forging a friendship with the settlers.

✳ STORMALONG
Read by John Candy; music by NRBQ

Captain Stormalong commands the biggest ship in the world, the *Cursor*, so huge its sides had to be soaped to get it through the English Channel, leaving the white marks of the soap on the Cliffs of Dover. Stormalong loves the sea so much that once, when he was in Utah, he cried so hard that his tears created the Great Salt Lake.

✳ THE TALKING EGGS
Read by Sissy Spacek; music by Michael Doucet with BeauSoleil

In this Cajun folktale, a girl who befriends a mysterious old woman is rewarded with magical talking eggs.

Storybook Classics

✳ THE ELEPHANT'S CHILD
Read by Jack Nicholson; music by Bobby McFerrin

Jack Nicholson reads Kipling's glorious prose (remember the "great, green greasy Limpopo River"?) accompanied by Bobby McFerrin (who produces every one of the sounds with his own hands and mouth). In this most famous of the "Just So" stories, a curious little elephant emerges from an encounter with a crocodile with a long nose that turns out to be very useful.

✳ THE EMPEROR AND THE NIGHTINGALE
Read by Glenn Close; music by Mark Isham

An emperor thinks that he can improve on a live nightingale by making one of jewels and clockworks, but finds that it cannot match the original.

✳ THE EMPEROR'S NEW CLOTHES
Read by Sir John Gielgud; music by Mark Isham

Two tricksters fool the emperor into thinking he is wearing the finest cloth in the land, when in fact he is wearing nothing at all.

✳ THE FISHERMAN AND HIS WIFE
Read by Jodie Foster; music by Van Dyke Parks
  When a fisherman is given three wishes, he and his wife manage to come away with nothing.

✳ HOW THE LEOPARD GOT HIS SPOTS
Read by Danny Glover; music by Ladysmith Black Mambazo
  In Kipling's "Just So" story, we learn how the leopard had to adapt after he moved to the forest, where his light fur no longer camouflaged him.

✳ HOW THE RHINOCEROS GOT HIS SKIN & HOW THE CAMEL GOT HIS HUMP
Read by Jack Nicholson; music by Bobby McFerrin
  In both of these "Just So" stories arrogant animals learn their lesson in a way they and their descendants will never forget.

✳ RED RIDING HOOD and GOLDILOCKS
Read by Meg Ryan; music by Art Lande
  Two spunky heroines get into trouble when they go off on their own, but they find a way out.

✳ THE STEADFAST TIN SOLDIER
Read by Jeremy Irons; music by Mark Isham
  The loyalty of the tin soldier and his willingness to endure any hardship for love make this poignant story a classic. NOTE: The sad ending may upset some children.

✳ THE TALE OF PETER RABBIT and THE TALE OF MR. JEREMY FISHER
Read by Meryl Streep; music by Lyle Mays
  Two of Beatrix Potter's classic stories about the little creatures in the garden: Peter Rabbit finds trouble when he goes too far from home. Mr. Jeremy Fisher turns out not to deserve his name when he has one fishing mishap after another, but he ends up having a very enjoyable evening with his understanding friends in spite of it.

✳ THE THREE BILLY GOATS GRUFF and THE THREE LITTLE PIGS
Read by Holly Hunter; music by Art Lande

In both stories, three siblings must figure out a way to protect themselves from being devoured.

✳ THUMBELINA

Read by Kelly McGillis; music by Mark Isham

The tiny heroine kidnapped by a toad has a number of adventures before finding happiness with a handsome king.

✳ THE UGLY DUCKLING

Read by Cher; music by Patrick Ball

All children feel like ugly ducklings sometimes, and this story should remind them that all of us have a swan inside.

✳ THE VELVETEEN RABBIT

Read by Meryl Streep; music by George Winston

A toy rabbit becomes "real" by being loved.

We All Have Tales

✳ ALADDIN AND THE MAGIC LAMP

Read by John Hurt; music by Mickey Hart

Perhaps the most famous of the stories from the Middle Eastern Thousand and One Night tales, this is the classic about the boy who finds the lamp with the genie and wins the love of the Sultan's daughter.

✳ ANANSI

Read by Denzel Washington; music by UB40

Anansi, the spider of Jamaican folklore, spins stories as well as webs, and loves to make himself the hero.

✳ THE BOY WHO DREW CATS

Read by William Hurt; music by Mark Isham

A Japanese boy will only draw cats, so everyone makes fun of him. But it turns out that his skill is the one that will save them all.

✳ THE BREMEN TOWN MUSICIANS

Read by Bob Hoskins; music by Eugene Friesen

A dog, cat, rooster, and donkey must adapt when they are no longer needed, and they decide to try to become musicians. This comic tale from Germany has an important message about persistence, cooperation, and following your dreams.

✳ EAST OF THE SUN, WEST OF THE MOON
Read by Max von Sydow; music by Lyle Mays

This is a Norwegian tale about a girl who goes to live with a white bear so that her family will be wealthy. But when she ignores his advice, she must travel to the castle of the Troll Queen.

✳ FINN MCCOUL
Read by Catherine O'Hara; music by Boys of the Lough

Ireland's most famous champion has to use his brain (and his wife's cooking) to help him defeat the giant.

✳ THE FIREBIRD
Read by Susan Sarandon; music by Mark Isham

The Tsar of Russia tells an archer he must bring him the mythical firebird and the Princess Vassilia so he can marry her. But the archer wants to marry Vassilia himself and must find a way to outsmart the tsar.

✳ THE FIVE CHINESE BROTHERS
Read by John Lone; music by Bill Douglass and David Austin

Each of the five brothers has one special power, and all are necessary to outwit the cruel emperor.

✳ **CONNECTIONS:** Compare this to *The Fool and the Flying Ship*, which also involves a variety of individuals with special powers.

✳ JACK AND THE BEANSTALK
Read by Michael Palin; music by David A. Stewart

Monty Python alumnus Michael Palin stresses the comedy in the English story of Jack and the giant he found at the top of the beanstalk.

✳ KING MIDAS AND THE GOLDEN TOUCH
Read by Michael Caine; music by Ellis Marsalis, featuring Yo-Yo Ma

The ancient Greek story about a king who wished to have anything he touched turn to gold teaches us an important lesson when he finds that he has destroyed the thing he loved most.

❄ KOI AND THE KOLA NUTS

Read by Whoopi Goldberg; music by Herbie Hancock

The son of the chief wants to be honored, in this African folktale, but he must prove that he deserves it, and in doing so finds that he must rely on some unexpected friends.

❄ THE MONKEY PEOPLE

Read by Raul Julia, music by Lee Ritenour

In this story set in South America, lazy people are delighted when a man brings them monkeys to do all their work, until they discover that the monkeys have gone too far.

❄ PEACHBOY

Read by Sigourney Weaver; music by Ryuichi Sakamoto

A little boy found inside a peach becomes the courageous hero who defeats the ogres and teaches his friends to cooperate in this Japanese folktale.

❄ PINOCCHIO

Read by Danny Aiello; music by Les Miserables Blues Band

The puppet boy's nose grows when he tells a lie in this Italian story, and he must learn many lessons about honesty and devotion before he can become a real boy.

❄ PUSS IN BOOTS

Read by Tracey Ullman; music by Jean Luc Ponty

In this French folktale, the youngest son of a miller feels cheated when his father leaves him nothing but a cat. But the cat turns out to be clever enough to save himself by finding a way to make his master wealthy. NOTE: Parents may want to discuss this story, in which a young man is rewarded without any justification.

❄ RUMPELSTILTSKIN

Read by Kathleen Turner; music by Tangerine Dream

A German folktale from the Brothers Grimm, this is the story of a young woman whose father brags that she can spin straw into gold. She is told by the king to prove it or she will die. She is helped by a mysterious little man who demands her first child as payment. Years later, when she is happily married to the prince, he returns, demanding her son, and she must find a way to outsmart him.

❋ THE TIGER AND THE BRAHMIN

Read by Ben Kingsley; music by Ravi Shankar

In this Indian tale, a holy man learns some lessons that were not in his books.

❋ TOM THUMB

Read by John Cleese; music by Elvis Costello

In this version, read by Monty Python alumnus John Cleese, Tom Thumb's accomplishments bring him to the Court of King Arthur, where he becomes a knight.

❋ **CONNECTIONS:** Compare to *tom thumb,* with Russ Tamblyn.

❋ THE WHITE CAT

Read by Emma Thompson; music by Joe Jackson

A young prince befriends a cat-queen, and she helps him meet the challenges set by his father, in this French fairytale with a romantic happily-ever-after conclusion.

CLASSIC TELEVISION CARTOONS

❋ BEANY AND CECIL

Many parents will remember fondly the cartoon series about the seasick sea serpent and will enjoy watching it again with their children.

❋ ROCKY AND BULLWINKLE

Rocky the Flying Squirrel and his big, lovably dumb pal Bullwinkle Moose are back on video, with their friends Mr. Peabody and Sherman (who travel back in time on the Wayback machine), Dudley Do-Right (the dim Mountie), and the Fractured Fairy Tales narrated by Edward Everett Horton. Jay Ward's wickedly subversive humor and wild puns make these just as much fun as they were in the 1960s.

❋ **CONNECTIONS:** Ward produced the *George of the Jungle* series, also available on video.

FEATURE FILMS FOR FAMILIES

The slogan of this Utah-based company (1-800-347-2833) is "strengthening traditional values through entertainment." Their videos, while often not up to Hollywood or broadcast standards of acting, writing, or production values, are wholesome and enjoyable. Each video box includes a list of questions about the story that are worthwhile for family discussion.

✳ THE BUTTERCREAM GANG
1991, 95 min, NR, 8 and up
Dir: Bruce Neibaur

When a boy leaves his old friends to join an unfriendly gang, his old friends demonstrate "unconditional love" and loyalty in bringing him back to his original values.

✳ IN YOUR WILDEST DREAMS
1991, 87 min, NR, 8 and up
Dir: Bruce Neibaur

A teenage boy "accidentally" makes $1 million in the stock market, and finds out what his "wildest dreams" really are. Mark stumbles into a complex insider trading scheme when he mistakenly places a real stock purchase order in a classroom simulation. He is even more tempted by the chance to give his family the things they have wished for than he is for making his own dream of owning a Ferrari come true. He has to think about whether something is right just because it is legal, and to compare the examples of his hardworking and honest father, boss, and girlfriend with the amoral and sybaritic Justin.

✳ JACOB'S HARVEST
1995, 95 min, NR, 8 and up
Dir: Michael Scott

Jacob walks away without a word of explanation the day before his planned wedding to Maddy. He returns twenty years later to find Maddy married to his brother Dan. Jacob's father is overjoyed to see him, but Dan and Maddy have mixed feelings. They must all learn to resolve their feelings and find a way to work together.

✳ RIGOLETTO
1993, 98 min, NR, 8 and up
Dir: Leo D. Paur

A disfigured man moves into a mysterious mansion in this mystical tale. He evicts a local family, but he agrees they may stay if the daughter, Bonnie, will be his servant. She is drawn to his music and, despite his bitterness, they become friends. The prejudice of other members of the community destroys him, but Bonnie sees that he has been released from his burdens, and may now be reborn, whole in heart and body.

✳ **CONNECTIONS:** Compare this to *Beauty and the Beast* and listen to the music from the opera *Rigoletto*.

✳ THE ROGUE STALLION

1990, 96 min, NR, 8 and up
Dir: Henri Safran

After her father dies, Anna and her mother and brother must leave Australia to return to New Zealand. But a greedy neighbor tries to drive them off their land. He also wants to destroy the beautiful wild stallion named Wildfire. Anna and the community work together to overcome prejudice and hate.

✳ SEASONS OF THE HEART

1993, 94 min, NR, 8 and up
Dir: T. C. Christiansen

A bereaved pioneer mother, whose daughters died on the trek West, has a hard time allowing herself to love her awkward adopted son, until Christmas Eve, when he finds a way to reach her.

✳ SPLIT INFINITY

1992, 90 min, NR, 8 and up
Dir: Stan Ferguson

Teen entrepreneur A. J. Knowlton thinks she knows what's important; she hopes to make a lot of money. But when she goes back in time to 1929 and meets her grandfather as a young man, she discovers that some things are even more important. NOTE: This movie unintentionally conveys something of a mixed message on the subject of money, as part of the happy ending involves profiting from the stock tips A. J. was able to give her grandfather before returning to the present.

✳ WILLY THE SPARROW

1993, 74 min, NR, 6 and up
Dir: Jozef Gemes

In this animated film, a boy who shoots a BB gun at sparrows is turned into a sparrow. He develops respect for all living creatures, and helps his new sparrow friends by teaching one to read and leading them in reclaiming their home in the barn from the cat.

THE BELL TELEPHONE SCIENCE SERIES

Some parents may remember these as the highlight of grade school science classes. Made for television in the 1960s by some of Hollywood's greatest talents, the science may be a bit out of date (to say nothing of the all-white and all-male scientists), but the tapes are still an outstanding introduction not just to the topics addressed but to the wonders of curiosity and the passion for solving mysteries that is the core of scientific inquiry.

✳ THE ALPHABET CONSPIRACY

This is the story of words and language, as a little girl discovers how language was developed, and how humans learn to speak.

✳ HEMO THE MAGNIFICENT

An introduction to blood and the circulatory system. Written and directed by Oscar-winning director Frank Capra (*It's a Wonderful Life* and many others), this is one of the highlights of the series. In addition to interesting information, presented with exceptional creativity, this even includes a discussion of the different (and similar) roles of science and art. This would make a great double feature with *Fantastic Voyage*.

✳ IT'S ABOUT TIME

This introduces the origins of time and time measurement, basic concepts of relativity, and an appearance by Nobel Prize–winner (and bestselling author) Richard Feynman. Older kids who enjoy this movie may like to read some of the essays in his book *Surely You're Joking, Mr. Feynman*, especially the ones about his youth and education, and his secrets for cracking all the combination locks while he was working on the atomic bomb at Los Alamos.

✳ **CONNECTIONS:** Mature teens will enjoy *Infinity*, with Matthew Broderick as Feynman in the early days of his career, working on the atomic bomb and deeply in love with his terminally ill wife.

✳ OUR MR. SUN

Written and directed by Frank Capra, this is the story of the sun, what it is made from, and how it is essential for life on Earth. NOTE: The movie begins and ends with biblical references, which some families will appreciate as providing context, but others will find irrelevant or annoying.

✳ THE THREAD OF LIFE

An introduction to genetics and DNA, this movie should prompt some home experiments in tracking tongue curling and attached earlobes through the family tree.

YOUNG PEOPLE'S CONCERTS WITH LEONARD BERNSTEIN

This award-winning series, hosted by conductor-composer Leonard Bernstein, introduces children to music. In "The Sound of the Orchestra," he begins with a passage from Haydn, and then explains that even though all the notes were played correctly, it was played all wrong. And in each episode, he makes clear how many choices are involved—for the composer, for the musician, for the conductor, for the listener—and how those choices are made. The tapes are in black and white, with no glitzy special effects, which may take getting used to, but kids who are patient enough to give them a try will learn a lot, and have a lot of fun, too. Kids will enjoy knowing that the host is the same man who wrote the music for *West Side Story, On the Waterfront,* and *On the Town.*

OTHER EDUCATIONAL VIDEOS

✳ DONALD IN MATHMAGICLAND

Donald Duck gets a fast-paced and fun introduction to mathematics, and the role it plays in art, sports, and music.

✳ THE MAGIC SCHOOL BUS

The outstanding series of science books for kids became a PBS series, and is now available on video. Ms. Frizzle (the voice of Lily Tomlin) takes her lucky students everywhere from inside the human body to outside the solar system to teach them how things work and why things are the way they are. Though produced for kids from 6–9, these are also immensely popular with kids from 3–6 and 9–12 as well.

STORIES BY FIRELIGHT

✳ TALES OF WONDER

1998, 60 min, NR, 6 and up
Dir: Chip Richie. Gregg Howard
This quiet, gentle video features Storyteller of the Year Gregg Howard telling eight traditional Cherokee and Chocktaw folk tales, (sometimes remi-

niscent of the stories of Aesop and Uncle Remus) to an enthralled group of children. The group sits before a cozy fire, listening to traditional Indian flute music and looking at simple pencil illustrations of the animal characters Howard describes. Some of the stories describe origins ("How the Deer Got Antlers") while others describe courage, folly, or problem-solving. This video is a real treasure as an antidote to hyperactive, MTV-style children's programs, and as a rare resource for Indian tradition and culture.

BILLY BUDD FAMILY VIDEO SERIES

✳ GOD'S TROMBONES
James Earl Jones and Dorian Harewood read poems by James Weldon Johnson.

✳ THE LITTLE PRINCE
In Antonine de St. Exupery's classic story, the little prince from another planet meets an aviator in the desert.

✳ MICHAEL THE VISITOR
A shoemaker takes in a homeless youth who turns out to be an angel, in this story by Leo Tolstoy.

THE BEST MOVIES
FOR PARENTS ABOUT
BEING A PARENT

After the kids go to bed, parents will enjoy these movies about all aspects of parenting: struggling to find the patience and wisdom necessary to handle a toddler or a teenager; resolving the conflicting demands of work and family; resolving the conflicting demands of children and spouse; trying to date as a single parent; dealing with in-laws, baby-sitters, and ex-spouses; and caring for aging parents. These movies are funny, touching, and bittersweet, just like being a parent.

✳ THE COURTSHIP OF EDDIE'S FATHER
1963, 117 min, NR
Dir: Vincente Minnelli. Glenn Ford, Shirley Jones, Ron Howard

When his wife dies, Tom Corbett (Glenn Ford) must deal with his own grief and with his bereft son, Eddie (Ronny Howard). The women in his life include his nurse neighbor (Shirley Jones), sweet beauty queen (and percussionist) Stella Stevens, and elegant executive Dina Merrill. A bit dated by today's standards, it is still a warm and sensitive comedy-drama. The relationship between the father and son is exceptionally well-handled, including Tom's feelings of conflict and inadequacy as he struggles to give Eddie what he needs while still feeling the loss of his wife.

✳ **CONNECTIONS:** Tom's best friend is played by Jerry Van Dyke, brother of Dick Van Dyke, and costar of television's *Coach*.

✳ DIVORCE, AMERICAN STYLE
1967, 118 min, NR
Dir: Bud Yorkin. Dick Van Dyke, Debbie Reynolds, Van Johnson, Jason Robards, Jean Simmons

The middle-American appeal of the leads (Dick Van Dyke and Debbie Reynolds) and the sitcom premise (divorcing couple realizes they really love each other) is the spoonful of sugar that helps the medicine of caustic satire and genuine subversiveness go down in this comedy by the team that went on to create television's *All in the Family*.

Richard and Barbara Harmon (Van Dyke and Reynolds), heads of a very traditional suburban family, impetuously decide to divorce following a silly argument. They then become the pawns of their well-meaning (and sometimes less well-meaning) friends. Jason Robards (of *A Thousand Clowns*) plays a divorced man trying to find someone to marry his ex-wife (Jean Simmons, of *Guys and Dolls*), so he can stop paying alimony, which will enable him to marry his new girlfriend (thus enabling her ex-husband to stop paying alimony). Some of the highlights include the community-wide weekend exchange of custody ("No, this weekend you go with *Uncle Daddy!*"), and the meeting with the lawyers, who skewer the Harmons as they set up a golf date.

✳ FATHER OF THE BRIDE
1950, 93 min, NR, b&w
Dir: Vincente Minnelli. Elizabeth Taylor, Spencer Tracy
(remade in 1991, 113 min, PG, directed by Charles Shyer, starring Steve Martin and Diane Keaton)

Within this gentle satire of middle-class life and the wedding that takes over the family is a tender story of a father who can't quite figure out how his daughter grew up so fast. In the original version, Elizabeth Taylor is Kay Banks, the heart-stoppingly beautiful bride, and Spencer Tracy (Stanley Banks) and Joan Bennett are her parents. The scene in which Stanley tries to comfort Kay as she explains why she wants to call off the wedding is a masterpiece.

✳ **CONNECTIONS:** The bride's younger brother is played by Russ Tamblyn of *Seven Brides for Seven Brothers, tom thumb,* and *West Side Story*. The 1991 remake, with Diane Keaton and Steve Martin as the parents and pretty Kimberly Williams as the bride, has more slapstick and less feeling, but Martin and Williams are superb, and the emphasis on the relationship between father and daughter is even stronger. Both movies have sequels about the daughter's first baby; in the Keaton-Martin sequel, the mother gets pregnant again and has a baby at the same time their daughter does.

✳ I NEVER SANG FOR MY FATHER

1970, 93 min, PG
Dir: Gilbert Cates. Gene Hackman, Melvyn Douglas

The problems of the parent as child and the child as parent are sensitively explored in this story of a man (Gene Hackman) who must deal directly with his difficult father (Melvyn Douglas) for the first time after his mother's death. Similar issues are handled well in *Nothing in Common* (Tom Hanks and Jackie Gleason), and *Dad* (Ted Danson and Jack Lemmon).

✳ KRAMER VS. KRAMER

1979, 104 min, PG
Dir: Robert Benton. Dustin Hoffman, Meryl Streep, Jane Alexander

Oscars for Best Picture, Director, Screenwriter, Actor, and Supporting Actress went to this movie about a father's relationship with his son. Dustin Hoffman plays Ted Kramer, whose focus on his career in advertising left him barely aware of his wife, Joanna (Meryl Streep), and six-year-old son, Billy (Justin Henry). When Joanna leaves him, Ted first sees it primarily as an inconvenience and embarrassment, but ultimately becomes so deeply involved in his relationship with his son that he loses his job. Then Joanna returns and sues for custody.

The scenes of parenting are brilliantly handled—the race to the emergency room for stitches after a fall at the playground, the school Halloween pageant, two-wheeler bicycle lessons, Billy's insisting on disobeying to see if his father will leave as his mother did, Ted's being late to pick Billy up at a birthday party. Three different scenes of Ted and Billy sharing breakfast define the stages of their relationship: the first panicky morning after Joanna's departure ("That's not the way Mom does it!"), the silent but comfortable and companionable routine of their partnership, and the loving transition to Joanna's reinvolvement.

✳ LORENZO'S OIL

1992, 135m, PG-13
Dir: George Miller. Susan Sarandon, Nick Nolte, Peter Ustinov

Lorenzo, the son of Michaela and Augusto Odone (Susan Sarandon and Nick Nolte), was diagnosed with adrenoleukodystrophy, an incurable degenerative disease. The Odones refused to accept the prognosis, and found themselves fighting not only the medical establishment but the "support group" of other parents (who did not believe a cure was possible) and their own friends and family (who urged them to get on with their lives). Instead, the Odones learned as much as they could about the disease and developed a theory that ultimately led to the first successful treatment. While their own son remains severely disabled, they have kept him from getting worse, and have kept many other boys from the effects of the disease.

✳ MILDRED PIERCE

1949, 109 min, NR, b&w
Dir: Michael Curtiz. Joan Crawford, Ann Blyth, Jack Carson, Zachery Scott

A woman (Joan Crawford, in a role that won her an Oscar) sacrifices everything for her daughter, who becomes one of the meanest and most selfish children in all of filmdom. A similar story about a father and son is *Edward, My Son*, with Spencer Tracy and Deborah Kerr as the parents who raise a monster.

✳ MR. BLANDINGS BUILDS HIS DREAM HOUSE

1948, 93 min, NR, b&w
Dir: H. C. Potter. Cary Grant, Myrna Loy, Melvyn Douglas, Louise Beavers

The ultimate movie about construction and redecorating, this movie features Cary Grant and Myrna Loy as the Blandings, who decide to move to the country. When their new home has to be torn down, they embark upon the nightmare of designing and presiding over the construction of a new one. Wry bachelor Melvyn Douglas (of **Ninotchka**) is their best friend (and a former beau of Mrs. Blandings), who enjoys the chance to comment sardonically on the proceedings. The scene in which Loy explains exactly the shade of blue she has in mind to the painters is priceless. NOTE: The portrayal of the black housekeeper (Louise Beavers), while not intended to be condescending, is insensitive by today's standards. Interestingly, she solves the main character's biggest problem (though he gives her only a token reward while he gets the credit).

✳ MR. HOBBS TAKES A VACATION

1962, 116 min, NR, b&w
Dir: Henry Koster. Jimmy Stewart, Maureen O'Hara

Though it is a bit dated, this movie still has a lot of relevance to anyone who has ever been on a multigenerational family vacation. Jimmy Stewart stays remarkably calm as he copes with catastrophes ranging from an extremely uncooperative beach-house boiler to a couple of even more uncooperative teenagers. In the meantime, one daughter has a husband out of work (the effort to entertain the stuffy prospective new boss is hilariously disastrous), another has a husband who is intrigued by a pretty neighbor, the teenage daughter is too self-conscious about her new braces to smile at a local dance, and the son doesn't want to do anything but watch television. With the help of the movies's most ravishing grandmother (Maureen O'Hara), Hobbs manages to handle it all and still find time for a couple of songs by Fabian.

❋ OUR VINES HAVE TENDER GRAPES

1945, 105 min, NR, b&w
Dir: Dalton Trumbo. Edward G. Robinson, Margaret O'Brien, Agnes Moorehead

In an uncharacteristic role, tough guy Edward G. Robinson plays a kind Norwegian farmer trying to be a good father to his adored little girl, played by Margaret O'Brien. Every parent will identify with his struggle to understand the right way to combine discipline and understanding.

❋ PARENTHOOD

1989, 124 min, PG-13
Dir: Ron Howard. Steve Martin, Tom Hulce, Jason Robards, Mary Steenburgen, Rick Moranis, Keanu Reeves

Every possible aspect of being a parent or a child is reflected in this movie about four grown children and their family struggles. Dianne Wiest plays a divorced mother with a rebellious teenage daughter and a withdrawn and angry son. Her sister, a teacher, is played by Harley Jane Kozak, married to a man who is determined to make their preschool daughter a prodigy by constantly drilling her. Brother Gil (Steve Martin) is happily married to Mary Steenburgen but is worried about his anxious eight-year-old, an unexpected new baby, a demanding boss, and unresolved conflicts with his own father (Jason Robards). The youngest brother (Tom Hulce, of **Amadeus**) is the irresponsible dreamer whose parents still worry about what to do with him. Funny, touching, insightful, and meaningful, this movie seems to bloom a bit more on each watching.

❋ SEARCHING FOR BOBBY FISCHER

1993, 111 min, PG
Dir: Steven Zaillian. Joe Mantegna, Joan Allen, Ben Kingsley, Laurence Fishburne

Brilliantly written, directed, and performed, this movie is based on the true story of chess prodigy Josh Waitzkin (played by real-life chess champion Max Pomeranc), his sportswriter father (Joe Mantegna), wise mother (Joan Allen), chess master tutor (Ben Kingsley as Bruce Pandolfini), and street-player friend (Laurence Fishburne). Josh's parents must find a way to support his interest, challenge his extraordinary ability, and make sure that he has as normal a childhood as possible. Should you teach a child to be as singlemindedly competitive as is necessary to be a champion? Can you relish a child's achievements without confusing them with your own? Even parents without prodigies will identify with Josh's father as he tells Josh's teacher that his son is better at chess than he will ever be at anything. This movie is perfect in every detail (one of the most authentically messy family dwellings in the movies), and magnificently performed.

❋ **CONNECTIONS:** A movie that deals with similar issues is *Little Man Tate,* in which Jodie Foster (who also directed) plays a waitress whose son is a genius. Like the Waitzkins, she must cope with his need for intellectual stimulation while protecting his need to be a child. As the Waitzkins struggle with Pandolfini over what is best for their child, Dede Tate struggles with the director of a school for gifted children, played by Dianne Wiest.

✳ SMALL CHANGE

1976, 104 min, PG
Dir: Francois Truffaut. Geory Desmouceaux, Philippe Goldman, Claudio Deluca
   This episodic collection of tales about children and the grace, vulnerability, and resilience of childhood is a poignant delight. A boy named Patrick has his first tentative encounters with the opposite sex. A child cuts his brother's hair. A toddler falls out of a window, terrorizing his mother, but lands safely and sees the whole thing as an adventure. A little girl insists on taking her ratty old purse when the family goes out to dinner. Her exasperated parents leave her at home, and while they are gone she manages to have the entire community rally to bring her a feast.

✳ THE TURNING POINT

1977, 119 min, PG
Dir: Herbert Ross. Shirley MacLaine, Anne Bancroft, Leslie Browne, Mikhail Baryshnikov, Tom Skerritt
   DeeDee (Shirley MacLaine) and Emma (Anne Bancroft), two young ballerinas who were close friends, took different paths. One married, had children, and taught dance in a small town. The other became a star and spent her life on the road, with no family ties. Years later, they confront the consequences of their choices as Amelia (Leslie Browne), DeeDee's daughter, joins the ballet company and has to make her own choices. The demanding world of ballet is an ideal setting for an insightful look at the stage of life when we really start to understand that we can't do it all—and it gives us an excuse for glorious ballet performances (featuring Mikhail Baryshnikov) as well. The conflict between family and career, the difficulty of letting children become independent, and the temptation to try to have your child fulfill your dreams are all sensitively handled.

✳ 35 UP

1991, 128 min, NR
Dir: Michael Apted
   In 1963, a British television crew filmed a documentary (*7 Up*) about seven-year-olds from a variety of different backgrounds, including students from both public and private schools. Every seven years since, the filmmakers have returned to the same group to document their lives and their perspectives. What was once an interesting cultural artifact has become a

riveting, longitudinal epic. Parents today will identify with the subjects of the film as they face the challenges of family and professional life.

More important, the movie is impossible to watch without being humbled by the strength of personality in these seven-year-olds who predict, sometimes with astonishing accuracy, what direction their lives will take. At age seven, one boy says he wants to be a jockey—and he becomes one before moving on to drive his own taxi. Another wants to become a scientist—and he becomes one, a professor at an American university. Their lives are defined by the opportunities presented to them; the class distinctions in the United Kingdom may be more clearly drawn than they are in the United States, but the differences of culture and money have an enormous impact that will seem familiar to Americans as well. Watching this movie will make you impatient for the next installment—you will become as curious about what will happen to its subjects as you are about your high school or college classmates. And it will leave you even more respectful of the dreams of your own children, and of those who may not have the same opportunities to achieve them.

✳ TWO FOR THE ROAD

1967, 112 min, NR
Dir: Stanley Donen. Audrey Hepburn, Albert Finney

A rare movie about marriage, this movie cuts back and forth among a couple's four trips through Europe, defining the stages of their relationship. They meet as students and fall in love, they vacation together as newlyweds with an excruciatingly unbearable American family, they cope with professional success. They argue, they disappoint each other, they disappoint themselves, they fall in love all over again. A brilliant screenplay by Frederic Raphael (an Oscar-winner for *Darling*) and breathtaking performances by Audrey Hepburn and Albert Finney, plus sparkling direction by Stanley Donen, a romantic Henry Mancini score, and spectacular Riviera scenery make this a bittersweet romantic classic.

The Movie Mom's Television and Video Watching Guidelines

- Watching television or videos is a treat, not a right. It's a good idea to make sure that it comes only after homework, chores, other kinds of play, and family time. Make sure there is some quiet time each day as well. The spirit is nourished by silence. All too often we try to drown out our unsettled or lonely feelings in noise instead of allowing them to resolve themselves. Just as important, the best and most meaningful family communication flourishes only in quiet.

- Plan with your child what he or she is going to watch. You might say something like, "We should have time for one hour of television today." Or, "Let's get a video to watch on Sunday afternoon." Then look at the newspaper or television guide listing together or look through a movie guide like this one to see the options and pick which ones you think are worthwhile. Try to avoid the "let's see if there's anything on television" channel-surf, which has a tendency to be numbing rather than engaging or relaxing. Distract the kids with crayons or toys, not television and videos. The Washington-based Center for Media Education estimates that preschoolers watch four hours of television a day. Most educators think that anything over two hours at that age takes too much time away from the important "work" of playing, learning to interact with others, learning to amuse themselves, and developing their imaginations. School-age kids should spend even less time with television.

- Turn the television set off when the program or video is over, unless there is something else you've planned to watch next. This discourages the idea that we "watch television" instead of watching particular programs.

- Watch with the kids whenever possible, and comment on what you see. Encourage them to comment, too: "What do you think he will do next?" Or, "She looks sad. I think they hurt her feelings." Or, "He's having a hard time feeling good about himself, isn't he?" Or, "If you were that kid, what would you do?" Or, "If someone said that to you, how would you feel?"

- Look for positive role models for girls. Children's shows produced for commercial networks tend to ignore girls. Producers are asked for shows with "boy appeal" because the numbers show that girls will watch shows produced for boys, but boys won't watch shows produced for girls. There is a lot of what I call "the Smurfette syndrome," a reference to the once-popular cartoon show that featured ninety-nine highly varied male characters, and one girl character whose sole and defining characteristic was that she was a female. Whether you have daughters or sons, help them to be sensitive to these concerns and ask questions like, "Do you think it's fair there are no girls on that team?" Or, "How come only the boys get to go on that adventure?" And comment positively on good female role models: "She's brave!" and, "That's what I call persistence!"

- Be alert for issues of race, religion, ethnicity, and class. The media tends to feature Dick and Jane/Ozzie and Harriet suburban families, where Dad works and Mom stays home and does housework and everyone is white and Christian. Nonwhites are often portrayed condescendingly or stereotypically. Make sure your children know there are many different kinds of families, and many different kinds of homes. Make an effort to be sure they see diverse families in what they watch.

- Set a good example. Don't let the kids see you veg out in front of the television, aimlessly clicking the remote. Don't tell them not to talk to you so you can watch some sitcom. Do let them see you reading, and enjoying what you read.

- Don't ever let anyone—parent, grandparent, sibling, or friend—tell a child that a program or video he or she wants to watch is "too babyish." Respect children's interests and affection for the shows they like, and their need to return to old comforts.

- Make sure children understand the difference between programs and commercials. Saturday morning cartoon commercials are particularly troublesome, with a sort of hip-hop precocity that shows grade-school kids acting like hyperactive miniteenagers.

- If you find you have made a mistake and have taken your children to a film you find inappropriate, leave the theater. You can get your money back. And you communicate an important lesson to your children about your commitment to protecting them. The same is true, of course, for a video you have brought home.

- Do not be shy about setting television limits with baby-sitters, friends' parents, or grandparents. Never leave your children with anyone without being clear about your rules.

- Be careful with tie-ins, especially cartoons based on movie characters. Just because a Saturday morning cartoon like *Beetlejuice* or *The Mask* or some fast-food gizmo is geared for children does not mean that the associated movie is appropriate for them as well.
- Use movies as a starting point for developing interests. Go to the library to check out a book or a video relating to what you have seen. Read the newspaper for stories relating to what you have seen. Make a craft project inspired by the show. ("Can you draw Mickey carrying the buckets of water?" Or, "Let's try to find on a map where Indiana Jones went.")
- When in doubt, turn it off. Remember, there is no reason to watch any video unless you genuinely feel it is the best use of your child's time.
- Every month or so, try a "television diet" day without any television at all, and use the extra time for special family activities.
- When an older sibling is watching a video that is not appropriate for a younger child, make sure the younger child has an appealing alternative. It's a good time for you to do something special together, even if it is just sorting laundry or setting the table.
- Establish strict limits on viewing, but try not to use limits as a punishment, unless the offense relates to television itself (watching without permission, for example) or time management: "If you don't finish cleaning up by three o'clock, you won't have time to watch the movie." This reinforces the message that we make decisions about television and videos based only on the merits of the shows.
- Let them know why you like (or don't like) particular shows. Try not to say that something is "too old" for them, as this will just make them more interested in seeing what it is about. Sometimes it works better to say (truthfully) that it is "too stupid." Compare it to food: Some shows are like healthful food, some are like candy, some are like poison. Model good television behavior yourself: Don't keep it on as background noise. Don't watch anything you don't want them to see if they are around (you'd be amazed—and appalled—at what a three-year-old can pick up).
- Never put a television set or VCR in a child's bedroom, unless he or she is sick in bed. Not only is it isolating, it makes establishing limits impossible.
- Never, never, never have the television set on during family meals. That is your most precious time to share the day's experiences, challenges, and thoughts, and to let children know how important they are to you. The same goes for rides in the car, minivan, or RV.

Film Lingo

A few quick facts about the vocabulary of those who make and watch movies and the people behind the scenes will help your family appreciate and enjoy what you watch even more.

Close-up

This is a shot that shows only the face of one or more of the characters. As standard as it is now, it is hard to believe that it was the innovation of silent movie director D. W. Griffith, who turned an industry that had not done much more than produce filmed plays into one that made movies.

Flip books

You can't see it on video, but if you look at a strip of film, you will see that the pictures don't actually move; rather, a movie is merely a series of still pictures that go by so fast (twenty-four frames a second), it seems we are watching moving pictures. This is because of "persistence of vision," which means that our eyes (actually our brains) hold an image for a split second after the image is gone. A famous optical illusion illustrates this: The disk with the bird on one side and the cage on the other, when flipped around quickly on a string, appears to us as a bird in a cage.

A great project for kids that will teach them this lesson is to give them each a small pad of paper and have them create a "flip book," making the same drawing over and over on each page, changing it very slightly each time. Have them make an egg with a chicken hatching out of it, or a firecracker exploding, or a bouncing ball. It may be easiest if they begin with the first and the last pictures, and then fill in all the pictures on the pages in between. When they are done they can flip the pages and see a "movie."

F/X

F/X stands for "special effects," and kids who enjoy special effects may want to go to the library to research how they are done, or watch the Discovery Channel's *Movie Magic* television program. The first real special effects wizard was director Georges Méliès, whose background was as a stage magician and master of illusion. His 1902 silent film, *A Trip to the Moon*, is still delightful viewing.

Surprisingly, some of the effects that appear most difficult are easiest, and vice versa. The oldest and easiest effect to reproduce in family home videos is that of appearing and disappearing. Just stop the camera (making sure nothing moves—*especially the camera*—but the person who is doing the trick, and have someone come into (or leave) the scene; then start shooting again. Presto!

Fruit carts and other perennials

Siskel and Ebert have immortalized the fruit cart, which they say is inevitably overturned in any major chase scene, leaving the owner standing in the street shaking his fist vengefully in the air. This is such a well-established cliché that college students often call out, "Fruit cart!" when they see it, and some filmmakers (perhaps hoping for a "thumbs-up") insert a fruit cart as a tribute to these powerful critics.

Critics and other movie lovers often compare notes on their favorite clichés. My own are two lines that—separately or sometimes together—seem to appear in just about every movie: "Why don't you try to get some rest," and, "Please, try to understand."

Gaffer, key grip, and best boy

Inveterate credit-readers often wonder what these mysterious people do. Grips are the handymen, and the key grip is the one in charge. The gaffer is the chief electrician. The best boy (yes, it can be a female) is an apprentice or assistant.

Homage

"Homage" (pronounced "oh-MAJZE," as the French do) means "homage" and in movies it means paying tribute to an admired film, or, sometimes it is just a fancy name for copying it.

Kuleshov

Lev Kuleshov was a Russian filmmaker who pioneered the use of editing to tell the story. He did a famous experiment in the early days of film. He took a picture of a man's face, telling him to be as expressionless as possible. Then he inserted the picture in a film, between shots of a pretty woman, some food, and a child. Audiences exclaimed at his acting artistry—how hungry he was for the food, how enticed by the lady, how caring for the child! This shows us about the way our brains impose linearity and connection, and how strongly we project aspects of ourselves onto the screen. The best filmmakers are able to understand and use these qualities to involve us in the stories they want to tell.

Long shot

This is a shot big enough so that you can see full figures and scenery. When it is used to help the audience know where the characters are at the beginning of a scene, it is called an "establishing shot."

MacGuffin

Alfred Hitchcock used this term to describe whatever it is that the hero and heroine are trying to find or do—whether it's finding the hidden jewels or the secret formula, or foiling the plot to take over the world.

Medium shot

This is a shot in which characters fill the frame, often from the waist up.

Montage

Montage just means editing, but the term is often used to mean a group of short scenes, usually wordless, with some music, giving an overall if shorthand impression of some development in the movie. A frequent example is when our hero and heroine go on their first date, and we see shots of them riding bicycles, walking on the beach, exclaiming over oddities in an open-air market, and kissing in the twilight. Indeed, this technique is so popular, it is often parodied.

Pan and scan

The proportion of length and height of a film screen (called the aspect ratio) is different from those of a television. When films are adapted for videos or broadcast, the sides of the frame are cut out of the picture. In order to let you see as much as possible of what was on the screen, the adapters use "pan and scan" —they show one side of what was on the original frame, and then move the viewer sideways so that you can see the other side. It often creates a real problem, as when you can see only five of the brides in *Seven Brides for Seven Brothers* dancing at once.

POV

This stands for "point of view" and it is an important way for a writer or filmmaker to engage the audience and affect its reaction to the movie. As you watch the movies in this book, ask yourself whose POV you are seeing. In some, it will be the POV of one of the characters, and you will see and know only what they do. In others, you may switch from one character to another, or have a more general and objective POV. Compare the way POV is handled in movies to the way it is handled in books.

Vorkapich

Slavko Vorkapich was the man who invented a number of visual cues for conveying information—like tearing off calendar pages to show time passing—that were so popular, they became clichés.

The Westmores

An amazing Hollywood story, the Westmore family all but invented the way makeup was used in the movies, and that had an enormous impact on cosmetics of all kinds. Before their era, ladies seldom even admitted wearing makeup, which consisted mostly of a little color for their lips and cheeks. The Westmores used makeup to enhance the best features of the stars and minimize their flaws. At one time, a different Westmore brother headed the makeup department of each of the major studios, including Warner Brothers, Universal, Paramount, and 20th Century Fox. Look in the credits of movies from the 1930s to the 1950s, to see how many Westmores you can find, and look in the credits of today's movies to find the third generation.

Winsor McCay and animation

Winsor McCay, one of the first comic strip artists, was also the person who realized he could make a series of drawings into a movie through what came to be known as "animation." The first animated movie was McCay's *Gertie the Dinosaur,* which caused almost as much of a sensation when it was first shown as if Gertie were a real dinosaur brought back to life. McCay personally drew every one of the thousands of drawings for that movie. Even with photocopiers and computers, animation still works essentially the same way. Claymation (as in the Wallace and Gromit and Will Vinton movies) is just as painstaking, with tiny adjustments of the clay figures for each frame.

Sources for Hard-to-Find Videos

Start with your public library, which is an outstanding source for classic videos that can be checked out at no charge. Libraries often have video-only releases, documentaries, and award-winning independent films that are hard to find anywhere else, and many libraries will use interlibrary loans to help you track down a video you want. Most cable TV systems carry American Movie Classics and Turner Classic Movies, both of which are terrific sources for family films.

If you can't find what you are looking for there or at your local video store, try *http://www.reel.com* or *http://www.amazon.com*. Both make an effort to make available every tape in print.

Other sources for videos:

Great Tapes for Kids (888) KID-TAPES
Video Yesteryear (800) 243-0987 *video@yesteryear.com*
Captain Bijou (256) 852-0198 *(lots of old TV shows)*
Facets (800) 532-2387
Video Library (800) 669-7157
Critic's Choice Video Search Line (800) 729-0833
Westwood Studios—for Children's Circle videos (800) 243-5020
Rabbit Ears (800) 334-2722 *http://www.rabbitears.com*
Schoolhouse Videos (888) 724-6654 *school@nando.net*

Recommended Reading

A Biographical Dictionary of Film by David Thomson
This is the most insightful and comprehensive encyclopedia of actors, actresses, directors, and producers.

The Filmgoer's Companion by Leslie Halliwell
This has been my favorite film encyclopedia for more than twenty years. It is comprehensive enough to answer all questions and is personal (even quirky) enough to feel like a letter from a delightful and knowledgeable friend. There's a new edition each year.

Hitchcock by Francois Truffaut
This book-length interview of Alfred Hitchcock by film critic–director François Truffaut is great fun to read and an outstanding introduction to the art and craft of filmmaking.

Internet Movie Database (http://us.imdb.com/search)
The engaging quirkiness of this astonishingly comprehensive resource now owned by Amazon reflects its creation by a group of volunteers. Anyone can add comments or information or post reviews.

Leonard Maltin's Movie and Video Guide by Leonard Maltin
Indispensible. I have copies at arm's length by the sofa and on my desk. This is the most complete and reliable of the thumbnail-sketch encyclopedias of movies and videos and is updated annually.

Lunatics and Lovers: A Tribute to the Giddy and Glittering Era of the Screen's "Screwball" and Romantic Comedies by Ted Sennett
This is a delightful guide to a delightful genre: the screwball romantic comedy.

Making Movies by Sidney Lumet
> The director of such movies as *12 Angry Men* and *Murder on the Orient Express* talks about his approach to making movies in this very lively and informative book.

The Movie Mom http://www.moviemom.com
> This is the Movie Mom's own Web site, with reviews of current releases and videos.

Past Imperfect: History According to the Movies by Mark C. Carnes, ed.
> This is an outstanding collection of essays by prominent historians on the historical accuracy of movies, from *Jurassic Park* to *Malcolm X.*

rec.arts.movies.past-films
> This Internet "newsgroup" is an ongoing discussion of all matters pertaining to movies other than current releases.

Rent Two Films and Let's Talk in the Morning by John W. Hesley and Jan G. Hesley
> Although designed for therapists to help them use movies to reach patients, this insightful book has a great deal of applicability for families. The Hesleys' web site is *http:///www.hesley.com.*

Screen It (http://www.screenit.com)
> This web site has detailed reviews of movies and videos with information on every aspect of concern to parents.

The Smart Parent's Guide to Kids' TV by Milton Chen, Ph.D.
> This is an excellent guide for parents on establishing appropriate limits and making the best use of the television children do watch.

Stay Tuned! Raising Media-Savvy Kids in the Age of the Channel-Surfing Couch Potato by Jane Murphy and Karen Tucker

VideoHound's Golden Movie Retriever by Martin Connors and Julia Furtaw, editors
> This is not as insightful as Maltin, but it's broader in scope and has some irresistible categories for the true lovers of trivia, including an index of songs from movies. Also available on CD-ROM.

Wings video *http://www.wingsvideo.com*
> Training, support, and distribution for kids who want to make their own movies.

Acknowledgments

Thanks and love to the people who knew this was a book even before I did, especially Judy Viorst, the book's very elegant fairy godmother, who made my dream come true. The idea really began when I told Tom Dunkel and Peter Bernstein about the MomFest. Thanks to both of them for getting me started, and especially to Peter and his coauthor, Chris Ma, for including the Movie Mom's recommendations in their wonderful *Practical Guide to Practically Everything* books. Thanks to Bob Lescher and Rachel Klayman for understanding what this book could be and making it possible. Thanks to Sally Waters for her encyclopedic knowledge and invaluable feedback and to Gabriel London, a gentleman and a scholar, for tireless fact-checking and help with research, and Paula Reedy for knowledgeable editing. Thanks to Tia Maggini for batting cleanup.

Thanks to the kids who watched movies and told me what they thought, including my forever Webelos: Aris Panapoulos, Bobby Blau, Curt White, and Matt Joseph; the kids and teachers from Burgundy Farm Country Day School, especially Nadiya Mahmood, Reid Swanson, Beverly Bell, Alex and Ben Parker, Yusef Harden, Bryan Fleming, Liz Miller, and Claire Paisley-Jones (who wrote a magnificent essay on *Glory*); as well as Claire, Julia, and Nora Riesenberg, Harrison Fahn, Sophie and Teddy Klein, Jackson Marlette, Sam, Toby, Theo, and Charles Leiss, Sam and Nell Norman, Claire, John Patrick, and Elizabeth Adams, Gregory and Emily Morris, Alex, Zach, and Claire Prosperi, Ian Sterne (and his parents), movie experts Mike Stacey and Victoria Wong, Alex and Claire Apatoff, Mira Singer, Lorenzo Acciai, William and Emily Stephen, Laura and Katy Rosen, Amaya and Walker Whitworth, and Sandy and Ellen Twaddell. Thanks to the many people who responded to frantic questions via e-mail, especially Sarah Kleinstock, Movie Trivia Czar J. M. Streep, and those stalwarts in rec.arts.movies.past-films. Thanks also to the editors at *Family Fun* and *Child* magazines, where portions of the Introduction originally appeared.

I don't think I could write a book without the friendship and support of Kit Bingham and Michael Deal. I hope I never have to find out. Experts in both movies and corporate governance, they were, as always, never-failing sources of feedback, fact-checking, and funny e-mails. Thanks to my beloved partner, Bob Monks, who gave me some time off to write a non-corporate-governance book, and whose influence is on every page. Thanks, too, to my other partners, Barbara Sleasman, Bob Holmes, Charles Woodworth, and John Higgins, for their support and consideration and for taking such good care of things while I was busy with the book, without making me worry that they could get along too well without me.

Thanks to the authors who taught me about the movies, including François Truffaut, Leslie Halliwell, and Stanley Cavell; to my teachers, including Paddy Whannel; and especially to the people who made the movies I never get tired of watching. Thanks to the authors who taught me about being a parent, especially Benjamin Spock, Penelope Leach, Haim Ginott, Adele Faber and Elaine Mazlish, and Marguerite Kelly, and to my best teachers, my parents and my children.

Thanks to my *mishpocha,* the family who feel like friends, and the friends who feel like family: Kathy and Andrew Stephen, Kristie Miller, Tom Dunkel, all the Caplins, Vicki Apatoff, David Drew, Stuart Brotman, Deborah Baughman, John Adams, Shannon Hackett, Henry Geller, Nadine Prosperi, Patty Marx, Steve Friess and Jim Richter, Faith Falkner, Bill Pedersen, Michael Kinsley, Alan Kahn (a real movie maven), Rosemary Brown, Ellen Burka, Gail Ifshin, Martha and Mary Minow, Ralph and Wendy Whitworth, Joe and Victoria Klein, Laurence and Celia Beasley, Noël and Frances Yauch, Sophie L'Helias, Judy Pomeranz, Kayla Gillan, Lynda Robb, Jesse Norman and Kate Bingham, Jane Leavy, Duncan Clark, Noel Gunther, T. L. Hawkins, Terry Savage, Elaine Levis, Paula Trienens, Renée Crown, Laurie Lipper, Cindy Perry, Parvané Hashemi, Sarah Teslik, Amy Castel, Tim Brooks, Isabel Elliott, and all the Renaissancers. Thanks to my family, including all the Minows, Apatoffs, Baskins, Frankels, Browns, Resnicks, Greenes, and Tierneys. Thanks especially to my mother, who told me when a great movie would be on "The Late Show" and then stayed up with me to watch, and to my dad, who left my sisters and mom at home to take just me to see **Around the World in Eighty Days** and **The Wonderful World of the Brothers Grimm.** Thanks to Fran Apatoff, who taught me to look for poetry in everything, even movies. Thanks to those I miss every day, especially Bill Apatoff (his favorite movie is on page 508) and Burt Minow (his favorite movie is on page 607) and Beth Tierney. Thanks to my children, Benjamin and Rachel, who wanted me to write something they would enjoy for a change, and cheered me on every step of the way.

And thanks most of all to David Apatoff, still the best person I know.

Title Index

Please note that only movies with descriptive entries—either full-length or brief—are included in this index.

A Big Hand for the Little Lady (10 and up), 505

A Charlie Brown Christmas (3 and up), 615–16

A Christmas Carol (several versions) 6 and up, 236, 617–18

A Christmas Memory (8 and up), 287, 616

A Christmas Story (8 and up), 258–59, 618

A Close Shave (6 and up), 635

A Doll's House (12 and up), 333

A Grand Day Out (6 and up), 635

A Hard Day's Night (8 and up), 563–64

A League of Their Own (12 and up), 133, 214, 305, 336, 591, 608

A Little Princess (6 and up), 55, 473–74, 642

A Man for All Seasons (10 and up), 183–84

A Night at the Opera (8 and up), 501–2

A Raisin in the Sun (12 and up), 134, 286

A River Runs Through It (high schoolers), 272–73

A Room With a View (10 and up), 406–7

A Soldier's Story (12 and up), 133

A Tale of Two Cities (10 and up), 305

A Thousand Clowns (high schoolers), 38–40, 288

A Tree Grows in Brooklyn (10 and up), 275–76, 492

Abe Lincoln in Illinois (8 and up), 427, 603

The Absent Minded Professor (4 and up), 534, 589

Adam's Rib (10 and up), 106–7, 336

Adventures of Milo and Otis (4 and up), 436–37

The Adventures of Robin Hood (6 and up), 135–38, 421, 623

Advise & Consent (12 and up), 613

The African Queen (8 and up), 290–92, 620

Airplane! (high schoolers), 514, 619

Airport (high schoolers), 620

Aladdin (4 and up), 454–55

Aladdin and His Wonderful Lamp (6 and up), 637

Aladdin and the Magic Lamp (6 and up), 647

Alexander and the Terrible, Horrible, No Good, Very Bad Day (3 and up), 626

Alice Adams (12 and up), 358–59

Alice in Wonderland (4 and up), 465, 466–67, 542

All About Eve (12 and up), 201–3

All About Helicopters (2 and up), 626

All the King's Men (12 and up), 203–5

All My Sons (12 and up), 195, 312

All the President's Men (12 and up), 169–70, 305, 432, 615

All the Way Home (12 and up), 312, 313–15

Almost Angels (8 and up), 338–39

The Alphabet Conspiracy (6 and up), 653

Amadeus (12 and up), 213

Amazing Grace and Other Stories (4 and up), 133, 627

American Graffiti (12 and up), 359–61

Amistad (high schoolers), 74–76

An Affair to Remember (10 and up), 409–10

An American in Paris (8 and up), 551–52

An American Tail (5 and up), 455

Anansi (6 and up), 647

Anastasia (5 and up), 456

Anatomy of a Murder (12 and up), 76–77

Anchors Aweigh (6 and up), 552

Andre (6 and up), 441–42

The Andromeda Strain (10 and up), 414–15

Angels in the Outfield (6 and up), 591, 607

Anne of Green Gables (6 and up), 287, 485

Annie (6 and up), 561

Annie Get Your Gun (6 and up), 213

Annie Oakley (6 and up), 336, 432, 642–43

The Apartment (mature high schoolers), 196

Apollo 13 (8 and up), 238–39, 432

Arabesque (12 and up), 572–73

The Aristocats (4 and up), 456

Around the World in 80 Days (8 and up), 415

Arsenic and Old Lace (12 and up), 280, 514

Au Revoir, Les Enfants (Good-Bye, Children) (12 and up), 196

Auntie Mame (12 and up), 280–81

The Autobiography of Miss Jane Pittman (8 and up), 601–2

Awakenings (10 and up), 98, 388–89

Babe (4 and up), 65–67, 437

Babes in Toyland (6 and up), 561–62

Baby...Secret of the Lost Legend (8 and up), 435

The Baby-Sitter's Club (8 and up), 485

Bach's Fight for Freedom (6 and up), 638

Back to the Future (8 and up), 534

Bad Day at Black Rock (10 and up), 133, 292–93

Ball of Fire (8 and up), 312, 581–82

Balto (5 and up), 457

The Band Wagon (6 and up), 548

The Barkleys of Broadway (8 and up), 544

The Barretts of Wimpole Street (12 and up), 281

Baseball (8 and up), 588

Beany and Cecil (6 and up), 650

Beauty and the Beast (4 and up), 457, 637

Becket (high schoolers), 621

Bedknobs and Broomsticks (6 and up), 468–69

Bedtime for Bonzo (6 and up), 444, 505

Bell, Book and Candle (high schoolers), 621

The Bell Telephone Science series (6 and up), 653–54

The Bellboy, 513

The Belles of St. Trinian's (8 and up), 348–49

Belles on Their Toes (6 and up), 432

Bells are Ringing (6 and up), 89–91, 566

Ben Hur (10 and up), 604

Benny & Joon (high schoolers), 281

The Best Little Girl in the World (12 and up), 333

The Best Man (12 and up), 613–14

The Best Years of Our Lives (12 and up), 239–41

The Big Adventure series (2 and up), 627

Big Bird in China and *Big Bird in Japan* (4 and up), 632

The Big Sleep (12 and up), 575

Billy Rose's Jumbo (6 and up), 562

The Bingo Long Traveling All-Stars & Motor Kings (12 and up), 107–9, 591

Birdman of Alcatraz (10 and up), 427–28

Bizet's Dream (6 and up), 639

The Black Stallion (8 and up), 438–39, 491

The Blackboard Jungle (12 and up), 349

Blazing Saddles, 513

Body and Soul (8 and up), 590

Born Free (6 and up), 440–41

Born Yesterday (10 and up), 149–51, 336, 586, 621

The Borrowers (8 and up), 485–86

The Boy Who Could Fly (8 and up), 516–17

The Boy Who Drew Cats (6 and up), 647

The Boy Who Left Home to Find Out About the Shivers (6 and up), 637

Boyz N the Hood (mature high schoolers), 281–82

The Brave Little Toaster (6 and up), 457–58

The Breakfast Club (high schoolers), 354

Breakfast at Tiffany's (12 and up), 390–92

Breaking Away (12 and up), 148, 214, 361–63

The Bremen Town Musicians (6 and up), 647–48

Brer Rabbit and Boss Lion (6 and up), 643

Brer Rabbit and the Wonderful Tar Baby (6 and up), 643

Brewster's Millions (8 and up), 231–32

Brian's Song (10 and up), 214, 432, 591

Bridge to Terabithia (10 and up), 486

Brigadoon (8 and up), 552

Bright Road (10 and up), 349

Bringing Up Baby (6 and up), 495–96

Brooks, Mel, films, 513

The Browning Version (mature high schoolers), 349

The Buddy Holly Story (12 and up), 129–30, 432

Bus Stop (10 and up), 99–100, 586

Butch Cassidy and the Sundance Kid (12 and up), 250

The Buttercream Gang (8 and up), 651

Bye Bye Birdie (8 and up), 363–65, 566

Cabin in the Sky (8 and up), 562

The Caine Mutiny (12 and up), 138–39

The Candidate (12 and up), 614

Can't Buy Me Love (high schoolers), 234

The Canterville Ghost (6 and up), 63, 542

Captain Blood (7 and up), 148, 415

Captain January (6 and up), 253–54

Captains Courageous (7 and up), 101–2

Carefree (6 and up), 545

Carousel (10 and up), 555

Casablanca (10 and up), 40, 198, 293–95

Cat Ballou (8 and up), 295–96, 336, 598

Cat on a Hot Tin Roof (12 and up), 254–55

The Chalk Garden (14 and up), 380–81

Chariots of Fire (8 and up), 209–11, 229, 591

Charlotte's Web (6 and up), 437, 465, 486

Cheaper by the Dozen (6 and up), 255–58, 432, 491

The Chocolate War (mature high schoolers), 170–72, 353

The Chronicles of Narnia (6 and up), 641

Cinderella (4 and up), 446–48, 556, 637

Citizen Kane (10 and up), 216–19

Clash of the Titans (8 and up), 518–19
Close Encounters of the Third Kind (8 and up), 520–21
Clueless (mature high schoolers), 354
Coal Miner's Daughter (12 and up), 428
Conrack (12 and up), 350
Cool Runnings (8 and up), 590
The Corn Is Green (10 and up), 151–53
The Cosmic Eye (6 and up), 458
The Court Jester (6 and up), 496–97, 625
The Courtship of Eddie's Father (parents), 656
The Creation (6 and up), 611
The Crimson Pirate (8 and up), 415–16
Crisis at Central High (10 and up), 621
The Curse of the Cat People (10 and up), 219–20
Cyrano (6 and up), 641

Daddy Long Legs (8 and up), 549–50
Damn Yankees (10 and up), 566, 591, 606
The Dancing Princesses (6 and up), 637–38
Darby O'Gill and the Little People (8 and up), 603
The Dark Crystal (8 and up), 534–35
Dark Victory (12 and up), 307–8
Davy Crockett (6 and up), 643
The Day the Earth Stood Still (8 and up), 156–57, 542
The Day Jimmy's Boa Ate the Wash and Other Stories (3 and up), 627
Dead Man Walking (mature high schoolers), 140–41
Dead Poets Society (12 and up), 339–41
The Defiant Ones (12 and up), 109–11
Destry Rides Again (8 and up), 157–59, 598
The Devil and Daniel Webster (10 and up), 195
The Diary of Anne Frank (12 and up), 251, 259–61, 491
Disney Sing-Along series (2 and up), 627–28
The Disorderly Orderly, 513
Divorce, American Style (parents), 657
Doctor Doolittle (4 and up), 486
Dominick and Eugene (mature high schoolers), 282
Donald in Mathmagicland (6 and up), 654
Don't Eat the Pictures: Sesame Street at the Metropolitan Museum of Art, 632
Dr. Strangelove or: How I Learned to Stop Worrying and Love the Bomb, 497–99, 622
Dragonslayer (10 and up), 521–23
Dragonworld (4 and up), 535
Duck Soup (6 and up), 505–6
Dumbo (5 and up), 448–49

E. T. the Extra-Terrestrial (6 and up), 535
East of the Sun, West of the Moon (6 and up), 648
Easter Parade (6 and up), 549, 555
Edison the Man (10 and up), 422–24
Educating Rita (mature high schoolers), 153, 353
Eight Men Out (10 and up), 198, 588

The Elephant's Child (6 and up), 645
Emma (8 and up), 55
The Emperor and the Nightingale (6 and up), 645
The Emperor's New Clothes (6 and up), 48, 234, 638, 645
The Enchanted Cottage (10 and up), 582–83
Enemy Mine (12 and up), 111–12
The Ernest Green Story (10 and up), 620

Faerie Tale Theater series (6 and up), 542, 637–38
Fail-Safe (12 and up), 622
The Fallen Idol (12 and up), 47, 579
Fame (mature high schoolers), 354
Fancy Pants (6 and up), 506
Fantasia (4 and up), 436, 465, 536
Fantastic Voyage (8 and up), 416
Father of the Bride (parents), 657
Fear Strikes Out (10 and up), 428
Ferdinand the Bull (4 and up), 159–60, 491
Ferngully: The Last Rainforest (6 and up), 458, 465
Fiddler on the Roof (6 and up), 112–13, 251, 287, 566
Field of Dreams (12 and up), 221–22, 591, 608
Finian's Rainbow (6 and up), 549
Finn McCoul (6 and up), 648
The Firebird (6 and up), 648
The First of May (8 and up), 282–83
The Fisherman and His Wife (6 and up), 646
The Five Chinese Brothers (6 and up), 648
The Five Pennies (8 and up), 428
The 5,000 Fingers of Dr. T (6 and up), 536
The Flamingo Kid (high schoolers), 287, 365–67
Flipper (8 and up), 443
Flower Drum Song (6 and up), 556
Fly Away Home (8 and up), 323, 437–38
Flying Down to Rio (6 and up), 545
Follow the Drinking Ground—A Story of the Underground Railroad (6 and up), 643
Follow the Fleet (6 and up), 545–46
Forbidden Planet (6 and up), 523–25
Four Clowns (4 and up), 506
Four Feathers (8 and up), 304, 421
Frankenstein (12 and up), 622, 641
Freaky Friday (6 and up), 55, 542
Free Willy (10 and up), 443
Friendly Persuasion (8 and up), 166, 172–74, 288
From the Mixed-Up Files of Mrs. Basil E. Frankweiler (8 and up), 487
Funny Face (8 and up), 549–50
Funny Girl (8 and up), 104, 326–27, 432, 566

Gaslight (10 and up), 308–10
The Gay Divorcee (6 and up), 546
The General (6 and up), 506–7
Gentleman's Agreement (10 and up), 55, 113–15

Gentlemen Prefer Blondes (6 and up), 562
Geo Kids: Bear Cubs, Baby Ducks, and Kooky
    Kookaburras (4 and up), 631
Geo Kids: Cool Cats, Raindrops, and Things that
    Live in Holes (4 and up), 631
Geo Kids: Flying, Trying, and Honking Around (4
    and up), 631
Getting Ready for School (3 and up), 632
The Getting of Wisdom (high schoolers), 341–43
Gidget (10 and up), 381
Girl Crazy (8 and up), 554
The Girl Who Spelled Freedom (8 and up),
    428–29
The Glass Menagerie (12 and up), 228
Glory (14 and up), 115–17
The Gods Must be Crazy (6 and up), 49–51,
    166
Goldilocks and the Three Bears (6 and up), 638
Gone with the Wind (10 and up), 241–44
Good News (6 and up), 562–63
Good Will Hunting (mature high schoolers),
    381–82
Goodbye, Mr. Chips (10 and up), 350
The Goofy Movie (8 and up), 283–84
The Gospel According to St. Matthew (8 and up),
    604
The Grapes of Wrath (12 and up), 261–62
The Great Escape (8 and up), 244–46
The Great Hair Argument (6 and up), 634
The Great McGinty (12 and up), 614
The Great Mouse Detective (6 and up), 465,
    575–76
The Great Muppet Caper (4 and up), 636
The Great Race (6 and up), 211–13, 623
The Great Train Robbery (10 and up), 577–78
The Great White Hope (10 and up), 429
Gregory's Girl (12 and up), 382, 586
Groundhog Day (mature high schoolers), 602
Guess Who's Coming to Dinner (10 and up),
    130
Gulliver's Travels (6 and up), 160–62, 465
The Gunfighter (10 and up), 174–76, 598
Guys and Dolls (8 and up), 176–78

Hamlet (animated) (6 and up), 639–40
Handel's Last Chance (6 and up), 639
Hans Christian Andersen (6 and up), 563
Hansel and Gretel (6 and up), 638
The Happiest Days of Your Life (8 and up), 350
Happy Birthday Moon and Other Stories (3 and
    up), 628
Harold and the Purple Crayon (3 and up), 628
Harriet the Spy (8 and up), 487
Harvey (12 and up), 228
The Harvey Girls (8 and up), 554
Hatari (8 and up), 441
Heart Like a Wheel (12 and up), 429
Heidi (6 and up), 488
Hello, Dolly! (6 and up), 98, 557–58
Help! (6 and up), 507
Hemo the Magnificent (6 and up), 653
Henry V (two versions) (12 and up), 622

Hercules (6 and up), 458–59
Here Comes Mr. Jordan (8 and up), 542, 590
High Anxiety, 513
High Noon (10 and up), 64, 178–80, 598
High Society (6 and up), 564
His Girl Friday (10 and up), 410, 507
The Hoboken Chicken Emergency (6 and up),
    641
Holiday (10 and up), 205–6, 410, 601
Holiday Inn (6 and up), 550
Home of the Brave (10 and up), 117–18
Homer Price Stories (4 and up), 628
Honey, I Shrunk the Kids (6 and up), 507–8
Hoop Dreams (14 and up), 214, 432, 589
Hoosiers (10 and up), 589
Houdini (10 and up), 429
The Hound of the Baskervilles (8 and up), 576
Houseboat (10 and up), 288, 315–17
How to Be a Perfect Person in Just Three Days
    (6 and up), 641
How the Leopard Got His Spots (6 and up), 646
How the Rhinoceros Got His Skin & How the
    Camel Got His Hump (6 and up), 646
How to Steal a Million (8 and up), 578
The Hunt for Red October (10 and up), 305,
    416
The Hustler (14 and up), 296–98

I Know Where I'm Going! (10 and up), 392–93,
    586
I Love You Again (8 and up), 393–95
I Never Sang for My Father (parents), 658
I Remember Mama (6 and up), 492, 605–6
I'm Glad I'm Me (2 and up), 632
The Importance of Being Earnest (10 and up),
    508
In and Out (12 and up), 130–31
In the Good Old Summertime (8 and up), 554
In the Heat of the Night (14 and up), 119–20
In Your Wildest Dreams (8 and up), 651
Include Me! (2 and up), 131
The Incredible Shrinking Man (8 and up), 536
Independence Day (10 and up), 537
The Indian in the Cupboard (8 and up), 488
Inherit the Wind (10 and up), 77–81
The Inspector General (6 and up), 508
Invasion of the Body Snatchers (12 and up),
    56–58, 542
It Happened One Night (8 and up), 583–85
It Happens Every Spring (6 and up), 591, 607
It Should Happen to You (8 and up), 104
It's About Time (6 and up), 653
It's Always Fair Weather (8 and up), 553
It's a Mad Mad Mad Mad World (6 and up),
    236, 509, 625
It's a Wonderful Life (10 and up), 33–35, 618
Ivanhoe (6 and up), 417

Jack and the Beanstalk (6 and up), 638, 648
The Jackie Robinson Story (8 and up), 429, 591
Jacob Have I Loved (6 and up), 312, 642
Jacob's Harvest (8 and up), 651

James and the Giant Peach (6 and up), 482

Jane Eyre (12 and up), 488–89

Jason and the Argonauts (6 and up), 537

Jezebel (10 and up), 367–69

John Henry (6 and up), 643

Johnny Appleseed (6 and up), 643

Johnny Belinda (12 and up), 102–4, 133

Johnny Tremain (8 and up), 492, 609

Jonah and the Whale (6 and up), 611

Journey to the Center of the Earth (6 and up), 417

The Journey of Natty Gann (10 and up), 336, 421, 444–45

Judgment at Nuremberg (high schoolers), 40, 87–88, 198

Julia (high schoolers), 141–42, 305, 336

Julius Caesar (animated) 6 and up, 640

The Jungle Book (8 and up), 441, 469–70

Jurassic Park (10 and up), 418, 436

The Karate Kid (14 and up), 591

Keeper of the Flame (12 and up), 48, 195

Kids for Character (2 and up), 628

Kim (8 and up), 470–72

King of Hearts (high schoolers), 162–63

The King and I (8 and up), 133, 343–45, 557

King Midas and the Golden Touch (6 and up), 236, 648

King Solomon's Mines (8 and up), 413–14, 441

King: A Filmed Record...Montgomery to Memphis (8 and up), 432–33, 602

Kiss Me Kate (6 and up), 564, 624

Knute Rockne, All American (high schoolers), 622–23

Koi and the Kola Nuts (6 and up), 649

Kramer vs. Kramer (parents), 658

Kukla, Fran, and Ollie (3 and up), 628–29

Labyrinth (10 and up), 537–38

The Lady from Shanghai (12 and up), 573

Lady and the Tramp (4 and up), 449–50

The Lady Vanishes (10 and up), 568–69

Ladyhawke (10 and up), 538

The Ladykillers (10 and up), 514, 578

Lamb Chop in the Land of No Manners (3 and up), 632–33

Lamb Chop's Play-Along (3 and up), 633

The Land Before Time (5 and up), 436, 460

Lassie Come Home (6 and up), 436

The Last Starfighter (10 and up), 299–300

Laura (10 and up), 574

The Lavender Hill Mob (8 and up), 578–79

The Lawrenceville Stories (8 and up), 351

The Learning Tree (high schoolers), 133, 369–71

The Legend of Sleepy Hollow (6 and up), 644

Lewis, Jerry, films, 513

Life with Father (8 and up), 608

Lifeboat (10 and up), 569

Li'l Abner (6 and up), 564

Lili (6 and up), 395–97

Lilies of the Field (10 and up), 91–93

The Lion King (5 and up), 460

The Lion in Winter (high schoolers), 621

Liszt's Rhapsody (6 and up), 639

The Little Foxes (12 and up), 284

Little Lord Fauntleroy (6 and up), 472–73

The Little Mermaid (5 and up), 460–61

Little Nemo: Adventures in Slumberland (5 and up), 461

Little Women (8 and up), 284, 492

Local Hero (12 and up), 397–98

Long Day's Journey Into Night (mature high schoolers), 285

The Long Walk Home (10 and up), 131, 602

Lord of the Flies (12 and up), 250–51

Lorenzo's Oil (parents), 658

Lost Horizon (8 and up), 222–24

Lucas (high schoolers), 353, 371–73

Lyle, Lyle Crocodile (4 and up), 629

Macbeth (animated) (6 and up), 640

The Magic School Bus (6 and up), 654

Magnificent Obsession (10 and up), 93–94

The Magnificent Seven (8 and up), 59–61, 598

Major Barbara (10 and up), 98, 180–81, 208

Malcolm X (high schoolers), 153–54, 305, 433

The Maltese Falcon (10 and up), 181–82, 577

The Man from Snowy River (8 and up), 418

The Man that Corrupted Hadleyburg (12 and up), 235

The Man Who Shot Liberty Valance (10 and up), 42–44, 166, 198

The Man Who Would Be King (10 and up), 418

The Manhattan Project (12 and up), 382

The Many Adventures of Winnie the Pooh (4 and up), 489

The Mark of Zorro (8 and up), 419, 623

Mary Poppins (6 and up), 474–75

The Mask (10 and up), 538

Mask (high schoolers), 133, 262–64, 385

Matilda (8 and up), 482–83

Maurice Sendak's Really Rosie (3 and up), 625, 629

Max's Chocolate Chicken and Other Stories for Young Children (2 and up), 629

Meet Me in St. Louis (6 and up), 264–66

Men in Black (10 and up), 539

Mike Mulligan and His Steam Shovel (3 and up), 251

Mike Mulligan and His Steam Shovel and Other Stories (3 and up), 629

Mildred Pierce (parents), 659

Miracle on 34th Street (6 and up), 225–26, 618

The Miracle Worker (10 and up), 424–25

Mister Roberts (12 and up), 143–44

Misty (6 and up), 439–40, 492

Modern Times (6 and up), 499–501

Monkey Business (6 and up), 509–10

The Monkey People (6 and up), 649

Monkey Trouble (6 and up), 444

Mose the Fireman (6 and up), 644

Moses in Egypt (6 and up), 605

Moses the Lawgiver (6 and up), 605

The Mouse that Roared (6 and up), 510
Mr. Blandings Builds His Dream House (parents), 659
Mr. Deeds Goes to Town (10 and up), 55, 94–95, 208, 236
Mr. Hobbs Takes a Vacation (parents), 659
Mr. Hulot's Holiday (6 and up), 509
Mr. Magoo's Christmas Carol (6 and up), 618
Mr. Smith Goes to Washington (8 and up), 184–86, 615
Mrs. Doubtfire (10 and up), 285
Mulan (6 and up), 332–33
The Muppet Christmas Carol (6 and up), 618, 637
The Muppet Movie (4 and up), 636
Muppet Treasure Island (8 and up), 489, 637
The Muppets Take Manhattan (4 and up), 636
Murder Most Foul (10 and up), 576
Murder on the Orient Express (10 and up), 576
The Music Man (6 and up), 229, 399–401
Mutiny on the Bounty (8 and up), 144–46
My Bodyguard (10 and up), 345–47, 385
My Brilliant Career (10 and up), 334
My Darling Clementine (8 and up), 597
My Fair Lady (6 and up), 67–70
My Friend Flicka (6 and up), 440
My Girl (12 and up), 334
My Life as a Dog (12 and up), 317–18
My Man Godfrey (8 and up), 510–11
Mystery Meal (6 and up), 634

Naked Gun series, 514
The Nasty Girl (mature high schoolers), 47, 64, 336
National Velvet (6 and up), 266–70, 336, 440, 492
The NeverEnding Story (6 and up), 229, 492, 539
New Pajamas (6 and up), 635
Night of the Hunter (12 and up), 574
Ninotchka (10 and up), 401–3, 586, 621
Norma Rae (mature high schoolers), 304–5, 433, 610
North by Northwest (10 and up), 569–70
Nothing but a Man (mature high schoolers), 120–22
Notorious (10 and up), 570
Now, Voyager (10 and up), 40, 288, 310–12
The Nutty Professor, 513

Oklahoma! (8 and up), 556
Old Yeller (8 and up), 318–19, 436
Oliver (8 and up), 559–60
Oliver & Company (5 and up), 461–62
On a Clear Day You Can See Forever (8 and up), 564–65
On the Town (8 and up), 553–54
On the Waterfront (high schoolers), 186–88
One Hundred and One Dalmations (5 and up), 462
101 Things to Do (3 and up), 633
Ordinary People (12 and up), 270–72

Our Mr. Sun (6 and up), 653
Our Vines Have Tender Grapes (parents), 660
The Ox-Bow Incident (10 and up), 81–83

The Pajama Game (8 and up), 566, 610
The Parent Trap (6 and up), 511
Parenthood (parents), 660
Pat and Mike (8 and up), 328–29, 410
Paul Bunyan (6 and up), 644
Peachboy (6 and up), 649
Pecos Bill (6 and up), 642
Perfect Day/Bad Day (6 and up), 635
Perfect Harmony (8 and up), 122–23, 312
Permanent Record (high schoolers), 323, 382–83
Peter Pan (4 and up), 450–51
The Phantom Tollbooth (6 and up), 133, 465, 489–90, 542
The Philadelphia Story (10 and up), 51–53, 410
Pinocchio (6 and up), 44–45, 465, 641, 649
The Pirate (10 and up), 229
The Pirates of Penzance (6 and up), 35–36
The Point (6 and up), 131, 465
Pollyanna (6 and up), 476–77
Poor Little Rich Girl (4 and up), 235
Powder (high schoolers), 383
Pretty in Pink (mature high schoolers), 354–55
Pride of the Yankees (8 and up), 430, 591, 608
The Prime of Miss Jean Brodie (high schoolers), 347–48
The Prince and the Pauper (6 and up), 53–55
The Princess Bride (8 and up), 419
Princess Scargo & the Birthday Pumpkin (6 and up), 644
The Prisoner of Zenda (8 and up), 40, 421
Puss in Boots (6 and up), 649

The Quiet Man (8 and up), 403–5, 604
Quiz Show (12 and up), 188–90

Raiders of the Lost Ark (8 and up), 419–20
Rain Man (mature high schoolers), 285–86
The Rainmaker (10 and up), 229, 329–32
The Ramona series (6 and up), 288, 492, 634–35
Ramona: The Patient (6 and up), 625
Rear Window (8 and up), 570–71
Rebel Without a Cause (12 and up), 373–75
The Red Badge of Courage (12 and up), 62–63, 305
The Red Balloon (3 and up), 539
Red Riding Hood and Goldilocks (6 and up), 646
Red River (12 and up), 208, 592–94
The Red Shoes (high schoolers), 623
The Rescuers (5 and up), 462
Return to Oz (8 and up), 525–26
Rhubarb (8 and up), 434–35
The Right Stuff (12 and up), 430
Rigoletto (8 and up), 651
Rip Van Winkle (6 and up), 644
The Road to Bali (6 and up), 511–12
The Robe (10 and up), 605

Roberta (8 and up), 546
The Robert McCloskey Library (3 and up), 630
Robin Hood: Men in Tights, 513
Robin and the Seven Hoods (8 and up), 565
The Rocketeer (8 and up), 420
Rocky (8 and up), 226–28, 591
Rocky and Bullwinkle (6 and up), 650
The Rogue Stallion (8 and up), 652
Roman Holiday (8 and up), 36–38
Romeo and Juliet (12 and up), 384, 586, 623
Rookie of the Year (6 and up), 588
Rossini's Ghost (6 and up), 639
Royal Wedding (6 and up), 550–51
Rudy (11 and up), 207–8, 622–23
Rumpelstiltskin (6 and up), 649
The Russians are Coming! The Russians are Coming! (6 and up), 123–24, 625

Sabrina (10 and up), 585
The Sandlot (6 and up), 589
The Santa Clause (8 and up), 616
Sarah, Plain and Tall (8 and up), 490
The Savior is Born (5 and up), 617
Say Anything (high schoolers), 376–77, 586
The Scarlet and the Black (10 and up), 190–91
The Scarlet Pimpernel (10 and up), 420, 623
Schindler's List (mature high schoolers), 196
School Ties (12 and up), 124–25, 353
Schoolhouse Rock (3 and up), 631
Scrooge (6 and up), 618
The Searchers (12 and up), 597
Searching for Bobby Fischer (parents), 660–61
Seasons of the Heart (8 and up), 652
The Secret Garden (8 and up), 478–79
The Secret of Roan Inish (8 and up), 539–40
Sense and Sensibility (10 and up), 410
Sergeant York (8 and up), 305, 431
Sesame Street Presents Follow that Bird (3 and up), 132
Seven Brides for Seven Brothers (6 and up), 560–61
7 Faces of Dr. Lao (6 and up), 526–27, 542
The Seven-Per-Cent Solution (12 and up), 576–77
1776 (8 and up), 433, 609–10
Shadow of a Doubt (10 and up), 571
The Shadow of Hate (12 and up), 132–33
Shadowlands (high schoolers), 585–86
The Shaggy Dog (4 and up), 436, 540
Shall We Dance (6 and up), 546–47
Shalom Sesame (3 and up), 632
Shane (8 and up), 492, 594–97
Shipwrecked (6 and up), 300–1
The Shop Around the Corner (10 and up), 586
Show Boat (10 and up), 565
Siblingitis (6 and up), 635
Sidekicks (10 and up), 591
Silent Movie, 513
Silk Stockings (8 and up), 551
Silverado (12 and up), 598
Sinbad the Sailor (8 and up), 421

Singin' in the Rain (6 and up), 246–48, 554, 625
Sixteen Candles (high schoolers), 355
Skin Game (10 and up), 126–27
Sleeping Beauty (5 and up), 312, 451–53
Small Change (parents), 661
Smile for Auntie and Other Stories (3 and up), 630
Smooth Talk (mature high schoolers), 335
The Sneetches (3 and up), 132–33
Snow White and the Seven Dwarfs (5 and up), 453–54
Snowplows at Work (2 and up), 626
So Dear to My Heart (5 and up), 437
The Solid Gold Cadillac (10 and up), 48, 336, 512
Some Kind of Wonderful (mature high schoolers), 355
Some Like It Hot (10 and up), 502–3, 623
The Song of Sacajawea (6 and up), 644
The Sound of Music (6 and up), 251, 407–9, 557
Sounder (8 and up), 286
South Pacific (8 and up), 556–57
Spartacus (high schoolers), 148, 191–94
The Spirit of St. Louis (8 and up), 431
Splendor in the Grass (high schoolers), 378–79
Split Infinity (8 and up), 236, 652
Squanto and the First Thanksgiving (6 and up), 645
Squeakerfoot/Goodbye, Hello (6 and up), 635
Stagecoach (10 and up), 598
Stalag 17 (12 and up), 248–50
Stand and Deliver (12 and up), 351, 433
Stand By Me (10 and up), 148, 384–85
Star Trek II: The Wrath of Khan (12 and up), 196
Star Wars (6 and up), 301–3, 542
State Fair (8 and up), 557
State of the Union (10 and up), 614–15
The Steadfast Tin Soldier (6 and up), 646
The Sting (10 and up), 579
Stop! Look! and Listen!, 514
Stories From the Black Tradition (4 and up), 630
Stories From the Jewish Tradition (4 and up), 615
Stormalong (6 and up), 645
Stormy Weather (10 and up), 565
The Story of Alexander Graham Bell (8 and up), 431–32
The Story of Vernon and Irene Castle (8 and up), 547
Strauss: The King of Three-Quarter Time (6 and up), 639
Strega Nonna and Other Stories (3 and up), 630
Sullivan's Travels (10 and up), 96–97, 410, 514
Summer Magic (6 and up), 566
Summer Stock (8 and up), 555
Sunrise at Campobello (10 and up), 426–27
Superman (4 and up), 540
The Sure Thing (mature high schoolers), 196, 385
The Swan Princess (5 and up), 462–63

Swing Time (6 and up), 547
Swiss Family Robinson (6 and up), 251, 492
The Sword in the Stone (4 and up), 303–4, 465

The Tale of Peter Rabbit and The Tale of Mr. Jeremy Fisher (6 and up), 646
Tales of Wonder (6 and up), 654–55
The Talking Eggs (6 and up), 645
The Taming of the Shrew (10 and up), 335, 624
Tea and Sympathy (high schoolers), 352
The Ten Commandments (8 and up), 605
Tex (high schoolers), 273–75, 385
That Darn Cat (8 and up), 435
That's Entertainment! (6 and up), 566
These Three (12 and up), 45–47
The Thief of Bagdad (8 and up), 528–29
The Thief and the Cobbler (5 and up), 463
The Thin Man (10 and up), 577
35 Up (parents), 661–62
The 39 Steps (10 and up), 571–72
The Thread of Life (6 and up), 653–54
The Three Billy Goats Gruff and The Three Little Pigs (6 and up), 646–47
The Three Lives of Thomasina (8 and up), 320–21, 435
The Three Musketeers (8 and up), 421
Three Stooges films, 514
Thumbelina (6 and up), 647
The Tiger and the Brahmin (6 and up), 649
Time Bandits (8 and up), 540–41
The Time Machine (8 and up), 541
Titanic (12 and up), 194–95
To Catch a Thief (8 and up), 572
To Have and Have Not (10 and up), 146–48
To Hell and Back (10 and up), 432
To Kill a Mockingbird (10 and up), 70–72, 134, 608
To Sir, With Love (mature high schoolers), 72, 353
Toby Tyler (6 and up), 444
tom thumb (6 and up), 541, 650
Top Hat (6 and up), 548
Topkapi (10 and up), 579
Touch of Evil (12 and up), 573–74
Toy Story (5 and up), 463–64
Treasure Island (8 and up), 490
The Treasure of the Sierra Madre (12 and up), 232–34, 312
The Trouble with Angels (8 and up), 352
Truly, Madly, Deeply (12 and up), 322–23
Tuck Everlasting (10 and up), 490
The Turning Point (high schoolers and parents), 623, 661
Twelfth Night (animated) (6 and up), 640
12 Angry Men (10 and up), 84–85
20,000 Leagues Under the Sea (8 and up), 163–65, 492
Two for the Road (parents), 662
2001: A Space Odyssey (10 and up), 529–31

The Ugly Duckling (6 and up), 647
The Ugly Duckling and Other Classic Fairy Tales (4 and up), 630
Unstrung Heroes (12 and up), 277–78, 323
Up the Down Staircase (mature high schoolers), 352–53

The Velveteen Rabbit (6 and up), 647
Vertigo (high schoolers), 621

War Games (10 and up), 165–66
We're Back: A Dinosaur's Story (5 and up), 436
West Side Story (10 and up), 127–29, 623
What a Way to Go! (8 and up), 235–36
What's Eating Gilbert Grape (mature high schoolers), 286–87
What's Up, Doc? (6 and up), 504–5
Where the Boys Are (12 and up), 385
Where the Lilies Bloom (10 and up), 288, 323, 336, 490–91
Where the Red Fern Grows (8 and up), 323, 491
Where's Spot?, Spot Goes to the Farm, and Spot Goes to a Party (2 and up), 633
The White Cat (6 and up), 650
White Christmas (4 and up), 98, 617
White Fang (10 and up), 445, 492
White Hunter, Black Heart (high schoolers), 620
Who Framed Roger Rabbit? (6 and up), 531–32
Who's Minding the Mint? (8 and up), 512–13
Wild Hearts Can't be Broken (8 and up), 335–36
The William Steig Library (4 and up), 631
Willie Wonka and the Chocolate Factory (6 and up), 483
Willow (8 and up), 533
Willy the Sparrow (6 and up), 652
Wilson (12 and up), 432
The Winslow Boy (10 and up), 86–87
The Witches (8 and up), 483–85
Witness for the Prosecution (10 and up), 88, 579
The Wiz (8 and up), 624
The Wizard of Oz (6 and up), 479–82, 542, 555, 624
The Wonderful World of the Brothers Grimm (6 and up), 541–42
The World of Henry Orient (12 and up), 379–80
The Wrong Trousers (6 and up), 636

Yankee Doodle Dandy (8 and up), 610
The Yearling (8 and up), 321–22, 492
Yellow Submarine (4 and up), 464–65, 625
You Can't Take It With You (8 and up), 278–80
Young Frankenstein (12 and up), 513, 622
Young People's Concerts with Leonard Bernstein series (6 and up), 654
Yours, Mine and Ours (8 and up), 287

Zebra in the Kitchen (5 and up), 445
Zucker, Abrahams, Zucker and Their Imitators films, 514

Age Group Index

Please bear in mind that the age categories in this index overlap. Any movie that is suitable for children ages 6 and up is also appropriate for children ages 8 and up or 10 and up. However, in order to avoid pages of repeat listings, each movie is listed only once, for the earliest appropriate age. For example, if you are looking for a movie suitable for your twelve-year-old son or daughter, you will want to peruse the movies in the category Ages 12 and Up, *and all the preceding age categories.*

Ages 2 and Up
All About Helicopters and *Snowplows at Work*, 625–26
The Big Adventure series, 627
Disney Sing-Along series, 627–28
I'm Glad I'm Me, 632
Include Me!, 131
Kids for Character, 628
Max's Chocolate Chicken and Other Stories for Young Children, 629
Where's Spot?, Spot Goes to the Farm, & Spot Goes to a Party, 633

Ages 3 and Up
A Charlie Brown Christmas, 615–16
Alexander and the Terrible, Horrible, No Good, Very Bad Day, 626
The Day Jimmy's Boa Ate the Wash and Other Stories, 627
Getting Ready for School, 632
Happy Birthday Moon and Other Stories, 628
Harold and the Purple Crayon, 628
Kukla, Fran, and Ollie, 628–29
Lamb Chop in the Land of No Manners, 632–33
Lamb Chop's Play-Along, 633
Maurice Sendak's Really Rosie, 625, 629
Mike Mulligan and His Steam Shovel, 251
Mike Mulligan and His Steam Shovel and Other Stories, 629
101 Things to Do, 633
The Red Balloon, 539

The Robert McCloskey Library, 630
Schoolhouse Rock, 631
Sesame Street Presents Follow that Bird, 132
Shalom Sesame, 632
Smile for Auntie and Other Stories, 630
The Sneetches, 132–33
Strega Nonna and Other Stories, 630

Ages 4 and Up
The Absent Minded Professor, 534, 589
Adventures of Milo and Otis, 436–37
Aladdin, 454–55
Alice in Wonderland, 465, 466–67, 542
Amazing Grace and Other Stories, 133, 627
The Aristocats, 456
Babe, 65–67, 437
Beauty and the Beast, 457, 636
Big Bird in China and *Big Bird in Japan*, 632
Cinderella, 446–48, 556, 637
Doctor Doolittle, 486
Don't Eat the Pictures, 632
Dragonworld, 535
Fantasia, 436, 465, 536
Ferdinand the Bull, 159–60, 491
Four Clowns, 506
Geo Kids: Bear Cubs, Baby Ducks, and Kooky Kookaburras, 631
Geo Kids: Cool Cats, Raindrops, & Things That Live in Holes, 631
Geo Kids: Flying, Trying, and Honking Around, 631

The Great Muppet Caper, 636
Homer Price Stories, 628
Lady and the Tramp, 449–50
Lyle, Lyle Crocodile, 629
The Many Adventures of Winnie the Pooh, 489
The Muppet Movie, 636
The Muppets Take Manhattan, 636
Peter Pan, 450–51
Poor Little Rich Girl, 235
The Shaggy Dog, 436, 540
Stories from the Black Tradition, 630
Stories from the Jewish Tradition, 615
Superman, 540
The Sword in the Stone, 303–4, 465
The Ugly Duckling and Other Classic Fairy Tales,
    630
White Christmas, 98, 617
The William Steig Library, 631
Yellow Submarine, 464–65, 625

Ages 5 and Up
An American Tail, 455
Anastasia, 456
Balto, 457
Dumbo, 448–49
The Land Before Time, 436, 460
The Lion King, 460
The Little Mermaid, 460–61
Little Nemo: Adventures in Slumberland, 461
Oliver & Company, 461–62
One Hundred and One Dalmations, 462
The Rescuers, 462
The Savior is Born, 617
Sleeping Beauty, 312, 451–53
Snow White and the Seven Dwarfs, 453–54
So Dear to My Heart, 437
The Swan Princess, 462–63
The Thief and the Cobbler, 463
Toy Story, 463–64
We're Back: A Dinosaur's Story, 436
Zebra in the Kitchen, 445

Ages 6 and Up
A Christmas Carol (several versions), 236,
    617–18
A Close Shave, 635
A Grand Day Out, 635
A Little Princess, 55, 473–74, 640
The Adventures of Robin Hood, 135–38, 421,
    623
Aladdin and His Wonderful Lamp, 637
Aladdin and the Magic Lamp, 647
The Alphabet Conspiracy, 653
Anansi, 647
Anchors Aweigh, 552
Andre, 441–42
Angels in the Outfield, 591, 607
Anne of Green Gables, 287, 485
Annie, 561
Annie Get Your Gun. 213
Annie Oakley, 336, 432, 642–43
Babes in Toyland, 561–62

Bach's Fight for Freedom, 638
The Band Wagon, 548
Beany and Cecil, 650
Bedknobs and Broomsticks, 468–69
Bedtime for Bonzo, 444, 505
The Bell Telephone Science series, 653
Belles on Their Toes, 432
Bells are Ringing, 89–91, 566
Billy Rose's Jumbo, 562
Bizet's Dream, 639
Born Free, 440–41
The Boy Who Drew Cats, 647
*The Boy Who Left Home to Find Out About the
    Shivers,* 637
The Brave Little Toaster, 457–58
The Bremen Town Musicians, 647–48
Brer Rabbit and Boss Lion, 643
Brer Rabbit and the Wonderful Tar Baby, 643
Bringing Up Baby, 495–96
The Canterville Ghost, 63, 542
Captain January, 253–54
Carefree, 545
Charlotte's Web, 437, 465, 486
Cheaper by the Dozen, 255–58, 432, 491
The Chronicles of Narnia, 641
The Cosmic Eye, 458
The Court Jester, 496–97, 625
The Creation, 611
Cyrano, 641
The Dancing Princesses, 637–38
Davy Crockett, 643
Donald in Mathmagicland, 654
Duck Soup, 505–6
E. T. the Extra-Terrestrial, 535
East of the Sun, West of the Moon, 648
Easter Parade, 549, 555
The Elephant's Child, 645
The Emperor and the Nightingale, 645
The Emperor's New Clothes, 48, 234, 537, 645
Faerie Tale Theater series, 542, 637–38
Fancy Pants, 506
Ferngully: The Last Rainforest, 458, 465
Fiddler on the Roof, 112–13, 251, 287, 566
Finian's Rainbow, 549
Finn McCoul, 648
The Firebird, 648
The Fisherman and His Wife, 646
The Five Chinese Brothers, 648
The 5,000 Fingers of Dr. T, 536
Flower Drum Song, 556
Flying Down to Rio, 545
Follow the Drinking Ground, 643
Follow the Fleet, 545–46
Forbidden Planet, 523–25
Freaky Friday, 55, 542
The Gay Divorcee, 546
The General, 506–7
Gentlemen Prefer Blondes, 562
The Gods Must be Crazy, 49–51, 166
Goldilocks and the Three Bears, 537
Good News, 562–63
The Great Hair Argument, 634

The Great Mouse Detective, 465, 575–76
The Great Race, 211–13, 623
Gulliver's Travels, 160–62, 465
Hamlet (animated), 639–40
Handel's Last Chance, 639
Hans Christian Andersen, 563
Hansel and Gretel, 638
Heidi, 488
Hello, Dolly!, 98, 557–58
Help!, 507
Hemo the Magnificent, 653
Hercules, 458–59
High Society, 564
The Hoboken Chicken Emergency, 641
Holiday Inn, 550
Honey, I Shrunk the Kids, 507–8
How to be a Perfect Person in Just Three Days,
    641
How the Leopard Got His Spots, 646
How the Rhinoceros Got His Skin & How the
    Camel Got His Hump, 646
I Remember Mama, 492, 605–6
The Inspector General, 508
It Happens Every Spring, 591, 607
It's About Time, 653
It's a Mad Mad Mad Mad World, 236, 509, 625
Ivanhoe, 417
Jack and the Beanstalk, 638, 648
Jacob Have I Loved, 312, 642
James and the Giant Peach, 482
Jason and the Argonauts, 537
John Henry, 643
Johnny Appleseed, 643
Jonah and the Whale, 611
Journey to the Center of the Earth, 417
Julius Caesar (animated), 640
King Midas and the Golden Touch, 236, 648
Kiss Me Kate, 564, 624
Koi and the Kola Nuts, 649
Lassie Come Home, 436
The Legend of Sleepy Hollow, 644
Li'l Abner, 564
Lili, 395–97
Liszt's Rhapsody, 639
Little Lord Fauntleroy, 472–73
Macbeth (animated), 640
The Magic School Bus, 654
Mary Poppins, 474–75
Meet Me in St. Louis, 264–66
Miracle on 34th Street, 225–26, 618
Misty, 439–40, 492
Modern Times, 499–501
Monkey Business, 509–10
The Monkey People, 649
Monkey Trouble, 444
Mose the Fireman, 644
Moses in Egypt, 605
Moses the Lawgiver, 604
The Mouse that Roared, 510
Mr. Hulot's Holiday, 509
Mr. Magoo's Christmas Carol, 615
Mulan, 332–33

The Muppet Christmas Carol, 618, 637
The Music Man, 229, 399–401
My Fair Lady, 67–70
My Friend Flicka, 440
Mystery Meal, 634
National Velvet, 266–70, 336, 440, 492
The NeverEnding Story, 229, 492, 539
New Pajamas, 635
Our Mr. Sun, 653
The Parent Trap, 511
Paul Bunyan, 644
Peachboy, 649
Pecos Bill, 644
Perfect Day/Bad Day, 635
The Phantom Tollbooth, 133, 465, 489–90, 542
Pinocchio, 44–45, 465, 641, 649
The Pirates of Penzance, 35–36
The Point, 131, 465
Pollyanna, 476–77
The Prince and the Pauper, 53–55
Princess Scargo & the Birthday Pumpkin, 644
Puss in Boots, 649
The Ramona series, 288, 492, 634–35
Ramona: The Patient, 625
Red Riding Hood and Goldilocks, 646
Rip Van Winkle, 644
The Road to Bali, 511–12
Rocky and Bullwinkle, 650
Rookie of the Year, 588
Rossini's Ghost, 639
Royal Wedding, 550–51
Rumpelstiltskin, 649
The Russians are Coming! The Russians are Com-
    ing!, 123–24, 624
The Sandlot, 589
Scrooge, 618
Seven Brides for Seven Brothers, 560–61
7 Faces of Dr. Lao, 526–27, 542
Shall We Dance, 546–47
Shipwrecked, 300–1
Siblingitis, 635
Singin' in the Rain, 246–48, 554, 625
The Song of Sacajawea, 644
The Sound of Music, 251, 407–9, 557
Squanto and the First Thanksgiving, 645
Squeakerfoot/Goodbye, Hello, 635
Star Wars, 301–3, 542
The Steadfast Tin Soldier, 646
Stormalong, 645
Strauss: The King of Three-Quarter Time, 639
Summer Magic, 566
Swing Time, 547
Swiss Family Robinson, 251, 492
The Tale of Peter Rabbit and The Tale of Mr. Jer-
    emy Fisher, 646
Tales of Wonder, 654–55
The Talking Eggs, 645
That's Entertainment!, 566
The Thread of Life, 653–54
The Three Billy Goats Gruff and The Three Little
    Pigs, 646–47
Thumbelina, 647

The Tiger and the Brahmin, 650
Toby Tyler, 444
tom thumb, 541, 650
Top Hat, 548
Twelfth Night (animated), 640
The Ugly Duckling, 647
The Velveteen Rabbit, 647
What's Up, Doc?, 504–5
The White Cat, 650
Who Framed Roger Rabbit?, 531–32
Willie Wonka and the Chocolate Factory, 483
Willy the Sparrow, 652
The Wizard of Oz, 479–82, 542, 555, 624
The Wonderful World of the Brothers Grimm,
    541–42
The Wrong Trousers, 636
Young People's Concerts with Leonard Bernstein,
    654

Ages 7 and Up
Captain Blood, 148, 415
Captains Courageous, 101–2

Ages 8 and Up
A Christmas Memory, 287, 616
A Christmas Story, 258–59, 618
A Hard Day's Night, 563–64
A Night at the Opera, 501–2
Abe Lincoln in Illinois, 427, 603
The African Queen, 290–92, 620
Almost Angels, 338–39
An American in Paris, 552
Apollo 13, 238–39, 432
Around the World in 80 Days, 415
The Autobiography of Miss Jane Pittman, 601–2
Baby...Secret of the Lost Legend, 435
The Baby-Sitter's Club, 485
Back to the Future, 534
Ball of Fire, 312, 581–82
The Barkleys of Broadway, 544
The Belles of St. Trinian's, 348–49
The Black Stallion, 438–39, 491
Body and Soul, 590
The Borrowers, 485–86
The Boy Who Could Fly, 516–17
Brewster's Millions, 231–32
Brigadoon, 552–53
The Buttercream Gang, 651
Bye Bye Birdie, 363–65, 566
Cabin in the Sky, 562
Cat Ballou, 295–96, 336, 598
Chariots of Fire, 209–11, 229, 591
Clash of the Titans, 518–19
Close Encounters of the Third Kind, 520–21
Cool Runnings, 590
The Crimson Pirate, 415–16
Daddy Long Legs, 548–49
Darby O'Gill and the Little People, 603–4
The Dark Crystal, 534–35
The Day the Earth Stood Still, 156–57, 542
Destry Rides Again, 157–59, 598
Emma, 55

Fantastic Voyage, 416
The First of May, 282–83
The Five Pennies, 428
Flipper, 443
Fly Away Home, 323, 437–38
Four Feathers, 304, 421
Friendly Persuasion, 166, 172–74, 288
From the Mixed-Up Files of Mrs. Basil E.
    Frankweiler, 487
Funny Face, 549–50
Funny Girl, 104, 326–27, 432, 566
Girl Crazy, 554
The Girl Who Spelled Freedom, 428–29
The Goofy Movie, 283–84
The Gospel According to St. Matthew, 604
The Great Escape, 244–46
Guys and Dolls, 176–78
The Happiest Days of Your Life, 350
Harriet the Spy, 487
The Harvey Girls, 554
Hatari, 441
Here Comes Mr. Jordan, 542, 590
The Hound of the Baskervilles, 576
How to Steal a Million, 578
I Love You Again, 393–95
In the Good Old Summertime, 554
In Your Wildest Dreams, 651
The Incredible Shrinking Man, 536
The Indian in the Cupboard, 488
It Happened One Night, 583–85
It Should Happen to You, 104
It's Always Fair Weather, 553
The Jackie Robinson Story, 429, 591
Jacob's Harvest, 651
Johnny Tremain, 492, 609
The Jungle Book, 441, 469–70
Kim, 470–72
The King and I, 133, 343–45, 557
King Solomon's Mines, 413–14, 441
King: A Filmed Record...Montgomery to Memphis,
    432–33, 602
The Lavender Hill Mob, 578–79
The Lawrenceville Stories, 351
Life with Father, 608
Little Women, 284, 492
Lost Horizon, 222–24
The Magnificent Seven, 59–61, 598
The Man from Snowy River, 418
The Mark of Zorro, 419, 623
Matilda, 482–83
Mr. Smith Goes to Washington, 184–86, 614
Muppet Treasure Island, 489, 637
Mutiny on the Bounty, 144–46
My Darling Clementine, 597
My Man Godfrey, 510–11
Oklahoma!, 556
Old Yeller, 318–19, 436
Oliver!, 559–60
On a Clear Day You Can See Forever, 564–65
On the Town, 553–54
The Pajama Game, 566, 610
Pat and Mike, 328–29, 410

Perfect Harmony, 122–23, 312
Pride of the Yankees, 430, 591, 608
The Princess Bride, 419
The Prisoner of Zenda, 40, 421
The Quiet Man, 403–5, 604
Raiders of the Lost Ark, 419–20
Rear Window, 570–71
Return to Oz, 525–26
Rhubarb, 434–35
Rigoletto, 651–52
Roberta, 546
Robin and the Seven Hoods, 565
The Rocketeer, 420
Rocky, 226–28, 591
The Rogue Stallion, 652
Roman Holiday, 36–38
The Santa Clause, 616
Sarah, Plain and Tall, 490
Seasons of the Heart, 652
The Secret Garden, 478–79
The Secret of Roan Inish, 539–40
Sergeant York, 305, 431
1776, 433, 609–10
Shane, 492, 594–97
Silk Stockings, 551
Sinbad the Sailor, 421
Sounder, 286
South Pacific, 556–57
The Spirit of St. Louis, 431
Split Infinity, 236, 652
State Fair, 557
The Story of Alexander Graham Bell, 431–32
The Story of Vernon and Irene Castle, 547
Summer Stock, 555
The Ten Commandments, 605
That Darn Cat, 435
The Thief of Bagdad, 528–29
The Three Lives of Thomasina, 320–21, 435
The Three Musketeers, 421
Time Bandits, 540–41
The Time Machine, 541
To Catch a Thief, 572
Treasure Island, 490
The Trouble with Angels, 352
20,000 Leagues Under the Sea, 163–65, 492
What a Way to Go!, 235–36
Where the Red Fern Grows, 323, 491
Who's Minding the Mint?, 512–13
Wild Hearts Can't be Broken, 335–36
Willow, 533
The Witches, 483–85
The Wizard of Oz, 624
Yankee Doodle Dandy, 610
The Yearling, 321–22, 492
You Can't Take It With You, 278–80
Yours, Mine and Ours, 287

Ages 10 and Up
A Big Hand for the Little Lady, 505
A Man for All Seasons, 183–84
A Room with a View, 406–7
A Tale of Two Cities, 305

A Tree Grows in Brooklyn, 275–76, 492
Adam's Rib, 106–7, 336
An Affair to Remember, 409–10
The Andromeda Strain, 414–15
Awakenings, 98, 388–89
Bad Day at Black Rock, 133, 292–93
Ben-Hur, 604
Birdman of Alcatraz, 427–28
Born Yesterday, 149–51, 336, 586, 621
Brian's Song, 214, 432, 591
Bridge to Terabithia, 486
Bright Road, 349
Bus Stop, 99–100, 586
Carousel, 555
Casablanca, 40, 198, 293–95
Citizen Kane, 216–19
The Corn is Green, 151–53
Crisis at Central High, 621
The Curse of the Cat People, 219–20
Damn Yankees, 566, 591, 607
The Devil and Daniel Webster, 196–97
Dragonslayer, 521–23
Edison the Man, 422–24
Eight Men Out, 198, 588
The Enchanted Cottage, 582–83
The Ernest Green Story, 621
Fear Strikes Out, 428
Free Willy, 443
Gaslight, 308–10
Gentleman's Agreement, 55, 113–15
Gidget, 381
Gone with the Wind, 241–44
Goodbye, Mr. Chips, 350
The Great Train Robbery, 577–78
The Great White Hope, 429
Guess Who's Coming to Dinner, 130
The Gunfighter, 174–76, 598
High Noon, 64, 178–80, 598
His Girl Friday, 410, 507
Holiday, 205–6, 410, 601
Home of the Brave, 117–18
Hoosiers, 589
Houdini, 429
Houseboat, 288, 315–17
The Hunt for Red October, 305, 416
I Know Where I'm Going!, 392–93, 586
The Importance of Being Earnest, 508
Independence Day, 537
Inherit the Wind, 77–81
It's a Wonderful Life, 33–35, 618
Jezebel, 367–69
The Journey of Natty Gann, 336, 421, 444–45
Jurassic Park, 418, 436
Labyrinth, 537–38
The Lady Vanishes, 568–69
Ladyhawke, 538
The Ladykillers, 514, 578
The Last Starfighter, 299–300
Laura, 574
Lifeboat, 569
Lilies of the Field, 91–93
The Long Walk Home, 131, 602

Magnificent Obsession, 93–94
Major Barbara, 98, 180–81, 208
The Maltese Falcon, 181–82, 577
The Man Who Shot Liberty Valance, 42–44,
    166, 198
The Man Who Would be King, 418
The Mask, 538
Men in Black, 539
The Miracle Worker, 424–25
Mr. Deeds Goes to Town, 55, 94–95, 208, 236
Mrs. Doubtfire, 285
Murder Most Foul, 576
Murder on the Orient Express, 576
My Bodyguard, 345–47, 385
My Brilliant Career, 334
Ninotchka, 401–3, 586, 621
North by Northwest, 569–70
Notorious, 570
Now, Voyager, 40, 288, 310–12
The Ox-Bow Incident, 81–83
The Philadelphia Story, 51–53, 410
The Pirate, 229
The Rainmaker, 229, 329–32
The Robe, 605
Sabrina, 585
The Scarlet and the Black, 190–91
The Scarlet Pimpernel, 420, 623
Sense and Sensibility, 410
Shadow of a Doubt, 571
The Shop Around the Corner, 596
Show Boat, 565
Sidekicks, 591
Skin Game, 126–27
The Solid Gold Cadillac, 48, 336, 512
Some Like It Hot, 502–3, 623
Stagecoach, 598
Stand By Me, 148, 384–85
State of the Union, 614–15
The Sting, 579
Stormy Weather, 565–66
Sullivan's Travels, 96–97, 410, 514
Sunrise at Campobello, 426–27
The Taming of the Shrew, 335, 624
The Thin Man, 577
The 39 Steps, 571–72
To Have and Have Not, 146–48
To Hell and Back, 432
To Kill a Mockingbird, 70–72, 134, 608
Topkapi, 579
Tuck Everlasting, 490
12 Angry Men, 84–85
2001: A Space Odyssey, 529–31
War Games, 165–66
West Side Story, 127–29, 623
Where the Lilies Bloom, 288, 323, 336, 490–91
White Fang, 445, 492
The Winslow Boy, 86–87
Witness for the Prosecution, 88, 579

Ages 11 and Up
Rudy, 207–8, 622–23

Ages 12 and Up
A Doll's House, 332
A League of Their Own, 133, 214, 305, 336,
    591, 608
A Raisin in the Sun, 134, 286
A Soldier's Story, 133
Advise & Consent, 613
Alice Adams, 358–59
All About Eve, 201–3
All the King's Men, 203–5
All My Sons, 195, 312
All the President's Men, 169–70, 305, 432, 615
All the Way Home, 312, 313–15
Amadeus, 213
American Graffiti, 359–61
Anatomy of a Murder, 76–77
Arabesque, 572–73
Arsenic and Old Lace, 280, 514
Au Revoir, Les Enfants (Good-Bye, Children), 196
Auntie Mame, 280–81
The Barretts of Wimpole Street, 281
The Best Little Girl in the World, 332
The Best Man, 613–14
The Best Years of Our Lives, 239–41
The Big Sleep, 575
The Bingo Long Traveling All-Stars & Motor
    Kings, 107–9, 591
The Blackboard Jungle, 349
Breakfast at Tiffany's, 390–92
Breaking Away, 148, 214, 361–63
The Buddy Holly Story, 129–30, 432
Butch Cassidy and the Sundance Kid, 250
The Caine Mutiny, 138–39
The Candidate, 614
Cat on a Hot Tin Roof, 254–55
Coal Miner's Daughter, 428
Conrack, 350
Dark Victory, 307–8
Dead Poets Society, 339–41
The Defiant Ones, 109–11
The Diary of Anne Frank, 251, 259–61, 491
Dr. Strangelove, 622
Enemy Mine, 111–12
Fail-Safe, 622
The Fallen Idol, 47, 579
Field of Dreams, 221–22, 591, 608
Frankenstein, 622, 641
The Glass Menagerie, 228
The Grapes of Wrath, 261–62
The Great McGinty, 614
Gregory's Girl, 382, 586
Harvey, 228
Heart Like a Wheel, 429
Henry V (two versions), 622
In and Out, 130–31
Invasion of the Body Snatchers, 56–58, 542
Jane Eyre, 488–89
Johnny Belinda, 102–4, 133
Keeper of the Flame, 48, 197
The Lady from Shanghai, 573
The Little Foxes, 284
Local Hero, 397–98

Lord of the Flies, 250–51
The Man that Corrupted Hadleyburg, 235
The Manhattan Project, 382
Mister Roberts, 143–44
My Girl, 334
My Life as a Dog, 317–18
Night of the Hunter, 574
Ordinary People, 270–72
Quiz Show, 188–90
Rebel Without a Cause, 373–75
The Red Badge of Courage, 62–63, 305
Red River, 208, 592–94
The Right Stuff, 430
Romeo and Juliet, 384, 586, 623
School Ties, 124–25, 353
The Searchers, 597
The Seven-Per-Cent Solution, 576–77
The Shadow of Hate, 132
Silverado, 598
Stalag 17, 248–50
Stand and Deliver, 351, 433
Star Trek II: The Wrath of Khan, 197–98
These Three, 45–47
Titanic, 194–95
Touch of Evil, 573–74
The Treasure of the Sierra Madre, 232–34, 312
Truly, Madly, Deeply, 322–23
Unstrung Heroes, 277–78, 323
Where the Boys Are, 385
Wilson, 432
The World of Henry Orient, 379–80
Young Frankenstein, 513, 622

Ages 14 and Up
The Chalk Garden, 380–81
Glory, 115–17
Hoop Dreams, 214, 432, 589
The Hustler, 296–98
In the Heat of the Night, 119
The Karate Kid, 591

High Schoolers
A River Runs Through It, 272–73
A Thousand Clowns, 38–40, 288
Airplane!, 514, 620
Airport, 620
Amistad, 74–76
Becket, 621
Bell, Book and Candle, 621
Benny & Joon, 281
The Breakfast Club, 354
Can't Buy Me Love, 234
Dr. Strangelove, 497–99
The Flamingo Kid, 287, 365–67
The Getting of Wisdom, 341–43
Judgment at Nuremberg, 40, 87–88, 198
Julia, 141–42, 305, 336
King of Hearts, 162–63
Knute Rockne, All American, 622–23
The Learning Tree, 133, 369–71
The Lion in Winter, 621

Lucas, 353, 371–73
Malcolm X, 153–54, 305, 433
Mask, 133, 262–64, 385
On the Waterfront, 186–88
Permanent Record, 323, 382–83
Powder, 383
The Prime of Miss Jean Brodie, 347–48
The Red Shoes, 623
Say Anything, 376–77, 586
Shadowlands, 585–86
Sixteen Candles, 355
Spartacus, 148, 191–94
Splendor in the Grass, 378–79
Tea and Sympathy, 352
Tex, 273–75, 385
The Turning Point, 623, 661
Vertigo, 621
White Hunter, Black Heart, 620

High Schoolers, Mature
The Apartment, 196
Boyz N the Hood, 281–82
The Browning Version, 349
The Chocolate War, 170–72, 353
Clueless, 354
Dead Man Walking, 140–41
Dominick and Eugene, 282
Educating Rita, 153, 353
Fame, 354
Good Will Hunting, 381–82
Groundhog Day, 602
Long Day's Journey into Night, 285
The Nasty Girl, 47, 64, 336
Norma Rae, 304–5, 433, 610
Nothing but a Man, 120–22
Pretty in Pink, 354–55
Rain Man, 285–86
Schindler's List, 197
Smooth Talk, 335
Some Kind of Wonderful, 355
The Sure Thing, 198, 385
To Sir, With Love, 72, 353
Up the Down Staircase, 352–53
What's Eating Gilbert Grape, 286–87

Parents
The Courtship of Eddie's Father, 656
Divorce, American Style, 657
Father of the Bride, 657
I Never Sang for My Father, 658
Kramer vs. Kramer, 658
Lorenzo's Oil, 658
Mildred Pierce, 659
Mr. Blandings Builds His Dream House, 659
Mr. Hobbs Takes a Vacation, 659
Our Vines Have Tender Grapes, 660
Parenthood, 660
Searching for Bobby Fischer, 660–61
Small Change, 661
35 Up, 661–62
The Turning Point, 623, 661
Two for the Road, 662